LANDMARKS IN Rhetoric and Public Address

LANDMARKS IN Rhetoric and Public Address

David Potter, GENERAL EDITOR

THE Philosophy of Rhetoric

BY

George Campbell

EDITED BY

Lloyd F. Bitzer

FOREWORD BY

David Potter

Southern Illinois University Press · CARBONDALE

LIBRARY OF CONGRESS CATALOG CARD NO. 63–14291
PRINTED IN THE UNITED STATES OF AMERICA

DESIGNED BY ANDOR BRAUN

FOREWORD

By David Potter

FIRST PUBLISHED in 1776, George Campbell's *Philosophy of Rhetoric* was adopted as a textbook in many of our early colleges. Its popularity in the classroom was lessened considerably by the appearance of Blair's *Lectures on Rhetoric and Belles Lettres* in 1783 and Whately's *Elements of Rhetoric* in 1828 but throughout the nineteenth century new editions of the book and reprints of old editions continued to appear and influence scholars. However, despite general acknowledgment that the *Philosophy of Rhetoric* is a, if not *the,* major contribution of its period to rhetorical theory, no complete edition of the work has been published in the twentieth century. And copies that infrequently appear for sale are usually reprints or reissues of the error-ridden American edition of 1844. This photo-offset reproduction of the edition of 1850 (London: William Tegg & Co.), made possible by the co-operation of the Princeton University Library, will make the best edition of the *Philosophy of Rhetoric* generally available for the first time in over one hundred years.

The introductory essay in our Landmarks edition is the work of Professor Lloyd F. Bitzer of the University of Wisconsin. Dr. Bitzer's concern with eighteenth century philosophers and rhetoricians stems from an academic specialization in rhetoric and philosophy and the study of contemporary philosophical influences upon Campbell's *Philosophy of Rhetoric.* The essay itself is the culmination of three years of intensive research. The consequence should be a clarification of the thinking of a new generation of rhetoricians.

CONTENTS

BOOK II

The Foundations and Essential Properties of Elocution

BOOK III

The Discriminating Properties of Elocution

EDITOR'S INTRODUCTION

By Lloyd F. Bitzer

WITH THE PUBLICATION of this volume, the complete text of *The Philosophy of Rhetoric,* which George Saintsbury called "the most important treatise on the New Rhetoric that the eighteenth century produced,"[1] is newly available for the first time in more than seventy-five years. George Campbell's *Rhetoric* was reprinted at least forty-two times after its initial publication in 1776. All but two editions (the original one and the 1911 Kleiser condensation) appeared in the nineteenth century. During this period the book was highly favored as a text for students of oratory, composition, and criticism; in addition, it was common stock for many writers on rhetoric—among them Richard Whately, John Bascom, and Henry Day—whose works gradually superseded it.[2]

A general surge of interest in the study of human communication is partially responsible for renewed interest in *The Philosophy of Rhetoric* during recent years. However, the greatest stimulation to new interest in the *Rhetoric* results from a growing opinion among scholars that Campbell's work is an important contribution to rhetorical theory—a contribution which deserves study along with such traditionally honored works as Aristotle's *Rhetoric,* Cicero's *De Oratore,* Quintilian's *Institutes of Oratory,* and Longinus' *On the Sublime.* The locus of the recent revival of interest and hence the sphere of influence of the book have been confined principally to the field of speech. With the publication of this edition, both locus of interest and sphere of influence may be expected to enlarge, for *The Philosophy of Rhetoric* is actually what its title announces, a *philosophy* of rhetoric in the broad sense, not a textbook on the art of speaking. All students of the theory of language and of the language arts should find it provocative and fruitful both as a treatment of rhetorical phenomena, ranging from sentence structure to tragic pleasure,

1. *A History of Criticism and Literary Taste in Europe* (3 vols.; New York: Dodd, Mead, and Co., 1905), II, 470.
2. Warren Guthrie, "The Development of Rhetorical Theory in America, 1635–1850," *Speech Monographs,* XV (1948), 61–71.

and as a model of the purposes and productions of a philosophical rhetorician.

The Rev. Dr. George Campbell was a clergyman and theologian of the Church of Scotland, a teacher and principal of Aberdeen's Marischal College, and a rhetorician. Moreover, in both learning and temper he was a philosopher. The fact that he wrote the *Rhetoric* as a philosopher, or as a philosophical rather than a practical rhetorician, is significant, because the book's distinctive contributions to the literature on rhetoric result from the encounter of a philosophic mind with materials in the discipline of rhetoric. Campbell permitted fundamental issues of metaphysics and epistemology to spill over into the theory of rhetoric; he believed, furthermore, that discussions of rhetorical phenomena are fragmentary when they lack philosophical explication. As a result, questions concerning the existence of external objects, the kinds of mental contents, the possibility of certain knowledge, the sources of knowledge, and the laws of both thought and feeling are entwined in his book with questions concerning belief and persuasion, method in discourse, logical and ethical proof, language and style, tragic pleasure, laughter, qualities of effective discourse, and other elements of rhetoric. *The Philosophy of Rhetoric* should be understood as a manifestation of Campbell's purposes and materials and insights as a philosopher of rhetoric.

Life and Writings

Born at Aberdeen on the 25th of December 1719, George Campbell was the youngest son among the six children of Rev. Colin Campbell and Margaret Walker Campbell. He received his first years of education at the grammar school in Aberdeen and later received instruction at Marischal College in the same town. Intending to pursue a career in law, he served an apprenticeship in Edinburgh until he became convinced that the church rather than the law was his calling. In 1741, while still an apprentice in Edinburgh, he began attending lectures on divinity. Shortly thereafter he returned to Aberdeen and began studies at both King's and Marischal College to prepare for the ministry. He was licensed to preach in 1746 and two years later secured a pastorate at Banchory Ternan, a town seventeen miles west of Aberdeen. There he remained for nine years, during which time he married Grace Farquharson. Campbell returned to Aberdeen as a minister in 1757, and two years later became Principal of Marischal College. In addition to this office, he was elected Professor of Divinity in 1771, replacing Alexander Gerard who had transferred to King's. He continued to preach regularly and to serve as both Principal and Professor of Divinity until 1795 when he resigned his positions after a period of ill health and certain decline. He died in 1796.

The move from Banchory Ternan to Aberdeen in 1757 was a significant event in Campbell's career. His new position as an Aberdeen minister was an immediate professional advancement, one which opened the way for later appointments as Principal and Professor at Marischal College. At Marischal, he gained stature as an educator and theologian; in the course of his responsibilities there, he prepared lectures on theology, church history, and pulpit eloquence which were published after his death. Moreover, his move to Aberdeen marked the beginning of several years of intensive philosophical thinking and writing, the fruits of which were *A Dissertation on Miracles* (1762) and *The Philosophy of Rhetoric* (1776). Although Campbell had written the first two chapters of the *Rhetoric* by 1750 (this he asserts in the Preface), he did nothing more until 1757. After the move to Aberdeen, he resumed his writing in earnest, producing in five years not only the remainder of Book One and probably a portion of Book Two, but also the whole of the *Dissertation on Miracles.* The *Dissertation,* a lengthy 288 pages in the original edition, was his first major work. In it he boldly attacked an essay penned by David Hume,[3] whose reputation as historian, essayist, and philosopher was unequalled at that time in Britain. The *Dissertation* firmly established Campbell's reputation as an able philosopher, disputant, and defender of religion.

Campbell's particular intellectual environment in Aberdeen both stimulated and influenced his thought and writing. In 1758 he had helped found the Philosophical Society of Aberdeen, the organization he identifies in his Preface as a "private literary society" whose members induced him to resume work on the *Rhetoric.* Besides Campbell, the Society's most active members were Thomas Reid, John Stewart, Alexander Gerard, John Gregory, and James Beattie. Total membership from 1758 to 1773 was fifteen, although the usual complement was seven or eight; as some members departed, others were added. Campbell was an active member during the fifteen years of the Society's existence. The purpose of the Society was defined in its Rules: the group would meet twice monthly to hear and comment on a "discourse" presented by one of its members or to discuss a "question" formally proposed at a previous meeting.

> The subject of the discourses and questions shall be philosophical. . . . And philosophical matters are understood to comprehend: every principle of science which may be deduced by just and lawful induction from the phenomena either of the human mind or of the material world; all observations and experiments that may furnish materials for

3. Hume's essay, "Of Miracles," originally intended as a part of *A Treatise of Human Nature* (1739–40), appeared as Section X of *An Enquiry Concerning Human Understanding* (1748).

> such induction; the examination of false schemes of philosophy and false methods of philosophizing; the subserviency of philosophy to arts, the principles they borrow from it, and the means of carrying them to their perfection.[4]

The last lines of this definition clearly allow discourses and questions on the art of eloquence, and Campbell provided them. Nearly all of the papers which later formed *The Philosophy of Rhetoric* were prepared as discourses for the Society. Born in the same manner were several other works, most notably Thomas Reid's *An Inquiry into the Human Mind on the Principles of Common Sense* (1764)[5] and James Beattie's *Essay on the Nature and Immutability of Truth; in Opposition to Sophistry and Scepticism* (1770).[6] Of the fifteen members of the Society, these three were to achieve wide reputation: Campbell for his *Dissertation* and *Rhetoric,* Reid for his *Inquiry,* and Beattie for his *Essay on Truth.* It is true of each man that his first important work resulted from inquiries stimulated by participation in the Philosophical Society. Furthermore, it is true of each man that he wrote his first work in response to the philosophy of David Hume.

Hume was not a member of the Society, but his writings—chiefly *A Treatise of Human Nature* (1739–40) and later philosophical essays—provided its members with materials for debate and criticism, praise and censure. In March 1763, Reid addressed a letter to Hume, part of which indicates the Society's estimation of Hume and its indebtedness to him.

> Your Friendly Adversaries Drs Campbell & Gerard as well as Dr Gregory return their compliments to you respectfully. A little Philosophical Society here of which all the three are members, is much indebted to you for its entertainment. Your company would, although we are all good Christians, be more acceptable than that of Saint Athanasius. And since we cannot have you upon the bench, you are brought

4. Minutes of the Philosophical Society of Aberdeen, 1758–1771; Aberdeen University Library, MS 539. To this document are appended the Rules. (On microfilm in the library of the State University of Iowa.) This document breaks off abruptly in the middle of an account of the meeting of March 12, 1771 and therefore fails to report the meetings which occurred during the remainder of 1771 and the two following years.

5. A. Campbell Fraser compared Reid's "discourses" with his *Inquiry,* "in which I find them mostly embodied." Fraser's *Thomas Reid* (Edinburgh: Oliphant Anderson and Ferrier, 1898), p. 52.

6. Beattie, writing to Sir William Forbes in 1766, said that he recently delivered a "discourse" which furnished groundwork for a major work, two-thirds finished. He referred probably to the *Essay on the Nature and Immutability of Truth.* Margaret Forbes, *Beattie and His Friends* (Westminster: Archibald Constable and Co., Ltd., 1904), p. 42.

> oftener than any other man to the bar, accused and defended with great zeal but without bitterness. If you write no more in morals politicks or metaphysics, I am affraid we shall be at a loss for subjects.[7]

Reid later identified Hume as the philosopher who caused him to suspect and reject the philosophical framework he had previously embraced and who stimulated him to original efforts in philosophy.[8] Campbell publicly expressed his indebtedness to Hume in the Advertisement to the *Dissertation on Miracles:* "I have not only been much entertained and instructed by his works; but, if I am possessed of any talent in abstract reasoning, I am not a little indebted to what he hath written on *human nature,* for the improvement of that talent."[9] The most striking evidence of Hume's influence on Campbell, however, is to be found in *The Philosophy of Rhetoric* itself. Campbell's philosophy and his theory of human nature, both of which profoundly affect his treatment of rhetoric, are drawn mainly from Hume.[10] Thus, the philosophy of Hume was pre-eminent not only in the private discussions of the Society's members, but in their public utterances as well. Hume, who was in a sense the absent member of the Philosophical Society of Aberdeen, was the leading figure in the intellectual environment in which Campbell conceived and tested nearly the whole of his *Philosophy of Rhetoric.*

Three of Campbell's major works were published during his lifetime. The first two were *Dissertation on Miracles* and *The Philosophy of Rhetoric.* The third was *New Testament, Gospels: The Four Gospels Translated from the Greek, with Preliminary Dissertations and Notes* (1789). Three sets of lectures to students of Marischal College were published posthumously in two volumes: *Lectures on Ecclesiastical History* (1800) and *Lectures on Systematic Theology and Pulpit Eloquence* (1807). To the first volume George Skene Keith added "Some Account of the Life and Writings of Dr. George Campbell," which is an invaluable source. Campbell's additional publications consist of a number of sermons and addresses.

Campbell's conduct in literary disputes plus evidence from his writings and from Keith's biography furnish insight into

7. J. Y. T. Greig, *The Letters of David Hume* (2 vols.; Oxford: The Clarendon Press, 1932), I, 376, n. 4.
8. See Reid's Dedication to *An Inquiry into the Human Mind* (2nd ed.; Edinburgh: A. Kincaid and J. Bell, 1765), p. v.
9. *A Dissertation on Miracles: Containing, An Examination of the Principles Advanced by David Hume, Esq. in an Essay on Miracles* (3rd ed.; Philadelphia: Thomas Dobson, 1790), p. vi.
10. See Lloyd F. Bitzer, "The Lively Idea: A Study of Hume's Influence on George Campbell's *Philosophy of Rhetoric*" (unpublished Ph.D. dissertation, State University of Iowa, 1962).

his character. As a clergyman he was a moderate, shunning extreme dogmatism on the one hand and rationalistic theology on the other. In matters of both religion and philosophy he was cautious in his own views and tolerant of the reasoned opinions of others. In conversation he was pleasant and entertaining, but sometimes lapsed into periods of reflective absence. In Keith's firsthand account of Campbell's character are these comments:

> He was uncommonly liberal to those who differed from him in religious opinions; so liberal, indeed, that he did not approve of considering some modern writers as infidels, who profess to be Christians, though they have written rather freely on certain articles. . . . He proceeded, with great caution, in forming his own opinion upon any subject, and without suspecting the veracity, or good sense, of others, took nothing upon trust; but even in matters of science, wished to consider every thing himself. [xliv] . . . The most prominent feature, in his moral character, was his love of truth. No man was ever more strict in speaking truth; and the least deviation from it was accompanied with the strongest marks of his disapprobation. [xlvii]

The Philosophy of Rhetoric

Campbell's definitions of rhetoric, or eloquence, clearly indicate the breadth of his conception of the art. According to one definition, rhetoric is "that art or talent by which the discourse is adapted to its end." According to another, it is "the grand art of communication, not of ideas only, but of sentiments, passions, dispositions, and purposes." At one point, Campbell refers to rhetoric as "the art of speaking, in the extensive sense in which I employ the term." (xlix, 1) By these definitions, any instance of written or oral discourse which aims to inform, convince, please, move, or persuade and which has as its communicative substance some passion, idea, sentiment, disposition, or purpose is an instance of rhetorical discourse. The materials of rhetoric consist of all the principles, concepts, rules, and techniques by means of which discourse of nearly every kind may be managed and thereby improved. Rhetoric, therefore, is a general art of discourse; it comprehends tragedy as well as private conversation, poetry as well as oratory, the purest expository writing as well as the most sublime oral persuasion.

Although it contains lengthy discussions of rhetorical materials, *The Philosophy of Rhetoric* is not a definitive treatment of the art of rhetoric. Hugh Blair, in his *Lectures on Rhetoric and Belles Lettres* (1783), treats many more rhetorical topics than does Campbell, who is not concerned primarily with practical rhetoric. Campbell's central subject matter is the philosophy of rhetoric, and he generally discusses those rhetorical materials which permit an exposition and confirmation of his views.

In his Introduction, Campbell says that the philosophy of rhetoric is the fourth and ultimate stage in the development of the art. The first and primitive stage consists of whatever rules and procedures a man may derive from an awareness of "what operates on his own mind, aided by the sympathetic feelings, and by that practical experience of mankind, which individuals, even in the rudest state of society, are capable of acquiring." The second stage marks the beginning of rhetoric as a critical science, for in this stage men distinguish types of discourse and arguments. In the third stage, practical rhetoric is formalized and perfected through scientific investigation.

> [Men] compare, with diligence, the various effects, favourable or unfavourable, of those attempts, carefully taking into consideration every attendant circumstance by which the success appears to have been influenced, and by which one may be enabled to discover to what particular purpose each attempt is adapted, and in what circumstances only to be used.

These three stages comprise practical rhetoric, which provides subject matter for the philosophy of rhetoric. The two are not coincident, however, and the primary task of the philosophical rhetorician does not consist in repeating the rules for invention, disposition, style, and delivery or in proposing major innovations in these traditional branches of rhetoric. Campbell had only a peripheral interest in practical rhetoric; he had little new to say about traditional rhetorical materials and maintained that the moderns made little or no improvement over the ancients in this area. His interest lay in the fourth and final stage, the philosophy of rhetoric, which he described as a "new country" explored only partially by a few of his predecessors. (l–li)

The philosophy of rhetoric, in Campbell's view, is the area of relationships between the art of rhetoric and its foundation-science, human nature, a new "science" in the eighteenth century. To illuminate this area is the philosophical rhetorician's task; to establish the art of rhetoric in the science of human nature is his ultimate purpose. In order to do this, Campbell intended to discover in human nature the principles which *explain* the art of rhetoric; he thus began with the conviction that the science of man supplies the principles by which rhetorical phenomena are fully explained. This does not mean that the philosopher of rhetoric establishes the soundness of rhetorical rules, techniques, and procedures—

the materials of practical rhetoric—by deducing them from the science of human nature. On the contrary, Campbell insisted that evidence for the soundness of such materials comes from the actual practice of the art and from the observations of rhetoricians who function at the third—the scientific—stage of rhetoric. To prove that the presence of certain conditions hinders or helps a particular kind of discourse is the task of the scientific rhetorician; to explain why the facts are so, is the task of the philosopher of rhetoric. The exploration of human nature, which Campbell considered an essential part of his task, consists chiefly in the exploration of the human mind; the leading explanatory principles of rhetoric are therefore principles of mind. The union of rhetoric and human nature and the central task of the philosophy of rhetoric are clearly implied in this declaration of purpose from the Preface:

> It is his purpose in this Work, on the one hand, to exhibit, he does not say, a correct map, but a tolerable sketch of the human mind; and, aided by the lights which the Poet and the Orator so amply furnish, to disclose its secret movements, tracing its principal channels of perception and action, as near as possible, to their source: and, on the other hand, from the science of human nature, to ascertain with greater precision, the radical principles of that art, whose object it is, by the use of language, to operate on the soul of the hearer, in the way of informing, convincing, pleasing, moving, or persuading. [xliii]

As this declaration indicates, Campbell aimed not only to uncover in human nature the principles that explain rhetoric, but also to use rhetorical data in his exploration of human nature. Throughout his book, the art of rhetoric and the science of human nature are made to illumine one another. Indeed, his exploration of human nature is hardly distinguishable at times from his treatment of rhetorical materials. In the second chapter of Book One, for example, the treatment of wit, humor, and ridicule serves two purposes: it explains the kinds of wit, humor, and ridicule and their manner of operation; at the same time, it confirms a very important doctrine in the theory of human nature—the doctrine of the association of ideas. Similarly, his discussion of tragic pleasure in Chapter Eleven of Book One serves not only to explain a perplexing point but also to confirm two elements of his theory—that the passions, like ideas, are connected by principles of association, and that the compelling power of ideas and passions is a function of their close relationship to impressions of sense. Some of Campbell's discussions—especially Chapters Five and Seven in Book One—are primarily attempts to uncover the principles of human nature. Other chapters—several in Book Two and all in Book Three—clearly illustrate Campbell's use of the principles of human nature to explain a variety of topics in rhetoric.

The view that a principal function of philosophy is to ground the arts and sciences in human nature was not unique with Campbell; he shared it with many eighteenth century writers. Lord Kames announces in the early pages of *Elements of Criticism* (1762) that his task is "to examine the sensitive branch of human nature, to trace the objects that are naturally agreeable, as well as those that are naturally disagreeable; and by these means to discover, if we can, what are the genuine principles of the fine arts." [11] Hume—whose *A Treatise of Human Nature* strongly influenced numerous theorists including Campbell and the other major Scottish critics, Kames and Blair—had claimed that the study of human nature is the condition of success in all fields of learning. In the Introduction to the *Treatise* he says,

> Here then is the only expedient, from which we can hope for success in our philosophical researches, to leave the tedious lingring method, which we have hitherto followed, and instead of taking now and then a castle or village on the frontier, to march up directly to the capital or center of these sciences, to human nature itself; which being once masters of, we may every where else hope for an easy victory.[12]

Hume understood this assault to be no less than revolutionary; the result would be "a compleat system of the sciences, built on a foundation almost entirely new." Campbell was less vocal in his enthusiasm, but he was not less confident of his philosophic endeavor and its potential result—the perfection of rhetoric, or eloquence, through its relationship to its foundation, human nature.

Campbell, in presenting his views, leaves much for his reader to supply. The significance of a number of discussions and the purpose of others are not immediately apparent. Moreover, no section or chapter contains a definitive statement of his philosophical framework and theory of human nature. There is, of course, an explanation for these inconveniences. All but three of the essays which comprise his book were prepared not for public reading but for presentation to members of the Philosophical Society of Aberdeen—men who were well acquainted with Campbell's views and able to supply the ideas which render his discussions completely intelligible. Most modern readers will find that some understanding of Campbell's philosophy, and of the theory of human nature

11. *Elements of Criticism* (New York: F. J. Huntington and Co., 1838), p. 13.
12. *A Treatise of Human Nature,* ed. L. A. Selby-Bigge (Oxford: The Clarendon Press, 1888), p. xx.

which is so prominent in that philosophy, is a prerequisite to full understanding and appreciation of his work.

Two of Campbell's general aims as a philosopher of rhetoric have been identified already: (1) He wanted to provide a theory of human nature; (2) he wanted to discover in human nature the explanatory principles of rhetoric and thus establish the art of rhetoric upon human nature. Attending these two purposes are others. (3) He hoped to develop a systematic theory of rhetoric, one which would provide consistent and interdependent explanations of rhetorical materials based on a single set of explanatory principles. (4) Furthermore, he intended to save rhetoric from the scorn of philosophers from Plato to Locke who regarded rhetoric as lacking the conditions of science or art. Locke, whom Campbell studied and respected, had characterized rhetoric as "that powerful instrument of error and deceit,"[13] a judgment shared with other men. Campbell resolved to elevate rhetoric, not only by establishing it as a discipline with roots in the new science of man, but, what is even more important, by providing machinery which, at least in theory, would tend to promote good discourse and hinder bad, thus encouraging truth and forthrightness and discouraging deceit and equivocation. (5) Finally, he aimed to elevate rhetoric in another, very specific way. For centuries rhetoric had been treated as an art which, although useful, is inferior to the art of the logician or scientist. Campbell attempted to provide a philosophical framework in which rhetoric and logic (and scientific inquiry) share the same methodology. In his view, the logical machinery of modern sciences does not differ in kind from the machinery of rhetorical proof.

Philosophy and Human Nature

GENERAL FEATURES OF CAMPBELL'S PHILOSOPHY

Campbell's philosophy was shaped by his response to two fundamental questions. The first is a question of metaphysics: What is the nature of the objects with which we are acquainted and about which we possess knowledge? The second is one of method: What are the processes by which we gain this acquaintance and knowledge? The following broad features of Campbell's response constitute a general and preliminary description of his philosophy.

Phenomenalism. His answer to the first question is that we are acquainted only with our own mental contents; we do not know external and independent objects. He does claim that we are compelled by nature to believe in the existence of an external and material world (40), but this view does not conflict with his analysis of sensation. Acts of sensing—the

13. *Essay Concerning Human Understanding*, III, X, 34.

source of all knowledge about matters of fact—have subjective mental contents as their objects; the contents of sensation, he says, are "my own present feelings, whose essence consists in being felt, and of which I am at present conscious" (41). Sensation, then, does not reveal external objects. Those things with which we are directly acquainted and from which all of our knowledge of fact is generated are mental entities, or perceptions.

Empiricism. Campbell's answer to the second question is that we acquire knowledge of real objects (things such as books, animals, and trees in contradistinction to mathematical statements, for instance) by direct inspection of particulars (mental entities) and by inference from particulars via the natural process of experience (47–48). The method of observation and experience (terms defined technically) is the method of science (52–53); use of this method, he implies, places him in company with the empirics rather than with the visionaries, or rationalists (xlvi–xlvii). He rejects the rival method of demonstration, employed by such rationalists as Descartes, Leibnitz, and Spinoza, on the ground that it fails to produce knowledge of real objects (40, 42); he rejects syllogistic logic on the same ground (61–70). All significant knowledge originates from the mind's direct acquaintance with particles, rather than with concepts or general truths; all inferential knowledge about real objects is constructed from particles through the process of experience, rather than through deduction by means of either strict demonstration or the syllogism.

Scepticism. Whether Campbell's scepticism preceded his phenomenalism and empiricism is a purely conjectural point; whichever feature came first, the three are comfortable together. His scepticism functions in all of his inquiries to assure careful scrutiny of assumptions and beliefs and utmost caution in accepting propositions. Furthermore, it encourages consistent use of the method of observation and experience, the logical method which best withstands sceptical criticism. Scepticism is apparent in Campbell's view that the mind never knows external objects and in his suspicion of pure reason as an instrument of knowledge; at one point, it is used in a specific and very important way—to destroy the efficacy of demonstration. Its ultimate expression, however, is found in Campbell's admission that the "common sense axioms"—general principles of knowledge and being—may be the opposite of what he and all mankind believe them to be (41).

Sensationalism. Sensation, the source of all knowledge about real objects, is also the source of that power or energy which, as a constituent of perceptions, compels in the mind some degree of attention or assent. The power of general conclusions to produce conviction results from the combined power of the sense perceptions which serve as evidence; the energy of a piece of fiction derives primarily from its likeness to impressions of sense; the compelling quality of any single idea varies according to its close or remote relation to sensation. Campbell usually calls this felt quality or energy in ideas "vivacity."

Naturalism. The study of human nature is very important not only because it yields principles which underlie rhetoric, but also because nature—especially human nature—confers values on whatever springs from it or accords with it. A "natural" emotional response is a correct response. The good practitioner of rhetoric is likely to communicate more effectivly than the deceiver because the former's processes of communication are "natural" and the latter's are "unnatural." The mental processes which operate instinctively to produce judgments are nearly infallible because they are "natural." Human nature, rather than reason, assures the truth of common sense axioms and supplies the machinery which makes the world of perceptions an intelligible one. Nature, rather than reason, finally overcomes the objections of radical scepticism.

THEORY OF HUMAN NATURE

Campbell's theory of human nature—actually a theory of mind—exhibits the foregoing general features. A statement of the main elements of his theory should be prefaced, perhaps, with the observation that his interest in the science of mind cannot be considered mere interest in the relationship between rhetoric and psychology. For a phenomenalist such as Campbell, the sum total of knowable reality is indistinguishable from the world of perceptions; the exploration of reality is the same as the exploration of perceptions, their relations, qualities, and behavior. The study of the mind and its contents is, in a very significant sense, the study of everything that can be known through natural processes.

Mental Contents. In his exploration of human nature, Campbell begins with entities which we cannot question—perceptions immediately present to the mind. He divides these into three classes. Sensations, the first class, reveal either internal states such as pleasures and pains, or qualities, such as color and figure, in seemingly external objects. All other legitimate perceptions originate in sensations. Ideas of memory, the second class, are derived exclusively from sensations; they are "prints that have been left by sensible impressions" (47). Ideas of imagination, the third class, are complex ideas whose constituents are derived from memory and ultimately from sensation; as totalities, however, they are not copies of either sensations or ideas of memory, and they may or may not correspond to observable objects. This class is extremely broad; it includes ideas of golden cities and centaurs—unreal things never observed—as well as all judgments about the real existence of things not presently sensed or remembered. All men are mortal, someone is knocking on the door, this page would burn if touched by a flame, a man is circling the earth in a space capsule—these and similar judgments express ideas of imagination, complex ideas neither sensed nor remembered. Campbell mentions one other class of perceptions, actually a pseudo-class. It consists of abstract or general ideas, which he analyzes as particular ideas employed by the mind to represent classes (260–61).

Vivacity. If we perceive a pencil on the desk, is this perception a sensation, an idea of memory, or an idea of imagination? How can it be identified? Campbell apparently holds that the mind distinguishes among kinds of perceptions by their relative degrees of vivacity. Thus, the perception of the pencil will be identified as a sensation, if such it is, because we feel the compelling degree of vivacity, or liveliness, which accompanies perceptions of sense. Nature has determined that perceptions of sense are accompanied by an almost unmistakable degree of vivacity, ideas of memory by a lesser degree of vivacity, and ideas of imagination by the least degree of vivacity.

Precisely what is vivacity? We must answer from our own experience, for Campbell never defines it, perhaps because as a feeling it is impossible to define. He remarks that to define the difference between "those lively signatures of memory, which command an unlimited assent, and those fainter traces which raise opinion only, or even doubt, is perhaps impracticable; but no man stands in need of such assistance to enable him in fact to distinguish them, for the direction of his own judgment and conduct" (41). Campbell uses the following terms to signify the quality of vivacity: liveliness, force, energy, brightness, brilliancy, steadiness, and lustre. He describes ideas lacking vivacity or possessing it in small degree as faint, languid, or feeble. Although difficult to define, vivacity is unmistakable in its effects. It commands attention and is therefore prerequisite to nearly every significant mental activity (73, 75). It arouses emotion: "passion must be awakened by communicating lively ideas of the object" (81). Vivacity is also largely responsible for assent, or belief (73).[14] Because they possess strong vivacity, sensations readily command assent from the mind. Most ideas of imagination do not secure assent readily, since they possess little or no vivacity. Sometimes, however, they do require

14. Belief and vivacity, although closely related, are not identical: vivacity is usually a factor in belief, but either can occur in the absence of the other. See pp. 73–74 where Campbell chides Hume for saying that "Belief consisteth in the liveliness of our ideas."

belief as readily as sensations because they somehow become infused with vivacity: as energy passes from one body to another, so vivacity apparently transfers from lively ideas of sense or memory to languid ideas of imagination. The methods by which ideas of imagination can be infused with vivacity and thereby made to compel attention and induce belief are of great interest to Campbell. The reason for his interest? Discourse deals almost entirely with ideas of imagination.

The Association of Ideas. Of the multitudes of perceptions that appear in consciousness, some vanish, others reappear frequently, a few reappear with perfect regularity; some are vague and fleeting, others generate a degree of attention, a few overpower the mind. These perceptions are of three kinds—sensations, ideas of memory, and ideas of imagination; furthermore, the degree of attention and belief which they require of the mind is determined chiefly by the vivacity they possess. Before Campbell can progress further in his study of mind and of nature, he must attempt to establish general laws governing the occurrence of perceptions. If there were no observable patterns or relationships among perceptions, significant generalizations and predictions—both of which require that relevant perceptions occur regularly—would be impossible, knowledge would be limited to acquaintance with particulars only, and the sequence of perceptions (hence, our universe) would be chaotic. We know from introspection, of course, that perceptions do not occur randomly; although some perceptions seem to be loosely joined, others seem inseparable. The philosopher of mind is vitally interested in the patterns among perceptions because they suggest the presence of laws or principles which govern the association of ideas and which do no less than hold together the world of ideas. As Hume aptly remarked in his *Abstract,* the natural principles of association are really "*to us* the cement of the universe." [15]

Although a number of relations among ideas are mentioned by Campbell (76–77, 81–90, 258), the three most important natural principles of association are resemblance, contiguity, and causation: the mind tends to associate ideas which are similar, ideas which are contiguous in space or time, and ideas related as causes and effects. Mind passes easily from the idea of a bird to that of an airplane by the principle of resemblance, from the idea of a candle to that of a flame by the associative principle of contiguity, and from the idea of lightning to that of thunder by the principle of causation (and perhaps by the principle of contiguity). These principles are not absolutely binding, of course. The mind is able to join

15. *An Abstract of A Treatise of Human Nature*, reprinted and with introduction by J. M. Keynes and P. Sraffa (Cambridge: The University Press, 1938), p. 32.

with some effort ideas which are dissimilar (the ideas of a candle and of a three-legged stool, for example); it can join ideas that are remote in both space and time; it can conceive of any idea as the cause or effect of any other. These natural principles thus seem to be general tendencies of mind rather than absolute laws of thought.

Experience and Method. Most important of these associative principles is causation, since this relation among ideas is the basis of everything we know *by inference* about real existence. In reasoning properly about things, the mind passes via the causal relation from ideas conceived as causes to ideas conceived as effects of those causes, or vice versa. However, the causal connection is not sensed; that is, ideas do not present themselves as causes or as effects. The causal relation between thunder and lightning, for instance, is not itself perceived; "all that comes under the cognizance of our senses, in the operations either of Nature or of Art, is the causes which precede, and the effects which follow" (366). How, then, does the mind supply the relation? The explanation lies in a natural process of mind which Campbell calls *experience* and which he defines as "the tendency of the mind to associate ideas under the notion of causes, effects, or adjuncts" (50). The mind observes the constant or frequent conjunction of perceptions (x and y); as a result, it acquires a habit or determination to conceive of one (y) when the other (x) is newly given. For example, after numerous observations of the constant conjunction of lightning and thunder, we begin to expect that a present perception of lightning will be followed by a perception of thunder; that is, upon perceiving one member of the pair, we imaginatively perceive the other, which is not actually given. This habit or determination to pass from one perception to the other is the causal relation. The strength of this relation depends upon the number of times we witness a conjunction, the constancy of the conjunction (whether frequent or invariable), and the similarity of the perceptions thought to be repeated—variables which account for the degree of probability afforded by the varieties of experience identified by Campbell. The complete explanation of this process appears under the heading "The Nature and Origin of Experience," in Chapter Five of Book One.

The pervasive influence of experience must not be underestimated. Experience, as the vehicle of all reliable inferences regarding "actual truth, or matter of fact," is the heart of the logical method used by natural sciences—even by natural theology. It is the method of inference which produces nearly all common judgments in everyday life and which underlies logical proof in rhetorical discourse. In other words, it is probably the foundation and unmistakably "the criterion of all moral reasoning whatever" (52). There must be no misconceptions regarding the nature of experience. It is a basically mechanical operation of the mind which functions best—automatically and infallibly—when the mind is least aware of it. Nature controls it as surely as she controls digestion and respiration, and she has given this process of experience (reasoning, "if you please to call it so") to the beasts as well as to man.

This conception of experience acquires added importance when coupled with Campbell's attack both on syllogistic logic and on the rationalists' method of strict demonstration. He maintains that syllogistic logic functions mainly to clarify language. Because it fails to uncover real knowledge, he rejects it. He attacks strict demonstration in two ways: first, he limits it to the realm of abstract ideas and their necessary relations—chiefly to mathematics and geometry (40, 42); second, through his sceptical attack on it (58–61), he actually makes the method of demonstration subservient to moral reasoning and experience. These attacks result in the downfall of both syllogistic logic and strict demonstration as infallible instruments of "actual truth." Experience (and the forms of moral reasoning based upon it) emerges as the fundamental method of inquiry and proof.

Other Elements. Campbell discusses other elements of the theory of mind—among them *sympathy, the association of passions,* and *the view that emotions ultimately determine human conduct.* Sympathy, like experience, is a term which refers to a definite process of mind—that operation by which passion is communicated from one person to another. One person, when he experiences fear, exhibits signs which another perceives; these perceptions trigger fear in the second person. "It is by sympathy we *rejoice with them that rejoice, and weep with them that weep*" (131). Sympathy is universally important because it "attacheth us to the concerns of others" (89). It is important in rhetoric because it is "one main engine by which the orator operates on the passions" (96). The doctrine that passions (emotions), like ideas, are associated appears in Campbell's discussion of tragic pleasure. He uses it as part of his explanation of tragic pleasure, but the doctrine itself is a basic one. The final element in Campbell's theory of mind to be mentioned here is the view that feeling, not reason, ultimately rules human conduct. Moral reasoning does function in discovering means, but the ends of conduct are determined by feeling. Emotional responses to objects both great and small may be described as natural or unnatural, but not as reasonable or unreasonable. Campbell maintains that it is not "by any reasoning we are ever taught that such an object ought to awaken such a passion. This we must learn originally from feeling, not from argument" (92, 80). Strictly speaking, there are no rational appeals in rhetorical persuasion.

Of the philosophers who might have influenced Campbell, only one expounded a correspondent philosophy and theory of human nature. In Hume's *Treatise* can be found Campbell's division of mental contents, the association of ideas, the principle of vivacity, the process of experience, plus other elements in the theory of human nature. On philosophical matters, Campbell cites Hume more often than he cites any other writer. Even his terminology at times is Hume's: For instance, Campbell says, "There is an attraction or association among the passions, as well as among the ideas of the mind" (129); Hume, in the *Treatise,* had said, "There is an attraction or association among impressions, as well as among ideas" (283). Abundant evidence indicates that Hume was the primary influence on Campbell's philosophy, including his philosophy of rhetoric.

The Theory of Rhetoric

The core of Campbell's theory of rhetoric is a cluster of notions, derived from his theory of human nature, which may be expressed in three propositions and accompanying explanations.

1. *The vivacity or liveliness of ideas is the quality primarily responsible for attention and belief.* Vivacity (liveliness, energy, force, brilliancy) is a felt quality in ideas to which we give attention and in most ideas which we believe; the amount of vivacity in an idea chiefly determines the degree of attention or belief which it compels. As a general rule, effective rhetorical discourse must compel attention and belief. Therefore, the rhetor—whether he proposes to inform, convince, please, arouse passion, or persuade—must communicate ideas which feel lively and vivid to his hearers or readers. Vivacity must permeate discourse; the effectiveness of nearly all instances of rhetorical discourse depends upon its presence. Vivacity, or the lively idea, is without doubt the key concept in Campbell's theory of rhetoric—the concept which fixes the character of his theory.

2. *Of the kinds of perceptions, sensations are typically most vivid, ideas of memory are less vivid, and ideas of imagination are least vivid.* The ideas that rhetors attempt to communicate are usually ideas of imagination for the hearers or readers (often, too, for the rhetor). Sensations cannot be communicated directly; a moment after entering consciousness, they actually become ideas of memory. Ideas of memory are occasionally communicated by the rhetor, but ideas of imagination are his chief stock. The tragedian's presentation, the statesman's expression of his country's destiny, the crusader's description of future blessings or evils, the physicist's account of infinitesimal matter and energy—these are not objects of sensation or memory for the audience. Rhetorical

discourse, then, is typically imaginative, a fact which creates the central and persistent problem of practical rhetoric: How can the rhetor infuse vivacity into ideas of imagination, which possess the least natural vivacity? He must find ways to make his ideas as lively and vivid as sensations or ideas of memory, because ideas of imagination, when given the power (vivacity) of sensible impressions or ideas of memory, will tend to compel attention, induce belief, and arouse passion (81, 119).

3. *"There is an attraction or association among . . . the ideas of the mind."* Another element of the theory of human nature—the doctrine of the association of ideas—is involved in several methods given by Campbell for infusing vivacity into ideas. It seems to be Campbell's view (it undoubtedly was Hume's) that not only do the laws of association govern or describe the behavior of ideas, but they also provide routes for the transfer of energy. Resemblance, contiguity, causation, and other relations among ideas can become circuits through which vivacity transfers from an already lively idea to a languid one. The remembrance of a childhood home is not only aroused upon seeing a photograph of the home (by the principle of resemblance), but the present lively perception (of the photograph) also leads to a more lively and vivid remembrance. A present sensation of blinding lightning not only leads to an imaginative perception of thunder, but the present sensation transfers such a quantity of vivacity to the imaginative idea that we are compelled to predict with absolute confidence that the sensation of thunder is imminent. If typically languid ideas of imagination—the usual stuff of discourse—are enlivened by relating them to perceptions which already possess vivacity, then the rhetor's success largely depends upon discovering and employing methods which will enliven his ideas through their relationship with other lively perceptions.

The rhetorical topics in Book One concern ideas, not their mode of expression. Books Two and Three deal with the expression of ideas through language. According to Campbell, we learn a language in the same manner that we learn about things—through experience. Knowledge of the connection between words and their referents is the product of observing the frequent or constant conjunction of these objects (258). This word-idea relation is crucial, because the communication of lively ideas requires finding in language the words which stand for the ideas, although the possibilities for failure are numerous. Such faults as barbarism, solecism, and impropriety impair this relation and hinder the communication of lively ideas; upon removal of these faults, discourse exhibits "purity." Such faults as obscurity, double meaning, and unintelligibility also destroy the relation between language and thought; upon their removal, discourse exhibits "perspicuity." Purity and perspicuity, the chief subjects of Book Two, are prerequisites for compelling discourse; their presence does not assure it, but their absence prevents it. Finally, the relation between language and thought is itself a source of energy, or vivacity. Ideas of imagination may be enlivened not only through their relationship with other already vivid ideas, but through stylistic devices as well. Campbell treats style as exclusively functional. Skillfully employed, it serves not merely to clothe thought but rather to infuse energy into discourse.

One or more of the foregoing elements of Campbell's theory underlie virtually all his discussions of rhetorical topics. For instance, beneath his analysis of wit, humor, and ridicule lies the doctrine of the association of ideas. Association, particularly the causal relation, and the principle of vivacity underlie his explanation of experience, the logical method that generates lively ideas. Campbell asserts that the syllogism operates in opposition to the production of vivacity, and consequently in opposition to belief. Two very important discussions in Chapter Seven of Book One are Campbell's analysis of persuasion and his enumeration of seven "circumstances which are chiefly instrumental in operating on the passions." The communication of "lively and glowing ideas" is essential in persuasion, and the seven "circumstances" are ways to enliven ideas by relating them to other ideas which already possess vivacity. His explanation of tragic pleasure (Chapter Eleven, Book One) is based on the doctrine of the association of passions, and also upon his view that tragedy, like other forms of "oratory," must present objects which produce in the mind so much vivacity that they approximate reality. Both association and experience underlie his theory of signs (256–60) and his standard of language usage. Book Three contains the most clear-cut illustration of Campbell's application of his theory: the entire book is devoted to explaining how lively ideas are produced through the choice, number, and arrangement of words, and through the use of connectives.

Some important constituents of Campbell's theory of rhetoric have been incorporated into the works of later rhetoricians and are well known to students of rhetoric: his classification of the ends of rhetoric (informing, convincing, pleasing, moving, persuading) and the manner in which these ends serve one another; his statement of factors for the analysis of discourse (in terms of the communicator, audience, subject, occasion, and end); his view concerning the relation of rhetoric to logic, the science of thought, and to grammar, the science of language; finally, his definition of rhetoric and his broad conception of the art.

Campbell's theory of rhetoric has three major deficiencies.

in some detail by the editor; a single asterisk indicates that libraries or private owners provided information permitting collation on selected items.

** A	1776	London. 2 vols. W. Strahan; and T. Cadell, in the Strand; and W. Creech at Edinburgh. I: xv, 511. II: vi, 445.
** B	1801	London. 2 vols. A. Strahan, T. Cadell, Jun. and W. Davies; and William Creech at Edinburgh. I: xvi, xxi, [23]–431. II: vii, 385. This edition is derived from A and does not incorporate Campbell's additions and corrections.
** C	1808	Edinburgh. 2 vols. William Creech, Edinburgh; and T. Cadell and W. Davies, London. I: xvi, 429. II: vi, 420. Campbell's additions and corrections appear for the first time in this edition.
** D	1816	Edinburgh. 2 vols. Archibald Constable & Co. and John Fairbairn (Successor to Mr Creech), Edinburgh; and T. Cadell and W. Davies, London. I: xvi, 429. II: vi, 420. Derived from C. Although editions C and D are similar in pagination, they are not printed from the same plates.
** E	1818	Boston. Wells and Lilly. xii, 445.
** F	1818	Philadelphia. Mitchell, Ames, and White. xii, 445. All collative evidence indicates that editions E and F were printed from the same plates. Derived from C, or from H, I, J, or K (see remarks under K).
** G	1819	Edinburgh. Thomas Turnbull. xii, 566. Derived from D.
** H	(*n.d.*)	Baltimore and Boston. Feilding Lucas, Jun, and P. H. Nicklin, Baltimore; and by T. B. Wait, & Co., Boston. xii, 517.
* I	——	Boston. Thomas B. Wait and Co. xii, 517.
* J	——	Boston and Newburyport. Thomas B. Wait and Co., Boston; and Thomas and Whipple, Newburyport. xii, 517.
* K	——	Boston and Newhaven. Thomas B. Wait and Co., Boston; and Beers and How, Newhaven. xii, 517. Partial collation suggests that one set of plates produced all four Wait editions—H, I, J, K. The editor was unable to find any solid evidence for establishing the year of publication of these editions, although a copy of H bears on its title page an owner's signature and the year 1819. It is possible that one or more of the Wait editions appeared sometime

before 1818, because collative evidence suggests that E and F (both 1818) may be derived from H, I, J, or K.

** L	1823	Boston. Charles Ewer. 21, [23]–475. Derived from E–F.
** M	1823	London. Seventh Edition. William Baynes and Son. xv, 447. Derived from D or G.
N	1823	London. Abridged for . . . schools . . . by A. Jamieson. G. & W. B. Whittaker. xviii, 401. Authority: Catalog of the British Museum. Another Jamieson abridgment, presumably a reprint of N, appeared in 1833, London. Authority: Catalog of The Advocates Library, Edinburgh.
** O	1834	New York. Jona. Leavitt, Jos. B. Collins, N. & J. White, Geo. Long, G. & C. & H. Carvill, D. Appleton, Peter Hill, Roe Lockwood, Moore & Payne. viii, 396. Derived from E–F or L.
* P	1835	Boston. J. H. Wilkins & Co., Hilliard, Gray, & Co., and Gould, Lincoln, & Kendall. viii, 396. Partial collation suggests that this edition is from the same plates that produced O.
** Q	1838	Oxford. Thomas Tegg and Son, London; Griffin and Co., Glasgow; Tegg and Co., Dublin; and J. & S. A. Tegg, Sydney and Hobart Town. xx, 426. Derived from G.
** R	1841	London. Eleventh Edition. Thomas Tegg. xx, 415. Derived from G or Q.
** S	1841	New York. Harper & Brothers. viii, 396. Derived from O–P.
** T	1844	New York. Harper & Brothers. xii, [13]–435. Derived from S. Reprints of T appeared in the following years.

* 18— (n.d.)	* 1851	* 1858	* 1873
* 1845	* 1854	* 1859	* 1877
* 1846	* 1855	* 1860	* 1881
* 1849	* 1856	** 1868	** 1885
* 1850	* 1857	** 1871	* 1887

** U	1850	London. William Tegg & Co. xvi, 415. Derived from R.
* V	1911	New York and London. Condensed by Grenville Kleiser. Funk & Wagnalls Company. vii, 177. Reprinted in 1912.

NOTES TO THE PRESENT EDITION: CORRECTIONS, ADDITIONS

Corrections

The prototype of the present edition is the 1850 London edition published by William Tegg and Company. It was chosen as the best single-volume edition, when judged by the combined standards of typographical quality and textual accuracy. However, because the Tegg edition is not perfect, users of the present volume will want to correct a number of misprints and word/phrase substitutions and omissions which affect either the sense or the clarity of expression. Accuracy of the text was determined through a line-by-line comparison with the 1808 edition, which was chosen as the base edition because it was prepared with considerable care and was the first to contain Campbell's own corrections and additions. The table of corrections given below will allow the user to mark significant variations between the present edition and the base edition. The table does not record the numerous insignificant variations—in spelling, punctuation, single words (further-farther, hath-has, in-on, etc.), and word arrangement—which in no way affect meaning or clarity.

Page	Para. (or N.)	Line	
xlv	2	4	For "sprung" read "sprang"
xlv	3	9	For "mechanist" read "machinist"
xlvi		3	For "marshalling affairs" read "marshalling of affairs"
xlvii	1	20	For "affected" read "effected"
xlviii	2	13	For "work" read "works"
l	2	9–10	For "is nature" read "is from nature"
li	1	9	For "not only the" read "not only in the"
li	2	11	For "found pretty" read "found a pretty"
3	2	26	For "manner" read "manners"
4	1	5	For "distinguished" read "distinguishing"
4	N. 5	6	For "could not have" read "could have"
7		9	For "at the same" read "in the same"
11	N. 4		For "Canto 3" read "Canto 2"
14	N. 7		For "Canto 2" read "Canto 3"
15	1	3	For "sign" read "signs"

Page	Para. (or N.)	Line	
22		3	For "improvement of the three lighter" read "improvement of morals; of the three lighter"
25		22	For "working our" read "working out"
30		5	For "where is" read "where there is"
31		1	For "a laughter" read "the laughter"
38		5	For "notions and ideas" read "notions or ideas"
46	1	35	For "and this" read "that this"
52		2–3	For "the others noway" read "the other parts noway"
53	3	1	For "that an analogical" read "that analogical"
57	1	7–8	For "produce a similar effect" read "produce one effect"
61	1	13	For "close candid" read "close and candid"
81	2	4	Insert footnote symbol "9" after "consequences"
85	1	3	For "daughter" read "daughters"
104	1	6	For "person" read "persons"
104	2	6	For "great" read "greater"
104	2	18	For "more question" read "more a question"
107	1	1	The word is "circumstance"
107	1	8–9	For "with equal terms" read "on equal terms"
109	2	13	For "cheap rate" read "cheap a rate"
113	1	2	For "sixth" read "seventh"
116	1	29	For "sentiment of feeling" read "sentiment or feeling"
118	1	10	Delete quotation marks after "sorrow"
119	N. 4		For "Chap. vi" read "Chap. vii"
130	2	4	For "present" read "pleasant"
134	1	14	For "some calamitous" read "some present calamitous"
134	2	9	For "predominate" read "predominant"
135	1	6	For "ingredient" read "ingredients"
138		11	For "on by" read "on himself by"
142	1	12	For "language" read "knowledge"
154	N. 7	1	For "to Johnson" read "with Johnson"
165			In the quotation from *Dunciad,* for "hand" read "hang"
181	2	1	For "The first kind of this" read "The first of this kind"
184		2	The word is "conjunction"

Page	Para. (or N.)	Line	
187	2	4	For "particle" read "participle"
188	N. 6		For "Spect. No. 409 T" read "Spect. No. 490 T"
189	2	5	Insert quotation marks after "was"
189	3	2	Insert quotation marks before "Micaiah"
191	1	5	For "of proximity" read "or proximity"
192	1	4	In "latter of a Platonic" delete "of"
193	1	2	For "raiseth" read "ariseth"
194	3	5	Insert footnote symbol "2" after "masters"
194	3	8	For "particle" read "participle"
195	1	11	For "name" read "names"
211	1	16	For "against any" read "against by any"
214	1	1–2	Quotation marks should enclose *"being observed* . . . nouns."
219	1	3–4	For "offends vivacity" read "offends against vivacity"
224		14	The word is "pronoun"
234	2	12	For "of using" read "of using it"
235		13	For "is apt" read "is very apt"
239		37	Insert quotation marks after "debauched"
245	2	16	For "wits" read "wit"
246	1	3	For "extravagant" read "extraordinary"
246	2	6	Insert quotation marks before "If the savour"
249		21	Most editions (the first included) read "tritical essay" rather than "critical essay." *Tritical*—derived from *trite.*
252	N. 1		For "15" read "51"
256	2	19	"In reading" should begin a new sentence
257	N. 2		Note should read "Vol. I, Book i, Part i, Sect. 7."
268	2	3	For "involved" read "revolved"
274	N. 9		Note should read "Book I, Chap. VII, Sect. 4."
289	1	5	After "red-fingered" substitute footnote symbol "6"
295	N. 9	3	Insert quotation marks after "petebat"
296	N. 1	2	For "Malade" read "Medecin"
297		9	Delete "any"
304	3	2	For "mention the method" read "mention, as a method"
306	N. 2		The note should read "Deut. xxxii. 25."
319	1	10	For "from Dryden" read "from the same author." Reference is to Pope.

Page	Para. (or N.)	Line	
339		10	For "is" read "his"
361	1	18	For "light" read "slight"
366		13–14	For "sentest thy" read "sentest forth thy"
373	2	16	For "knave employ" read "knave may employ"
376	3	12	Insert footnote symbol "6" after "May"
398	1	6	For "many, if not" read "many, not"
401	2	14	The word is "artisan"
403	2	7	For "that is" read "that it is"
406		21	For "probably" read "properly"
410	N. 7	2	For "there" read "their"

Campbell's Additions

After the *Rhetoric* was first published (1776), Campbell prepared corrections and additions. For reasons unknown, these did not appear in the second edition (1801). They did appear in the third (1808) and in all subsequent editions. His numerous corrections are mostly stylistic. His additions, few in number, serve usually to elaborate points through examples or explanations. Neither corrections nor additions represent any change in doctrine. The additions—notes, sentences, paragraphs—are identified in the following table.

Page	Para. (or N.)	Line	
21	N. 7		Concluding sentence
101	1		Entire paragraph ("It ought not to be overlooked" etc.)
101	N. 3		Entire note
121	N. 9	4	"Ubi vero atrocitate . . . cap. 3."
141	N. 4		Entire note
148	N. 8		Entire note
155		1	Three sentences ("*Besides* and *beside* . . . as the preposition.")
155	N. 9		Second sentence ("*Holden* . . . meetings.")
165	1	19	The sentence commencing "*Coaction* and coactive"
165	1	29	The sentence commencing "In the same way"
167	2		Entire paragraph ("Nothing can be . . . declivity")
175	N. 2		Entire note

Page	Para. (or N.)	Line	
192	3		Entire paragraph ("To *demean* . . . noble or mean.")
193	1		Entire paragraph ("There is . . . discovery.")
194	1		Entire paragraph ("*Apparent* for *certain* . . . what it is.")
233	N. 7	10	Last seven sentences of the note ("In some instances . . . into books.")
254	N. 6		Entire note
254	N. 7		Entire note
266–68			Two and a half paragraphs commencing near the bottom of page 266 ("There is, in respect") and concluding on page 268, line 10 (". . . with justice be applied.")
296	N. 9	3	Concluding sentence and reference ("In the ancient . . . ed. 2, p. 212.")
357	N. 4	27	Two sentences ("The like may be urged . . . plus attentif.")
363	1		Entire paragraph ("I shall add . . . *to sin.*")
363	N. 1		Entire note

SELECTED BIBLIOGRAPHY

Published and Unpublished Materials on Campbell, on Hume, and on the Period

Bate, Walter Jackson. *From Classic to Romantic: Premises of Taste in Eighteenth-Century England.* Cambridge: Harvard University Press, 1946.

Becker, Carl L. *The Heavenly City of the Eighteenth Century Philosophers.* New Haven: Yale University Press, 1932.

Bitzer, Lloyd F. "A Re-evaluation of Campbell's Doctrine of Evidence," *Quarterly Journal of Speech,* XLVI (April 1960), 135–40.

———. "The Lively Idea: A Study of Hume's Influence on George Campbell's *Philosophy of Rhetoric.*" Unpublished Ph.D. dissertation, State University of Iowa, 1962.

Bryan, W. F. "A Late Eighteenth-Century Purist," *Studies in Philology,* XXIII (1926), 358–70.

Carpenter, Richard. "Three Scottish Critics: An Essay in the History of Ideas." Unpublished Ph.D. dissertation, Boston University, 1951.

Chambers, Robert (ed.). *Biographical Dictionary of Eminent*

Scotsmen. 4 vols. Glasgow, Edinburgh, and London: Blackie and Son, 1855.

Crawford, John. "The Rhetoric of George Campbell." Unpublished Ph.D. dissertation, Northwestern University, 1947.

Edney, Clarence W. "George Campbell's Theory of Logical Truth," *Speech Monographs,* XV (1948), 19–32.

———. "George Campbell's Theory of Public Address." Unpublished Ph.D. dissertation, State University of Iowa, 1946.

Ehninger, Douglas. "George Campbell and the Revolution in Inventional Theory," *Southern Speech Journal,* XV (May 1950), 270–76.

———. "Selected Theories of *Inventio* in English Rhetoric, 1759–1828." Unpublished Ph.D. dissertation, Ohio State University, 1949.

Graves, S. A. *The Scottish Philosophy of Common Sense.* Oxford: The Clarendon Press, 1960.

Hall, Alta. "George Campbell's *Philosophy of Rhetoric.*" Unpublished Ph.D. dissertation, Cornell University, 1934.

Harding, Harold. "English Rhetorical Theory, 1750–1800." Unpublished Ph.D. dissertation, Cornell University, 1937.

Jessop, T. E. *A Bibliography of David Hume and of Scottish Philosophy from Francis Hutcheson to Lord Balfour.* London: A. Brown and Sons, Ltd., 1938.

Laing, B. M. *David Hume.* London: Ernest Benn, Ltd., 1932.

Laird, John. *Hume's Philosophy of Human Nature.* London: Methuen and Co., Ltd., 1932.

McCosh, James. *Scottish Philosophy: Biographical, Expository, Critical, from Hutcheson to Hamilton.* New York: Robert Carter and Brothers, 1875.

Monk, Samuel H. *The Sublime: A Study of Critical Theories in XVIII–Century England.* New York: Modern Language Association of America, 1935.

Mossner, Ernest Campbell. *The Life of David Hume.* Austin: University of Texas Press, 1954.

Passmore, J. A. *Hume's Intentions.* Cambridge: The University Press, 1952.

Sandford, William P. *English Theories of Public Address, 1530–1828.* Columbus, Ohio: H. L. Hedrick, 1931.

Smith, Norman Kemp. *The Philosophy of David Hume.* London: Macmillan and Co., 1941.

Stephen, Leslie. *History of English Thought in the Eighteenth Century.* 2 vols. London: Smith, Elder, and Co., 1902.

Willey, Basil. *The Eighteenth Century Background: Studies on the Idea of Nature in the Thought of the Period.* New York: Columbia University Press, 1941.

Williams, A. M. "The Scottish School of Rhetoric," *Education,* XIII (1892–93), 142–50, 220–27, 281–90, 344–54, 427–34, 488–96.

ACKNOWLEDGMENTS

To the many libraries and individuals who supplied information and who loaned copies of Campbell's *Rhetoric*; to my wife, who helped extensively in collation of texts; to the Graduate School of the University of Wisconsin, which granted summer research time during which most of the work on this edition was completed.

THE

PHILOSOPHY OF RHETORIC.

BY GEORGE CAMPBELL, D.D., F.R.S., EDIN.

PRINCIPAL OF THE MARISCHAL COLLEGE, ABERDEEN.

CERTO SCIANT HOMINES, ARTES INVENIENDI SOLIDAS ET VERAS ADOLESCERE ET INCREMENTA SUMERE CUM IPSIS INVENTIS.

BAC. DE AUGM. SCIENT. L. V. C. S.

NEW EDITION.

LONDON:
WILLIAM TEGG & CO., 85, QUEEN STREET, CHEAPSIDE.
MDCCCL.

PREFACE.

There are several reasons which have induced the Author of the following sheets to give the Public some account of their origin and progress, previously to their coming under its examination. They are a series of Essays closely connected with one another, and written on a subject, in the examination of which he has at intervals employed himself for a considerable part of his life. Considered separately, each may justly be termed a whole, and complete in itself; taken together, they are constituent parts of one work. The Author entered on this inquiry as early as the year 1750; and it was then that the two first Chapters of the first Book were composed. These he intended as a sort of groundwork to the whole. And the judicious Reader will perceive that, in raising the superstructure, he has entirely conformed to the plan there delineated. That first outline he showed soon after to several of his acquaintance, some of whom are still living. In the year 1757 it was read to a private literary society, of which the Author had the honour to be a member. It was a difference in his situation at that time, and his connexion with the gentlemen of that society, some of whom have since honourably distinguished themselves in the republic of letters, that induced him to resume a subject which he had so long laid aside. The three following years all the other chapters of that Book, except the third, the sixth, and the tenth, which have been but lately added (rather as illustrations and confirmations of some parts of the work, than as essential to it) were composed, and submitted to the judgment of the same ingenious friends. All that follows on the subject of Elocution hath also undergone the same review.

Nor has there been any material alteration made on these, or any addition to them, except in a few instances of notes, examples, and verbal corrections, since they were composed.

It is also proper to observe here, that since transcribing the present Work for the press, a manuscript was put into his hands by Doctor Beattie, at the very time that, in order to be favoured with the Doctor's opinion of this performance, the Author gave him the first Book for his perusal. Doctor Beattie's Tract is called *An Essay on Laughter and Ludicrous Writing.* Whilst the Author carefully perused that Essay, it gave him a very agreeable surprise to discover that, on a question so nice and curious, there should, without any previous communication, be so remarkable a coincidence of sentiments in every thing wherein their subjects coincide. A man must have an uncommon confidence in his own faculties (I might have said in his own infallibility) who is not sensibly more satisfied of the justness of their procedure, especially in abstract matters, when he discovers such a concurrence with the ideas and reasoning of writers of discernment. The subject of that piece is indeed Laughter in general, with an inquiry into those qualities in the object by which it is excited. The investigation is conducted with the greatest accuracy, and the theory confirmed and illustrated by such a variety of pertinent examples, as enable us to scrutinize his doctrine on every side, and view it in almost every possible light. He does not enter into the specific characters whereby wit and humour are discriminated, which are the chief considerations here. His design leads him to consider rather those particulars wherein they all agree, than those wherein they differ. He treats of ludicrous objects and ludicrous writing, with a view to account for the superior copiousness and refinement of modern ridicule. When philosophical acuteness is happily united with so great richness of fancy and mastery in language, the obscurity in which a subject was formerly involved vanishes entirely, and a reader unacquainted with all other theories and hypotheses can hardly be persuaded that there was ever any difficulty in the question. But there is one reason to think, that the world will soon be favoured with an opportunity of judging for itself, in regard to the merits of that performance.

One reason, though not the only one, which the Author has for mentioning the manner wherein the composition of this

Work has been conducted, and the time it has taken, is, not to enhance its value with the Public, but to apologize in some measure for that inequality in the execution and the style, with which he is afraid it will be thought chargeable. It is his purpose in this Work, on the one hand, to exhibit, he does not say, a correct map, but a tolerable sketch of the human mind; and, aided by the lights which the Poet and the Orator so amply furnish, to disclose its secret movements, tracing its principal channels of perception and action, as near as possible, to their source: and, on the other hand, from the science of human nature, to ascertain with greater precision, the radical principles of that art, whose object it is, by the use of language, to operate on the soul of the hearer, in the way of informing, convincing, pleasing, moving, or persuading. In the prosecution of a design so extensive, there are two extremes to be shunned. One is, too much abstraction in investigating causes; the other, too much minuteness in specifying effects. By the first, the perspicuity of a performance may be endangered; by the second, its dignity may be sacrificed. The Author does not flatter himself so far as to imagine that he hath succeeded perfectly in his endeavours to avoid either extreme. In a work of this kind it is impossible that every thing should be alike perspicuous to every reader, or that all the parts should be equally elevated. Variety in this respect, as well as in others, is perhaps, on the whole, more pleasing and more instructive than too scrupulous an uniformity. To the eye the interchange of hill and dale beautifies the prospect; and to the ear there is no music in monotony. The Author can truly say, that he has endeavoured, as much as he could, in the most abstruse questions, to avoid obscurity; and in regard to such of his remarks as may be thought too minute and particular, if just, they will not, he hopes, on a re-examination, be deemed of no consequence. Those may serve to illustrate a general observation, which are scarcely worth notice as subjects either of censure or of praise. Nor is there any thing in this Book which, in his opinion, will create even the smallest difficulty to persons accustomed to inquire into the faculties of the mind. Indeed, the much greater part of it will, he is persuaded, be level to the capacity of all those readers (not perhaps the most numerous class) who think reflection of some use in reading, and who do not read merely with the intention of killing time.

He begs leave to add, that though his subject be Eloquence, yet, as the nature of his work is didactical, wherein the understanding only is addressed, the style in general admits no higher qualities than purity and perspicuity. These were therefore his highest aim. The best ornaments out of place are not only unbecoming but offensive. Nor can any thing be further from his thoughts than to pretend an exemption from such positive faults in expression, as, on the article of Elocution, he hath so freely criticized in the best English authors. He is entirely sensible, that an impropriety or other negligence in style will escape the notice of the writer, which hardly escapes that of any body else. Next to the purpose of illustrating the principles and canons which he here submits to the judgment of the Public, the two following motives weighed most with the Author in inducing him to use so much freedom in regard to the writings of those for whom he has the highest veneration. One is, to show that we ought in writing, as in other things, carefully to beware of implicit attachment and servile imitation, even when they seem to be claimed by the most celebrated names. The other is, to evince that we are in danger of doing great injustice to a work by deciding hastily on its merit from a collection of such oversights. If the critic be rigorous in marking whatever is amiss in this way, what author may abide the trial? But though such slips are not to be regarded as the sole or even principal test of demerit in literary productions, they ought not to be altogether overlooked. Whatever is faulty in any degree it were better to avoid. And there are consequences regarding the language in general, as well as the success of particular works, which should preserve verbal criticism from being considered as beneath the attention of any author. An author, so far from having reason to be offended, is doubtless obliged to the man who, free from captious petulance, candidly points out his errors of what kind soever they be.

INTRODUCTION.

ALL art is founded in science, and the science is of little value which does not serve as a foundation to some beneficial art. On the most sublime of all sciences, *theology* and *ethics*, is built the most important of all arts, *the art of living*. The abstract mathematical sciences serve as a ground-work to the arts of the land-measurer and the accountant; and in conjunction with natural philosophy, including geography and astronomy, to those of the architect, the navigator, the dialist, and many others. Of what consequence anatomy is to surgery, and that part of physiology which teaches the laws of gravitation and of motion is to the artificer, is a matter too obvious to need illustration. The general remark might, if necessary, be exemplified throughout the whole circle of arts, both useful and elegant. Valuable knowledge, therefore, always leads to some practical skill, and is perfected in it. On the other hand, the practical skill loses much of its beauty and extensive utility, which does not originate in knowledge. There is by consequence a natural relation between the sciences and the arts, like that which subsists between the parent and the offspring.

I acknowledge indeed that these are sometimes unnaturally separated; and that by the mere influence of example on the one hand, and imitation on the other, some progress may be made in an art, without the knowledge of the principles from which it sprung. By the help of a few rules, which men are taught to use mechanically, a good practical arithmetician may be formed, who neither knows the reasons on which the rules he works by were first established, nor ever thinks it of any moment to inquire into them. In like manner, we frequently meet with expert artisans, who are ignorant of the six mechanical powers, which, though in the exercise of their profession they daily employ, they do not understand the principles whereby, in any instance, the result of their application is ascertained. The propagation of the arts may therefore be compared more justly to that variety which takes place in the vegetable kingdom, than to the uniformity which obtains universally in the animal world; for, as to the anomalous race of zoophytes, I do not comprehend them in the number. It is not always necessary that the plant spring from the seed, a slip from another plant will often answer the purpose.

There is, however, a very considerable difference in the expectations that may justly be raised from the different methods followed in the acquisition of the art. Improvements, unless in extraordinary instances of genius and sagacity, are not to be expected from those who have acquired all their dexterity from imitation and habit. One who has had an education no better than that of an ordinary mechanic, may prove an excellent manual operator; but it is only in the well instructed mechanician that you would expect to find a good mechanist. The analogy to vegetation, above suggested, holds here also. The offset is commonly no more than a mere copy of the parent plant. It is from the seed only you can expect, with the aid of proper culture, to produce new varieties, and even to make improvements on the species. "Expert men," says Lord Bacon, "can execute and judge of particulars, one by one; but the general counsels, and the plots and marshalling affairs, come best from those that are learned."

Indeed, in almost every art, even as used by mere practitioners, there are certain rules, as hath been already hinted, which must carefully be followed, and which serve the artist instead of principles. An acquaintance with these is one step, and but one step towards science. Thus in the common books of arithmetic, intended solely for practice, the rules laid down for the ordinary operations, as for numeration, or numerical notation, addition, subtraction, multiplication, division, and a few others, which are sufficient for all the purposes of the accountant, serve instead of principles; and, to a superficial observer, may be thought to supersede the study of any thing further. But their utility reaches a very little way, compared with that which results from the knowledge of the foundations of the art, and of what has been, not unfitly, styled *arithmetic universal.* It may be justly said that, without some portion of this knowledge, the practical rules had never been invented. Besides, if by these the particular questions which come exactly within the description of the rule may be solved; by the other, such general rules themselves, as serve for the solution of endless particulars, may be discovered.

The case I own is somewhat different with those arts which are entirely founded on experiment and observation, and are not derived, like pure mathematics, from abstract and universal axioms. But even in these, when we rise from the individual to the species, from the species to the genus, and thence to the most extensive orders and classes, we arrive, though in a different way, at the knowledge of general truths, which, in a certain sense, are also scientific, and answer a similar purpose. Our acquaintance with nature and its laws is so much extended, that we shall be enabled, in numberless cases, not only to apply to the most profitable purposes the knowledge we have thus acquired, but to determine beforehand, with sufficient certainty, the success of every new application. In this progress we are like people who, from a low and narrow bottom, where the view is confined to a few acres, gradually ascend a lofty peak or promontory. The prospect is perpetually enlarging as we mount, and when we reach the summit, the boundless horizon, comprehending all the variety of sea and land, hill and valley, town and country, arable and desert, lies under the eye at once.

Those who in medicine have scarcely risen to the discernment of any general principles, and have no other directory but the experiences gained in the first and lowest stage, or as it were at the foot of the mountain, are commonly distinguished by the name of *empirics.* Something similar may be said to obtain in the other liberal arts; for in all of them more enlargement of mind is necessary than is required for the exercise of those called mechanical. The character directly opposite to the *empiric* is the *visionary;* for it is not in theology only that there are visionaries. Of the two extremes I acknowledge that the latter is the worse. The first founds upon facts, but the facts are few, and commonly in his reasonings, through his imperfect knowledge of the subject, misapplied. The second often argues very consequentially from principles which, having no foundation in nature, may justly be denominated the illegitimate issue of his own imagination. He in this resembles the man of science, that he acts systematically, for there are false as well as true theorists, and is influenced by certain general propositions, real or imaginary. But the difference lies here, that in the one they are real, in the other imaginary. The system of the one is reared on the firm basis of experience, the theory of the other is no better than a castle in the air. I mention characters only in the extreme, because in this manner they are best discriminated. In real life, however, any two of these, sometimes all the three, in various proportions, may be found blended in the same person.

The arts are frequently divided into the useful, and the polite, fine, or elegant; for these words are, in this application, used synonymously. This division is not coincident with that into the mechanical and the liberal. Physic, navigation, and the art of war, though properly liberal arts, fall entirely under the denomination of the useful; whereas painting and sculpture, though requiring a good deal of manual labour, and in that respect more nearly related to the mechanical, belong to the class denominated elegant. The first division arises purely from the consideration of the end to be attained; the second from the consideration of the means to be employed. In respect of the end, an art is either useful or elegant; in respect of the means, it is either mechanical or liberal. The true foundation of the former distribution is, that certain arts are manifestly and ultimately calculated for profit or use; whilst others, on the contrary, seem to terminate in pleasing. The one supplies a real want, the other only gratifies some mental taste. Yet, in strictness, in the execution of the useful arts there is often scope for elegance, and the arts called elegant are by no means destitute of use. The principal difference is, that use is the direct and avowed purpose of the former, whereas it is more latently and indirectly affected by the latter. Under this class are commonly included, not only the arts of the painter and statuary, but those also of the musician and the poet. Eloquence and architecture, by which last term is always understood more than building merely for accommodation, are to be considered as of a mixed nature, wherein utility and beauty have almost equal influence.

The elegant arts, as well as the useful, are founded in experience, but from the difference of their nature there arises a considerable difference both in their origin and in their growth. Necessity, the mother of invention, drives men, in the earliest state of society, to the study and cultivation of the useful arts; it is always leisure and abundance which lead men to seek gratifications no way conducive to the preservation either of the individual or of the species. The elegant arts, therefore, are doubtless to be considered as the younger sisters. The progress of the former towards perfection is, however, much slower than that of the latter. Indeed, with regard to the first, it is impossible to say, as to several arts, what is the perfection of the art; since we are incapable of conceiving how far the united discernment and industry of men, properly applied, may yet carry them.

For some centuries backwards, the men of every age have made great and unexpected improvements on the labours of their predecessors. And it is very probable that the subsequent age will produce discoveries and acquisitions, which we of this age are as little capable of foreseeing, as those who preceded us in the last century were capable of conjecturing the progress that would be made in the present. The case is not entirely similar in the fine arts. These, though later in their appearing, are more rapid in their advancement. There may, indeed, be in these a degree of perfection beyond what we have experienced; but we have some conception of the very utmost to which it can proceed. For instance, where resemblance is the object, as in a picture or statue, a perfect conformity to its archetype is a thing at least conceivable. In like manner, the utmost pleasure of which the imagination is susceptible, by a poetical narrative or exhibition, is a thing, in my judgment, not inconceivable. We Britons, for example, do, by immense degrees, excel the ancient Greeks in the arts of navigation and ship-building; and how much further we may still excel them in these, by means of discoveries and improvements yet to be made, it would be the greatest presumption in any man to say. But as it requires not a prophetic spirit to discover, it implies no presumption to affirm, that we shall never excel them so far in poetry and eloquence, if ever in these respects we come to equal them. The same thing might probably be affirmed in regard to painting, sculpture, and music, if we had here as ample a fund of materials for forming a comparison.

But let it be observed, that the remarks now made regard only the advancement of the arts themselves; for though the useful are of slower growth than the other, and their utmost perfection cannot always be so easily ascertained, yet the acquisition of any one of them by a learner in the perfection which it has reached at the time, is a much easier matter than the acquisition of any of the elegant arts; —besides that the latter require much more of a certain happy combination in the original frame of spirit, commonly called genius, than is necessary to the other.

Let it be observed further, that as the gratification of taste is the immediate object of the fine arts, their effect is in a manner instantaneous, and the quality of any new production in these is immediately judged by every body; for all have in them some rudiments of taste, though in some they are improved by a good, in others corrupted by a bad education, and in others almost suppressed by a total want of education. In the useful arts, on the contrary, as more time and experience are requisite for discovering the means by which our accommodation is effected, so it generally requires examination, time, and trial, that we may be satisfied of the fitness of the work for the end proposed. In these we are not near so apt to consider ourselves as judges, unless we be either artists, or accustomed to employ and examine the work of artists in that particular profession.

I mentioned some arts that have their fundamental principles in the abstract sciences of geometry and arithmetic, and some in the doctrine of gravitation and motion. There are others, as the medical and chirurgical arts, which require a still broader foundation of science and anatomy, the animal economy, natural history, diseases, and remedies.—Those arts which, like poetry, are purely to be ranked among the elegant, as their end is attained by an accommodation to some internal taste, so the springs by which alone they can be regulated must be sought for in the nature of the human mind, and more especially in the principles of the imagination. It is also in the human mind that we must investigate the source of some of the useful arts. Logic, whose end is the discovery of truth, is founded in the doctrine of the understanding: and ethics (under which may be comprehended economics, politics, and jurisprudence) are founded in that of the will.

This was the idea of Lord Verulam,[1] perhaps the most comprehensive genius in philosophy that has appeared in modern times. But these are not the only arts which have their foundation in the science of human nature. Grammar too, in its general principles, has a close connexion with the understanding, and the theory of the association of ideas.

But there is no art whatever that hath so close a connexion with all the faculties and powers of the mind, as eloquence, or the art of speaking, in the extensive sense in which I employ the term. For in the first place, that it ought to be ranked among the polite or fine arts, is manifest from this, that in all its exertions, with little or no exception, (as will appear afterwards,) it requires the aid of the imagination. Thereby it not only pleases, but by pleasing commands attention, rouses the passions, and often at last subdues the most stubborn resolution. It is also a useful art. This is certainly the case if the power of speech be a useful faculty, as it professedly teaches us how to employ that faculty with the greatest probability of success. Further, if the logical art, and the ethical, be useful, eloquence is useful, as it instructs us how these arts must be applied for the conviction and the persuasion of others. It is indeed the grand art of communication, not of ideas only, but of sentiments, passions, dispositions, and purposes. Nay, without this, the greatest talents, even wisdom itself, lose much of their lustre, and still more of their usefulness. "The wise in heart," saith Solomon, "shall be called prudent, but the sweetness of the lips increaseth learning."[2] By the former a man's own conduct may be well regulated, but the latter is absolutely necessary for diffusing valuable knowledge, and enforcing right rules of action upon others.

Poetry indeed is properly no other than a particular mode or form of certain branches of oratory. But of this more afterwards. Suffice it only to remark at present, that the direct end of the former, whether to delight the fancy as in epic, or to move the passions as in tragedy, is avowedly in part the aim, and sometimes the immediate and proposed aim, of the orator. The same medium, language, is made use of; the same general rules of composition, in narration, description, argumentation, are observed; and the same tropes and figures, either for beautifying or for invigorating the diction, are employed by both. In regard to versification, it is

[1] Doctrina circa *intellectum*, atque illa altera circa *voluntatem* hominis, in natalibus suis tanquam gemellæ sunt. Etenim *illuminationis puritas* et *arbitrii libertas* simul inceperunt, simul corruerunt. Neque datur in universitate rerum tam intima sympathia quam illa *Veri* et *Boni*.—Venimus jam ad doctrinam circa usum et objecta facultatum animæ humanæ. Illa duas habet partes easque notissimas, et consensu receptas, *Logicam* et *Ethicam*.—— Logica de intellectu et ratione: Ethica de voluntate, appetitu, et affectibus disserit. Altera decreta, altera actiones progignit. De Aug. Sci. l. v., c. 1.

[2] Prov. xvi. 21.

more to be considered as an appendage, than as a constituent of poetry. In this lies what may be called the more mechanical part of the poet's work, being at most but a sort of garnishing, and by far too unessential to give a designation to the kind. This particularity in form, to adopt an expression of the naturalists, constitutes only variety, and not a different species.

Now, though a considerable proficiency in the practice of the oratorical art may be easily and almost naturally attained, by one in whom clearness of apprehension is happily united with sensibility of taste, fertility of imagination, and a certain readiness in language, a more thorough investigation of the latent energies, if I may thus express myself, whereby the instruments employed by eloquence produce their effect upon the hearers, will serve considerably both to improve the taste, and to enrich the fancy. By the former effect we learn to amend and avoid faults in composing and speaking, against which the best natural but uncultivated parts give no security; and by the latter, the proper mediums are suggested, whereby the necessary aids of topics, arguments, illustrations, and motives, may be procured. Besides, this study, properly conducted, leads directly to an acquaintance with ourselves; it not only traces the operations of the intellect and imagination, but discloses the lurking springs of action in the heart. In this view it is perhaps the surest and the shortest, as well as the pleasantest way of arriving at the science of the human mind. It is as an humble attempt to lead the mind of the studious inquirer into this tract, that the following sheets are now submitted to the examination of the public.

When we consider the manner in which the rhetorical art hath arisen, and been treated in the schools, we must be sensible that in this, as in the imitative arts, the first handle has been given to criticism by actual performances in the art. The principles of our nature will, without the aid of any previous and formal instruction, sufficiently account for the first attempts. As speakers existed before grammarians, and reasoners before logicians, so doubtless there were orators before there were rhetoricians, and poets before critics. The first impulse towards the attainment of every art is Nature. The earliest assistance and direction that can be obtained in the rhetorical art, by which men operate on the minds of others, arises from the consciousness a man has of what operates on his own mind, aided by the sympathetic feelings, and by that practical experience of mankind, which individuals, even in the rudest state of society, are capable of acquiring. The next step is to observe and discriminate, by proper appellations, the different attempts, whether modes of arguing, or forms of speech, that have been employed for the purposes of explaining, convincing, pleasing, moving, and persuading. Here we have the beginnings of the critical science. The third step is to compare, with diligence, the various effects, favourable or unfavourable, of those attempts, carefully taking into consideration every attendant circumstance by which the success appears to have been influenced, and by which one may be enabled to discover to what particular purpose each attempt is adapted, and in what circumstances only to be used. The fourth and last is to canvass those principles in our nature to which the various attempts are adapted, and by which, in any instance, their success or want of success may be accounted for. By the first step the critic is supplied with materials. By the second, the materials are distributed and classed, the forms of argument, the tropes and figures of speech, with their divisions and subdivisions, are explained. By the third, the rules of composition are discovered, or the method of combining and disposing the several materials, so as that they may be perfectly adapted to the end in view. By the fourth, we arrive at that knowledge of human nature which, besides its other advantages, adds both weight and evidence to all precedent discoveries and rules.

The second of the steps above mentioned, which, by the way, is the first of the rhetorical art, for all that precedes is properly supplied by Nature, appeared to the author of Hudibras the utmost pitch that had even to his time been attained:

> For all a rhetorician's rules
> Teach nothing but to name his tools.[3]

In this, however, the matter has been exaggerated by the satirist. Considerable progress had been made by the ancient Greeks and Romans, in devising the proper rules of composition, not only the two sorts of poesy, epic and dramatic, but also in the three sorts of orations which were in most frequent use among them, the deliberative, the judiciary, and the demonstrative. And I must acknowledge that, as far as I have been able to discover, there has been little or no improvement in this respect made by the moderns. The observations and rules transmitted to us from these distinguished names in the learned world, Aristotle, Cicero, and Quintilian, have been for the most part only translated by later critics, or put into a modish dress and new arrangement. And as to the fourth and last step, it may be said to bring us into a new country, of which, though there have been some successful incursions occasionally made upon its frontiers, we are not yet in full possession.

The performance which, of all those I happen to be acquainted with, seems to have advanced farthest in this way, is the *Elements of Criticism.* But the subject of the learned and ingenious author of that work is rather too multifarious to admit so narrow a scrutiny as would be necessary for a perfect knowledge of the several parts. Every thing that is an object of taste, *sculpture*, *painting*, *music*, *architecture*, and *gardening*, as well as *poetry* and *eloquence*, come within his plan. On the other hand, though his subject be more multiform, it is, in respect of its connexion with the mind, less extensive than that here proposed. All those particular arts are examined only on that side wherein there is found pretty considerable coincidence with one another; namely, as objects of taste, which, by exciting sentiments of grandeur, beauty, novelty, and the like, are calculated to delight the imagination. In this view, eloquence comes no further under consideration, than as a fine art, and adapted, like the others above mentioned, to please the fancy, and to move the passions. But to treat it also as a useful art, and closely connected with the understanding and the will, would have led to a discussion foreign to his purpose.

I am aware that, from the deduction given above, it may be urged, that the fact, as here represented, seems to subvert the principle formerly laid down, and that as practice in the art has given the first scope for criticism, the former cannot justly be considered as

[3] Part i. Canto 1.

deriving light and direction from the latter; that, on the contrary, the latter ought to be regarded as merely affording a sort of intellectual entertainment to speculative men. It may be said that this science, however entertaining, as it must derive all its light and information from the actual examples in the art, can never in return be subservient to the art, from which alone it has received whatever it has to bestow. This objection, however specious, will not bear a near examination. For let it be observed, that though in all the arts the first rough drafts, or imperfect attempts, that are made, precede every thing that can be termed criticism, they do not precede every thing that can be termed knowledge, which every human creature that is not an idiot, is every day from his birth acquiring by experience and observation. This knowledge must of necessity precede even those rudest and earliest essays; and if, in the imperfect and indigested state in which knowledge must always be found in the mind that is rather self-taught than totally untaught, it deserves not to be dignified with the title of Science, neither does the first awkward attempt in practice merit to be honoured with the name of Art. As is the one, such is the other. It is enough for my purpose that something must be known, before any thing in this way, with a view to an end, can be undertaken to be done.

At the same time it is acknowledged, that as man is much more an active than a contemplative being, and as generally there is some view to action, especially in uncultivated minds, in all their observations and inquiries, it cannot be doubted that, in composition, the first attempts would be in the art, and that afterwards, from the comparison of different attempts with one another, and the consideration of the success with which they had been severally attended, would arise gradually the rules of criticism. Nor can it, on the other hand, be pleaded with any appearance of truth, that observations derived from the productions of an art can be of no service for the improvement of that art, and consequently of no benefit to future artists. On the contrary, it is thus that every art, liberal or mechanical, elegant or useful, except those founded in pure mathematics, advances towards perfection. From observing similar but different attempts and experiments, and from comparing their effects, general remarks are made, which serve as so many rules for directing future practice; and from comparing such general remarks together, others still more general are deduced. A few individual instances serve as a foundation to those observations, which, when once sufficiently established, extend their influence to instances innumerable. It is in this way that, on experiments comparatively few, all the physiological sciences have been reared; it is in this way that those comprehensive truths were first discovered, which have had such an unlimited influence on the most important arts, and given man so vast a dominion over the elements, and even the most refractory powers of nature. It is evident, therefore, that the artist and the critic are reciprocally subservient, and the particular province of each is greatly improved by the assistance of the other.

But it is not necessary here to enter further into this subject; what I shall have occasion afterwards to advance on the acquisition of experience, and the manner of using it, will be a sufficient illustration.

THE

PHILOSOPHY OF RHETORIC.

BOOK I.

THE NATURE AND FOUNDATIONS OF ELOQUENCE.

CHAPTER I.

Eloquence in the largest acceptation defined, its more general forms exhibited, with their different objects, ends, and characters.

In speaking there is always some end proposed, or some effect which the speaker intends to produce on the hearer. The word *eloquence* in its greatest latitude denotes, "That art or talent by which the discourse is adapted to its end[1]."

All the ends of speaking are reducible to four; every speech being intended to enlighten the understanding, to please the imagination, to move the passions, or to influence the will.

Any one discourse admits only one of these ends as the principal. Nevertheless, in discoursing on a subject, many things may be introduced, which are more immediately and apparently directed to some of the other ends of speaking, and not to that which is the chief intent of the whole. But then these other and immediate ends are in effect but means, and must be rendered conducive to that which is the primary intention. Accordingly, the propriety or the impropriety of the introduction of such secondary ends, will always be inferred from their subserviency or want of subserviency to that end, which is, in respect of them, the ultimate. For example, a discourse addressed to the understanding, and calculated to illustrate or evince some point purely speculative, may borrow aid from the imagination, and admit metaphor and comparison, but not the bolder and more striking figures, as that called

1 "Dicere secundum virtutem orationis. Scientia bene dicendi." Quintilian The word *eloquence*, in common conversation, is seldom used in such a comprehensive sense. I have, however, made choice of this definition on a double account: 1st. It exactly corresponds to Tully's idea of a perfect orator; "Optimus est orator qui dicendo animos audientium et docet, et delectat, et permovet." 2dly. It is best adapted to the subject of these papers. See the note on page 4.

vision or fiction[2], prosopopœia, and the like, which are not so much intended to elucidate a subject, as to excite admiration. Still less will it admit an address to the passions, which, as it never fails to disturb the operation of the intellectual faculty, must be regarded by every intelligent hearer as foreign at least, if not insidious. It is obvious, that either of these, far from being subservient to the main design, would distract the attention from it.

There is indeed one kind of address to the understanding, and only one, which, it may not be improper to observe, disdains all assistance whatever from the fancy. The address I mean is mathematical demonstration. As this does not, like moral reasoning, admit degrees of evidence, its perfection, in point of eloquence, if so uncommon an application of the term may be allowed, consists in perspicuity. Perspicuity here results entirely from propriety and simplicity of diction, and from accuracy of method, where the mind is regularly, step by step, conducted forwards in the same track, the attention no way diverted, nothing left to be supplied, no one unnecessary word or idea introduced[3]. On the contrary, an harangue framed for affecting the hearts or influencing the resolves of an assembly, needs greatly the assistance both of intellect and of imagination.

In general it may be asserted, that each preceding species, in the order above exhibited, is preparatory to the subsequent; that each subsequent species is founded on the preceding; and that thus they ascend in a regular progression. Knowledge, the object of the intellect, furnisheth materials for the fancy; the fancy culls, compounds, and, by her mimic art, disposes these materials so as to affect the passions; the passions are the natural spurs to volition or action, and so need only to be right directed. This connexion and dependency will better appear from the following observations.

When a speaker addresseth himself to the understanding, he proposes the *instruction* of his hearers, and that, either by explaining some doctrine unknown, or not distinctly comprehended by them, or by proving some position disbelieved or doubted by them.—In other words, he proposes either to dispel ignorance or to vanquish error. In the one, his aim is their *information;* in the other, their *conviction.* Accordingly the predominant quality of the former is *perspicuity;* of the

[2] By vision or fiction is understood, that rhetorical figure of which Quintilian says, "Quas φαντασιας Græci vocant, nos sane *visiones* appellamus, per quas imagines rerum absentium ita repræsentantur animo, ut eas cernere oculis ac præsentes habere videamur."

[3] Of this kind Euclid hath given us the most perfect models, which have not, I think, been sufficiently imitated by later mathematicians. In him you find the exactest arrangement inviolably observed, the properest and simplest, and by consequence the plainest expressions constantly used, nothing deficient, nothing superfluous; in brief, nothing which in more, or fewer, or other words, or words otherwise disposed, could have been better expressed.

latter, *argument*. By that we are made to know, by this to believe.

The imagination is addressed by exhibiting to it a lively and beautiful representation of a suitable object. As in this exhibition, the task of the orator may, in some sort, be said, like that of the painter, to consist in imitation, the merit of the work results entirely from these two sources; dignity, as well in the subject or thing imitated, as in the manner of imitation; and resemblance, in the portrait or performance. Now the principal scope for this class being in narration and description, poetry, which is one mode of oratory, especially epic poetry, must be ranked under it. The effect of the dramatic, at least of tragedy, being upon the passions, the drama falls under another species, to be explained afterwards. But that kind of address of which I am now treating, attains the summit of perfection in the *sublime*, or those great and noble images, which, when in suitable colouring presented to the mind, do, as it were, distend the imagination with some vast conception, and quite ravish the soul.

The sublime, it may be urged, as it raiseth admiration, should be considered as one species of address to the passions. But this objection, when examined, will appear superficial. There are few words in any language (particularly such as relate to the operations and feelings of the mind) which are strictly univocal. Thus admiration, when persons are the object, is commonly used for a high degree of esteem; but when otherwise applied, it denotes solely an internal taste. It is that pleasurable sensation which instantly ariseth on the perception of magnitude, or of whatever is great and stupendous in its kind. For there is a greatness in the degrees of quality in spiritual subjects, analagous to that which subsists in the degrees of quantity in material things. Accordingly, in all tongues, perhaps without exception, the ordinary terms, which are considered as literally expressive of the latter, are also used promiscuously to denote the former. Now admiration, when thus applied, doth not require to its production, as the passions generally do, any reflex view of motives or tendencies, or of any relation either to private interest, or to the good of others; and ought therefore to be numbered among those original feelings of the mind, which are denominated by some the reflex senses, being of the same class with a taste for beauty, an ear for music, or our moral sentiments. Now, the immediate view of whatever is directed to the imagination (whether the subject be things inanimate or animal forms, whether characters, actions, incidents, or manner, terminates in the gratification of some internal taste: as a taste for the wonderful, the fair, the good; for elegance, for novelty, or for grandeur.

But it is evident, that this creative faculty, the fancy, frequently lends her aid in promoting still nobler ends. From her exuberant stores most of those tropes and figures are extracted, which, when properly employed, have such a marvellous efficacy in rousing the passions, and by some secret, sudden, and inexplicable association, awakening all the tenderest emotions of the heart. In this case, the address of the orator is not ultimately intended to astonish by the loftiness of his images, or to delight by the beauteous resemblance which his painting bears to nature; nay, it will not permit the hearers even a moment's leisure for making the comparison, but as it were by some magical spell, hurries them, ere they are aware, into love, pity, grief, terror, desire, aversion, fury, or hatred. It therefore assumes the denomination of *pathetic*[4], which is the characteristic of the third species of discourse, that addressed to the passions.

Finally, as that kind, the most complex of all, which is calculated to influence the will, and persuade to a certain conduct, is in reality an artful mixture of that which proposes to convince the judgment, and that which interests the passions, its distinguished excellency results from these two, the argumentative and the pathetic incorporated together. These acting with united force, and, if I may so express myself, in concert, constitute that passionate eviction, that *vehemence* of contention, which is admirably fitted for persuasion, and hath always been regarded as the supreme qualification in an orator[5]. It is this

[4] I am sensible that this word is commonly used in a more limited sense, for that which only excites commiseration. *Perhaps* the word *impassioned* would answer better.

[5] This animated reasoning the Greek rhetoricians termed δεινοτης, which from signifying the principal excellency in an orator, came at length to denote oratory itself. And as vehemence and eloquence became synonymous, the latter, suitably to this way of thinking, was sometimes defined the *art of persuasion*. But that this definition is defective, appears even from their own writings, since in a consistency with it, their rhetorics could not have comprehended those orations called *demonstrative*, the design of which was not to persuade but to please. Yet it is easy to discover the origin of this defect, and that both from the nature of the thing, and from the customs which obtained among both Greeks and Romans. First, from the nature of the thing, for to persuade presupposes in some degree, and therefore may be understood to imply, all the other talents of an orator, to enlighten, to evince, to paint, to astonish, to inflame; but this doth not hold inversely; one may explain with clearness, and prove with energy, who is incapable of the sublime, the pathetic, and the vehement: besides, this power of persuasion, or, as Cicero calls it, "Posse voluntates hominum impellere quo velis, unde velis, deducere," as it makes a man master of his hearers, is the most considerable in respect of consequences. Secondly, from ancient customs. All their public orations were ranked under three classes, the demonstrative, the judiciary, and the deliberative. In the two last it was impossible to rise to eminence, without that important talent, the power of persuasion. These were in much more frequent use than the first, and withal the surest means of advancing both the fortune and the fame of the orator; for as on the judiciary the lives and estates of private persons depended, on the deliberative hung the resolves of senates, the fate of kingdoms, nay, of the most renowned republics the world ever knew. Consequently, to excel in these, must have been the direct road to riches, honours, and preferment. No wonder, then, that persuasion should almost wholly engross the rhetorician's notice.

which bears down every obstacle, and procures the speaker an irresistible power over the thoughts and purposes of his audience. It is this which hath been so justly celebrated as giving one man an ascendant over others, superior even to what despotism itself can bestow; since by the latter the more ignoble part only, the body and its members are enslaved; whereas from the dominion of the former, nothing is exempted, neither judgment nor affection, not even the inmost recesses, the most latent movements of the soul. What opposition is he not prepared to conquer, on whose arms reason hath conferred solidity and weight, and passion such a sharpness as enables them, in defiance of every obstruction, to open a speedy passage to the heart?

It is not, however, every kind of pathos, which will give the orator so great an ascendancy over the minds of his hearers. All passions are not alike capable of producing this effect. Some are naturally inert and torpid; they deject the mind, and indispose it for enterprise. Of this kind are sorrow, fear, shame, humility. Others, on the contrary, elevate the soul, and stimulate to action. Such are hope, patriotism, ambition, emulation, anger. These, with the greatest facility, are made to concur in direction with arguments exciting to resolution and activity: and are, consequently, the fittest for producing, what for want of a better term in our language, I shall henceforth denominate the *vehement*. There is, besides, an intermediate kind of passions, which do not so congenially and directly either restrain us from acting, or incite us to act; but, by the art of the speaker, can, in an oblique manner, be made conducive to either. Such are joy, love, esteem, compassion. Nevertheless, all these kinds may find a place in suasory discourses, or such as are intended to operate on the will. The first is properest for dissuading; the second, as hath been already hinted, for persuading; the third is equally accommodated to both.

Guided by the above reflections, we may easily trace that connexion in the various forms of eloquence, which was remarked on, distinguishing them by their several objects. The imagination is charmed by a finished picture, wherein even drapery and ornament are not neglected; for here the end is pleasure. Would we penetrate further, and agitate the soul, we must exhibit only some vivid strokes, some expressive features, not decorated as for show (all ostentation being both despicable and hurtful here), but such as appear the natural exposition of those bright and deep impressions, made by the subject upon the speaker's mind; for here the end is not pleasure, but emotion. Would we not only touch the heart, but win it entirely to co-operate with our views, those affecting lineaments must be so interwoven with our argument, as that, from the passion excited our reasoning may derive importance, and so be fitted for commanding attention; and by the justness of the reasoning the passion may be more deeply rooted and enforced; and that thus both may be made to conspire in effectuating that persuasion which is the end proposed. For here, if I may adopt the schoolmen's language, we do not argue to gain barely the assent of the understanding, but, which is infinitely more important, the consent of the will[6].

To prevent mistakes, it will not be beside my purpose further to remark, that several of the terms above explained are sometimes used by rhetoricians and critics in a much larger and more vague signification, than has been given them here. Sublimity and vehemence, in particular, are often confounded, the latter being considered as a species of the former. In this manner has this subject been treated by that great master Longinus, whose acceptation of the term *sublime* is extremely indefinite, importing an eminent degree of almost any excellence of speech, of whatever kind. Doubtless, if things themselves be understood, it does not seem material what names are assigned them. Yet it is both more accurate, and proves no inconsiderable aid to the right understanding of things, to discriminate by different signs such as are truly different. And that the two qualities above mentioned are of this number is undeniable, since we can produce passages full of vehemence, wherein no image is presented, which, with any propriety, can be termed great or sublime[7]. In matters of criticism, as in the abstract sciences, it is of the utmost consequence to ascertain, with precision, the meanings of words,

[6] This subordination is beautifully and concisely expressed by Hersan in Rollin, "Je conclus que la veritable eloquence est celle qui persuade; qu'elle ne persuade ordinairement qu'en touchant; qu'elle ne touche que par des choses et par des idées palpables."

[7] For an instance of this, let that of Cicero against Antony suffice. "Tu istis faucibus, istis lateribus, ista gladiatoria totius corporis firmitate, tantum vini in Hippiæ nuptiis exhauseras, ut tibi necesse esset in populi Romani conspectu vomere postridie. O rem non modo visu fœdam, sed etiam auditu! Si hoc tibi inter cœnam, in tuis immanibus illis poculis accidisset, quis non turpe duceret? In cœtu vero populi Romani, negotium publicum gerens, magister equitum, cui ructare turpe esset, is vomens, frustis esculentis vinum redolentibus gremium suum et totum tribunal implevit." Here the vivacity of the address, in turning from the audience to the person declaimed against, the energy of the expressions, the repetition, exclamation, interrogation, and climax of aggravating circumstances, accumulated with rapidity upon one another, display in the strongest light the turpitude of the action, and thus at once convince the judgment and fire the indignation. It is therefore justly styled vehement. But what is the image it presents? The reverse in every respect of the sublime; what, instead of gazing on with admiration, we should avert our eyes from with abhorrence. For, however it might pass in a Roman senate, I question whether Ciceronian eloquence itself could excuse the uttering of such things in any modern assembly, not to say a polite one. With vernacular expressions, answering to these, "vomere, ructare, frustis esculentis vinum redolentibus," our more delicate ears would be immoderately shocked. In a case of this kind the more lively the picture is, so much the more abominable it is.

and, as nearly as the genius of the language in which one writes will permit, to make them correspond to the boundaries assigned by Nature to the things signified. That the lofty and the vehement, though still distinguishable, are sometimes combined, and act with united force, is not to be denied. It is then only that the orator can be said to fight with weapons which are at once sharp, massive, and refulgent, which, like heaven's artillery, dazzle while they strike, which overpower the sight and the heart at the same instant. How admirably do the two forenamed qualities, when happily blended, correspond in the rational, to the thunder and lightning in the natural world, which are not more awfully majestical in sound and aspect, than irresistible in power[8].

Thus much shall suffice for explaining the spirit, the intent, and the distinguishing qualities of each of the forementioned sorts of address; all of which agree in this, an accommodation to affairs of a serious and important nature.

[8] A noted passage in Cicero's oration for Cornelius Balbus will serve as an example of the union of sublimity with vehemence. Speaking of Pompey, who had rewarded the valour and public services of our orator's client, by making him a Roman citizen, he says, "Utrum enim inscientem vultis contra fœdera fecisse, an scientem? Si scientem, O nomen nostri imperii, O populi Romani excellens dignitas, O Cneii Pompeii sic late longeque diffusa laus, ut ejus gloriæ domicilium communis imperii finibus terminetur: O nationes, urbes, populi, reges, tetrarchæ, tyranni, testes Cneii Pompeii non solum virtutis in bello, sed etiam religionis in pace: vos denique mutæ regiones imploro, et sola terrarum ultimarum, vos maria, portus, insulæ, littoraque; quæ est enim ora, quæ sedes, qui locus, in quo non extent hujus cum fortitudinis, tum vero humanitatis, tum animi, tum consilii, impressa vestigia! Hunc quisquam incredibili quâdam atque inauditâ gravitate, virtute, constantiâ præditum fœdera scientem neglexisse, violâsse, rupisse, dicere audebit?" Here every thing conspires to aggrandize the hero, and exalt him to something more than mortal in the minds of the auditory; at the same time, every thing inspires the most perfect veneration for his character, and the most entire confidence in his integrity and judgment. The whole world is exhibited as no more than a sufficient theatre for such a superior genius to act upon. How noble is the idea! All the nations and potentates of the earth are, in a manner, produced as witnesses of his valour and his truth. Thus the orator at once fills the imagination with the immensity of the object, kindles in the breast an ardour of affection and gratitude, and, by so many accumulated evidences, convinces the understanding, and silences every doubt. Accordingly, the effect which the words above quoted, and some other things advanced in relation to the same personage, had upon the audience, as we learn from Quintilian, was quite extraordinary. They extorted from them such demonstrations of their applause and admiration, as he acknowledges to have been but ill-suited to the place and the occasion. He excuses it, however, because he considers it, not as a voluntary, but as a necessary consequence of the impression made upon the minds of the people. His words are remarkable, "Atque ego illos credo qui aderant, nec sensisse quid facerent, nec sponte judicioque plausisse; sed velut mente captos, et quo essent in loco ignaros, erupisse in hunc voluntatis affectum," lib. viii. cap. 3. Without doubt, a considerable share of the effect ought to be ascribed to the immense advantage which the action and pronunciation of the orator would give to his expression.

CHAPTER II.

Of wit, humour, and ridicule.

This article, concerning eloquence in its largest acceptation, I cannot properly dismiss without making some observations on another genus of oratory, in many things similar to the former, but which is naturally suited to light and trivial matters.

This also may be branched into three sorts, corresponding to those already discussed, directed to the fancy, the passions, and the will; for that which illuminates the understanding serves as a common foundation to both, and has here nothing peculiar. This may be styled the eloquence of conversation, as the other is more strictly the eloquence of declamation[9]. Not, indeed, but that wit, humour, ridicule, which are the essentials of the former, may often be successfully admitted into public harangues. And, on the other hand, sublimity, pathos, vehemence, may sometimes enter the precincts of familiar converse. To justify the use of such distinctive appellations, it is enough that they refer to those particulars which are predominant in each, though not peculiar to either.

SECTION I.—*Of wit.*

To consider the matter more nearly, it is the design of wit to excite in the mind an agreeable surprise, and that arising, not from any thing marvellous in the subject, but solely from the imagery she employs, or the strange assemblage of related ideas presented to the mind. This end is effected in one or other of these three ways: first in debasing things pompous or seemingly grave: I say *seemingly* grave, because to vilify what is *truly* grave has something shocking in it, which rarely fails to counteract the end: secondly, in aggrandizing things little and frivolous: thirdly, in setting ordinary objects, by means not only remote, but apparently contrary, in a particular and uncommon point of view[1]. This will be better understood from the following observations and examples.

[9] In the latter of these the ancients excel; in the former the moderns. Demosthenes and Cicero, not to say Homer and Virgil, to this day remain unrivalled; and in all antiquity, Lucian himself not excepted, we cannot find a match for Swift and Cervantes.

[1] I know no language which affords a name for this species of imagery, but the English. The French *esprit* or *bel esprit*, though on some occasions rightly translated *wit*, hath commonly a signification more extensive and generical. It must be owned, indeed, that in conformity to the style of French critics, the term *wit*, in English writings, hath been sometimes used with equal latitude. But this is certainly a perversion of the word from its ordinary sense, through

The materials employed by wit in the grotesque pieces she exhibits, are partly derived from those common fountains of whatever is directed to the imaginative powers, the ornaments of elocution, and the oratorical figures, simile, apostrophe, antithesis, metaphor; partly from those she in a manner appropriates to herself, irony, hyperbole, allusion, parody, and (if the reader will pardon my descending so low) paronomasia[2], and pun. The limning of wit differs from the rhetorical painting above described in two respects. One is, that in the latter there is not only a resemblance requisite in that particular on which the comparison is founded, but there must also be a general similitude, in the nature and quality of that which is the basis of the imagery, to that which is the theme of discourse. In respect of dignity, or the impression they make upon the mind, they must be things homogeneous. What has magnificence, must invariably be portrayed by what is magnificent; objects of importance by objects important; such as have grace by things graceful: Whereas the witty, though requiring an exact likeness in the first particular, demands, in the second, a contrariety rather, or remoteness. This enchantress exults in reconciling contradictions, and in hitting on that special light and attitude, wherein you can discover an unexpected similarity in objects, which, at first sight, appear the most dissimilar and heterogeneous. Thus high and low are coupled, humble and superb, momentous and trivial, common and extraordinary. Addison, indeed, observes[3], that wit is often produced, not by the resemblance, but by the opposition of ideas. But this, of which, however, he hath not given us an instance, doth not constitute a different species, as the repugnancy in that case will always be found between objects in other respects resembling; for it is to the contrast of

an excessive deference to the manner and idiom of our ingenious neighbours. Indeed, when an author varies the meaning in the same work, he not only occasions perplexity to his reader, but falls himself into an apparent inconsistency. An error of this kind, in Mr. Pope, has been lately pointed out by a very ingenious and judicious critic. "In the Essay on Criticism it is said,

True wit is nature to advantage dress'd:

But immediately after this the poet adds,

For works may have more wit than does 'em good.

Now let us substitute the definition in the place of the thing, and it will stand thus: A work may have more of *nature dressed to advantage*, than will do it good. This is impossible; and it is evident, that the confusion arises from the poet's having annexed two different ideas to the same word." Webb's Remarks on the Beauties of Poetry, Dialogue ii.

[2] Paronomasia is properly that figure which the French call *jeu de mots*. Such as "Inceptio est amentium, haud amantium." Ter. Andr. "Which tempted our attempt." Milt. B. i. "To begird the Almighty's throne, beseeching or besieging." B. v.

[3] Spectator.

dissimilitude and likeness, remoteness and relation, in the same objects, that its peculiar effect is imputable. Hence we hear of the flashes and the sallies of wit, phrases which imply suddenness, surprise, and contrariety. These are illustrated in the first by a term which implies an instantaneous emergence of light in darkness: in the second, by a word which denotes an abrupt transition to things distant. For we may remark in passing, that though language be older than criticism, those expressions adopted by the former, to elucidate matters of taste, will be found to have a pretty close conformity to the purest discoveries of the latter.

Nay, of so much consequence here are surprise and novelty, that nothing is more tasteless, and sometimes disgusting, than a joke that has become stale by frequent repetition. For the same reason, even a pun or a happy allusion will appear excellent when thrown out extempore in conversation, which would be deemed execrable in print. In like manner, a witty repartee is infinitely more pleasing than a witty attack. For though, in both cases, the thing may be equally new to the reader or hearer, the effect on him is greatly injured, when there is ground to suppose that it may be the slow production of study and premeditation. This, however, holds most with regard to the inferior tribes of witticisms, of which their readiness is the best recommendation.

The other respect in which wit differs from the illustrations of the graver orator, is the way wherein it affects the hearer. Sublimity elevates, beauty charms, wit diverts. The first, as hath been already observed, enraptures, and as it were, dilates the soul; the second diffuseth over it a serene delight; the third tickles the fancy, and throws the spirits into an agreeable vibration.

To these reflections I shall subjoin examples in each of the three sorts of wit above explained.

It will, however, be proper to premise, that if the reader should not at first be sensible of the justness of the solutions and explications to be given, he ought not hastily to form an unfavourable conclusion. Wherever there is taste, the witty and the humorous make themselves perceived, and produce their effect instantaneously; but they are of so subtle a nature, that they will hardly endure to be touched, much less to undergo a strict analysis and scrutiny. They are like those volatile essences, which, being too delicate to bear the open air, evaporate almost as soon as they are exposed to it. Accordingly, the wittiest things will sometimes be made to appear insipid, and the most ingenious frigid, by scrutinizing them too narrowly. Besides, the very frame of spirit proper for being diverted with the laughable in objects, is so different from that which is necessary for philosophizing on them, that there is a risk, that when we are most disposed to inquire into the cause, we are least capable of feeling the effect; as it is certain, that when the effect hath its full influence on us, we have little inclination for investigating the cause. For these reasons, I have resolved to be brief in my illustrations, having often observed that, in such nice and abstract inquiries, if a proper hint do not suggest the matter to the reader, he will be but more perplexed by long and elaborate discussions.

Of the first sort, which consists in the debasement of things great and eminent, Butler, amongst a thousand other instances, hath given us those which follow:

> And now had Phœbus in the lap
> Of Thetis taken out his nap;
> And, like a lobster boil'd, the morn
> From black to red began to turn[4].

Here the low allegorical style of the first couplet, and the simile used in the second, afford us a just notion of this lowest species, which is distinguished by the name of *the ludicrous*. Another specimen from the same author you have in these lines:

> Great on the bench, great in the saddle,
> That could as well bind o'er as swaddle,
> Mighty he was at both of these,
> And styled of *war*, as well as *peace:*
> So some rats of amphibious nature,
> Are either for the *land* or *water*[5].

In this coarse kind of drollery, those laughable translations or paraphrases of heroic and other serious poems, wherein the authors are said to be travestied, chiefly abound.

To the same class those instances must be referred, in which, though there is no direct comparison made, qualities of real dignity and importance are degraded, by being coupled with things mean and frivolous, as in some respect standing in the same predicament. An example of this I shall now give from the same hand.

> For when the restless Greeks sat down
> So many years, before Troy town,
> And were renown'd, as Homer writes,
> For well-soled boots[6], no less than fights[7].

I shall only observe further, that this sort, whose aim is to debase, delights in the most homely expressions, provincial idioms, and cant phrases.

[4] Hudibras, Part ii. Canto 3.
[5] Ibid. Part i. Canto 1.
[6] In allusion to the εὐκνήμιδες Ἀχαιοί, an expression which frequently occurs, both in the Iliad and in the Odyssey.
[7] Hudibras, Part i. Canto 2.

The second kind, consisting of the aggrandizement of little things, which is by far the most splendid, and displays a soaring imagination, these lines of Pope will serve to illustrate:

As Berecynthia, while her offspring vie
In homage to the mother of the sky,
Surveys around her in the blest abode,
An hundred sons, and every son a god:
Not with less glory mighty Dulness crown'd,
Shall take thro' Grub-street her triumphant round;
And her Parnassus glancing o'er at once,
Behold an hundred sons, and each a dunce[8].

This whole similitude is spirited. The parent of the celestials is contrasted by the daughter of Night and Chaos; heaven by Grub-street; gods by dunces. Besides, the parody it contains on a beautiful passage in Virgil, adds a particular lustre to it[9]. This species we may term *the thrasonical*, or *the mock-majestic*. It affects the most pompous language, and sonorous phraseology, as much as the other affects the reverse, the vilest and most grovelling dialect.

I shall produce another example from the same writer, which is, indeed, inimitably fine. It represents a lady employed at her toilet, attended by her maid, under the allegory of the celebration of some solemn and religious ceremony. The passage is rather long for a quotation, but as the omission of any part would be a real mutilation, I shall give it entire.

And now unveil'd the toilet stands display'd,
Each silver vase in mystic order laid.
First, rob'd in white, the nymph intent adores,
With head uncovered, the cosmetic powers.
A heavenly image in the glass appears,
To that she bends, to that her eyes she rears;
Th' inferior priestess, at her altar's side,
Trembling begins the sacred rites of pride;
Unnumbered treasures ope at once, and here
The various offerings of the world appear;
From each she nicely culls with curious toil,
And decks the goddess with the glittering spoil.
This casket India's glowing gems unlocks,
And all Arabia breathes from yonder box.
The tortoise here and elephant unite,
Transform'd to combs, the speckled and the white.
Here files of pins extend their shining rows,
Puffs, powders, patches, bibles, billet-doux.
Now awful beauty puts on all its arms,
The fair each moment rises in her charms,

---

[8] Dunciad, B.

[9] The passage is this,

Felix prole virûm, qualis Berecynthia mater
Invehitur curru Phrygias turrita per urbes,
Læta deûm partu, centum complexa nepotes,
Omnes cœlicolas, omnes supera alta tenentes. ÆNEIS.

Repairs her smiles, awakens every grace,
And calls forth all the wonders of her face;
Sees by degrees a purer blush arise,
And keener lightnings quicken in her eyes[1].

To this class also we must refer the application of grave reflections to mere trifles. For that *great* and *serious* are naturally associated by the mind, and likewise little and trifling, is sufficiently evinced by the common modes of expression on these subjects used in every tongue. An apposite instance of such an application we have from Philips,

My galligaskins, that have long withstood
The winter's fury and encroaching frosts,
By time subdued, *(what will not time subdue?)*
A horrid chasm disclose[2].

Like to this, but not equal, is that of Young,

One day his wife *(for who can wives reclaim?)*
Levell'd her barbarous needle at his fame[3].

To both the preceding kinds the term *burlesque* is applied, but especially to the first.

Of the third species of wit, which is by far the most multifarious, and which results from what I may call the queerness or singularity of the imagery, I shall give a few specimens that will serve to mark some of its principal varieties. To illustrate all would be impossible.

The first I shall exemplify is where there is an apparent contrariety in the things she exhibits as connected. This kind of contrast we have in these lines of Garth,

Then Hydrops next appears amongst the throng;
Bloated and big she slowly sails along;
But, like a miser, in excess she's poor;
And pines for thirst amidst her watery store[4].

The wit in these lines doth not so much arise from the comparison they contain of the dropsy to a miser, (which falls under the description that immediately succeeds,) as from the union of contraries they present to the imagination, poverty in the midst of opulence, and thirst in one who is already drenched in water.

A second sort is where the things compared are what with dialecticians would come under the denomination of *disparates*, being such as can be ranked under no common genus. Of this I shall subjoin an example from Young,

[1] Rape of the Lock, Canto 1.
[2] Splendid Shilling,
[3] Universal Passion.
[4] Dispensary.

Health chiefly keeps an Atheist in the dark,
A fever argues better than a *Clarke:*
Let but the logic in his pulse decay,
The Grecian he'll renounce, and learn to pray[5].

Here, by implication, health is compared to a sophister, or darkener of the understanding, a fever to a metaphysical disputant, a regular pulse to false logic, for the word logic in the third line is used ironically. In other words, we have here modes and substances, the affections of body, and the exercise of reason, strangely, but not insignificantly linked together; strangely, else the sentiment, however just, could not be denominated witty; significantly, because an unmeaning jumble of things incongruous would not be wit, but nonsense.

A third variety in this species springs from confounding artfully the proper and metaphorical sense of an expression. In this way, one would assign as a motive what is discovered to be perfectly absurd, when but ever so little attended to; and yet, from the ordinary meaning of the words, hath a specious appearance on a single glance. Of this kind you have an instance in the subsequent lines,

While thus the lady talk'd, the knight
Turn'd th' outside of his eyes to white,
As men of inward light are wont
To turn their optics in upon't[6].

For whither can they turn their eyes more properly than to the light?

A fourth variety, much resembling the former, is when the argument or comparison (for all argument is a kind of comparison) is founded on the supposal of corporeal or personal attributes in what is strictly not susceptible of them, as in this,

But Hudibras gave him a twitch
As quick as lightning in the breech,
Just in the place where honour's lodg'd,
As wise philosophers have judg'd;
Because a kick in that place more
Hurts honour than deep wounds before[7].

Is demonstration itself more satisfactory? Can any thing be hurt, but where it is? However, the mention of this as the sage deduction of philosophers, is no inconsiderable addition to the wit. Indeed, this particular circumstance belongs properly to the first species mentioned, in which high and low, great and little, are coupled. Another example, not unlike the preceding, you have in these words,

[5] Universal Passion.
[6] Hudibras, Part iii. Canto 1.
[7] Ibid. Part ii. Canto 2.

What makes morality a crime,
The most notorious of the time;
Morality which both the saints
And wicked too cry out against?
'Cause grace and virtue are within
Prohibited decrees of kin:
And therefore no true saint allows
They shall be suffer'd to espouse[8].

When the two foregoing instances are compared together we should say of the first, that it has more of simplicity and nature, and is therefore more pleasing; of the second, that it has more of ingenuity and conceit, and is consequently more surprising.

The fifth and only other variety I shall observe, is that which ariseth from a relation not in the things signified, but in the sign, of all relations, no doubt, the slightest. Identity here gives rise to puns and clinches: resemblance to quibbles, cranks, and rhymes: Of these, I imagine, it is quite unnecessary to exhibit specimens. The wit here is so dependent on the sound, that it is commonly incapable of being transfused into another language, and as, among persons of taste and discernment, it is in less request than the other sorts above enumerated, those who abound in this, and never rise to any thing superior, are distinguished by the diminutive appellation of witlings.

Let it be remarked in general, that from one or more of the three last-mentioned varieties, those plebeian tribes of witticism, the conundrums, the rebuses, the riddles, and some others, are lineally, though perhaps not all legitimately descended. I shall only add, that I have not produced the forenamed varieties as an exact enumeration of all the subdivisions of which the third species of wit is susceptible. It is capable, I acknowledge, of being almost infinitely diversified; and it is principally to its various exhibitions that we apply the epithets *sportive*, *sprightly*, *ingenious*, according as they recede more or less from those of the declaimer.

SECTION II.—*Of Humour.*

As wit is the painting, humour is the pathetic, in this inferior sphere of eloquence. The nature and efficacy of humour may be thus unravelled. A just exhibition of any ardent or durable passion, excited by some adequate cause, instantly attacheth sympathy, the common tie of human souls, and thereby communicates the passion to the breast of the hearer. But when the emotion is either not violent or not durable, and the motive not any thing real, but imaginary, or at least quite disproportionate to the effect; or when the passion displays itself preposterously, so as rather to obstruct than to promote its aim,

8 Hudibras, Part iii. Canto 1.

in these cases a natural representation, instead of fellow-feeling, creates amusement, and universally awakens contempt. The portrait in the former case we call *pathetic*, in the latter *humorous*[9]. It was said that the emotion must be either not violent or not durable. This limitation is necessary, because a passion extreme in its degree, as well as lasting, cannot yield diversion to a well-disposed mind, but generally affects it with pity, not seldom with a mixture of horror and indignation. The sense of the ridiculous, though invariably the same, is in this case totally surmounted by a principle of our nature, much more powerful.

The passion which humour addresseth as its object, is, as hath been signified above, contempt. But it ought carefully to be noted, that every address, even every pertinent address to contempt, is not humorous. This passion is not less capable of being excited by the severe and tragic, than by the merry and comic manner. The subject of humour is always character, but not every thing in character; its foibles generally, such as caprices, little extravagances, weak anxieties, jealousies, childish fondness, pertness, vanity, and self-conceit. One finds the greatest scope for exercising this talent in telling familiar stories, or in acting any whimsical part in an assumed character. Such an one, we say, has the talent of humouring a tale, or any queer manner which he chooseth to exhibit. Thus we speak of the passions in tragedy, but of the humours in comedy; and even to express passion as appearing in the more trivial occurrences of life, we commonly use this term, as when we talk of good humour, ill humour, peevish or pleasant humour; hence it is that a capricious temper we call humorsome, the person possessed of it a humorist, and such facts or events as afford subject for the humours, we denominate comical.

[9] It ought to be observed, that this term is also used to express any lively strictures of such specialities in temper and conduct, as have neither moment enough to interest sympathy, nor incongruity enough to excite contempt. In this case, humour, not being addressed to passion, but to fancy, must be considered as a kind of moral painting, and differs from wit only in these two things; first, in that character alone is the subject of the former, whereas all things whatever fall within the province of the latter; secondly, humour paints more simply by direct imitation, wit more variously by illustration and imagery. Of this kind of humour, merely graphical, Addison hath given us numberless examples in many of the characters he hath so finely drawn, and little incidents he hath so pleasantly related in his Tatlers and Spectators. I might remark of the word *humour*, as I did of the term *wit*, that we scarcely find in other languages a word exactly corresponding. The Latin *facetiæ* seems to come the nearest. Thus Cicero, "Huic generi orationis aspergentur etiam sales, qui in dicendo mirum quantum valent: quorum duo genera sunt, unum facetiarum, alterum dicacitatis: utetur utroque, sed altero in narrando aliquid venuste, altero in jaciendo mittendoque ridiculo; cujus genera plura sunt." Orator. 48. Here one would think, that the philosopher must have had in his eye the different provinces of wit and humour, calling the former *dicacitas*, and the latter *facetiæ*. It is plain, however, that, both by him and other Latin authors, these two words are often confounded. There appears indeed, to be more uniformity in the use that is made of the second term, than in the application of the first.

Indeed, comedy is the proper province of humour. Wit is called in solely as an auxiliary, humour predominates. The comic poet bears the same analogy to the author of the mock-heroic, that the tragic poet bears to the author of the epic. The epos recites, and advancing with a step majestic and sedate, engageth all the nobler powers of imagination, a sense of grandeur, of beauty, and of order; tragedy personates, and thus employing a more rapid and animated diction, seizeth directly upon the heart. The little epic, a narrative intended for amusement, and addressed to all the lighter powers of fancy, delights in the excursions of wit: the production of the comic muse, being a representation, is circumscribed by narrower bounds, and is all life and activity throughout. Thus Buckingham says with the greatest justness, of comedy,

> *Humour* is *all*. *Wit* should be only brought
> To turn agreeably some proper thought[1].

The pathetic and facetious differ not only in subject and effect, as will appear upon the most superficial review of what hath been said, but also in the manner of imitation. In this the man of humour descends to a minuteness which the orator disdains. The former will often successfully run into downright mimicry, and exhibit peculiarities in voice, gesture, and pronunciation, which in the other would be intolerable. The reason of the difference is this: That we may divert, by exciting scorn and contempt, the individual must be exposed; that we may move, by interesting the more generous principles of humanity, the language and sentiments, not so much of the individual, as of human nature, must be displayed. So very different, or rather opposite, are these two in this respect, that there could not be a more effectual expedient for undoing the charm of the most affecting representation, than an attempt in the speaker to mimic the personal singularities of the man for whom he desires to interest us. On the other hand, in the humorous, where the end is diversion, even overacting, if moderate, is not improper.

It was observed already, that though contempt be the only passion addressed by humour, yet this passion may with propriety and success be assailed by the severer eloquence, where there is not the smallest tincture of humour. This it will not be beside our purpose to specify, in order the more effectually to show the difference.—Lord Bolingbroke, speaking of the state of these kingdoms from the time of Restoration, has these words: "The two brothers, Charles, and James, when in exile, became infected with popery to such degrees as their different

[1] Essay on Poetry.

characters admitted of. Charles had parts; and his good understanding served as an antidote to repel the poison. James, the simplest man of his time, drank off the whole chalice. The poison met, in his composition, with all the fear, all the credulity, and all the obstinacy of temper proper to increase its virulence, and to strengthen its effect.——Drunk with superstitious, and even enthusiastic zeal, he ran headlong into his own ruin, whilst he endeavoured to precipitate ours. His parliament and his people did all they could to save themselves, by winning him. But all was vain. He had no principle on which they could take hold. Even his good qualities worked against them; and his love of his country went halves with his bigotry. How he succeeded we have heard from our fathers. The Revolution of one thousand six hundred and eighty-eight saved the nation, and ruined the king[2]."—Nothing can be more contemptuous, and, at the same time, less derisive, than this representation. We should readily say of it, that it is strongly animated, and happily expressed; but no man who understands English would say it is humorous. I shall add one example from Dr. Swift. "I should be exceedingly sorry to find the legislature make any new laws against the practice of duelling, because the methods are easy and many for a wise man to avoid a quarrel with honour, or engage in it with innocence. And I can discover no political evil in suffering bullies, sharpers, and rakes, to rid the world of each other by a method of their own, where the law hath not been able to find an expedient[3]."

For a specimen of the humorous, take as a contrast to the two last examples, the following delineation of a fop:

Sir Plume (of amber snuff-box justly vain,
And the nice conduct of a clouded cane)
With earnest eyes and round unthinking face,
He first the snuff-box open'd, then the case,
And thus broke out, "My Lord, why,—what the devil?
Z—ds!—damn the lock!—'fore Gad, you must be civil!
Plague on't!—'tis past a jest,—nay prithee,—pox!
Give her the hair."—He spoke and rapp'd his box.
"It grieves me much," replied the peer again,
"Who speaks so well, should ever speak in vain:
But"——————[4]

This, both in the descriptive and the dramatic part, particularly in the draught it contains of the baronet's mind, aspect, manner, and eloquence, (if we except the sarcastic term *justly*, the double sense of the word *open'd*, and the fine irony couched in the reply) is purely facetious. An instance of wit and humour combined, where they reciprocally set off and enliven

[2] A Letter to Sir William Wyndham.
[3] Swift on Good Manners.
[4] Rape of the Lock, Canto 4.

each other, Pope hath also furnished us with in another part of the same exquisite performance.

> Whether the nymph shall break Diana's law,
> Or some frail china jar receive a flaw;
> Or stain her honour, or her new brocade;
> Forget her prayers, or miss a masquerade;
> Or lose her heart, or necklace, at a ball;
> Or whether heaven has doom'd that Shock must fall[5].

This is humorous, in that it is a lively sketch of the female estimate of mischances, as our poet's commentator rightly terms it, marked out by a few striking lineaments. It is likewise witty, for, not to mention the play on words like that remarked in the former example, a trope familiar to this author, you have here a comparison of—a woman's chastity to a piece of porcelain,—her honour to a gaudy robe,—her prayers to a fantastical disguise,—her heart to a trinket; and all these together to her lap-dog, and that founded on one lucky circumstance (a malicious critic would perhaps discern or imagine more) by which these things, how unlike soever in other respects, may be compared, the impression they make on the mind of a fine lady.

Hudibras, so often above quoted, abounds in wit in almost all its varieties; to which the author's various erudition hath not a little contributed. And this, it must be owned, is more suitable to the nature of his poem. At the same time, it is by no means destitute of humour, as appears particularly in the different exhibitions of character given by the knight and his squire. But in no part of the story is this talent displayed to greater advantage than in the consultation of the lawyer[6], to which I shall refer the reader, as the passage is too long for my transcribing. There is, perhaps, no book in any language, wherein the humorous is carried to a higher pitch of perfection, than in the adventures of the celebrated knight of La Mancha. As to our English dramatists, who does not acknowledge the transcendent excellence of Shakspeare in this province, as well as in the pathetic? Of the later comic writers, Congreve has an exuberance of wit, but Farquhar has more humour. It may, however, with too much truth, be affirmed of English comedy in general, (for there are some exceptions,) that, to the discredit of our stage, as well as of the national delicacy and discernment, obscenity is made too often to supply the place of wit, and ribaldry the place of humour.

Wit and humour, as above explained, commonly concur in a tendency to provoke laughter, by exhibiting a curious and unexpected affinity; the first generally by comparison, either

[5] Rape of the Lock, Canto 2.
[6] Part iii. Canto 3.

direct or implied, the second by connecting in some other relation, such as causality or vicinity, objects apparently the most dissimilar and heterogeneous; which incongruous affinity, we may remark by the way, gives the true meaning of the word *oddity*, and is the proper object of laughter.

The difference between these and that grander kind of eloquence treated in the first part of this chapter, I shall, if possible, still further illustrate, by a few similitudes borrowed from the optical science. The latter may be conceived as a plane mirror, which faithfully reflects the object, in colour, figure, size, and posture. Wit, on the contrary, Proteus-like, transforms itself into a variety of shapes. It is now a convex speculum, which gives a just representation in form and colour, but withal reduces the greatest objects to the most despicable littleness: now a concave speculum, which swells the smallest trifles to an enormous magnitude; now again a speculum of a cylindrical, a conical, or an irregular make, which, though in colour, and even in attitude, it reflects a pretty strong resemblance, widely varies the proportions. Humour, when we consider the contrariety of its effects, contempt and laughter, (which constitute what in one word is termed *derision*,) to that sympathy and love often produced by the pathetic, may in respect of these be aptly compared to a concave mirror, when the object is placed beyond the focus; in which case it appears, by reflection, both diminished and inverted, circumstances which happily adumbrate the contemptible and the ridiculous.

SECTION III.—*Of Ridicule.*

The intention of raising a laugh is either merely to divert by that grateful titillation which it excites, or to influence the opinions and purposes of the hearers. In this also, the risible faculty, when suitably directed, hath often proved a very potent engine. When this is the view of the speaker, as there is always an air of reasoning conveyed under that species of imagery, narration, or description, which stimulates laughter, these, thus blended, obtain the appellation of *ridicule*, the poignancy of which hath a similar effect in futile subjects, to that produced by what is called *the vehement* in solemn and important matters.

Nor doth all the difference between these lie in the dignity of the subject. Ridicule is not only confined to questions of less moment, but is fitter for refuting error than for supporting truth, for restraining from wrong conduct, than for inciting to the practice of what is right. Nor are these the sole restrictions; it is not properly levelled at the false, but at the *absurd* in tenets; nor can the edge of ridicule strike with equal force every species of misconduct: it is not the criminal part which it attacks, but that which we denominate silly or foolish. With regard to doctrine, it is evident that it is not falsity or mistake, but palpable error or absurdity (a thing hardly confutable by mere argument), which is the object of contempt; and consequently those dogmas are beyond the reach of cool reasoning which are within the rightful confines of ridicule. That they are generally conceived to be so, appears from the sense universally assigned to expressions like these, 'Such a position is ridiculous—It doth not deserve a serious answer.' Every body knows that they import more than 'It is false,' being, in other words, 'This is such an extravagance as is not so much a subject of argument as of laughter.' And that we may discover what it is, with regard to conduct, to which ridicule is applicable, we need only consider the different departments of tragedy and of comedy. In the last, it is of mighty influence; into the first it never legally obtains admittance. Those things which principally come under its lash are awkwardness, rusticity, ignorance, cowardice, levity, foppery, pedantry, and affectation of every kind. But against murder, cruelty, parricide, ingratitude, perfidy[7], to attempt to raise a laugh, would show such an unnatural insensibility in the speaker as would be excessively disgustful to any audience. To punish such enormities the tragic poet must take a very different route.

Now, from this distinction of vices or faults into two classes, there hath sprung a parallel division in all the kinds of poesy which relate to manners. The epopée, a picturesque, or graphical poem, is either heroic, or what is called mock-heroic, and by Aristotle iambic[8], from the measure in which poems of this kind were at first composed. The drama, an animated poem, is either in the buskin or in the sock; for farce deserves not a place in the subdivision, being at most but a kind of dramatical apologue, whereof the characters are monstrous, the intrigue unnatural, the incidents often impossible, and which, instead of humour, has adopted a spurious bantling called *fun.* To satisfy us that satire, whose end is persuasion, admits also the like distribution, we need only recur to the different methods pursued by the two famous Latin satirists, Juvenal and Horace. The one declaims, the other derides. Accordingly, as Dryden justly observes[9], vice is the quarry of the

[7] To this black catalogue an ancient Pagan of Athens or of Rome would have added *adultery*, but the modern refinements of us Christians (if without profanation we can so apply the name) absolutely forbid it, as nothing on our theatre is a more common subject of laughter than this. Nor is the laugh raised against the adulterer, else we might have some plea for our morals, if none for our taste; but, to the indelible reproach of the taste, the sense, and the virtue of the nation, in his favour. How much degenerated from our worthier, though unpolished, ancestors, of whom Tacitus affirms, "Nemo illic vitia ridet; nec corrumpere et corrumpi sæculum vocatur." De Mor. Germ. c. 19.

[8] Poet. 4.

[9] Origin and Progress of Satire.

former, folly of the latter[1]. Thus, of the three graver forms, the aim, whether avowed or latent, always is, or ought to be, the improvement of the three lighter, the refinement of manners[2]. But though the latter have for their peculiar object manners, in the limited and distinctive sense of that word, they may, with propriety, admit many things which directly conduce to the advancement of morals, and ought never to admit any thing which hath a contrary tendency. Virtue is of primary importance, both for the happiness of individuals, and for the well-being of society; an external polish is at best but a secondary accomplishment, ornamental indeed when it adds a lustre to virtue, pernicious when it serves only to embellish profligacy, and in itself comparatively of but little consequence, either to private or to public felicity[3].

Another remarkable difference, the only one which remains to be observed, between the vehement or contentious and

[1] The differences and relations to be found in the several forms of poetry mentioned, may be more concisely marked by the following scheme, which brings them under the view at once.

The object.	Serious.	The end morals.	Facetious.	The end manners.	The means,	The Poet,
Fancy	—Great epic		—Little epic	—	Insinuation	Narrator,
Passion	—Tragedy		—Comedy	—	Conformation	Representer,
Will	—High satire		—Low satire	—	Persuasion	Reasoner.

[2] These observations will enable us to understand that of the poet,

——————Ridiculum acri
Fortius et melius magnas plerumque secat res. HOR.

Great and signal, it must be owned, are the effects of ridicule; but the subject must always appear to the ridiculer, and to those affected by his pleasantry, under the notion of littleness and futility, two essential requisites in the object of contempt and risibility.

[3] Whether this attention has been always given to morals, particularly in comedy, must be left to the determination of those who are most conversant in that species of scenic representations. One may, however, venture to prognosticate, that if in any period it shall become fashionable to show no regard to virtue in such entertainments, if the hero of the piece, a fine gentleman to be sure, adorned as usual with all the superficial and exterior graces which the poet can confer, and crowned with success in the end, shall be an unprincipled libertine, a man of more spirit, forsooth, than to be checked in his pursuits by the restraints of religion, by a regard to the common rights of mankind, or by the laws of hospitality and private friendship, which were accounted sacred among the Pagans and those whom we denominate Barbarians; then, indeed, the stage will become merely the school of gallantry and intrigue; thither the youth of both sexes will resort, and will not resort in vain, in order to get rid of that troublesome companion modesty, intended by Providence as a guard to virtue, and a check against licentiousness; there vice will soon learn to provide herself in a proper stock of effrontery, and a suitable address for effecting her designs, and triumphing over innocence; then, in fine, if religion, virtue, principle, equity, gratitude, and good faith, are not empty sounds, the stage will prove the greatest of nuisances, and deserve to be styled the principal corrupter of the age. Whether such an era hath ever happened in the history of the theatre, in this or any other country, or is likely to happen, I do not take upon me to decide.

the derisive, consists in the manner of conducting them. As in each there is a mixture of argument, this in the former ought, in appearance at least, to have the ascendant, but not in the latter. The attack of the declaimer is direct and open; argument therefore is his avowed aim. On the contrary, the passions which he excites ought never to appear to the auditors as the effects of his intention and address, but both in him and them, as the native, the unavoidable consequences of the subject treated, and of that conviction which his reasoning produces in the understanding. Although, in fact, he intends to move his auditory, he only declares his purpose to convince them. To reverse this method, and profess an intention to work upon their passions, would be in effect to tell them that he meant to impose upon their understandings, and to bias them by his art, and consequently, would be to warn them to be on their guard against him. Nothing is better founded than the famous aphorism of rhetoricians, that the perfection of art consists in concealing art[4]. On the other hand, the assault of him who ridicules is, from its very nature, covert and oblique. What we profess to contemn, we scorn to confute. It is on this account that the reasoning in ridicule, if at all delicate, is always conveyed under a species of disguise. Nay, sometimes, which is more astonishing, the contempt itself seems to be dissembled, and the rallier assumes an air of arguing gravely in defence of that which he actually exposeth as ridiculous. Hence, undoubtedly, it proceeds, that a serious manner commonly adds energy to a joke. The fact, however, is, that in this case the very dissimulation is dissembled. He would not have you think him in earnest, though he affects the appearance of it; knowing that otherwise his end would be frustrated. He wants you should perceive that he is dissembling, which no real dissembler ever wanted. It is, indeed, this circumstance alone, which distinguishes an ironical expression from a lie. Accordingly, through the thinness of the veil employed, he takes care that the sneer shall be discovered. You are quickly made to perceive his aim, by means of the strange arguments he produces, the absurd consequences he draws, the odd embarrassments which in his personated character he is involved in, and the still odder methods he takes to disentangle himself. In this manner doctrines and practices are treated, when exposed by a continued run of irony; a way of refutation which bears a strong analogy to that species of demonstration termed by mathematicians apagogical, as reducing the adversary to what is contradictory or impracticable. This method seems to have been first introduced into moral subjects, and employed with success, by the father of ancient wisdom, Socrates. As the attack

[4] Artis est celare artem.

of ridicule, whatever form it adopts, is always indirect, that of irony may be said to be reverted. It resembles the manner of fighting ascribed to the ancient Parthians, who were ever more formidable in flight than in onset; who looked towards one quarter, and fought towards the opposite; whose bodies moved in one direction, and their arrows in the contrary[5].

It remains now to confirm and illustrate this branch of the theory, by suitable examples. And, not to encumber the reader with a needless multiplicity of excerptions, I shall first recur to those already produced. The first, second, and the fifth passages from Butler, the first from Young, and the quotation from the Dispensary, though witty, have no ridicule in them. Their whole aim is to divert by the oddness of the imagery. This merits a careful and particular attention, as on the accuracy of our conceptions here, depends, in a great measure, our forming a just notion of the relation which ridicule bears to wit, and of the distinction that subsists between them. Let this, therefore, be carefully remembered, that where nothing reprehensible, or supposed to be reprehensible, either in conduct or in sentiment, is struck at, there is properly no satire (or as it is sometimes termed emphatically enough, pointed wit), and consequently no ridicule.

The example that first claims particular notice here is one from Young's Satires,

> Health chiefly keeps an Atheist in the dark, &c.

The wittiness of this passage was already illustrated: I shall now endeavour to show the argument couched under it, both which together constitute the ridicule. "Atheism is unreasonable." Why? "The Atheist neither founds his unbelief on reason, nor will attend to it. Was ever an Infidel in health convinced by reasoning; or did he ever in sickness need to be reasoned with on this subject? The truth then is that the daring principles of the libertine are solely supported by the vigour and healthiness of his constitution, which incline him to pleasure, thoughtlessness, and presumption; accordingly you find that, when this foundation is subverted, the whole fabric of infidelity falls to pieces." There is rarely, however, so much of argument in ridicule as may be discovered in this passage. Generally, as was observed already, it is but hinted in a single word or phrase, or appears to be glanced at occasionally, without any direct intention. Thus, in the third quotation from Butler, there is an oblique thrust at Homer, for his manner of recurring so often, in poems of so great dignity, to such mean and trifling epithets. The

[5] Miles sagittas et celerem fugam
Parthi ——————— perhorrescit. HOR.

Fidentemque fuga Parthum versisque sagittis. VIRG.

fourth and sixth satirize the particular fanatical practice, and fanatical opinion, to which they refer. To assign a preposterous motive to an action, or to produce an absurd argument for an opinion, is an innuendo, that no good motive or argument can be given[6]. The citations from the Rape of the Lock are no otherwise to be considered as ridicule, than as a lively exhibition of some follies, either in disposition or in behaviour, is the strongest dissuasive from imitating them. In this way, humour rarely fails to have some raillery in it, in like manner as the pathetic often persuades without argument, which, when obvious, is supplied by the judgment of the hearer[7]. The second example seems intended to disgrace the petty quaintness of a fop's manner, and the emptiness of his conversation, as being a huddle of oaths and nonsense. The third finely satirizes the value which the ladies too often put upon the merest trifles. To these I shall add one instance more from Hudibras, where it is said of priests and exorcists,

> Supplied with spiritual provision,
> And magazines of ammunition,
> With crosses, relics, crucifixes,
> Beads, pictures, rosaries, and pixes,
> The tools of working our salvation,
> By mere mechanic operation[8].

The reasoning here is sufficiently insinuated by the happy application of a few words, such as mechanic tools to the work of salvation; crosses, relics, beads, pictures, and other such trumpery, to spiritual provision. The justness of the representation of their practice, together with the manifest incongruity of the things, supply us at once with the wit and the argument. There is in this poem a great deal of ridicule; but the author's quarry is the frantic excesses of enthusiasm, and the base artifices of hypocrisy; he very rarely, as in the above passage, points to the idiot gewgaws of superstition. I shall only add one instance from Pope, which has something peculiar in it,

> Then sighing thus, "And am I now threescore?
> Ah! why, ye gods! should two and two make four[9]?"

This, though not in the narrative, but in the dramatic style, is more witty than humorous. The absurdity of the exclamation in the second line is too gross to be natural to any but a

[6] We have an excellent specimen of this sort of ridicule in Montesquieu's Spirit of Laws, b. xv. c. 5, where the practice of Europeans, in enslaving the negroes, is ironically justified, in a manner which does honour to the author's humanity and love of justice, at the same time that it displays a happy talent in ridicule.

[7] Ridicule resulting from a simple, but humorous narration, is finely illustrated in the first ten or twelve Provincial Letters.

[8] Part iii. Canto 1. [9] Dunciad.

madman, and therefore hath not humour. Nevertheless, its resemblance to the common complaint of old age, contained in the first, of which it may be called the analysis, renders it at once both an ingenious exhibition of such complaint in its real import, and an argument of its folly. But notwithstanding this example, it holds in general, that when any thing nonsensical in principle is to be assailed by ridicule, the natural ally of reason is wit; when any extravagance or impropriety in conduct, humour seldom fails to be of the confederacy. It may be further observed, that the words *banter* and *raillery* are also used to signify ridicule of a certain form, applied, indeed, more commonly to practices than to opinions, and oftener to the little peculiarities of individuals, than to the distinguishing customs or usages of sects and parties. The only difference in meaning, as far as I have remarked, between the two terms, is, that the first generally denotes a coarser, the second a finer sort of ridicule; the former prevails most among the lower classes of the people, the latter only among persons of breeding.

I shall conclude this chapter with observing, that though the gayer and more familiar eloquence, now explained, may often properly, as was remarked before, be admitted into public orations on subjects of consequence, such, for instance, as are delivered in the senate or at the bar, and even sometimes, though more sparingly, on the bench; it is seldom or never of service in those which come from the pulpit. It is true, that an air of ridicule in disproving or dissuading, by rendering opinions or practices contemptible, hath occasionally been attempted, with approbation, by preachers of great name. I can only say, that when this airy manner is employed, it requires to be managed with the greatest care and delicacy, that it may not degenerate into a strain but ill adapted to so serious an occupation. For the reverence of the place, the gravity of the function, the solemnity of worship, the severity of the precepts, and the importance of the motives of religion; above all, the awful presence of God, with a sense of which the mind, when occupied in religious exercises, ought eminently to be impressed; all these seem utterly incompatible with the levity of ridicule. They render jesting impertinence, and laughter madness. Therefore, any thing in preaching which might provoke this emotion, would justly be deemed an unpardonable offence against both piety and decorum.

In the two preceding chapters I have considered the nature of oratory in general, its various forms, whether arising from difference in the object, understanding, imagination, passion, will; or in the subject, eminent and severe, light and frivolous, with their respective ends and characters. Under these are included all the primary and characteristical qualities of whatever can pertinently find a place either in writing or in discourse, or can truly be termed fine in the one, or eloquent in the other.

CHAPTER III.

The Doctrine of the preceding Chapter defended.

BEFORE I proceed to another topic, it will perhaps be thought proper to inquire how far the theory, now laid down and explained, coincides with the doctrines on this article to be found in the writings of philosophers and critics. Not that I think such inquiries and discussions always necessary; on the contrary, I imagine they often tend but to embarrass the reader, by distracting his attention to a multiplicity of objects, and so to darken and perplex a plain question. This is particularly the case on those points on which there hath been a variety of jarring sentiments. The simplest way and the most perspicuous, and generally that which best promotes the discovery of truth, is to give as distinct and methodical a delineation as possible of one's own ideas, together with the grounds on which they are founded, and to leave it to the doubtful reader (who thinks it worth the trouble) to compare the theory with the systems of other writers, and then to judge for himself. I am not, however, so tenacious of this method, as not to allow that it may sometimes, with advantage, be departed from. This holds especially when the sentiments of an author are opposed by inveterate prejudices in the reader, arising from contrary opinions early imbibed, or from an excessive deference to venerable names and ancient authorities.

SECTION I.—*Aristotle's account of* the Ridiculous *explained.*

Some, on a superficial view, may imagine that the doctrine above expounded is opposed by no less authority than that of Aristotle. If it were, I should not think that equivalent to a demonstration of its falsity. But let us hear; Aristotle hath observed, that "the ridiculous implies something deformed, and consists in those smaller faults, which are neither painful nor pernicious, but unbeseeming: thus a face excites laughter wherein there is deformity and distortion without pain." For my part, nothing can appear more coincident than this, as far as it goes, with the principles which I have endeavoured to establish. The Stagyrite here speaks of ridicule, not of laughter in general, and not of every sort of ridicule, but solely of the ridiculous in manners, of which he hath in few words given a very apposite description. To take notice of any other laughable object, would have been foreign to his purpose. Laughter is not his theme, but comedy, and laughter only so far as comedy is concerned with it. Now, the concern of comedy reaches no further than that kind of ridicule which, as I said, relates to manners. The very words, with which the above quotation is introduced, evince the truth of this. "Comedy," says he, "is, as we remarked, an imitation of things that are amiss; yet it does not level at every vice.[1]" He had remarked in the preceding chapter, that its means of correction are "not reproach, but ridicule[2]." Nor does the clause in the end of the sentence, concerning a countenance which raises laughter, in the least invalidate what I have now affirmed; for it is plain that this is suggested in the way of similitude, to illustrate what he had advanced, and not as a particular instance of the position he had laid down. For we can never suppose that he would have called distorted features "a certain fault or slip[3]," and still less that he would have specified this, as what might be corrected by the art of the comedian. As an instance, therefore, it would have confuted his definition, and shown that his account of the object of laughter must be erroneous, since this emotion may be excited, as appears from the example produced by himself, where there is nothing faulty or vicious in any kind or degree. As an illustration it was extremely pertinent. It showed that the ridiculous in manners (which was all that his definition regarded) was, as far as the different nature of the things would permit, analogous to the laughable in other subjects, and that it supposed an incongruous combination, where there is nothing either calamitous or destructive. But that in other objects, unconnected with either character or conduct, with either the body or the soul, there might not be images or exhibitions presented to the mind which would naturally provoke laughter, the philosopher has nowhere, as far as I know, so much as insinuated.

SECTION II.—*Hobbes's account of* Laughter *examined.*

From the founder of the peripatetic school, let us descend to the philosopher of Malmesbury, who hath defined laughter "a sudden glory, arising from a sudden conception of some eminency in ourselves, by comparison with the infirmity of others, or with our own formerly[4]." This account is, I ac-

[1] The whole passage runs thus, Ἡ δε κωμωδια εστιν, ὥσπερ ειπομεν, μιμησις φαυλοτερων μεν, ου μεντοι κατα πασαν κακιαν, αλλα του αισχρου εστι το γελοιον μοριον· το γαρ γελοιον εστιν ἁμαρτημα τι και αισχος ανωδυνον και ου φθαρτικον· οἱον ευθυς το γελοιον προσωπον αισχρον τι και διεστραμμενον ανευ οδυνης. Poet. 5.

[2] Ου ψογον αλλα το γελοιον δραματοποιησας.

[3] Ἁμαρτημα τι.

[4] Human Nature, Chap. ix. § 13.

knowledge, incompatible with that given in the preceding pages, and, in my judgment, results entirely from a view of the subject, which is in some respect partial, and in some respect false. It is in some respect partial. When laughter is produced by ridicule, it is, doubtless, accompanied with some degree of contempt. Ridicule, as hath been observed already, has a double operation, first on the fancy, by presenting to it such a group as constitutes a laughable object; secondly, on the passion mentioned, by exhibiting absurdity in human character, in principles or in conduct: and contempt always implies a sense of superiority. No wonder then that one likes not to be ridiculed or laughed at. Now, it is this union which is the great source of this author's error, and of his attributing to one of the associated principles, from an imperfect view of the subject, what is purely the effect of the other.

For that the emotion called laughter doth not result from the contempt, but solely from the perception of oddity, with which the passion is occasionally, not necessarily, combined, is manifest from the following considerations. First, contempt may be raised in a very high degree, both suddenly and unexpectedly, without producing the least tendency to laugh. Of this instances have been given already from Bolingbroke and Swift, and innumerable others will occur to those who are conversant in the writings of those authors. Secondly, laughter may be, and is daily, produced by the perception of incongruous association, when there is no contempt. And this shows that Hobbes's view of the matter is false as well as partial. "Men," says he, "laugh at jests, the wit whereof always consisteth in the elegant discovering and conveying to our minds some absurdity of another[5]." I maintain, that men also laugh at jests, the wit whereof doth not consist in discovering any absurdity of another; for all jests do not come within his description. On a careful perusal of the foregoing sheets, the reader will find that there have been several instances of this kind produced already, in which it hath been observed that there is wit, but no ridicule. I shall bring but one other instance. Many have laughed at the queerness of the comparison of these lines,

> For rhyme the rudder is of verses,
> With which like ships they steer their courses[6];

who never dreamt that there was any person or party, practice or opinion, derided in them. But as people are often very ingenious, in their manner of defending a favourite hypothesis, if any admirer of the Hobbesian philosophy should pretend to

[5] Human Nature, Chap. ix. § 13.
[6] Hudibras, Part i. Canto 1.

discover some class of men whom the poet here meant to ridicule, he ought to consider that if any one hath been tickled with the passage, to whom the same thought never occurred, that single instance would be sufficient to subvert the doctrine, as it would show that there may be laughter, where is no triumph or glorying over any body, and consequently no conceit of one's own superiority. So that there may be, and often is, both contempt without laughter, and laughter without contempt.

Besides, where wit is really pointed, which constitutes ridicule, that it is not from what gives the conceit of our own eminence by comparison, but purely from the odd assemblage of ideas, that the laughter springs, is evident from this, that if you make but a trifling alteration in the expression, so as to destroy the wit (which often turns on a very little circumstance), without altering the real import of the sentence (a thing not only possible but easy), you will produce the same opinion, and the same contempt; and consequently will give the same subject of triumph, yet without the least tendency to laugh: and conversely, in reading a well written satire, a man may be much diverted by the wit, whose judgment is not convinced by the ridicule or insinuated argument, and whose former esteem of the object is not in the least impaired. Indeed, men's telling their own blunders, even blunders recently committed, and laughing at them, a thing not uncommon in very risible dispositions, is utterly inexplicable on Hobbes's system. For, to consider the thing only with regard to the laugher himself, there is to him no subject of glorying, that is not counterbalanced by an equal subject of humiliation (he being both the person laughing, and the person laughed at), and these two subjects must destroy one another. With regard to others, he appears solely under the notion of inferiority, as the person triumphed over. Indeed, as in ridicule, agreeably to the doctrine here propounded, there is always some degree, often but a very slight degree, of contempt, it is not every character, I acknowledge, that is fond of presenting to others such subjects of mirth. Wherever one shows a proneness to it, it is demonstrable that on that person sociality and the love of laughter have much greater influence than vanity or self-conceit: since for the sake of sharing with others in the joyous entertainment, he can submit to the mortifying circumstance of being the subject. This, however, is in effect no more than enjoying the sweet which predominates, notwithstanding a little of the bitter with which it is mingled. The laugh in this case is so far from being expressive of the passion, that it is produced in spite of the passion which operates against it, and if strong enough would effectually restrain it.

But it is impossible that there could be any enjoyment to

him on the other hypothesis, which makes a laughter merely the expression of a triumph, occasioned by the sudden display of one's own comparative excellence, a triumph in which the person derided could not partake. In this case, on the contrary, he must undoubtedly sustain the part of the weeper, (according to the account which the same author hath given of that opposite passion[7], as he calls it,) and "suddenly fall out with himself, on the sudden conception of defect." To suppose that a person in laughing enjoys the contempt of himself as a matter of exultation over his own infirmity, is of a piece with Cowley's description of envy exaggerated to absurdity, wherein she is said

To envy at the praise herself had won[8].

In the same way, a miser may be said to grudge the money that himself hath got, or a glutton the repast; for the lust of praise as much terminates in self, as avarice or gluttony. It is a strange sort of theory, which makes the frustration of a passion and the gratification the same thing.

As to the remark, that wit is not the only cause of this emotion, that men laugh at indecencies and mischances; nothing is more certain. A well-dressed man falling into the kennel, will raise in the spectators a peal of laughter. But this confirms, instead of weakening, the doctrine here laid down. The genuine object is always things grouped together, in which there is some striking unsuitableness. The effect is much the same, whether the things themselves are presented to the senses by external accident, or the ideas of them are presented to the imagination by wit and humour; though it is only with the latter that the subject of eloquence is concerned.

In regard to Hobbes's system, I shall only remark further, that according to it, a very risible man, and a very self-conceited supercilious man, should imply the same character, yet, in fact, perhaps, no two characters more rarely meet in the same person. Pride, and contempt, its usual attendant, considered in themselves, are unpleasant passions, and tend to make men fastidious, always finding ground to be dissatisfied with their situation and their company. Accordingly, those who are most addicted to these passions are not generally the happiest of mortals. It is only when the last of these hath gotten for an alloy a considerable share of sensibility in regard to wit and humour, which serves both to moderate and to sweeten the passion, that it can be termed in any degree sociable or agreeable. It hath been often remarked of very proud persons, that they disdain to

[7] Hobbes's Hum. Nat. Chap. ix. § 14.
[8] Davideis, Book i.

laugh, as thinking that it derogates from their dignity, and levels them too much with the common herd. The merriest people, on the contrary, are the least suspected of being haughty and contemptuous people. The company of the former is generally as much courted as that of the latter is shunned. To refer ourselves to such universal observations, is to appeal to the common sense of mankind. How admirably is the height of pride and arrogance touched in the character which Cæsar gives of Cassius!

> ———— He loves no plays
> As thou dost, Antony; he hears no music;
> Seldom he smiles, and smiles in such a sort,
> As if he mock'd himself, and scorn'd his spirit,
> That could be mov'd to smile at any thing[9].

I should not have been so particular in the refutation of the English philosopher's system in regard to laughter, had I not considered a careful discussion of this question as one of the best means of developing some of the radical principles of this inquiry.

CHAPTER IV.

Of the relation which eloquence bears to logic and to grammar.

In contemplating a human creature, the most natural division of the subject is the common division into soul and body, or into the living principle of perception and of action, and that system of material organs by which the other receives information from without, and is enabled to exert its powers, both for its own benefit and for that of the species. Analogous to this, there are two things in every discourse which principally claim our attention, the sense and the expression; or in other words, the thought and the symbol by which it is communicated. These may be said to constitute the soul and the body of an oration, or indeed of whatever is signified to another by language. For, as in man, each of these constituent parts hath its distinctive attributes, and as the perfection of the latter consisteth in its fitness for serving the purposes of the former, so it is precisely with those two essential parts of every speech, the sense and the expression. Now, it is by the sense that rhetoric holds of logic, and by the expression that she holds of grammar.

[9] Shakspeare's Julius Cæsar.

The sole and ultimate end of logic is the eviction of truth; one important end of eloquence, though, as appears from the first chapter, neither the sole, nor always the ultimate, is the conviction of the hearers. Pure logic regards only the subject, which is examined solely for the sake of information. Truth, as such, is the proper aim of the examiner. Eloquence not only considers the subject, but also the speaker and the hearers, and both the subject and the speaker for the sake of the hearers, or rather for the sake of the effect intended to be produced in them. Now, to convince the hearers is always either proposed by the orator, as his end in addressing them, or supposed to accompany the accomplishment of his end. Of the five sorts of discourses above mentioned, there are only two wherein conviction is the avowed purpose. One is that addressed to the understanding, in which the speaker proposeth to prove some position disbelieved or doubted by the hearers; the other is that which is calculated to influence the will, and persuade to a certain conduct; for it is by convincing the judgment that he proposeth to interest the passions and fix the resolution. As to the three other kinds of discourses enumerated, which address the understanding, the imagination, and the passions, conviction, though not the end, ought ever to accompany the accomplishment of the end. It is never formally proposed as an end where there are not supposed to be previous doubts or errors to conquer. But when due attention is not paid to it, by a proper management of the subject, doubts, disbelief, and mistake will be raised by the discourse itself, where there were none before, and these will not fail to obstruct the speaker's end, whatever it be. In explanatory discourses, which are of all kinds the simplest, there is a certain precision of manner which ought to pervade the whole, and which, though not in the form of argument, is not the less satisfactory, since it carries internal evidence along with it. In harangues pathetic or panegyrical, in order that the hearers may be moved or pleased, it is of great consequence to impress them with the belief of the reality of the subject. Nay, even in those performances where truth, in regard to the individual facts related, is neither sought nor expected, as in some sorts of poetry, and in romance, truth still is an object to the mind, the general truths regarding character, manners, and incidents. When these are preserved, the piece may justly be denominated true, considered as a picture of life; though false, considered as a narrative of particular events. And even these untrue events must be counterfeits of truth, and bear its image; for in cases wherein the proposed end can be rendered consistent with unbelief, it cannot be rendered compatible with incredibility. Thus, in order to satisfy the mind, in most cases, truth, and in every case, what bears the semblance of truth, must be presented to it. This holds equally, whatever be the declared aim of the speaker. I need scarcely add, that to prove a particular point is often occasionally necessary in every sort of discourse, as a subordinate end conducive to the advancement of the principal. If then it is the business of logic to evince the truth, to convince an auditory, which is the province of eloquence, is but a particular application of the logician's art. As logic therefore forges the arms which eloquence teacheth us to wield, we must first have recourse to the former, that being made acquainted with the materials of which her weapons and armour are severally made, we may know their respective strength and temper, and when and how each is to be used.

Now, if it be by the sense or soul of the discourse that rhetoric holds of logic, or the art of thinking and reasoning, it is by the expression or body of the discourse that she holds of grammar, or the art of conveying our thoughts in the words of a particular language. The observation of one analogy naturally suggests another. As the soul is of heavenly extraction and the body of earthly, so the sense of the discourse ought to have its source in the invariable nature of truth and right, whereas the expression can derive its energy only from the arbitrary conventions of men, sources as unlike, or rather as widely different, as the breath of the Almighty and the dust of the earth. In every region of the globe we may soon discover, that people feel and argue in much the same manner, but the speech of one nation is quite unintelligible to another. The art of the logician is accordingly, in some sense, universal; the art of the grammarian is always particular and local. The rules of argumentation laid down by Aristotle, in his Analytics, are of as much use for the discovery of truth in Britain or China as they were in Greece; but Priscian's rules of inflection and construction can assist us in learning no language but Latin. In propriety there cannot be such a thing as an universal grammar, unless there were such a thing as an universal language. The term hath sometimes, indeed, been applied to a collection of observations on the similar analogies that have been discovered in all tongues, ancient and modern, known to the authors of such collections. I do not mention this liberty in the use of the term with a view to censure it. In the application of technical or learned words, an author hath greater scope than in the application of those which are in more frequent use, and is only then thought censurable when he exposeth himself to be misunderstood. But it is to my purpose to observe that, as such collections convey the knowledge of no tongue whatever, the name *grammar*, when applied to them, is used in a sense quite different from that which it has in the common acceptation; perhaps as different, though the subject be language, as when it is applied to a system of geography.

Now, the grammatical art hath its completion in syntax; the oratorical, as far as the body or expression is concerned, in style. Syntax regards only the composition of many words into one sentence; style, at the same time that it attends to this, regards further the composition of many sentences into one discourse. Nor is this the only difference; the grammarian, with respect to what the two arts have in common, the structure of sentences, requires only purity; that is, that the words employed belong to the language, and that they be construed in the manner, and used in the signification, which custom hath rendered necessary for conveying the sense. The orator requires also beauty and strength. The highest aim of the former is the lowest aim of the latter; where grammar ends eloquence begins.

Thus the grammarian's department bears much the same relation to the orator's which the art of the mason bears to that of the architect. There is, however, one difference that well deserves our notice. As in architecture it is not necessary that he who designs should execute his own plans, he may be an excellent artist in this way who would handle very awkwardly the hammer and the trowel. But it is alike incumbent on the orator to design and to execute. He must, therefore, be master of the language he speaks or writes, and must be capable of adding to grammatic purity those higher qualities of elocution which will render his discourse graceful and energetic.

So much for the connexion that subsists between rhetoric and these parent arts, logic and grammar.

CHAPTER V.

Of the different sources of Evidence, and the different Subjects to which they are respectively adapted.

LOGICAL truth consisteth in the conformity of our conceptions to their archetypes in the nature of things. This conformity is perceived by the mind, either immediately on a bare attention to the ideas under review, or mediately by a comparison of these with other related ideas. Evidence of the former kind is called intuitive; of the latter, deductive.

SECTION I.— *Of Intuitive Evidence.*

PART I.—*Mathematical Axioms.*

Of intuitive evidence there are different sorts. One is that which results purely from *intellection.*[1] Of this kind is the evidence of these propositions: "One and four make five—

[1] I have here adopted the term *intellection* rather than *perception*, because, though not so usual, it is both more apposite and less equivocal. *Perception*

Things equal to the same thing are equal to one another—The whole is greater than a part;" and, in brief, all axioms in arithmetic and geometry. These are, in effect, but so many different expositions of our own general notions, taken in different views. Some of them are no other than definitions, or equivalent to definitions. To say, "One and four make *five*," is precisely the same as to say, "We give the name of *five* to one added to four." In fact, they are all, in some respect, reducible to this axiom, "Whatever is, is." I do not say they are deduced from it, for they have in like manner that original and intrinsic evidence, which makes them, as soon as the terms are understood, to be perceived intuitively. And if they are not thus perceived, no deduction of reason will ever confer on them any additional evidence. Nay, in point of time, the discovery of the less general truths has the priority, not from their superior evidence, but solely from this consideration, that the less general are sooner objects of perception to us, the natural progress of the mind, in the acquisition of its ideas, being from particular things to universal notions, and not inversely. But I affirm that, though not deduced from that axiom, they may be considered as particular exemplifications of it, and coincident with it, inasmuch as they are all implied in this, that the properties of our clear and adequate ideas can be no other than what the mind clearly perceives them to be.

But, in order to prevent mistakes, it will be necessary further to illustrate this subject. It might be thought that if axioms were propositions perfectly identical, it would be impossible to advance a step, by their means, beyond the simple ideas first perceived by the mind. And it must be owned, if the predicate of the proposition were nothing but a repetition of the subject, under the same aspect, and in the same or synonymous terms, no conceivable advantage could be made of it for the furtherance of knowledge. Of such propositions as these for instance, "Seven are seven," "eight are eight," and "ten added to eleven, are equal to ten added to eleven," it is manifest, that we could never avail ourselves of them for the improvement of science. Nor does the change of the name make any alteration in point of utility. The propositions, "Twelve are a dozen," "twenty are a score," unless considered as explications of the words *dozen* and *score*, are equally insignificant with the former. But when the thing,

is employed alike to denote every immediate object of thought, or whatever is apprehended by the mind, our sensations themselves, and those qualities in body suggested by our sensations, the ideas of these upon reflection, whether remembered or imagined, together with those called general notions, or abstract ideas. It is only the last of these kinds which are considered as peculiarly the object of the understanding, and which, therefore, require to be distinguished by a peculiar name. Obscurity arising from an uncommon word is easily surmounted, whereas ambiguity, by misleading us, ere we are aware, confounds our notion of the subject altogether.

though in effect coinciding, is considered under a different aspect; when what is single in the subject is divided in the predicate, and conversely; or when what is a whole in the one is regarded as a part of something else in the other; such propositions lead to the discovery of innumerable and apparently remote relations. One added to four may be accounted no other than a definition of the word *five*, as was remarked above. But when I say, "Two added to three are equal to five," I advance a truth, which, though equally clear, is quite distinct from the preceding. Thus, if one should affirm, "Twice fifteen make thirty," and again, "Thirteen added to seventeen make thirty," nobody would pretend that he had repeated the same proposition in other words. The cases are entirely similar. In both, the same thing is predicated of ideas which, taken severally, are different. From these again result other equations, as, "One added to four are equal to two added to three," and "twice fifteen are equal to thirteen added to seventeen."

Now, it is by the aid of such simple and elementary principles, that the arithmetician and the algebraist proceed to the most astonishing discoveries. Nor are the operations of the geometrician essentially different. By a very few steps you are made to perceive the equality, or rather the coincidence, of the sum of the two angles formed by one straight line falling on another, with two right angles. By a process equally plain you are brought to discover, first, that if one side of a triangle be produced, the external angle will be equal to both the internal and opposite angles, and then, that all the angles of a triangle are equal to two right angles. So much for the nature and use of the first kind of intuitive evidence, resulting from pure intellection.

PART II.—*Consciousness.*

The next kind is that which ariseth from *consciousness.* Hence every man derives the perfect assurance that he hath of his own existence. Nor is he only in this way assured that he exists, but that he thinks, that he feels, that he sees, that he hears, and the like. Hence his absolute certainty in regard to the reality of his sensations and passions, and of every thing whose essence consists in being perceived. Nor does this kind of intuition regard only the truth of the original feelings or impressions, but also many of the judgments that are formed by the mind, on comparing these one with another. Thus the judgments we daily and hourly form, concerning resemblances or disparities in visible objects, or size in things tangible, where the odds is considerable, darker or lighter tints in colours, stronger or weaker tastes or smells, are all self-evident, and discoverable at once. It is from the same principle that, in regard to ourselves, we judge infallibly concerning the feelings, whether pleasant or painful, which we derive from what are called the internal senses, and pronounce concerning beauty or deformity, harmony or discord, the elegant or the ridiculous. The difference between this kind of intuition and the former will appear on the slightest reflection. The former concerns only abstract notions and ideas, particularly in regard to number and extension, the objects purely of the understanding; the latter concerns only the existence of the mind itself, and its actual feelings, impressions or affections, pleasures or pains, the immediate subjects of sense, taking that word in the largest acceptation. The former gives rise to those universal truths, first principles or axioms, which serve as the foundation of abstract science; whereas the latter, though absolutely essential to the individual, yet as it only regards particular perceptions, which represent no distinct genus or species of objects, the judgments resulting thence cannot form any general positions to which a chain of reasoning may be fastened, and consequently are not of the nature of axioms, though both similar and equal in respect of evidence.

PART III.—*Common Sense.*

The third sort is that which ariseth from what hath been termed properly enough, *common sense*,[2] as being an original

[2] The first among the moderns who took notice of this principle, as one of the genuine springs of our knowledge, was Buffier, a French philosopher of the present century, in a book entitled *Traité des premières Vérités;* one who to an uncommon degree of acuteness in matters of abstraction added that solidity of judgment which hath prevented in him, what had proved the wreck of many great names in philosophy, his understanding becoming the dupe of his ingenuity. This doctrine hath lately, in our own country, been set in the clearest light, and supported by invincible force of argument, by two very able writers in the science of man, Dr. Reid, in his *Inquiry into the Human Mind*, and Dr. Beattie, in his *Essay on the Immutability of Truth.* I beg leave to remark in this place, that, though for distinction's sake, I use the term *common sense* in a more limited signification than either of the authors last mentioned, there appears to be no real difference in our sentiments of the thing itself. I am not ignorant that this doctrine has been lately attacked by Dr. Priestley in a most extraordinary manner, a manner which no man, who has any regard to the name either of Englishman or of philosopher, will ever desire to see imitated, in this or any other country. I have read the performance, but have not been able to discover the author's sentiments in relation to the principal point in dispute. He says expressly, [Examination of Dr. Reid's Inquiry, &c. p. 119,] "Had these writers," Messieurs Reid, Beattie, and Oswald, "assumed as the elements of their common sense certain truths which are so plain that no man could doubt of them, (without entering into the ground of our assent to them,) their conduct would have been liable to very little objection." And is not this the very thing which these writers have done? What he means to signify by the parenthesis, "(without entering into the ground of our assent to them,)" it is not easy to guess. By a ground of assent to any proposition is commonly understood a reason or argument in support of it. Now, by his own hypothesis, there are truths so plain, that no man can doubt of them. If so, what ground of assent beyond their own plainness ought we to seek; what beside this can we ever hope to find, or what better reason needs be given for denominating such truths the dictates of common sense? If something plainer could be found to serve as evidence of any of them, then this plainer truth would be admitted as the first principle, and the other would be considered as deduced by rea-

source of knowledge common to all mankind. I own, indeed, that in different persons it prevails in different degrees of strength; but no human creature hath been found originally and totally

soning. But notwithstanding the mistake in the instance, the general doctrine of primary truths would remain unhurt. It seems, however, that though their conduct would have been liable to very little, it would have been liable to some objection. "All that could have been said would have been, that, without any necessity, they had made an innovation in the received use of the term." I have a better opinion of these gentlemen than to imagine, that if the thing which they contend for be admitted, they will enter into a dispute with any person about the name: though, in my judgment, even as to this, it is not they, but he, who is the innovator. He proceeds, "For no person ever denied that there are self-evident truths, and that these must be assumed, as the foundation of all our reasoning. I never met with any person who did not acknowledge this, or heard of any argumentative treatise that did not go on the supposition of it." Now, if this be the case, I would gladly know what is the great point he controverts. Is it, whether such self-evident truths shall be denominated principles of Common Sense, or be distinguished by some other appellation? Was it worth any man's while to write an octavo of near 400 pages, for the discussion of such a question as this? And if, as he assures us, they have said more than is necessary, in proof of a truth which he himself thinks indisputable, was it no more than necessary in Dr. Priestley to compose so large a volume, in order to convince the world that too much had been said already on the subject? I do not enter into the examination of his objections to some of the particular principles produced as primary truths. An attempt of this kind would be foreign to my purpose; besides that the authors he has attacked are better qualified for defending their own doctrine, and no doubt will do it, if they think there is occasion. I shall only subjoin two remarks on this book. The first is, that the author, through the whole, confounds two things totally distinct, certain associations of ideas, and certain judgments implying belief, which, though in some, are not in all cases, and therefore not necessarily, connected with association. And if so, merely to account for the association is in no case to account for the belief with which it is attended. Nay, admitting his plea, [page 86,] that by the principle of association not only the ideas but the concomitant belief may be accounted for, even this does not invalidate the doctrine he impugns. For, let it be observed that it is one thing to assign a cause which, from the mechanism of our nature, has given rise to a particular tenet or belief, and another thing to produce a reason by which the understanding has been convinced. Now, unless this be done as to the principles in question, they must be considered as primary truths, in respect of the understanding, which never deduced them from other truths, and which is under a necessity, in all moral reasonings, of founding upon them. In fact, to give any other account of our conviction of them is to confirm instead of confuting the doctrine, that in all argumentation they must be regarded as primary truths, or truths which reason never inferred, through any medium, from other truths previously perceived. My second remark is, that though this examiner has, from Dr. Reid, given us a catalogue of first principles, which he deems unworthy of the honourable place assigned them, he has no where thought proper to give us a list of those self-evident truths which, by his own account, and in his own express words, "must be assumed as the foundation of all our reasoning." How much light might have been thrown upon the subject by the contrast! Perhaps we should have been enabled, on the comparison, to discover some distinctive characters in his genuine axioms, which would have preserved us from the danger of confounding them with their spurious ones. Nothing is more evident than that, in whatever regards matter of fact, the mathematical axioms will not answer. These are purely fitted for evolving the abstract relations of quantity. This he in effect owns himself [page 39]. It would have been obliging, then, and would have greatly contributed to shorten the controversy, if he had given us at least a specimen of those self-evident principles, which, in his estimation, are the *ne plus ultra* of moral reasoning.

destitute of it, who is not accounted a monster in his kind; for such, doubtless, are all idiots and changelings. By madness, a disease which makes terrible havoc on the faculties of the mind, it may be in a great measure, but is never entirely lost.

It is purely hence that we derive our assurance of such truths as these: "Whatever has a beginning has a cause"—"When there is in the effect a manifest adjustment of the several parts to a certain end, there is intelligence in the cause." "The course of nature will be the same to-morrow that it is to-day; or, the future will resemble the past"—"There is such a thing as body; or, there are material substances independent of the mind's conceptions"—"There are other intelligent beings in the universe besides me"—"The clear representations of my memory, in regard to past events, are indubitably true." These, and a great many more of the same kind, it is impossible for any man by reasoning to evince, as might easily be shown, were this a proper place for the discussion. And it is equally impossible, without a full conviction of them, to advance a single step in the acquisition of knowledge, especially in all that regards mankind, life, and conduct.

I am sensible that some of these, to men not accustomed to inquiries of this kind, will appear at first not to be primary principles, but conclusions from other principles; and some of them will be thought to coincide with the other kinds of intuition above mentioned. Thus the first, "Whatever hath a beginning hath a cause," may be thought to stand on the same footing with mathematical axioms. I acknowledge that in point of evidence they are equal, and it is alike impossible, in either case, for a rational creature to withhold his assent. Nevertheless, there is a difference in kind. All the axioms in mathematics are but the enunciations of certain properties in our abstract notions, distinctly perceived by the mind, but have no relation to any thing without themselves, and can never be made the foundation of any conclusion concerning actual existence; whereas, in the axiom last specified, from the existence of one thing we intuitively conclude the existence of another. This proposition, however, so far differs, in my apprehension, from others of the same order, that I cannot avoid considering the opposite assertion as not only false but contradictory; but I do not pretend to explain the ground of this difference.

The faith we give to memory may be thought, on a superficial view, to be resolvable into consciousness, as well as that we give to the immediate impressions of sense. But on a little attention one may easily perceive the difference. To believe the report of our senses doth indeed commonly imply to believe the existence of certain external and corporeal objects, which give rise to our particular sensations. This, I acknowledge, is a principle which doth not spring from consciousness, (for consciousness cannot extend beyond sensation,) but from common sense, as well as the assurance we have in the report of memory. But this was not intended to be included under the second branch of intuitive evidence. By that firm belief in sense, which I there resolved into consciousness, I meant no more than to say, I am certain that I see, and feel, and think, what I actually see, and feel, and think. As in this I pronounce only concerning my own present feelings, whose essence consists in being felt, and of which I am at present conscious, my conviction is reducible to this axiom, or coincident with it, "It is impossible for a thing to be and not to be at the same time." Now when I say, I trust entirely to the clear report of my memory, I mean a good deal more than, "I am certain that my memory gives such a report, or represents things in such a manner," for this conviction I have indeed from consciousness; but I mean, "I am certain that things happened heretofore at such a time, in the precise manner in which I now remember that they then happened." Thus there is a reference in the ideas of memory to former sensible impressions, to which there is nothing analogous in sensation. At the same time it is evident, that remembrance is not always accompanied with this full conviction. To describe, in words, the difference between those lively signatures of memory, which command an unlimited assent, and those fainter traces which raise opinion only, or even doubt, is perhaps impracticable; but no man stands in need of such assistance to enable him in fact to distinguish them, for the direction of his own judgment and conduct. Some may imagine that it is from experience we come to know what faith in every case is due to memory. But it will appear more fully afterwards, that unless we had implicitly relied on the distinct and vivid informations of that faculty, we could not have moved a step towards the acquisition of experience. It must, however, be admitted, that experience is of use in assisting us to judge concerning the more languid and confused suggestions of memory; or, to speak more properly, concerning the reality of those things, of which we ourselves are doubtful whether we remember them or not.

In regard to the primary truths of this order, it may be urged that it cannot be affirmed of them all at least, as it may of the axioms in mathematics, or the assurances we have from consciousness, that the denial of them implies a manifest contradiction. It is, perhaps, physically possible that the course of nature will be inverted the very next moment; that my memory is no other than a delirium, and my life a dream; that all is mere illusion; that I am the only being in the universe, and that there is no such thing as body. Nothing can be juster than the reply given by Buffier, "It must be owned," says he,[3] "that to maintain propositions, the reverse of the primary truths of common sense, doth not imply a contradiction; it only implies insanity." But if any person, on account of this difference in the nature of these two classes of axioms, should not think the term intuitive so properly applied to the evidence of the last mentioned, let him denominate it, if he please, instinctive: I have no objection to the term; nor do I think it derogates in the least from the dignity, the certainty, or the importance of the truths themselves. Such instincts are no other than the oracles of eternal wisdom.

For, let it be observed further, that axioms of this last kind are as essential to moral reasoning, to all deductions concerning life and existence, as those of the first kind are to the sciences of arithmetic and geometry. Perhaps it will appear afterwards that, without the aid of some of them, these sciences themselves would be utterly inaccessible to us. Besides, the mathematical axioms can never extend their influence beyond the precincts of abstract knowledge, in regard to number and extension, or assist us in the discovery of any matter of fact: whereas, with knowledge of the latter kind, the whole conduct and business of human life is principally and intimately connected. All reasoning necessarily supposes that there are certain principles in which we must acquiesce, and beyond which we cannot go—principles clearly discernible by their own light, which can derive no additional evidence from any thing besides. On the contrary supposition, the investigation of truth would be an endless and a fruitless task; we should be eternally proving, whilst nothing could ever be proved; because, by the hypothesis, we could never ascend to premises which require no proof. "If there be no first truths," says the author lately quoted,[4] "there can be no second truths, nor third, nor indeed any truth at all."

So much for intuitive evidence, in the extensive meaning which hath here been given to that term, as including every thing whose evidence results from the simple contemplation of the ideas or perceptions which form the proposition under consideration, and requires not the intervention of any third idea as a medium of proof. This, for order's sake, I have distributed into three classes, the truths of pure intellection, of consciousness, and of common sense. The first may be denominated metaphysical, the second physical, the third moral; all of them natural, original, and unaccountable.

[3] Premières Vérités, Part i. Chap. xi.
[4] Ib. Dessein de l'Ouvrage.

SECTION II.—*Of deductive evidence.*

PART I.—*Division of the subject into scientific and moral, with the principal distinctions between them.*

All rational or deductive evidence is derived from one or other of these two sources: from the invariable properties or relations of general ideas; or from the actual, though perhaps variable connexions subsisting among things. The former we call demonstrative, the latter moral. Demonstration is built on pure intellection, and consisteth in an uninterrupted series of axioms. That propositions formerly demonstrated are taken into the series, doth not in the least invalidate this account; inasmuch as these propositions are all resolvable into axioms, and are admitted as links in the chain; not because necessary, but merely to avoid the useless prolixity which frequent and tedious repetition of proofs formerly given would occasion. Moral evidence is founded on the principles we have from consciousness and common sense, improved by experience; and as it proceeds on this general presumption or moral axiom, that the course of nature in time to come will be similar to what it hath been hitherto, it decides, in regard to particulars, concerning the future from the past, and concerning things unknown from things familiar to us. The first is solely conversant about number and extension, and about those other qualities which are measurable by these. Such are duration, velocity, and weight. With regard to such qualities as pleasure and pain, virtue and vice, wisdom and folly, beauty and deformity, though they admit degrees, yet, as there is no standard or common measure, by which their differences and proportions can be ascertained and expressed in numbers, they can never become the subject of demonstrative reasoning. Here rhetoric, it must be acknowledged, hath little to do. Simplicity of diction, and precision in arrangement, whence results perspicuity, are, as was observed already,[5] all the requisites. The proper province of rhetoric is the second, or moral evidence; for to the second belong all decisions concerning fact, and things without us.

But that the nature of moral evidence may be better understood, it will not be amiss to remark a few of the most eminent differences between this and the demonstrative.

The first difference that occurs is in their subjects. The subject of the one is, as hath been observed, abstract independent truth, or the unchangeable and necessary relations of ideas; that of the other, the real but often changeable and contingent connexions that subsist among things actually existing. Ab-

[5] Chap. i.

stract truths, as the properties of quantity, have no respect to time or to place, no dependence on the volition of any being, or on any cause whatever, but are eternally and immutably the same. The very reverse of all this generally obtains with regard to fact. In consequence of what has been now advanced, assertions opposite to truths of the former kind, are not only false, but absurd. They are not only not true, but it is impossible they should be true, whilst the meanings of the words (and consequently the ideas compared) remain the same. This doth not hold commonly in any other kind of evidence. Take, for instance, of the first kind, the following affirmations, "The cube of two is the half of sixteen,"—"The square of the hypothenuse is equal to the sum of the squares of the sides,"—"If equal things be taken from equal things, the remainders will be equal." Contrary propositions, as, "The cube of two is more than the half of sixteen,"—"The square of the hypothenuse is less than the sum of the squares of the sides," —"If equal things be taken from equal things, the remainders will be unequal," are chargeable, not only with falsity, but with absurdity, being inconceivable and contradictory. Whereas, to these truths which we acquire by moral evidence, "Cæsar overcame Pompey,"—"The sun will rise to-morrow,"—"All men will die,"—the opposite assertions, though untrue, are easily conceivable without changing, in the least, the import of the words, and therefore do not imply a contradiction.

The second difference I shall remark is, that moral evidence admits degrees, demonstration doth not. This is a plain consequence of the preceding difference. Essential or necessary truth, the sole object of the latter, is incompatible with degree. And though actual truth, or matter of fact, be the ultimate aim of the former, likelihood alone, which is susceptible of degree, is usually the utmost attainment. Whatever is exhibited as demonstration is either mere illusion, and so no evidence at all, or absolutely perfect. There is no medium. In moral reasoning we ascend from possibility, by an insensible gradation, to probability, and thence, in the same manner, to the summit of moral certainty. On this summit, or on any of the steps leading to it, the conclusion of the argument may rest. Hence the result of that is, by way of eminence, denominated science, and the evidence itself is termed scientific; the result of this is frequently (not always) entitled to no higher denomination than opinion. Now, in the mathematical sciences, no mention is ever made of opinions.

The third difference is, that in the one there never can be any contrariety of proofs; in the other, there not only may be, but almost always is. If one demonstration were ever capable of being refuted, it could be solely by another demonstration, this being the only sort of evidence adapted to the subject, and the only sort by which the former could be matched. But to suppose that contraries are demonstrable, is to suppose that the same proposition is both true and false, which is a manifest contradiction. Consequently, if there should ever be the appearance of demonstration on opposite sides, that on one side must be fallacious and sophistical. It is not so with moral evidence, for, unless in a few singular instances, there is always real, not apparent evidence on both sides. There are contrary experiences, contrary presumptions, contrary testimonies, to balance against one another. In this case, the probability, upon the whole, is in the proportion which the evidence on the side that preponderates bears to its opposite. We usually say, indeed, that the evidence lies on such a side of the question, and not on the reverse; but by this expression is only meant the overplus of evidence, on comparing both sides. In like manner, when we affirm of an event, that it is probable, we say the contrary is only possible, although, when they are severally considered, we do not scruple to say, This is more probable than that; or, The probabilities on one side outweigh those on the other.

The fourth and last difference I shall observe is, that scientific evidence is simple, consisting of only one coherent series, every part of which depends on the preceding, and, as it were, suspends the following: moral evidence is generally complicated, being in reality a bundle of independent proofs. The longest demonstration is but one uniform chain, the links whereof, taken severally, are not to be regarded as so many arguments, and consequently when thus taken, they conclude nothing; but taken together, and in their proper order, they form one argument, which is perfectly conclusive. It is true, the same theorem may be demonstrable in different ways, and by different mediums; but as a single demonstration, clearly understood, commands the fullest conviction, every other is superfluous. After one demonstrative proof, a man may try a second, purely as an exercise of ingenuity, or the better to assure himself that he hath not committed an oversight in the first. Thus it may serve to warrant the regular procedure of his faculties, but not to make an addition to the former proof, or supply any deficiency perceived in it. So far is it from answering this end, that he is no sooner sensible of a defect in an attempt of this nature, than the whole is rejected as good for nothing, and carrying with it no degree of evidence whatever. In moral reasoning, on the contrary, there is often a combination of many distinct topics of argument, no way dependent on one another. Each hath a certain portion of evidence belonging to itself, each bestows on the conclusion a particular degree of likelihood, of all which accumulated the credibility of the fact is compounded. The former may be compared to an arch, no part of which can subsist independently of the rest. If you make any breach in it, you destroy the whole. The latter may be compared to a tower, the height whereof is but the aggregate of the heights of the several parts reared above one another, and so may be gradually diminished, as it was gradually raised.

So much for the respective natures of scientific and of moral evidence, and those characteristical qualities which discriminate them from each other. On a survey of the whole, it seems indubitable, that if the former is infinitely superior in point of authority, the latter no less excels in point of importance. Abstract truth, as far as it is the object of our faculties, is almost entirely confined to quantity, concrete or discrete. The sphere of Demonstration is narrow, but within her sphere she is a despotic sovereign, her sway is uncontrollable. Her rival, on the contrary, hath less power but wider empire. Her forces, indeed, are not always irresistible; but the whole world is comprised in her dominions. Reality or fact comprehends the laws and the works of nature, as well as the arts and the institutions of men; in brief, all the beings which fall under the cognizance of the human mind, with all their modifications, operations, and effects. By the first, we must acknowledge, when applied to things, and combined with the discoveries of the second, our researches into nature in a certain line are facilitated, the understanding is enlightened, and many of the arts, both elegant and useful, are improved and perfected. Without the aid of the second, society must not only suffer but perish. Human nature itself could not subsist. This organ of knowledge, which extends its influence to every precinct of philosophy, and governs in most, serves also to regulate all the ordinary but indispensable concernments of life. To these it is admirably adapted, notwithstanding its inferiority in respect of dignity, accuracy, and perspicuity. For it is principally to the acquisitions procured by experience that we owe the use of language, and the knowledge of almost every thing that makes the soul of a man differ from that of a new-born infant. On the other hand, there is no despot so absolute as not to be liable to a check on some side or other; and that the prerogatives of demonstration are not so very considerable, as on a cursory view one is apt to imagine; and this, as well as every other operation of the intellect, must partake in the weakness incident to all our mental faculties, and inseparable from our nature, I shall afterwards take an opportunity particularly to evince.

PART. II.—*The nature and origin of Experience.*

I should now consider the principal tribes comprehended under the general name of moral evidence; but, that every difficulty may be removed, which might retard our progress in the proposed discussion, it will be necessary, in the first place, to explore more accurately those sources in our nature which give being to experience, and consequently to all those attainments, moral and intellectual, that are derived from it. These sources are two, sense and memory. The senses, both external and internal, are the original inlets of perception. They inform the mind of the facts, which in the present instant are situated within the sphere of their activity, and no sooner discharge their office in any particular instance than the articles of information exhibited by them are devolved on the memory. Remembrance instantly succeeds sensation, insomuch that the memory becomes the sole repository of the knowledge received from sense; knowledge which, without this repository, would be as instantaneously lost as it is gotten, and could be of no service to the mind. Our sensations would be no better than the fleeting pictures of a moving object on a camera obscura, which leave not the least vestige behind them. Memory, therefore, is the only original voucher extant of those past realities for which we had once the evidence of sense. Her ideas are, as it were, the prints that have been left by sensible impressions. But from these two faculties, considered in themselves, there results to us the knowledge only of individual facts, and only of such facts as either heretofore have come, or at present do come, under the notice of our senses.

Now, in order to render this knowledge useful to us, in discovering the nature of things, and in regulating our conduct, a further process of the mind is necessary, which deserves to be carefully attended to, and may be thus illustrated. I have observed a stone fall to the ground when nothing intervened to impede its motion. This single fact produces little or no effect on the mind beyond a bare remembrance. At another time, I observe the fall of a tile, at another of an apple, and so of almost every kind of body in the like situation. Thus my senses first, and then my memory, furnish me with numerous examples, which, though different in every other particular, are similar in this, that they present a body moving downwards, till obstructed either by the ground or by some intervenient object. Hence my first notion of gravitation. For, with regard to the similar circumstances of different facts, as by the repetition such circumstances are more deeply imprinted, the mind acquires a habit of retaining them, omitting those circumstances peculiar to each wherein their differences consist. Hence, if objects of any kind, in a particular manner circumstanced, are remembered to have been usually, and still more if uniformly, succeeded by certain particular consequences, the idea of the former, in the supposed circumstance introduced into the mind, immediately associates the idea of the latter;

and if the object itself, so circumstanced, be presented to the senses, the mind instantly anticipates the appearance of the customary consequence. This holds also inversely. The retention and association above explained are called Experience. The anticipation is in effect no other than a particular conclusion from that experience. Here we may remark by the way, that though memory gives birth to experience, which results from the comparison of facts remembered, the experience or habitual association remains, when the individual facts on which it is founded are all forgotten. I know from an experience which excludes all doubt, the power of fire in melting silver, and yet may not be able at present to recollect a particular instance in which I have seen this effect produced, or even in which I have had the fact attested by a credible witness.

Some will perhaps object that the account now given makes our experimental reasoning look like a sort of mechanism, necessarily resulting from the very constitution of the mind. I acknowledge the justness of the remark, but do not think that it ought to be regarded as an objection. It is plain that our reasoning in this way, if you please to call it so, is very early, and precedes all reflection on our faculties, and the manner of applying them. Those who attend to the progress of human nature through its different stages, and through childhood in particular, will observe that children make great acquisitions in knowledge from experience long before they attain the use of speech. The beasts also, in their sphere, improve by experience, which hath in them just the same foundations of sense and memory as in us, and hath, besides, a similar influence on their actions. It is precisely in the same manner, and with the same success, that you might train a dog, or accustom a child to expect food on your calling to him in one tone of voice, and to dread your resentment when you use another. The brutes have evidently the rudiments of this species of rationality, which extends as far in them as the immediate purposes of self-preservation require, and which, whether you call it reason or instinct, they both acquire and use in the same manner as we do. That it reaches no further in them, seems to arise from an original incapacity of classing, and (if I may use the expression) generalizing their perceptions; an exercise which to us very quickly becomes familiar, and is what chiefly fits us for the use of language. Indeed, in the extent of this capacity, as much, perhaps, as in any thing, lies also the principal natural superiority of one man over another.

But that we may be satisfied, that to this kind of reasoning, in its earliest or simplest form, little or no reflection is necessary, let it be observed, that it is now universally admitted by opticians, that it is not purely from sight, but from sight aided by experience, that we derive our notions of the distance of visible objects from the eye. The sensation, say they, is instantaneously followed by a conclusion or judgment founded on experience. The point is determined from the different phases of the object found, in former trials, to be connected with different distances, or from the effort that accompanies the different conformations we are obliged to give the organs of sight, in order to obtain a distinct vision of the object. Now, if this be the case, as I think hath been sufficiently evinced of late, it is manifest that this judgment is so truly instantaneous, and so perfectly the result of feeling and association, that the forming of it totally escapes our notice. Perhaps in no period of life will you find a person, that, on the first mention of it, can be easily persuaded that he derives this knowledge from experience. Every man will be ready to tell you that he needs no other witnesses than his eyes, to satisfy him that objects are not in contact with his body, but are at different distances from him as well as from one another. So passive is the mind in this matter, and so rapid are the transitions which, by this ideal attraction, she is impelled to make, that she is, in a manner, unconscious of her own operations. There is some ground to think, from the exact analogy which their organs bear to ours, that the discovery of distance from the eye is attained by brutes in the same manner as by us. As to this, however, I will not be positive. But though, in this way, the mind acquires an early perception of the most obvious and necessary truths, without which the bodily organs would be of little use; in matters less important her procedure is much slower, and more the result of voluntary application; and as the exertion is more deliberate, she is more conscious of her own activity, or, at least, remembers it longer. It is then only that in common style we honour her operation with the name of *reasoning;* though there is no essential difference between the two cases. It is true, indeed, that the conclusions in the first way, by which also in infancy we learn language, are commonly more to be regarded as infallible, than those effected in the second.

PART III.—*The subdivisions of Moral Reasoning.*

But to return to the proposed distribution of moral evidence. Under it I include these three tribes, experience, analogy, and testimony. To these I shall subjoin the consideration of a fourth, totally distinct from them all, but which appears to be a mixture of the demonstrative and the moral; or rather a particular application of the former, for ascertaining the precise force of the latter. The evidence I mean is that resulting from calculations concerning chances.

I.—*Experience.*

The first of these I have named peculiarly the evidence of experience, not with philosophical propriety, but in compliance with common language, and for distinction's sake. Analogical reasoning is surely reasoning from a more indirect experience. Now, as to this first kind, our experience is either uniform or various. In the one case, provided the facts on which it is founded be sufficiently numerous, the conclusion is said to be morally certain. In the other, the conclusion, built on the greater number of instances, is said to be probable, and more or less so, according to the proportion which the instances on that side bear to those on the opposite. Thus we are perfectly assured that iron thrown into the river will sink, that deal will float; because these conclusions are built on a full and uniform experience. That in the last week of December next, it will snow in any part of Britain specified, is perhaps probable; that is, if, on inquiry or recollection, we are satisfied that this hath more frequently happened than the contrary; that some time in that month it will snow, is more probable, but not certain, because, though this conclusion is founded on experience, that experience is not uniform; lastly, that it will snow some time during winter will, I believe, on the same principles, be pronounced certain.

It was affirmed that experience, or the tendency of the mind to associate ideas under the notion of causes, effects, or adjuncts, is never contracted by one example only. This assertion, it may be thought, is contradicted by the principle on which physiologists commonly proceed, who consider one accurate experiment in support of a particular doctrine as sufficient evidence. The better to explain this phenomenon, and the further to illustrate the nature of experience, I shall make the following observations. First, whereas sense and memory are conversant only about individuals, our earliest experiences imply, or perhaps generate, the notion of a species, including all those individuals which have the most obvious and universal resemblance. From Charles, Thomas, William, we ascend to the idea of man; from Britain, France, Spain, to the idea of kingdom. As our acquaintance with nature enlarges, we discover resemblances, of a striking and important nature, between one species and another, which naturally begets the notion of a genus. From comparing men with beasts, birds, fishes, and reptiles, we perceive that they are all alike possessed of life, or a principle of sensation and action, and of an organized body, and hence acquire the idea of animal: in like manner, from comparing kingdoms with republics and aristocracies, we obtain the idea of nation, and thence again rise in the same track to ideas still more comprehensive. Further, let it be remembered, that by experience we not only decide concerning the future from the past, but concerning things uncommon from things familiar which resemble them.

Now, to apply this observation: a botanist, in traversing the fields, lights on a particular plant, which appears to be of a species he is not acquainted with. The flower, he observes, is monopetalous, and the number of flowers it carries is seven. Here are two facts that occur to his observation; let us consider in what way he will be disposed to argue from them. From the first he does not hesitate to conclude, not only as probable, but as certain, that this individual, and all of the same species, invariably produce monopetalous flowers. From the second, he by no means concludes, as either certain, or even probable, that the flowers which either this plant, or others of the same species, carry at once, will always be seven. This difference, to a superficial inquirer, might seem capricious, since there appears to be one example, and but one in either case, on which the conclusion can be founded. The truth is, that it is not from this example only that he deduces these inferences. Had he never heretofore taken the smallest notice of any plant, he could not have reasoned at all from these remarks. The mind recurs instantly from the unknown to all the other known species of the same genus, and thence to all the known genera of the same order or tribe; and having experienced in the one instance, a regularity in every species, genus, and tribe, which admits no exception; in the other a variety as boundless as that of season, soil, and culture, it learns hence to mark the difference.

Again, we may observe that, on a closer acquaintance with those objects wherewith we are surrounded, we come to discover that they are mostly of a compound nature, and that not only as containing a complication of those qualities called accidents, as gravity, mobility, colour, extension, figure, solidity, which are common almost to all matter, not only as consisting of different members, but as comprehending a mixture of bodies, often very different in their nature and properties, as air, fire, water, earth, salt, oil, spirit, and the like. These, perhaps, on deeper researches, will be found to consist of materials still simpler. Moreover, as we advance in the study of nature, we daily find more reason to be convinced of her constancy in all her operations, that like causes, in like circumstances, always produce like effects, and inversely, like effects always flow from like causes. The inconstancy which appears at first in some of nature's works, a more improved experience teacheth us to account for in this manner. As most of the objects we know are of a complex nature, on a narrower scrutiny we find, that the effects ascribed to them ought often solely to be ascribed to one or more of the component parts; that the others noway contribute to the production: that, on the contrary, they sometimes tend to hinder it. If the parts in the composition of similar objects were always in equal quantity, their being compounded would make no odds; if the parts, though not equal, bore always the same proportion to the whole, this would make a difference: but such as in many cases might be computed. In both respects, however, there is an immense variety. Perhaps every individual differs from every other individual of the same species, both in the quantities and in the proportions of its constituent members and component parts. This diversity is also found in other things, which, though hardly reducible to species, are generally known by the same name. The atmosphere in the same place at different times, or at the same time in different places, differs in density, heat, humidity, and the number, quality, and proportion of the vapours or particles with which it is loaden. The more then we become acquainted with elementary natures, the more we are ascertained by a general experience of the uniformity of their operations. And though perhaps it be impossible for us to attain the knowledge of the simplest elements of any body, yet when any thing appears so simple, or rather so exactly uniform, as that we have observed it invariably to produce similar effects; on discovering any new effects, though but by one experiment, we conclude, from the general experience of the efficient, a like constancy in this energy as in the rest. Fire consumes wood, melts copper, and hardens clay. In these instances it acts uniformly, but not in these only. I have always experienced hitherto, that whatever of any species is consumed by it once, all of the same species it will consume upon trial at any time. The like may be said of what is melted, or hardened, or otherwise altered by it. If then, for the first time, I try the influence of fire on any fossil, or other substance, whatever be the effect, I readily conclude that fire will always produce a similar effect on similar bodies. This conclusion is not founded on this single instance, but on this instance compared with a general experience of the regularity of this element in all its operations.

So much for the first tribe, the evidence of experience, on which I have enlarged the more, as it is, if not the foundation, at least the criterion of all moral reasoning whatever. It is, besides, the principal organ of truth in all the branches of physiology (I use the word in its largest acceptation), including natural history, astronomy, geography, mechanics, optics, hydrostatics, meteorology, medicine, chemistry. Under the general term I also comprehend natural theology and psychology, which, in my opinion, have been most unnaturally disjoined by philosophers. Spirit, which here comprises only the Supreme Being and the human soul, is surely as much included under the notion of natural object as body is, and is knowable to the philosopher purely in the same way, by observation and experience.

II.—*Analogy*.

The evidence of analogy, as was hinted above, is but a more indirect experience, founded on some remote similitude. As things, however, are often more easily comprehended by the aid of example than by definition, I shall in that manner illustrate the difference between experimental evidence and analogical. The circulation of the blood in one human body is, I shall suppose, experimentally discovered. Nobody will doubt of this being a sufficient proof from experience, that the blood circulates in every human body. Nay, further, when we consider the great similarity which other animal bodies bear to the human body, and that both in the structure and in the destination of the several organs and limbs; particularly when we consider the resemblance in the blood itself, and blood-vessels, and in the fabric and pulsation of the heart and arteries, it will appear sufficient experimental evidence of the circulation of the blood in brutes, especially in quadrupeds. Yet, in this application, it is manifest, that the evidence is weaker than in the former. But should I from the same experiment infer the circulation of the sap in vegetables, this would be called an argument only from analogy. Now, all reasonings from experience are obviously weakened in proportion to the remoteness of the resemblance subsisting between that on which the argument is founded, and that concerning which we form the conclusion.

The same thing may be considered in a different way. I have learnt from experience, that like effects sometimes proceed from objects which faintly resemble, but not near so frequently as from objects which have a more perfect likeness. By this experience I have been enabled to determine the degrees of probability from the degrees of similarity in the different cases. It is presumable that the former of these ways has the earliest influence, when the mind, unaccustomed to reflection, forms but a weak association, and consequently but a weak expectation of a similar event from a weak resemblance. The latter seems more the result of thought, and is better adapted to the ordinary forms of reasoning.

It is allowed that an analogical evidence is at best but a feeble support, and is hardly ever honoured with the name of proof. Nevertheless, when the analogies are numerous, and the subject admits not evidence of another kind, it doth not want efficacy. It must be owned, however, that it is generally more successful in silencing objections than in evincing truth, and on this account may more properly be styled the defensive arms of the orator than the offensive. Though it rarely refutes, it frequently repels refutation, like those weapons which, though they cannot kill the enemy, will ward his blows.[6]

III.—*Testimony.*

The third tribe is the evidence of testimony, which is either oral or written. This also hath been thought by some, but unjustly, to be solely and originally derived from the same source, experience.[7] The utmost in regard to this, that can be affirmed with truth, is that the evidence of testimony is to be considered as strictly logical, no further than human veracity in general, or the veracity of witnesses of such a character, and in such circumstances in particular, is supported, or perhaps more properly, hath not been refuted, by experience. But that testimony, antecedently to experience, hath a natural influence on belief, is undeniable. In this it resembles memory; for though the defects and misrepresentations of memory are corrected by experience, yet that this faculty hath an innate evidence of its own we know from this, that if we had not previously given an implicit faith to memory, we had never been able to acquire experience. This will appear from the revisal of its nature, as explained above. Nay, it must be owned, that in what regards single facts, testimony is more adequate evidence than any conclusions from experience. The immediate conclusions from experience are general, and run thus: "This is the ordinary course of nature;"—"Such an event may reasonably be expected, when all the attendant circumstances are similar." When we descend to particulars, the conclusion necessarily becomes weaker, being more indirect. For though all the *known* circumstances be similar, all the *actual* circumstances may not be similar; nor is it possible in any case to be assured, that all the actual circumstances are known to us. Accordingly, experience is the foundation of philosophy; which consists in a collection of general truths, systematically digested. On the contrary, the direct conclusion from testimony is particular, and runs thus: "This is the fact in the instance specified." Testimony, therefore, is the foundation of

[6] Dr. Butler, in his excellent treatise called *The Analogy of Religion natural and revealed, to the Constitution and Course of Nature*, hath shown us how useful this mode of reasoning may be rendered, by the application he hath so successfully made of it for refuting the cavils of infidelity.

[7] I had occasion to make some reflections on this subject formerly. See Dissertation on Miracles, Part i. Sect. 1. There are several ingenious observations on the same subject in Reid's Inquiry, Ch. vi. Sect. 23.

history, which is occupied about individuals. Hence we derive our acquaintance with past ages, as from experience we derive all that we can discover of the future. But the former is dignified with the name of knowledge, whereas the latter is regarded as matter of conjecture only. When experience is applied to the discovery of the truth in a particular incident, we call the evidence presumptive; ample testimony is accounted a positive proof of the fact. Nay, the strongest conviction built merely on the former is sometimes overturned by the slightest attack of the latter. Testimony is capable of giving us absolute certainty (Mr. Hume himself being judge[8]) even of the most miraculous fact, or of what is contrary to uniform experience. For, perhaps, in no other instance can experience be applied to individual events with so much certainty, as in what relates to the revolutions of the heavenly bodies. Yet, even this evidence, he admits, may not only be counterbalanced, but destroyed by testimony.

But to return. Testimony is a serious intimation from another, of any fact or observation, as being what he remembers to have seen or heard or experienced. To this, when we have no positive reasons of mistrust or doubt, we are, by an original principle of our nature (analogous to that which compels our faith in memory), led to give an unlimited assent. As on memory alone is founded the merely personal experience of the individual, so on testimony in concurrence with memory is founded the much more extensive experience which is not originally our own, but derived from others.[9] By the first, I question not, a man might acquire all the knowledge necessary for mere animal support, in that rudest state of human nature (if ever such a state existed) which was without speech and without society; to the last, in conjunction with the other, we are indebted for every thing which distinguishes the man from the brute, for language, arts, and civilization. It hath been observed, that from experience we learn to confine our belief in human testimony within the proper bounds. Hence we are taught to consider many attendant circumstances, which serve either to corroborate or to invalidate its evidence. The reputation of the attester, his manner of address, the nature of the fact attested, the occasion of giving the testimony, the possible or probable design in giving it, the disposition of the hearers to whom it was given, and several other circumstances, have all considerable influence in fixing the degree of credibility. But of these I shall have occasion to take notice afterwards. It deserves likewise to be attended to on this subject, that in a number of concurrent testimonies (in cases wherein there could have been no previous concert), there is a probability distinct

8 Essay on Miracles, p. 2.
9 Dissertation on Miracles, Part i. Sect. 2.

from that which may be termed the sum of the probabilities resulting from the testimonies of the witnesses, a probability which would remain even though the witnesses were of such a character as to merit no faith at all. This probability arises purely from the concurrence itself. That such a concurrence should spring from chance is as one to infinite; that is, in other words, morally impossible. If therefore concert be excluded, there remains no other cause but the reality of the fact.

Now to this species of evidence, testimony, we are first immediately indebted for all the branches of philology, such as, history, civil, ecclesiastic, and literary; grammar, languages, jurisprudence, and criticism; to which I may add revealed religion, as far as it is to be considered as a subject of historical and critical inquiry, and so discoverable by natural means: and secondly, to the same source we owe, as was hinted above, a great part of that light which is commonly known under the name of experience, but which is, in fact, not founded on our own personal observations, or the notices originally given by our own senses, but on the attested experiences and observations of others. So that as hence we derive entirely our knowledge of the actions and productions of men, especially in other regions and in former ages, hence also we derive, in a much greater measure than is commonly imagined, our acquaintance with Nature and her works.—Logic, rhetoric, ethics, economics, and politics are properly branches of pneumatology, though very closely connected with the philological studies above enumerated.

IV.—*Calculations of Chances.*

The last kind of evidence I proposed to consider, was that resulting from calculations of chances. Chance is not commonly understood, either in philosophic or in vulgar language, to imply the exclusion of a cause, but our ignorance of the cause. It is often employed to denote a bare possibility of an event, when nothing is known either to produce or to hinder it. But in this meaning it can never be made the subject of calculation. It then only affords scope to the calculator, when a cause is known for the production of an effect, and when that effect must necessarily be attended with this or that or the other circumstance; but no cause is known to determine us to regard one particular circumstance in preference to the rest, as that which shall accompany the supposed effect. The effect is then considered as necessary, but the circumstance as only casual or contingent. When a die is thrown out of the hand, we know that its gravity will make it fall; we know also that this, together with its cubical figure, will make it lie so, when intercepted by the table, as to have one side facing upwards. Thus far we proceed on the certain principles of a uniform experience; but there is no principle which can lead me to conclude that one side rather than another will be turned up. I know that this circumstance is not without a cause; but is, on the contrary, as really effected by the previous tossing which it receives in the hand or in the box, as its fall and the manner of its lying are by its gravity and figure. But the various turns or motions given it, in this manner, do inevitably escape my notice; and so are held for nothing. I say, therefore, that the chance is equal for every one of the six sides. Now, if five of these were marked with the same figure, suppose a dagger [†], and only one with an asterisk [*], I should in that case say, there were five chances that the die would turn up the dagger, for one that it would turn up the asterisk. For the turning up each of the six sides being equally possible, there are five cases in which the dagger, and only one in which the asterisk would be uppermost.

This differs from experience, inasmuch as I reckon the probability here, not from numbering and comparing the events after repeated trials, but without any trial, from balancing the possibilities on both sides. But though different from experience, it is so similar, that we cannot wonder that it should produce a similar effect upon the mind. These different positions being considered as equal, if any of five shall produce a similar effect, and but the sixth another, the mind, weighing the different events, resteth in an expectation of that in which the greater number of chances concur; but still accompanied with a degree of hesitancy, which appears proportioned to the number of chances on the opposite side. It is much after the same manner that the mind, on comparing its own experiences, when five instances favour one side to one that favours the contrary, determines the greater credibility of the former. Hence, in all complicated cases, the very degree of probability may be arithmetically ascertained. That two dice marked in the common way will turn up seven, is thrice as probable as that they will turn up eleven, and six times as probable as that they will turn up twelve.[1] The degree of probability is here determined demonstratively. It is indeed true that such mathematical calculations may be founded on experience, as well as upon chances. Examples of this we have in the computations that have been made of the value of annuities, insurances, and several other commercial articles. In such cases a great number of instances

[1] Call one die A, the other B. The chances for 7 are

A 1. B 6.	A 4. B 3.
A 2. B 5.	A 5. B 2.
A 3. B.4.	A 6. B 1.

The chances for eleven are

A 6. B 5.
A 5. B 6.

The only chance for 12 is A 6. B 6. The 1st is to the 2nd as 6 to 2; to the 3rd, as 6 to 1.

is necessary, the greatest exactness in collecting them on each side, and due care that there be no discoverable peculiarity in any of them, which would render them unfit for supporting a general conclusion.

PART IV.—*The superiority of Scientific Evidence re-examined.*

After the enumeration made in the first part of this section, of the principal differences between scientific evidence and moral, I signified my intention of resuming the subject afterwards, as far at least as might be necessary to show, that the prerogatives of demonstration are not so considerable, as on a cursory view one is apt to imagine. It will be proper now to execute this intention. I could not attempt it sooner, as the right apprehension of what is to be advanced will depend on a just conception of those things which have lately been explained. In the comparison referred to, I contrasted the two sorts of evidence, as they are in themselves, without considering the influence which the necessary application of our faculties in using both, has, and ought to have, on the effect. The observations then made in that abstracted view of the subject, appear to be well founded. But that view, I acknowledge, doth not comprehend the whole with which we are concerned.

It was observed of memory, that as it instantly succeeds sensation, it is the repository of all the stores from which our experience is collected, and that without an implicit faith in the clear representations of that faculty, we could not advance a step in the acquisition of experimental knowledge. Yet we know that memory is not infallible: nor can we pretend that in any case there is not a physical possibility of her making a false report. Here, it may be said, is an irremediable imbecility in the very foundation of moral reasoning. But is it less so in demonstrative reasoning? This point deserves a careful examination.

It was remarked concerning the latter, that it is a proof consisting of an uninterrupted series of axioms. The truth of each is intuitively perceived as we proceed. But this process is of necessity gradual, and these axioms are all brought in succession. It must then be solely by the aid of memory, that they are capable of producing conviction in the mind. Nor by this do I mean to affirm, that we can remember the preceding steps with their connexions, so as to have them all present to our view at one instant; for then we should, in that instant, perceive the whole intuitively. Our remembrance, on the contrary, amounts to no more than this, that the perception of the truth of the axiom to which we are advanced in the proof, is accompanied with a strong impression on the memory of the satisfaction that the mind received from the justness and regularity of what preceded. And in this we are under a necessity of acquiescing; for the understanding is no more capable of contemplating and perceiving at once the truth of all the propositions in the series, than the tongue is capable of uttering them at once. Before we make progress in geometry, we come to demonstrations, wherein there is a reference to preceding demonstrations; and in these perhaps to others that preceded them. The bare reflection, that as to these we once were satisfied, is accounted by every learner, and teacher too, as sufficient. And if it were not so, no advancement at all could be made in this science. Yet, here again, the whole evidence is reduced to the testimony of memory. It may be said that, along with the remembrance now mentioned, there is often in the mind a conscious power of recollecting the several steps, whenever it pleases; but the power of recollecting them severally, and successively, and the actual instantaneous recollection of the whole, are widely different. Now, what is the consequence of this induction? It is plainly this, that, in spite of the pride of mathesis, no demonstration whatever can produce, or reasonably ought to produce, a higher degree of certainty than that which results from the vivid representations of memory, on which the other is obliged to lean. Such is here the natural subordination, however rational and purely intellectual the former may be accounted, however mysterious and inexplicable the latter. For it is manifest, that without a perfect acquiescence in such representations, the mathematician could not advance a single step beyond his definitions and axioms. Nothing therefore is more certain, however inconceivable it appeared to Dr. Priestley, than what was affirmed by Dr. Oswald, that *the possibility of error attends the most complete demonstration.*

If from theory we recur to fact, we shall quickly find, that those most deeply versed in this sort of reasoning are conscious of the justness of the remark now made. A geometrician, I shall suppose, discovers a new theorem, which, having made a diagram for the purpose, he attempts to demonstrate, and succeeds in the attempt. The figure he hath constructed is very complex, and the demonstration long. Allow me now to ask, Will he be so perfectly satisfied on the first trial as not to think it of importance to make a second, perhaps a third, and a fourth? Whence arises this diffidence? Purely from the consciousness of the fallibility of his own faculties. But to what purpose, it may be said, the reiterations of the attempt, since it is impossible for him, by any efforts, to shake off his dependence on the accuracy of his attention and fidelity of his memory? Or, what can he have more than reiterated testimonies of his memory, in support of the truth of its former testimony? I acknowledge, that after a hundred attempts he can have no more. But even this is a great deal. We learn from experience, that the mistakes or oversights committed by the mind in one operation, are sometimes, on a review, corrected on the second, or perhaps on a third. Besides, the repetition, when no error is discovered, enlivens the remembrance, and so strengthens the conviction. But, for this conviction, it is plain that we are in a great measure indebted to memory, and in some measure even to experience.

Arithmetical operations, as well as geometrical, are in their nature scientific; yet the most accurate accountants are very sensible of the possibility of committing a blunder, and therefore rarely fail, for securing the matter, when it is of importance, to prove what they have done, by trying to effect the same thing another way. You have employed yourself, I suppose, in resolving some difficult problem by algebra, and are convinced that your solution is just. One whom you know to be an expert algebraist, carefully peruses the whole operation, and acquaints you that he hath discovered an error in your procedure. You are that instant sensible that your conviction was not of such an impregnable nature, but that his single testimony, in consequence of the confidence you repose in his experienced veracity and skill, makes a considerable abatement in it.

Many cases might be supposed, of belief founded only on moral evidence, which it would be impossible thus to shake. A man of known probity and good sense, and (if you think it makes an addition of any moment in this case) an astronomer and philosopher, bids you look at the sun as it goes down, and tells you, with a serious countenance, that the sun which sets to-day will never again rise upon the earth. What would be the effect of this declaration? Would it create in you any doubts? I believe it might, as to the soundness of the man's intellects, but not as to the truth of what he said. Thus, if we regard only the effect, demonstration itself doth not always produce such immovable certainty, as is sometimes consequent on merely moral evidence. And if there are, on the other hand, some well known demonstrations, of so great authority, that it would equally look like lunacy to impugn, it may deserve the attention of the curious to inquire how far, with respect to the bulk of mankind, these circumstances, their having stood the test of ages, their having obtained the universal suffrage of those who are qualified to examine them (things purely of the nature of moral evidence), have contributed to that unshaken faith with which they are received.

The principal difference then, in respect of the result of both kinds, is reduced to this narrow point. In mathematical reasoning, provided you are ascertained of the regular procedure of the mind, to affirm that the conclusion is false implies a contradiction; in moral reasoning, though the procedure of the mind were quite unexceptionable, there still remains a physical possibility of the falsity of the conclusion. But how small this difference is in reality, any judicious person who but attends a little may easily discover. The geometrician, for instance, can no more doubt whether the book called Euclid's Elements is a human composition, whether its contents were discovered and digested into the order in which they are there disposed, by human genius and art, than he can doubt the truth of the propositions therein demonstrated. Is he in the smallest degree surer of any of the properties of the circle, than that if he take away his hand from the compasses with which he is describing it on the wall, they will immediately fall to the ground. These things affect his mind, and influence his practice, precisely in the same manner.

So much for the various kinds of evidence, whether intuitive or deductive; intuitive evidence, as divided into that of pure intellection, of consciousness, and of common sense, under the last of which that of memory is included; deductive evidence, as divided into scientific and moral, with the subdivisions of the latter into experience, analogy, and testimony, to which hath been added the consideration of a mixed species concerning chances. So much for the various subjects of discourse, and the sorts of eviction of which they are respectively susceptible. This, though peculiarly the logician's province, is the foundation of all conviction, and consequently of persuasion too. To attain either of these ends, the speaker must always assume the character of the close candid reasoner: for though he may be an acute logician who is no orator, he will never be a consummate orator who is no logician.

CHAP. VI.

Of the Nature and Use of the scholastic art of Syllogizing.

HAVING in the preceding chapter endeavoured to trace the outlines of natural logic, perhaps with more minuteness than in such an inquiry as this was strictly necessary, it might appear strange to pass over in silence the dialectic of the schools; an art which, though now fallen into disrepute, maintained, for a tract of ages, the highest reputation among the learned. What was so long regarded as teaching the only legitimate use and application of our rational powers in the acquisition of knowledge, ought not surely, when we are employed in investigating the nature and the different sorts of evidence, to be altogether overlooked.

It is long since I was first convinced, by what Mr. Locke had said on the subject, that the syllogistic art, with its figures and moods, serves more to display the ingenuity of the inventor, and to exercise the address and fluency of the learner, than to assist the diligent inquirer in his researches after truth. The method of proving by syllogism, appears, even on a superficial review, both unnatural and prolix. The rules laid down for distinguishing the conclusive from the inconclusive forms of argument, the true syllogism from the various kinds of sophism, are at once cumbersome to the memory, and unnecessary in practice. No person, one may venture to pronounce, will ever be made a reasoner, who stands in need of them. In a word, the whole bears the manifest indications of an artificial and ostentatious parade of learning, calculated for giving the appearance of great profundity to what in fact is very shallow. Such, I acknowledge, have been, for a long time, my sentiments on the subject. On a nearer inspection, I cannot say I have found reason to alter them, though I think I have seen a little further into the nature of this disputative science, and consequently into the grounds of its futility. I shall, therefore, as briefly as possible, lay before the reader a few observations on the subject, and so dismiss this article.

Permit me only to premise in general, that I proceed all along on the supposition, that the reader hath some previous acquaintance with school logic. It would be extremely superfluous, in a work like this, to give even the shortest abridgment that could be made of an art so well known, and which is still to be found in many thousand volumes. On the other hand, it is not necessary that he be an adept in it; a mere smattering will sufficiently serve the present purpose.

My first observation is, that this method of arguing has not the least affinity to moral reasoning, the procedure in the one being the very reverse of that employed in the other. In moral reasoning we proceed by analysis, and ascend from particulars to universals; in syllogizing we proceed by synthesis, and descend from universals to particulars. The analytic is the only method which we can follow, in the acquisition of natural knowledge, or whatever regards actual existences; the synthetic is more properly the method that ought to be pursued, in the application of knowledge already acquired. It is for this reason it has been called the didactic method, as being the shortest way of communicating the principles of a science. But even in teaching, as often as we attempt, not barely to inform, but to convince, there is a necessity of recurring to the track in which the knowledge we would convey was first attained. Now, the method of reasoning by syllogism more resembles mathematical demonstration, wherein, from universal principles, called axioms, we deduce many truths, which, though general in their nature, may, when compared with those first principles, be justly styled particular. Whereas in all kinds of knowledge, wherein experience is our only guide, we can proceed to general truths solely by an induction of particulars.

Agreeably to this remark, if a syllogism be regular in mood and figure, and if the premises be true, the conclusion is infallible. The whole foundation of the syllogistic art lies in these two axioms: "Things which coincide with the same thing, coincide with one another;" and "Two things, whereof one does, and one does not coincide with the same thing, do not coincide with one another." On the former rest all the affirmative syllogisms, on the latter all the negative. Accordingly, there is no more mention here of probability and of degrees of evidence, than in the operations of geometry and algebra. It is true, indeed, that the term *probable* may be admitted into a syllogism, and make an essential part of the conclusion, and so it may also in an arithmetical computation; but this does not in the least affect what was advanced just now; for in all such cases, the probability itself is assumed in one of the premises: whereas, in the inductive method of reasoning, it often happens, that from certain facts we can deduce only probable consequences.

I observe secondly, that though this manner of arguing has more of the nature of scientific reasoning than of moral, it has, nevertheless, not been thought worthy of being adopted by mathematicians, as a proper method of demonstrating their theorems. I am satisfied that mathematical demonstration is capable of being moulded into the syllogistic form, having made the trial with success on some propositions. But that this form is a very incommodious one, and has many disadvantages, but not one advantage of that commonly practised, will be manifest to every one who makes the experiment. It is at once more indirect, more tedious, and more obscure. I may add, that if into those abstract sciences one were to introduce some specious fallacies, such fallacies could be much more easily sheltered under the awkward verbosity of this artificial method, than under the elegant simplicity of that which has hitherto been used.

My third remark, which, by the way, is directly consequent on the two former, shall be, that in the ordinary application of this art to matters with which we can be made acquainted only by experience, it can be of little or no utility. So far from leading the mind, agreeably to the design of all argument and investigation, from things known to things unknown, and by things evident to things obscure; its usual progress is, on the contrary, from things less known to things better known, and by things obscure to things evident. But that it may not be thought that I do injustice to the art by this representation, I must entreat that the few following considerations may be attended to.

When, in the way of induction, the mind proceeds from individual instances to the discovery of such truths as regard a species, and from these again to such as comprehend a genus, we may say with reason, that as we advance, there may be in every succeeding step, and commonly is, less certainty than in the preceding; but in no instance whatever can there be more. Besides, as the judgment formed concerning the less general was anterior to that formed concerning the more general, so the conviction is more vivid arising from both circumstances, that, being less general, it is more distinctly conceived, and being earlier, it is more deeply imprinted. Now, the customary procedure in the syllogistic science is, as was remarked, the natural method reversed, being from general to special, and consequently from less to more obvious. In scientific reasoning the case is very different, as the axioms, or universal truths from which the mathematician argues, are so far from being the slow result of induction and experience, that they are self-evident. They are no sooner apprehended than necessarily assented to.

But to illustrate the matter by examples, take the following specimen in *Barbara*, the first mood of the first figure:—

All animals feel;
All horses are animals;
Therefore all horses feel.

It is impossible that any reasonable man, who really doubts whether a horse has feeling or is a mere automaton, should be convinced by this argument. For, supposing he uses the names *horse* and *animal*, as standing in the same relation of species and genus which they bear in the common acceptation of the words, the argument you employ is, in effect, but an affirmation of the point which he denies, couched in such terms as include a multitude of other similar affirmations, which, whether true or false, are nothing to the purpose. Thus *all animals feel*, is only a compendious expression, for *all horses feel, all dogs feel, all camels feel, all eagles feel*, and so through the whole animal creation. I affirm, besides, that the procedure here is from things less known to things better known. It is possible that one may believe the conclusion who denies the major: but the reverse is not possible; for, to express myself in the language of the art, that may be predicated of the species, which is not predicable of the genus; but that can never be predicated of the genus, which is not predicable of the species. If one, therefore, were under such an error in regard to the brutes, true logic, which is always coincident with good sense, would lead our reflections to the indications of perception and feeling, given by these animals, and the remarkable conformity which in this respect, and in respect to their bodily organs, they bear to our own species.

It may be said, that if the subject of the question were a creature much more ignoble than the horse, there would be no scope for this objection to the argument. Substitute, then, the word *oysters* for horses in the minor, and it will stand thus,

All animals feel;
All oysters are animals;
Therefore all oysters feel.

In order to give the greater advantage to the advocate for this scholastic art, let us suppose the antagonist does not maintain the opposite side from any favour to Descartes' theory concerning brutes, but from some notion entertained of that particular order of beings which is the subject of dispute. It is evident, that though he should admit the truth of the major, he would regard the minor as merely another manner of expressing the conclusion; for he would conceive an animal no otherwise than as a body endowed with sensation or feeling.

Sometimes, indeed, there is not in the premises any position more generic, under which the conclusion can be comprised. In this case you always find that the same proposition is exhibited in different words; insomuch that the stress of the argument lies in a mere synonyma or something equivalent. The following is an example:—

The Almighty ought to be worshipped;
God is the Almighty;
Therefore God ought to be worshipped.

It would be superfluous to illustrate that this argument could have no greater influence on the Epicurean, than the first mentioned one would have on the Cartesian. To suppose the contrary is to suppose the conviction effected by the charm of a sound, and not by the sense of what is advanced. Thus also the middle term and the subject frequently correspond to each other, as the definition, description, or circumlocution, and the name. Of this I shall give an example in *Disamis*, as in the technical dialect the third mood of the third figure is denominated,—

Some men are rapacious;
All men are rational animals;
Therefore some rational animals are rapacious.

Who does not perceive that "rational animals" is but a periphrasis for men?

It may be proper to subjoin one example at least, in negative syllogisms. The subsequent is one in *Celarent*, the second mood of the first figure:—

Nothing violent is lasting;
But tyranny is violent;
Therefore tyranny is not lasting.

Here a *thing violent* serves for the genus of which *tyranny* is a species; and nothing can be clearer than that it requires much less experience to discover whether shortness of duration be justly attributed to tyranny the species, than whether it be justly predicated of every violent thing. The application of what was said on the first example, to that now given, is so obvious that it would be losing time to attempt further to illustrate it.

Logicians have been at pains to discriminate the regular and consequential combinations of the three terms, as they are called, from the irregular and inconsequent. A combination of the latter kind, if the defect be in the form, is called a paralogism; if in the sense, a sophism; though sometimes these two appellations are confounded. Of the latter, one kind is denominated *petitio principii*, which is commonly rendered in English, *a begging of the question*, and is defined the proving of a thing by itself, whether expressed in the same or in different words, or which amounts to the same thing, assuming in the proof the very opinion or principle proposed to be proved. It is surprising that this should ever have been by those artists styled a sophism, since it is in fact so essential to the art, that there is always some radical defect in a syllogism which is not chargeable with this. The truth of what I now affirm will appear to any one, on the slightest review of what has been evinced in the preceding part of this chapter.

The fourth and last observation I shall make on this topic is, that the proper province of the syllogistical science is rather the adjustment of our language, in expressing ourselves on subjects previously known, than the acquisition of knowledge in things themselves. According to M. du Marsais, "Reasoning consists in deducing, inferring, or drawing a judgment from other judgments already known; or rather in showing that the judgment in question has been already formed implicitly, insomuch that the only point is to develope it, and show its identity with some anterior judgment."[2] Now I affirm that the former part of this definition suits all deductive reasoning, whether scientifical or moral, in which the principle deduced is distinct from, however closely related to, the principles from which the deduction is made. The latter part of

[2] Le raisonnement consiste à déduire, à inférer, à tirer un jugement d'autres jugemens déjà connus; ou plutôt à faire voir que le jugement dont il s'agit, a déjà été porté d'une manière implicite; de sorte qu'il n'est plus question que de le développer, et d' en faire voir l'identité avec quelque jugement anterieur. Logique Art. 7.

the definition, which begins with the words *or rather*, does not answer as an explication of the former, as the author seems to have intended, but exactly hits the character of syllogistic reasoning, and indeed of all sorts of controversy merely verbal. If you regard only the thing signified, the argument conveys no instruction, nor does it forward us in the knowledge of things a single step. But if you regard principally the signs, it may serve to correct misapplications of them, through inadvertency or otherwise.

In evincing the truth of this doctrine, I shall begin with a simple illustration from what may happen to any one in studying a foreign tongue. I learn from an Italian and French dictionary, that the Italian word *pecora* corresponds to the French word *brebis*, and from a French and English dictionary, that the French *brebis* corresponds to the English *sheep*. Hence I form this argument,

Pecora is the same with *brebis;*
Brebis is the same with *sheep;*
Therefore *pecora* is the same with *sheep*.

This, though not in mood and figure, is evidently conclusive. Nay, more, if the words *pecora*, *brebis*, and *sheep*, under the notion of signs, be regarded as the terms, it has three distinct terms, and contains a direct and scientifical deduction from this axiom, "Things coincident with the same thing are coincident with one another." On the other hand, let the things signified be solely regarded, and there is but one term in the whole, namely, the species of quadruped denoted by the three names above mentioned. Nor is there, in this view of the matter, another judgment in all the three propositions, but this identical one, "A sheep is a sheep."

Nor let it be imagined that the only right application can be in the acquisition of strange languages. Every tongue whatever gives scope for it, inasmuch as in every tongue the speaker labours under great inconveniences, especially on abstract questions, both from the paucity, obscurity, and ambiguity of the words on the one hand; and from his own misapprehensions, and imperfect acquaintance with them on the other. As a man may, therefore, by an artful and sophistical use of them, be brought to admit, in certain terms, what he would deny in others, this disputatious discipline may, under proper management, by setting in a stronger light the inconsistencies occasioned by such improprieties, be rendered instrumental in correcting them. It was remarked above,[3] that such propositions as these, "Twelve are a dozen," "Twenty are a score," unless considered as explications of the words *dozen* and

[3] Chap. v. Sect. 1. Part 1.

score, are quite insignificant. This limitation, however, it was necessary to add; for those positions which are identical when considered purely as relating to the things signified, are nowise identical when regarded purely as explanatory of the names. Suppose that through the imperfection of a man's knowledge in the language, aided by another's sophistry, and perhaps his own inattention, he is brought to admit of the one term, what he would refuse of the other, such an argument as this might be employed,

> Twelve, you allow, are equal to the fifth part of sixty;
> Now a dozen are equal to twelve;
> Therefore a dozen are equal to the fifth part of sixty.

I mark the case rather strongly, for the sake of illustration; for I am sensible, that in what regards things so definite as all names of number are, it is impossible for any one, who is not quite ignorant of the tongue, to be misled. But the intelligent reader will easily conceive, that in abstruse and metaphysical subjects, wherein the terms are often both extensive and indefinite in their signification, and sometimes even equivocal, the most acute and wary may be entangled in them.

In further confirmation of my fourth remark, I shall produce an example in *Camestres*, the second mood of the second figure:

> All animals are mortal;
> But angels are not mortal;
> Therefore angels are not animals.

When the antagonist calls an angel an animal, it must proceed from one or other of these two causes, either from an error in regard to the nature of the angelic order, or from a mistake as to the import of the English word *animal*. If the first be the case,—namely, some erroneous opinion about angels, as that they are embodied spirits, generated and corruptible like ourselves,—it is evident that the forementioned syllogism labours under the common defect of all syllogisms. It assumes the very point in question. But if the difference between the disputants be, as it frequently happens, merely verbal, and the opponent uses the word *animal* as another name for living creature, and as exactly corresponding to the Greek term,[4] arguments of this sort may be of service, for setting the impropriety of such a misapplication of the English name in a clearer light. For let it be observed, that though Nature hath strongly marked the principal differences to be found in different orders of beings, a procedure which hath suggested to men the manner of classing things into genera and species, this does not hold

[4] Ζῶον.

equally in every case. Hence it is, that the general terms in different languages do not always exactly correspond. Some nations, from particular circumstances, are more affected by one property in objects, others by another. This leads to a different distribution of things under their several names. Now, though it is not of importance that the words in one tongue exactly correspond to those in another, it is of importance that in the same tongue uniformity in this respect be, as much as is possible, observed. Errors in regard to the signs tend not only to retard the progress of knowledge, but to introduce errors in regard to the things signified. Now, by suggesting the different attributes comprised in the definition of the term, as so many mediums in the proof, an appeal is made to the adversary's practice in the language. In this way such mediums may be presented as will satisfy a candid adversary, that the application he makes of the term in question is not conformable to the usage of the tongue.

On the other hand, it is certain, that in matters of an abstract and complex nature, where the terms are comprehensive, indefinite, not in frequent use, and consequently not well ascertained, men may argue together eternally, without making the smallest impression on each other, not sensible, all the while, that there is not at bottom any difference between them, except as to the import of words and phrases. I do not say, however, that this is a consequence peculiar to this manner of debating, though perhaps oftener resulting from it, on account of its many nice distinctions, unmeaning subtleties, and mazy windings, than from any other manner. For it must be owned, that the syllogistic art has at least as often been employed for imposing fallacies on the understanding, as for detecting those imposed. And though verbal controversy seems to be its natural province, it is neither the only method adapted to such discussions, nor the most expeditious.

To conclude then; what shall we denominate the artificial system, or organ of truth, as it has been called, of which we have been treating? Shall we style it the art of reasoning? So honourable an appellation it by no means merits, since, as hath been shown, it is ill adapted to scientific matters, and for that reason never employed by the mathematician; and is utterly incapable of assisting us in our researches into nature. Shall we then pronounce it the science of *logomachy*, or in plain English, the art of fighting with words, and about words? And in this wordy warfare, shall we say that the rules of syllogizing are the tactics? This would certainly hit the matter more nearly; but I know not how it happens, that to call any thing *logomachy* or *altercation*, would be considered as giving bad names; and when a good use may be made of an invention, it seems unreasonable to fix an odious name upon it, which ought only to discriminate the abuse. I shall therefore only title it the scholastic art of disputation.[5] It is the schoolmen's science of defence.

When all erudition consisted more in an acquaintance with words, and an address in using them, than in the knowledge of things, dexterity in this exercitation conferred as much lustre on the scholar, as agility in the tilts and tournaments added glory to the knight. In proportion as the attention of mankind has been drawn off to the study of nature, the honours of this contentious art have faded, and it is now almost forgotten. There is no reason to wish its revival, as eloquence seems to have been very little benefited by it, and philosophy still less.

Nay, there is but good reason to affirm, that there are two evils at least which it has gendered. These are, first, an itch of disputing on every subject, however uncontrovertible; the other, a sort of philosophic pride, which will not permit us to think that we believe any thing, even a self-evident principle, without a previous reason or argument. In order to gratify this passion, we invariably recur to words, and are at immense pains to lose ourselves in clouds of our own raising. We imagine we are advancing and making wonderful progress, while the mist of words in which we have involved our intellects, hinders us from discerning that we are moving in a circle all the time.[6]

[5] It answers to that branch of logic which Lord Verulam styles *Doctrina de elenchis hermeniæ;* concerning which he affirms, "Dedimus ei nomen ex usu, quia verus ejus usus est plane redargutio, et cautio circa usum verborum. Quinimo partem illam de prædicamentis, si recte instituator, circa cautiones, de non confundendis aut transponendis definitionum et divisionum terminis, præcipuum usum sortiri existimamus, et huc etiam referri malumus." De Aug. Scient. L. v. c. 4.

[6] How ridiculous are the efforts which some very learned and judicious men have made, in order to evince that whatever begins to exist must have a cause. One argues, "There must have been a cause to determine the time and place," as though it were more evident that the accidents could not be determined without a cause, than that the existence of the thing could not be so determined. Another insists very curiously, that if a thing had no cause, it must have been the cause of itself; a third, with equal consistency, that nothing must have been the cause. Thus, by always assuming *the absolute necessity of a cause,* they demonstrate *the absolute necessity of a cause.* For a full illustration of the futility of such pretended reasonings, see the Treatise of Human Nature, B. i. Part iii. Sect. 3. I do not think they have succeeded better, who have attempted to assign a reason for the faith we have in this principle, that *the future will resemble the past.* A late author imagines that he solves the difficulty at once, by saying, that what is now time past, was once future; and that though no man has had experience of what *is* future, every man has had experience of what *was* future." Would it then be more perspicuous to state the question thus: "How come we to believe that *what is future,* not *what was future,* will resemble the past?" Of the first he says expressly, that no man has had experience, though almost in the same breath he tells us, not very consistently, "The answer is sufficient, have we not always found it to be so?" an answer which appears to me not more illogical than ungrammatical. But admitting with him, that to consider time as past or future (though no distinction can be more precise) is only puzzling the

CHAPTER VII.

Of the Consideration which the Speaker ought to have of the Hearers, as men in general.

RHETORIC, as was observed already, not only considers the subject, but also the hearers and the speaker.[7] The hearers must be considered in a twofold view, as men in general, and as such men in particular.

As men in general, it must be allowed there are certain principles in our nature, which, when properly addressed and managed, give no inconsiderable aid to reason in promoting belief. Nor is it just to conclude from this concession, as some have hastily done, that oratory may be defined, "The art of deception." The use of such helps will be found, on a stricter examination, to be in most cases quite legitimate, and even necessary, if we would give reason herself that influence which is certainly her due. In order to evince the truth considered by itself, conclusive arguments alone are requisite; but in order to convince me by these arguments, it is moreover requisite that they be understood, that they be attended to,

question; let us inquire whether a reason can be assigned for judging that the unknown time will resemble the known. Suppose our whole time divided into equal portions. Call these portions A, B, C, D, E, F, G. Of these the three first have been experienced, the remaining four are not. The three first I found to resemble one another, but how must I argue with regard to the rest? Shall I say B was like A, therefore D will be like C; or, if you think it strengthens the argument, shall I say, C resembled A and B, therefore D will resemble A, B, and C. I would gladly know what sort of reasoning, scientifical or moral, this could be denominated; or what is the medium by which the conclusion is made out? Suppose, further, I get acquainted with D, formerly unknown, and find that it actually resembles A, B, and C, how can this furnish me with any knowledge of E, F, and G, things totally distinct? The resemblance I have discovered in D, to A, B, and C, can never be extended to any thing that is not D, nor any part of D, namely to E, F, and G; unless you assume this as the medium, that the unknown will resemble the known; or, which is equivalent, that the future will resemble the past. So far is this principle, therefore, from being deduced from particular experience, that it is fundamental to all particular deductions from experience, in which we could not advance a single step without it. We are often misled, in cases of this nature, by a vague and popular use of words, not attending to the nicer differences in their import in different situations. If one were to ask me, "Have you, then, no reason to believe that the future will resemble the past?" I should certainly answer, "I have the greatest reason to believe it." And if the question had been concerning a geometrical axiom, I should have returned the same answer. By *reason* we often mean, not an argument, or medium of proving, but a ground in human nature on which a particular judgment is founded. Nay further, as no progress in reasoning can be made where there is no foundation, (and first principles are here the sole foundation,) I should readily admit, that the man who does not believe such propositions, if it were possible to find such a man, is perfectly irrational, and consequently not to be argued with.

7 Chap. iv.

that they be remembered by me; and in order to persuade me by them to any particular action or conduct, it is further requisite, that by interesting me in the subject, they may, as it were, be felt. It is not therefore the understanding alone that is here concerned. If the orator would prove successful, it is necessary that he engage in his service all these different powers of the mind, the imagination, the memory, and the passions. These are not the supplanters of reason, or even rivals in her sway; they are her handmaids, by whose ministry she is enabled to usher truth into the heart, and procure it there a favourable reception. As handmaids they are liable to be seduced by sophistry in the garb of reason, and sometimes are made ignorantly to lend their aid in the introduction of falsehood. But their service is not on this account to be dispensed with; there is even a necessity of employing it, founded on our nature. Our eyes and hands and feet will give us the same assistance in doing mischief as in doing good; but it would not therefore be better for the world, that all mankind were blind and lame. Arms are not to be laid aside by honest men, because carried by assassins and ruffians; they are to be used the rather for this very reason. Nor are those mental powers, of which eloquence so much avails herself, like the art of war or other human arts, perfectly indifferent to good and evil, and only beneficial as they are rightly employed. On the contrary, they are by nature, as will perhaps appear afterwards, more friendly to truth than to falsehood, and more easily retained in the cause of virtue, than in that of vice.[8]

SECTION I.—*Men considered as endowed with Understanding.*

But to descend to particulars; the first thing to be studied by the speaker is, that his arguments may be understood. If they be unintelligible, the cause must be either in the sense or

[8] "Notandum est enim, affectus ipsos ad bonum apparens semper ferri, atque hac ex parte aliquid habere cum ratione commune; verum illud interest, quod *affectus intuentur præcipue bonum in præsentia; ratio prospiciens in longum, etiam futurum, et in summa*. Ideoque cum quæ in præsentia obversentur, impleant phantasiam fortius, succumbit plerumque ratio et subjugatur. Sed postquam eloquentiâ et suasionum vi effectum sit, ut futura et remota constituantur et conspiciantur tanquam præsentia, tum demum abeunte in partes rationis, phantasia ratio fit superior. Concludamus igitur, non deberi magis vitio verti *Rhetoricæ*, quod deteriorem partem cohonestare sciat quam *Dialecticæ*, quod sophismata concinnare doceat. Quis enim nescit contrariorum eandem rationem esse, licet usu opponantur?" De Aug. Scient. L. vi. c. 3. Τα ὑποκειμενα πραγματα ουχ ὁμοιως εχει, αλλ' αιει τ' αληθη και τα βελτιω τη φυσει ευσυλλογιστοτερα και πιθανωτερα, ὡς ἁπλως ειπειν.—ει δ' ὁτι μεγαλα βλαψειεν αν ὁ χρωμενος αδικως τῃ τοιαυτῃ δυναμει των λογων, τουτο τε κοινον εστι κατα παντων των αγαθων, πλην αρετης, και μαλιστα κατα των χρησιμωτατων, οἱον ισχυος, ὑγιειας, πλουτου, στρατηγιας· τοιουτοις γαρ αν τις ωφελησειε τα μεγιστα, χρωμενος δικαιως, και βλαψειεν αδικως. Arist. Rhet. L. i. c. 1.

in the expression. It lies in the sense if the mediums of proof be such as the hearers are unacquainted with; that is, if the ideas introduced be either without the sphere of their knowledge, or too abstract for their apprehension and habits of thinking. It lies in the sense likewise, if the train of reasoning (though no unusual ideas should be introduced) be longer, or more complex, or more intricate, than they are accustomed to. But as the fitness of the arguments, in these respects, depends on the capacity, education, and attainments of the hearers, which in different orders of men are different, this properly belongs to the consideration which the speaker ought to have of his audience, not as men in general, but as men in particular. The obscurity which ariseth from the expression will come in course to be considered in the sequel.

SECTION II.—*Men considered as endowed with Imagination.*

The second thing requisite is that his reasoning be attended to; for this purpose the imagination must be engaged. Attention is prerequisite to every effect of speaking, and without some gratification in hearing, there will be no attention, at least of any continuance. Those qualities in ideas which principally gratify the fancy, are vivacity, beauty, sublimity, novelty. Nothing contributes more to vivacity than striking resemblances in the imagery, which convey, besides, an additional pleasure of their own.

But there is still a further end to be served by pleasing the imagination, than that of awakening and preserving the attention, however important this purpose alone ought to be accounted. I will not say with a late subtle metaphysician,[9] that "Belief consisteth in the liveliness of our ideas." That this doctrine is erroneous, it would be quite foreign to my purpose to attempt here to evince.[1] Thus much however is indubitable, that belief commonly enlivens our ideas; and that lively ideas have a stronger influence than faint ideas to induce belief. But so far are these two from being coincident, that even this connexion between them, though common, is not necessary. Vivacity of ideas is not always accompanied with faith, nor is faith always able to produce vivacity. The ideas raised in my mind by the Œdipus Tyrannus of Sophocles, or the Lear of Shakespeare, are incomparably more lively than those excited by a cold but faithful historiographer. Yet I may give full credit to the languid narrative of the latter, though I believe not a single sentence in those tragedies. If a proof were asked of

[9] The author of a Treatise of Human Nature, in 3 vols.

[1] If one is desirous to see a refutation of this principle, let him consult Reid's Inquiry, Chap. ii. Sect. 5.

the greater vivacity in the one case than in the other (which, by the way, must be finally determined by consciousness), let these effects serve for arguments. The ideas of the poet give greater pleasure, command closer attention, operate more strongly on the passions, and are longer remembered. If these be not sufficient evidences of greater vivacity, I own I have no apprehension of the meaning which that author affixes to the term. The connexion, however, that generally subsisteth between vivacity and belief will appear less marvellous, if we reflect that there is not so great a difference between argument and illustration as is usually imagined. The same ingenious writer says, concerning moral reasoning, that it is but a kind of comparison. The truth of this assertion any one will easily be convinced of, who considers the preceding observations on that subject.

Where then lies the difference between addressing the judgment and addressing the fancy? and what hath given rise to the distinction between ratiocination and imagery? The following observations will serve for an answer to this query. It is evident, that though the mind receives a considerable pleasure from the discovery of resemblance, no pleasure is received when the resemblance is of such a nature as is familiar to every body. Such are those resemblances which result from the specific and generic qualities of ordinary objects. What gives the principal delight to the imagination, is the exhibition of a strong likeness, which escapes the notice of the generality of people. The similitude of man to man, eagle to eagle, sea to sea, or in brief, of one individual to another individual of the same species, affects not the fancy in the least. What poet would ever think of comparing a combat between two of his heroes to a combat between other two? Yet no where else will he find so strong a resemblance. Indeed, to the faculty of imagination, this resemblance appears rather under the notion of identity; although it be the foundation of the strongest reasoning from experience. Again, the similarity of one species to another of the same genus, as of the lion to the tiger, of the alder to the oak, though this too be a considerable fund of argumentation, hardly strikes the fancy more than the preceding, inasmuch as the generical properties, whereof every species participates, are also obvious. But if from the experimental reasoning we descend to the analogical, we may be said to come upon a common to which reason and fancy have an equal claim. "A comparison," says Quintilian,[2] "hath almost the effect of an example." But what are rhetorical comparisons, when brought to illustrate any point inculcated on the hearers,—what are they, I say, but arguments from analogy? In proof of

[2] Instit. lib. v. cap. 11. Proximas exempli vires habet similitudo.

this let us borrow an instance from the forementioned rhetorician, "Would you be convinced of the necessity of education for the mind, consider of what importance culture is to the ground: the field which, cultivated, produceth a plentiful crop of useful fruits, if neglected, will be overrun with briars and brambles, and other useless or noxious weeds."[3] It would be no better than trifling to point out the argument couched in this passage. Now if comparison, which is the chief, hath so great an influence upon conviction, it is no wonder that all those other oratorical tropes and figures addressed to the imagination, which are more or less nearly related to comparison, should derive hence both life and efficacy.[4] Even antithesis implies comparison. Simile is a comparison in epitome.[5] Metaphor is an allegory in miniature. Allegory and prosopopeia are comparisons conveyed under a particular form.

SECTION III.—*Men considered as endowed with Memory.*

Further, vivid ideas are not only more powerful than languid ideas in commanding and preserving attention, they are not only more efficacious in producing conviction, but they are also more easily retained. Those several powers, understanding, imagination, memory, and passion, are mutually subservient. That it is necessary for the orator to engage the help of memory, will appear from many reasons, particularly from what was remarked above, on the fourth difference between moral reasoning and demonstrative.[6] It was there observed, that in the former the credibility of the fact is the sum of the evidence of all the arguments, often independent of one another, brought to support it. And though it was shown that demonstration itself, without the assistance of this faculty, could never produce conviction; yet here it must be owned, that the natural connexion of the several links in the chain renders the remembrance easier. Now, as nothing can operate on the mind which is not in some respect present to it, care must be taken by the orator that, in introducing new topics, the vestiges left by the former on the minds of the hearers may not be effaced. It is the sense of this necessity which hath given rise to the rules of composition.

Some will perhaps consider it as irregular, that I speak here

[3] Ibid. Ut si animum dicas excolendum, similitudine utaris terræ, quæ neglecta sentes atque dumos, exculta fructus creat.

[4] Præterea, nescio quomodo etiam credit facilius, quæ audienti jucunda sunt, et voluptate ad fidem ducitur. Quint. L. iv. c. 2.

[5] Simile and comparison are in common language frequently confounded. The difference is this: Simile is no more than a comparison suggested in a word or two; as, He fought like a lion: His face shone as the sun. Comparison is a simile circumstantiated and included in one or more separate sentences.

[6] Chap. v. Sect. ii. P. 1.

of addressing the memory, of which no mention at all was made in the first chapter, wherein I considered the different forms of eloquence, classing them by the different faculties of the mind addressed. But this apparent irregularity will vanish, when it is observed, that, with regard to the faculties there mentioned, each of them may not only be the direct, but even the ultimate object of what is spoken. The whole scope may be at one time to inform or convince the understanding, at another to delight the imagination, at a third to agitate the passions, and at a fourth to determine the will. But it is never the ultimate end of speaking to be remembered, when what is spoken tends neither to instruct, to please, to move, nor to persuade. This therefore is of necessity no more on any occasion than a subordinate end; or, which is precisely the same thing, the means to some further end; and as such, it is more or less necessary on every occasion. The speaker's attention to this subserviency of memory is always so much the more requisite, the greater the difficulty of remembrance is, and the more important the being remembered is to the attainment of the ultimate end. On both accounts, it is of more consequence in those discourses whose aim is either instruction or persuasion, than in those whose design is solely to please the fancy, or to move the passions. And if there are any which answer none of those ends, it were better to learn to forget them than to teach the method of making them to be retained.

The author of the treatise above quoted hath divided the principles of association in ideas into resemblance, contiguity, and causation. I do not here inquire into all the defects of this enumeration, but only observe that, even on his own system, order both in space and time ought to have been included. It appears at least to have an equal title with causation, which, according to him, is but a particular modification and combination of the other two. Causation, considered as an associating principle, is, in his theory, no more than the contiguous succession of two ideas, which is more deeply imprinted on the mind by its experience of a similar contiguity and succession of the impressions from which they are copied. This therefore is the result of resemblance and vicinity united. Order in place is likewise a mode of vicinity, where this last tie is strengthened by the regularity and simplicity of figure; which qualities arise solely from the resemblance of the corresponding parts of the figure; or the parts similarly situated. Regular figures, besides the advantages they derive from simplicity and uniformity, have this also, that they are more familiar to the mind than irregular figures, and are therefore more easily conceived. Hence the influence which order in place hath upon the memory. If any person question this influence, let him but reflect, how much easier it is to remember a considerable number of persons, whom one hath seen ranged on benches or chairs, round a hall, than the same number seen standing promiscuously in a crowd: and how natural it is, for assisting the memory in recollecting the persons, to recur to the order wherein they were placed.

As to order in time, which in composition is properly styled Method, it consisteth principally in connecting the parts in such a manner as to give vicinity to things in the discourse which have an affinity; that is, resemblance, causality, or other relation in nature; and thus making their customary association and resemblance, as in the former case, co-operate with their contiguity in duration, or immediate succession in the delivery. The utility of method for aiding the memory, all the world knows. But besides this, there are some parts of the discourse, as well as figures of speech, peculiarly adapted to this end. Such are the division of the subject, the rhetorical repetitions of every kind, the different modes of transition and recapitulation.

SECTION IV.—*Men considered as endowed with Passions.*

To conclude; when persuasion is the end, passion also must be engaged. If it is fancy which bestows brilliancy on our ideas, if it is memory which gives them stability, passion doth more, it animates them. Hence they derive spirit and energy. To say that it is possible to persuade without speaking to the passions, is but at best a kind of specious nonsense. The coolest reasoner always in persuading addresseth himself to the passions some way or other. This he cannot avoid doing, if he speak to the purpose. To make me believe it is enough to show me that things are so; to make me act, it is necessary to show that the action will answer some end. That can never be an end to me which gratifies no passion or affection in my nature. You assure me, "It is for my honour." Now you solicit my pride, without which I had never been able to understand the word. You say, "It is for my interest." Now you bespeak my self-love. "It is for the public good." Now you rouse my patriotism. "It will relieve the miserable." Now you touch my pity. So far therefore it is from being an unfair method of persuasion to move the passions, that there is no persuasion without moving them.

But if so much depend on passion, where is the scope for argument? Before I answer this question, let it be observed that, in order to persuade, there are two things which must be carefully studied by the orator. The first is, to excite some desire or passion in the hearers; the second is to satisfy their judgment that there is a connexion between the action to which he would persuade them, and the gratification of the desire or passion which he excites. This is the analysis of persuasion. The former is effected by communicating lively and glowing ideas of the object; the latter, unless so evident of itself as to supersede the necessity, by presenting the best and most forcible arguments which the nature of the subject admits. In the one lies the pathetic, in the other the argumentative. These incorporated together (as was observed in the first chapter) constitute that vehemence of contention, to which the greatest exploits of eloquence ought doubtless to be ascribed. Here then is the principal scope for argument, but not the only scope, as will appear in the sequel. When the first end alone is attained, the pathetic without the rational, the passions are indeed roused from a disagreeable languor by the help of the imagination, and the mind is thrown into a state which, though accompanied with some painful emotions, rarely fails, upon the whole, to affect it with pleasure. But, if the hearers are judicious, no practical effect is produced. They cannot by such declamation be influenced to a particular action, because not convinced that that action will conduce to the gratifying of the passion raised. Your eloquence hath fired my ambition, and makes me burn with public zeal. The consequence is, there is nothing which at present I would not attempt for the sake of fame, and the interest of my country. You advise me to such a conduct; but you have not shown me how that can contribute to gratify either passion. Satisfy me in this, and I am instantly at your command. Indeed, when the hearers are rude and ignorant, nothing more is necessary in the speaker than to inflame their passions. They will not require that the connexion between the conduct he urges and the end proposed be evinced to them. His word will satisfy. And therefore bold affirmations are made to supply the place of reasons. Hence it is that the rabble are ever the prey of quacks and impudent pretenders of every denomination.

On the contrary, when the other end alone is attained, the rational without the pathetic, the speaker is as far from his purpose as before. You have proved, beyond contradiction, that acting thus is the sure way to procure such an object. I perceive that your reasoning is conclusive: but I am not affected by it. Why? I have no passion for the object. I am indifferent whether I procure it or not. You have demonstrated that such a step will mortify my enemy. I believe it; but I have no resentment, and will not trouble myself to give pain to another. Your arguments evince that it would gratify my vanity. But I prefer my ease. Thus passion is the mover to action, reason is the guide. Good is the object of the will, truth is the object of the understanding.[7]

[7] Several causes have contributed to involve this subject in confusion. One is the ambiguity and imperfection of language. Motives are often

It may be thought that when the motive is the equity, the generosity, or the intrinsic merit of the action recommended,

called arguments, and both motives and arguments are promiscuously styled reasons. Another is, the idle disputes that have arisen among philosophers concerning the nature of good, both physical and moral. "Truth and good are one," says the author of the Pleasures of Imagination, an author whose poetical merit will not be questioned by persons of taste. The expression might have been passed in the poet, whose right to the use of *catachresis*, one of the many privileges comprehended under the name of *poetic license*, prescription hath fully established. But by philosophizing on this passage in his notes, he warrants us to canvass his reasoning, for no such privilege hath as yet been conceded to philosophers. Indeed, in attempting to illustrate, he has, I think, confuted it, or, to speak more properly, shown it to have no meaning. He mentions two opinions concerning the connexion of truth and beauty, which is one species of good. "Some philosophers," says he, "assert an independent and invariable law in nature, in consequence of which *all rational beings must alike perceive beauty in some certain proportions, and deformity in the contrary.*" Now, though I do not conceive what is meant either by an *independent law*, or by *contrary proportions*, this, if it proves any thing, proves as clearly that deformity and truth are one, as that beauty and truth are one; for those *contrary proportions* are surely as much proportions, or, if you will, as true proportions, as *some certain proportions* are. Accordingly, if, in the conclusion deduced, you put the word *deformity* instead of *beauty*, and the word *beauty* instead of *deformity*, the sense will be equally complete. "Others," he adds, "there are, who believe beauty to be merely a relative and arbitrary thing; and that it is not impossible, in a physical sense, that two beings of equal capacities for truth, should perceive, one of them beauty, and the other deformity, in the same relations. And upon this supposition, by that truth which is always connected with beauty, nothing more can be meant than the conformity of any object to those proportions, upon which, after a careful examination, the beauty of that species is found to depend." This opinion, if I am able to comprehend it, differs only in one point from the preceding. It supposes the standard or law of beauty not invariable or universal. It is liable to the same objection, and that rather more glaringly; for if the same relations must be always equally *true relations*, deformity is as really one with truth as beauty is, since the very same relations can exhibit both appearances. In short, no hypothesis hitherto invented hath shown that by means of the discursive faculty, without the aid of any other mental power, we could ever obtain a notion of either the beautiful or the good; and till this be shown, nothing is shown to the purpose. The author aforesaid, far from attempting this, proceeds on the supposition, that we first perceive beauty, he says not how, and then having, by a careful examination, discovered the proportions which give rise to the perception, denominate them *true;* so that all those elaborate disquisitions with which we are amused, amount only to a few insignificant identical propositions very improperly expressed. For out of a vast profusion of learned phrase, this is all the information we can pick, that "Beauty is—*truly* beauty," and that "Good is—*truly* good." "Moral good," says a celebrated writer, "consisteth in *fitness.*" From this account any person would at first readily conclude, that morals, according to him, are not concerned in the ends which we pursue, but solely in the choice of means for attaining our ends; that if this choice be judicious the conduct is moral; if injudicious, the contrary. But this truly pious author is far from admitting such an interpretation of his words. *Fitness* in this sense hath no relation to a further end. It is an absolute fitness, a fitness in itself. We are obliged to ask, What then is that fitness, which you call absolute? for the application of the word in every other case invariably implying the proper direction of means to an end, far from affording light to the meaning it has here, tends directly to mislead us. The only answer, as far as I can learn, that hath ever been given to this question, is neither more nor less than this, "That alone is absolutely fit which is morally good:" so that in saying moral good consisteth in fitness, no more is meant than that it consisteth in moral good. Another moralist appears, who hath made a most wonderful discovery. It is, that argument may be employed to evince the reasonableness of the end, as well as the fitness of the means. But this way of speaking suits better the popular dialect than the philosophical. The term *reasonableness*, when used in this manner, means nothing but the goodness, the amiableness, or moral excellency. If therefore the hearer hath no love of justice, no benevolence, no regard to right, although he were endowed with the perspicacity of a cherub, your harangue could never have any influence on his mind. The reason is, when you speak of the fitness of the means, you address yourself only to the head; when you speak of the goodness of the end, you address yourself to the heart, of which we supposed him destitute. Are we then to class the virtues among the passions? By no means. But without entering into a discussion of the difference, which would be foreign to our purpose, let it suffice to observe, that they have this in common with passion. They necessarily imply an habitual propensity to a certain species of conduct, an habitual aversion to the contrary: a veneration for such a character, an abhorrence of such another. They are, therefore, though not passions, so closely related to them, that they are properly considered as motives to action, being equally capable of giving an impulse to the will. The difference is akin to that, if not the same, which rhetoricians observe between *pathos* and *ethos*, passion and disposition.[8] Accordingly, what is addressed solely to the moral powers of the mind, is not so properly denominated the pathetic, as the *sentimental*. The term, I own, is rather modern, but is nevertheless convenient, as it fills a vacant room, and doth not, like most of our new-fangled words, justle out older and worthier occupants, to the no small detriment of the language. It occupies, so to speak, the middle place between the pathetic and that which is addressed to the imagination, and partakes of both, adding to the warmth of the former the grace and attractions of the latter.

there is not a vice in the world but lying, and that acting virtuously in any situation is but one way or other of telling truth. When this curious theory comes to be explained, we find the practical lie results solely from acting contrary to what those moral sentiments dictate, which, instead of deducing, he everywhere presupposeth to be known and acknowledged by us. Thus he reasons perpetually in a circle, and without advancing a single step beyond it, makes the same things both causes and effects reciprocally. Conduct appears to be false for no other reason than because it is immoral, and immoral for no other reason but because it is false. Such philosophy would not have been unworthy those profound ontologists, who have blest the world with the discovery that "One being is but *one* being," that "A being is *truly* a being," and that "Every being has all the *properties* that it has," and who, to the unspeakable increase of useful knowledge, have denominated these the general attributes of being, and distinguished them by the titles, *unity*, *truth*, and *goodness*. This, if it be any thing, is the very sublimate of science.

[8] This seems to have been the sense which Quintilian had of the difference between παθος and ηθος, when he gave *amor* for an example of the first, and *charitas* of the second. The word ηθος is also sometimes used for moral sentiment. Inst. L. vi. c. 2.

Now, the principal questions on this subject are these two:—How is a passion or disposition that is favourable to the design of the orator, to be excited in the hearers? How is an unfavourable passion or disposition to be calmed? As to the first it was said already in general, that passion must be awakened by communicating lively ideas of the object. The reason will be obvious from the following remarks: A passion is most strongly excited by sensation. The sight of danger, immediate or near, instantly rouseth fear; the feeling of an injury, and the presence of the injurer, in a moment kindle anger. Next to the influence of sense is that of memory, the effect of which upon passion, if the fact be recent, and remembered distinctly and circumstantially, is almost equal. Next to the influence of memory is that of imagination; by which is here solely meant the faculty of apprehending what is neither perceived by the senses, nor remembered. Now, as it is this power of which the orator must chiefly avail himself, it is proper to inquire what those circumstances are, which will make the ideas he summons up in the imaginations of his hearers, resemble, in lustre and steadiness, those of sensation and remembrance. For the same circumstances will infallibly make them resemble also in their effects; that is, in the influence they will have upon the passions and affections of the heart.

SECTION V.—*The circumstances that are chiefly instrumental in operating on the Passions.*

These are perhaps all reducible to the seven following, probability, plausibility, importance, proximity of time, connexion of place, relation of the actors or sufferers to the hearers or speaker, interest of the hearers or speaker in the consequences.

PART I.—*Probability.*

The first is *probability*, which is now considered only as an expedient for enlivening passion. Here again there is commonly scope for argument.[1] Probability results from evidence, and begets belief. Belief invigorates our ideas. Belief raised to the highest becomes certainty. Certainty flows either from the force of the evidence, real or apparent, that is produced: or

[9] I am not quite positive as to the accuracy of this enumeration, and shall therefore freely permit my learned and ingenious friend Dr. Reid, to annex the *et cætera* he proposes in such cases, in order to supply all defects. See Sketches of the History of Man, B. iii. Sk. 1. Appendix, c. ii. sect. 2.

[1] In the judiciary orations of the ancients, this was the principal scope for argument. That to condemn the guilty, and to acquit the innocent, would gratify their indignation against the injurious, and their love of right, was too manifest to require a proof. The fact that there was guilt in the prisoner, or that there was innocence, did require it. It was otherwise in deliberative orations, as the conduct recommended was more remotely connected with the emotions raised.

without any evidence produced by the speaker, from the previous notoriety of the fact. If the fact be notorious, it will not only be superfluous in the speaker to attempt to prove it, but it will be pernicious to his design. The reason is plain. By proving he supposeth it questionable, and by supposing actually renders it so to his audience: he brings them from viewing it in the stronger light of certainty, to view it in the weaker light of probability: in lieu of sunshine he gives them twilight. Of the different means and kinds of probation I have spoken already.

PART II.—*Plausibility*.

The second circumstance is *plausibility*, a thing totally distinct from the former, as having an effect upon the mind quite independent of faith or probability. It ariseth chiefly from the consistency of the narration, from its being what is commonly called natural and feasible. This the French critics have aptly enough denominated in their language *vraisemblance*, the English critics more improperly in theirs *probability*. In order to avoid the manifest ambiguity there is in this application of the word, it had been better to retain the word *verisimilitude*, now almost obsolete. That there is a relation between those two qualities must, notwithstanding, be admitted. This, however, is an additional reason for assigning them different names. An homonymous term, whose different significations have no affinity to one another, is very seldom liable to be misunderstood.

But as to the nature and extent of this relation, let it be observed, that the want of plausibility implies an internal improbability, which it will require the stronger external evidence to surmount. Nevertheless, the implausibility may be surmounted by such evidence, and we may be fully ascertained of what is in itself exceedingly implausible. Implausibility is, in a certain degree, positive evidence against a narrative; whereas plausibility implies no positive evidence for it. We know that fiction may be as plausible as truth. A narration may be possessed of this quality to the highest degree, which we not only regard as improbable, but know to be false. Probability is a light darted on the object, from the proofs, which for this reason are pertinently enough styled *evidence*. Plausibility is a native lustre issuing directly from the object. The former is the aim of the historian, the latter of the poet. That every one may be satisfied that the second is generally not inferior to the first, in its influence on the mind, we need but appeal to the effects of tragedy, of epic, and even of romance, which, in its principal characters, participates of the nature of poesy, though written in prose.

It deserves, however, to be remarked, that though plausibility alone hath often greater efficacy in rousing the passions than probability, or even certainty; yet, in any species of composition wherein truth, or at least probability, is expected, the mind quickly nauseates the most plausible tale, which is unsupported by proper arguments. For this reason it is the business of the orator, as much as his subject will permit, to avail himself of both qualities. There is one case, and but one, in which plausibility itself may be dispensed with; that is, when the fact is so incontestible that it is impossible to entertain a doubt of it; for when implausibility is incapable of impairing belief, it hath sometimes, especially in forensic causes, even a good effect. By presenting us with something monstrous in its kind, it raiseth astonishment, and thereby heightens every passion which the narrative is fitted to excite.

But to return to the explication of this quality. When I explained the nature of experience, I showed that it consisteth of all the general truth collected from particular facts remembered; the mind forming to itself, often insensibly, and as it were mechanically, certain maxims, from comparing, or rather associating the similar circumstances of different incidents.[2] Hence it is, that when a number of ideas relating to any fact or event are successively introduced into my mind by a speaker; if the train he deduceth coincide with the general current of my experience; if in nothing it thwart those conclusions and anticipations which are become habitual to me, my mind accompanies him with facility, glides along from one idea to another, and admits the whole with pleasure. If, on the contrary, the train he introduceth run counter to the current of my experience; if in many things it shock those conclusions and anticipations which are become habitual to me, my mind attends him with difficulty, suffers a sort of violence in passing from one idea to another, and rejects the whole with disdain:

For while upon such monstrous scenes we gaze,
They shock our faith, our indignation raise.[3]
FRANCIS.

In the former case I pronounce the narrative natural and credible, in the latter I say it is unnatural and incredible, if not impossible; and, which is particularly expressive of the different appearances in respect of connexion made by the ideas in my mind, the one tale I call coherent, the other incoherent. When therefore the orator can obtain no direct aid from the memory of his hearers, which is rarely to be obtained, he must, for the sake of brightening, and strengthening, and if I may be permitted to use so bold a metaphor, cementing his ideas, bespeak the assistance of experience. This, if properly employed,

[2] Chap. V. Sect. ii. Part 2.
[3] Quodcunque ostendis mihi sic, incredulus odi.
Hor. De Arte Poet.

will prove a potent ally, by adding the grace of *verisimilitude* to the whole. It is therefore first of all requisite, that the circumstances of the narration, and the order in which they are exhibited, be what is commonly called natural, that is, congruous to general experience.

Where passion is the end, it is not a sufficient reason for introducing any circumstance that it is natural; it must also be pertinent. It is pertinent, when either necessary for giving a distinct and consistent apprehension of the object, at least for obviating some objection that may be started, or doubt that may be entertained concerning it; or when such as, in its particular tendency, promotes the general aim. All circumstances, however plausible, which serve merely for decoration, never fail to divert the attention, and so become prejudicial to the proposed influence on passion.

But I am aware that, from the explication I have given of this quality, it will be said, that I have run into the error, if it be an error, which I intended to avoid, and have confounded it with probability, by deriving it solely from the same origin, experience. In answer to this, let it be observed, that in every plausible tale which is unsupported by external evidence, there will be found throughout the whole, when duly canvassed, a mixture of possibilities and probabilities, and that not in such a manner as to make one part or incident probable, another barely possible, but so blended as equally to affect the whole, and every member. Take the Iliad for an example. That a haughty, choleric, and vindictive hero, such as Achilles is represented to have been, should, upon the public affront and injury he received from Agamemnon, treat that general with indignity, and form a resolution of withdrawing his troops, remaining thenceforth an unconcerned spectator of the calamities of his countrymen, our experience of the baleful influences of pride and anger renders in some degree probable; again, that one of such a character as Agamemnon, rapacious, jealous of his pre-eminence as commander-in-chief, who envied the superior merit of Achilles, and harboured resentment against him—that such a one, I say, on such an occurrence as is related by the poet, should have given the provocation, will be acknowledged also to have some probability. But that there were such personages, of such characters, in such circumstances, is merely possible. Here there is a total want of evidence. Experience is silent. Properly indeed the case comes not within the verge of its jurisdiction. Its general conclusions may serve in confutation, but can never serve in proof of particular or historical facts. Sufficient testimony, and that only, will answer here. The testimony of the poet in this case goes for nothing. His object we know is not truth but likelihood. Experience, however, advances nothing against those allegations of the poet, therefore we call them possible; it can say nothing for them, therefore we do not call them probable. The whole at most amounts to this—if such causes existed, such effects probably followed. But we have no evidence of the existence of the causes; therefore we have no evidence of the existence of the effects. Consequently, all the probability implied in this quality is a hypothetical probability, which is in effect none at all. It is an axiom among dialecticians, in relation to the syllogistic art, that the conclusion always follows the weaker of the premises. To apply this to the present purpose, an application not illicit, though unusual,—if one of the premises, suppose the major, contain an affirmation that is barely possible, the minor, one that is probable, possibility only can be deduced in the conclusion.

These two qualities, therefore, PROBABILITY and PLAUSIBILITY, (if I may be indulged a little in the allegoric style), I shall call sister-graces, daughter of the same father *Experience*, who is the progeny of *Memory*, the first-born and heir of *Sense*. These daughters *Experience* had by different mothers. The elder is the offspring of *Reason*, the younger is the child of *Fancy*. The elder, regular in her features, and majestic both in shape and mien, is admirably fitted for commanding esteem, and even a religious veneration: the younger, careless, blooming, sprightly, is entirely formed for captivating the heart, and engaging love. The conversation of each is entertaining and instructive, but in different ways. Sages seem to think that there is more instruction to be gotten from the just observations of the elder; almost all are agreed that there is more entertainment in the lively sallies of the younger. The principal companion and favourite of the first is *Truth*, but whether *Truth* or *Fiction* share most in the favour of the second it were often difficult to say. Both are naturally well-disposed, and even friendly to *Virtue*, but the elder is by much the more steady of the two; the younger, though perhaps not less capable of doing good, is more easily corrupted, and hath sometimes basely turned procuress to *Vice*. Though rivals, they have a sisterly affection to each other, and love to be together. The elder, sensible that there are but few who can for any time relish her society alone, is generally anxious that her sister be of the party; the younger, conscious of her own superior talents in this respect, can more easily dispense with the other's company. Nevertheless, when she is discoursing on great and serious subjects, in order to add weight to her words, she often quotes her sister's testimony, which she knows is better credited than her own, a compliment that is but sparingly returned by the elder. Each sister hath her admirers. Those of the younger are more numerous, those of the elder more constant. In the retinue of the former you will find the young, the gay, the dissipated; but these are not her only attendants. The middle-aged, however, and the thoughtful, more commonly attach themselves to the latter. To conclude; as something may be learned of characters from the invectives of enemies, as well as from the encomiums of friends, those who have not judgment to discern the good qualities of the first-born, accuse her of dulness, pedantry, and stiffness; those who have not taste to relish the charms of the second, charge her with folly, levity, and falseness. Meantime, it appears to be the universal opinion of the impartial, and such as have been best acquainted with both, that though the attractives of the younger be more irresistible at sight, the virtues of the elder will be longer remembered.

So much for the two qualities *probability* and *plausibility*, on which I have expatiated the more, as they are the principal, and in some respect, indispensable. The others are not compatible with every subject; but as they are of real moment, it is necessary to attend to them, that so they may not be overlooked in cases wherein the subject requires that they be urged.

PART III.—*Importance.*

The third circumstance I took notice of was *importance*, the appearance of which always tends, by fixing attention more closely, to add brightness and strength to the ideas. The importance in moral subjects is analagous to the quantity of matter in physical subjects, as on quantity the moment of moving bodies in a great degree depends. An action may derive importance from its own nature, from those concerned in it as acting or suffering, or from its consequences. It derives importance from its own nature, if it be stupendous in its kind, if the result of what is uncommonly great, whether good or bad, passion or invention, virtue or vice, as what in respect of generosity is godlike, what in respect of atrocity is diabolical: it derives importance from those concerned in it, when the actors or the sufferers are considerable, on account either of their dignity or of their number, or of both: it derives importance from its consequences, when these are remarkable in regard to their greatness, their multitude, their extent, and that either as to the many and distant places affected by them, or as to the future and remote periods to which they may reach, or as to both.

All the four remaining circumstances derive their efficacy purely from one and the same cause, the connexion of the subject with those occupied, as speaker or hearers, in the discourse. *Self* is the centre here, which hath a similar power in the ideal world to that of the sun in the material world, in communicating both light and heat to whatever is within the sphere of its activity, and in a greater or less degree according to the nearness or remoteness.

PART IV.—*Proximity of Time.*

First, as to *proximity of time*, every one knows that any melancholy incident is the more affecting that it is recent. Hence it is become common with story-tellers, that they may make a deeper impression on the hearers, to introduce remarks like these; that the tale which they relate is not old, that it happened but lately, or in their own time, or that they are yet living who had a part in it, or were witnesses of it. Proximity of time regards not only the past but the future. An event that will probably soon happen hath greater influence upon us than what will probably happen a long time hence. I have hitherto proceeded on the hypothesis, that the orator rouses the passions of his hearers by exhibiting some past transaction; but we must acknowledge that passion may be as strongly excited by his reasonings concerning an event yet to come. In the judiciary orations there is greater scope for the former, in the deliberative for the latter; though in each kind there may occasionally be scope for both. All the seven circumstances enumerated are applicable, and have equal weight, whether they relate to the future or to the past. The only exception that I know of is, that probability and plausibility are scarcely distinguishable, when used in reference to events in futurity. As in these there is no access for testimony, what constitutes the principal distinction is quite excluded. In comparing the influence of the past upon our minds, with that of the future, it appears in general, that if the evidence, the importance, and the distance of the objects be equal, the latter will be greater than the former. The reason, I imagine, is, we are conscious that as every moment, the future, which seems placed before us, is approaching; and the past, which lies, as it were, behind, is retiring, our nearness or relation to the one constantly increaseth as the other decreaseth. There is something like attraction in the first case, and repulsion in the second. This tends to interest us more in the future than in the past, and consequently to the present view aggrandizes the one and diminishes the other.

What, nevertheless, gives the past a very considerable advantage, is its being generally susceptible of much stronger evidence than the future. The lights of the mind are, if I may so express myself, in an opposite situation to the lights of the body. These discover clearly the prospect lying before us, but not the ground we have already passed. By the memory, on the contrary, that great luminary of the mind, things past are exhibited in retrospect: we have no correspondent faculty to irradiate the future: and even in matters which fall not within the reach of our memory, past events are often clearly discoverable by testimony, and by effects at present existing; whereas we have nothing equivalent to found our arguments upon in reasoning about things to come. It is for this reason, that the future is considered as the province of conjecture and uncertainty.

PART V.—*Connexion of Place.*

Local *connexion*, the fifth in the above enumeration, hath a more powerful effect than proximity of time. Duration and space are two things, (call them entities or attributes, or what you please,) in some respects the most like, and in some respects the most unlike to one another. They resemble in continuity, divisibility, infinity, in their being deemed essential to the existence of other things, and in the doubts that have been raised as to their having a real or independent existence of their own. They differ, in that the latter is permanent, whereas the very essence of the former consisteth in transitoriness; the parts of the one are all successive, of the other all co-existent. The greater portions of time are all distinguished by the memorable things which have been transacted in them, the smaller portions by the revolutions of the heavenly bodies: the portions of place, great and small, (for we do not here consider the regions of the fixed stars and planets,) are distinguished by the various tracts of land and water, into which the earth is divided and subdivided; the one distinction intelligible, the other sensible; the one chiefly known to the inquisitive, the other in a great measure obvious to all.

Hence perhaps it arises, that the latter is considered as a firmer ground of relation than the former. Who is not more curious to know the notable transactions which have happened in his own country from the earliest antiquity, than to be acquainted with those which have happened in the remotest regions of the globe, during the century wherein he lives? It must be owned, however, that the former circumstance is more frequently aided by that of personal relation than the latter. Connexion of place not only includes vicinage, but every other local relation, such as being in a province under the same government with us, in a state that is in alliance with us, in a country well known to us, and the like. Of the influence of this connexion in operating on our passions we have daily proofs. With how much indifference, at least with how slight and transient emotion, do we read in newspapers the accounts of the most deplorable accidents in countries distant and unknown! How much, on the contrary, are we alarmed and agitated on being informed that any such accident hath happened in our neighbourhood, and that even though we be totally unacquainted with the persons concerned!

PART VI.—*Relation to the Persons concerned.*

Still greater is the power of *relation* to the persons concerned, which was the sixth circumstance mentioned, as this tie is more direct than that which attacheth us to the scene of action. It is the persons, not the place, that are the immediate objects of the passions love or hatred, pity or anger, envy or contempt. Relation to the actors commonly produces an effect contrary to that produced by relation to the sufferers, the first in extenuation, the second in aggravation of the crime alleged. The first makes for the apologist, the second for the accuser. This I say is commonly the case, not always. A remote relation to the actors, when the offence is heinous, especially if the sufferers be more nearly related, will sometimes rather aggravate than extenuate the guilt in our estimation. But it is impossible with any precision to reduce these effects to rules; so much depending on the different tempers and sentiments of different audiences. Personal relations are of various kinds. Some have generally greater influence than others; some again have greater influence with one person, others with another. They are consanguinity, affinity, friendship, acquaintance, being fellow-citizens, countrymen, of the same surname, language, religion, occupation, and innumerable others.

PART VII.—*Interest in the Consequences.*

But of all the connective circumstances, the most powerful is *interest*, which is the last. Of all relations, personal relation, by bringing the object very near, most enlivens that sympathy which attacheth us to the concerns of others; interest in the effects brings the object, if I may say so, into contact with us, and makes the mind cling to it as a concern of its own. Sympathy is but a reflected feeling, and therefore, in ordinary cases, must be weaker than the original. Though the mirror be ever so true, a lover will not be obliged to it for presenting him with the figure of his mistress when he hath an opportunity of gazing on her person. Nor will the orator place his chief confidence in the assistance of the social and sympathetic affections, when he hath it in his power to arm the selfish.

Men universally, from a just conception of the difference, have, when self is concerned, given a different name to what seems originally the same passion in a higher degree. Injury, to whomsoever offered, is to every man that observes it, and whose sense of right is not debauched by vicious practice, the natural object of *indignation*. Indignation always implies *resentment*, or a desire of retaliating on the injurious person, so far at least as to make him repent the wrong he hath committed. This indignation in the person injured is, from our knowledge of mankind, supposed to be, not indeed universally, but generally so much stronger, that it ought to be distinguished by another appellation, and is, accordingly, denominated *revenge*. In like manner beneficence, on whomsoever exercised, is the natural object of our *love;* love always implies *benevolence*, or a desire of promoting the happiness of the beneficent person; but this passion in the person benefited is conceived to be so much greater, and to infer so strong an obligation to a return of good offices to his benefactor, that it merits to be distinguished by the title *gratitude*. Now by this circumstance of *interest* in the effects, the speaker, from engaging *pity* in his favour, can proceed to operate on a more powerful principle, *self-preservation*. The *benevolence* of his hearers he can work up into *gratitude*, their *indignation* into *revenge*.

The two last-mentioned circumstances, personal relation and interest, are not without influence, as was hinted in the enumeration, though they regard the speaker only, and not the hearers. The reason is, a person present with us, whom we see and hear, and who, by words, and looks, and gestures, gives the liveliest signs of his feelings, has the surest and most immediate claim upon our sympathy. We become infected with his passions. We are hurried along by them, and not allowed leisure to distinguish between his relation and our relation, his interest and our interest.

SECTION VI.—*Other Passions, as well as Moral Sentiments, useful auxiliaries.*

So much for those circumstances in the object presented by the speaker, which serve to awaken and inflame the passions of the hearers.[4] But when a passion is once raised, there are

[4] To illustrate most of the preceding circumstances, and show the manner of applying them, I shall take an example from Cicero's last oration against Verres, where, after relating the crucifixion of Gavius, a Roman citizen, he exclaims, "1. O nomen dulce libertatis! O jus eximium nostræ civitatis! O lex Porcia, legesque Semproniæ! O graviter desiderata, et aliquando reddita plebi Romanæ tribunitia potestas! 2. Huccine tandem omnia reciderunt, ut civis Romanus in provincia populi Romani, in oppido fœderatorum, ab eo qui beneficio populi Romani fasces et secures haberet, deligatus in foro virgis cæderetur?——3. Sed quid ego plura de Gavio? quasi tu Gavio tum fueris infestus, ac non nomini, generi, juri civium hostis, non illi inquam homini, sed causæ communi libertatis inimicus fuisti. 4. Quid enim attinuit, cum Mamertini more atque instituto suo, crucem fixissent post urbem, in via Pompeia; te jubere in ea parte figere, quæ ad fretum spectat; et hoc addere, quod negare nullo modo potes, quod omnibus audientibus dixisti palam, te idcirco illum locum deligere, ut ille qui se civem Romanum esse diceret, ex cruce Italiam cerneret, ac domum suam prospicere posset? 5. Itaque illa crux sola, judices, post conditam Messanam illo in loco fixa est. 6. Italiæ conspectus ad eam rem ab isto delectus est, ut ille in dolore cruciatuque moriens, perangusto freto divisa servitutis ac libertatis jura cognosceret; Italia autem

also other means by which it may be kept alive, and even augmented. Other passions or dispositions may be called in as auxiliaries. Nothing is more efficacious in this respect than a

alumnum suum, servitutis extremo summoque supplicio affectum videret. 7. Facinus est vincire civem Romanum, scelus verberare, prope parricidium necare, quid dicam, in crucem tollere? verbo satis digno tam nefaria res appellari nullo modo potest. 8. Non fuit his omnibus iste contentus. Spectet, inquit, patriam; in conspectu legum libertatisque moriatur. 9. Non tu hoc loco Gavium, non unum hominem, nescio quem, civem Romanum, sed communem libertatis et civitatis causam in illum cruciatum et crucem egisti. 10. Jam vero videte hominis audaciam! Nonne enim graviter tulisse arbitramini, quod illam civibus Romanis crucem non posset in foro, non in comitio, non in rostris defigere? 11. Quod enim his locis in provincia sua celebritate simillimum, regione proximum, potuit, elegit. 12. Monumentum sceleris —audaciæque suæ voluit esse in conspectu Italiæ, prætervectione omnium qui ultro citroque navigarent. 13. Paulo ante, judices, lacrymas in morte miserâ atque indignissimâ navarchorum non tenebamus: et recte de merito sociorum innocentium miseriâ commovebamur. 14. Quid nunc in nostor sanguine tandem facere debemus? nam civium Romanorum sanguis conjunctus existimandus est.———15. Omnes hoc loco cives Romani, et qui adsunt et qui ubicunque sunt, vestram severitatem desiderant, vestram fidem implorant, vestrum auxilium requirunt. 16. Omnia sua jura, commoda, auxilia, totam denique libertatem in vestris sententiis versari arbitrantur."———I shall point out the pathetic circumstances exemplified in this passage, observing the order wherein they were enumerated. I have numbered the sentences in the quotation to prevent repetition on referring to them. It must be remarked, first of all, that in judiciary orations, such as this, the proper place for plausibility is the narration; for probability, the confirmation or proof: the other five, though generally admissible into either of those places, shine principally in peroration. I shall show how the orator hath availed himself of these in the passage now cited. First, *importance;* and that first in respect of the enormity of the action, No. 7; of the disposition of the actor, No. 3, 9, 10; and to render probable what might otherwise appear merely conjectural, No. 4, 5, 8, 11, 12; in respect of consequences, their greatness, No. 1, 2: where the crime is most artfully though implicitly represented as subversive of all that was dear to them, liberty, the right of citizens, their most valuable laws, and that idol of the people, the tribunitian power; their extent, No. 15, 16. Secondly, *proximity of time;* there is but an insinuation of this circumstance in the word *tandem*, No. 2. There are two reasons which probably induced the orator in this particular to be so sparing. One is, the recency of the crime, as if the criminal's prætorship was notorious; the other and the weightier is, that of all relations this is the weakest; and even what influence it hath, reflection serves rather to correct than to confirm. In appearing to lay stress on so slight a circumstance, a speaker displays rather penury of matter than abundance. It is better, therefore, in most cases, to suggest it as it were by accident, than to insist on it as of design. It deserves also to be remarked, that the word here employed is very emphatical, as it conveys at the same time a tacit comparison of their so recent degeneracy with the freedom, security, and glory which they had long enjoyed. The same word is again introduced, No. 14, to the same intent. Thirdly, *local connexion;* in respect of vicinage, how affectingly, though indirectly, is it touched, No. 4, 6, 8, 11, 12! indirectly, for reasons similar to those mentioned on the circumstance of time; as to other local connexions, No. 2, "in provincia populi Romani, in oppido fœderatorum." Fourthly, *personal relation;* first of the perpetrator, No. 2, "ab eo qui beneficio," &c. his crime therefore more atrocious and ungrateful, the most sacred rights violated by one who ought to have protected them; next of the sufferer, No. 2, "civis Romanus." This is most pathetically urged, and, by a comparison introduced, greatly heightened, No. 13, 14. Fifthly, the *interest*, which not the hearers only, but all who bear the Roman name, have in the consequences, No. 15, 16. We see, in the above example, with what uncommon address and delicacy those circumstances ought to be sense of justice, a sense of public utility, a sense of glory; and nothing conduceth more to operate on these, than the sentiments of sages whose wisdom we venerate, the example of heroes whose exploits we admire. I shall conclude what relates to the exciting of passion when I have remarked, that pleading the importance and the other pathetic circumstances, or pleading the authority of opinions or precedents, is usually considered, and aptly enough, as being likewise a species of reasoning.

This concession, however, doth not imply, that by any reasoning we are ever taught that such an object ought to awaken such a passion. This we must learn originally from feeling, not from argument. No speaker attempts to prove it; though he sometimes introduceth moral considerations, in order to justify the passion when raised, and to prevent the hearers from attempting to suppress it. Even when he is enforcing their regard to the pathetic circumstances above mentioned, it is not so much his aim to show that these circumstances ought to augment the passion, as that these circumstances are in the object. The effect upon their minds he commonly leaves to nature; and is not afraid of the conclusion, if he can make every aggravating circumstance be, as it were, both perceived and felt by them. In the enthymeme, (the syllogism of orators, as Quintilian[5] terms it,) employed in such cases, the sentiment that such a quality or circumstance ought to rouse such a passion, though the foundation of all, is generally assumed without proof, or even without mention. This forms the major proposition, which is suppressed as obvious. His whole art is exerted in evincing the minor, which is the antecedent in his argument, and which maintains the reality of those attendant circumstances in the case in hand. A careful attention to the examples of vehemence in the first chapter, and the quotation in the foregoing note, will sufficiently illustrate this remark.

sometimes blended, sometimes but insinuated, sometimes, on the contrary, warmly urged, sometimes shaded a little, that the art may be concealed; and, in brief; the whole conducted so as that nothing material may be omitted, that every sentiment may easily follow that which precedes, and usher that which follows it, and that every thing said may appear to be the language of pure nature. The art of the rhetorician, like that of the philosopher, is analytical; the art of the orator is synthetical. The former acts the part of the skilful anatomist, who, by removing the teguments, and nicely separating the parts, presents us with views at once naked, distinct, and hideous, now of the structure of the bones, now of the muscles and tendons, now of the arteries and veins, now of the bowels, now of the brain and nervous system. The latter imitates Nature in the constructing of her work, who, with wonderful symmetry, unites the various organs, adapts them to their respective uses, and covers all with a decent veil, the skin. This, though she hide entirely the more minute and the interior parts, and show not to equal advantage even the articulations of the limbs, and the adjustment of the larger members, adds inexpressible beauty, and strength, and energy to the whole.

[5] Instit. l. i. c. 9.

SECTION VII.—*How an Unfavourable Passion must be calmed.*

I come now to the second question on the subject of passion. How is an unfavourable passion, or disposition, to be calmed? The answer is, either, first, by annihilating, or at least diminishing the object which raised it; or secondly, by exciting some other passion which may counterwork it.

By proving the falsity of the narration, or the utter incredibility of the future event, on the supposed truth of which the passion was founded, the object is annihilated. It is diminished by all such circumstances as are contrary to those by which it is increased. These are, improbability, implausibility, insignificance, distance of time, remoteness of place, the persons concerned such as we have no connexion with, the consequences such as we have no interest in. The method recommended by Gorgias, and approved by Aristotle, though peculiar in its manner, is, in those cases wherein it may properly be attempted, coincident in effect with that now mentioned. "It was a just opinion of Gorgias, that the serious argument of an adversary should be confounded by ridicule, and his ridicule by serious argument."[6] For this is only endeavouring, by the aid of laughter and contempt, to diminish, or even quite undo, the unfriendly emotions that have been raised in the minds of the hearers; or, on the contrary, by satisfying them of the seriousness of the subject, and of the importance of its consequences, to extinguish the contempt, and make the laughter, which the antagonist wanted to excite, appear when examined, no better than madness.

The second way of silencing an unfavourable passion or disposition, is by conjuring up some other passion or disposition, which may overcome it. With regard to conduct, whenever the mind deliberates, it is conscious of contrary motives impelling it in opposite directions; in other words, it finds that acting thus would gratify one passion; not acting, or acting otherwise, would gratify another. To take such a step, I perceive, would promote my interest, but derogate from my honour. Such another will gratify my resentment, but hurt my interest. When this is the case, as the speaker can be at no loss to discover the conflicting passions, he must be sensible that whatever force he adds to the disposition that favours his design, is in fact so much subtracted from the disposition that opposeth it, and conversely; as in the two scales of a balance,

[6] Δειν, εφη Γοργιας, την μεν σπουδην διαφθειρειν των εναντιων γελωτι, τον δε γελωτα σπουδῃ· ορθως λεγων. Rhet. l. iii. c. 18.

it is equal in regard to the effect, whether you add so much weight to one scale, or take it from the other.

Thus we have seen in what manner passion to an absent object may be excited by eloquence, which, by enlivening and invigorating the ideas of imagination, makes them resemble the impressions of sense and the traces of memory; and in this respect hath an effect on the mind similar to that produced by a telescope on the sight; things remote are brought near, things obscure rendered conspicuous. We have seen also in what manner a passion already excited may be calmed; how, by the oratorical magic, as by inverting the telescope, the object may be again removed and diminished.

It were endless to enumerate all the rhetorical figures that are adapted to the pathetic. Let it suffice to say, that most of those already named may be successfully employed here. Of others the principal are these, correction, climax, vision, exclamation, apostrophe, and interrogation. The three first, correction, climax, and vision, tend greatly to enliven the ideas, by the implicit, but animated comparison and opposition conveyed in them. Implicit and indirect comparison is more suitable to the disturbed state of mind required by the pathetic, than that which is explicit and direct. The latter implies leisure and tranquillity, the former rapidity and fire. Exclamation and apostrophe operate chiefly by sympathy, as they are the most ardent expressions of perturbation in the speaker. It at first sight appears more difficult to account for the effect of interrogation, which, being an appeal to the hearers, though it might awaken a closer attention, yet could not, one would imagine, excite in their minds any emotion that was not there before. This, nevertheless, it doth excite, through an oblique operation of the same principle. Such an appeal implies in the orator the strongest confidence in the rectitude of his sentiments, and in the concurrence of every reasonable being. The auditors, by sympathizing with this frame of spirit, find it impracticable to withhold an assent which is so confidently depended on. But there will be occasion afterwards for discussing more particularly the rhetorical tropes and figures, when we come to treat of elocution.

Thus I have finished the consideration which the speaker ought to have of his hearers as men in general; that is, as thinking beings endowed with understanding, imagination, memory, and passions, such as we are conscious of in ourselves, and learn from the experience of their effects to be in others. I have pointed out the arts to be employed by him in engaging all those faculties in his service, that what he advanceth may not only be understood, not only command attention, not only be remembered, but, which is the chief point of all, may interest the heart.

CHAPTER VIII.

Of the Consideration which the Speaker ought to have of the Hearers, as such men in particular.

It was remarked in the beginning of the preceding chapter, that the hearers ought to be considered in a twofold view, as men in general, and as such men in particular. The first consideration I have despatched, I now enter on the second.

When it is affirmed that the hearers are to be considered as such men in particular, no more is meant, than that regard ought to be had by the speaker to the special character of the audience, as composed of such individuals; that he may suit himself to them, both in his style and in his arguments.[7] Now, the difference between one audience and another is very great, not only in intellectual but in moral attainments. That may be clearly intelligible to a House of Commons, which would appear as if spoken in an unknown tongue to a conventicle of enthusiasts. That may kindle fury in the latter, which would create no emotion in the former but laughter and contempt. The most obvious difference that appears in different auditories, results from the different cultivation of the understanding; and the influence which this, and their manner of life, have both upon the imagination and upon the memory.

But even in cases wherein the difference in education and moral culture hath not been considerable, different habits afterwards contracted, and different occupations in life, give different propensities, and make one incline more to one passion, another to another. They consequently afford the intelligent speaker an easier passage to the heart, through the channel of the favourite passion. Thus liberty and independence will ever be prevalent motives with republicans, pomp and splendour with those attached to monarchy. In mercantile states, such as Carthage among the ancients, or Holland among the moderns, interest will always prove the most cogent argument; in states solely or chiefly composed of soldiers, such as Sparta and ancient Rome, no inducement will be found a counterpoise to glory. Similar differences are also to be made in addressing different classes of men. With men of genius the most successful topic will be fame; with men of industry, riches; with men of fortune, pleasure.

[7] He must be "Orpheus in sylvis, inter delphinas Arion." Virg.

But as the characters of audiences may be infinitely diversified, and as the influence they ought to have respectively upon the speaker must be obvious to a person of discernment, it is sufficient here to have observed thus much in the general concerning them.

CHAPTER IX.

Of the Consideration which the Speaker ought to have of Himself.

THE last consideration I mentioned, is that which the speaker ought to have of himself. By this we are to understand, not that estimate of himself which is derived directly from consciousness or self-acquaintance, but that which is obtained reflexively from the opinion entertained of him by the hearers, or the character which he bears with them. Sympathy is one main engine by which the orator operates on the passions.

> With them who laugh, our social joy appears;
> With them who mourn, we sympathize in tears;
> If you would have me weep, begin the strain,
> Then I shall feel your sorrows, feel your pain.[8]
> FRANCIS.

Whatever, therefore, weakens that principle of sympathy, must do the speaker unutterable prejudice in respect of his power over the passions of his audience, but not in this respect only. One source, at least, of the primary influence of testimony on faith, is doubtless to be attributed to the same communicative principle. At the same time it is certain, as was remarked above, that every testimony doth not equally attach this principle; that in this particular the reputation of the attester hath a considerable power. Now, the speaker's apparent conviction of the truth of what he advanceth, adds to all his other arguments an evidence, though not precisely the same, yet near akin to that of his own testimony.[9] This hath some weight even with the wisest hearers, but is every thing with

[8] Ut ridentibus arrident, ita flentibus adflent
Humani vultus. Si vis me flere, dolendum est
Primum ipsi tibi: tunc tua me infortunia lædent.
Hor. De Arte Poet.

[9] Ne illud quidem præteribo, quantam afferat fidem expositioni narrantis auctoritas. QUINT. lib. iv. cap. 2.

the vulgar. Whatever therefore lessens sympathy, must also impair belief.

Sympathy in the hearers to the speaker may be lessened several ways, chiefly by these two; by a low opinion of his intellectual abilities, and by a bad opinion of his morals. The latter is the more prejudicial of the two. Men generally will think themselves in less danger of being seduced by a man of weak understanding, but of distinguished probity, than by a man of the best understanding who is of a profligate life. So much more powerfully do the qualities of the heart attach us, than those of the head. This preference, though it may be justly called untaught and instinctive, arising purely from the original frame of the mind, reason, or the knowledge of mankind acquired by experience, instead of weakening, seems afterwards to corroborate. Hence it hath become a common topic with rhetoricians, that, in order to be a successful orator, one must be a good man; for to be good is the only sure way of being long esteemed good, and to be esteemed good is previously necessary to one's being heard with due attention and regard. Consequently, the topic hath a foundation in human nature. There are indeed other things in the character of the speaker, which, in a less degree, will hurt his influence; youth, inexperience of affairs, former want of success, and the like.

But of all the prepossessions in the minds of the hearers which tend to impede or counteract the design of the speaker, party-spirit, where it happens to prevail, is the most pernicious, being at once the most inflexible and the most unjust. This prejudice I mention by itself, as those above recited may have place at any time, and in any national circumstances. This hath place only when a people is so unfortunate as to be torn by faction. In that case, if the speaker and the hearers, or the bulk of the hearers, be of contrary parties, their minds will be more prepossessed against him, though his life were ever so blameless, than if he were a man of the most flagitious manners, but of the same party. This holds but too much alike of all parties, religious and political. Violent party-men not only lose all sympathy with those of the opposite side, but contract an antipathy to them. This, on some occasions, even the divinest eloquence will not surmount.

As to personal prejudices in general, I shall conclude with two remarks. The first is, the more gross the hearers are, so much the more susceptible they are of such prejudices. Nothing exposes the mind more to all their baneful influences than ignorance and rudeness; the rabble chiefly consider who speaks, men of sense and education what is spoken. Nor are the multitude, to do them justice, less excessive in their love than in their hatred, in their attachments than in their aversions. From a consciousness, it would seem, of their own incapacity to guide themselves, they are ever prone blindly to submit to the guidance of some popular orator, who hath had the address first, either to gain their approbation by his real or pretended virtues, or, which is the easier way, to recommend himself to their esteem by a flaming zeal for their favourite distinctions, and afterwards by his eloquence to work upon their passions. At the same time it must be acknowledged, on the other hand, that even men of the most improved intellects, and most refined sentiments, are not altogether beyond the reach of preconceived opinion, either in the speaker's favour or to his prejudice.

The second remark is, that when the opinion of the audience is unfavourable, the speaker hath need to be much more cautious in every step he takes, to show more modesty, and greater deference to the judgment of his hearers; perhaps in order to win them, he may find it necessary to make some concessions in relation to his former principles or conduct, and to entreat their attention from pure regard to the subject; that, like men of judgment and candour, they would impartially consider what is said, and give a welcome reception to truth, from what quarter soever it proceed. Thus he must attempt, if possible, to mollify them, gradually to insinuate himself into their favour, and thereby imperceptibly to transfuse his sentiments and passions into their minds.

The man who enjoys the advantage of popularity needs not this caution. The minds of his auditors are perfectly attuned to his. They are prepared for adopting implicitly his opinions, and accompanying him in all his most passionate excursions. When the people are willing to run with you, you may run as fast as you can, especially when the case requires impetuosity and despatch. But if you find in them no such ardour, if it is not even without reluctance that they are induced to walk with you, you must slacken your pace and keep them company, lest they either stand still or turn back. Different rules are given by rhetoricians as adapted to different circumstances. Differences in this respect are numberless. It is enough here to have observed those principles in the mind on which the rules are founded.

CHAPTER X.

The different kinds of public speaking in use among the moderns compared, with a view to their different advantages in respect of eloquence.

THE principal sorts of discourses which here demand our notice, and on which I intend to make some observations, are the three following: orations delivered at the bar, those pronounced in the senate, and those spoken from the pulpit. I do not make a separate article of the speeches delivered by judges to their colleagues on the bench; because, though there be something peculiar here, arising from the difference in character that subsists between the judge and the pleader, in all the other material circumstances, the persons addressed, the subject, the occasion, and the purpose in speaking, there is in these two sorts a perfect coincidence. In like manner, I forbear to mention the theatre, because so entirely dissimilar, both in form and in kind, as hardly to be capable of a place in the comparison. Besides, it is only a cursory view of the chief differences, and not a critical examination of them all, that is here proposed; my design being solely to assist the mind both in apprehending rightly, and in applying properly, the principles above laid down. In this respect, the present discussion will serve to exemplify and illustrate those principles. Under these five particulars, therefore, the speaker, the hearers or persons addressed, the subject, the occasion, and the end in view, or the effect intended to be produced by the discourse, I shall arrange, for order's sake, the remarks I intend to lay before the reader.

SECTION I.—*In regard to the Speaker.*

The first consideration is that of the character to be sustained by the speaker. It was remarked in general, in the preceding chapter, that for promoting the success of the orator, (whatever be the kind of public speaking in which he is concerned,) it is a matter of some consequence that, in the opinion of those whom he addresseth, he is both a wise and a good man. But though this in some measure holds universally, nothing is more certain than that the degree of consequence which lies in their opinion, is exceedingly different in the different kinds. In each it depends chiefly on two circumstances, the nature of his profession as a public speaker, and the character of those to whom his discourses are addressed.

As to the first, arising from the nature of the profession, it will not admit a question, that the preacher hath in this respect the most difficult task; inasmuch as he hath a character to support, which is much more easily injured than that either of the senator, or the speaker at the bar. No doubt the reputation of capacity, experience in affairs, and as much integrity as is thought attainable by those called men of the world, will add weight to the words of the senator; that of skill in his profession, and fidelity in his representation, will serve to recommend what is spoken by the lawyer at the bar; but if these characters in general remain unimpeached, the public will be sufficiently indulgent to both in every other respect. On the contrary, there is little or no indulgence, in regard to his own failings, to be expected by the man who is professedly a sort of authorized censor, who hath it in charge to mark and reprehend the faults of others. And even in the execution of this so ticklish a part of his office, the least excess on either hand exposeth him to censure and dislike. Too much lenity is enough to stigmatize him as lukewarm in the cause of virtue, and too much severity as a stranger to the spirit of the gospel.

But let us consider more directly what is implied in the character, that we may better judge of the effect it will have on the expectations and demands of the people, and consequently on his public teaching. First, then, it is a character of some authority, as it is of one educated for a purpose so important as that of a teacher of religion. This authority, however, from the nature of the function, must be tempered with moderation, candour, and benevolence. The preacher of the gospel, as the very terms import, is the minister of grace, the herald of divine mercy to ignorant, sinful, and erring men. The magistrate, on the contrary, (under which term may be included secular judges and counsellors of every denomination,) is the minister of divine justice and of wrath. *He beareth not the sword in vain.*[1] He is on the part of heaven the avenger of the society with whose protection he is intrusted, against all who invade its rights. The first operates chiefly on our love, the second on our fear. *Minister of religion*, like angel of God, is a name that ought to convey the idea of something endearing and attractive; whereas the title *minister of justice* invariably suggests the notion of something awful and unrelenting. In the former, even his indignation against sin ought to be surmounted by his pity of the condition, and concern for the recovery, of the sinner. Though firm in declaring the will of God, though steady in maintaining the cause of truth, yet mild in his addresses to the people, condescending to the weak, using rather entreaty than command, beseeching them by the lowliness and gentleness of Christ, knowing that "the servant of the Lord must not strive, but be gentle to all men, apt to teach, patient, in meekness instructing those that oppose themselves."[2] He must be grave without moroseness, cheerful without levity. And even in setting before his people the terrors of the Lord, affection ought manifestly to predominate in the warning which he is compelled to give. From these few hints it plainly appears, that there is a certain delicacy in the character of a preacher, which he is never at liberty totally to overlook, and to which, if there appear any thing incongruous, either in his conduct or in his public performances, it will never fail to injure their effect. On the contrary, it is well known, that as, in the other professions, the speaker's pri-

[1] Romans xiii. 4. [2] 2 Tim. ii. 24, 25.

vate life is but very little minded, so there are many things which, though they would be accounted nowise unsuitable from the bar or in the senate, would be deemed altogether unbefitting the pulpit.

It ought not to be overlooked, on the other hand, that there is one peculiarity in the lawyer's professional character, which is unfavourable to conviction, and consequently gives him some disadvantage both of the senator and the preacher. We know that he must defend his client, and argue on the side on which he is retained. We know also that a trifling and accidental circumstance, which nowise affects the merit of the cause, such as a prior application from the adverse party, would probably have made him employ the same acuteness, and display the same fervour, on the opposite side of the question. This circumstance, though not considered as a fault in the character of the man, but a natural, because an ordinary, consequent of the office, cannot fail, when reflected on, to make us shyer of yielding our assent. It removes entirely what was observed in the preceding chapter to be of great moment, our belief of the speaker's sincerity. This belief can hardly be rendered compatible with the knowledge that both truth and right are so commonly and avowedly sacrificed to interest. I acknowledge that an uncommon share of eloquence will carry off the minds of most people from attending to this circumstance, or at least from paying any regard to it. Yet Antony is represented by Cicero,[3] as thinking the advocate's reputation so delicate, that the practice of amusing himself in philosophical disputations with his friends is sufficient to hurt it, and consequently to affect the credibility of his pleadings. Surely the barefaced prostitution of his talents, (and in spite of his commonness, what else can we call it?) in supporting indifferently, as pecuniary considerations determine him, truth or falsehood, justice or injustice, must have a still worse effect on the opinion of his hearers.

It was affirmed that the consequence of the speaker's own character, in furthering or hindering his success, depends in some measure on the character of those whom he addresseth. Here indeed it will be found, on inquiry, that the preacher labours under a manifest disadvantage. Most congregations are of that kind, as will appear from the article immediately succeeding, which, agreeably to an observation made in the former chapter, very much considers who speaks; those addressed from the bar, or in the senate, consider more what is spoken.

[3] De Orat. Lib. 2. Ego ista studia non improbo, moderata modo sint. Opinionem istorum studiorum, et suspicionem omnium artificii apud eos qui res judicent, oratori adversariam esse arbitror. Imminuit enim et oratoris auctoritatem, et orationis fidem.

SECTION II.—*In regard to the Persons addressed.*

The second particular mentioned as a ground of comparison, is the consideration of the character of the hearers, or more properly the persons addressed. The necessity which a speaker is under of suiting himself to his audience, both that he may be understood by them, and that his words may have influence upon them, is a maxim so evident as to need neither proof nor illustration.

Now, the first remark that claims our attention here is, that the more mixed the auditory is, the greater is the difficulty of speaking to them with effect. The reason is obvious—what will tend to favour your success with one, may tend to obstruct it with another. The more various therefore the individuals are, in respect of age, rank, fortune, education, prejudices, the more delicate must be the art of preserving propriety in an address to the whole. The pleader has, in this respect, the simplest and the easiest task of all; the judges, to whom his oration is addressed, being commonly men of the same rank, of similar education, and not differing greatly in respect of studies or attainments. The difference in these respects is much more considerable when he addresses the jury. A speaker in the house of peers hath not so mixed an auditory as one who harangues in the house of commons. And even here, as all the members may be supposed to have been educated as gentlemen, the audience is not nearly so promiscuous as were the popular assemblies of Athens and of Rome, to which their demagogues declaimed with so much vehemence, and so wonderful success. Yet, even of these, women, minors, and servants made no part.

We may therefore justly reckon a christian congregation in a populous and flourishing city, where there is a great variety in rank and education, to be of all audiences the most promiscuous. And though it is impossible that, in so mixed a multitude, every thing that is advanced by the speaker should, both in sentiment and in expression, be adapted to the apprehension of every individual hearer, and fall in with his particular prepossessions, yet it may be expected, that whatever is advanced shall be within the reach of every class of hearers, and shall not unnecessarily shock the innocent prejudices of any. This is still, however, to be understood with the exception of mere children, fools, and a few others who, through the total neglect of parents or guardians in their education, are grossly ignorant. Such, though in the audience, are not to be considered as constituting a part of it. But how great is the attention requisite in the speaker in such an assembly, that, whilst on the one hand he avoids, either in style or in sentiment, soaring above the capacity of the lower class, he may not, on the other, sink below the regard of the higher. To attain simplicity without flatness, delicacy without refinement, perspicuity without recurring to low idioms and similitudes, will require his utmost care.

Another remark on this article that deserves our notice is, that the less improved in knowledge and discernment the hearers are, the easier it is for the speaker to work upon their passions, and by working on their passions, to obtain his end. This, it must be owned, appears, on the other hand, to give a considerable advantage to the preacher, as in no congregation can the bulk of the people be regarded as on a footing, in point of improvement, with either house of parliament, or with the judges in a court of judicature. It is certain, that the more gross the hearers are, the more avowedly may you address yourself to their passions, and the less occasion there is for argument; whereas, the more intelligent they are, the more covertly must you operate on their passions, and the more attentive must you be in regard to the justness, or at least the speciousness of your reasoning. Hence some have strangely concluded, that the only scope for eloquence is in haranguing the multitude; that in gaining over to your purpose men of knowledge and breeding, the exertion of oratorical talents hath no influence. This is precisely as if one should argue, because a mob is much easier subdued than regular troops, there is no occasion for the art of war, nor is there a proper field for the exertion of military skill, unless when you are quelling an undisciplined rabble. Every body sees in this case, not only how absurd such a way of arguing would be, but that the very reverse ought to be the conclusion. The reason why people do not so quickly perceive the absurdity in the other case is, that they affix no distinct meaning to the word *eloquence*, often denoting no more by that term than simply the power of moving the passions. But even in this improper acceptation, their notion is far from being just; for wherever there are men, learned or ignorant, civilized or barbarous, there are passions; and the greater the difficulty is in affecting these, the more art is requisite. The truth is, eloquence, like every other art, proposeth the accomplishment of a certain end. Passion is for the most part but the means employed for effecting the end, and therefore, like all other means, will no further be regarded in any case, than it can be rendered conducible to the end.

Now the preacher's advantage even here, in point of facility, at least in several situations, will not appear, on reflection, to be so great as on a superficial view it may be thought. Let it be observed, that in such congregations as were supposed, there is a mixture of superior and inferior ranks. It is therefore the business of the speaker, so far only to accommodate himself to one class, as not wantonly to disgust another. Besides, it will scarcely be denied that those in the superior walks of life, however much by reading and conversation improved in all genteel accomplishments, often have as much need of religious instruction and moral improvement, as those who in every other particular are acknowledged to be their inferiors. And doubtless the reformation of such will be allowed to be, in one respect, of greater importance, (and therefore never to be overlooked,) that in consequence of such an event, more good may redound to others, from the more extensive influence of their authority and example.

SECTION III.—*In regard to the Subject.*

The third particular mentioned was the subject of discourse. This may be considered in a twofold view; first, as implying the topics of argument, motives, and principles, which are suited to each of the different kinds, and must be employed in order to produce the intended effect on the hearers; secondly, as implying the person or things in whose favour, or to whose prejudice, the speaker purposes to excite the passions of the audience, and thereby to influence their determinations.

On the first of these articles, I acknowledge the preacher hath incomparably the advantage of every other public orator. At the bar, critical explications of dark and ambiguous statutes, quotations of precedents sometimes contradictory, and comments on jarring decisions and reports, often necessarily consume the great part of the speaker's time. Hence the mixture of a sort of metaphysics and verbal criticism, employed by lawyers in their pleadings, hath come to be distinguished by the name *chicane*, a species of reasoning too abstruse to command attention of any continuance even from the studious, and consequently not very favourable to the powers of rhetoric. When the argument doth not turn on the common law, or on nice and hypercritical explications of the statute, but on the great principles of natural right and justice, as sometimes happens, particularly in criminal cases, the speaker is much more advantageously situated for exhibiting his rhetorical talents than in the former case. When, in consequence of the imperfection of the evidence, the question happens to be more question of fact than either of municipal law or of natural equity, the pleader hath more advantages than in the first case, and fewer than in the second.

Again, in the deliberations in the senate, the utility or the disadvantages that will probably follow on a measure proposed, if it should receive the sanction of the legislature, constitute the principal topics of debate. This, though it sometimes leads to a kind of reasoning rather too complex and involved for ordinary apprehension, is in the main more favourable to the display of pathos, vehemence, and sublimity than the much greater part of the forensic causes can be said to be. That these qualities have been sometimes found in a very high degree in the orations pronounced in a British senate, is a fact incontrovertible.

But beyond all question, the preacher's subject of argument, considered in itself, is infinitely more lofty and more affecting. The doctrines of religion are such as relate to God, the adorable Creator and Ruler of the world, his attributes, government, and law. What science to be compared with it in sublimity? It teaches also the origin of man, his primitive dignity, the source of his degeneracy, the means of his recovery, the eternal happiness that awaits the good, and the future misery of the impenitent. Is there any kind of knowledge in which human creatures are so deeply interested? In a word, whether we consider the doctrines of religion or its documents, the examples it holds forth to our imitation, or its motives, promises, and threatenings, we see on every hand a subject that gives scope for the exertion of all the highest powers of rhetoric. What are the sanctions of any human laws, compared with the sanctions of the divine law, with which we are brought acquainted by the gospel? Or where shall we find instructions, similitudes, and examples, that speak so directly to the heart, as the parables and other divine lessons of our blessed Lord?

In regard to the second thing which I took notice of as included under the general term *subject*, namely the persons or things in whose favour, or to whose prejudice the speaker intends to excite the passions of the audience, and thereby to influence their determinations, the other two have commonly the advantage of the preacher. The reason is, that his subject is generally things; theirs, on the contrary, is persons. In what regards the painful passions, indignation, hatred, contempt, abhorrence, this difference invariably obtains. The preacher's business is solely to excite your detestation of the crime; the pleader's business is principally to make you detest the criminal. The former paints vice to you in all its odious colours; the latter paints the vicious. There is a degree of abstraction, and consequently a much greater degree of attention, requisite to enable us to form just conceptions of the ideas and sentiments of the former; whereas, those of the latter, referring to an actual, perhaps a living, present, and well-known subject, are much more level to common capacity, and therefore not only are more easily apprehended by the understanding, but take a stronger hold of the imagination. It would have been impossible even for Cicero to inflame the minds of the people to so high a pitch against *oppression*, considered in the abstract, as he actually did inflame them against Verres the *oppressor*;

nor could he have incensed them so much against *treason* and *conspiracy*, as he did incense them against Catiline the *traitor* and *conspirator*. The like may be observed of the effects of his orations against Antony, and in a thousand other instances.

Though the occasions in this way are more frequent at the bar, yet, as the deliberations in the senate often proceed on the reputation and past conduct of individuals, there is commonly here also a much better handle for rousing the passions than that enjoyed by the preacher. How much advantage Demosthenes drew from the known character and insidious arts of Philip king of Macedon, for influencing the resolves of the Athenians, and other Grecian states, those who are acquainted with the Philippics of the orator, and the history of that period, will be very sensible. In what concerns the pleasing affections, the preacher may sometimes, not often, avail himself of real human characters, as in funeral sermons, and in discourses on the patterns of virtue given us by our Saviour, and by those saints of whom we have the history in the sacred code. But such examples are comparatively few.

SECTION IV.—*In regard to the Occasion.*

The fourth circumstance mentioned as a ground of comparison, is the particular occasion of speaking. And in this I think it evident, that both the pleader and the senator have the advantage of the preacher. When any important cause comes to be tried before a civil judicatory, or when any important question comes to be agitated in either house of parliament, as the point to be discussed hath generally for some time before been a topic of conversation in most companies, perhaps throughout the kingdom, (which of itself is sufficient to give consequence to any thing,) people are apprized beforehand of the particular day fixed for the discussion. Accordingly, they come prepared with some knowledge of the case, a persuasion of its importance, and a curiosity which sharpens their attention, and assists both their understanding and their memory.

Men go to church without any of these advantages. The subject of the sermon is not known to the congregation, till the minister announce it just as he begins, by reading the text. Now, from our experience of human nature, we may be sensible that whatever be the comparative importance of the things themselves, the generality of men cannot here be wrought up, in an instant, to the like anxious curiosity about what is to be said, nor can be so well prepared for hearing it. It may indeed be urged, in regard to those subjects which come regularly to be discussed at stated times, as on public festivals, as well as in regard to assize-sermons, charity-sermons, and other occasional discourses, that these must be admitted as exceptions. Perhaps in some degree they are, but not altogether: for first, the precise point to be argued, or proposition to be evinced, is very rarely known. The most that we can say is, that the subject will have a relation (sometimes remote enough) to such an article of faith, or to the obligations we lie under to the practice of such a duty. But further, if the topic were ever so well known, the frequent recurrence of such occasions, once a year at least, hath long familiarized us to them, and, by destroying their novelty, hath abated exceedingly of that ardour which ariseth in the mind for hearing a discussion, conceived to be of importance, which one never had access to hear before, and probably never will have access to hear again.

I shall here take notice of another circumstance, which, without great stretch, may be classed under this article, and which likewise gives some advantage to the counsellor and the senator. It is the opposition and contradiction which they expect to meet with. Opponents sharpen one another, as iron sharpeneth iron. There is not the same spur either to exertion in the speaker, or to attention in the hearer, where there is no conflict, where you have no adversary to encounter with equal terms. Mr. Bickerstaff would have made but small progress in the science of defence, by pushing at the human figure which he had chalked upon the wall,[4] in comparison of what he might have made by the help of a fellow combatant of flesh and blood. I do not, however, pretend that these cases are entirely parallel. The whole of an adversary's plea may be perfectly known, and may, to the satisfaction of every reasonable person, be perfectly confuted, though he hath not been heard by the counsel at the bar.

SECTION V.—*In regard to the End in view.*

The fifth and last particular mentioned, and indeed the most important of them all, is the effect in each species intended to be produced. The primary intention of preaching is the reformation of mankind. "The grace of God, that bringeth salvation, hath appeared to all men, teaching us that, denying ungodliness and worldly lusts, we should live soberly, righteously, and godly in this present world."[5] Reformation of life and manners—of all things that which is the most difficult by any means whatever to effectuate; I may add, of all tasks ever attempted by persuasion, that which has the most frequently baffled its power.

What is the task of any other orator compared with this?

[4] Tatler. [5] Tit. ii. 11, 12.

It is really as nothing at all, and hardly deserves to be named. An unjust judge, gradually worked on by the resistless force of human eloquence, may be persuaded, against his inclination, perhaps against a previous resolution, to pronounce an equitable sentence. All the effect on him, intended by the pleader, was merely momentary. The orator hath had the address to employ the time allowed him in such a manner as to secure the happy moment. Notwithstanding this, there may be no real change wrought upon the judge. He may continue the same obdurate wretch he was before. Nay, if the sentence had been delayed but a single day after hearing the cause, he would perhaps have given a very different award.

Is it to be wondered at, that when the passions of the people were agitated by the persuasive powers of a Demosthenes, whilst the thunder of his eloquence was yet sounding in their ears, the orator should be absolute master of their resolves? But an apostle or evangelist (for there is no anachronism in a bare supposition) might have thus addressed the celebrated Athenian, "You do, indeed, succeed to admiration, and the address and genius which you display in speaking justly entitle you to our praise. But however great the consequences may be of the measures to which, by your eloquence, they are determined, the change produced in the people is nothing, or next to nothing. If you would be ascertained of the truth of this, allow the assembly to disperse immediately after hearing you; give them time to cool, and then collect their votes, and it is a thousand to one you shall find that the charm is dissolved."

But very different is the purpose of the christian orator. It is not a momentary, but a permanent effect at which he aims. It is not an immediate and favourable suffrage, but a thorough change of heart and disposition, that will satisfy his view. That man would need to be possessed of oratory superior to human, who would effectually persuade him that stole to steal no more, the sensualist to forego his pleasures, and the miser his hoards, the insolent and haughty to become meek and humble, the vindictive forgiving, the cruel and unfeeling merciful and humane.

I may add to these considerations, that the difficulty lies not only in the permanency, but in the very nature of the change to be effected. It is wonderful, but it is too well vouched to admit of a doubt, that by the powers of rhetoric you may produce in mankind almost any change more easily than this. It is not unprecedented that one should persuade a multitude, from mistaken motives of religion, to act the part of ruffians, fools, or madmen; to perpetrate the most extravagant, nay, the most flagitious actions; to steel their hearts against humanity, and the loudest calls of affection: but where is the eloquence that will gain such an ascendant over a multitude, as to persuade them, for the love of God, to be wise, and just, and good? Happy the preacher whose sermons, by the blessing of Heaven, have been instrumental in producing even a few such instances! Do but look into the annals of church history, and you will soon be convinced of the surprising difference there is in the two cases mentioned—the amazing facility of the one, and the almost impossibility of the other.

As to the foolish or mad extravagances, hurtful only to themselves, to which numbers may be excited by the powers of persuasion, the history of the flagellants, and even the history of monachism, afford many unquestionable examples. But what is much worse, at one time you see Europe nearly depopulated at the persuasion of a fanatical monk, its inhabitants rushing armed into Asia, in order to fight for Jesus Christ, as they termed it, but as it proved in fact, to disgrace, as far as lay in them, the name of Christ and of Christian amongst infidels; to butcher those who never injured them, and to whose lands they had at least no better title than those whom they intended, by all possible means, to dispossess; and to give the world a melancholy proof, that there is no pitch of brutality and rapacity to which the passions of avarice and ambition, consecrated and inflamed by religious enthusiasm, will not drive mankind. At another time you see multitudes, by the like methods, worked up into a fury against innocent countrymen, neighbours, friends, and kinsmen, glorying in being most active in cutting the throats of those who were formerly held dear to them.

Such were the crusades preached up but too effectually, first against the Mahometans in the East, and next against Christians whom they called heretics, in the heart of Europe. And even in our own time, have we not seen new factions raised by popular declaimers, whose only merit was impudence, whose only engine of influence was calumny and self-praise, whose only moral lesson was malevolence? As to the dogmas whereby such have at any time affected to discriminate themselves, these are commonly no other than the *shibboleth*, the watchword of the party, worn, for distinction's sake, as a badge, a jargon unintelligible alike to the teacher and to the learner. Such apostles never fail to make proselytes. For who would not purchase heaven at so cheap rate? There is nothing that people can more easily afford. It is only to think very well of their leader and of themselves, to think very ill of their neighbour, to calumniate him freely, and to hate him heartily.

I am sensible that some will imagine that this account itself throws an insuperable obstacle in our way, as from it one will naturally infer, that oratory must be one of the most dangerous things in the world, and much more capable of doing ill than good. It needs but some reflection to make this mighty obstacle entirely vanish.—Very little eloquence is necessary for persuading people to a conduct to which their own depravity hath previously given them a bias. How soothing is it to them not only to have their minds made easy under the indulged malignity of their disposition, but to have that very malignity sanctified with a good name! So little of the oratorical talent is required here, that those who court popular applause, and look upon it as the pinnacle of human glory to be blindly followed by the multitude, commonly recur to defamation, especially of superiors and brethren, not so much for a subject on which they may display their eloquence, as for a succedaneum to supply their want of eloquence, a succedaneum which never yet was found to fail. I knew a preacher who, from this expedient alone, from being long the aversion of the populace, on account of his dulness, awkwardness, and coldness, all of a sudden became their idol. Little force is necessary to push down heavy bodies placed on the verge of a declivity, but much force is requisite to stop them in their progress, and push them up.

If a man should say, that because the first is more frequently effected than the last, it is the best trial of strength, and the only suitable use to which it can be applied, we should at least not think him remarkable for distinctness in his ideas. Popularity alone, therefore, is no test at all of the eloquence of the speaker, no more than velocity alone would be of the force of the external impulse originally given to the body moving. As in this the direction of the body, and other circumstances, must be taken into the account; so in that, you must consider the tendency of the teaching, whether it favours or opposes the vices of the hearers. To head a sect, to infuse party-spirit, to make men arrogant, uncharitable, and malevolent, is the easiest task imaginable, and to which almost any blockhead is fully equal. But to produce the contrary effect, to subdue the spirit of faction, and that monster spiritual pride, with which it is invariably accompanied, to inspire equity, moderation, and charity into men's sentiments and conduct with regard to others, is the genuine test of eloquence. Here its triumph is truly glorious, and in its application to this end lies its great utility:

> The gates of hell are open night and day;
> Smooth the descent, and easy is the way:
> But to return and view the cheerful skies,
> In this the task and mighty labour lies.[6]
>
> DRYDEN.

Now in regard to the comparison, from which I fear I shall be thought to have digressed, between the forensic and sena-

[6] ——— Facilis descensus Averni:
Noctes atque dies patet atri janua Ditis:
Sed revocare gradum, superasque evadere ad auras,
Hic labor, hoc opus est. VIRG. ÆN. lib vi.

torian eloquence, and that of the pulpit, I must not omit to observe, that in what I say of the difference of the effect to be produced by the last mentioned species, I am to be understood as speaking of the effect intended by preaching in general, and even of that which, in whole or in part, is, or ought to be, either more immediately or more remotely, the scope of all discourses proceeding from the pulpit. I am, at the same time, sensible that in some of these, beside the ultimate view, there is an immediate and outward effect which the sermon is intended to produce. This is the case particularly in charity-sermons, and perhaps some other occasional discourses. Now of these few, in respect of such immediate purpose, we must admit, that they bear a pretty close analogy to the pleadings of the advocate, and the orations of the senator.

Upon the whole of the comparison I have stated, it appears manifest that, in most of the particulars above enumerated, the preacher labours under a very great disadvantage. He hath himself a more delicate part to perform than either the pleader or the senator, and a character to maintain which is much more easily injured. The auditors, though rarely so accomplished as to require the same accuracy of composition, or acuteness of reasoning, as may be expected in the other two, are more various in age, rank, taste, inclinations, sentiments, prejudices, to which he must accommodate himself. And if he derives some advantages from the richness, the variety, and the nobleness of the principles, motives, and arguments with which his subject furnishes him, he derives also some inconveniences from this circumstance, that almost the only engine by which he can operate on the passions of his hearers, is the exhibition of abstract qualities, virtues, and vices, whereas that chiefly employed by other orators is the exhibition of real persons, the virtuous and the vicious. Nor are the occasions of his addresses to the people equally fitted with those of the senator and of the pleader for exciting their curiosity and riveting their attention. And, finally, the task assigned him, the effect which he ought ever to have in view, is so great, so important, so durable, as seems to bid defiance to the strongest efforts of oratorical genius.

Nothing is more common than for people, I suppose without reflecting, to express their wonder that there is so little eloquence amongst our preachers, and that so little success attends their preaching. As to the last, their success, it is a matter not to be ascertained with so much precision as some appear fondly to imagine. The evil prevented, as well as the good promoted, ought here, in all justice, to come into the reckoning. And what that may be, it is impossible in any supposed circumstances to determine. As to the first, their eloquence, I acknowledge that for my own part, considering how rare the talent is among men in general, considering all the disadvantages preachers labour under, not only those above enumerated, but others, arising from their different situations, particularly considering the frequency of this exercise, together with the other duties of their office, to which the fixed pastors are obliged, I have been for a long time more disposed to wonder, that we hear so many instructive and even eloquent sermons, than that we hear so few.

CHAPTER XI.

Of the cause of that pleasure which we receive from objects or representations that excite pity and other painful feelings.

It hath been observed already,[7] that without some gratification in hearing, the attention must inevitably flag. And it is manifest from experience that nothing tends more effectually to prevent this consequence, and keep our attention alive and vigorous, than the pathetic, which consists chiefly in exhibitions of human misery. Yet that such exhibitions should so highly gratify us, appears somewhat mysterious. Every body is sensible, that of all qualities in a work of genius, this is that which endears it most to the generality of readers. One would imagine, on the first mention of this, that it were impossible to account for it otherwise than from an innate principle of malice, which teacheth us to extract delight to ourselves from the sufferings of others, and as it were to enjoy their calamities. A very little reflection, however, would suffice for correcting this error; nay, without any reflection, we may truly say, that the common sense of mankind prevents them effectually from falling into it. Bad as we are, and prone as we are to be hurried into the worst of passions by self-love, partiality, and pride, malice is a disposition which, either in the abstract, or as it discovers itself in the actions of an indifferent person, we can never contemplate without feeling a just detestation and abhorrence, being ready to pronounce it the ugliest of objects. Yet this sentiment is not more universal than is the approbation and even love that we bestow on the tender-hearted, or those who are most exquisitely susceptible of all the influence of the pathetic. Nor are there any two dispositions of which human

[7] Chapter iv.

nature is capable, that have ever been considered as further removed from each other, than the malicious and the compassionate are. The fact itself, that the mind derives pleasure from representations of anguish, is undeniable: the question about the cause is curious, and hath a manifest relation to my subject.

I purposed, indeed, at first, to discuss this point in that part of the sixth chapter which relates to the means of operating on the passions, with which the present inquiry is intimately connected. Finding afterwards that the discussion would prove rather too long an interruption, and that the other points which came naturally to be treated in that place could be explained with sufficient clearness independently of this, I judged it better to reserve this question for a separate chapter. Various hypotheses have been devised by the ingenious, in order to solve the difficulty. These I shall first briefly examine, and then lay before the reader what appears to me to be the true solution. Of all that have entered into the subject, those who seem most to merit our regard are two French critics and one of our own country.

SECTION I.—*The different solutions hitherto given by philosophers examined.*

PART I.—*The first hypothesis.*

Abbé du Bos begins his excellent reflections on poetry and painting, with that very question which is the subject of this chapter, and in answer to it supports at some length[8] a theory, the substance of which I shall endeavour to comprise in a few words. Few things, according to him, are more disagreeable to the mind, than that listlessness into which it falls, when it has nothing to occupy it, or to awake the passions. In order to get rid of this most painful situation, it seeks with avidity every amusement and pursuit; business, gaming, news, shows, public executions, romances; in short, whatever will rouse the passions, and take off the mind's attention from itself. It matters not what the emotion be, only the stronger it is, so much the better. And for this reason, those passions which, considered in themselves, are the most afflicting and disagreeable, are preferable to the pleasant, inasmuch as they most effectually relieve the soul from that oppressive languor which preys upon

[8] Reflexions critiques sur la Poesie et sur la Peinture, Sect. i. ii. iii.

it in a state of inactivity. They afford it ample occupation, and, by giving play to its latent movements and springs of action, convey a pleasure which more than counterbalances the pain.

I admit, with Mr. Hume,[9] that there is some weight in these observations, which may sufficiently account for the pleasure taken in gaming, hunting, and several other diversions and sports. But they are not quite satisfactory, as they do not assign a sufficient reason why poets, painters, and orators, exercise themselves more in actuating the painful passions, than in exciting the pleasant. These, one would think, ought in every respect to have the advantage, because, at the same time that they preserve the mind from a state of inaction, they convey a feeling that is allowed to be agreeable. And though it were granted, that passions of the former kind are stronger than those of the latter (which doth not hold invariably, there being perhaps more examples of persons who have been killed with joy, than those who have died of grief), strength alone will not account for the preference. It by no means holds here, that the stronger the emotion is, so much the fitter for this purpose. On the contrary, if you exceed but ever so little a certain measure, instead of that sympathetic delightful sorrow, which makes affliction itself wear a lovely aspect, and engages the mind to hug it, not only with tenderness, but with transport, you only excite horror and aversion. "It is certain," says the author last quoted, very justly,[1] "that the same object of distress which pleases in a tragedy, were it really set before us, would give the most unfeigned uneasiness, though it be then the most effectual cure of languor and indolence." And it is more than barely possible, even in the representations of the tragedian, or in the descriptions of the orator or the poet, to exceed that measure. I acknowledge, indeed, that this measure or degree is not the same to every temper. Some are much sooner shocked with mournful representations than others. Our mental, like our bodily appetites and capacities, are exceedingly various. It is, however, the business of both the speaker and the writer, to accommodate himself to what may be styled the common standard; for there is a common standard, in what regards the faculties of the mind, as well as in what concerns the powers of the body. Now, if there be any quality in the afflictive passions, besides their strength, that renders them peculiarly adapted to rescue the mind from that torpid but corrosive rest which is considered as the greatest of evils, that quality ought to have been pointed out: for till then the phenomenon under examination is not accounted for. The most that can be concluded

[9] Essay on Tragedy.

[1] Ibid.

from the Abbé's premises is the utility of exciting passion of some kind or other, but nothing that can evince the superior fitness of the distressful affections.

PART II.—*The second hypothesis.*

The next hypothesis is Fontenelle's.[2] Not having the original at hand at present, I shall give Mr. Hume's translation of the passage, in his Essay on Tragedy above quoted. "Pleasure and pain, which are two sentiments so different in themselves, differ not so much in their cause. From the instance of tickling it appears that the movement of pleasure, pushed a little too far, becomes pain; and that the movement of pain, a little moderated, becomes pleasure. Hence it proceeds, that there is such a thing as a sorrow soft and agreeable. It is a pain weakened and diminished. The heart likes naturally to be moved and affected. Melancholy objects suit it, and even disastrous and sorrowful, provided they are softened by some circumstance. It is certain that, on the theatre, the representation has almost the effect of reality; but yet it has not altogether that effect. However we may be hurried away by the spectacle, whatever dominion the senses and imagination may usurp over the reason, there still lurks at the bottom a certain idea of falsehood in the whole of what we see. This idea, though weak and disguised, suffices to diminish the pain which we suffer from the misfortunes of those whom we love, and to reduce that affliction to such a pitch as converts it into a pleasure. We weep for the misfortunes of a hero to whom we are attached. In the same instant we comfort ourselves by reflecting that it is nothing but a fiction: and it is precisely that mixture of sentiments which composes an agreeable sorrow, and tears that delight us. But as that affliction which is caused by exterior and sensible objects is stronger than the consolation which arises from an internal reflection, they are the effects and symptoms of sorrow which ought to prevail in the composition."

I cannot affirm that this solution appears to me so just and convincing as it seems it did to Mr. Hume. If this English version, like a faithful mirror, reflect the true image of the French original, I think the author in some degree chargeable with what in that language is emphatically enough styled *verbiage*, a manner of writing very common with those of his nation, and with their imitators in ours. The only truth that I can discover in his hypothesis, lies in one small circumstance, which is so far from being applicable to the whole case under

[2] Reflexions sur la Poetique, Sect. xxxvi.

consideration, that it can properly be applied but to a very few particular instances, and is therefore no solution at all. That there are at least many cases to which it cannot be applied, the author last mentioned declares himself to be perfectly sensible.

But let us examine the passage more narrowly. He begins with laying it down as a general principle, that however different the feelings of pleasure and of pain are in themselves, they differ not much in their cause; that the movement of pleasure pushed a little too far becomes pain; and that the movement of pain a little moderated becomes pleasure. For an illustration of this he gives an example in tickling. I will admit that there are several other similar instances, in which the observation to appearance holds. The warmth received from sitting near the fire, by one who hath been almost chilled with cold, is very pleasing; yet you may increase this warmth, first to a disagreeable heat, and then to burning, which is one of the greatest torments. It is nevertheless extremely hazardous, on a few instances, and those not perfectly parallel to the case in hand, to found a general theory. Let us make the experiment, how the application of this doctrine to the passions of the mind will answer. And for our greater security against mistake, let us begin with the simplest cases in the direct, and not in the reflex or sympathetic passions, in which hardly ever any feeling or affection comes alone. A merchant loseth all his fortune by a shipwreck, and is reduced at one stroke from opulence to indigence. His grief, we may suppose, will be very violent. If he had lost half his stock only, it is natural to think he would have borne the loss more easily, though still he would have been affected; perhaps the loss of fifty pounds he would have scarcely felt: but I should be glad to know how much the movement or passion must be moderated; or, in other words, as the difference ariseth solely from the different degrees of the cause, how small the loss must be when the sentiment of feeling of it begins to be converted into a real pleasure: for to me it doth not appear natural that any the most trifling loss, were it of a single shilling, should be the subject of positive delight.

But to try another instance, a gross and public insult commonly provokes a very high degree of resentment, and gives a most pungent vexation to a person of sensibility. I would gladly know whether a smaller affront, or some slight instance of neglect or contempt, gives such a person any pleasure. Try the experiment also on friendship and hatred, and you will find the same success. As the warmest friendship is highly agreeable to the mind, the slightest liking is also agreeable, though in a less degree. Perfect hatred is a kind of torture to the breast that harbours it, which will not be found capable of being mitigated into pleasure; for there is no degree of ill-will without pain. The gradation in the cause and in the effect are entirely correspondent.

Nor can any just conclusion be drawn from the affections of the body, as in these the consequence is often solely imputable to a certain proportion of strength, in the cause that operates, to the present disposition of the organs. But though I cannot find that in any uncompounded passion the most remote degrees are productive of such contrary effects, I do not deny that when different passions are blended, some of them pleasing and some painful, the pleasure or the pain of those which predominate may, through the wonderful mechanism[3] of our mental frame, be considerably augmented by the mixture.

The only truth which, as I hinted already, I can discover in the preceding hypothesis, is, that the mind in certain cases avails itself of the notion of falsehood, in order to prevent the representation or narrative from producing too strong an effect upon the imagination, and consequently to relieve itself from such an excess of passion as could not otherwise fail to be painful. But let it be observed, that this notion is not a necessary concomitant of the pleasure that results from pity and other such affections, but is merely accidental. It was remarked above, that if the pathetic exceeds a certain measure, from being very pleasant it becomes very painful. Then the mind recurs to every expedient, and to disbelief amongst others, by which it may be enabled to disburden itself of what distresseth it. And, indeed, whenever this recourse is had by any, it is a sure indication that, with regard to such, the poet, orator, or historian hath exceeded the proper measure.

But that this only holds when we are too deeply interested by the sympathetic sorrow, will appear from the following considerations: first, from the great pains often taken by writers (whose design is certainly not to shock, but to please their readers) to make the most moving stories they relate be firmly believed; secondly, from the tendency, nay fondness, of the generality of mankind to believe what moves them, and their averseness to be convinced that it is a fiction. This can result only from the consciousness that, in ordinary cases, disbelief, by weakening their pity, would diminish, instead of increasing, their pleasure. They must be very far then from entertaining Fontenelle's notion, that it is necessary to the producing of that pleasure; for we cannot well suspect them of a plot against their own enjoyment. Thirdly, and lastly, from the delight which we take in reading or hearing the most tragical narra-

[3] The word *mechanism*, applied to the mind, ought not reasonably to give offence to any. I only use the term metaphorically, for those effects in the operation of the mental faculties produced in consequence of such fixed laws as are independent of the will. It hath here therefore no reference to the doctrine of the materialist, a system which, in my opinion, is not only untenable, but absurd.

tions of orators and historians, of the reality of which we entertain no doubt; I might add, in revolving in our own minds, and in relating to others, disastrous incidents which have fallen within the compass of our own knowledge, and as to which, consequently, we have an absolute assurance of the fact.

PART III.—*The third hypothesis.*

The third hypothesis which I shall produce on this subject, is Mr. Hume's. Only it ought to be remarked previously, that he doth not propose it as a full solution of the question, but rather as a supplement to the former two, in the doctrine of both which he, in a great measure, acquiesces. Take his theory in his own words. He begins with putting the question, "What is it, then, which, in this case," that is, when the sorrow is not softened by fiction, "raises a pleasure from the bosom of uneasiness, so to speak; and a pleasure which still retains all the features and outward symptoms of distress and sorrow?" I answer: This extraordinary effect proceeds from that very eloquence with which the melancholy scene is represented. The genius required to paint objects in a lively manner, the art employed in collecting all the pathetic circumstances, the judgment displayed in disposing them; the exercise, I say, of these noble talents, together with the force of expression, and beauty of oratorial numbers, diffuse the highest satisfaction on the audience, and excite the most delightful movements. By this means, the uneasiness of the melancholy passions is not only overpowered and effaced by something stronger of an opposite kind, but the whole movement of those passions is converted into pleasure, and swells the delight which the eloquence raises in us. The same force of oratory, employed on an uninteresting subject, would not please half so much, or rather would appear altogether ridiculous; and the mind, being left in absolute calmness and indifference, would relish none of those beauties of imagination or expression which, if joined to passion, give it such exquisite entertainment. The impulse or vehemence arising from sorrow, compassion, indignation, receives a new direction from the sentiments of beauty. The latter, being the predominant emotion, seize the whole mind, and convert the former into themselves, or at least tincture them so strongly, as totally to alter their nature: and the soul being, at the same time, roused by passion and charmed by eloquence, feels on the whole a strong movement which is altogether delightful."

I am sorry to say, but truth compels me to acknowledge, that I have reaped no more satisfaction from this account of the matter, than from those which preceded it. I could have wished, indeed, that the author had been a little more explicit in his manner of expressing himself; for I am not certain that

I perfectly comprehend his meaning. At one time he seems only to intend to say, that it is the purpose of eloquence, to the promoting of which its tropes and figures are wonderfully adapted, to infuse into the mind of the hearer such compassion, sorrow, indignation, and other passions, as are, notwithstanding their original character, when abstractly considered, accompanied with pleasure. At another time it appears rather his design to signify, though he doth not plainly speak it out, that the discovery made by the hearer, of the admirable art and ingenuity of the speaker, and of the elegance and harmony of what is spoken, gives that peculiar pleasure to the mind which makes even the painful passions become delightful.

If the first of these be all that he intended to affirm, he hath told us indeed a certain truth, but nothing new or uncommon; nay more, he hath told us nothing that can serve in the smallest degree for a solution of the difficulty. Who ever doubted, that it is the design and work of eloquence to move the passions, and to please? The question which this naturally gives rise to is, How doth eloquence produce this effect? This, I believe, it will be acknowledged to do principally, if not solely, agreeably to the doctrine explained above,[4] by communicating lively, distinct, and strong ideas of the distress which it exhibits. By a judicious yet natural arrangement of the most affecting circumstances, by a proper selection of the most suitable tropes and figures, it enlivens the ideas raised in the imagination to such a pitch as makes them strongly resemble the perceptions of the senses, or the transcripts of the memory. The question, then, with which we are immediately concerned, doth obviously recur, and seems, if possible, more mysterious than before: for how can the aggravating of all the circumstances of misery in the representation, make it be contemplated with pleasure? One would naturally imagine that this must be the most effectual method for making it give still greater pain. How can the heightening of grief, fear, anxiety, and other uneasy sensations, render them agreeable?

Besides, this ingenious author has not adverted, that his hypothesis, instead of being supplementary to Fontenelle's, as he appears to have intended, is subversive of the principles on which the French critic's theory is founded. The effect, according to the latter, results from moderating, weakening, softening, and diminishing the passion: according to the former, it results from what is directly opposite, from the arts employed by the orator for the purpose of exaggerating, strengthening, heightening, and inflaming the passion. Indeed, neither of these writers seems to have attended suffi-

[4] Chap. vi.

ciently to one particular, which of itself might have shown the insufficiency of their systems. The particular alluded to is, that pity, if it exceed not a certain degree, gives pleasure to the mind, when excited by the original objects in distress, as well as by the representations made by poets, painters, and orators: and, on the contrary, if it exceed a certain degree, it is on the whole painful, whether awakened by the real objects of pity, or roused by the exhibitions of the historian or of the poet. Indeed, as sense operates much more strongly on the mind than imagination does, the excess is much more frequent in the former case than in the latter.

Now, in attempting to give a solution of the difficulty, it is plain, that all our theorists ought regularly and properly to begin with the former case. If in that, which is the original and the simplest, the matter is sufficiently accounted for, it is accounted for in every case, it being the manifest design both of painting and of oratory, as nearly as possible, to produce the same affections which the very objects represented would have produced in our minds: whereas, though Mr. Hume should be admitted to have accounted fully for the impression made by the poet and the orator, we are as far as ever from the discovery of the cause why pity excited by the objects themselves, when it hath no eloquence to recommend it, is on the whole, if not excessive, a pleasant emotion.

But if this celebrated writer intended to assert that the discovery of the oratory, that is, of the address and talents of the speaker, is what gives the hearer a pleasure, which, mingling itself with pity, fear, indignation, converts the whole, as he expresseth it, into one strong movement, which is altogether delightful: if this be his sentiment, he hath indeed advanced something extraordinary, and entirely new. And that this is his opinion, appears, I think, obliquely, from the expressions which he useth. "The genius required, the art employed, the judgment displayed, along with force of expression, and beauty of oratorial numbers, diffuse the highest satisfaction on the audience."—Again, "The impulse or vehemence arising from sorrow, compassion, indignation, receives a new direction from the sentiments of beauty." If this then be a just solution of the difficulty, and the detection of the speaker's talents and address be necessary to render the hearer susceptible of this charming sorrow, this delightful anguish, how grossly have all critics and rhetoricians been deceived hitherto. These, in direct opposition to this curious theory, have laid it down in their rhetorics as a fundamental maxim, that "it is essential to the art to conceal the art;"[5] a maxim, too, which, in their estimation, the orator, in no part of his province, is obliged to such

[5] Artis est celare artem.

a scrupulous observance of, as in the pathetic.[6] In this the speaker, if he would prove successful, must make his subject totally engross the attention of the hearers; insomuch that he himself, his genius, his art, his judgment, his richness of language, his harmony of numbers, are not minded in the least.[7]

Never does the orator obtain a nobler triumph by his eloquence than when his sentiments and style and order appear so naturally to arise out of the subject, that every hearer is inclined to think, he could not have either thought or spoken otherwise himself; when every thing, in short, is exhibited in such a manner,

> As all might hope to imitate with ease;
> Yet while they strive the same success to gain,
> Should find their labour and their hopes are vain.[8]

As to the harmony of numbers, it ought no further to be the speaker's care, than that he may avoid an offensive dissonance or halting in his periods, which, by hurting the ear, abstracts the attention from the subject, and must by consequence serve to obstruct the effect. Yet, even this, it may be safely averred, will not tend half so much to counteract the end, as an elaborate harmony, or a flowing elocution, which carries along with it the evident marks of address and study.[9]

Our author proceeds all along on the supposition that there are two distinct effects produced by the eloquence on the hearers; one the sentiment of beauty, or (as he explains it more particularly) of the harmony of oratorial numbers, of the exercise of these noble talents, genius, art, and judgment; the other the passion which the speaker purposeth to raise in their minds. He maintains, that when the first predominates, the mixture of the two effects becomes exceedingly pleasant,

[6] Effugienda igitur in hac præcipue parte omnis calliditatis suspicio: nihil videatur fictum, nihil solicitum: omnia potius a causa quam ab oratore profecta credantur. Sed hoc pati non possumus, et perire artem putamus, nisi appareat: cum desinat ars esse, si apparet.—QUINT. Instit. lib. iv. cap. 2.

[7] Ubi res agitur, et vera dimicatio est, ultimus sit famæ locus. Propterea non debet quisquam, ubi maxima rerum momenta versantur, de verbis esse solicitus. Neque hoc eo pertinet, ut in his nullus sit ornatus, sed uti pressior et severior, minus confessus, præcipue ad materiam accommodatus.—QUINT. Instit. lib. viii. cap. 3.

[8] ——————— Ut sibi quivis
Speret idem; sudet multum, frustraque laboret,
Ausus idem. HOR. De Arte Poet.

[9] Commoveaturne quisquam ejus fortunâ, quem tumidum ac sui jactantem, et ambitiosum institorem eloquentiæ in ancipiti forte videat? Non: imo oderit reum verba aucupantem, et anxium de fama ingenii, et cui esse diserto vacet. QUINT. l. xi. cap. 1. Ubi vero atrocitate, invidiâ, miseratione pugnandum est, quis ferat contrapositis et pariter cadentibus, et consimilibus, irascentem, flentem, rogantem? cum in his rebus cura verborum deroget affectibus fidem; et ubicunque ars ostentatur, veritas abesse videatur, cap. 3.

and the reverse when the second is superior. At least, if this is not what he means to assert and vindicate, I despair of being able to assign a meaning to the following expressions: "The genius required to paint,—the art employed in collecting,—the judgment displayed in disposing—diffuse the highest satisfaction on the audience, and excite the most delightful movements. By this means the uneasiness of the melancholy passions is not only overpowered and effaced by something stronger of an opposite kind, but the whole movement of those passions is converted into pleasure, and swells the delight which the eloquence raises in us." Again, "The impulse or vehemence arising from sorrow—receives a new direction from the sentiments of beauty. The latter being the predominant emotion, seize the whole mind, and convert the former——" Again, "The soul, being at the same time roused with passion and charmed by eloquence, feels on the whole——" And in the paragraph immediately succeeding, "It is thus the fiction of tragedy softens the passion, by an infusion of a new feeling, not merely by weakening or diminishing the sorrow——" Now to me it is manifest, that this notion of two distinguishable, and even opposite effects, as he terms them, produced in the hearer by the eloquence, is perfectly imaginary; that, on the contrary, whatever charm or fascination, if you please to call it so, there is in the pity excited by the orator, it ariseth not from any extrinsic sentiment of beauty blended with it, but intimately from its own nature, from those passions which pity necessarily associates, or, I should rather say, includes.

But do we not often hear people speak of eloquence as moving them greatly, and pleasing them highly at the same time? Nothing more common. But these are never understood by them as two original, separate, and independent effects, but as essentially connected. Push your inquiries but ever so little, and you will find all agree in affirming, that it is by being moved, and by that solely, that they are pleased: in philosophical strictness, therefore, the pleasure is the immediate effect of the passion, and the passion the immediate effect of the eloquence.

But is there then no pleasure in contemplating the beauty of composition, the richness of fancy, the power of numbers, and the energy of expression? There is undoubtedly. But so far is this pleasure from commixing with the pathos, and giving a direction to it, that, on the contrary, they seem to be in a great measure incompatible. Such indeed is the pleasure which the artist or the critic enjoys, who can coolly and deliberately survey the whole; upon whose passions the art of the speaker hath little or no influence, and that purely for this reason, because he discovers that art. The bulk of hearers know no further than to approve the man who affects them, who speaks to their heart, as they very properly and emphatically term it, and to commend the performance by which this is accomplished. But how it is accomplished, they neither give themselves the trouble to consider, nor attempt to explain.[1]

PART IV.—*The fourth hypothesis.*

Lastly, To mention only one other hypothesis; there are who maintain that compassion is "an example of unmixed selfishness and malignity," and may be "resolved into that power of imagination by which we apply the misfortunes of others to ourselves;" that we are said "to pity no longer than we fancy ourselves to suffer, and to be pleased only by reflecting that our sufferings are not real; thus indulging a dream of distress, from which we can awake whenever we please, to exult in our security, and enjoy the comparison of the fiction with truth."[2]

This is no other than the antiquated doctrine of the philosopher of Malmesbury, rescued from oblivion, to which it had been fast descending, and republished with improvements. Hobbes indeed thought it a sufficient stretch, in order to render the sympathetic sorrow purely selfish, to define it, "imagination or fiction of future calamity to ourselves, proceeding from the sense of another man's calamity."[3] But in the first quotation we have another kind of fiction; namely, that we are at present the very sufferers ourselves, the identical persons whose cases are exhibited as being so deplorable, and whose calamities we so sincerely lament. There were some things hinted in the beginning of the chapter, in relation to this paradoxical conceit, which I should not have thought it necessary to resume, had it not been adopted by a late author, whose periodical

[1] The inquiry contained in this chapter was written long before I had an opportunity of perusing a very ingenious English commentary and notes on Horace's Epistles to the Pisos and to Augustus, in which Mr. Hume's sentiments on this subject are occasionally criticized. The opinions of that commentator, in regard to Mr. Hume's theory, coincide in every thing material with mine. This author considers the question no further than it relates to the representations of tragedy, and hath, by confining his view to this single point, been led to lay greater stress on Fontenelle's hypothesis than, for the solution of the general phenomenon, it is entitled to. It is very true that our theatrical entertainments commonly exhibit a degree of distress which we could not bear to witness in the objects represented. Consequently the consideration that it is but a picture, and not the original, a fictitious exhibition, and not the reality, which we contemplate, is essential for rendering the whole, I may say, supportable as well as pleasant. But even in this case, when it is necessary to our repose to consider the scenical misery before us as mere illusion, we are generally better pleased to consider the things represented as genuine fact. It requires, indeed, but a further degree of affliction to make us even pleased to think that the copy never had any archetype in nature. But when this is the case we may truly say, that the poet hath exceeded and wrought up pity to a kind of horror.

[2] Adventurer, No. 110.

[3] Hum. Nat. chap. ix. sect. 10.

essays seemed to entitle him to the character of an ingenious, moral, and instructive writer.[4] For though he hath declined entering formally into the debate, he hath sufficiently shown his sentiments on this article, and hath endeavoured indirectly to support them.

I doubt not that it will appear to many of my readers as equally silly to refute this hypothesis and to defend it. Nothing could betray reasonable men into such extravagances, but the dotage with which one is affected towards every appendage of a favourite system. And this is an appendage of that system which derives all the affections and springs of action in the human mind from self-love. In almost all system-builders of every denomination, there is a vehement desire of simplifying their principles, and reducing all to one. Hence in medicine, the passion for finding a catholicon, or cure of all diseases; and in chemistry, for discovering the true alcahest, or universal dissolvent. Nor have our moralists entirely escaped the contagion. One reduceth all the virtues to *prudence*, and is ready to make it clear as sunshine that there neither is nor can be another source of moral good, but a right conducted self-love: another is equally confident that all the virtues are but different modifications of disinterested *benevolence:* a third will demonstrate to you that *veracity* is the whole duty of man: a fourth, with more ingenuity, and much greater appearance of reason, assures you that the true system of ethics is comprised in one word, *sympathy*.

But to the point in hand: it appears a great objection to the selfish system, that in pity we are affected with a real sorrow for the sufferings of others, or at least that men have universally understood this to be the case, as appears from the very words and phrases expressive of this emotion to be found in all known languages. But to one who has thoroughly imbibed the principles and spirit of a philosophic sect, which hath commonly as violent an appetite for mystery (though under different name, for with the philosopher it is paradox) as any religious sect whatever, how paltry must an objection appear, which hath nothing to support it but the conviction of all mankind, those only excepted whose minds have been perverted by scholastic sophistry!

It is remarkable, that though so many have contended that some fiction of the imagination is absolutely necessary to the production of pity, and though the examples of this emotion are so frequent (I hope, in the theorists themselves no less than in others) as to give ample scope for examination, they are so little agreed what this fiction is. Some contend only, that in witnessing tragedy one is under a sort of momentary

[4] Hawkesworth.

deception, which a very little reflection can correct, and imagines that he is actually witnessing those distresses and miseries which are only represented in borrowed characters, and that the actors are the very persons whom they exhibit. This supposition, I acknowledge, is the most admissible of all. That children and simple people, who are utter strangers to theatrical amusements, are apt at first to be deceived in this manner, is undeniable. That, therefore, through the magical power (if I may call it so) of natural and animated action, a transient illusion somewhat similar may be produced in persons of knowledge and experience, I will not take upon me to controvert. But this hypothesis is not necessarily connected with any particular theory of the passions. The persons for whom we grieve, whether the real objects or only their representatives mistaken for them, are still other persons, and not ourselves. Besides, this was never intended to account but for the degree of emotion in one particular case only.

Others, therefore, who refer every thing to self, will have it, that by a fiction of the mind we instantly conceive some future and similar calamity as coming upon ourselves; and that it is solely this conception, and this dread, which call forth all our sorrow and our tears. Others, not satisfied with this, maintain boldly, that we conceive ourselves to be the persons suffering the miseries related or represented, at the very instant that our pity is raised. When nature is deserted by us, it is no wonder that we should lose our way in the devious tracks of imagination, and not know where to settle.

The first would say, "When I see Garrick in the character of King Lear in the utmost agony of distress, I am so transported with the passions raised in my breast, that I quite forget the tragedian, and imagine that my eyes are fixed on that much injured and most miserable monarch." Says the second, "I am not in the least liable to so gross a blunder; but I cannot help, in consequence of the representation, being struck with the impression that I am soon to be in the same situation, and to be used with the like ingratitude and barbarity." Says the third, "The case is still worse with me; for I conceive myself, and not the player, to be that wretched man at the very time that he is acted. I fancy that I am actually in the midst of the storm, suffering all his anguish, that my daughters have turned me out of doors, and treated me with such unheard-of cruelty and injustice." It is exceeding lucky that there do not oftener follow terrible consequences from these misconceptions. It will be said, "They are transient, and quickly cured by recollection." But however transient, if they really exist, they must exist for some time. Now, if unhappily a man had two of his daughters sitting near him at the very instant he was under this delusion, and if, by a very natural and consequential fiction, he fancied them to be Goneril and Regan, the effects might be fatal to the ladies, though they were the most dutiful children in the world.

It hath never yet been denied (for it is impossible to say what will be denied) that pity influences a person to contribute to relieve the object when it is in his power. But if there is a mistake in the object, there must of necessity be a mistake in the direction of the relief. For instance, you see a man perishing with hunger, and your compassion is raised; now you will pity no longer, say these acute reasoners, than you fancy yourself to suffer. You yourself properly are the sole object of your own pity, and as you desire to relieve the person only whom you pity, if there be any food within your reach, you will no doubt devour it voraciously, in order to allay the famine which you fancy you are enduring; but you will not give one morsel to the wretch who really needs your aid, but who is by no means the object of your regret, for whom you can feel no compunction, and with whose distress (which is quite a foreign matter to you) it is impossible you should be affected, especially when under the power of a passion consisting of unmixed selfishness and malignity. For though, if you did not pity him, you would, on cool reflection, give him some aid, perhaps from principle, perhaps from example, or perhaps from habit, unluckily this accursed pity, this unmixed malignant selfishness, interposeth, to shut your heart against him, and to obstruct the pious purpose.

I know no way of eluding this objection but one, which is indeed a very easy way. It is to introduce another fiction of the imagination, and to say, that when this emotion is raised, I lose all consciousness of my own existence and identity, and fancy that the pitiable object before me is my very self; and that the real I, or what I formerly mistook for myself, is some other body, a mere spectator of my misery, or perhaps nobody at all. Thus unknowingly I may contribute to his relief, when under the strange illusion which makes me fancy that, instead of giving to another, I am taking to myself. But if the man be scrupulously honest, he will certainly restore to me, when I am awake, what I gave him unintentionally in my sleep.

That such fictions may sometimes take place in madness, which almost totally unhinges our mental faculties, I will not dispute; but that such are the natural operations of the passions in a sound state, when the intellectual powers are unimpaired, is what no man would have ever either conceived or advanced, that had not a darling hypothesis to support. And by such arguments, it is certain that every hypothesis whatever may equally be supported. Suppose I have taken it into my head to write a theory of the mind: and, in order to give unity and simplicity to my system, as well as to recommend it by the grace of novelty, I have resolved to deduce all the actions, all the pursuits, and all the passions of men from self-hatred, as the common fountain. If to degrade human nature be so great a recommendation as we find it is to many speculators, as well as to all atheists and fanatics, who happen, on this point, I know not how, to be most cordially united, the theory now suggested is by no means deficient in that sort of merit from which one might expect to it the very best reception. Self-love is certainly no vice, however justly the want of love to our neighbour be accounted one; but if any thing can be called vicious, self-hatred is undoubtedly so.

Let it not be imagined that nothing specious can be urged in favour of this hypothesis; what else, it may be pleaded, could induce the miser to deny himself not only the comforts, but even almost the necessaries of life, to pine for want in the midst of plenty, to live in unintermitted anxiety and terror? All the world sees that it is not to procure his own enjoyment, which he invariably and to the last repudiates. And can any reasonable person be so simple as to believe that it is for the purpose of leaving a fortune to his heir, a man whom he despises, for whose deliverance from perdition he would not part with half-a-crown, and whom of all mankind next to himself he hates the most? What else could induce the sensualist to squander his all in dissipation and debauchery; to rush on ruin certain and foreseen? You call it pleasure. But is he ignorant that his pleasures are more than ten times counterbalanced by the plagues and even torments which they bring? Does the conviction, or even the experience of this deter him? On the contrary, with what steady perseverance, with what determined resolution doth he proceed in his career, not intimidated by the haggard forms which stare him in the face, poverty and infamy, disease and death? What else could induce the man who is reputed covetous, not of money but of fame, that is of wind, to sacrifice his tranquillity, and almost all the enjoyments of life; to spend his days and nights in fruitless disquietude and endless care? Has a bare name, think you, an empty sound, such inconceivable charms? Can a mere nothing serve as a counterpoise to solid and substantial good? Are we not rather imposed upon by appearances, when we conclude this to be his motive? Can we be senseless enough to imagine that it is the bubble reputation (which, were it any thing, a dead man surely cannot enjoy) that the soldier is so infatuated as to seek even in the cannon's mouth? Are not these, therefore, but the various ways of self-destroying, to which, according to their various tastes, men are prompted, by the same universal principle of self-hatred?

If you should insist on certain phenomena, which appear to be irreconcilable to my hypothesis, I think I am provided with an answer. You urge our readiness to resent an affront or injury, real or imagined, which we receive, and which ought to gratify instead of provoking us, on the supposition that we hate ourselves. But may it not be retorted, that its being a gratification is that which excites our resentment, inasmuch as we are enemies to every kind of self-indulgence? If this answer will not suffice, I have another which is excellent. It lies in the definition of the word revenge. Revenge, I pronounce, may be justly "deemed an example of unmixed self-abhorrence and benignity, and may be resolved into that power of imagination, by which we apply the sufferings that we inflict on others to ourselves; we are said to wreak our vengeance no longer than we fancy ourselves to suffer, and to be satiated by reflecting that the sufferings of others are not really ours; that we have been but indulging a dream of self-punishment, from which, when we awake and discover the fiction, our anger instantly subsides, and we are meek as lambs." Is this extravagant? Compare it, I pray you, with the preceding explication of compassion, to which it is a perfect counterpart. Consider seriously, and you will find that it is not in the smallest degree more manifest, that another and not ourselves is the object of our resentment when we are angry, than it is that another and not ourselves is the object of our compassion when we are moved with pity. Both indeed have a self-evidence in them, which, whilst our minds remain unsophisticated by the dogmatism of system, extorts from us an unlimited assent.

SECTION II.—*The author's hypothesis on this subject.*

Where so many have failed of success, it may be thought presumptuous to attempt a decision. But despondency in regard to a question which seems to fall within the reach of our faculties, and is entirely subjected to our observation and experience, must appear to the inquisitive and philosophic mind a still greater fault than even presumption. The latter may occasion the introduction of a false theory, which must necessarily come under the review and correction of succeeding philosophers. And the detection of error proves often instrumental to the discovery of truth. Whereas the former quashes curiosity altogether, and influences one implicitly to abandon an inquiry as utterly undeterminable. I shall therefore now offer a few observations concerning the passions, which, if rightly apprehended and weighed, will, I hope, contribute to the solution of the present question.

My first observation shall be, that almost all the simple passions of which the mind is susceptible may be divided into two classes, the *pleasant* and the *painful.* It is at the same time acknowledged, that the pleasures and the pains created by the different passions, differ considerably from one another, both in kind and degree. Of the former class are love, joy, hope, pride, gratitude; of the latter, hatred, grief, fear, shame, anger. Let it be remarked, that by the name *pride* in the first class, (which I own admits a variety of acceptations,) no more is meant here than the feeling which we have on obtaining the merited approbation of other men, in which sense it stands in direct opposition to *shame* in the second class, or the feeling which we have when conscious of incurring the deserved blame of others. In like manner *gratitude*, or the resentment of favour, is opposed to *anger*, or the resentment of injury. To the second class I might have added *desire* and *aversion*, which give the mind some uneasiness or dissatisfaction with its present state; but these are often the occasion of pleasure, as they are the principal spurs to action, and perhaps more than any other passion relieve the mind from that languor which, according to the just remark of Abbé du Bos, is perfectly oppressive. Besides, as they are perpetually accompanied with some degree of either *hope* or *fear*, generally with both, they are either pleasant or painful as the one or the other preponderates. For these reasons they may be considered as in themselves of an indifferent or intermediate kind.

The second observation is, that there is an attraction or association among the passions, as well as among the ideas of the mind. Rarely any passion comes alone. To investigate the laws of this attraction would be indeed a matter of curious inquiry, but it doth not fall within the limits of the present question. Almost all the other affections attract or excite desire or aversion of some sort or other. The passions which seem to have the least influence on these are joy and grief; and of the two, joy, I believe, will be acknowledged to have less of the attractive power than grief. Joy is the end of desire and the completion of hope; therefore when attained, it not only excludes occasion for the others, but seems, for a while at least, to repel them, as what would give an impertinent interruption to the pleasure resulting from the contemplation of present felicity, with which the mind, under the influence of joy, is engrossed. Grief hath a like tendency. When the mind is overwhelmed by this gloomy passion, it resists the instigations of desire, as what would again, to no purpose, rouse its activity; it disdains hope, it even loathes it as a vain and a delusive dream. The first suggestions of these passions seem but as harbingers to the cutting recollection of former flattering prospects, once too fondly entertained, now utterly extinct, and succeeded by an insupportable and irremediable disappointment, which every recollection serves but to aggravate. Nay, how unaccountable soever it may appear, the mind seems to have a mournful satisfaction in being allowed to indulge its anguish, and to immerse itself wholly in its own afflictions. But this can be affirmed of sorrow only in the extreme. When it begins to subside, or when originally but in a weak degree, it leads the mind to seek relief from desire, and hope, and other passions.—Love naturally associates to it benevolence, which is one species of desire, for here no more is meant by it than a desire of the happiness of the person loved. Hatred as naturally associates malevolence or malice, which is the desire of evil to the person hated.[6]

My third observation is, that pain of every kind generally makes a deeper impression on the imagination than pleasure does, and is longer retained by the memory. It is a common remark of every people and of every age, and consequently hath some foundation in human nature, that benefits are sooner forgotten than injuries, and favours than affronts. Those who are accustomed to attend the theatre will be sensible, that the plots of the best tragedies which they have witnessed are better remembered by them than those of the most celebrated comedies. And indeed every body that reflects may be satisfied that no story takes a firmer hold of the memory than a tale of woe. In civil history, as well as in biography, it is the disastrous, and not the joyous events, which are oftenest recollected and retailed.

The fourth observation is, that from a group of passions (if I may so express myself) associated together, and having the same object, some of which are of the pleasant, others of the painful kind, if the present predominate, there ariseth often a greater and a more durable pleasure to the mind than would result from these, if alone and unmixed. That the case is so,

[6] The ambiguity and even penury of all languages, in relation to our internal feelings, make it very difficult, in treating of them, to preserve at once perspicuity and accuracy. Benevolence is sometimes used, perhaps with little variation from its most common import, for charity or universal love; and love itself will be thought by some to be properly defined by the desire or wish of the happiness of its object. As to the first, it is enough that I have assigned the precise meaning in which I use the term; and in regard to the second, those who are duly attentive to what passes within their own breasts will be sensible, that by love, in the strictest acceptation, is meant a certain pleasurable emotion excited in the mind by a suitable object, to which the desire of the happiness of the object is generally consequent. The felicity of the object may however be such as to leave no room for any desire or wish of ours in regard to it. This holds particularly in our love to God. Besides, there may be a desire of the happiness of others, arising from very different causes, where there is nothing of that sentiment or feeling which is strictly called *love*. I own, at the same time, that the term love is also often used to denote simply benevolence or good-will; as when we are commanded to love all men, known and unknown, good and bad, friendly and injurious. To that tender emotion which qualities supposed amiable alone can excite, the precept surely doth not extend. These things I thought it necessary to observe, in order to prevent mistakes in a case which requires so much precision.

will, I believe, on a careful inquiry, be found to be a matter of experience; how it happens to be so, I am afraid human sagacity will never be able to investigate.

This observation holds especially when the emotions and affections raised in us are derived from sympathy, and have not directly self for the object. Sympathy is not a passion, but that quality of the soul which renders it susceptible of almost any passion, by communication from the bosom of another. It is by sympathy we *rejoice with them that rejoice, and weep with them that weep*. This faculty, however, doth not act with equal strength in these opposite cases, but is much weaker in the first than in the second. It would perhaps be easier to assign the intention of nature in this difference, than the cause of the difference. The miserable need the aid and sympathy of others; the happy do not. I must further observe on this subject, what I believe was hinted once already, that sympathy may be greatly strengthened or weakened by the influence of connected passions. Thus love associates to it benevolence, and both give double force to sympathy. Hatred, on the contrary, associates to it malice, and destroys sympathy.

There are consequently several reasons why a scene of pure unmixed joy, in any work of genius, cannot give a great or lasting pleasure to the mind. First, sympathetic joy is much fainter and more transient than sympathetic grief, and they are generally the sympathetic passions which are infused by poets, orators, painters, and historians: secondly, joy is the least attractive of all the affections. It perhaps can never properly be said to associate to it desire, the great spring of action. The most we can say is, that when it begins to subside it again gives place to desire, this passion being of such a nature, as that it can hardly for any time be banished from the soul. Hence it is that the joy, which has no other foundation but sympathy, quickly tires the mind and runs into satiety. Hence it is, also, that dramatic writers, and even romance writers, make a scene of pure joy always the last scene of the piece, and but a short one. It may just be mentioned, thirdly, not indeed as an argument, (for of its weakness in this respect I am very sensible,) but as an illustration from analogy, that every thing in nature is heightened and set off by its contrary, which, by giving scope for comparison, enhances every excellence. The colours in painting acquire a double lustre from the shades; the harmony in music is greatly improved by a judicious mixture of discords. The whole conduct of life, were it necessary, might exemplify the position. A mixture of pain, then, seems to be of consequence to give strength and stability to pleasure.

The fifth observation is, that under the name *pity* may be

included all the emotions excited by tragedy. In common speech all indeed are included under this name that are excited by that species of eloquence which is denominated the pathetic. The passions moved by tragedy have been commonly said to be *pity* and *terror*. This enumeration is more popular than philosophical, even though adopted by the Stagyrite himself. For what is pity but a participation by sympathy in the woes of others, and the feelings naturally consequent upon them, of whatever kind they be, their fears as well as sorrows? whereas, this way of contradistinguishing terror from pity, would make one who knew nothing of tragedy but from the definition, imagine that it were intended to make us compassionate others in trouble, and dread mischief to ourselves. If this were really the case, I believe there are few or none who would find any pleasure in this species of entertainment. Of this there occurs an example, when, as hath sometimes happened, in the midst of the performance, the audience are alarmed with the sudden report that the house hath taken fire, or when they hear a noise which makes them suspect that the roof or walls are falling. Then, indeed, terror stares in every countenance; but such a terror as gives no degree of pleasure, and is so far from coalescing with the passions raised by the tragedy, that, on the contrary, it expels them altogether, and leaves not in the mind, for some time at least, another idea or reflection but what concerns personal safety.

On the other hand, if all the sympathetic affections excited by the theatrical representation were to be severally enumerated, I cannot see why hope, indignation, love and hatred, gratitude and resentment, should not be included as well as fear. To account then for the pleasure which we find in pity, is, in a great measure, to give a solution of the question under review. I do not say that this will satisfy in every case. On the contrary, there are many cases in which Abbé du Bos's account above recited, of the pleasure arising from the agitation and fluctuation of the passions, is the only solution that can be given.

My sixth and last observation on this head is, that pity is not a simple passion, but a group of passions, strictly united by association, and as it were blended by centring in the same object. Of these some are pleasant, some painful; commonly the pleasant preponderate. It hath been remarked already, that love attracts benevolence, benevolence quickens sympathy. The same attraction takes place inversely, though not, perhaps, with equal strength. Sympathy engages benevolence, and benevolence love. That benevolence, or the habit of wishing happiness to another, from whatever motive it hath originally sprung, will at length draw in love, might be proved from a thousand instances.

In the party divisions which obtain in some countries, it often happens, that a man is at first induced to take a side, purely from a motive of interest; for some time, from this motive solely, he wishes the success of the party with which he is embarked. From a habit of wishing this, he will continue to wish it, when, by a change of circumstances, his own interest is no longer connected with it; nay, which is more strange, he will even contract such a love and attachment to the party, as to promote their interest in direct opposition to his own. That commiseration or sympathy in woe hath still a stronger tendency to engage our love is evident.

This is the only rational account that can be given, why mothers of a humane disposition generally love most the sickliest child in the family, though perhaps far from being the loveliest in respect either of temper or of other qualities. The habit of commiseration habituates them to the feeling and exertion of benevolence. Benevolence, habitually felt and exerted, confirms and augments their love. "Nothing," says Mr. Hume,[6] "endears so much a friend as sorrow for his death. The pleasure of his company hath not so powerful an influence." Distress to the pitying eye diminishes every fault, and sets off every good quality in the brightest colours. Nor is it a less powerful advocate for the mistress than for the friend: often does the single circumstance of misfortune subdue all resentment of former coldness and ill usage, and make a languid and dying passion revive and flame out with a violence which it is impossible any longer to withstand. Every body acknowledges that beauty is never so irresistible as in tears. Distress is commonly sufficient, with those who are not very hard-hearted or pitiless (for these words are nearly of the same import), to make even enmity itself relent.

There are, then, in *pity* these three different emotions, first, *commiseration*, purely painful; secondly, *benevolence*, or a desire of the relief and happiness of the object pitied, a passion, as was already observed, of the intermediate kind; thirdly, *love*, in which is always implied one of the noblest and most exquisite pleasures whereof the soul is susceptible, and which is itself, in most cases, sufficient to give a counterpoise of pleasure to the whole.

For the further confirmation of this theory, let it be remarked, that orators and poets, in order to strengthen this association and union, are at pains to adorn the character of him for whom they would engage our pity, with every amiable quality which, in a consistency with probability, they can crowd into it. On the contrary, when the character is hateful, the person's misfortunes are unpitied. Sometimes they even occasion a pleasure

[6] Essay on Tragedy.

of a very different kind; namely, that which the mind naturally takes in viewing the just punishment of demerit. When the character has such a mixture of good and odious qualities, as that we can neither withhold our commiseration, nor bestow our love; the mind is then torn opposite ways at once, by passions which, instead of uniting, repel one another. Hence the piece becomes shocking and disgustful. Such, to a certain degree, in my judgment, the tragedy of *Venice Preserved*, wherein the hero, notwithstanding several good qualities, is a villain and a traitor, will appear to every well disposed mind. All the above cases, if attended to, will be found exactly to tally with the hypothesis here suggested.

All the answer then which I am able to produce, upon the whole, and which results from the foregoing observations, is this: the principal pleasure in pity ariseth from its own nature, or from the nature of those passions of which it is compounded, and not from any thing extrinsic or adventitious. The tender emotions of love which enter into the composition, sweeten the commiseration or sympathetic sorrow; the commiseration gives a stability to those emotions, with which otherwise the mind would soon be cloyed, when directed towards a person, imaginary, unknown, or with whom we are totally unacquainted. The very benevolence or wish of contributing to his relief, affords an occupation to the thoughts, which agreeably rouses them. It impels the mind to devise expedients by which the unhappy person (if our pity is excited by some calamitous incident) may be, or (if it is awaked by the art of the poet, the orator, or the historian) might have been, relieved from his distress. Yet the whole movement of the combined affections is not converted into pleasure; for though the uneasiness of the melancholy passions be overpowered, it is not effaced by something stronger of an opposite kind.

Mr. Hume, indeed, in his manner of expressing himself on this article, hath not observed either an entire uniformity, or his usual precision. I should rather say, from some dubiousness in relation to the account he was giving, he seems to have, in part, retracted what he had been establishing, and thus leaves the reader with an alternative in the decision. First he tells us, that "the whole movement of those [melancholy] passions is converted into pleasure." Afterwards, "the latter [the sentiments of beauty] being the predominate emotion, seize the whole mind, and convert the former [the impulse or vehemence arising from sorrow, compassion, indignation] into themselves;" he adds, by way of correction, "or at least tincture them so strongly, as totally to alter their nature." Again, "the soul feels, on the whole, a strong movement, which is altogether delightful." All this, I acknowledge, appears to me to be neither sufficiently definite, nor quite intelligible.

But passing that, I shall only subjoin, that the combination of the passions in the instance under our examination, is not like the blending of colours, two of which will produce a third, wherein you can discern nothing of the original hues united in producing it; but it rather resembles a mixture of tastes, when you are quite sensible of the different savours of the ingredient. Thus blue and yellow mingled make green, in which you discover no tint of either; and all the colours of a rainbow, blended, constitute a white, which appears to the eye as simple and original as any of them, and perfectly unlike to each. On the other hand, in eating meat with salt, for instance, we taste both distinctly; and though the latter singly would be disagreeable, the former is rendered more agreeable by the mixture than it would otherwise have been.

I own, indeed, that certain adventitious circumstances may contribute to heighten the effect. But these cannot be regarded as essential to the passion. They occur occasionally. Some of them actually occur but seldom. Of this sort is the satisfaction which ariseth from a sense of our own ease and security, compared with the calamity and the danger of another.

> 'Tis pleasant, safely to behold from shore
> The rolling ship, and hear the tempest roar:
> Not that another's pain is our delight,
> But pains unfelt produce the pleasing sight.
> 'Tis pleasant also to behold from far
> The moving legions mingled in the war. [7]

The poet hath hit here on some of the very few circumstances in which it would be natural to certain tempers, not surely the most humane, to draw comfort in the midst of sympathetic sorrow, from such a comparison. The reflection, in my opinion, occurs almost only when a very small change in external situation, as a change in place to the distance of a few furlongs, would put us into the same lamentable circumstances which we are commiserating in others. Even something of this kind will present itself to our thoughts, when there is no particular object to demand our pity. A man who, in tempestuous weather, sits snug in a close house, near a good fire, and hears the wind and rain beating upon the roof and windows, will naturally think of his own comfortable situation, compared with that of a traveller, who, perhaps, far from shelter, is exposed to all the violence of the tempest. But in such cases, a difference, as I said, in a single accidental circumstance, which may happen at any time, is

[7] Suave mari magno, turbantibus æquora ventis,
E terra magnum alterius spectare laborem,
Non quia vexari quenquam 'st jucunda voluptas,
Sed quibus ipse malis careas, quia cernere suave 'st:
Suave etiam belli certamina magna tueri,
Per campos instructa, tua sine parte perîcli. LUCRET. l. 2.

all that is necessary to put a man in the same disastrous situation, wherein he either sees or conceives others to be. And the very slightness of the circumstance which would have been sufficient to reverse the scene, makes him so ready to congratulate with himself on his better luck. Whereas nothing is less natural, and I will venture to say, less common, than such a reflection, when the differences are many, and of a kind which cannot be reckoned merely accidental; as when the calamity is what the person pitying must consider himself as not liable to, or in the remotest hazard of. A man who, with the most undissembled compassion, bewails the wretched and undeserved fate of Desdemona, is not apt to think of himself, how fortunate he is in not being the wife of a credulous, jealous, and revengeful husband; though perhaps a girl who hath lately rejected a suitor of this character, will reflect with great complacency on the escape she has made.

Another adventitious source of pleasure is the satisfaction that results from the conscious exercise of the humane affections, which it is our duty to cherish and improve. I mention this as adventitious, because, though not unnatural, I do not imagine that the sensations of sympathetic sorrow, either always or immediately, give rise to this reflection. Children, and even savages, are susceptible of pity, who think no more of claiming any merit to themselves on this score, than they think of claiming merit from their feeling the natural appetites of hunger and thirst. Nay, it is very possible that persons may know its power and sweetness too, when, through the influence of education and bad example, they consider it as a weakness or blemish in their disposition, and as such endeavour to conceal and stifle it. A certain degree of civilization seems to be necessary to make us thoroughly sensible of its beauty and utility, and consequently that it ought to be cultivated. Bigotry may teach a man to think inhumanity, in certain circumstances, a virtue. Yet nature will reclaim, and may make him, in spite of the dictates of a misguided conscience, feel all the tenderness of pity to the heretic, who, in his opinion, has more than merited the very worst that can be inflicted on him.

I acknowledge that, on the other hand, when the sentiment comes generally to prevail, that compassion is in itself praiseworthy, it may be rendered a source of much more self-satisfaction to the vain-glorious, than reasonably it ought to yield. Such persons gladly lay hold of every handle which serves to raise them in their own esteem. And I make no doubt that several, from this very motive, have exalted this principle as immoderately as others have vilified it. Every good man will agree, that this is the case when people consider it as either a veil for their vices, or an atonement for the neglect of their duty. For my own part, I am inclined to think, that those who are most ready to abuse it thus, are not the most remarkable for any exercise of it by which society can be profited. There is a species of deception in the case, which it is not beside the purpose briefly to unravel.

It hath been observed that sense invariably makes a stronger impression than memory, and memory a stronger than imagination; yet there are particular circumstances which appear to form an exception, and to give an efficacy to the ideas of imagination, beyond what either memory or sense can boast. So great is the anomaly which sometimes displays itself in human characters, that it is not impossible to find persons who are quickly made to cry at seeing a tragedy, or reading a romance, which they know to be fictions, and yet are both inattentive and unfeeling in respect of the actual objects of compassion who live in their neighbourhood, and are daily under their eye. Nevertheless, this is an exception from the rule, more in appearance than in reality. The cases are not parallel: there are certain circumstances which obtain in the one, and have no place in the other; and to these peculiarities the difference in the effect is solely imputable. What follows will serve fully to explain my meaning.

Men may be of a selfish, contracted, and even avaricious disposition, who are not what we should denominate hard-hearted, or insusceptible of sympathetic feeling. Such will gladly enjoy the luxury of pity (as Hawkesworth terms it) when it nowise interferes with their more powerful passions; that is, when it comes unaccompanied with a demand upon their pockets. With the tragic or the romantic hero or heroine they most cordially sympathize, because the only tribute which wretches of their dignity exact from them is sighs and tears. And of these their consciences inform them, to their inexpressible consolation, that they are no niggards. But the case is totally different with living objects. Barren tears and sighs will not satisfy these. Hence it is that people's avarice, a most formidable adversary to the unhappy, is interested to prevent their being moved by such, and to make them avoid, as much as possible, every opportunity of knowing or seeing them.[8] But as that cannot always be

[8] In the parable of the compassionate Samaritan, Luke x. 30, &c. this disposition to shun the sight of misery, which one is resolved not to redress, is finely touched in the conduct of the priest and the Levite, who, when they espied a person naked, wounded, and almost expiring on the road, are said to have "passed by on the other side." Indeed, in the account given of the Levite in our version, there is a something which, to me, has a contradictory appearance. He "came and looked on him, and passed by on the other side." There is not a vestige of this inconsistency in the original, which says simply, ελθων και ιδων αντιπαρηλθεν, the meaning of which plainly is, "travelling that way, and seeing one in this wretched plight, he kept on the other side of the road, and passed on." In such a case, a man who is not quite obdurate, would avoid the cutting reflection, that he knows any thing of the matter. And though he must be conscious that he knew a little, and might have known

done, as commiseration is attended with benevolence, and as benevolence itself, if not gratified, by our giving relief when it is in our power, embitters the pleasure which would otherwise result from pity, as the refusal is also attended with self-reproach; a person of such a temper, strongly, and for the most part effectually, resists his being moved. He puts his ingenuity to the rack, in order to satisfy himself that he ought not to be affected. He is certain that the person is not a proper object of beneficence, he is convinced that his distress is more pretended than real; or, if that cannot be alleged, the man hath surely brought it on by his vices, therefore he deserves to suffer, and is nowise entitled to our pity; or at least he makes not a good use of what may charitably, but injudiciously, be bestowed upon him. Such are the common shifts by which selfishness eludes the calls of humanity, and chooses to reserve all its worthless stock of pity for fictitious objects, or for those who, in respect of time, or place, or eminence, are beyond its reach.

For these reasons, I am satisfied that compassion alone, especially that displayed on occasion of witnessing public spectacles, is at best but a very weak evidence of philanthropy. The only proof that is entirely unequivocal, is actual beneficence, when one seeks out the real objects of commiseration, not as a matter of self-indulgence, but in order to bring relief to those who need it, to give hope to the desponding, and comfort to the sorrowful, for the sake of which one endures the sight of wretchedness, when, instead of giving pleasure, it distresseth every feeling heart. Such, however, enjoy at length a luxury far superior to that of pity, the godlike luxury of dispelling grief, communicating happiness, and doing good.

more if he would, he is glad to gloss his inhumanity even to himself, with some pretext of hurry or thoughtlessness, or anything that may conceal the naked truth,—a truth which he is as averse to discover in himself, as he is to see in another the misery which he is determined not to relieve.

THE

PHILOSOPHY OF RHETORIC.

BOOK II.

THE FOUNDATIONS AND ESSENTIAL PROPERTIES OF ELOCUTION.

CHAPTER I.

The Nature and Characters of the Use which gives Law to Language.

ELOQUENCE hath always been considered, and very justly, as having a particular connexion with language. It is the intention of eloquence to convey our sentiments into the minds of others, in order to produce a certain effect upon them. Language is the only vehicle by which this conveyance can be made. The art of speaking, then, is not less necessary to the orator than the art of thinking. Without the latter, the former could not have existed. Without the former, the latter would be ineffective. Every tongue whatever is founded in use or custom,

> ——— Whose arbitrary sway
> Words and the forms of language must obey.[9] FRANCIS.

Language is purely a species of fashion (for this holds equally of every tongue) in which, by the general but tacit consent of the people of a particular state or country, certain sounds come to be appropriated to certain things, as their signs, and certain ways of inflecting and combining those sounds come to be established, as denoting the relations which subsist among the things signified.

It is not the business of grammar, as some critics seem preposterously to imagine, to give law to the fashions which regulate our speech. On the contrary, from its conformity to these, and from that alone, it derives all its authority and value. For, what is the grammar of any language? It is no other than

[9] ——————— Usus,
Quem penes arbitrium est et jus et norma loquendi.
HOR. De Arte Poet.

a collection of general observations methodically digested, and comprising all the modes previously and independently established, by which the significations, derivations, and combinations of words in that language are ascertained. It is of no consequence here to what causes originally these modes or fashions owe their existence, to imitation, to reflection, to affectation, or to caprice; they no sooner obtain and become general, than they are laws of the language, and the grammarian's only business is to note, collect, and methodize them. Nor does this truth concern only those more comprehensive analogies or rules, which affect whole classes of words, such as nouns, verbs, and the other parts of speech; but it concerns every individual word, in the inflecting or the combining of which a particular mode hath prevailed. Every single anomaly, therefore, though departing from the rule assigned to the other words of the same class, and on that account called an exception, stands on the same basis on which the rules of the tongue are founded, custom having prescribed for it a separate rule.[1]

The truth of this position hath never, for aught I can remember, been directly controverted by anybody; yet it is certain, that both critics and grammarians often argue in such a way as is altogether inconsistent with it. What, for example, shall we make of that complaint of Doctor Swift, "that our language, in many instances, offends against every part of grammar?"[2] Or what could the doctor's notion of grammar be, when expressing himself in this manner? Some notion, possibly, he had of grammar in the abstract, an universal archetype by which the particular grammars of all different tongues ought to be regulated. If this was his meaning, I cannot say whether he is in the right or in the wrong in this accusation. I acknowledge myself to be entirely ignorant of this ideal grammar; nor can I form a conjecture where its laws are to be learnt. One thing, indeed, every smatterer in philosophy will tell us, that there can be no natural connexion between the sounds of any language, and the things signified, or between the modes of inflection and combination and the relations they are intended to express. Perhaps he meant the grammar of some other language; if so, the charge was certainly true, but not to the purpose, since we can say with equal truth, of every language, that it offends against the grammar of every other language whatsoever. If he meant the English

[1] Thus in the two verbs *call* and *shall*, the second person singular of the former is *callest*, agreeably to the general rule, the second person singular of the latter is *shalt*, agreeably to a particular rule affecting that verb. To say *shallest* for *shalt*, would be as much a barbarism, though according to the general rule, as to say *calt* for *callest*, which is according to no rule.

[2] Letter to the Lord High Treasurer, &c.

grammar, I would ask, whence has that grammar derived its laws? If from general use, (and I cannot conceive another origin,) then it must be owned, that there is a general use in that language as well as in others; and it were absurd to accuse the language which is purely what is conformable to general use in speaking and writing, as offending against general use. But if he meant to say, that there is no fixed, established, or general use in the language, that it is quite irregular, he hath been very unlucky in his manner of expressing himself. Nothing is more evident, than that where there is no law there is no transgression. In that case, he ought to have said that it is not susceptible of grammar; which, by the way, would not have been true of English, or indeed of any the most uncultivated language on the earth.

It is easy then to assign the reason, why the justness of the complaint, as Doctor Lowth observes,[3] has never yet been questioned; it is purely because, not being understood, it hath never been minded. But if, according to this ingenious gentleman, the words *our language*, have, by a new kind of trope, been used to denote those who speak and write English, and no more have been intended than to signify, that our best speakers and most approved authors frequently offend against the rules of grammar, that is, against the general use of language, I shall not here enter on a discussion of the question. Only let us rest in these as fixed principles, that use, or the custom of speaking, is the sole original standard of conversation, as far as regards the expression, and the custom of writing is the sole standard of style: that the latter comprehends the former, and something more; that to the tribunal of use, as to the supreme authority, and consequently, in every grammatical controversy, the last resort, we are entitled to appeal from the laws and the decisions of grammarians; and that this order of subordination ought never, on any account, to be reversed.[4]

But if use be here a matter of such consequence, it will be necessary, before advancing any further, to ascertain precisely what it is. We shall otherwise be in danger, though we agree about the name, of differing widely in the notion that we assign to it.

SECTION I.—*Reputable Use.*

In what extent then must the word be understood? It is sometimes called *general use;* yet is it not manifest that the

[3] Preface to his Introduction to English Grammar.

[4] Non ratione nititur analogia, sed exemplo: nec lex est loquendi, sed observatio: ut ipsam analogiam nulla res alia fecerit quam consuetudo. QUINT. Inst. l. i. c. 6.

generality of people speak and write very badly? Nay, is not this a truth that will be even generally acknowledged? It will be so; and this very acknowledgment shows that many terms and idioms may be common, which nevertheless, have not the general sanction, no, nor even the suffrage of those that use them. The use here spoken of, implies not only *currency*, but *vogue*. It is properly *reputable custom*.

This leads to a distinction between good use and bad use in language, the former of which will be found to have the approbation of those who have not themselves attained it. The far greater part of mankind, perhaps ninety-nine of a hundred, are, by reason of poverty and other circumstances, deprived of the advantages of education, and condemned to toil for bread, almost incessantly, in some narrow occupation. They have neither the leisure nor the means of attaining any knowledge, except what lies within the contracted circle of their several professions. As the ideas which occupy their minds are few, the portion of the language known to them must be very scanty. It is impossible that our language of words should outstrip our knowledge of things. It may, and often doth, come short of it. Words may be remembered as sounds, but cannot be understood as signs, whilst we remain unacquainted with the things signified.

Hence it will happen, that in the lower walks of life, from the intercourse which all ranks occasionally have with one another, the people will frequently have occasion to hear words of which they never had occasion to learn the meaning. These they will pick up and remember, produce and misapply. But there is rarely any uniformity in such blunders, or any thing determinate in the senses they give to words which are not within their sphere. Nay, they are not themselves altogether unconscious of this defect. It often ariseth from an admiration of the manner of their superiors, and from an ill-judged imitation of their way of speaking, that the greatest errors of the illiterate, in respect of conversation, proceed. And were they sensible how widely different their use and application of such words is, from that of those whom they affect to imitate, they would renounce their own immediately.

But it may be said, and said with truth, that in such subjects as are within their reach, many words and idioms prevail among the populace which, notwithstanding a use pretty uniform and extensive, are considered as corrupt, and like counterfeit money, though common, not valued. This is the case particularly with those terms and phrases which critics have denominated *vulgarisms*. Their use is not reputable. On the contrary, we always associate with it such notions of meanness, as suit those orders of men amongst whom chiefly the use is found. Hence it is that many, who have contracted a habit of employing such idioms, do not approve them; and though, through negligence, they frequently fall into them in conversation, they carefully avoid them in writing, or even in a solemn speech on any important occasion. Their currency, therefore, is without authority and weight. The tattle of children hath a currency, but, however universal their manner of corrupting words may be among themselves, it can never establish what is accounted use in language. Now, what children are to men, that precisely the ignorant are to the knowing.

From the practice of those who are conversant in any art, elegant or mechanical, we always take the sense of the terms and phrases belonging to that art; in like manner, from the practice of those who have had a liberal education, and are therefore presumed to be best acquainted with men and things, we judge of the general use in language. If in this particular there be any deference to the practice of the great and rich, it is not ultimately because they are greater and richer than others, but because, from their greatness and riches, they are imagined to be wiser and more knowing. The source, therefore, of that preference which distinguisheth good use from bad in language, is a natural propension of the human mind to believe that those are the best judges of the proper signs, and of the proper application of them, who understand best the things which they represent.

But who are they that in the public estimation are possessed of this character? This question is of the greatest moment for ascertaining that use which is entitled to the epithets reputable and good. Vaugelas makes them in France to be "the soundest part of the court, and the soundest part of the authors of the age."[5] With us Britons, the first part at least of this description will not answer. In France, which is a pure monarchy, as the dependence of the inferior orders is much greater, their submission to their superiors, and the humble respect which in every instance they show them, seem, in our way of judging, to border even upon adoration. With us, on the contrary, who in our spirit, as well as in the constitution of our government, have more of the republican than of the monarchical, there is no remarkable partiality in favour of courtiers. At least their being such rarely enhanceth our opinion either of their abilities or of their virtues.

I would not by this be understood to signify, that the primary principle which gives rise to the distinction between good use and bad in language, is different in different countries. It is not originally, even in France, a deference to power, but to

5 "Voici comme on definit le bon usage. C'est la façon de parler de la plus saine partie de la cour, conformément à la façon d'écrire de la plus saine partie des auteurs du tems." Preface aux Remarques sur la Langue Françaíse.

wisdom. Only it must be remarked, that the tendency of the imagination is to accumulate all great qualities into the same character. Wherever we find one or two of these, we naturally presume the rest. This is particularly true of those qualities, which by their immediate consequences strongly affect the external senses. We are in a manner dazzled by them.—Hence it happens, that it is difficult even for a man of discernment, till he be better instructed by experience, to restrain a veneration for the judgment of a person of uncommon splendour and magnificence; as if one who is more powerful and opulent than his neighbours were of necessity wiser too. Now, this original bias of the mind some political constitutions serve to strengthen, others to correct.

But without resting the matter entirely on the difference in respect of government between France and Britain, the British court is commonly too fluctuating an object. Use in language requires firmer ground to stand upon. No doubt, the conversation of men of rank and eminence, whether of the court or not, will have its influence. And in what concerns merely the pronunciation, it is the only rule to which we can refer the matter in every doubtful case; but in what concerns the words themselves, their construction and application, it is of importance to have some certain, steady, and well-known standard to recur to, a standard which every one hath access to canvass and examine.

And this can be no other than authors of reputation. Accordingly, we find that these are, by universal consent, in actual possession of this authority; as to this tribunal, when any doubt arises, the appeal is always made.

I choose to name them authors of reputation, rather than good authors, for two reasons: first, because it is more strictly conformable to the truth of the case. It is solely the esteem of the public, and not their intrinsic merit (though these two go generally together), which raises them to this distinction, and stamps a value on their language. Secondly, this character is more definitive than the other, and therefore more extensively intelligible. Between two or more authors, different readers will differ exceedingly, as to the preference in point of merit, who agree perfectly as to the respective places they hold in the favour of the public. You may find persons of a taste so particular as to prefer Parnell to Milton; but you will hardly find a person that will dispute the superiority of the latter in the article of fame. For this reason, I affirm that Vaugelas' definition labours under an essential defect; inasmuch as it may be difficult to meet with two persons whose judgments entirely coincide in determining who are the sounder part of the court, or of the authors of the age. I need scarcely add, that when I speak of reputation, I mean not only in regard to knowledge, but in regard to the talent of communicating knowledge. I could name writers, who, in respect of the first, have been justly valued by the public, but who, on account of a supposed deficiency in respect of the second, are considered as of no authority in language.

Nor is there the least ground to fear that we should be cramped here within too narrow limits. In the English tongue there is a plentiful supply of noted writings in all the various kinds of composition, in prose and verse, serious and ludicrous, grave and familiar. Agreeably then to this first qualification of the term, we must understand to be comprehended under general use, *whatever modes of speech are authorized as good by the writings of a great number, if not the majority, of celebrated authors.*

SECTION II.—*National Use.*

Another qualification of the term *use* which deserves our attention, is that it must be *national.* This I consider in a twofold view, as it stands opposed both to *provincial* and to *foreign.*

In every province there are peculiarities of dialect which affect not only the pronunciation and the accent, but even the inflection and the combination of words, whereby their idiom is distinguished both from that of the nation and from that of every other province. The narrowness of the circle to which the currency of the words and phrases of such dialects is confined, sufficiently discriminates them from that which is properly styled the language, and which commands a circulation incomparably wider. This is one reason, I imagine, why the term *use,* on this subject, is commonly accompanied with the epithet *general.* In the use of provincial idioms, there is, it must be acknowledged, a pretty considerable concurrence both of the middle and of the lower ranks. But still this use is bounded by the province, county, or district, which gives name to the dialect, and beyond which its peculiarities are sometimes unintelligible, and always ridiculous. But the language, properly so called, is found current, especially in the upper and the middle ranks, over the whole British empire. Thus, though in every province they ridicule the idiom of every other province, they all vail to the English idiom, and scruple not to acknowledge its superiority over their own.

For example, in some parts of Wales, (if we may credit Shakspeare,[5]) the common people say *goot* for good; in the south of Scotland they said *gude,* and in the north *gueed.* Wherever one of these pronunciations prevails, you will never

[5] Fluellen in Henry V.

hear from a native either of the other two; but the word *good* is to be heard every where from natives as well as strangers; nor do the people ever dream that there is any thing laughable in it, however much they are disposed to laugh at the county-accents and idioms which they discern in one another. Nay more, though the people of distant provinces do not understand one another, they mostly all understand one who speaks properly. It is a just and curious observation of Dr. Kenrick, that "the case of languages, or rather speech, being quite contrary to that of science, in the former the ignorant understand the learned better than the learned do the ignorant; in the latter, it is otherwise."[6]

Hence it will perhaps be found true, upon inquiry, notwithstanding its paradoxical appearance, that though it be very uncommon to speak or write pure English, yet, of all the idioms subsisting amongst us, that to which we give the character of purity is the commonest. The faulty idioms do not jar more with true English, than they do with one another; so that, in order to our being satisfied of the truth of the apparent paradox, it is requisite only that we remember that these idioms are diverse one from another, though they come under the common denomination of *impure*. Those who wander from the road may be incomparably more than those who travel in it; and yet, if it be into a thousand different bypaths that they deviate, there may not in any one of these be found so many as those whom you will meet upon the king's highway.

What hath been now said of provincial dialects, may, with very little variation, be applied to professional dialects, or the cant which is sometimes observed to prevail among those of the same profession or way of life. The currency of the latter cannot be so exactly circumscribed as that of the former, whose distinction is purely local; but their use is not on that account either more extensive or more reputable. Let the following serve as instances of this kind. *Advice*, in the commercial idiom, means information or intelligence; *nervous*, in open defiance of analogy, doth in the medical cant, as Johnson expresseth it, denote, having weak nerves; and the word *turtle*, though pre-occupied time immemorial by a species of dove, is, as we learn from the same authority, employed by sailors and gluttons to signify a tortoise.[7]

It was remarked, that national might also be opposed to foreign. I imagine it is too evident to need illustration, that the introduction of extraneous words and idioms, from other languages and foreign nations, cannot be a smaller transgression against the established custom of the English tongue,

[6] Rhet. Gram. chap. ii. sect. 4.
[7] See those words in the English Dictionary.

than the introduction of words and idioms peculiar to some precincts of England, or at least somewhere current within the British pale. The only material difference between them is, that the one is more commonly the error of the learned, the other of the vulgar. But if, in this view, the former is entitled to greater indulgence from the respect paid to learning; in another view, it is entitled to less, as it is much more commonly the result of affectation. Thus two essential qualities of usage, in regard to language, have been settled, that it be both *reputable* and *national.*

SECTION III.—*Present Use.*

But there will naturally arise here another question, "Is not use, even good and national use, in the same country, different in different periods? And if so, to the usage of what period shall we attach ourselves, as the proper rule? If you say *the present*, as it may reasonably be expected that you will, the difficulty is not entirely removed. In what extent of signification must we understand the word *present?* How far may we safely range in quest of authorities? or, at what distance backwards from this moment are authors still to be accounted as possessing a legislative voice in language?" To this I own it is difficult to give an answer with all the precision that might be desired. Yet it is certain, that when we are in search of precedents for any word or idiom, there are certain mounds which we cannot overleap with safety. For instance, the authority of Hooker or of Raleigh, however great their merit and their fame be, will not now be admitted in support of a term or expression not to be found in any good writer of a later date.

In truth, the boundary must not be fixed at the same distance in every subject. Poetry hath ever been allowed a wider range than prose; and it is but just that, by an indulgence of this kind, some compensation should be made for the peculiar restraints she is laid under by the measure. Nor is this only a matter of convenience to the poet; it is also a matter of gratification to the reader. Diversity in the style relieves the ear, and prevents its being tired with the too frequent recurrence of the rhymes, or sameness of the metre. But still there are limits to this diversity. The authority of Milton and of Waller, on this article, remains as yet unquestioned. I should not think it prudent often to introduce words or phrases of which no example could be produced since the days of Spenser and of Shakspeare.

And even in prose, the bounds are not the same for every kind of composition. In matters of science, for instance, whose terms, from the nature of the thing, are not capable of such a currency as those which belong to ordinary subjects, and are within the reach of ordinary readers, there is no necessity of confining an author within a very narrow circle. But in composing pieces which come under this last denomination, as history, romance, travels, moral essays, familiar letters, and the like, it is safest for an author to consider those words and idioms as obsolete, which have been disused by all good authors for a longer period than the age of man extends to. It is not by ancient, but by present use, that our style must be regulated. And that use can never be denominated present, which hath been laid aside time immemorial, or, which amounts to the same thing, falls not within the knowledge or remembrance of any now living.[8]

This remark not only affects terms and phrases, but also the declension, combination, and the construction of words. Is it not then surprising to find, that one of Lowth's penetration should think a single person entitled to revive a form of inflection in a particular word, which had been rejected by all good writers, of every denomination, for more than a hundred and fifty years?[9] But if present use is to be denounced for ancient, it will be necessary to determine at what precise period antiquity is to be regarded as a rule. One inclines to remove the standard to the distance of a century and a half; another may, with as good reason, fix it three centuries backwards, and another six. And if the language of any of these periods is to be judged by the use of any other, it will be found, no doubt, entirely barbarous. To me it is so evident, either that the present use must be the standard of the present language, or that the language admits no standard whatsoever, that I cannot conceive a clearer or more indisputable principle, from which to bring an argument to support it.

Yet it is certain, that even some of our best critics and grammarians talk occasionally as if they had a notion of some other standard, though they never give us a single hint to direct us where to search for it. Dr. Johnson, for example, in the preface to his very valuable dictionary, acknowledges properly the absolute dominion of custom over language, and yet, in the explanation of particular words, expresseth himself sometimes

[8] Nam fuerit pene ridiculum malle sermonem quo locuti sunt homines, quam quo loquantur. QUINT. Inst. l. i. cap. 6.

[9] Introd. &c. In a note on the irregular verb *sit*, he says, "Dr. Middleton hath, with great propriety, restored the true participle *sitten*." Would he not have acted with as great propriety, had he restored the true participles, *pight* for *pitched*, *raught* for *reached*, *blent* for *blended*, and *shright* for *shrieked*, on full as good authority, the authority of Spenser, one of the sweetest of our ancient bards? And why might not Dr. Lowth himself have, with great propriety, restored the true participles *hitten*, *casten*, *letten*, *putten*, *setten*, *shutten*, *slitten*, *splitten*, *founden*, *grounden*, of the verbs *hit*, *cast*, *let*, *put*, *set*, *shut*, *slit*, *split*, *find*, *grind*: for it would not be impossible to produce antiquated authors in support of all these.—Besides, they are all used to this day in some provincial dialects.

in a manner that is inconsistent with this doctrine, "This word," says he in one place, "though common, and used by the best writers, is perhaps barbarous."[1] I have always understood a barbarism in speech to be a term or expression totally unsupported by the present usage of good writers in the language. A meaning very different is suggested here, but what that meaning is it will not be easy to conjecture. Nor has this celebrated writer given us, on the word *barbarous*, any definition of the term which will throw light on his application of it in the passage quoted. I entirely agree with Doctor Priestley, that it will never be the arbitrary rules of any man, or body of men whatever, that will ascertain the language,[2] there being no other dictator here but use.

It is indeed easier to discover the aim of our critics in their observations on this subject, than the meaning of the terms which they employ. These are often employed without precision; their aim, however, is generally good. It is, as much as possible, to give a check to innovation. But the means which they use for this purpose have sometimes even a contrary tendency. If you will replace what hath been long since expunged from the language, and extirpate what is firmly rooted, undoubtedly you yourself become an innovator. If you desert the present use, and by your example at least, establish it as a maxim, that every critic may revive at pleasure old-fashioned terms, inflections, and combinations, and make such alterations on words as will bring them nearer to what he supposeth to be the etymon, there can be nothing fixed or stable on the subject. Possibly you prefer the usage that prevailed in the reign of Queen Elizabeth; another may, with as good reason, have a partiality for that which subsisted in the days of Chaucer. And with regard to etymology, about which grammarians make so much useless bustle, if every one hath a privilege of altering words, according to his own opinion of their origin, the opinions of the learned being on this subject so various, nothing but a general chaos can ensue.

On the other hand, it may be said, "Are we to catch at every new-fashioned term and phrase which whim or affectation may invent, and folly circulate? Can this ever tend to give either dignity to our style, or permanency to our language?" It cannot, surely. This leads to a further explanation and limitation of the term *present use*, to prevent our being misled by a mere name. It is possible, nay, it is common, for men, in avoiding one error, to run into another and a worse.[3] There is a mean in every thing. I have purposely avoided the expressions *recent use* and *modern use*, as these seem to stand in direct

[1] See the word *Nowadays*.
[2] Preface to his Rudiments of English Grammar.
[3] In vitium ducit culpæ fuga, si caret arte. Hor. De Arte Poet.

opposition to what is *ancient*. But I have used the word *present* which, in respect of place, is always opposed to *absent*, and in respect of time, to *past* or *future*, that now have no existence. When, therefore, the word is used of language, its proper contrary is not ancient but *obsolete*. Besides, though I have acknowledged language to be a species of *mode* or *fashion*, as doubtless it is, yet, being much more permanent than articles of apparel, furniture, and the like, that, in regard to their form, are under the dominion of that inconstant power, I have avoided also using the words *fashionable* and *modish*, which but too generally convey the ideas of novelty and levity. Words, therefore, are by no means to be accounted the worse for being old, if they are not obsolete; neither is any word the better for being new. On the contrary, some time is absolutely necessary to constitute that custom or use, on which the establishment of words depends.

If we recur to the standard already assigned, namely, the writings of a plurality of celebrated authors; there will be no scope for the comprehension of words and idioms which can be denominated novel and upstart. It must be owned that we often meet with such terms and phrases in newspapers, periodical pieces, and political pamphlets. The writers to the times rarely fail to have their performances studded with a competent number of these fantastic ornaments. A popular orator in the House of Commons hath a sort of patent from the public, during the continuance of his popularity, for coining as many as he pleases. And they are no sooner issued, than they obtrude themselves upon us from every quarter, in all the daily papers, letters, essays, addresses, &c. But this is of no significancy. Such words and phrases are but the insects of a season at the most. The people, always fickle, are just as prompt to drop them, as they were to take them up. And not one of a hundred survives the particular occasion or party-struggle which gave it birth. We may justly apply to them what Johnson says of a great number of the terms of the laborious and mercantile part of the people, "This fugitive cant cannot be regarded as any part of the durable materials of a language, and therefore must be suffered to perish, with other things unworthy of preservation."[4]

As use, therefore, implies duration, and as even a few years are not sufficient for ascertaining the characters of authors, I have, for the most part, in the following sheets, taken my prose examples, neither from living authors, nor those who wrote before the Revolution; not from the first, because an author's fame is not so firmly established in his lifetime; nor from the last, that there may be no suspicion that the style is super-

[4] Preface to his Dictionary.

annuated. The vulgar translation of the Bible I must indeed except from this restriction. The continuance and universality of its use throughout the British dominions affords an obvious reason for the exception.

Thus I have attempted to explain what that *use* is, which is the sole mistress of language, and to ascertain the precise import and extent of these her essential attributes, *reputable*, *national*, and *present*, and to give the directions proper to be observed in searching for the laws of this empress. In truth, grammar and criticism are but her ministers; and though, like other ministers, they would sometimes impose the dictates of their own humour upon the people, as the commands of their sovereign, they are not so often successful in such attempts as to encourage the frequent repetition of them.

CHAPTER II.

The nature and use of verbal Criticism, with its principal Canons.

THE first thing in elocution that claims our attention is purity; all its other qualities have their foundation in this. The great standard of purity is use, whose essential properties, as regarding language, have been considered and explained in the preceding chapter. But before I proceed to illustrate and specify the various offences against purity, or the different ways in which it may be violated, it will be proper to inquire so much further into the nature of the subject, as will enable us to fix on some general rules or canons, by which, in all our particular decisions, we ought to be directed. This I have judged the more necessary, as many of the verbal criticisms which have been made on English authors, since the beginning of the present century (for in this island we had little or nothing of the kind before), seem to have proceeded either from no settled principles at all, or from such as will not bear a near examination. There is this further advantage in beginning with establishing certain canons, that, if they shall be found reasonable, they will tend to make what remains of our road both shorter and clearer than it would otherwise have been. Much in the way of illustration and eviction may be saved, on the particular remarks. And if, on the contrary, they should not be reasonable, and consequently the remarks raised on them should not be well founded, no way that I can think of bids fairer for detecting the fallacy, and preventing every reader from being misled. A fluent and specious, but superficial manner of criticizing, is very apt to take at first, even with readers whom a deliberate examination into the principles on which the whole is built, would quickly undeceive.

"But," it may be said, "if custom, which is so capricious and unaccountable, is every thing in language, of what significance is either the grammarian or the critic?" Of considerable significance notwithstanding; and of most then when they confine themselves to their legal departments, and do not usurp an authority that doth not belong to them. The man who, in a country like ours, should compile a succinct, perspicuous, and faithful digest of the laws, though no lawgiver, would be universally acknowledged to be a public benefactor. How easy would that important branch of knowledge be rendered by such a work, in comparison of what it must be, when we have nothing to have recourse to, but a labyrinth of statutes, reports, and opinions. That man also would be of considerable use, though not in the same degree, who should vigilantly attend to every illegal practice that was beginning to prevail, and evince its danger, by exposing its contrariety to law. Of similar benefit, though in a different sphere, are grammar and criticism. In language, the grammarian is properly the compiler of the digest; and the verbal critic, the man who seasonably notifies the abuses that are creeping in. Both tend to facilitate the study of the tongue to strangers, and to render natives more perfect in the knowledge of it, to advance general use into universal, and to give a greater stability at least, if not a permanency, to custom, the most mutable thing in nature. These are advantages which, with a moderate share of attention, may be discovered from what hath been already said on the subject: but they are not the only advantages. From what I shall have occasion to observe afterwards, it will probably appear, that these arts, by assisting to suppress every unlicensed term, and to stigmatize every improper idiom, tend to give greater precision, and consequently more perspicuity and beauty to our style.

The observations made in the preceding chapter, might easily be converted into so many canons of criticism, by which, whatever is repugnant to reputable, to national, or to present use, in the sense wherein these epithets have been explained, would be condemned as a transgression of the radical laws of the language. But on this subject of use, there arise two eminent questions, the determination of which may lead to the establishment of other canons not less important. The first question is this, "Is reputable, national, and present use, which, for brevity's sake, I shall hereafter simply denominate good use, always uniform in her decisions?" The second is, "As no term, idiom, or application, that is totally unsupported by her, can be admitted to be good, is every term, idiom, and application that is countenanced by her, to be esteemed good, and therefore worthy to be retained?"

SECTION I.—*Good use not always uniform in her decisions.*

In answer to the former of these questions, I acknowledge, that in every case there is not a perfect uniformity in the determinations, even of such use as may justly be denominated good. Wherever a considerable number of authorities can be produced in support of two different though resembling modes of expression for the same thing, there is always a divided use, and one cannot be said to speak barbarously, or to oppose the usage of the language, who conforms to either side.[5] This divided use hath place sometimes in single words, sometimes in construction, and sometimes in arrangement. In all such cases there is scope for choice; and it belongs, without question, to the critical art, to lay down the principles by which, in doubtful cases, our choice should be directed.

There are, indeed, some differences in single words, which ought still to be retained. They are a kind of synonymas, and afford a little variety, without occasioning any inconvenience whatever.[6] In arrangement, too, it certainly holds that various manners suit various styles, as various styles suit various subjects, and various sorts of composition. For this reason, unless when some obscurity, ambiguity, or inelegance is created, no disposition of words which hath obtained the public approbation ought to be altogether rejected. In construction the case is somewhat different. Purity, perspicuity, and elegance generally require, that in this there be the strictest uniformity. Yet differences here are not only allowable, but even convenient,

[5] The words *nowise*, *noway*, and *noways*, afford a proper instance of this divided use. Yet our learned and ingenious lexicographer hath denominated all those who either write or pronounce the word *noways*, ignorant barbarians. These ignorant barbarians (but he hath surely not adverted to this circumstance) are only Pope, and Swift, and Addison, and Locke, and several others of our most celebrated writers. This censure is the more astonishing, that even in this form which he has thought fit to repudiate, the meaning assigned to it is strictly conformable to that which etymology, according to his own explication, would suggest. See Johnson's Dictionary on the words *nowise* and *way*, particularly the senses of *way*, marked with these numbers, 15, 16, 18, and 19.

[6] Such are, subterranean and subterraneous, homogeneal and homogeneous, authentic and authentical, isle and island, mount and mountain, clime and climate, near and nigh, betwixt and between, amongst and among, amidst and amid. Nor do I see any hurt that would ensue from adding *nowise* and *noway* to the number.

when attended with correspondent differences in the application. Thus the verb *to found,* when used literally, is more properly followed by the preposition *on,* as, "The house was *founded on* a rock;" in the metaphorical application, it is often better with *in,* as in this sentence, "They maintained, that dominion is *founded in* grace." Both sentences would be badly expressed, if these prepositions were transposed, though there are perhaps cases wherein either would be good. In those instances, therefore, of divided use, which give scope for option, the following canons are humbly proposed, in order to assist us in assigning the preference. Let it, in the mean time, be remembered, as a point always presupposed, that the authorities on the opposite sides are equal, or nearly so. When those of one side greatly preponderate, it is in vain to oppose the prevailing usage. Custom, when wavering, may be swayed, but when reluctant, will not be forced. And in this department a person never effects so little, as when he attempts too much.[7]

Canon the first.

The first canon, then, shall be, When use is divided as to any particular word or phrase, and the expression used by one part hath been pre-occupied, or is in any instance susceptible of a different signification, and the expression employed by the other part never admits a different sense, both perspicuity and variety require, that the form of expression which is in every instance strictly univocal be preferred.

For this reason *aught,* signifying any thing, is preferable to *ought,* which is one of our defective verbs: *by consequence,* meaning consequently, is preferable to *of consequence;* as this expression is often employed to denote momentous or important. In the preposition *toward* and *towards,* and the adverbs *forward* and *forwards, backward* and *backwards,* the two forms are used indiscriminately. But as the first form in all these is also an adjective, it is better to confine the particles to the second. Custom, too, seems at present to lean this way. *Be-*

[7] For this reason it is to no purpose to Johnson to pronounce the word *news* a plural, (whatever it might have been in the days of Sidney and Raleigh,) since custom hath evidently determined otherwise. Nor is the observation on the letter [*s*] in his Dictionary well founded, that "it seems to be established as a rule, that no noun singular should end with [*s*] single;" the words *alms, amends, summons, sous, genus, species, genius, chorus,* and several others, show the contrary. For the same reason the words *averse* and *aversion* are more properly construed with *to* than with *from.* The examples in favour of the latter preposition are beyond comparison outnumbered by those in favour of the former. The argument from etymology is here of no value, being taken from the use of another language. If by the same rule we were to regulate all nouns and verbs of Latin original, our present syntax would be overturned. It is more conformable to English analogy with *to;* the words *dislike* and *hatred,* nearly synonymous, are thus construed.

sides and *beside* serve both as conjunctions and as prepositions.[8] There appears some tendency at present to assign to each a separate province. This tendency ought to be humoured by employing only the former as the conjunction, the latter as the preposition.

This principle likewise leads me to prefer *extemporary* as an adjective to *extempore*, which is properly an adverb, and ought, for the sake of precision, to be restrained to that use. It is only of late that this last term begins to be employed adjectively. Thus we say, with equal propriety, an *extemporary prayer*, an *extemporary sermon*, and, he *prays extempore*, he *preaches extempore*. I know not how Dr. Priestley hath happened to mention the term *extemporary*, in a way which would make one think he considered it as a word peculiar to Mr. Hume. The word hath evidently been in good use for a longer time than one thinks of searching back in quest of authorities, and remains in good use to this day. By the same rule we ought to prefer *scarcely*, as an adverb, to *scarce*, which is an adjective; and *exceedingly*, as an adverb, to *exceeding*, which is a participle. For the same reason also I am inclined to prefer that use, which makes *ye* invariably the nominative plural of the personal pronoun *thou*, and *you* the accusative, when applied to an actual plurality. When used for the singular number, custom hath determined that it shall be *you* in both cases. This renders the distinction rather more important, as for the most part it would show directly, whether one or more were addressed; a point in which we are often liable to mistake in all modern languages. From the like principle, in those verbs which have for the participle passive both the preterite form and one peculiar, the peculiar form ought to have the preference. Thus, I have *gotten*, I have *hidden*, I have *spoken*, are better than I have *got*, I have *hid*, I have *spoke*.[9] From the same principle I think *ate* is preferable in the preterite tense, and *eaten* in the participle, to *eat*, which is the constant form of the present, though sometimes also used for both the others.

But though in this judgment concerning the participles I agree entirely with all our approved modern grammarians, I can by no means concur with some of them in their manner of supporting it. "We should be immediately shocked," says one of the best of them,[1] "at *I have knew*, *I have saw*, *I have gave*, &c., but our ears are grown familiar with *I have wrote*, *I have drank*, *I have bore*, &c. which are altogether as barbarous." Nothing

[8] These nearly correspond to the conjunction *præterea* and the preposition *præter* in Latin.

[9] Yet I should prefer, "I have *held, helped, melted*," to "I have *holden, holpen, molten*," these last participles being now obsolete. *Holden* is indeed still used when we speak formally of courts or public meetings.

[1] Lowth's Introduction to English Grammar.

can be more inconsistent, in my opinion, with the very first principles of grammar than what is here advanced. This ingenious gentleman surely will not pretend, that there is a barbarism in every word which serves for preterite and participle both, else the far greater part of the preterites and participles of our tongue are barbarous. If not, what renders many of them, such as *loved*, *hated*, *sent*, *brought*, good English when employed either way? I know no answer that can be given, but custom; that is, in other words, our ears are familiarized to them by frequent use. And what was ever meant by a barbarism in speech, but that which shocks us by violating the constant usage in speaking or in writing? If so, to be equally barbarous and to be equally shocking are synonymous; whereas to be barbarous, and to be in familiar use, are a contradiction in terms. Yet in this manner does our author often express himself. "No authority," says he in another place, "is sufficient to justify so manifest a solecism." No man needed less to be informed that authority is every thing in language, and that it is the want of it alone that constitutes both the barbarism and the solecism.

Canon the second.

The second canon is, In doubtful cases regard ought to be had in our decisions to the analogy of the language.

For this reason I prefer *contemporary* to *cotemporary*. The general use in words compounded with the inseparable preposition *con*, is to retain the (n) before a consonant, and to expunge it before a vowel or an (h) mute. Thus we say *condisciple*, *conjuncture*, *concomitant;* but *co-equal*, *co-eternal*, *co-incide*, *co-heir*. I know but one exception, which is *co-partner*. But in dubious cases we ought to follow the rule, and not the exception. If by the former canon the adverbs *backwards* and *forwards* are preferable to *backward* and *forward;* by this canon, from the principle of analogy, *afterwards* and *homewards* should be preferred to *afterward* and *homeward*. Of the two adverbs *thereabout* and *thereabouts*, compounded of the particle *there* and the preposition, the former alone is analogical, there being no such word in the language as *abouts*. The same holds of *hereabout* and *whereabout*. In the verbs *to dare*, and *to need*, many say in the third person present singular, *dare* and *need*, as "he *need* not go; he *dare* not do it." Others say, *dares* and *needs*. As the first usage is exceedingly irregular, hardly any thing less than uniform practice could authorize it. This rule supplies us with another reason for preferring *scarcely* and *exceedingly* as adverbs to *scarce* and *exceeding*. The phrases *Would to God*, and *Would God*, can both plead the authority of custom; but the latter is strictly analogical, the former is not. It is an established idiom in the English tongue that any of the auxiliaries *might*, *could*, *would*, *should*, *did*, and *had*, with the nominative subjoined, should express sometimes a supposition, sometimes a wish: which of the two it expresses in any instance is easily discovered from the context. Thus the expression, "*Would he* but ask it of me," denotes either, "*If he would*, or *I wish that he would* but ask it of me." *Would God*, then is properly, *I wish that God would*, or, *O that God would*. The other expression it is impossible to reconcile to analogy any way.[2] For a like reason the phrase *ever so*, as when we say, "though he were *ever so* good," is preferable to *never so*. In both these decisions I subscribe to the judgment of Dr. Johnson. Of the two phrases *in no wise* in three words, and *nowise* in one, the last only is conformable to the present genius of the tongue. The noun *wise*, signifying manner, is quite obsolete. It remains now only in composition, in which, along with an adjective or other substantive, it forms an adverb or conjunction. Such are *sidewise*, *lengthwise*, *coastwise*, *contrariwise*, *likewise*, *otherwise*. These always preserve the compound form, and never admit a preposition; consequently *nowise*, which is an adverb of the same order, ought analogically to be written in one word, and not to be preceded by *in*. In every ancient style all these words were uncompounded, and had the preposition. They said *in like wise*, and *in other wise*.[3] And even at present if custom were uniform, as it is divided, in admitting *in* before *nowise*, it ought to be followed, though anomalous. In these matters it is foolish to attempt to struggle against the stream. All that I here plead for is, that when custom varies, analogy should decide the question. In the determination of this particular instance I differ from Dr. Priestley. Sometimes *whether* is followed by *no*, sometimes by *not*. For instance some would say, "*Whether* he will or *no*;" others, "*Whether* he will or *not*." Of these it is the latter only that is analogical. There is an ellipsis of the verb in the last clause, which when you supply, you find it ne-

[2] What has given rise to it is evidently the French *Plût à Dieu*, of the same import. But it has not been adverted to (so servile commonly are imitators), that the verb *plaire* is impersonal, and regularly construed with the preposition *à*; neither of which is the case with the English *will* and *would*.

[3] In proof of this I shall produce a passage taken from the Prologue of the English translation of the Legenda Aurea, which seems to have been made towards the end of the fifteenth century. "I haue submysed my selfe to translate into Englysshe the legende of sayntes whyche is called legenda aurea in latyn; That is to saye, the golden legende. For in lyke wyse as golde is moost noble aboue all other metallys; in lyke wise is thys legende holden moost noble aboue all other werkes." About the time that our present version of the Scriptures was made, the old usage was wearing out. The phrase *in like wise* occurs but once (Matt. xxi. 24), whereas the compound term *likewise* occurs frequently.—We find in several places, *on this wise*, *in any wise*, and *in no wise*. The two first phrases are now obsolete, and the third seems to be in the state which Dr. Johnson calls *obsolescent*.

cessary to use the adverb *not*, "*Whether* he will or will *not*." I shall only add, that by both the preceding canons we ought always to say *rend* in the present of the indicative and of the infinitive, and never *rent*, as is sometimes done. The latter term hath been pre-occupied by the preterite and the participle passive, besides that it is only in this application that it can be said to be used analogically. For this reason, the active participle ought always to be *rending* and not *renting*.

Canon the third.

The third canon is, When the terms or expressions are in other respects equal, that ought to be preferred which is most agreeable to the ear.

This rule hath perhaps a greater chance of being observed than any other, it having been the general bent for some time to avoid harsh sounds and unmusical periods. Of this we have many examples. *Delicateness* hath very properly given way to *delicacy;* and for a like reason *authenticity* will probably soon displace *authenticalness*, and *vindictive* dispossess *vindicative* altogether. Nay, a regard to sound hath, in some instances, had an influence on the public choice, to the prejudice of both the former canons, which, one would think, ought to be regarded as of more importance. Thus the term *ingenuity* hath obtained a preference to *ingeniousness*, though the former cannot be deduced analogically from *ingenious*, and had besides been pre-occupied, and consequently would be equivocal, being a regular derivative from the term *ingenuous*, if the newer acceptation had not before now supplanted the other altogether.

Canon the fourth.

The fourth canon is, In cases wherein none of the foregoing rules gives either side a ground of preference, a regard to simplicity (in which I include etymology when manifest) ought to determine our choice.

Under the name simplicity, I must be understood to comprehend also brevity; for that expression is always the simplest which, with equal purity and perspicuity, is the briefest. We have, for instance, several active verbs which are used either with or without a preposition indiscriminately. Thus we say either *accept* or *accept of*, *admit* or *admit of*, *approve* or *approve of;* in like manner *address* or *address to*, *attain* or *attain to*. In such instances it will hold, I suppose, pretty generally, that the simple form is preferable. This appears particularly in the passive voice, in which every one must see the difference. "His present was *accepted of* by his friend." —"His excuse was *admitted of* by his master."—"The magistrates were *addressed to* by the townsmen," are evidently much worse than, "His present was *accepted* by his friend." —"His excuse was *admitted* by his master."—"The magistrates were *addressed* by the townsmen." We have but too many of this awkward, disjointed sort of compounds, and therefore ought not to multiply them without necessity. Now, if once the preposition should obtain in the active voice, the rules of syntax will absolutely require it in the passive. Sometimes, indeed, the verb hath two regimens, and then the preposition is necessary to one of them, as, "I address myself to my judges."—"They addressed their vows to Apollo." But of such cases I am not here speaking.

Both etymology and analogy, as well as euphony and simplicity, determine us in preferring *subtract* to *substract*, and consequently *subtraction* to *substraction*.[4]

Canon the fifth.

The fifth and only other canon that occurs to me on the subject of divided use is, In the few cases wherein neither perspicuity nor analogy, neither sound nor simplicity assists us in fixing our choice, it is safest to prefer that manner which is most conformable to ancient usage.

This is founded on a very plain maxim, that in language, as in several other things, change itself, unless when it is clearly advantageous, is ineligible. This affords another reason for preferring that usage which distinguishes *ye* as the nominative plural of *thou*, when more than one are addressed, from *you* the accusative. For it may be remarked, that this distinction is very regularly observed in our translation of the Bible, as well as in all our best ancient authors. Milton, too, is particularly attentive to it. The words *causey* and *causeway* are at present used promiscuously, though I do not know whether there be any difference but in the spelling. The old way is *causey*, which, as there appears no good reason for altering it,

[4] *Subtract* is regularly deduced from the supine *subtractum* of the Latin verb *subtraho*, in the same way as *act* from *actum*, the supine of *ago*, and *translate* from *translatum*, the supine of *transfero*. But it would be quite unexampled to derive the English verb from the French *soustraire*. Besides, there is not another instance in the language of a word beginning with the Latin preposition *sub*, where the *sub* is followed by an *s*, unless when the original word compounded with the preposition begins with an *s*. Thus we say *subscribe* from *sub* and *scribo*, *subsist* from *sub* and *sisto*, *substitute* from *sub* and *statuo*. But we cannot say *substract* from *sub* and *straho*, there being no such word. There can be no doubt, therefore, that a mistaken etymology, arising from an affinity to the French term, not in the verb, but in the verbal noun, has given rise to this harsh anomaly.

ought to be held the best. The alteration, I suppose, hath sprung from some mistaken notion about the etymology; but if the notion had been just, the reason would not have been sufficient. It tends, besides, either to introduce a vitiated pronunciation, or to add to the anomalies in orthography (by far too numerous already), with which the language is encumbered. Much the same may be said of *jail* and *gaol*, *jailer* and *gaoler*. That *jail* and *jailer* have been first used, is probable, from the vulgar translation of the Bible.[5] The quotations on the other side from Shakspeare are not much to be minded, as it is well known that his editors have taken a good deal of freedom with his orthography. The argument, from its derivation from the French *geole*, is very puerile. For the same reason we ought to write *jarter*, and not *garter*, and plead the spelling of the French primitive *jartiere*. Nor would it violate the laws of pronunciation in English, more to sound the [ja] as though it were written [ga], than to sound the [ga] as though it were written [ja].

SECTION II.—*Every thing favoured by good use not on that account worthy to be retained.*

I come now to the second question for ascertaining both the extent of the authority claimed by custom, and the rightful prerogatives of criticism. As no term, idiom, or application, that is totally unsupported by use, can be admitted to be good; is every term, idiom, and application, that is countenanced by use, to be esteemed good, and therefore worthy to be retained? I answer, that though nothing in language can be good from which use withholds her approbation, there may be many things to which she gives it that are not in all respects good, or such as are worthy to be retained and imitated. In some instances *custom* may very properly be checked by *criticism*, which hath a sort of negative, and though not the censorian power of instant degradation, the privilege of remonstrating, and by means of this, when used discreetly, of bringing what is bad into disrepute, and so cancelling it gradually; but which hath no positive right to establish any thing. Her power too is like that of eloquence; she operates on us purely by persuasion, depending for success on the solidity, or at least the speciousness of her arguments; whereas custom hath an unaccountable and irresistible influence over us, an influence which is prior to persuasion, and independent of it, nay, sometimes even in contradiction to it. Of different modes of expression, that which comes to be favoured by general practice may be

[5] Acts xvi. 23..

denominated best, because established; but it cannot always be said with truth, that it is established because best. And, therefore, though I agree in the general principles maintained by Priestley[6] on this subject, I do not concur in this sentiment as holding universally, that "the best forms of speech will, in time, establish themselves by their own superior excellence." Time and chance have an influence on all things human, and on nothing more remarkably than on language; insomuch that we often see that, of various forms, those will recommend themselves, and come into general use, which, if abstractedly considered, are neither the simplest nor the most agreeable to the ear, nor the most conformable to analogy. And though we cannot say properly of any expression which has the sanction of good use, that it is barbarous, we must admit that, in other respects, it may be faulty.

It is therefore, I acknowledge, not without meaning, that Swift, in the proposal above quoted,[7] affirms that, "there are many gross improprieties, which, though authorized by practice, ought to be discarded." Now, in order to discard them, nothing more is necessary than to disuse them. And to bring us to disuse them, both the example and the arguments of the critic will have their weight. A very little attention will satisfy every reasonable person of the difference there is between the bare omission, or rather the not employing of what is used, and the introduction of what is unusual. The former, provided what you substitute in its stead be proper, and have the authority of custom, can never come under the observation, or at least the reprehension of a reader; whereas the latter shocks our ears immediately. Here, therefore, lies one principal province of criticism, to point out the characters of those words and idioms which deserve to be disfranchised and consigned to perpetual oblivion. It is by carefully filing off all roughnesses and inequalities that languages, like metals, must be polished. This, indeed, is an effect of taste. And hence it happens, that the first rudiments of taste no sooner appear in any people, than the language begins, as it were of itself, to emerge out of that state of rudeness in which it will ever be found in uncivilized nations. As they improve in arts and sciences their speech refines; it not only becomes richer and more comprehensive, but acquires greater precision, perspicuity, and harmony. This effect taste insensibly produces among the people long before the language becomes the object of their attention. But when criticism hath called forth their attention to this object, there is a probability that the effect will be accelerated.

It is, however, no less certain, on the other hand, that in

[6] Preface to the Rudiments of English Grammar.

[7] For ascertaining the English tongue; see the Letter to the Lord High Treasurer.

the declension of taste and science language will unavoidably degenerate, and though the critical art may retard a little, it will never be able to prevent this degeneracy. I shall therefore subjoin a few remarks under the form of canons, in relation to those words or expressions which may be thought to merit degradation from the rank they have hitherto maintained, submitting these remarks entirely, as every thing of the kind must be submitted, to the final determination of the impartial public.

Canon the sixth.

The first canon on this subject is, All words and phrases which are remarkably harsh and unharmonious, and not absolutely necessary, may justly be judged worthy of this fate.

I call a word or phrase absolutely necessary, when we have no synonymous words, in the event of a dismission, to supply its place, or no way of conveying properly the same idea without the aid of circumlocution. The rule, with this limitation, will, I believe, be generally assented to. The only difficulty is, to fix the criteria by which we may discriminate the obnoxious words from all others.

It may well be reckoned that we have lighted on one criterion, when we have found a decompound or term composed of words already compounded, whereof the several parts are not easily, and therefore not closely united. Such are the words, *bare-faced-ness*, *shame-faced-ness*, *un-success-ful-ness*, *dis-interest-ed-ness*, *wrong-headed-ness*, *tender-hearted-ness*. They are so heavy and drawling, and withal so ill compacted, that they have not more vivacity than a periphrasis, to compensate for the defect of harmony.

Another criterion is, when a word is so formed and accented as to render it of difficult utterance to the speaker, and consequently disagreeable in sound to the hearer. This happens in two cases; first, when the syllables, which immediately follow the accented syllable, are so crowded with consonants, as of necessity to retard the pronunciation. The words *quéstionless*, *chrróniclers*, *convénticlers*, *concúpiscence*, *remémbrancer*, are examples of this. The accent in all these is on the antepenultimate, for which reason the last two syllables ought to be pronounced quick; a thing scarcely practicable, on account of the number of consonants which occur in these syllables. The attempt to quicken the pronunciation, though familiar to Englishmen, exhibits to strangers the appearance of awkward hurry, instead of that easy fluency to be found in those words wherein the unaccented syllables are naturally short. Such are *lévity*, *vánity*, *avídity*, all accented in like manner on the antepenultimate. The second case in which a similar dissonance is found, is when too many syllables follow the accented syllable. For though these be naturally short, their number, if they exceed two, makes a disagreeable pronunciation. Examples of this are the words *prímarily*, *cúrsorily*, *súmmarily*, *perémptorily*, *perémptoriness*, *víndicative;* all of which are accented on the fourth syllable from the end. It were to be wished that the use which now prevails, in regard to the manner of accenting some words, would alter, as we cannot afford to part with every term that is liable to exception in this respect. Nor is a change here to be despaired of, since we find it hath happened to several words already, as the places which they occupy in ancient poetry sufficiently evince.

A third criterion is, when a short or unaccented syllable is repeated, or followed by another short or unaccented syllable very much resembling. This always gives the appearance of stammering to the pronunciation. Such are the words *hólily*, *fárriering*, *síllily*. We have not many words chargeable with this fault: nay, so early have the people been sensible of the disagreeable sound occasioned by such recurrences, that it would appear they have added the adverbial termination to very few of our adjectives ending in *ly*. I believe there are no examples extant of *heavenlily*, *godlily*, *timelily*, *dailily*. Johnson hath given us, in his Dictionary, the word *lowlily*, which is as bad as any of them, but without quoting authorities. In these and such like, the simple forms, as *heavenly*, *godly*, *timely*, *daily*, *homely*, *courtly*, *comely*, seem always to have served both for adjective and adverb; though this too hath its inconvenience. It deserves our notice, that the repetition of a syllable is never offensive, when either one or both are long, as in *papa*, *mamma*, *murmur*, *tartar*, *barbarous*, *lily*.

Besides the cases aforesaid, I know of none that ought to dispose us to the total disuse of words really significant. A little harshness by the collision of consonants, which, nevertheless, our organs find no difficulty in articulating, and which do not suggest to the hearer the disagreeable idea either of precipitation or of stammering, are by no means a sufficient reason for the suppression of a useful term. The monosyllables *judg'd*, *drudg'd*, *grudg'd*, which some have thought very offensive, appear not in the least exceptionable compared with the words above mentioned. It would not do well to introduce such hard and strong sounds too frequently; but when they are used sparingly and properly, they have even a good effect. Variety in sound is advantageous to a language: and it is convenient that we should have some sounds that are rough and masculine, as well as some that are liquid and feminine.

I observe this the rather, because I think there is at present a greater risk of going too far in refining than of not going far enough. The ears of some critics are immoderately delicate.

A late essayist,[8] one who seems to possess a considerable share of ingenuity and taste, proposes the utter extirpation of *encroach*, *encroachment*, *inculcate*, *purport*, *methinks*, and some others, the precise meaning of which, we have no single words in English that perfectly express. An ear so nice as to be hurt by these, appears to me in the same light as a stomach so squeamish as to nauseate our beef and beer, the ordinary food of the country. Such ears, I should say, are not adapted to our speech, nor such stomachs to our climate. This humour, were it to become general, would have a very unfavourable aspect to the language; and it might admit a question whether, on such principles, if an expurgation of the vocabulary were attempted, there would remain one third of the whole stock, that would not be deemed worthy of excision. This would be particularly inconvenient, if every body were as much an enemy as this gentleman seems to be to all new-fashioned terms and phrases. We should hardly have words enow left for necessary purposes.[9]

Canon the seventh.

The second canon on this subject is, When etymology plainly points to a signification different from that which the

[8] Sketches by Launcelot Temple, Esq.—of late republished and owned by Dr. Armstrong.

[9] I shall only observe here, by the way, that those languages which are allowed to be the most susceptible of all the graces of harmony have admitted many ill-sounding words. Such are in Greek σπλαγχνιζεσθαι, προσφθεγξασθαι, εγχριμφθεις, κεκακοκα, μεμιμημενον. In the two last, one finds a dissonant recurrence of the same letter to a degree quite unexampled with us. There is, however, such a mixture of long and short syllables, as prevents that difficulty of utterance which was remarked in some English words. Such are also in Latin *dixisses*, *spississimus*, *percrebrescebantque*. The last of these words is very rough, and the two first have as much of the hissing letters as any English word whatever. The Italian is considered, and I believe justly, as the most musical of all languages, yet there are in it some sounds which even to us, accustomed to a dialect boisterous like our weather, appear harsh and jarring. Such are *incrocicchiare*, *sdrucciolo*so, *spregiatrice*. There is a great difference between words which sound harshly, but are of easy pronunciation to the natives, and those words which even to natives occasion difficulty in the utterance, and consequently convey some idea of awkwardness to the hearer, which is prejudicial to the design. There are in the languages of all countries many words which foreigners will find a difficulty in pronouncing, that the natives have no conception of. The Greeks could not easily articulate the Latin terminations in *ans* and *ens*. On the other hand, there were many sounds in Greek which appeared intolerable to the Latins, such as words beginning with μν, φθ, ψ, πτ, κτ, and many others. No people have so studiously avoided the collision of consonants as the Italians. To their delicate ears *pt*, *ct*, and *cs*, or *x*, though belonging to different syllables, and interposed between vowels, are offensive, nor can they easily pronounce them. Instead of *apto*, and *lecto*, and *Alexandro*, they must say *atto*, and *letto*, and *Alessandro*. But these very people begin some of their words with the three consonants *sdr*, which to our ears are perfectly shocking. It is not therefore so much harshness of sound, as difficulty of utterance, that should make some words be rejected altogether. The latter tends to divert our attention, and consequently to obstruct the effect. The former hath not this tendency, unless they be obtruded on us too frequently.

word commonly bears, propriety and simplicity both require its dismission.

I use the word *plainly*, because, when the etymology is from an ancient or foreign language, or from obsolete roots in our own language, or when it is obscure or doubtful, no regard should be had to it. The case is different when the roots either are, or strongly appear to be, English, are in present use, and clearly suggest another meaning. Of this kind is the word *beholden*, for obliged or indebted. It should regularly be the passive participle of the verb to *behold*, which would convey a sense totally different. Not that I consider the term as equivocal, for in the last acceptation it hath long since been disused, having been supplanted by *beheld*. But the formation of the word is so analogical, as to make it have at least the appearance of impropriety when used in a sense that seems naturally so foreign to it. The word *beholding*, to express the same thing, is still more exceptionable than the other, and includes a real impropriety, being an active form with a passive signification. *To vouchsafe*, as denoting *to condescend*, is liable to a similar exception, and for that reason, more than for its harshness, may be dispensed with. *Coaction* and *coactive*, as signifying *compulsion* and *compulsive*, though regularly deduced from the Latin *coactum*, have so much the appearance of being compounded of the English words *action* and *active*, with the inseparable preposition *co*, which would give them a meaning quite different, that one can scarcely hear them without some tendency to mistake the sense. The verb *to unloose* should analogically signify *to tie*, in like manner as *to untie* signifies *to loose*. To what purpose is it, then, to retain a term, without any necessity, in a signification the reverse of that which its etymology manifestly suggests? In the same way *to annul*, and *to disannul* ought by analogy to be contraries, though irregularly used as synonymous. The verb *to unravel* commonly indeed, as well as analogically, signifies *to disentangle*, *to extricate:* sometimes, however, it is absurdly employed to denote the contrary, *to disorder*, *to entangle*, as in these lines in the address to the goddess of Dulness,

> Or quite unravel all the reasoning thread,
> And hand some curious cobweb in its stead.[1]

All considerations of analogy, propriety, perspicuity, unite in persuading us to repudiate this preposterous application altogether.

[1] Dunciad, B. i.

Canon the eighth.

The third canon is, When any words become obsolete, or at least are never used, except as constituting part of particular phrases, it is better to dispense with their service entirely, and give up the phrases.

The reasons are; first, because the disuse in ordinary cases renders the term somewhat indefinite, and occasions a degree of obscurity: secondly, because the introduction of words which never appear but with the same attendants, gives the style an air of vulgarity and cant. Examples of this we have in the words *lief*, *dint*, *whit*, *moot*, *pro* and *con*, as, "*I had as lief* go myself," for "I should like as well to go myself." "He convinced his antagonist *by dint of argument*," that is, "by strength of argument." "He made them yield *by dint of arms*,"—"by force of arms." "He is *not a whit better*,"—"no better." "The case you mention is *a moot point*,"—"a disputable point." "The question was strenuously debated *pro and con*,"—"on both sides."

Canon the ninth.

The fourth and last canon I propose, is, All those phrases which, when analyzed grammatically, include a solecism, and all those to which use hath affixed a particular sense, but which, when explained by the general and established rules of the language, are susceptible either of a different sense or of no sense, ought to be discarded altogether.

It is this kind of phraseology which is distinguished by the epithet *idiomatical*, and hath been originally the spawn, partly of ignorance, and partly of affectation. Of the first sort, which includes a solecism, is the phrase, "*I had* rather *do* such a thing," for, "I would rather do it." The auxiliary *had* joined to the infinitive active *do*, is a gross violation of the rules of conjugation in our language, and though good use may be considered as protecting this expression from being branded with the name of a blunder, yet, as it is both irregular and unnecessary, I can foresee no inconvenience that will arise from dropping it. I have seen this idiom criticized in some essay, whose name I cannot now remember, and its origin very naturally accounted for, by supposing it to have sprung from the contraction *I'd*, which supplies the place both of *I had* and of *I would*, and which hath been at first ignorantly resolved into *I had* when it ought to have been *I would*. The phrase, thus frequently mistaken, hath come at length to establish itself, and to stand on its own foot.[2]

Of the second sort, which, when explained grammatically, leads to a different sense from what the words in conjunction commonly bear, is, "He sings a good song," for "he sings well." The plain meaning of the words as they stand connected is very different, for who sees not that a good song may be ill sung? Of the same stamp is, "He plays a good fiddle," for "he plays well on the fiddle." This seems also to involve a solecism. We speak indeed of playing a tune, but it is always *on* the instrument.

Nothing can be more common or less proper than to speak of a *river's emptying itself.* Dr. Johnson, in his dictionary, explains the verb *to empty*, as importing *to evacuate, to exhaust.* Amongst his authorities we have this sentence from Arbuthnot. "The Euxine sea is conveniently situated for trade, by the communication it has with Asia and Europe, and the great navigable *rivers* that *empty themselves* into it." Passing the word *rivers* as a metonymy for their *channels*, are these ever "evacuated or exhausted?" To say a *river falls* into the sea, or a ship falls down the river, is entirely proper, as the motion is no other than a fall down a real though gentle declivity.

Under the third sort, which can scarcely be considered as literally conveying any sense, may be ranked a number of vile, but common phrases, sometimes to be found in good authors, like *shooting at rovers*, *having a month's mind*, *currying favour*, *dancing attendance*, and many others. Of the same kind also, though not reprehensible in the same degree, is the idiomatical use that is sometimes made of certain verbs, as *stand*, for insist, "*he stands* upon security;" *take* for understand, in such phrases as these, "You *take* me," and "as I *take* it;" *hold* for continue, as, "he does not *hold* long in one mind." But of all kinds, the worst is that wherein the words, when construed, are susceptible of no meaning at all. Such an expression is the following, "There were seven ladies in the company, every one prettier than another," by which it is intended, I suppose, to denote that they were all very pretty. One prettier, implies that there is another less pretty, but where every one is prettier

[2] Whether with Johnson and Lowth we should consider the phrases *by this means*, *by that means*, *it is a means*, as liable to the same exception, is perhaps more doubtful. Priestley considers the word *means* as of both numbers, and of such nouns we have several examples in the language. But it may be objected, that as the singular form *mean* is still frequently to be met with, this must inevitably give to the above phrases an appearance of solecism in the judgment of those who are accustomed to attend to the rules of syntax. But however this may induce such critics to avoid the expressions in question, no person of taste, I presume, will venture so far to violate the present usage, and consequently to shock the ears of the generality of readers as to say, "By this mean," or "By that mean."

there can be none less, and consequently none more pretty. Such trash is the disgrace of any tongue. Ambitiously to display nonsensical phrases of this sort, as some writers have affected to do, under the ridiculous notion of a familiar and easy manner, is not to set off the riches of a language, but to expose its rags. As such idioms, therefore, err alike against purity, simplicity, perspicuity, and elegance, they are entitled to no quarter from the critic. A few of these, in the writings of good authors, I shall have occasion to point out when I come to speak of the solecism and the impropriety.

So much for the canons of verbal criticism, which properly succeed the characters of good use, proposed in the preceding chapter for the detection of the most flagrant errors in the choice, the construction, and the application of words. The first five of these canons are intended to suggest the principles by which our choice ought to be directed, in cases wherein use itself is wavering, and the four last to point out those further improvements which the critical art, without exceeding her legal powers, may assist in producing. There are, indeed, those who seem disposed to extend her authority much further.

But we ought always to remember, that as the principal mode of improving a language, which she is empowered to employ, is by condemning and exploding, there is a considerable danger lest she carry her improvements this way too far. Our mother-tongue, by being too much impaired, may be impoverished, and so more injured in copiousness and nerve than all our refinements will ever be able to compensate. For this reason there ought, in support of every sentence of proscription, to be an evident plea from the principles of perspicuity, elegance, or harmony.

If so, the want of etymology, whatever be the opinion of some grammarians, cannot be reckoned a sufficient ground for the suppression of a significant term which hath come into good use. For my part, I should think it as unreasonable to reject, on this account, the assistance of an expressive word, which opportunely offers its service, when perhaps no other could so exactly answer my purpose, as to refuse the needful aid of a proper person because he could give no account of his family or pedigree. Though what is called *cant* is generally, not necessarily nor always, without etymology, it is not this defect, but the baseness of the use which fixeth on it that disgraceful appellation. No absolute monarch hath it more in his power to nobilitate a person of obscure birth, than it is in the power of good use to ennoble words of low or dubious extraction; such, for instance, as have either arisen, nobody knows how, like *fib*, *banter*, *bigot*, *fop*, *flippant*, among the rabble, or like *flimsy*, sprung from the cant of manufacturers. It is never from an attention to etymology, which would frequently mislead us, but from custom, the only infallible guide in this matter, that the meanings of words in present use must be learnt. And, indeed, if the want in question were material, it would equally affect all those words, no inconsiderable part of our language, whose descent is doubtful or unknown. Besides, in no one case can the line of derivation be traced backwards to infinity. We must always terminate in some words of whose genealogy no account can be given.[3]

It ought, at the same time to be observed, that what hath been said on this topic relates only to such words as bear no distinguishable traces of the baseness of their source; the case is quite different in regard to those terms which may be said to proclaim their vile and despicable origin, and that either by associating disagreeable and unsuitable ideas, as *bellytimber*, *thorowstitch*, *dumfound;* or by betraying some frivolous humour in the formation of them, as *transmogrify*, *bamboozle*, *topsyturvy*, *pellmell*, *helterskelter*, *hurlyburly*. These may all find a place in burlesque, but ought never to show themselves in any serious performance. A person of no birth, as the phrase is, may be raised to the rank of nobility, and, which is more, may become it; but nothing can add dignity to that man, or fit him for the company of gentlemen, who bears indelible marks of the clown in his look, gait, and whole behaviour.

CHAPTER III.

Of Grammatical Purity.

It was remarked formerly,[4] that though the grammatical art bears much the same relation to the rhetorical, which the art of the mason bears to that of the architect, there is one very memorable difference between the two cases. In architecture it is not necessary that he who designs should execute his own

[3] Dr. Johnson, who, notwithstanding his acknowledged learning, penetration, and ingenuity, appears sometimes, if I may adopt his own expression, "lost in lexicography," hath declared the name *punch*, which signifies a certain mixed liquor very well known, a cant word, because, being to appearance without etymology, it hath probably arisen from some silly conceit among the people. The name *sherbet*, which signifies another known mixture, he allows to be good, because it is Arabic; though, for aught we know, its origin among the Arabs hath been equally ignoble or uncertain. By this way of reckoning, if the word *punch*, in the sense wherein we use it, should by any accident be imported into Arabia, and come into use there, it would make good Arabic, though it be but cant English; as their *sherbet*, though in all likelihood but cant Arabic, makes good English. This, I own, appears to me very capricious.

[4] Chap. ii.

plan; he may therefore be an excellent artist in this way who has neither skill nor practice in masonry; on the contrary, it is equally incumbent on the orator to design and to execute. He ought therefore to be master of the language which he speaks or writes, and to be capable of adding to grammatic purity those higher qualities of elocution which will give grace and energy to his discourse. I propose, then, in the first place, by way of laying the foundation,[5] to consider that purity which he hath in common with the grammarian, and then proceed to consider those qualities of speech which are peculiarly oratorical.

It was also observed before,[6] that the art of the logician is universal, the art of the grammarian particular. By consequence, my present subject being language, it is necessary to make choice of some particular tongue, to which the observations to be made will be adapted, and from which the illustrations to be introduced will be taken. Let English be that tongue. This is a preference to which it is surely entitled from those who write in it. Pure English, then, implies three things; *first*, that the words be English; *secondly*, that their construction, under which, in our tongue, arrangement also is comprehended, be in the English idiom; *thirdly*, that the words and phrases be employed to express the precise meaning which custom hath affixed to them.

From the definition now given, it will be evident, on reflection, that this is one of those qualities, of which, though the want exposes the writer to much censure, the possession hardly entitles him to any praise. The truth is, it is a kind of negative quality, as the name imports, consisting more in an exemption from certain blemishes, than in the acquisition of any excellence. It holds the same place among the virtues of elocution that justice holds among the moral virtues. The more necessary each is, and the more blameable the transgression is, the less merit has the observance. Grace and energy, on the contrary, are like generosity and public spirit. To be deficient in these virtues is not treated as criminal; but to be eminent for the practice of them is accounted meritorious. As, therefore, in what regards the laws of purity, the violation is much more conspicuous than the observance, I am under the disagreeable necessity of taking my illustrations on this article solely from the former.

Purity, it was said, implies three things. Accordingly, in three different ways it may be injured. First, the words used may not be English. This fault hath received from grammarians the denomination of *barbarism*. Secondly, the construction of

[5] Solum quidem et quasi fundamentum oratoris, vides locutionem emendatam et Latinam. Cic. De Clar. Orat. The same holds equally of any language which the orator is obliged to use.

[6] Book i. Chap. iv.

the sentence may not be in the English idiom. This hath gotten the name of *solecism*. Thirdly, the words and phrases may not be employed to express the precise meaning which custom hath affixed to them. This is termed *impropriety*.[7]

SECTION I.—*The Barbarism.*

The reproach of barbarism may be incurred by three different ways; by the use of words entirely obsolete, by the use of words entirely new, or by new formations and compositions from simple and primitive words in present use.

PART I.—*By the use of obsolete words.*

Obsolete words, though they once were English, are not so now; though they were both proper and expressive in the days of our forefathers, are become as strange to our ears as many parts of their garb would be to our eyes. And if so, such words have no more title than foreign words to be introduced at present; for though they are not so totally unknown as to occasion obscurity, a fault which I shall consider afterwards, their appearance is so unusual, and their form is so antiquated, that, if not perfectly ridiculous, they at least suggest the notion of stiffness and affectation. We ought, therefore, not only to avoid words that are no longer understood by any but critics and antiquarians, such as *hight*, *cleped*, *uneath*, *erst*, *whilom;* we must also, when writing in prose, and on serious subjects, renounce the aid of those terms, which, though not unintelligible, all writers of any name have now ceased to use. Such are *behest*, *fantasy*, *tribulation*, *erewhile*, *whenas*, *peradventure*, *self-same*, *anon*. All these offend more or less against the third criterion of good use formerly given,[8] that it be such as obtains at present.

Some indulgence, however, on this, as well as on several other articles, as was hinted already, must be given to poets, on many accounts; and particularly on account of the peculiar inconveniences to which the laws of versification subject them. Besides, in treating some topics, passages of ancient story, for example, there may be found sometimes a suitableness in the introduction of old words. In certain kinds of style, when used sparingly and with judgment, they serve to add the venerable air of antiquity to the narrative. In burlesque also,

7 Quintilian hath suggested this distribution. Instit. lib. i. cap. 5. Deprehendat quæ barbara, quæ impropria, quæ contra legem loquendi composita.

8 Book II. Chap. 1. Sect. iii.

they often produce a good effect. But it is admitted on all sides, that this species of writing is not strictly subjected to the laws of purity.

PART II.—*By the use of new words.*

Another tribe of barbarisms, much more numerous, is constituted by new words. Here indeed the hazard is more imminent, as the tendency to this extreme is more prevalent. Nay, our language is in greater danger of being overwhelmed by an inundation of foreign words than of any other species of destruction. There is, doubtless, some excuse for borrowing the assistance of neighbours, when their assistance is really wanted; that is, when we cannot do our business without it; but there is certainly a meanness in choosing to be indebted to others for what we can be easily supplied with out of our own stock. When words are introduced by any writer, from a sort of necessity, in order to avoid tedious and languid circumlocutions, there is reason to believe they will soon be adopted by others convinced of the necessity, and will at length be naturalized by the public. But it were to be wished, that the public would ever reject those which are obtruded on it merely through a licentious affectation of novelty. And of this kind certainly are most of the words and phrases which have, in this century, been imported from France. Are not *pleasure*, *opinionative*, and *sally*, as expressive as *volupty*, *opiniatre*, and *sortie?* Wherein is the expression *last resort* inferior to *dernier resort; liberal arts*, to *beaux arts;* and *polite literature*, to *belles lettres?* Yet some writers have arrived at such a pitch of futility as to imagine, that if they can but make a few trifling changes, like *aimable* for *amiable*, *politesse* for *politeness*, *delicatesse*, for *delicacy*, and *hauteur* for *haughtiness*, they have found so many gems which are capable of adding a wonderful lustre to their works. With such, indeed, it is in vain to argue; but to others, who are not quite so unreasonable, I beg leave to suggest the following remarks.

First, it ought to be remarked, that the rules of pronunciation and orthography in French are so different from those which obtain in English, that the far greater part of the French words lately introduced constitute so many anomalies with us, which, by loading the grammatical rules with exceptions, greatly corrupt the simplicity and regularity of our tongue.

Nor is this the only way in which they corrupt its simplicity; let it be observed further, that one of the principal beauties of any language, and the most essential to simplicity, results from this, That a few plain and primitive words called roots, have, by an analogy which hath insensibly established itself, given rise to an infinite number of derivative and compound words, between which and the primitive, and between the former and their conjugates, there is a resemblance in sense, corresponding to that which there is in sound. Hence it will happen that a word may be very emphatical in the language to which it owes its birth, arising from the light that is reflected on it by the other words of the same etymology; which, when it is transplanted into another language loses its emphasis entirely. The French word *eclaircissement*, for instance, is regularly deduced thus; *Eclaircissement*, *eclaircisse*, *eclaircir*, *eclair*, *clair*, which is the etymon, whence also are descended, *eclairement*, *clarté*, *clarifier*, *clairification*, *eclairer*. The like may be observed in regard to *connoisseur*, *reconnoitre*, *agrémens*, and a thousand others. Whereas such words with us look rather like strays than like any part of our own property. They are very much in the condition of exiles who, having been driven from their families, relations, and friends, are compelled to take refuge in a country where there is not a single person with whom they can claim a connexion, either by blood or by alliance.

But the patrons of this practice will probably plead, that as the French is the finer language, ours must certainly be improved by the mixture. Into the truth of the hypothesis from which they argue I shall not now enquire. It sufficeth for my present purpose, to observe, that the consequence is not logical, though the plea were just. A liquor produced by the mixture of two liquors of different qualities will often prove worse than either. The Greek is, doubtless, a language much superior, in riches, harmony, and variety, to the Latin; yet, by an affectation in the Romans of Greek words and idioms (like the passion of the English for whatever is imported from France) as much, perhaps, as by any thing, the Latin was not only vitiated, but lost almost entirely, in a few centuries, that beauty and majesty which we discover in the writings of the Augustan age. On the contrary, nothing contributed more to the preservation of the Greek tongue in its native purity for such an amazing number of centuries, unexampled in the history of any other language, than the contempt they had of this practice. It was in consequence of this contempt that they were the first who branded a foreign term in any of their writers with the odious name of *barbarism*.

But there are two considerations which ought especially to weigh with authors, and hinder them from wantonly admitting such extraneous productions into their performances. One is, if these foreigners be allowed to settle amongst us they will infallibly supplant the old inhabitants. Whatever ground is given to the one, is so much taken from the other. Is it then prudent in a writer to foment a humour of innovation which tends to make the language of his country still more changeable, and consequently to render the style of his own writings the sooner obsolete? Nor let it be imagined that this is not a necessary consequence. Nothing can be juster than Johnson's manner of arguing on this subject, in regard to what Swift a little chimerically proposeth, that though new words be introduced, none should be permitted to become obsolete.[9] For what makes a word obsolete but a general, though tacit agreement to forbear it? And what so readily produces this agreement, as another term which hath gotten a vogue and currency, and is always at hand to supply its place? And if thus, for some time, a word is overlooked or neglected, how shall it be recalled, when it hath once, by disuse, become unfamiliar, and, by unfamiliarity, unpleasing?

The other consideration is, that if he should not be followed in the use of those foreign words which he hath endeavoured to usher into the language, if they meet not with a favourable reception from the public, they will ever appear as spots in his work. Such is the appearance which the terms *opine*, *ignore*, *fraicheur*, *adroitness*, *opiniatry*, and *opiniatrety*, have at present in the writings of some ingenious men. Whether, therefore, he be, or be not, imitated, he will himself prove a loser at last. I might add to these, that as borrowing naturally exposeth to the suspicion of poverty, this poverty will much more readily, and more justly too, be imputed to the writer than to the language.

Inventors in the arts, and discoverers in science, have an indisputable title to give names to their own inventions and discoveries. When foreign inventions and discoveries are imported into this island, it is both natural and reasonable that the name should accompany the thing. Nay, in regard even to evils of foreign growth, I should not object to the observance of the same rule. Were any one to insist that we have not in our language words precisely corresponding to the French *galimatias*, *phebus*, *verbiage*, *gasconnade*, *rodomontade*, I should not contend with him about it; nor should I perhaps dislike, that the very name served to show that these plants are the natives of a ranker soil, and did not originally belong to us. But if the introduction of exotic words were never admitted, except in such cases, or in order to supply an evident want amongst ourselves, we should not at present have one such term where we have fifty. The advice of the poet, with regard to both the fore-mentioned sorts of barbarism, is extremely good.

> In words, as fashions, the same rule will hold;
> Alike fantastic, if too new or old:
> Be not the first by whom the new are tried,
> Nor yet the last to lay the old aside.[1]

[9] Preface to the Dictionary.

[1] Pope's Essay on Criticism.

PART III.—*By the use of good words new-modelled.*

The third species of barbarism is that produced by new formations and compositions from primitives in present use. I acknowledge that, when the English analogy is observed in the derivation or composition, and when the new-coined word is wanted in the language, greater liberty ought to be given on this article than on the former. The reason of the difference will appear from what hath been said already. But still this is a liberty which needs an excuse from necessity, and is in no case pardonable, unless the words be at least not disagreeable to the ear, and be so analogically formed that a reader, without the help of the context, may easily discover the meaning.[2]

Now, if the plea of necessity be requisite, what quarter is due to such frivolous innovations as these, *incumberment*,[3] *portic*,[3] *martyrised*,[3] *eucharisty*,[3] *analyse*,[3] *connexity*,[3] *stoician*,[3] *platonician*,[3] *peripatetician*,[3] *pythagorician*,[3] *fictious*,[4] *majestatic*,[5] *acception*,[6] which were intended solely to express what had always been at least as well expressed, by *encumberance*, *portico*, *martyr'd*, *eucharist*, *analysis*, *connexion*, *stoic*, *platonist*, *peripatetic*, *pythagorean*, *fictitious*, *majestic*, *acceptation*. And if any regard is due to the ear, what shall we say of—I cannot call it the composition, but the collision of—words which are naturally the most unfit for coalescing, like *saint-authors*, *saintprotectrices*, *architectcapacity*, *commentatorcapacity*, *authorcharacter*, and many others forged in the same taste, to be found in the pages of a late right honourable author?[7] And lastly, if the analogy of the language must be preserved in composition, to what kind of reception are the following entitled, all fabricated in the same shop, *selfend*, *selfpassion*, *selfaffections*, *selfpractice*, *homedialect*, *bellysense*, and *mirror-writing?*

It may, indeed, be urged, that the pronoun *self* is used in composition with such latitude that one can scarcely err in forming new words with its assistance. But this is a mistake. New words may be formed by it; but they must be formed analogically. And the analogy of these formations may be understood from observing, that when analyzed thus, they ought regularly to exhibit the same meaning. Make *one's self*, *himself*, *herself*, *itself*, or *themselves*, as the sense requires, follow the last word in the compound, with the preposition inter-

[2] There are some words of recent introduction, which come so much under this description, that it might be accounted too fastidious in the critic entirely to reject them. Such are *continental, sentimental, originality, criminality, capability, to originate, to figure, to adduce*, and perhaps a few others.

[3] Bolingbroke. [4] Prior. [5] Spectator, No. 580.

[6] Hammond. [7] Shaftesbury.

vening, with which the word, whether noun or participle, is usually construed. If the word be a substantive, the preposition is commonly *of*, if the passive participle, *by*, and if the active participle, no preposition is requisite. Thus *selflove* is the *love of one's self*. In the same way are resolved *selfhate*, *selfmurder*, *selfpreservation*. When we say of a man that he is *selfcondemned*, we mean, that he is *condemned by himself*. A *selfconsuming fire*, is a fire *consuming itself*.

Now, to apply this observation, what is the meaning of *the end of one's self*, *the passion of one's self*, *the affections of one's self*, and *the practice of one's self?* And if some meaning may be affixed to any of these expressions, it is easy to perceive that it is not the meaning of the author. Yet I can remember but two compounds that have obtained in English, which are not formed according to the analogy above explained. One is *selfwilled*, signifying *perverse*, and now little used; the other is *selfexistence*, a favourite word of some metaphysicians, which, if it signify any thing more than what is properly and clearly expressed by independency and eternity, signifies I know not what. In new formations, however, the rule ought to be followed, and not the exceptions. But what shall be said of such monsters as *selfpractice*, *bellysense*, and *mirrorwriting?* These, indeed, might have been regarded as flowers of rhetoric in the days of Cromwell, when a jargon of this sort was much in vogue, but are extremely unsuitable to the chaster language of the present age.

Again, under this class may be ranked another modern refinement. I mean the alterations that have been made by some later writers on proper names and some other words of foreign extraction, and on their derivatives, on pretence of bringing them nearer, both in pronunciation and in spelling, to the original names, as they appear in the language from which those words were taken. In order to answer this important purpose, several terms which have maintained their place in our tongue for many centuries, and which are known to every body, must be expelled, that room may be made for a set of uncouth and barbarous sounds, with which our ears are unacquainted, and to some of which it is impossible for us so to adapt our organs, accustomed only to English, as rightly to articulate them.

It hath been the invariable custom of all nations, as far as I know—it was particularly the custom of the Grecians and the Romans—when they introduced a foreign name into their language, to make such alterations on it as would facilitate the pronunciation to their own people, and render it more analogous to the other words of their tongue. There is an evident convenience in this practice; but where the harm of it is, I am not able to discover. No more can I divine what good reason can be alleged for proscribing the name *Zoroaster*, till of late universally adopted by English authors who had occasion to mention that eastern sage, and the same, except in termination, that is used in Greek and Latin classics. Is *Zerdusht*, which those people would substitute in its place, a more musical word? Or is it of any consequence to us, that it is nearer the Persian original? Will this sound give us a deeper insight than the other into the character, the philosophy, and the history of the man? On the same principles we are commanded by these refiners to banish *Confucius* for the sake of *Con-fut-cee*, and never again, on pain of the charge of gross ignorance, to mention *Mahomet*, *Mahometan*, *Mahometism*, since *Mohammed*, *Mohammedan*, *Mohammedism*, are ready to supply their room. *Mussulman* must give place to *moslem*, *hegira* to *hejra*, and *alcoran* to *koran*. The *dervis* too is turned a *dervesh*, and the *bashaw* is transformed into a *pacha*.

But why do our modern reformers stop here? Ought not this reformation, if good for any thing, to be rendered more extensively useful? How much more edifying would holy writ prove to readers of every capacity if, instead of those vulgar corruptions, *Jacob*, and *Judah*, and *Moses*, and *Elijah*, we had the satisfaction to find in our Bibles, as some assure us that the words ought to be pronounced, *Yagnhakob*, and *Yehudah*, and *Moscheh*, and *Eliyahu?* Nay, since it seems to be agreed amongst our oriental scholars that the Hebrew *jod* sounds like the English *y* before a vowel, and that their *vau* is the same with the German *w*, the word *Jehovah* ought also to be exploded, that we may henceforth speak of the Deity more reverently and intelligibly by the only authentic name, *Yehowah*. A reform of this kind was indeed, for the benefit of the learned, attempted abroad more than two centuries ago, by a kindred genius of those modern English critics, one Pagninus, a Dominican friar. In a translation which this man made of the scriptures, into a sort of monkish gibberish that he called Latin, he hath, in order to satisfy the world of the vast importance and utility of his work, instead of *Eve*, written *Chauva*, and for *Isaiah*, *Jeremiah*, *Ezekiel*—given us *Jesahiahu*, *Irmeiahu*, *Jechezechel*. But I know not how it hath happened, that in this he hath had no imitators among men of letters. Probably, upon the trial, people have discovered that they were just as much edified by the old names as by the new.

Again, why this reformation should be confined almost entirely to proper names, for my part, I can discover no good reason. Appellatives are doubtless entitled to a share. Critics of this stamp ought, for example, boldly to resolve, in spite of inveterate abuses and plebeian prejudices, never, whilst they breathe, either to write or to pronounce the words *pope*, *popery*, and *popedom*, but instead of them, *pape*, *papery*, and *papedom;* since whether we derive these words immediately from the French,[8] the Latin,[9] or the Greek,[1] still it appears that the *o* is but a base usurper of a place which rightfully belongs to the *a*. The reason assigned for saying *koran* and not *alcoran*, is truly curious. *Al*, say they, is the Arabic article, and signifies *the;* consequently, if we should say *the alcoran*, we should fall into a gross perissology. It is just as if we said *the the book*. A plain illiterate man would think it sufficient to reply, What though *al* signifies *the* in Arabic, it hath no signification in English, and is only here the first syllable of a name which use hath appropriated, no matter how, to a particular book. But if ye who are such deep scholars, and wonderful improvers of your mother-tongue, are determined to exclude this harmless syllable from *alcoran*, act at least consistently, and dismiss it also from *alchymy*, *alcove*, *alembic*, *algebra*, *almanac*, and all the other words in the language that are derived in the same way, and from the same source. Indeed, it is not easy to say where ye will stop, for if ye attend to it ye will find many words of Latin or French origin, which stand equally in need of reformation.[2]

It is necessary to add, that if the public give way to a humour of this kind, there will be no end of innovating. When some critics first thought of reforming the word *bashaw*, one would have it *bassa*, another *pacha*, and a third *pasha;* and how many more shapes it may yet be transformed into it is impossible to say. A late historiographer hath adopted just the half of Sale's reformation of the name Mahomet. He restores the vowels to the places which they formerly held, but admits his alteration of the consonants, never writing either Mahomet or Mohammed, but Mahommed. In regard to such foreign names of persons, offices, eras, and rites, it would be obliging in writers of this stamp to annex to their works a glossary, for the sake of the

[8] Pape. [9] Papa. [1] Παππας.

[2] Suppose one of these Aristarchs advancing in such ingenious refinements, and thus criticizing on the word *aversion:* "This substantive is by divers authors diversely construed. Some say *aversion to a change*, others *aversion from a change:* both, I affirm, from a blind attachment to vernacular idioms, have alike deviated into the most ugly and deformed faults. This judgment, how severe soever, I am able to support by an irrefragable argument. *Aversion*, according to its etymology, denotes *turning from*. The first syllable *a* is, in the original language, a preposition signifying *from*. It would therefore be absurd to conjoin in the same phrase with it the preposition *to*, which hath a contrary signification; and to use *from* after aversion, would render the expression hideously pleonastic. In defiance therefore of a habitude which, however ancient and universal, is the offspring of ignorance, we must, if we would speak correctly, either say *aversion a change*, the first syllable *a* having the force of the preposition, or, cutting off this prepositive, we must say *version from a change*." If any should think this representation exaggerated, let him compare the reasoning with that which hath been seriously used for mutilating the word *alcoran*, and he will find it in all respects the same. It is, I acknowledge, of no consequence whether we say *alcoran* or *koran;* but it is of consequence that such a silly argument shall not be held a sufficient ground for innovation.

unlearned, who cannot divine whether their newfangled terms belong to things formerly unknown, or are no more than the old names of things familiar to them newly vamped and dressed. Surely if any thing deserves to be branded with the name of pedantry, it is an ostentation of erudition, to the reproach of learning, by affecting singularity in trifles.

I shall just mention another set of barbarisms, which also comes under this class, and arises from the abbreviation of polysyllables, by lopping off all the syllables except the first, or the first and second. Instances of this are *hyp* for *hypochondriac*, *rep* for *reputation*, *ult* for *ultimate*, *penult* for *penultimate*, *incog* for *incognito*, *hyper* for *hypercritic*, *extra* for *extraordinary*. Happily all these affected terms have been denied the public suffrage. I scarcely know any such that have established themselves, except *mob* for *mobile*.[3] And this it hath effected at last, notwithstanding the unrelenting zeal with which it was persecuted by Dr. Swift, wherever he met with it. But as the word in question hath gotten use, the supreme arbitress of language, on its side, there would be as much obstinacy in rejecting it at present, as there was perhaps folly at first in ushering it upon the public stage.

As to the humour of abbreviating, we need say very little, as it seems hardly now to subsist amongst us. It only arose in this island about the end of the last century, and when, in the beginning of the present, it assumed to figure in conversation, and even sometimes to appear in print, it was so warmly attacked by Addison and Swift, and other writers of eminence, that since then it hath been in general disgrace, hardly daring to appear in good company, and never showing itself in books of any name.

The two classes of barbarisms, last mentioned, comprehending new words, and new formations from words still current, offend against use, considered both as reputable and as national. There are many other sorts of transgression which might be enumerated here, such as vulgarisms, provincial idioms, and the cant of particular professions. But these are more commonly ranked among the offences against elegance than among the violations of grammatical purity, and will therefore be considered afterwards.

SECTION II.—*The Solecism.*

I now enter on the consideration of the second way by which the purity of the style is injured, the *solecism*. This is accounted by grammarians a much greater fault than the former,

[3] As I am disposed to think that in matters of this kind the public is rarely in the wrong, it would not be difficult to assign a plausible reason for this preference. First, the word *mobile*, from which it is contracted, can scarcely be called English, and, I suspect, never had the sanction of the public voice. Secondly, there is not another word in the language that expresses precisely the

as it displays a greater ignorance of the fundamental rules of the language. The sole aim of grammar is to convey the knowledge of the language; consequently, the degree of grammatical demerit in every blunder can only be ascertained by the degree of deficiency in this knowledge which it betrays. But the aim of eloquence is quite another thing. The speaker or the writer doth not purpose to display his knowledge in the language, but only to employ the language which he speaks or writes in order to the attainment of some further end. This knowledge he useth solely as the instrument or means by which he intends to instruct, to please, to move, or to persuade. The degree of demerit, therefore, which, by the orator's account, is to be found in every blunder, must be ascertained by a very different measure. Such offence is more or less heinous, precisely in proportion as it proves a greater or smaller obstruction to the speaker's or writer's aim. Hence it happens, that when solecisms are not very glaring, when they do not darken the sense or suggest some ridiculous idea, the rhetorician regards them as much more excusable than barbarisms. The reason is, the former is accounted solely the effect of negligence, the latter of affectation. Negligence in expression, often the consequence of a noble ardour in regard to the sentiments, is at the worst a venial trespass, sometimes it is even not without energy; affectation is always a deadly sin against the laws of rhetoric.

It ought also to be observed, that in the article of solecisms, much greater indulgence is given to the speaker than to the writer; and to the writer who proposeth to persuade or move, greater allowances are made, than to him who proposeth barely to instruct or please. The more vehemence is required by the nature of the subject, the less correctness is exacted in the manner of treating it. Nay, a remarkable deficiency in this respect is not near so prejudicial to the scope of the orator, as a scrupulous accuracy which bears in it the symptoms of study and art. Æschines is said to have remarked, that the orations of his rival and antagonist Demosthenes smelled of the lamp; thereby intimating that their style and composition were too elaborate. If the remark is just, it contains the greatest censure that ever was passed upon that eminent orator. But, as the intermediate degrees between the two extremes are innumerable, both doubtless ought to be avoided.

Grammatical inaccuracies ought to be avoided by a writer for two reasons. One is, that a reader will much sooner discover them than a hearer, however attentive he be. The other is,

same idea, *a tumultuous and seditious rout:* the word *mobility*, adopted by some writers, is a gross misapplication of a philosophical term, which means only *susceptibility of motion;* lastly, the word *mob*, is fitter than either of those for giving rise, according to the analogy of our tongue, to such convenient derivatives as *to mob, mobbed, mobbish, mobber.*

as writing implies more leisure and greater coolness than is implied in speaking, defects of this kind when discovered in the former, will be less excused than they would be in the latter.

To enumerate all the kinds of solecism into which it is possible to fall, would be both a useless and an endless task. The transgression of any of the syntactic rules is a solecism; and almost every rule may be transgressed in various ways. But as novices only are capable of falling into the most flagrant solecisms, such, I mean, as betray ignorance in the rudiments of the tongue, I shall leave it to grammarians to exemplify and class the various blunders of this sort which may be committed by the learner. All I propose to do at present, is to take notice of a few less observable, which writers of great name, and even critical skill in the language, have slidden into through inattention; and which, though of the nature of solecism, ought perhaps to be distinguished by the softer name *inaccuracy*.[4]

The first kind of this I shall observe is a mistake of the plural number for the singular, "The zeal of the *seraphim* breaks forth in a becoming warmth of sentiments and expressions, as the character which is given us of *him* denotes that generous scorn and intrepidity which attends heroic virtue."[5] *Cherub* and *seraph* are two nouns in the singular number transplanted into our language directly from the Hebrew. In the plural we are authorized, both by use and by analogy, to say either *cherubs* and *seraphs*, according to the English idiom, or *cherubim* and *seraphim*, according to the oriental. The former suits better the familiar, the latter the solemn style. It is surprising that an author of Mr. Addison's discernment, did not, in criticizing Milton, take notice of a distinction which is everywhere so carefully observed by the poet. I shall add to this remark, that as the words *cherubim* and *seraphim* are plural, the terms *cherubims* and *seraphims*, as expressing the plural, are quite improper. Yet these barbarisms occur sometimes in our translation of the Bible; which, nevertheless, doth not once adopt the plural form *cherubim* and *seraphim*, to express the singular; though one would naturally imagine that this error must originally have given rise to the other.

Inaccuracies are often found in the way wherein the degrees

[4] I am sensible that in what concerns the subject of this section I have been in a great measure prevented by the remarks of Lowth and Priestley, and some other critics and grammarians who have lately favoured the world with their observations. Since reading their publications, I have curtailed considerably what I had prepared on this article; for though I rarely hit upon the same examples, there was often a coincidence in the matter, inasmuch as the species of fault animadverted on was frequently the same. I have now almost entirely confined myself to such slips as have been overlooked by others. I say *almost entirely;* for when any error begins to prevail, even a single additional remonstrance may be of consequence; and in points on which critics are divided, I thought it not unreasonable to offer my opinion.

[5] Spectator, No. 327.

of comparison are applied and construed. Some of these, I suspect, have as yet escaped the animadversion of all our critics. Before I produce examples it will be proper to observe, that the comparative degree implies commonly a comparison of one thing with one other thing; the superlative, on the contrary, always implies a comparison of one thing with many others. The former, consequently, requires to be followed by the singular number, the latter by the plural. In our language the conjunction *than* must be interposed between the things compared in the former case, the preposition *of* is always used in the latter.

The following is an example of wrong construction in the comparative: "This noble nation hath *of all others* admitted *fewer* corruptions."[6] The word *fewer* is here construed precisely as if it were the superlative. Grammatically thus: "This noble nation hath admitted *fewer* corruptions *than any other*." Sometimes indeed the comparative is rightly followed by a plural; as in these words, "He is wiser than we." But it cannot be construed with the preposition *of*, before that to which the subject is compared. There is one case, and but one, wherein the aforesaid preposition is proper after the comparative, and that is, when the words following the preposition comprehend both sides of the comparison; as, "He is the taller man of the two." In these words *the two* are included, he and the person to whom he is compared. It deserves our notice also, that in such cases, and only in such, the comparative has the definite article *the* prefixed to it, and is construed precisely as the superlative: nay, both degrees are in such cases used indiscriminately. We say rightly, either, "This is the weaker of the two," or—"the weakest of the two." If, however, we may form a judgment from the most general principles of analogy, the former is preferable because there are only two things compared.

I shall subjoin to this an inaccuracy in a comparison of equality, where, though the positive degree only is used, the construction must be similar to that of the comparative, both being followed by conjunctions which govern no case. "Such notions would be avowed at this time by none but Rosicrucians, and fanatics as mad *as them*."[7] Grammatically *they*, the verb *are* being understood.

That the particles, *as* after the positive, and *than* after the comparative, are conjunctions and not prepositions, seems never to have been questioned by any grammarian or critic before Dr. Priestley. I readily acknowledge that it is use which must decide the point; nor should I hesitate a moment in agreeing to the notion he suggests, if it were supported by what could be justly denominated general and reputable use. But to me

[6] Swift's Mechanical Operations.

[7] Bolingbroke's Ph. Fr. 24.

it is manifest that both the most numerous and the most considerable authorities are on the opposite side; and therefore, that those instances which he produceth in favour of that hypothesis ought to be regarded merely as negligences of style, into which (as I shall have occasion to observe more fully in the sequel) even the best writers will sometimes fall. That in the colloquial dialect, as Johnson calls it, such idioms frequently occur, is undeniable. In conversation you will perhaps ten times oftener hear people say, "There's the books you wanted," than "There are the books ——;" and "You was present," when a single person is addressed, than "You were present." Yet good use is always considered as declaring solely for the last mode of expression in both cases. The argument drawn from the French usage (which, by the way, hath no authority in our tongue), is not at all apposite.[8]

But supposing good use were divided on the present question, I acknowledge that the first and second canons proposed on this subject,[9] would determine me to prefer the opinion of those who consider the aforesaid particles as conjunctions. The first directs us in doubtful cases to incline to that side in which there is the least danger of ambiguity. In order to illustrate this point, it will be necessary to observe, that the doubt is not properly stated by saying, with Dr. Priestley, that the question is, whether the nominative or accusative ought to follow the particles *than* and *as;* but, whether these particles are, in such particular cases, to be regarded as conjunctions or prepositions. For on either supposition, it must be admitted, that in certain circumstances the accusative ought to follow, and not the nominative. But I insist, that as in such cases there is a difference in the sense, uniformly to consider those particles as conjunctions is the only way of removing ambiguity. Thus I say properly, "I esteem you more than they." I say pro-

[8] The oblique cases of their personal pronouns, answering to our *me, thee,* and *him,* are *me, te,* and *le,* not *moi, toi,* and *lui.* In these last we have the indefinite form, which serves indifferently, as occasion requires, for either nominative or accusative, and to which there is nothing in our language that exactly corresponds. Thus, to express in French, "He and I are relations," we must say, "Lui et moi, nous sommes parens." But in English, "Him and me, we are relations," would be insufferable. The nominatives, *je, tu, il,* are never used by them, but when immediately joined to the verb, prefixed in affirming, or affixed in interrogating. In every other situation the indefinite form must supply their place. *Le Clerc* thus renders a passage of Scripture (Rev. i. 18), "Moi qui vis présentement, j'ai été mort." But who that understands English would say, "Me who live at present, I have been dead." Let this serve also as an answer to the plea for these vulgar, but unauthorized idioms, *It is me, It is him,* from the *C'est moi, C'est lui,* of the French. I shall observe, in passing, that one of Priestley's quotations in support of these phrases is defensible on a different principle, and therefore not to his purpose. "It is not *me* you are in love with." The *me* is here governed by the preposition *with.* "It is not *with me* you are in love."—Such transpositions are frequent in our language.

[9] Book II. Chap. ii. Sect. 1.

perly also, "I esteem you more than them," but in a sense quite different. If *than* is understood as a conjnnction, there can be nothing ambiguous in either sentence. The case of the pronoun determines at once the words to be supplied. The first is, "I esteem you more than they *esteem you*." The second is, "I esteem you more than I *esteem* them." But this distinction is confounded, if you make *than* a preposition, which, as in every instance it will require the oblique case, will by consequence render the expression equivocal. For this reason, I consider that quotation from Smollet (who is, by the bye, the only authority alleged on this question),—"Tell the cardinal, that I understand poetry better than him," as chargeable not so much with inaccuracy as with impropriety. The sense it expresses is clearly, "I understand poetry better than I understand him." But this is not the sense of the author. The second canon leads directly to the same decision, as it teacheth us to prefer what is most agreeable to analogy. Now, that is always most repugnant to analogy, which tends most to multiply exceptions. Consequently, to consider the particles employed in this manner, of stating a comparison as conjunctions (which they are universally admitted to be in every other case), is more analogical than to consider them as changing their usual denomination and character in such instances.

But to proceed; incorrectness in using the superlative degree, appears in the subsequent quotation: "The vice of covetousness is what enters *deepest* into the soul *of any other*."[1] An instance of the same fault I shall give from a writer of no small merit for harmony and elegance. "We have a profession set apart for the purposes of persuasion, wherein a talent of this kind would prove *the likeliest* perhaps *of any other*."[2] I do not here criticize on the word *other* in those examples which, in my opinion, is likewise faulty, after the superlative; but this fault comes under another category. The error I mean at present to point out, is the superlative followed by the singular number, "the deepest of any other," "the likeliest of any other." We should not say, "the best of any man," or "the best of any other man," for "the best of men." We may indeed say, "He is the oldest of the family." But the word family is a collective noun, and equivalent to *all in the house*. In like manner it may be said, "The eyes are the worst of his face." But this expression is evidently deficient. The face is not the thing with which the eyes are compared, but contains the things with which they are compared. The sentence, when the ellipsis is supplied, stands thus, "Of all the features of his face, the eyes are the worst."

Both the expressions above censured may be corrected by substituting the comparative in room of the superlative. "The

[1] Guardian, No. 19. [2] Fitz-Osborn's Letters, B. i. L. 24.

vice of covetousness is what enters *deeper* into the soul *than any other;*" and "We have a profession set apart for the purposes of persuasion, wherein a talent of this kind would prove *likelier* perhaps *than any other.*" It is also possible to retain the superlative, and render the expression grammatical. "Covetousness is what *of all vices* enters *the deepest* into the soul;"——and "wherein a talent of this kind would perhaps *of all talents* prove the *likeliest.*"

In the following example we have a numeral adjective, which doth not belong to any entire word in the sentence as its substantive, but to a part of a word. "The first project was to shorten discourse by cutting polysyllables into one."[3] The term *one* relates to *syllable*, a part of the word polysyllables. This is quite ungrammatical. The expression is likewise exceptionable on the score of propriety, but of this afterwards.

There is an error of the same kind in the following passage from Addison, "My Christian and sirname begin and end with the same letters."[4] The word Christian is here an adjective, which hath for its substantive the last syllable of the word sirname. The expression is also exceptionable on the score of perspicuity, of which afterwards.

Sometimes the possessive pronoun does not suit the antecedent. "*Each* of the sexes," says Addison, "should keep within *its* particular bounds, and content *themselves* to exult within *their* respective districts."[5] *Themselves* and *their* cannot grammatically refer to *each*, as singular. Besides, the trespass here is the more glaring, that these pronouns are coupled with *its* referring to the same noun.

In no part of speech do good writers more frequently fall into mistakes than in the verbs. Of these I shall give some specimens out of a much greater number which might be collected. The first shall be of a wrong tense, "*Ye will* not come unto me, that ye *might* have life."[6] In two clauses thus connected, when the first verb is in the present or the future, the second, which is dependent on it, cannot be in the past. The words, therefore, ought to have been translated, "that ye *may* have life." On the contrary, had the first verb been in the preterite, the second ought to have been so too. Thus, "*Ye would* not come to me," or, "*Ye did* not come to me, that ye *might* have life," is entirely grammatical. In either of these instances, to use the present tense would be erroneous. When the first verb is in the preterperfect, or the present perfect, as some call it, because it hath a reference both to the past and to the present, the second, I imagine, may be either tense. Thus, "Ye *have* not *come* to me that ye *might,*"—or, "that ye *may*—have life," seem equally unexceptionable.

[3] Voyage to Laputa.
[4] Spectator, No. 505. O.
[5] Freeholder, No. 38.
[6] John v. 40.

Let it be observed, that in expressing abstract or universal truths, the present tense of the verb ought, according to the idiom of our language, and perhaps of every language, always to be employed. In such cases, the verb in that form has no relation to time, but serves merely as a copula to the two terms of the proposition. The case is different with the past and the future, in which the notion of time is always comprehended. Yet this peculiarity in the present hath sometimes been overlooked, even by good authors, who, when speaking of a past event which occasions the mention of some general truth, are led to use the same tense in enunciating the general truth, with that which has been employed in the preceding part of the sentence. Of this we have the following example from Swift, which shall serve for the second instance of inaccuracy in the verbs. "It is confidently reported, that two young gentlemen of real hopes, bright wit, and profound judgment, who, upon a thorough examination of causes and effects, and by the mere force of natural abilities, without the least tincture of learning, have made a discovery, that there *was* no God, and generously communicating their thoughts for the good of the public, were some time ago, by an unparalleled severity, and upon I know not what obsolete law, broke for blasphemy."[7] Properly—"have made a discovery that there *is* no God."

The third example shall be of a wrong mood. "*If* thou *bring* thy gift to the altar, and there *rememberest* that thy brother hath ought against thee."[8]——The construction of the two verbs *bring* and *rememberest* ought to be the same, as they are both under the regimen of the same conjunction *if*. Yet the one is in the subjunctive mood, the other in the indicative.

The fourth instance shall be the omission of an essential part of one of the complex tenses, the writer apparently referring to a part of the verb occurring in a former clause of the sentence, although the part referred to will not supply the defect, but some other part not produced. Of this the following is an example: "I shall do all I can to persuade others to *take* the same measures for their cure which I *have*."[9] Here we have a reference in the end to the preceding verb *take*. Yet it is not the word *take* which will supply the sense, but *taken*. This participle, therefore, ought to have been added.

The fifth specimen in the verbs shall be of a faulty reference to a part to be mentioned. "This dedication may serve for almost any book, that *has*, is, or shall be published." *Has* in this place being merely a part of a complex tense, means nothing without the rest of the tense. Yet the rest of the tense

[7] An Argument against abolishing Christianity. [8] Matt. v. 23.
[9] Guardian, No. 1.

is not to be found in the sentence. We cannot say, "any book that *has published*," no more can we say "that *has be published*." Corrected it would run thus, "that *has been*, or *shall be* published." The word *is* ought to be expunged, as adding nothing to the sense.

I shall next produce a few instances of inaccuracy, which result from coupling words together, and assigning to them a common regimen, when use will not admit that they be construed in the same manner. The following is an example in the construction of adjectives: "Will it be urged, that the four gospels are *as old* or even *older than* tradition?"[1] The words *as old* and *older* cannot have a common regimen; the one requires to be followed by the conjunction *as*, the other by *than*. If he had said, "*as old as* tradition, and even *older;*" there would have been no error. The comparative, in this case, is not construed with the preceding words, but with words which, being ascertained by the preceding, are properly enough understood.

I shall exemplify the same inaccuracy in the construction of verbs. "It requireth few talents *to which* most men are not *born*, or at least may not *acquire*."[2] Admitting that the words *to which* are rightly construed with the passive particle *born*, they cannot be construed with the active verb *acquire*. For it ought to be noted, that the connexion between the preposition and the noun or pronoun governed by it is so intimate, that there cannot be a reference to the one without the other. The last clause therefore, ought to run thus, "or *which* at least *they* may not acquire." The repetition of the relative makes the insertion of the personal pronoun necessary.

There is an error of the same kind in the sentence following: "The court of Chancery frequently *mitigates*, and breaks the teeth of common law."[3] What is the regimen of the active verb *mitigates?* Regularly it ought to be *the teeth of the common law*, as these words make the regimen of the active verb *breaks*, with which the former is coupled. But as this manner of construing the sentence would render the expression highly improper, if not nonsensical, it is evidently the author's view, that the verb *mitigates* should be construed with these words *the common law*, which being in construction with the preposition *of* (or, as some would call it, in the genitive) cannot serve grammatically as the regimen of an active verb.

"Give the Whigs," says the candid Dean of Saint Patrick's, "but power enough to insult their sovereign, engross his favours to themselves, and to oppress and plunder their fellow-subjects; they presently *grow into* good humour, and *good*

[1] Bolingb. Ph. Es. iv. S. 19.
[2] Swift on Conversation.
[3] Spectator, No. 564.

language towards the crown." [4] I do not like much *grow into good humour*, for growing good-humoured, but *grow into good language* is insufferable.

I shall add to these an instance in the syntax of nouns. "There is never wanting a set of evil instruments, who either *out of* mad zeal, private hatred, or *filthy lucre*, are always ready."[5]—We say properly, "A man acts *out of mad zeal*, or *out of private hatred*:" but we cannot say, if we would speak English, "He acts *out of filthy lucre*." He ought, therefore, to have substituted in the place of the two last words the term *avarice*, or *love of filthy lucre*, either of which expressions would have been rightly construed with the preposition.

Of the same kind nearly is the following specimen in the government of a substantive: "There is one that will think herself obliged to double her *kindness* and *caresses* of me." [6] The word *kindness* requires to be followed by either *to* or *for*, and cannot be construed with the preposition *of*.

We often find something irregular in the management of the prepositions; for instance, in the omission of one altogether: "He lamented the fatal mistake the world had been so long *in* using silk-worms." [7] Another *in* is necessary to complete the construction, whether we suppose the *in* mentioned to belong to the preceding words, or to the succeeding. But as it would have sounded harshly to subjoin another *in* immediately after the former, it would have been better to give the sentence another turn: as, "He lamented the fatal mistake *in* which the world have been so long, *in* using silk-worms." [8]

We have a similar omission, though not of a preposition, in the expression following: "That the discoursing on politics shall be looked upon *as* dull *as* talking on the weather." [9] Syntax absolutely requires, that the sentence in this form should have another *as* immediately before the first. At the same time it must be owned, that this would render the expression very inelegant. This dilemma might have been avoided by giving another turn to the concluding part, as thus, "—— shall be looked upon as equally dull with talking on the weather."

Of an error in the wrong choice of a preposition, these words of the same author will furnish an example: "The greatest masters of critical learning differ *among one another*." [1] Had he said, "differ *among themselves*," the expression would have been faultless. But the terms *themselves* and *one another*, though frequently synonymous, rarely admit the same construction. We cannot say, "one differs *among another*." But we may say, "one differs *from another*," or "*with another*;"

[4] Examiner, No. 35.
[5] Swift's Sermon on False Witness.
[6] Spect. No. 409. T.
[7] Voyage to Laputa.
[8] Voyage to Laputa.
[9] Freeholder, No. 38.
[1] Spectator, No. 321.

the former to express a difference in opinion, the latter a quarrel or breach. It ought, therefore, to have been in the above cited passage, "differ *from one another.*"

I shall only add an instance or two of inaccuracy in the conjunctions and the adverbs; first in the conjunctions: "A petty constable will *neither* act cheerfully *or* wisely."[2]—Properly—"act *neither* cheerfully *nor* wisely." *Neither* cannot grammatically be followed by *or*.

An example of incorrectness in the adverbs you have in the passage following; "Lest I should be charged for being worse than my word, I shall endeavour to satisfy my reader by pursuing my method proposed; *if peradventure* he can call to mind what that method was.[3] The adverb *peradventure*, expressing a degree of evidence or credibility, cannot regularly be construed with the hypothetical conjunction *if*. It is only to affirmations and negations, not to bare suppositions, that all the adverbs denoting certainty, probability, or possibility, properly belong.

The following passage in the common version of the Bible is liable to the same censure; Micaiah said, *if* thou *certainly* return in peace, then hath not the Lord spoken by me."[4] The translators in this, as in some other places, have been misled by a well-meant attempt to express the force of a hebraism, which in many cases cannot be expressed in our language.

I shall conclude this article with a quotation from an excellent author, of which, indeed, it would not be easy to say in what part the solecism may be discovered, the whole passage being so perfectly solecistical. "As he that would keep his house in repair, must attend every little breach or flaw, and supply it immediately, else time alone will bring all to ruin; how much more the common accidents of storms and rain? He must live in perpetual danger of his house falling about his ears; and will find it cheaper to throw it quite down, and build it again from the ground, perhaps upon a new foundation, or at least in a new form, which may neither be so safe nor so convenient as the old."[5] It is impossible to analyze this sentence grammatically, or to say whether it be one sentence or more. It seems by the conjunction *as*, to begin with a comparison, but we have not a single hint of the subject illustrated. Besides, the introducing of the interrogation, How much more—? after *else*, which could be regularly followed only by an affirmation or negation; and the incoherency of the next clause, *He must live*—render it indeed—all of a piece.

[2] Swift's Free Thoughts, &c.

[3] Shaftesbury, Vol. iii. Misc. ii. Ch. 3.

[4] 2 Chron. xviii. 27. Sacy, in his French translation, hath expressed the sense of the original with more simplicity and propriety. "Michée repartit, Si vous revenez en paix, le Seigneur n'a point parlé par ma bouche."

[5] Project for the Advancement of Religion. Last sentence.

So much for the solecism, of which examples might be multiplied almost without end. Let those produced suffice for a specimen. It is acknowledged, that such negligences are not to be considered as blemishes of any moment in a work of genius, since those, and even worse, may be discovered, on a careful examination, in the most celebrated writings. It is for this reason acknowledged also, that it is neither candid nor judicious to form an opinion of a book from a few such specks, selected perhaps from the distant parts of a large performance, and brought into our view at once. Yet, on the other hand, it is certain that an attention to these little things ought not to be altogether disregarded by any writer. Purity of expression hath but a small share of merit: it hath, however, some share. But it ought especially to be remembered that, on the account of purity, a considerable part of the merit discovered in the other virtues of elocution, to which it contributes, ought undoubtedly to be charged. The words of the language constitute the materials with which the orator must work; the rules of the language teach him by what management those materials are rendered useful. And what is purity but the right using of the words of the language by a careful observance of the rules? It is therefore justly considered as essential to all the other graces of expression. Hence, not only perspicuity and vivacity, but even elegance and animation derive a lustre.

SECTION III.—*The Impropriety.*

I come now to consider the third and last class of faults against purity, to which I gave the name of *impropriety*. The barbarism is an offence against etymology, the solecism against syntax, the impropriety against lexicography. The business of the lexicographer is to assign to every word of the language the precise meaning or meanings which use hath assigned to it. To do this is as really a part of the grammarian's province, though commonly executed by a different hand, as etymology and syntax. The end of every grammar is to convey the knowledge of that language of which it is the grammar. But the knowledge of all the rules, both of derivation, under which inflection is included, and of construction, nay, and of all the words in the language, is not the knowledge of the language. The words must be known, not barely as sounds, but as signs. We must know to what things respectively they are appropriated. Thus, in our own tongue, we may err egregiously against propriety, and consequently against purity, though all the words we employ be English, and though they be construed in the English idiom. The reason is evident; they may be misapplied; they may be employed as signs of things to which use hath not affixed them. This fault may be committed either in single words or in phrases.

PART I.—*Impropriety in single Words.*

I begin with single words. As none but those who are grossly ignorant of our tongue can misapply the words that have no affinity to those whose place they are made to occupy, I shall take notice only of such improprieties, as by some resemblance of proximity in sound, or sense, or both, a writer is apt unwarily to be seduced into.

It is by proximity in sound that several are misled to use the word *observation* for *observance*, as when they speak of the religious observation of a festival, for the religious observance of it. Both words spring from the root *observe*, but in different significations. When to observe signifies to *remark*, the verbal noun is *observation:* when it signifies to *obey* or to keep, the verbal is *observance*.

By a similar mistake *endurance* hath been used for *duration*, and confounded with it; whereas its proper sense is *patience*. It is derived from the active verb to endure, which signifies to *suffer*, and not from the neuter which signifies to *last*. In the days of Queen Elizabeth, the word endurance was synonymous with duration, whereas now it is in this acceptation obsolete. Nay, even in a later period, about the middle of the last century, several words were used synonymously which we now invariably discriminate. Such are the terms *state* and *estate*, *property* and *propriety*, *import* and *importance*, *conscience* and *consciousness*, *arrant* and *errant*.

Human and *humane* are sometimes confounded, though the only authorized sense of the former is, *belonging to man;* of the latter, *kind and compassionate*. *Humanly* is improperly put for *humanely* in these lines of Pope:

> Tho' learn'd, well-bred; and tho' well-bred, sincere:
> Modestly bold, and *humanly* severe.[6]

The abstract *humanity* is equally adapted to both senses.

By an error of the same kind with the former, the adjectives *ceremonious* and *ceremonial* are sometimes used promiscuously, though by the best and most general use they are distinguished. They come from the same noun *ceremony*, which signifies both a *form of civility*, and a *religious rite*. The epithet expressive of the first signification is *ceremonious*, of the second *ceremonial*.

The word *construction* serves as the verbal noun of two different verbs, to *construe* and to *construct*. The first is a grammatical term, relating solely to the disposition of words in

[6] Essay on Criticism.

a sentence; the second signifies to *fabricate* or *build.* The common relation in which the two verbs stand to the same appellative, hath misled some writers to confound them; so far at least as to use improperly the word *construct*, and speak of *constructing*, instead of construing, a sentence; for I have not observed the like misapplication of the other verb. We never read of *construing* a fabric or machine.

Academician is frequently to be found in Bolingbroke's works for *academic.* The former denotes solely with us a member of a French academy, or of one established on a similar footing; the latter of a Platonic philosopher, one of that sect which took its denomination from the Grecian academy; or more properly from the grove of Academus, where the principles of that philosophy were first inculcated.

By a like error, the words *sophist* and *sophister* are sometimes confounded; the proper sense of the former being a teacher of philosophy in ancient Greece; of the latter, a specious, but false reasoner.

"To *demean* one's self" has been improperly used by some writers, misled by the sound of the second syllable, for "to debase one's self," or "to behave meanly;" whereas the verb *to demean* implies no more than the verb *to behave.* Both require an adverb, or something equivalent, to enable them to express whether the demeanour or behaviour is good or bad, noble or mean.

E'er, a contraction of the adverb *ever*, hath, from a resemblance, or rather an identity in sound, been mistaken for the conjunction *ere*, before; and in like manner *it's*, the genitive of the pronoun *it*, for *'tis*, a contraction of *it is.*

In the same way *bad* is sometimes very improperly used for *bade*, the preterite of the verb *bid*, and *sate* for *sat*, the preterite of *sit.* The only proper use of the word *bad* is as a synonyma for *ill*; and to *sate* is the same in signification as to *glut.*

The word *genii* hath by some writers been erroneously adopted for *geniuses.* Each is a plural of the same word *genius*, but in different senses. When *genius* in the singular means a separate spirit or demon good or bad, the plural is *genii;* when it denotes mental abilities, or a person eminently possessed of these, the plural is *geniuses.* There are some similar instances in our tongue of different plurals belonging to the same singular in different significations. The word *brother* is one. The plural in modern language, when used literally for male children of the same parent or parents, is *brothers;* when used figuratively for people of the same profession, nation, religion, or people considered as related by sharing jointly in the same human nature, is *brethren.* Anciently this last term was the only plural.

I shall next specify improprieties arising from a similitude in sense, into which writers of considerable reputation have sometimes fallen. *Veracity* you will find, even among such, applied to things, and used for *reality;* whereas in strict propriety the word is only applicable to persons, and signifies not physical, but moral truth.

"*There* is no sort of joy," says Dr. Burnet,[7] "more grateful to the mind of man, than that which raiseth from the *invention* of truth." For *invention* he ought to have said *discovery.*

Epithet hath been used corruptly to denote *title* or *appellation;* whereas it only signifies some attribute expressed by an adjective.

In the same way, *verdict* hath been made to usurp the place of *testimony;* and the word *risible* hath of late been perverted from its original sense, which is *capable of laughing*, to denote *ridiculous*, *laughable*, or *fit to be laughed at.* Hence these newfangled phrases *risible jests*, and *risible absurdities.* The proper discrimination between *risible* and *ridiculous* is, that the former hath an active, the latter a passive signification. Thus we say, "Man is a *risible* animal."—"A fop is a *ridiculous* character." To substitute the former instead of the latter, and say, "A fop is a *risible* character," is, I suspect, no better English, than to substitute the latter instead of the former, and say, "Man is a *ridiculous* animal." In confirmation of this distinction it may be further remarked, that the abstract *risibility*, which analogically ought to determine the import of the concrete, is still limited to its original and active sense, the *faculty of laughter.* Where our language hath provided us with distinct names for the active verbal and the passive, as no distinction is more useful for preventing ambiguity, so no distinction ought to be more sacredly observed.

But to proceed; the word *together* often supplies the place of *successively*, sometimes awkwardly enough, as in the following sentence. "I do not remember that I ever spoke three sentences *together* in my whole life."[8] The resemblance which continuity in time bears to continuity in place is the source of this impropriety, which, by the way, is become so frequent, that I am doubtful whether it ought to be included in the number. Yet, should this application generally obtain, it would, by confounding things different, often occasion ambiguity. If, for example, one should say, "Charles, William, and David, lived *together* in the same house," in order to denote that William immediately succeeded Charles, and David succeeded William, every one would be sensible of the impropriety. But if such a use of the word be improper in one case, it is so in every case.

By an error not unlike, the word *everlasting* hath been em-

[7] Theory of the Earth, B. i. Ch 1.

[8] Spect. No. 1.

ployed to denote time without beginning, though the only proper sense of it be time without end; as in these words, "From *everlasting* to everlasting thou art God."[9] It may further be remarked of this term, that the true meaning is so strongly marked in its composition, that very frequent use will not be sufficient to prevent the misapplication from appearing awkward. I think, besides, that there is a want of correctness in using the word substantively. The proper expression is, "From *eternity* to eternity thou art God."

Apparent for *certain, manifest,* (as it has been sometimes employed by a very eminent author, the late Lord Lyttleton,) is often equivocal, and can hardly ever be accounted entirely proper. Both etymology and the most frequent use lead us so directly to the signification *seeming* as opposed to *real,* or *visible* as opposed to *concealed,* that at first we are always in hazard of mistaking it. For the same reason I do not like the phrase *to make appear* (though a very common one) for *to prove, to evince, to show.* By the aid of sophistry a man may *make* a thing *appear* to be what it is not. This is very different from showing what it is.

Abundance, in the following quotation, is, I imagine, improperly used for a *great deal.* "I will only mention that passage of the buskins, which, after *abundance* of persuasion, you would hardly suffer to be cut from your legs."[1]

The word *due,* in the citation subjoined, is not only improperly, but preposterously employed. "What right the first observers of nature, and instructors of mankind, had to the title of sages we cannot say. It was *due* perhaps more to the ignorance of the scholars, than to the knowledge of the masters." The author hath doubtless adopted the word *due* in this place, as preferable at least to the word *owing,* which, though an active particle, is frequently, and some think inaccurately, employed in a passive sense. Thus, in order to avoid a latent error, if it be an error, he hath run into a palpable absurdity; for what can be more absurd than to say, that the title of sages is due more to ignorance than to knowledge? It had been better to give the sentence another turn, and to say, "It took its rise perhaps more from the ignorance of the scholars, than from the knowledge of the masters."

I shall add the improper use of the word *surfeit,* in the following quotation from Anson's Voyage round the World: "We thought it prudent totally to abstain from fish, the few we caught at our first arrival having *surfeited* those who ate of them."[3] I should not have mentioned, indeed I should not have discovered, this impropriety in that excellent performance,

[9] Ps. xc. 2.
[1] Swift's Examiner, No. 27.
[2] Bolingb. Phil. Ess. ii. Sect. 1.
[3] Anson's Voyage, B. iii. C. 2.

which would have passed with me for an expression somewhat indefinite, had it not been for the following passage in a late publication. "Several of our people were so much disordered by eating of a very fine-looking fish, which we caught here, that their recovery was for a long time doubtful. The author of the account of Lord Anson's Voyage says, that the people on board the Centurion thought it prudent to abstain from fish, as the few which they caught at their first arrival surfeited those who ate of them. But not attending sufficiently to this caution, and too hastily taking the word *surfeit* in its literal and common acceptation, we imagined that those who tasted the fish, when Lord Anson first came hither, were made sick merely by eating too much; whereas, if that had been the case, there would have been no reason for totally abstaining, but only eating temperately. We, however, bought our knowledge by experience, which we might have had cheaper; for though all our people who tasted this fish ate sparingly, they were all soon afterwards dangerously ill."[4] I have given this passage entire, chiefly because it serves to show both that an inaccuracy, apparently trifling, may, by misleading the reader, be productive of very bad consequences; and that those remarks which tend to add precision and perspicuity to our language are not of so little moment as some, who have not duly considered the subject, would affect to represent them.

To this class we may reduce the *idiotism*, or the employing of an English word in a sense which it bears in some provincial dialect, in low and partial use, or which perhaps the corresponding word bears in some foreign tongue, but unsupported by general use in our own language. An example of this we have in the word *impracticable*, when it is used for *impassable*, and applied to roads; an application which suits the French idiom, but not the English. Of the same kind, are the following Gallicisms of Bolingbroke: "All this was done, at the time, on the occasion, and by the persons, I *intend*,"[5] properly *mean*. "When we learn the name of complex ideas and notions we should accustom the mind to *decompound* them, that we may verify them, and so make them our own, as well as to learn to compound others."[6] *Decompound* he hath used for *analyze*, misled by the meaning of the French word *decomposer*, which is not only different from the sense of the English word but contrary to it. *To decompound*, is to compound of materials already compounded.

The use made of the verb *arrive*, in the subsequent passage, is also exceptionable in the same way: "I am a man, and can-

[4] Byron's Voyage, Chap. xi. [5] Of the State of Parties.
[6] Phil. Ess. i. Sect. 4.

not help feeling any sorrow that can *arrive at* man."[7] In English, it should be, "*happen* to man."

To hold, signifying *to use*, and applied to language; *to give into*, signifying *to adopt*, in the figurative sense of that word; are other expressions frequently employed by this author, and of late by several others, which fall under the same censure. Even our celebrated translator of the Iliad hath not been clear of this charge. Witness the title he hath given to a small dissertation prefixed to that work. "A view," he calls it, "of *the* epic *poem*," in which short title there are two improprieties. First the word *poem*, which always denotes with us a particular performance, is here used, agreeably to the French idiom, for *poetry* in general, or the art which characterizes the performance; secondly, the definite article *the* is employed, which, though it be always given to abstracts in French, is never so applied in English, unless with a view to appropriate them to some subject. And this, by the way, renders the article with us more determinative than it is in French, or perhaps in any other tongue.[8] Accordingly, on the first hearing of the title above mentioned, there is no English reader who would not suppose, that it were a critical tract on some particular epic poem, and not on that species of poesy.

Another error of the same kind is the *Latinism*. Of this, indeed, the examples are not so frequent. Foppery is a sort of folly much more contagious than pedantry; but as they result alike from affectation, they deserve alike to be proscribed. An instance of the latter is the word *affection*, when applied to things inanimate, and signifying the state of being affected by any cause. Another instance is the word *integrity* when used, for entireness. But here, I think, a distinction ought to be made between the familiar style and that of philosophical disquisition. In the latter, it will be reasonable to allow a greater latitude, especially in cases wherein there may be a penury of proper terms, and wherein, without such indulgence, there would be a necessity of recurring too often to periphrasis. But the less, even here, this liberty is used, it is the better.

To these properly succeeds that sort of the *vulgarism*[9] in which only a low and partial use can be pleaded in support of the application that is made of a particular word. Of this you have an example in the following quotation: "'Tis my humble request you will be particular in speaking *to* the following

[7] Spectator, No. 502. T.

[8] Accordingly Bossu hath styled his performance on the same subject, *Traité du Poëme Epique*. It is this title, I suppose, which hath misled the English poet

[9] I say, that sort of the vulgarism, because, when the word is in no acceptation in good use, it is a sort that partakes of the barbarism; but when a particular application of a good word is current only among the lower classes, it belongs to the impropriety.

points."[1] The preposition ought to have been *on*. Precisely of the same stamp is the *on't* for *of it*, so much used by one class of writers. The pronoun *it* is by a like idiom made sometimes to follow neuter verbs, as in the following passage: "He is an assertor of liberty and property; he rattles *it* out against popery and arbitrary power, and priestcraft and high church."[2]

The auxiliaries *should*, *should have*, and *should be*, are sometimes used in the same improper manner. I am not sensible of the elegance which Dr. Priestley seems to have discovered in the expression—"The general report is that *he should have said*"—for "that *he said*." It appears to me not only as an idiomatical expression, but as chargeable both with pleonasm and with ambiguity. For what a man said is often very different from what he should have said.

I shall finish all that I propose to offer on the idiotism, when I have observed, that these remarks are not to be extended to the precincts of satire and burlesque. There indeed a vulgar, or even what is called a cant expression, will sometimes be more emphatical than any proper term whatsoever. The satirist may plead his privilege. For this reason the following lines are not to be considered as falling under this criticism.

> Whether the charmer sinner it, or saint it,
> If folly grows romantic, I must paint it.[3]

It remains to give some instances wherein sound and sense both concur in misleading us. Of this the word *enough* is an example, which is frequently confounded with *enow*, and used for it. Both denote sufficiency, the former in quantity or in degrees of quality, the latter in number. Thus we say properly, "We have courage *enough*, and ammunition *enough*; but we have not men *enow*."

The derivatives *falseness*, *falsity*, *falsehood*, from the root *false*, are often by mistake employed for one another, though in the best use they are evidently distinguished. The first, *falseness*, is properly used in a moral sense for want of veracity, and applied only to persons; the other two are applied only to things. *Falsity* denotes that quality in the abstract, which may be defined contrariety to truth. *Falsehood* is an untrue assertion. The word *negligence* is improperly used in the following passage: "The *negligence* of this leaves us exposed to an uncommon levity in our usual conversation."[4] He ought to have said *neglect*. The former implies the habit, the latter denotes the act; perhaps in this case I should say the instance;

[1] Guardian, No. 57.
[2] Swift's Project for the Advancement of Religion.
[3] Pope. [4] Spect. No. 76.

for an act of a habit of not doing, hath itself the appearance of impropriety.

Precisely of the same kind is the misapplication of the word *conscience* in this quotation. "The *conscience* of approving one's self a benefactor to mankind, is the noblest recompense for being so."[5] Properly the *consciousness;* the former denotes the faculty, the latter a particular exertion.

This impropriety is reversed in the citation following: "I apprehend that all the *sophism,* which has been, or can be employed, will not be sufficient to acquit this system at the tribunal of reason."[6] For *sophism* he should have said *sophistry;* this denotes fallacious reasoning, that only a fallacious argument. This error is of the same kind with *poem* for *poetry,* which was remarked above.

Sometimes the neuter verb is mistaken for the active. "What Tully says of war, may be applied to disputing; it should always be so managed, as to *remember,* that the only end of it is peace."[7] Properly *remind us.*

Sometimes again, the active verb is mistaken for the neuter. "I may say without vanity, that there is not a gentleman in England better read in tomb-stones than myself, my studies having *laid* very much in church-yards."[8] Properly *lien* or *lain.* The active verb *lay* for the neuter *lie,* is so frequently to be met with in some very modern compositions, as to give room for suspecting that it is an idiom of the cockney language, or of some provincial dialect. In that case it might have been classed under the idiotism.

Perhaps under the same predicament ought also to be ranked the word *plenty,* used adjectively for *plentiful,* which indeed appears to me so gross a vulgarism, that I should not have thought it worthy a place here, if I had not sometimes found it in works of considerable merit. The relative *whom,* in the following quotation, is improperly used for *which,* the former always regarding persons, the latter always things. "The exercise of reason appears as little in them, as in the beasts they sometimes hunt, and by *whom* they are sometimes hunted."[9]

I shall add but two more instances of impropriety in single words, instances which I have reserved for this place, as being somewhat peculiar, and therefore not strictly reducible to any of the classes above mentioned; instances too, from authors of such eminence in respect of style, as may fully convince us, if we are not already convinced, that infallibility is not more attainable here than in other articles. "As I firmly believe the divine *precept,* delivered by the Author of Christianity, 'There is not a sparrow falls to the ground without my Father,' and

[5] Spect. No. 588.
[6] Bol. Ph. Ess. 20.
[7] Pope's Thoughts on various Subjects.
[8] Spect. No. 518.
[9] Bolingb. Ph. Ess. ii. Sect. 2.

cannot admit the agency of chance in the government of the world, I must necessarily refer every event to one cause, as well the danger as the escape, as well the sufferings as the enjoyments of life."[1] There is very little affinity, either in sense or in sound, between *precept* and *doctrine;* and nothing but an oscitancy, from which no writer whatever is uniformly exempted, can account for so odd a misapplication of a familiar term. The words in connection might have shown the error. It is the *doctrines* of our religion that we are required to believe, and the *precepts* that we are required to obey. The other example is, "Their success may be compared to that of a certain prince, who placed, it is said, cats and other animals, adored by the Egyptians, in front of his army, when he invaded that people. A reverence for these *phantoms* made the Egyptians lay down their arms, and become an easy conquest."[2] What the author here intended to say, it is hard to conjecture; but it is unquestionable, that in no sense whatever can cats and other animals be called *phantoms*.

I shall now, before I proceed to consider impropriety, as it appears in phrases, make a few reflections on those principles which most frequently betray authors into such misapplications in the use of single words. As to that which hath been denominated the *vulgarism*, its genuine source seems to be the affectation of an easy, familiar, and careless manner. The writers who abound in this idiom generally imagine, that their style must appear the more natural, the less pains they bestow upon it. Addison hath exactly hit their notion of easy writing. "It is," says he, "what any man may easily write." But these people, it would seem, need to be informed, that ease is one thing, and carelessness is another; nay, that these two are so widely different, that the former is most commonly the result of the greatest care. It is like ease in motion, which, though originally the effect of discipline, when once it hath become habitual, has a more simple and more natural appearance than is to be observed in any manner which untutored Nature can produce. This sentiment is well expressed by the poet:

> But ease in writing flows from art, not chance;
> As those move easiest who have learnt to dance.[3]

True ease in composition, accompanied with purity, differs as much from that homely manner which affects the familiarity of low phrases and vulgar idioms, as the appearance of a woman that is plainly but neatly dressed, differs from that of a slattern. But this affectation is to be considered as the spring of one species of impropriety only.

[1] General Introduction to the Account of the Voyages of Commodore Byron, &c. by Hawkesworth.

[2] Bolingb. Ph. Ess. iv. Sect. 1.

[3] Pope's Imitations.

All the rest, unless when chargeable on inadvertency, as they sometimes doubtless are, seem naturally to flow from one or other of these two sources, which are almost diametrically opposite to the former. One is, the love of novelty; the other, a fondness for variety. The former, when excessive, tends directly to misguide us, by making us disdain the beaten track, for no other reason but because it is the beaten track. The idea of vulgarity, in the imaginations of those who are affected by this principle, is connected with every thing that is conceived as customary. The genuine issue of this extreme, much worse, I acknowledge, than the former, is not only improprieties, but even absurdities, and fustian, and bombast. The latter, to wit, a fondness for variety, produceth often the same effect, though more indirectly. It begets an immoderate dread of becoming tedious, by repeating too frequently the same sound. In order to avoid this, a writer resolves at any rate to diversify his style, let it cost what it will. And, indeed, this fancied excellence usually costs more than it is worth. Very often propriety and perspicuity both are sacrificed to it.

It is justly observed by Abbé Girard,[4] that when a performance grows dull through an excess of uniformity, it is not so much because the ear is tired by the frequent repetition of the same sound, as because the mind is fatigued by the frequent recurrence of the same idea. If, therefore, there be a remarkable paucity of ideas, a diversity of words will not answer the purpose, or give to the work the agreeable appearance of variety. On the contrary, when an author is at great pains to vary his expressions, and for this purpose even deserts the common road, he will, to an intelligent reader, but the more expose his poverty, the more he is solicitous to conceal it. And, indeed, what can more effectually betray a penury of words, than to be always recurring to such as custom hath appropriated to purposes different from those for which we use them? Would the glitter of jewels, which we know to be stolen, produce an opinion of the wearer's affluence? And must not such alienations of words, if I may be allowed the metaphor, awaken the suspicion of some original defects which have given occasion to them? We should hardly say that a house were richly furnished, I am sure we could not say that it were well furnished, where we found a superfluity of utensils for answering some purposes, and a total want of those adapted to other purposes not less necessary and important. We should think, on the contrary, that there were much greater appearance both of opulence and of taste where, though there were little or nothing superfluous, no vessel or piece of furniture useful in a family were wanting. When one is obliged to make some utensils

[4] Synonymes François. Preface.

supply purposes to which they were not originally destined; when for instance, "the copper pot boils milk, heats porridge, holds small beer, and, in case of necessity, serves for a jorden,"[5] there are always, it must be confessed, the strongest indications of indigence. On the contrary, when every real use hath some instrument or utensil adapted to it, there is the appearance, if not of profusion, of what is much more valuable, plenty.

In a language there may be great redundancies, and, at the same time, great defects. It is infinitely less important to have a number of synonymous words, which are even sometimes cumbersome, than to have very few that can be called homonymous, and, consequently, to have all the differences which there are in things, as much as possible, marked by corresponding differences in their signs. That this should be perfectly attained, I own is impossible. The varieties in things are infinite, whereas the richest language hath its limits. Indeed, the more a people improve in taste and knowledge, they come the more, though by imperceptible degrees, to make distinctions in the applications of words which were used promiscuously before. And it is by thus marking the delicate differences of things, which, in a ruder state, they overlooked, more than by any other means, that their language is refined and polished. Hence it acquires precision, perspicuity, vivacity, energy. It would be no difficult task to evince, as partly it may be collected from what hath been observed already, that our own language hath from this source received greater improvements in the course of the last century and of the present, than from the accession of new words, or perhaps from any other cause. Nothing then, surely, can serve more to corrupt it, than to overturn the barriers use hath erected, by confounding words as synonymous, to which distinct significations have been assigned. This conduct is as bad policy with regard to style, as it would be with regard to land to convert a great part of the property into a common. On the contrary, as it conduceth to the advancement of agriculture, and to the increase of the annual produce of a country, to divide the commons, and turn them into property, a similar conduct, in the appropriation of words, renders a language more useful and expressive.

PART II.—*Impropriety in Phrases.*

I come now to consider the improprieties which occur in phrases. The first of this kind of which I shall take notice is, when the expression, on being grammatically analyzed, is discovered to contain some inconsistency. Such is the phrase *of*

[5] Swift.

all others after the superlative, common with many English writers. Interpreted by the rules of syntax, it implies that a thing is different from itself. Take these words for an example, "It celebrates the church of England as the *most* perfect *of all others*."[6] Properly, either—"as more perfect than any other," or—"as the most perfect of all churches." This is precisely the same sort of impropriety into which Milton hath fallen in these words,

> ——————— Adam,
> The comeliest man of men *since born*
> *His sons.* The fairest of *her daughters* Eve.[7]

And in these,

> ——————— The loveliest pair
> That ever *since* in love's embraces met.[8]

Use, indeed, may be pleaded for such expressions, which, it must be acknowledged, use hath rendered intelligible. But still the general laws of the language, which constitute the most extensive and important use, may be pleaded against them. Now, it is one principal method of purifying a language, to lay aside such idioms as are inconsistent with its radical principles and constituent rules; or as, when interpreted by such principles and rules, exhibit manifest nonsense. Nor does the least inconvenience result from this conduct, as we can be at no loss to find expressions of our meaning altogether as natural, and entirely as unexceptionable.

Sometimes, indeed, through mere inattention, slips of this kind are committed, as in the following instance: "I do not reckon that we want a genius more than *the rest of* our neighbours."[9] The impropriety here is corrected by omitting the words in Italics.

Another oversight of much the same kind, and by the same author, we have in the following passage: "I had like to have gotten one or two broken heads for my impertinence."[1] This unavoidably suggests the question, How many heads was he possessed of?—Properly, "I was once or twice like to have gotten my head broken."

Another from the same work, being a passage formerly quoted for another purpose, is this, "The first project was to shorten discourse by cutting polysyllables into one."[2] One thing may be cut in two or more; but it is inconceivable that by cutting, two or more things should be made one.

Another, still from the same hand, "I solemnly declare, that

[6] Swift's Apology for the Tale of a Tub.
[7] Paradise Lost. [8] Ib. b. iv.
[9] Swift's Proposal for ascertaining the English Tongue.
[1] Voyage to Brobdignag. [2] Voyage to Laputa.

I have not *wilfully* committed the least *mistake*."[3] The words used here are incompatible. A wrong wilfully committed is no mistake.

Addison hath fallen into an inaccuracy of the same kind, in the following lines:

> So the *pure limpid* stream, when *foul with stains*
> Of rushing torrents and descending rains.[4]

A stream may doubtless be at one time limpid, and at another foul, which is all that the author meant; but we cannot properly call it a *pure limpid* stream, when it is *foul with stains.* So much for those improprieties which involve in them some absurdity.

I shall next illustrate those by which an author is made to say one thing when he means another. Of this kind I shall produce only one example at present, as I shall have occasion afterwards of considering the same fault under the article of perspicuity. "I will instance in one opinion, which I look upon every man obliged in conscience to quit, or in prudence to conceal; I mean, that whoever argues in defence of absolute power in a single person, though he offers the old plausible plea, that it is his opinion, which he cannot help, unless he be convinced, ought in all free states to be treated as the common enemy of mankind."[5] From the scope of the discourse, it is evident he means that whoever hath it for his opinion that a single person is entitled to absolute authority, ought to quit or conceal that opinion, because, otherwise, he will in a free state deserve to be treated as a common enemy. Whereas, if he says any thing, he says, that whoever thinks that the advocates for absolute power ought to be treated as common enemies, is obliged to quit or conceal that opinion; a sentiment very different from the former.

The only species of impropriety that remains to be exemplified, is that wherein there appears some slight incongruity in the combination of the words, as in the quotations following: "When you fall *into a man's conversation*, the first thing you should consider is——."[6] Properly, "fall *into conversation with a man*." "I wish, sir, you would animadvert frequently on the false taste *the town is in*, with relation to plays as well as operas."[7] Properly, "the false taste *of the town*."

"The presence of the Deity, and the *care* such an august *cause* is supposed to *take about any action*."[8] The impropriety here is best corrected by substituting the word *being* in the place of *cause;* for though there be nothing improper in calling

[3] Remarks on the Barrier Treaty. [4] Cato.
[5] Sentiments of a Church of England Man. [6] Spect. No. 49.
[7] Ib. No. 22. [8] Pope's View of the Epic Poem.

the Deity an august Cause, the author hath very improperly connected with this appellative some words totally unsuitable; for who ever heard of a *cause taking care about an action?*

I shall produce but one other instance:—"Neither implies that there are virtuous habits and accomplishments already *attained* by the *possessor*, but they certainly show an *unprejudiced* capacity *towards* them."[9] In the first clause of this sentence there is a gross inconsistency; we are informed of habits and accomplishments that are *possessed* but not *attained;* in the second clause there is a double impropriety, the participial adjective is not suited to the substantive with which it is construed; nor is the subsequent preposition expressive of the sense. Supposing then, that the word *possessor* hath been used inadvertently for *person*, or some other general term, the sense may be exhibited thus: "Neither implies that there are virtuous habits and accomplishments already attained by this person; but they certainly show that his mind is not prejudiced against them, and that it hath a capacity of attaining them."

Under this head I might consider that impropriety which results from the use of metaphors, or other tropes, wherein the similitude to the subject, or connexion with it, is too remote; also that which results from the construction of words with any trope which are not applicable in the literal sense. The former errs chiefly against vivacity, the latter against elegance. Of the one, therefore, I shall have occasion to speak, when I consider the *catachresis*, of the other when I treat of *mixed metaphor*.

I have now finished what was intended on the subject of grammatical purity; the first, and in some respects, the most essential of all the virtues of elocution. I have illustrated the three different ways in which it may be violated; the *barbarism*, when the words employed are not English; the *solecism*, when the construction is not English; the *impropriety*, when the meaning in which any English word or phrase is used, by a writer or speaker, is not the sense which good use hath assigned to it.

CHAPTER IV.

Some Grammatical Doubts in regard to English Construction stated and examined.

BEFORE I dismiss this article altogether, it will not be amiss to consider a little some dubious points in construction, on which our critics appear not to be agreed.

[9] Guardian, No. 34.

One of the most eminent of them makes this remark upon the neuter verbs: "A neuter verb cannot become a passive. In a neuter verb the agent and the object are the same, and cannot be separated even in imagination, as in the examples *to sleep, to walk;* but when the verb is passive, one thing is acted upon by another, really or by supposition different from it."[1] To this is subjoined in the margin the following note: "That some neuter verbs take a passive form, but without a passive signification, has been observed above. Here we speak of their becoming both in form and signification passive, and shall endeavour further to illustrate the rule by example. To *split*, like many other English verbs, has both an active and a neuter signification; according to the former we say, The force of gunpowder *split* the rock; according to the latter, The ship *split* upon the rock:—and converting the verb active into a passive, we may say, The rock was *split* by the force of gunpowder; or, The ship was *split* upon the rock. But we cannot say with any propriety, turning the verb neuter into a passive, The rock *was split* upon by the ship."

This author's reasoning, so far as concerns verbs properly neuter, is so manifestly just that it commands a full assent from every one that understands it. I differ from him only in regard to the application. In my apprehension, what may grammatically be named the neuter verbs, are not near so numerous in our tongue as he imagines. I do not enter into the difference between verbs absolutely neuter, and intransitively active. I concur with him in thinking, that this distinction holds more of metaphysics than of grammar. But by verbs grammatically neuter, I mean such as are not followed either by an accusative, or by a preposition and a noun; for I take this to be the only grammatical criterion with us. Of this kind is the simple and primitive verb *to laugh;* accordingly to say *he was laughed*, would be repugnant alike to grammar and to sense. But give this verb a regimen, and say, *to laugh at*, and you alter its nature, by adding to its signification. It were an abuse of words to call this a neuter, being as truly a compound active verb in English, as *deridere* is in Latin, to which it exactly corresponds in meaning. Nor doth it make any odds that the preposition in the one language precedes the verb, and is conjoined with it, and in the other follows it, and detached from it. The real union is the same in both. Accordingly *he was laughed at*, is as evidently good English, as *derisus fuit* is good Latin.

Let us hear this author himself, who, speaking of verbs compounded with a preposition, says expressly, "In English the preposition is more frequently placed after the verb, and sepa-

[1] Short Introduction, &c. Sentences.

rate from it, like an adverb; in which situation it is no less apt to affect the sense of it, and to give it a new meaning; and may still be considered as belonging to the verb, and a part of it. As, *to cast* is to throw; but *to cast up*, or to compute, *an account*, is quite a different thing; thus, *to fall on*, *to bear out*, *to give over*, &c." Innumerable examples might be produced, to show that such verbs have been always used as active or transitive compounds, call them which you please, and therefore as properly susceptible of the passive voice. I shall produce only one authority, which, I am persuaded, the intelligent reader will admit to be a good one. It is no other than this ingenious critic himself, and the passage of his which I have in view will be found in the very quotation above made. "When the verb is passive, one thing *is acted upon* by another." Here the verb *to act upon* is undoubtedly neuter, if the verb *to split upon* be neuter in the expression censured, and conversely, the verb *to split upon* is undoubtedly active, if the verb *to act upon* be active in the passage quoted. Nor can any thing be more similar than the construction: "One thing *is acted upon* by another"— "The rock *is split upon* by the ship."

After all, I am sensible that the latter expression is liable to an exception, which cannot be made against the former. I therefore agree with the author in condemning it, but not in the reason of pronouncing this sentence. The only reason that weighs with me is this: the active sense of the simple verb *to split*, and the sense of the compound *to split upon*, are, in such a phrase as that above mentioned, apt to be confounded Nay, what is more, the false sense is that which is first suggested to the mind, as if the rock and not the ship had been *split*. And though the subsequent words remove the ambiguity, yet the very hesitancy which it occasions renders the expression justly chargeable, though not with solecism, with what is perhaps worse, obscurity and inelegance.

That we may be satisfied that this and no other is the genuine cause of censure, let us borrow an example from some verb, which in the simple form is properly univocal. *To smile* is such a verb, being a neuter, which, in its primitive and uncompounded state, never receives an active signification; but *to smile on* is with us, according to the definition given above, a compound active verb, just as *arridere*[2] (to which it corresponds alike in etymology and meaning) is in Latin. Accordingly, we cannot say *he was smiled*, in any sense. But to say, *he was smiled on*, as in the following example, "He was *smiled on* by

[2] I know that the verb *arrideo* is accounted neuter by Latin lexicographers. The reason lies not in the signification of the word, but purely in this circumstance, that it governs the dative and not the accusative. But with this distinction we have no concern. That it is active in its import is evident from this, that it is used by good authors in the passive.

fortune in every stage of life," is entirely unexceptionable. Yet the only difference between this and the phrase above criticized, ariseth hence, that there is something ambiguous in the first appearance of the one, which is not to be found in the other. And, indeed, when the simple and primitive verb has both an active signification and a neuter, (as is the case with the verb *split,*) such an ambiguous appearance of the compound in the passive is an invariable consequence.

I shall observe further, in order to prevent mistakes on this subject, that there are also in our language compound neuter, as well as compound active verbs. Such are, *to go up, to come down, to fall out.* These properly have no passive voice; and though some of them admit a passive form, it is without a passive signification. Thus, *he is gone up,* and *he has gone up,* are nearly of the same import. Now, the only distinction in English between the active compound and the neuter compound is this; the preposition in the former, or more properly the compound verb itself, hath a regimen, in the latter it hath none. Indeed these last may be further compounded, by the addition of a preposition with a noun, in which case they also become active or transitive verbs; as in these instances, "He *went up to* her;" "She *fell out with* them." Consequently, in giving a passive voice to these there is no solecism. We may say, "She *was gone up to* by him," "They *were fallen out with* by her." But it must be owned, that the passive form, in this kind of decomposite verbs, ought always to be avoided as inelegant, if not obscure. By bringing three prepositions thus together, one inevitably creates a certain confusion of thought; and it is not till after some painful attention, that the reader discovers two of the prepositions to belong to the preceding verb, and the third to the succeeding noun. The principal scope of the foregoing observations on the passage quoted from Dr. Lowth, is to point out the only characteristical distinction between verbs neuter and verbs active, which obtains in our language.

To these I shall subjoin a few things, which may serve for ascertaining another distinction in regard to verbs. When a verb is used impersonally, it ought, undoubtedly, to be in the singular number, whether the neuter pronoun be expressed or understood; and when no nominative in the sentence can regularly be construed with the verb, it ought to be considered as impersonal. For this reason analogy, as well as usage, favour this mode of expression, "The conditions of the agreement were *as follows;*" and not *as follow.* A few late writers have inconsiderately adopted this last form through a mistake of the construction. For the same reason we ought to say, "I shall consider his censures so far only as *concerns* my friend's conduct:" and not "so far as *concern.*" It is manifest that the word *conditions* in the first case, and *censures* in the second, cannot serve as nominatives. If we give either sentence another turn, and instead of *as*, say *such as*, the verb is no longer impersonal. The pronoun *such* is the nominative, whose number is determined by its antecedent. Thus we must say, "They were such as follow,"—"such of his censures only as concern my friend." In this I entirely concur with a late anonymous remarker on the language.

I shall only add on this subject, that the use of impersonal verbs was much more frequent with us formerly than it is now. Thus, *it pleaseth me*, *it grieveth me*, *it repenteth me*, were a sort of impersonals, for which we should now say, *I please*, *I grieve*, *I repent*. *Methinks* and *methought* at present, as *meseemeth* and *meseemed* anciently, are, as Johnson justly supposes, remains of the same practice.[3] It would not be easy to conjecture what hath misled some writers so far as to make them adopt the uncouth term *methoughts*, in contempt alike of usage and of analogy, and even without any colourable pretext that I can think of, for *thoughts* is no part of the verb at all.

I shall now consider another suspected idiom in English, which is the indefinite use sometimes made of the pronoun *it*, when applied in the several ways following; first, to persons as well as to things; secondly, to the first person and the second, as well as to the third; and thirdly, to a plural as well as to a singular. Concerning the second application and the third, Dr. Johnson says in his Dictionary, "This mode of speech, though used by good authors, and supported by the *il y a* of the French, has yet an appearance of barbarism." Dr. Lowth doubts only of the third application. "The phrase," says he, "which occurs in the following examples, though pretty common, and authorized by custom, yet seems to be somewhat defective in the same way." He had been specifying inaccuracies arising from disagreement in number. The examples alluded to are,—

> '*Tis these* that early taint the female soul.[4]
>
> '*Tis they* that give the great Atrides' spoils;
> '*Tis they* that still renew Ulysses' toils.[5]
>
> ———————— Who was't came by?
> '*Tis two* or *three*, my Lord, that bring you word,
> Macduff is fled to England.[6]

Against the first application, to persons as well as to things, neither of these critics seems to have any objection; and it must be owned that they express themselves rather sceptically than dogmatically about the other two. Yet, in my judgment, if

[3] The similar use of impersonal verbs, and the *il me semble* of the French, render this hypothesis still more probable.

[4] Pope. [5] Prior. [6] Shakspeare.

one be censurable, they are all censurable, and if one be proper, they are all proper. The distinction of genders, especially with us, is as essential as the distinction of persons or that of numbers. I say, especially with us, because, though the circumstances be few wherein the gender can be marked, yet, in those few, our language, perhaps more than any other tongue, follows the dictates of pure nature. The masculine pronoun *he* in it applies always to males, or at least to persons (God and angels, for example) who in respect of dignity are conceived as males: the feminine *she* to females; and unless where the style is figurative, the neuter *it* to things either not susceptible of sex, or in which the sex is unknown. Besides, if we have recourse to the Latin syntax, the genuine source of most of our grammatical scruples, we shall find there an equal repugnancy to all the applications above rehearsed.[7]

But, to clear up this matter as much as possible, I shall recur to some remarks of the last-mentioned critic, concerning the significations and the uses of the neuter *it*. "The pronoun *it*," he tells us, "is sometimes employed to express, first, the subject of any inquiry or discourse; secondly, the state or condition of any thing or person; thirdly, the thing, whatever it be, that is the cause of any effect or event, or any person considered merely as a cause, without regard to proper personality." In illustration of the third use, he quotes these words,—

> You heard her say herself, *it was* not *I*———
> '*Twas* I that killed her———.[8]

The observations of this author concerning the neuter pronoun, are, as far as they go, unexceptionable. He ought to have added to the word *personality*, in the third use, the words *gender* or *number*. The example which he hath given shows that there is no more regard to *gender* than to *personality;* and that there ought to be no more regard *to number* than to either of the former, may be evinced from the considerations following.

When a personal pronoun must be used indefinitely, as in asking a question whereof the subject is unknown, there is a necessity of using one person for all the persons, one gender for all the genders, and one number for both numbers. Now in English, custom has consigned to this indefinite use, the third person, the neuter gender, and the singular number. Accordingly, in asking a question, nobody censures this use of the pronoun, as in the interrogation, *Who is it?* Yet by the answer it may be found to be *I* or *he*, *one* or *many*. But

[7] In Latin *id fuit ille* would be as gross a solecism, as *id fuit ego* or *id fuit vos*.
[8] Shakspeare.

whatever be the answer, if the question be proper, it is proper to begin the answer by expressing the subject of inquiry in the same indefinite manner wherein it was expressed in the question. The words *it is* are consequently pertinent here, whatever be the words which ought to follow, whether *I* or *he*, *we* or *they*.[9] Nay, this way of beginning the answer by the same indefinite expression of the subject that was used in the question, is the only method authorized in the language for connecting these two together, and showing that what is asserted is an answer to the question asked. And if there be nothing faulty in the expression, when it is an answer to a question actually proposed, there can be no fault in it, where no question is proposed. For every answer, that is not a bare assent or denial, ought, independently of the question, to contain a proposition grammatically enunciated, and every affirmation or negation ought to be so enunciated as that it might be an answer to a question. Thus by a very simple sorites it can be proved, that if the pronoun *it* may be used indefinitely in one case, it may in every case. Nor is it possible to conceive even the shadow of a reason, why one number may not as well serve indefinitely for both numbers, as one person for all the persons, and one gender for all the genders.

That which hath made more writers scrupulous about the first of these applications than about the other two, is, I imagine, the appearance not of the pronoun, but of the substantive verb in the singular adjoined to some term in the plural. In order to avoid this supposed incongruity, the translators of the Bible have in one place stumbled on a very uncouth expression. "Search the scriptures, for in them ye think ye have eternal life; and *they are they* which testify of me."[1] In the other applications they have not hesitated to use the indefinite pronoun *it*, as in this expression: "*It is I*, be not afraid."[2] Yet the phrase *they are they* in the first quotation, adopted to prevent the incongruous adjunction of the verb in the singular, and the subsequent noun or pronoun in the plural, is, I suspect, no better English than the phrase *I am I* would have been in the second, by which they might have prevented the adjunction not less incongruous of the third person of the verb to the first personal pronoun. If there be any difference in respect of congruity, the former is the less incongruous of the two. The latter never occurs but in such passages as those above quoted; whereas nothing is commoner than to use the substantive verb as a copula to two nouns differing in number; in which case it generally agrees with the first. "His *meat was locusts* and wild honey,"[3] is a sentence

[9] In this observation I find I have the concurrence of Dr. Priestley.

[1] John v. 39. [2] Matt. xiv. 27. [3] Matt. iii. 4.

which, I believe, nobody ever suspected to be ungrammatical. Now, as every noun may be represented by a pronoun, what is grammatical in those must, by a parity of reason, be grammatical in these also. Had the question been put, "What was his meat?" the answer had undoubtedly been proper, "It was locusts and wild honey." And this is another argument which in my apprehension is decisive.

But "this comes," as Dr. Lowth expresseth himself in a similar case, "of forcing the English under the rules of a foreign language, with which it has little concern."[4] A convenient mode of speech which custom hath established, and for which there is pretty frequent occasion, ought not to be hastily given up, especially when the language doth not furnish us with another equally simple and easy to supply its place. I should not have entered so minutely into the defence of a practice sufficiently authorized by use, but in order, if possible, to satisfy those critics who, though both ingenious and acute, are apt to be rather more scrupulous on the article of language than the nature of the subject will admit. In every tongue there are real anomalies which have obtained the sanction of custom; for this at most hath been reckoned only dubious. There are particularly some in our own, which have never, as far as I know, been excepted against any writer, and which, nevertheless, it is much more difficult to reconcile to the syntactic order than that which I have been now defending. An example of this is the use of the indefinite article, which is naturally singular, before adjectives expressive of number, and joined with substantives in the plural. Such are the phrases following, *a few persons*, *a great many men*, *a hundred* or *a thousand ships*.

There is another point on which, as both the practice of writers and the judgment of critics seem to be divided, it may not be improper to make a few remarks. It is the way of using the infinitive after a verb in the preterite. Some will have it that the verb governed ought to be in the past as well as the verb governing; and others that the infinitive ought to be in what is called the present, but what is in fact indefinite in regard to time. I do not think that on either side the different

[4] The English hath little or no affinity in structure either to the Latin or to the Greek. It much more resembles the modern European languages, especially the French. Accordingly we find in it an idiom very similar to that which hath been considered above, I do not mean the *il y a*, because the *a* is part of an active verb, and the words that follow in the sentence are its regimen; consequently no agreement in person and number is required. But the idiom to which I allude is the *il est*, as used in the following sentence, "*Il est des animaux* qui semblent reduits au toucher; *il en est qui semblent* participer à nôtre intelligence." Contemplation de la Nature, par Bonnet. I am too zealous an advocate for English independency to look on this argument as conclusive. But I think it more than a sufficient counterpoise to all that can be pleaded on the other side from the syntax of the learned languages.

cases have been distinguished with sufficient accuracy. A very little attention will, I hope, enable us to unravel the difficulty entirely.

Let us begin with the simplest case, the infinitive after the present of the indicative. When the infinitive is expressive of what is conceived to be either future in regard to the verb in the present, or contemporary, the infinitive ought to be in the present. Thus, "I intend *to write* to my father to-morrow." "He seems *to be* a man of letters." In the first example the verb *to write* expresses what is future in respect to the verb *intend.* In the second the verb *to be* expresses what is equally present with the verb *seems.* About the propriety of such expressions there is no doubt. Again, if the infinitive after the verb in the present be intended to express what must have been antecedent to that which is expressed by the governing verb, the infinitive must be in the preterperfect, even though the other verb be in the present. Thus, "From his conversation he appears *to have studied* Homer with great care and judgment." To use the present in this case, and say, "He appears *to study* Homer"——would overturn the sense.

The same rule must be followed when the governing verb is in the preterite; for let it be observed that it is the tense of the governing verb only that marks the absolute time; the tense of the verb governed marks solely its relative time with respect to the other. Thus I should say, "I always intended *to write* to my father, though I have not yet done it." "He seemed *to be* a man of letters." "From a conversation I once had with him, he appeared *to have studied* Homer with great care and judgment." Propriety plainly requires that in the first two instances the infinitive should be in the present tense, and in the third instance in the preterite.

Priestley has not expressed himself on this subject with precision. *I found him better than I expected to find him*, is the only proper analogical expression. *Expected to have found him* is irreconcileable alike to grammar and to sense. Indeed all verbs expressive of hope, desire, intention, or command, must invariably be followed by the present and not the perfect of the infinitive. Every body would perceive an error in this expression: "It is long since I commanded him to have done it." Yet *expected to have found* is no better. It is as clear that the *finding* must be posterior to the expectation, as that the *obedience* must be posterior to the command. But though the anonymous remarker formerly quoted is in the right as to the particular expressions criticized by him, he decides too generally, and seems to have imagined that in no case ought the preterperfect of the infinitive to follow the preterite of the indicative. If this was his opinion, he was egregiously mistaken. It is however agreed on both sides that, in order to express the past with the defective verb *ought*, we must use the perfect of the infinitive, and say for example, "he ought to *have done* it;" this in that verb being the only possible way of distinguishing the past from the present.

There is only one other observation of Dr. Lowth on which, before I conclude this article, I must beg leave to offer some remarks. "Phrases like the following, though very common, are improper: Much depends upon the *rule's being observed;* and error will be the consequence of *its being neglected.* For here is a noun and a pronoun representing it, each in the possessive case, that is, under government of another noun, but without other noun to govern it—for *being observed* and *being neglected* are not nouns: nor can you supply the place of the possessive case by the preposition *of* before the noun or pronoun."[5] For my part, notwithstanding what is here very speciously urged, I am not satisfied that there is any fault in the phrases censured. They appear to me to be perfectly in the idiom of our tongue, and such as on some occasions could not easily be avoided, unless by recurring to circumlocution, an expedient which invariably tends to enervate the expression. But let us examine the matter more nearly.

This author admits that the active participle may be employed as a noun, and has given some excellent directions regarding the manner in which it ought to be construed, that the proper distinction may be preserved between the noun and the gerund. Phrases like these, therefore, he would have admitted as unexceptionable: "Much depends upon *their observing* of the rule, and error will be the consequence of *their neglecting* of it." Now, though I allow both the modes of expression to be good, I think the first simpler and better than the second. Let us consider whether the former be liable to any objections, which do not equally affect the latter.

One principal objection to the first is, "You cannot supply the place of the possessive case by the preposition *of* before the noun or pronoun." Right; but before you draw any conclusion from this circumstance, try whether it will not equally affect both expressions; for if it does, both are on this account to be rejected, or neither. In the first, the sentence will be made to run thus, "Much depends upon *the being observed of* the rule, and error will be the consequence of *the being neglected of* it." Very bad, without question. In the second, thus, "Much depends upon *the observing of them* of the rule, and error will be the consequence of *the neglecting of them* of it." Still worse. But it may be thought that as, in the last example, the participial noun gets a double regimen, this occasions all the impropriety and confusion. I shall therefore make the

[5] Introduction, &c. Sentences, Note on the 6th Phrase.

experiment on a more simple sentence. "Much will depend on *your pupil's composing*, but more on *his reading* frequently." Would it be English to say, "Much will depend on *the composing of your pupil*, but more on *the reading of him* frequently?" No, certainly. If this argument then prove any thing, it proves too much, and consequently can be no criterion.

The only other objection mentioned is, that *being observed* and *being neglected* are not nouns. It is acknowledged that, in the common acceptation of the word, they are not nouns, but passive participles; neither is the active participle commonly a noun, neither is the infinitive of the verb active or passive a noun. Yet the genius of the tongue permits that all these may be construed as nouns in certain occurrences. The infinitive in particular is employed substantively when it is made either the nominative or the regimen of a verb. Now in this way not the infinitive only, but along with it all the words in construction are understood as one compound noun, as in the examples following: "*To love God and our neighbour* is a duty incumbent on us all," and "The gospel strongly inculcates on us this important lesson, *to love God and our neighbour*." But in no other situation can such clauses supply the place of nouns. They are never used in construction with other nouns followed by a preposition. The quotation brought from Spenser is, I suspect, a mere Grecism, which was not in his time more than it is at present conformable to the English idiom. *For* is the only preposition that seems ever to have been construed with such clauses after another verb. And even this usage is now totally laid aside.

I am of opinion, therefore, upon the whole, that as the idiom in question is analogical, supported by good use, and sometimes very expedient, it ought not to be entirely reprobated.

CHAPTER V.

Of the qualities of Style strictly rhetorical.

PURITY, of which I have treated at some length in the two preceding chapters, may justly be denominated grammatical truth. It consisteth in the conformity of the expression to the sentiment which the speaker or the writer intends to convey by it, as moral truth consisteth in the conformity of the sentiment intended to be conveyed, to the sentiment actually entertained by the speaker or the writer; and logical truth, as was hinted above, in the conformity of the sentiment to the nature of things. The opposite to logical truth is properly error; to moral truth, a lie; to grammatical truth, a blunder. Now, the only standard by which the conformity implied in grammatic truth must be ascertained in every language, is, as hath been evinced,[6] reputable, national, and present use, in that language.

But it is with the expression as with the sentiment, it is not enough to the orator that both be true. A sentence may be a just exhibition, according to the rules of the language, of the thought intended to be conveyed by it, and may therefore, to a mere grammarian, be unexceptionable; which to an orator may appear extremely faulty. It may, nevertheless, be obscure, it may be languid, it may be inelegant, it may be flat, it may be unmusical. It is not ultimately the justness either of the thought or of the expression, which is the aim of the orator; but it is a certain effect to be produced in the hearers. This effect as he purposeth to produce in them by means of language, which he makes the instrument of conveying his sentiments into their minds, he must take care in the first place that his style be perspicuous, that so he may be sure of being understood. If he would not only inform the understanding, but please the imagination, he must add the charms of vivacity and elegance, corresponding to the two sources from which, as was observed in the beginning of this work,[7] the merit of an address of this kind results. By vivacity, resemblance is attained; by elegance, dignity of manner. For as to the dignity of the subject itself, or thing imitated, it concerns solely the thought. If he purposes to work upon the passions, his very diction, as well as his sentiments, must be animated. Thus language and thought, like body and soul, are made to correspond, and the qualities of the one exactly to co-operate with those of the other.

But though the perfection of the body consists, as was formerly observed,[8] in its fitness for serving the purposes of the soul, it is at the same time capable of one peculiar excellence as a visible object. The excellence I mean is *beauty*, which evidently implies more than what results from the fitness of the several organs and members for answering their respective ends. That there is a beauty in the perceived fitness of means to their end, and instruments to their use, is uncontrovertible. All that I contend for here is, that this is not the whole of what is implied in the term *beauty*. The eyes of one person may be much inferior in this respect to those of another, though equally fit for all the purposes of vision. The like may be said of every other feature. Analogous to this there is an excellence of which language is susceptible as an audible object, distinct from its aptitude for conveying the sentiments of the orator with light and energy into the minds of the hearers. Now, as *music* is to the ear what *beauty* is to the eye, I shall, for want of a more

[6] Book II. Chap. i. [7] Book I. Chap. i. [8] Book I. Chap. iv.

proper term, denominate this excellence in style, its music; though I acknowledge the word is rarely used with so great latitude.

Thus it appears that beside *purity*, which is a quality entirely grammatical, the five simple and original qualities of style, considered as an object to the understanding, the imagination, the passions, and the ear, are *perspicuity*, *vivacity*, *elegance*, *animation*, and *music*.

CHAPTER VI.

Of Perspicuity.

OF all the qualities above mentioned the first and most essential is *perspicuity*.[9] Every speaker doth not propose to please the imagination, nor is every subject susceptible of those ornaments which conduce to this purpose. Much less is it the aim of every speech to agitate the passions. There are some occasions, therefore, on which vivacity, and many on which animation of style are not necessary; nay, there are occasions on which the last especially would be improper. But whatever be the ultimate intention of the orator, to inform, to convince, to please, to move, or to persuade, still he must speak so as to be understood, or he speaks to no purpose. If he do not propose to convey certain sentiments into the minds of his hearers, by the aid of signs intelligible to them, he may as well declaim before them in an unknown tongue. This prerogative the intellect has above all the other faculties, that whether it be or be not immediately addressed by the speaker, it must be regarded by him either ultimately or subordinately; ultimately, when the direct purpose of the discourse is information or conviction; subordinately, when the end is pleasure, emotion, or persuasion.

There is another difference also between perspicuity and the two last-mentioned qualities, vivacity and animation, which deserves to be remarked. In a discourse wherein either or both of these are requisite, it is not every sentence that requires, or even admits them; but every sentence ought to be perspicuous. The effect of all the other qualities of style is lost without this. This, being to the understanding what light is to the eye, ought to be diffused over the whole performance. In this respect it resembles grammatical purity, of which I have already treated,

[9] Prima est eloquentiæ virtus perspicuitas. QUINT.

but it is not in this respect only that it resembles it. Both are best illustrated by showing the different ways wherein they may be lost. It is for these reasons that, though perspicuity be more properly a rhetorical than a grammatical quality, I thought it better to include it in this book, which treats of the foundations and essential or universal properties of elocution, than to class it with those which are purely discriminative of particular styles.

Indeed, if language were capable of absolute perfection, which it evidently is not; if words and things could be rendered exact counterparts to each other; if every different thing in nature had a different symbol by which it were expressed; and every difference in the relations of things had a corresponding difference in the combinations of words, purity alone would secure perspicuity, or rather these two would entirely coincide. To speak grammatically would, in that case, convey infallibly and perspicuously the full meaning of the speaker, if he had any meaning, into the mind of every hearer who perfectly understands the language. There would not be even a possibility of mistake or doubt. But the case is widely different with all the languages that ever were, are, or will be in the world.

Grammatical purity, in every tongue, conduceth greatly to perspicuity, but it will by no means secure it. A man may in respect of it speak unexceptionably, and yet speak obscurely, or ambiguously; and though we cannot say that a man may speak properly, and at the same time speak unintelligibly, yet this last case falls more naturally to be considered as an offence against perspicuity than as a violation of propriety. For when the meaning is not discovered the particular impropriety cannot be pointed out. In the three different ways, therefore, just now mentioned, perspicuity may be violated.

SECTION I.—*The Obscure.*

PART I.—*From Defect.*

This is the first offence against perspicuity, and may arise from several causes. First, from some defect in the expression. There are in all languages certain elliptical expressions which use hath established, and which, therefore, very rarely occasion darkness. When they do occasion it, they ought always to be avoided. Such are, in Greek and Latin, the frequent suppression of the substantive verb, and of the possessive pronouns; I was going to add, and of the personal pronouns also: but, on reflection, I am sensible that, in the omission of them in the nominative, there is properly no ellipsis, as the verb, by its inflection actually expresses them. Accordingly, in these languages, the pronoun in the nominative is never rightly introduced, unless when it is emphatical. But the idiom of most modern tongues, English and French particularly, will seldom admit such ellipsis.[1] In Italian and Spanish they are pretty frequent.

Often, indeed, the affectation of conciseness, often the rapidity of thought natural to some writers, will give rise to still more material defects in the expression. Of these I shall produce a few examples: "He is inspired," says an eminent writer, "with a true *sense of that function*, when chosen from a regard to the interests of piety and virtue."[2] *Sense* in this passage denotes an inward feeling, or the impression which some sentiment makes upon the mind. Now, a function cannot be a sentiment impressed or felt. The expression is therefore defective, and ought to have been, "He is inspired with a true sense of the dignity or of the importance of that function."—"You ought to contemn all the wit in the world against you."[3] As the writer doth not intend to signify that all the wit in the world is actually exerted against the person whom he addresses, there is a defect in the expression, though perhaps it will be thought chargeable with redundancy at the same time. More plainly thus, "You ought to contemn all the wit that can be employed against you."—"He talks all the way up stairs to a visit."[4] There is here also a faulty omission, which, if it cannot be said to obscure the sense, doth at least withhold that light whereof it is susceptible. If the word *visit* ever meant person or people, there would be an ambiguity in the sentence, and we should imagine this the object talked to; but as that

[1] The French, I imagine, have gone to the other extreme. They require in many instances repetition of pronouns, prepositions, and articles, which, as they add nothing to the perspicuity, must render the expression languid. There are some cases in which this repetition is consequential on the very construction of their language. For example, we say properly in English, *my father and mother;* because the possessive pronoun, having no distinction of gender, and so having but one form, is alike applicable to both: the case being different with them renders it necessary to follow a different rule, and to say, *mon père et ma mère.* But it is not to instances of this sort that the rule is limited. Custom with them hath extended it to innumerable cases, wherein there is no necessity from construction. With us it is enough to say, "She was *robbed of her clothes and jewels.*" With them the preposition and the pronoun must both be repeated, *de ses habits et de ses joyaux.* Again, with them it is not sufficient to say, "The woman *whom you know and love,*" but *whom you know and whom you love—que vous connoissez et que vous aimez.* In like manner, the relatives in French must never be omitted. They often are in English, and when the omission occasions no obscurity it is not accounted improper. An expression like this would in their tongue be intolerable: "You are obliged *to say and do all you can.*" It must be "*to say and to do all that which you can,*"—de dire et de faire tout ce que vous savez. But though in several instances the critics of that nation have refined on their language to excess, and by needless repetitions have sometimes enervated the expression, their criticisms, when useful in assisting us to shun any obscurity or ambiguity, deserve to be adopted.

[2] Guardian, No. 13. [3] Ibid. No. 53. [4] Spect. No. 2.

cannot be the case, the expression is rather to be accounted lame, there being no verb in it with which the words *to a visit* can be construed. More explicitly thus, "He talks all the way as he walks up stairs to make a visit."—"Arbitrary power," says an elegant writer, "I look upon as a greater evil than anarchy itself, as much as a savage is a happier state of life than a slave at the oar."[5] Neither savage nor slave can be denominated a state of life, though the states in which they live may properly be compared.—"This courage among the adversaries of the court," says the same writer in another piece, "was inspired into them by various incidents, for every one of which, I think, the ministers, or, if that was the case, the minister alone is to answer."[6] *If that was the case*, pray, what is he supposing to have been the case? To the relative *that* I can find no antecedent, and am left to guess that he means, *if there was but one minister*.—"When a man considers not only an ample fortune, but even the very necessaries of life, his pretence to food itself, at the mercy of others, he cannot but look upon himself in the state of the dead, with his case thus much worse, that the last office is performed by his adversaries instead of his friends."[7] There is a double ellipsis in this sentence. You must first supply *as being* before the words *at the mercy*, and insert *as* before *in the state of the dead*.—"I beg of you," says Steele, "never let the glory of our nation, who made France tremble, and yet has the gentleness to be unable to bear opposition from the meanest of his own countrymen, be calumniated in so impudent a manner, as in the insinuation that he affected a perpetual dictatorship."[8] At first reading, one is at a loss to find an antecedent to the pronouns *who*, *his*, and *he*. On reflection one discovers that the phrase *the glory of our nation* is figurative, and denotes a certain illustrious personage. The trope is rather too adventurous, without some softening clause, to suit the idiom of our tongue. The sense would have appeared immediately, had he said, "Never let the man, who may justly be styled the glory of our nation——."

The instances now given will suffice to specify the obscurities in style which arise from deficiency. The same evil may also be occasioned by excess. But as this almost invariably offends vivacity, and only sometimes produceth darkness, there will be a more proper occasion of considering it afterwards. Another cause of obscurity is a bad choice of words. When it is this alone which renders the sentence obscure, there is always ground for the charge of impropriety, which hath been discussed already.

[5] Sentiments of a Church of England Man.
[6] Free Thoughts on the Present State of Affairs.
[7] Spectator, No. 456, T.
[8] Guardian, No. 53.

PART II.—*From bad Arrangement.*

Another source of obscurity is a bad arrangement of the words. In this case the construction is not sufficiently clear. One often, on first hearing the sentence, imagines, from the turn of it, that it ought to be construed one way, and on reflection finds that he must construe it another way. Of this, which is a blemish too common even in the style of our best writers, I shall produce a few examples: "It contained," says Swift, "a warrant for conducting me and my retinue to Traldragdubb or Trildrogdrib, for it is pronounced both ways, as near as I can remember, *by a party of ten horse*."[9] The words *by a party of ten horse* must be construed with the participle *conducting*, but they are placed so far from this word, and so near the verb *pronounced*, that at first they suggest a meaning perfectly ludicrous. "I had several men died in my ship *of* calentures."[1] The preposition *of* must be construed with the verb *died*, and not, as the first appearance would suggest, with the noun *ship* immediately preceding. More clearly thus, "I had several men in my ship who died of calentures." I shall remark, by the way, that though the relatives *who* and *which* may, agreeably to the English idiom, be sometimes omitted in the oblique cases, to omit them in the nominative, as in the passage last quoted, almost always gives a maimed appearance to the expression. "I perceived it had been scoured *with half an eye*."[2] The situation of the last phrase, which is besides a very bad one, is liable to the same exception. "I have hopes that when Will confronts him, and *all the ladies in whose behalf he engages him* cast kind looks and wishes of success at their champion, he will have some shame."[3] It is impossible not to imagine, on hearing the first part of the sentence, that Will is to confront all the ladies,—though afterwards we find it necessary to construe this clause with the following verb. This confusion is removed at once by repeating the adverb *when*, thus, "I have hopes that when Will confronts him, and when all the ladies cast kind looks——." The subsequent sentence is liable to the same exception: "He advanced against the fierce ancient, imitating his address, his pace, and career, *as well as the vigour of his horse* and his own skill would allow."[4] The clause *as well as the vigour of his horse* appears at first to belong to the former part of the sentence, and is afterwards found to belong to the latter. In all the above instances of bad arrangement, there is what may be justly termed a constructive

[9] Voyage to Laputa.
[1] Voyage to the Houyhnhyms.
[2] Guardian, No. 10.
[3] Spectator, No. 20.
[4] Battle of the Books.

ambiguity; that is, the words are so disposed in point of order as would render them really ambiguous if, in that construction which the expression first suggests, any meaning were exhibited. As this is not the case, the faulty order of the words cannot be properly considered as rendering the sentence ambiguous, but obscure.

It may indeed be argued that, in these and the like examples, the least reflection in the reader will quickly remove the obscurity. But why is there any obscurity to be removed? Or why does the writer require more attention from the reader, or the speaker from the hearer, than is absolutely necessary? It ought to be remembered that whatever application we must give to the words is, in fact, so much deducted from what we owe to the sentiments. Besides, the effort that is exerted in a very close attention to the language always weakens the effect which the thoughts were intended to produce in the mind. "By perspicuity," as Quintilian justly observes, "care is taken, not that the hearer *may* understand, if he will; but that he *must* understand, whether he will or not."[5] Perspicuity originally and properly implies *transparency*, such as may be ascribed to air, glass, water, or any other medium through which material objects are viewed. From this original and proper sense it hath been metaphorically applied to language, this being, as it were, the medium through which we perceive the notions and sentiments of a speaker. Now, in corporeal things, if the medium through which we look at any object be perfectly transparent, our whole attention is fixed on the object; we are scarcely sensible that there is a medium which intervenes, and can hardly be said to perceive it. But if there be any flaw in the medium, if we see through it but dimly, if the object be imperfectly represented, or if we know it to be misrepresented, our attention is immediately taken off the object, to the medium. We are then desirous to discover the cause either of the dim and confused representation, or of the misrepresentation of things which it exhibits, that so the defect in vision may be supplied by judgment. The case of language is precisely similar. A discourse, then, excels in perspicuity, when the subject engrosses the attention of the hearer, and the diction is so little minded by him that he can scarcely be said to be conscious that it is through this medium he sees into the speaker's thoughts. On the contrary, the least obscurity, ambiguity, or confusion in the style, instantly removes the attention from the sentiment to the expression, and the hearer endeavours, by the aid of reflection, to correct the imperfections of the speaker's language.

[5] Non ut intelligere possit, sed ne omnino possit non intelligere, curandum. Instit. Lib. viii. Cap. 2.

So much for obviating the objections which are frequently raised against such remarks as I have already made, and shall probably hereafter make, on the subject of language. The elements which enter into composition of the hugest bodies are subtle and inconsiderable. The rudiments of every art and science exhibit at first, to a learner, the appearance of littleness and insignificancy. And it is by attending to such reflections as to a superficial observer would appear minute and hypercritical, that language must be improved, and eloquence perfected.[6]

I return to the causes of obscurity, and shall only further observe, concerning the effect of bad arrangement, that it generally obscures the sense, even when it doth not, as in the preceding instances, suggest a wrong construction. Of this the following will suffice for an example: "The young man did not want natural talents; but the father of him was a coxcomb, who affected being a fine gentleman so unmercifully, that he could not *endure* in his sight, or the frequent *mention* of *one*, who was his son, growing into manhood, and thrusting him out of the gay world."[7] It is not easy to disentangle the construction of this sentence. One is at a loss at first to find any accusative to the active verb *endure;* on further examination it is discovered to have two, the word *mention*, and the word *one*, which is here closely combined with the preposition *of*, and makes the regimen of the noun *mention*. I might observe also the vile application of the word *unmercifully*. This, together with the irregularity of the reference, and intricacy of the whole, renders the passage under consideration one of those which may, with equal justice, be ranked under *solecism*, *impropriety*, *obscurity*, or *inelegance*.

PART III.—*From using the Same Word in Different Senses.*

Another source of obscurity is when the same word is in the same sentence used in different senses. This error is exemplified in the following quotation: "That he should be in earnest it is hard to conceive; since any reasons of doubt, which he might have in this case, would have been reasons of doubt in the case of other men, who may give *more*, but cannot give *more evident*, signs of thought than their fellow creatures."[8] This errs alike against perspicuity and elegance; the word *more* is first an adjective, the comparative of *many;* in an instant it is an adverb, and the sign of the comparative degree. As the reader is not apprised of this, the sentence must appear to him, on the first glance, a flat contradiction. Perspicuously either thus, "who may give *more numerous*, but cannot give

[6] The maxim *Natura se potissimum prodit in minimis*, is not confined to physiology. [7] Spect. No. 496. T. [8] Boling. Ph. Ess. i. Sect. 9.

more evident signs——," or thus, "who may give *more*, but cannot give *clearer* signs."

It is but seldom that the same pronoun can be used twice or oftener in the same sentence, in reference to different things, without darkening the expression. It is necessary to observe here that the signification of the personal, as well as of the relative pronouns, and even of the adverbs of place and time, must be determined by the things to which they relate. To use them, therefore, with reference to different things, is in effect to employ the same word in different senses; which, when it occurs in the same sentence, or in sentences closely connected, is rarely found entirely compatible with perspicuity. Of this I shall give some examples. "One may have an air *which* proceeds from a just sufficiency and knowledge of the matter before him, *which* may naturally produce some motions of his head and body, *which* might become the bench better than the bar."[9] The pronoun *which* is here thrice used in three several senses; and it must require reflection to discover that the first denotes an *air*, the second *sufficiency and knowledge*, and the third *motions of the head and body*. Such is the use of the pronouns *those* and *who* in the following sentence of the same writer: "The sharks, *who* prey upon the inadvertency of young heirs, are more pardonable than *those*, *who* trespass upon the good opinion of *those*, *who* treat with them upon the foot of choice and respect."[1] The same fault here renders a very short sentence at once obscure, inelegant and unmusical. The like use of the pronoun *they*, in the following sentence, almost occasions an ambiguity: "*They* were persons of such moderate intellects, even before *they* were impaired by *their* passions."[2]— The use made of the pronoun *it*, in the example subjoined, is liable to the same exception: "If *it* were spoken with never so great skill in the actor, the manner of uttering that sentence could have nothing in *it*, which could strike any but people of the greatest humanity, nay, people elegant and skilful in observations upon *it*."[3] To the preceding examples I shall add one wherein the adverb *when*, by being used in the same manner, occasions some obscurity: "He is inspired with a true sense of that function, *when* chosen from a regard to the interests of piety and virtue, and a scorn of whatever men call great in a transitory being, *when* it comes in competition with what is unchangeable and eternal."[4]

PART IV.—*From an uncertain reference in Pronouns and Relatives.*

A cause of obscurity also arising from the use of pronouns and relatives, is when it doth not appear at first to what they

[9] Guardian, No. 13. [1] Ibid. No. 73. [2] Spect. No. 30.
[3] Ibid. No. 502. [4] Guardian, No. 13.

refer. Of this fault I shall give the three following instances: "There are other examples," says Bolingbroke, "of the same kind, which cannot be brought without the utmost horror, because in them it is supposed impiously, against principles as self-evident as any of those necessary truths, which are *such* of all knowledge, that the supreme Being commands by one law, what he forbids by another."[5] It is not so clear as it ought to be what is the antecedent to *such*. Another from the same author: "The laws of Nature are truly what my Lord Bacon styles his aphorisms, laws of laws. Civil laws are always imperfect, and often false deductions from *them*, or applications of *them;* nay, *they* stand in many instances in direct opposition to *them*."[6] It is not quite obvious, on the first reading, that the prononn *them* in this passage doth always refer to the laws of Nature, and *they* to civil laws. "When a man considers the state of his own mind, about which every member of the Christian world is supposed at this time to be employed, he will find that the best defence against vice, is preserving the worthiest part of his own spirit pure from any great offence against it."[7] It must be owned that the darkness of this sentence is not to be imputed solely to the pronoun.

PART V.—*From too Artificial a Structure of the Sentence.*

Another cause of obscurity is when the structure of the sentence is too much complicated, or too artificial; or when the sense is too long suspended by parentheses. Some critics have been so strongly persuaded of the bad effect of parentheses on perspicuity, as to think they ought to be discarded altogether. But this, I imagine, is also an extreme. If the parenthesis be short, and if it be introduced in a proper place, it will not in the least hurt the clearness, and may add both to the vivacity and to the energy of the sentence. Others, again, have carried their dislike to the parenthesis only so far as to lay aside the hooks by which it is commonly distinguished, and to use commas in their place. But this is not avoiding the fault, if it be a fault; it is only endeavouring to commit it so as to escape discovery, and may therefore be more justly denominated a corruption in writing than an improvement. Punctuation, it will readily be acknowledged, is of considerable assistance to the reading and pronunciation. No part of a sentence requires to be distinguished, by the manner of pronouncing it, more than a parenthesis; and consequently, no part of a sentence ought to be more distinctly marked in the pointing.

[5] Bolingb. Phil. Fr. 20. [6] Ib. Fr. 9. [7] Guardian, No. 19.

PART VI.—*From technical Terms.*

Another source of darkness in composing is the injudicious introduction of technical words and phrases, as in the following passage:

> Tack to the larboard, and stand off to sea,
> Veer starboard sea and land———.[8]

What an absurd profusion, in an epic poem too, of terms which few beside seamen understand! In strict propriety, technical words should not be considered as belonging to the language; because not in current use, nor understood by the generality even of readers. They are but the peculiar dialect of a particular class. When those of that class only are addressed, as in treatises on the principles of their art, it is admitted that the use of such terms may be not only convenient, but even necessary. It is allowable also in ridicule, if used sparingly, as in comedy and romance.

PART VII.—*From long Sentences.*

The last cause of obscurity I shall take notice of is very long sentences. This rarely fails to be conjoined with some of the other faults before mentioned. The two subsequent quotations, from two eminent writers, will serve sufficiently to exemplify more than one of them. The first is from Bolingbroke's Philosophy: "If we are so, contrary to all appearances (for they denote plainly one single system, all the parts of which are so intimately connected and dependent one on another, that the whole begins, proceeds, and ends together,) this union of a body and a soul must be magical indeed, as Doctor Cudworth calls it; so magical, that the hypothesis serves to no purpose in philosophy, whatever it may do in theology; and is still less comprehensible than the hypothesis which assumes, that although our idea of thought be not included in the idea of matter or body, as the idea of figure is, for instance, in that of limited extension, yet the faculty of thinking, in all the modes of thought, may have been superadded by Omnipotence, to certain systems of matter: which it is not less than blasphemy to deny; though divines and philosophers, who deny it in terms, may be cited; and which, whether it be true or no, will never be proved false by a little metaphysical jargon about essences, and attributes, and modes."[9] The other quotation is from

[8] Dryden's Æneid.

[9] Essay i. Sect. 2.

Swift's letter to the Lord High Treasurer, containing a proposal for correcting, improving, and ascertaining the English tongue: "To this succeeded that licentiousness which entered with the Restoration, and from infecting our religion and morals, fell to corrupt our language, (which last was not like to be much improved by those who at that time made up the court of king Charles the Second; either such who had followed him in his banishment, or who had been altogether conversant in the dialect of those fanatic times; or young men who had been educated in the same company,) so that the court (which used to be the standard of propriety and correctness of speech) was then (and, I think, hath ever since continued) the worst school in England for that accomplishment; and so will remain, till better care be taken in the education of our young nobility, that they may set out into the world with some foundation of literature, in order to qualify them for patterns of politeness." There are, indeed, cases in which even a long period will not create obscurity. When this happens, it may almost always be remarked that all the principal members of the period are similar in their structure, and would constitute so many distinct sentences, if they were not united by their reference to some common clause in the beginning or the end.

SECTION II.—*The Double Meaning.*

It was observed that perspicuity might be violated, not only by obscurity, but also by double meaning. The fault in this case is not that the sentence conveys darkly or imperfectly the author's meaning, but that it conveys also some other meaning, which is not the author's. His words are susceptible of more than one interpretation. When this happens, it is always occasioned, either by using some expression which is equivocal; that is, hath more meanings than one affixed to it; or by ranging the words in such an order, that the construction is rendered equivocal, or made to exhibit different senses. To the former, for distinction's sake, I shall assign the name of equivocation; to the latter I shall appropriate that of ambiguity.

PART I.—*Equivocation.*

I begin with the first. When the word equivocation denotes, as in common language it generally denotes, the use of an equivocal word or phrase, or other ambiguity, with an intention to deceive, it doth not differ essentially from a lie. This offence falls under the reproof of the moralist, not the censure of the rhetorician. Again, when the word denotes, as agreeably to etymology it may denote, that exercise of wit which consists in the playful use of any term or phrase in different senses, and is denominated *pun*, it is amenable indeed to the tribunal of criticism, but cannot be regarded as a violation of the laws of perspicuity. It is neither with the liar nor with the punster that I am concerned at present. The only species of equivocation that comes under reprehension here, is that which takes place when an author undesignedly employs an expression susceptible of a sense different from the sense he intends to convey by it.

In order to avoid this fault, no writer or speaker can think of disusing all the homonymous terms of the language, or all such as have more than one signification. To attempt this in any tongue, ancient or modern, would be to attempt the annihilation of the greater part of the language; for in every language the words strictly univocal will be found to be the smaller number. But it must be admitted, as a rule in elocution, that equivocal terms ought ever to be avoided, unless where their connexion with the other words of the sentence instantly ascertains the meaning. This, indeed, the connexion is often so capable of effecting, that the hearer will never reflect that the word is equivocal, the true sense being the only sense which the expression suggests to his mind. Thus the word *pound* signifies both the sum of *twenty shillings sterling*, and the weight of *sixteen ounces avoirdupoise*. Now, if you should tell me that you rent a house at fifty *pounds*, or that you have bought fifty *pounds* of meat in the market, the idea of weight will never present itself to my mind in the one case, or the idea of money in the other. But it frequently happens, through the inadvertency of writers, that the connected words in the sentence do not immediately ascertain the sense of the equivocal term. And though an intelligent reader may easily find the sense on reflection, and with the aid of the context, we may lay it down as a maxim, that an author always offends against perspicuity when his style requires that reflection from his reader. But I shall proceed to illustrate, by examples, the fault of which I am treating. An equivocation, then, may be either in a single word or in a phrase.

As to the former, there is scarcely any of the parts of speech in which you will not find equivocal terms. To begin with particles; the preposition *of* denotes sometimes the relation which any affection bears to its subject; that is, the person whose affection it is; sometimes the relation which it bears to its object. Hence this expression of the apostle hath been observed to be equivocal: "I am persuaded that neither death nor life—shall be able to separate us from the love *of* God."[1] By *the love of God*, say interpreters, may be understood, either *God's*

[1] Romans viii. 38, &c.

love to us, or *our love to God.* It is remarkable that the genitive case in the ancient languages, and the prepositions corresponding to that case in the modern languages, are alike susceptible of this double meaning. Only as to our own language, we may observe in passing, that of late the preposition *of* is more commonly put before the subject, and *to* before the object of the passion. But this is not the only way in which the preposition *of* may be equivocal. As it sometimes denotes the relation of the effect to the cause, sometimes that of the accident to the subject, from this duplicity of signification there will also, in certain circumstances, arise a double sense. You have an example in these words of Swift: "A little after the reformation *of* Luther."[2]—It may indeed be doubted whether this should not rather be called an impropriety, since *the reformation of a man* will suggest much more readily a change wrought *on* the man, than a change wrought *by* him. And the former of these senses it could not more readily suggest, if the expression in that sense were not more conformable to use.

My next instance shall be in the conjunctions; "They were both much more ancient among the Persians than Zoroaster *or* Zerdusht."[3] The *or* here is equivocal. It serves either as a copulative to synonymous words, or as a disjunctive of different things. If, therefore, the reader should not know that Zoroaster and Zerdusht mean the same person, he will mistake the sense. In coupling appellatives there is not the same hazard, it being generally manifest to those who know the language, whether the words coupled have the same signification. If, nevertheless, in any case it should be doubtful, an attention to the ensuing rules may have its utility. If the first noun follows an article, or a preposition, or both, the article, or the preposition, or both, should be repeated before the second, when the two nouns are intended to denote different things; and should not be repeated when they are intended to denote the same thing. If there be neither article nor preposition before the first, and if it be the intention of the writer to use the particle *or* disjunctively, let the first noun be preceded by *either*, which will infallibly ascertain the meaning. On the contrary, if, in such a dubious case, it be his design to use the particle as a copulative to synonymous words, the piece will rarely sustain a material injury by his omitting both the conjunction and the synonyma.

The following is an example in the pronouns: "She united the great body of the people in *her* and their common interest."[4] The word *her* may be either the possessive pronoun or the accusative case of the personal pronoun. A very small

[2] Mechan. Operat. [3] Bol. Subst. of Letters to M. de Pouilly.
[4] Idea of a Patriot King.

alteration in the order totally removes the doubt. Say, "in their and *her* common interest." The word *her*, thus connected, can be only the possessive, as the author doubtless intended it should be, in the passage quoted.

An example in substantives: "Your majesty has lost all hopes of any future excises by their *consumption*."[5] The word *consumption* has both an active sense and a passive. It means either the act of consuming, or the state of being consumed. Clearly thus: "Your majesty has lost all hopes of levying any future excises on what they shall consume."

In adjectives: "As for such animals as are *mortal*, or noxious, we have a right to destroy them."[6] Here the false sense is suggested more readily than the true. The word *mortal*, therefore, in this sentence, might justly be considered as improper; for though it sometimes means destructive, or causing death, it is then almost invariably joined with some noun expressive of hurt or danger. Thus we say, a *mortal poison*, a *mortal wound*, a *mortal disease*, or a *mortal enemy;* but the phrases *mortal creature*, *mortal animal*, or *mortal man*, are always understood to imply creature, animal, or man *liable to death.*

In verbs: "The next refuge was to say, it was *overlooked* by one man, and many passages wholly written by another."[7] The word *overlooked* sometimes signifies *revised*, and sometimes *neglected.* As it seems to be in the former sense that this participle is used here, the word *revised* ought to have been preferred. Another instance in verbs: "I have furnished the house exactly according to your fancy, or, if you please, my own; for I have long since learnt to like nothing but what you *do*."[8] The word *do* in this passage may be either the auxiliary, or, as it might be termed, the supplementary verb, and be intended only to supersede the repetition of the verb *like;* or it may be the simple active verb, which answers to the Latin *facere*, and the French *faire.*

In the next quotation the homonymous term may be either an adjective or an adverb, and admits a different sense in each acceptation:

Not *only* Jesuits can equivocate.[9]

If the word *only* is here an adverb, the sense is, "To equivocate is not the only thing that Jesuits can do." This interpretation, though not the author's meaning, suits the construction. A very small alteration in the order gives a proper and unequivocal, though a prosaic expression of this sense:

[5] Guardian, No. 52. [6] Ibid. No. 61. [7] Spect. No. 19
[8] Ibid. No. 627. [9] Dryden's Hind and Panther.

"Jesuits can not only equivocate."——Again, if the word *only* is here an adjective (and this doubtless is the author's intention) the sense is, "Jesuits are not the only persons who can equivocate." But this interpretation suits ill the composition of the sentence. The only other instance of this error in single words I shall produce, is one in which, on the first glance, there appears room to doubt whether a particular term ought to be understood literally or metaphorically. The word *handled* in the following passage will illustrate what I mean: "Thus much I thought fit to premise before I resume the subject which I have already *handled*, I mean the naked bosoms of our British ladies."[1] Sometimes, indeed, a thing like this may be said archly and of design, in which case it falls not under this animadversion.

It was remarked above, that there are not only equivocal words in our language, but equivocal phrases. *Not the least*, and *not the smallest*, are of this kind. They are sometimes made to imply *not any;* as though one should say, *not even the least, not so much as the smallest;* and sometimes again to signify *a very great*, as though it were expressed in this manner, *far from being the least or smallest.* Thus they are susceptible of two significations, that are not only different but contrary. We have an instance in the following passage: "Your character of universal guardian, joined to the concern you ought to have for the cause of virtue and religion, assure me you will not think that clergymen, when injured, have *the least* right to your protection."[2] This sentence hath also the disadvantage taken notice of in some of the preceding quotations, that the sense not intended by the writer occurs to the reader much more readily than the author's real meaning. *Nothing less than* is another phrase, which, like the two former, is susceptible of opposite interpretations. Thus, "He aimed at *nothing less than* the crown," may denote either "Nothing was less aimed at by him than the crown;" or, "Nothing inferior to the crown could satisfy his ambition." All such phrases ought to be totally laid aside. The expression *will have mercy*, is equivocal in the following passage of the vulgar translation of the Bible: "I *will have mercy*, and not sacrifice."[3] The expression commonly denotes, "I will exercise mercy;" whereas it is in this place employed to signify, "I require others to exercise it." The sentiment, therefore, ought to have been rendered here, as we find it expressed in the prophetical book alluded to, "I desire mercy and not sacrifice."[4] When the phrase in question happens to be followed by the preposition *on* or *upon* before the object,

[1] Guardian, No. 116.
[2] Ibid. No. 80.
[3] Matt. ix. 13.
[4] Hos. vi. 6.

there is nothing equivocal in it, the sense being ascertained by the connexion.

So much for equivocal words and phrases.

PART II.—*Ambiguity.*

I come now to consider that species of *double meaning* which ariseth, not from the use of equivocal terms, but solely from the construction, and which I therefore distinguished by the name of *ambiguity.* This, of all the faults against perspicuity, it is in all languages the most difficult to avoid. There is not one of the parts of speech which may not be so placed, as that, agreeably to the rules of grammar, it may be construed with different parts of the sentence, and by consequence made to exhibit different senses. Besides, a writer, intent upon his subject, is less apt to advert to those imperfections in his style which occasion ambiguity, than to any other. As no term or phrase he employs doth of itself suggest the false meaning, a manner of construing his words different from that which is expressive of his sentiment will not so readily occur to his thoughts: and yet this erroneous manner of construing them may be the most obvious to the reader. I shall give examples of ambiguities in most of the parts of speech, beginning with the pronouns.

As the signification of the pronouns (which by themselves express only some relation) is ascertained merely by the antecedent to which they refer, the greatest care must be taken, if we would express ourselves perspicuously, that the reference be unquestionable. Yet the greatest care on this article will not always be effectual. There are no rules which either have been, or, I suspect, can be devised in any language, that will, in all circumstances, fix the relations of the pronouns in such a manner as to prevent ambiguity altogether. I shall instance first in the pronoun *who*, begging that the reader will observe its application in the two following sentences: "Solomon the son of David, *who* built the temple of Jerusalem, was the richest monarch that ever reigned over the people of God;" and "Solomon the son of David *who* was persecuted by Saul, was the richest monarch——." In these two sentences, the *who* is similarly situated; yet, in the former, it relates to the person first mentioned; in the latter, to the second. But this relation to the one or to the other it would be impossible for any reader to discover who had not some previous knowledge of the history of those kings. In such cases, therefore, it is better to give another turn to the sentence. Instead of the first, one might say, "Solomon the son of David, and the builder of the temple of Jerusalem, was the richest monarch." The conjunction *and* makes the following words relate entirely to Solomon, as nothing had been affirmed concerning David. It is more difficult to avoid the ambiguity in the other instance, without adopting some circumlocution that will flatten the expression. In the style that prevailed in this island about two centuries ago, they would have escaped the ambiguous construction in some such way as this, " Solomon, the son of David, even of him whom Saul persecuted, was the richest——." But this phraseology has, to modern ears, I know not what air of formality that renders it intolerable. Better thus, " Solomon, whose father David was persecuted by Saul, was the richest ——." The following quotation exhibits a triple sense, arising from the same cause, the indeterminate use of the relative :—

> Such were the centaurs of Ixion's race,
> *Who* a bright cloud for Juno did embrace. [5]

Was it *the centaurs*, or *Ixion*, or *his race*, that embraced the cloud? I cannot help observing further on this passage, that the relative ought grammatically, for a reason to be assigned afterwards, rather to refer to *centaurs* than to either of the other two, and least of all to *Ixion*, to which it was intended to refer.[6]

But there is often an ambiguity in the relatives *who*, *which*, *that*, *whose*, and *whom*, even when there can be no doubt in regard to the antecedent. This arises from the different ways wherein the latter is affected by the former. To express myself in the language of grammarians, these pronouns are sometimes explicative, sometimes determinative. They are explicative when they serve merely for the illustration of the subject, by pointing out either some property or some circumstance belonging to it, leaving it, however, to be understood in its full extent. Of this kind are the following examples: " Man, who is born of woman, is of few days and full of trouble." " Godliness, which with contentment is great gain, has the promise both of the

[5] Denham's Progress of Learning.

[6] Let it not be imagined that in this particular our tongue has the disadvantage of other languages. The same difficulty, as far as my acquaintance with them reaches, affects them all; and even some modern tongues in a higher degree than ours. In English, one is never at a loss to discover whether the reference be to persons or to things. In French and Italian the expression is often ambiguous in this respect also. In a French devotional book I find this pious admonition:—" Conservez-vous dans l'amour de Dieu, qui peut vous garantir de toute chute." I ask whether the antecedent here be *l'amour* or *Dieu*, since the relative *qui* is of such extensive import as to be applicable to either. The expression would be equally ambiguous in Italian, " Conservatevi nell' amor di Dio, che vi puo conservare senza intoppo." In English, according to the present use, there would be no ambiguity in the expression. If the author meant to ascribe this energy to the devout affection itself, he would say, " Keep yourselves in the love of God, *which* can preserve you from falling;" if to God the great object of our love, he would say, "*who* can preserve you."—This convenient distinction was not, however, uniformly observed with us till about the middle of the last century.

present life and of the future." The clause, "who is born of woman," in the first example, and "which with contentment is great gain," in the second, point to certain properties in the antecedents, but do not restrain their signification. For, should we omit these clauses altogether, we could say with equal truth, "Man is of few days and full of trouble." "Godliness has the promise both of the present life and of the future." On the other hand, these pronouns are determinative, when they are employed to limit the import of the antecedent, as in these instances: "The man that endureth to the end shall be saved." "The remorse, which issues in reformation, is true repentance." Each of the relatives here confines the signification of its antecedent to such only as are possessed of the qualification mentioned. For it is not affirmed of every man that he shall be saved; nor of all remorse, that it is true repentance.

From comparing the above examples, it may be fairly collected, that with us the definite article is of great use for discriminating the explicative sense from the determinative. In the first case it is rarely used, in the second it ought never to be omitted, unless when something still more definite, such as a demonstrative pronoun, supplies its place.[7] The following passage is faulty in this respect: "I know that *all words which* are signs of complex ideas, furnish matter of mistake and cavil."[8] As *words*, the antecedent, has neither the article nor a demonstrative pronoun to connect it with the subsequent relative, it would seem that the clause "which are signs of complex ideas," were merely explicative, and that the subject *words* were

7 In this respect the articles are more subservient to perspicuity in our tongue than in many others. In French, a writer must give the article indiscriminately in all the instances above specified. Thus, "L'homme, qui est né de la femme, vit très-peu de tems, et il est rempli de misères;" and "L'homme qui persévérera jusqu'à la fin, sera sauvé." In like manner, "La pieté, qui jointe avec le contentement est un grand gain, a les promesses de la vie présente, et de celle qui est à venir;" and "Le remors qui aboutit à la reformation, est le vrai repentir." The like indistinctness will be found to obtain in Italian and some other modern languages, and arises, in a great measure, from their giving the article almost invariably to abstracts. In some instances, there appears of late a tendency in writers, especially on politics, to give up this advantage entirely; not by adding the article to abstracts but (which equally destroys the distinction) by omitting it when the term has a particular application. How often do we now find, even in books, such phrases as the following! "This was an undertaking too arduous for private persons unaided by government." "It is hard to say what measure administration will next adopt." As in both cases it is the present government and the present administration of the country of the author that is meant, these nouns ought to have the definite article prefixed to them, and can scarcely be called English without it. The former of these words is indeed frequently used in the abstract, in which case it never has the article, as thus: "Government is absolutely necessary in all civilized societies." "He published tracts on various subjects, on religion, government, trade, &c." Abuses, such as that here criticized, greatly hurtful to perspicuity and precision, arise first in conversation, thence they creep into newspapers, thence into pamphlets, and at last unwarily find admission into books.

8 Bolingbroke's Dissertation on Parties, Let. 12.

to be understood in the utmost latitude. This could not be the writer's sense, as it would be absurd to affirm of all words, that they are signs of complex ideas. He ought therefore to have said either, "I know that all *the* words *which* are signs of complex ideas,"—or "I know that all *those* words *which* are signs——." Either of these ways makes the clause beginning with the relative serve to limit the import of the antecedent.

There are certain cases, it must be owned, wherein the antecedent would require the article, even though the relatives were intended solely for explication, as in these words of the Psalmist: "My goodness extendeth not to thee; but to the saints, and to the excellent ones, in whom is all my delight."[9] The last clause is probably not restrictive, the words *saints* and *excellent ones* necessarily requiring the article. Now, when such antecedents are followed by a determinative, they ought, for distinction's sake, to be attended with the demonstrative pronoun, as thus, "—but to *those* saints, and to *those* excellent ones in *whom*—."

Through not attending to this circumstance, the translators of the Bible have rendered the following passage ambiguous, even in regard to the antecedent: "There stood by me this night the angel of God, *whose* I am, and *whom* I serve."[1] The relatives here *whose* and *whom* refer more regularly to *angel* than to *God*. This, however, is not agreeable to the sense of the apostle. The words, therefore, ought to have been translated "— an angel of *the* God," or "— of *that* God *whose* I am, and *whom* I serve."[2] For though the term *God* in strict propriety can be applied only to one, and may therefore be thought to stand on the same footing with proper names, it is, in the common way of using, an appellative, and follows the construction of appellatives. Thus we say, "the God of Abraham," "the God of armies." Besides, Paul in the passage quoted was speaking to heathens; and this circumstance gives an additional propriety to the article.

For an instance of ambiguity in the construction of the pronoun *his*, I shall borrow an example from a French Grammarian;[3] for though an equivocal word can rarely be translated by an equivocal word, it is very easy, when two languages have a considerable degree of similarity in their structure and analogy, to transfer an ambiguity from one to the other. The instance I mean is this, "Lisias promised to his father never to abandon *his* friends." Were they his own friends, or his father's, whom Lisias promised never to abandon? This sentence rendered literally would be ambiguous in most modern tongues.[4]

[9] Psalm xvi. 2, 3.

[1] Acts xxvii. 23.

[2] Αγγελος του Θεου οὑ ειμι και ᾧ λατρευω.

[3] Buffier.

[4] It would not be ambiguous in Latin. The distinction which obtains in that tongue between the pronouns *suus* and *ejus* would totally preclude all doubt.

In the earliest and simplest times, the dramatic manner in which people were accustomed to relate the plainest facts, served effectually to exclude all ambiguities of this sort from their writings. They would have said, "Lisias gave a promise to his father in these words, I will never abandon *my friends*," if they were his own friends of whom he spoke; "*your friends*," if they were his father's. It is, I think, to be regretted, that the moderns have too much departed from this primitive simplicity. It doth not want some advantages, besides that of perspicuity. It is often more picturesque, as well as more affecting; though it must be owned, it requires so many words, and such frequent repetitions of *he said*, *he answered*, and the like, that the dialogue, if long, is apt to grow irksome. But it is at least pardonable to adopt this method occasionally, where it can serve to remove an ambiguity. As the turn which Buffier gives the sentence in French, in order to avoid the double meaning, answers equally well in English, I shall here literally translate it. On the first supposition, "Lisias, speaking of his friends, promised to his father never to abandon them." On the second supposition, "Lisias, speaking of his father's friends, promised to his father never to abandon them."[5]

It is easy to conceive that in numberless instances, the pronoun *he* will, in like manner, be ambiguous when two or more males happen to be mentioned in the same clause of a sentence. In such a case, we ought always either to give another turn to the expression, or to use the noun itself, and not the pronoun; for when the repetition of a word is necessary, it is not offensive. The translators of the Bible have often judiciously used this method; I say judiciously, because, though the other method be on some occasions preferable, yet, by attempting the other, they would have run a much greater risk of destroying that beautiful simplicity, which is an eminent characteristic of the language of holy writ. I shall take an instance from the speech

[5] I even think, that the turn of the sentence is easier in English than in French: "Lisias, parlant des amis de son père à son père même, lui promit de ne les abandonner jamais." It may be thought that, on the first supposition there is a shorter way of removing the doubt. *Ses propres amis* in French, and *his own friends* in English, would effectually answer the end. But let it be observed, that the introduction of this appropriating term hath an exclusive appearance with regard to others, that might be very unsuitable. I observe further, that the distinction in English between *his* and *her* precludes several ambiguities that affect most other European tongues. Suppose the promise had been made to the mother instead of the father, the simple enunciation of it would be equally ambiguous in French, as in the other case. "Lisias promit à sa mère de n'abandonner jamais *ses* amis," is their expression, whether they be *his* friends or *hers*, of whom he speaks. If it were a daughter to her father, the case would be the same with them, but different with us. I may remark here, by the way, how much more this small distinction in regard to the antecedent conduces to perspicuity, than the distinctions of gender and number in regard to the nouns with which they are joined. As to this last connexion, the place of the pronoun always ascertains it, so that, for this purpose at least, the change of termination is superfluous.

of Judah to his brother Joseph in Egypt: "We said to my lord, the lad cannot leave his father; for if he should leave his father, his father would die."[6] The words *his father* are in this short verse thrice repeated, and yet are not disagreeable, as they contribute to perspicuity. Had the last part of the sentence run thus, "If he should leave his father, he would die," it would not have appeared from the expression, whether it was the child or the parent that would die. Some have imagined that the pronoun ought always regularly to refer to the nearest preceding noun of the same gender and number. But this notion is founded in a mistake, and doth not suit the idiom of any language ancient or modern. From the rank that some words maintain in the sentence, if I may be allowed that expression, a reader will have a natural tendency to consider the pronoun as referring to them, without regard to their situation. In support of this observation, I shall produce two examples. The first shall be of the neuter singular of the third personal pronoun: "But I shall leave this subject to your management, and question not but you will throw *it* into such light, as shall at once improve and entertain your reader."[7] There is no ambiguity here, nor would it, on the most cursory reading, enter into the head of any person of common sense, that the pronoun *it* relates to *management*, which is nearer, and not to *subject*, which is more remote. Nor is it the sense only that directs us in this preference. There is another principle by which we are influenced. The accusative of the active verb is one chief object of attention in a sentence; the regimen of that accusative hath but a secondary value; it is regarded only as explanatory of the former, or at most as an appendage to it. This consideration doth not affect those only who understand grammar, but all who understand the language. The different parts of speech, through the power of custom, produce their effect on those who are ignorant of their very names, as much as on the grammarian himself; though it is the grammarian alone who can give a rational account of these effects. The other example I promised to give, shall be of the masculine of the same number and person, in the noted complaint of Cardinal Wolsey immediately after his disgrace:

> Had I but serv'd my God, with half the zeal
> I serv'd my king; *he* would not in mine age
> Have left me naked to mine enemies.[8]

Here, though the word *king* is adjoining, and the word *God* at some distance, the pronoun *he* cannot so regularly refer to that noun as to this. The reason is, the whole of the second clause beginning with these words, "with half the zeal," main-

[6] Gen. xliv. 22. [7] Spect. No. 628. [8] Shakspeare. Henry VIII.

tains but a subordinate rank in the sentence, as it is introduced in explication of the first, and might be omitted, not indeed without impairing, but without destroying the sense. Yet neither the rank in the sentence, nor the nearness of position, will invariably determine the import of the relative. Sometimes, indeed, as was observed by the French author last quoted, the sense of the words connected is sufficient to remove the ambiguity, though the reader should have no previous knowledge of the subject. And doubtless, it is equally reasonable to admit a construction which, though naturally equivocal, is fixed by the connexion, as to admit an equivocal term, the sense whereof is in this manner ascertained. Of an ambiguity thus removed, the following will serve for an example: "Alexander having conquered Darius, made himself master of *his* dominions." *His* may refer grammatically either to Alexander, or to Darius, but as no man is said to make himself master of what was previously his own, the words connected prevent the false sense from presenting itself to the reader.

But it is not the pronouns only that are liable to be used ambiguously. There is in adjectives particularly, a great risk of ambiguity, when they are not adjoined to the substantives to which they belong. This hazard, it must be owned, is greater in our language than in most others, our adjectives having no declension whereby case, number, and gender are distinguished. Their relation, therefore, for the most part, is not otherwise to be ascertained but by their place. The following sentence will serve for an example: "God heapeth favours on his servants ever liberal and faithful." Is it God or his servants that are liberal and faithful? If the former, say "God, ever liberal and faithful, heapeth favours on his servants." If the latter, say either, "God heapeth favours on his ever liberal and faithful servants," or—"his servants who are ever liberal and faithful." There is another frequent cause of ambiguity in the use of adjectives, which hath been as yet in our language, very little attended to. Two or more are sometimes made to refer to the same substantive, when, in fact, they do not belong to the same thing, but to different things, which, being of the same kind, are expressed by the same generic name. I explain myself by an example: "Both the ecclesiastic and secular powers concurred in those measures." Here the two adjectives ecclesiastic and secular relate to the same substantive, powers, but do not relate to the same individual things; for the powers denominated ecclesiastic are totally different from those denominated secular. Indeed, the reader's perfect knowledge of the difference may prevent his attending to this ambiguity, or rather impropriety of speech. But this mode of expression ought to be avoided, because, if admitted in one instance where the meaning perhaps is clear to the generality of readers, a writer will be apt inadvertently to fall into it in other instances, where the meaning is not clear, nay, where most readers will be misled. This too common idiom may be avoided either by repeating the substantive, or by subjoining the substantive to the first adjective, and prefixing the article to the second as well as to the first. Say either, "Both the ecclesiastical powers and the secular powers concurred in those measures;" or, which is perhaps preferable, "Both the ecclesiastic powers and the secular concurred in those measures." The substantive being posterior to the first adjective, and anterior to the second, the second, though it refers, cannot, according to grammatical order, belong to it. The substantive is therefore understood as repeated; besides, the repetition of the article has the force to denote that this is not an additional epithet to the same subject, but belongs to a subject totally distinct, though coming under the same denomination. There is, indeed, one phrase liable to the aforesaid objection, which use hath so firmly established, that, I fear, it would savour of affectation to alter. The phrase I mean is, "The lords spiritual and temporal in parliament assembled." Nevertheless, when it is not expected that we should express ourselves in the style of the law, and when we are not quoting either a decision of the house of peers, or an act of parliament, I imagine it would be better to say, "The spiritual lords and the temporal."—On the contrary, wherever the two adjectives are expressive of qualities belonging to a subject, not only specifically but individually the same, the other mode of speech is preferable, which makes them belong also to the same noun. Thus we say properly, "The high and mighty states of Holland," because it is not some of the states that are denominated *high*, and others of them *mighty*, but both epithets are given alike to all. It would therefore be equally faulty here to adopt such an arrangement as would make a reader conceive them to be different. In cases wherein the article is not used, the place of the substantive ought to show whether both adjectives belong to the same thing, or to different things having the same name. In the first case, the substantive ought either to precede both adjectives, or to follow both; in the second, it ought to follow the first adjective, and may be repeated after the second, or understood, as will best suit the harmony of the sentence, or the nature of the composition; for the second adjective cannot grammatically belong to the noun which follows the first, though that noun may properly suggest to the reader the word to be supplied. Thus I should say rightly, "It is the opinion of all *good and wise men*, that a vicious person cannot enjoy true happiness;" because I mean to signify, that this is the opinion of those to whom both qualities, goodness and wisdom, are justly attributed. But the following passage in our version of the sacred text is not so proper: "Every scribe instructed into the kingdom of heaven, is like an householder, who bringeth out of his treasure *things new and old*."[9] Both epithets cannot belong to the same things. Make but a small alteration in the order, and say *new things and old*, and you will add greatly both to the perspicuity and to the propriety of the expression. In cases similar to the example last quoted, if a preposition be necessary to the construction of the sentence, it ought to be repeated before the second adjective. Thus, "Death is the common lot of all, of good men and of bad." But when both adjectives express the qualities of an identical subject, it is better not to repeat the preposition. "The prince gave encouragement to *all honest and industrious artificers* of neighbouring nations to come and settle amongst his subjects." Here both qualities *honesty* and *industry* are required in every artificer encouraged by the prince. I shall observe lastly on this article, that though the adjectives relate to different things, if no substantive be expressed, it is not necessary to repeat the preposition. The reason is, that in such cases the adjectives are used substantively, or, to speak more properly, are real substantives. Thus we may say either, "Death is the inevitable fate of good and bad, rich and poor, wise and foolish," or—"of good and of bad, of rich and of poor."—When the definite article is prefixed to the first adjective, it ought to be repeated before the second, if the adjectives are expressive of qualities belonging to different subjects; but not if they refer to the same subject. Thus we say rightly, "How immense the difference between the pious and the profane." "I address myself only to the intelligent and attentive." In the former, the subjects referred to are manifestly different; in the latter, they coincide, as both qualities are required in every hearer. The following passage is by consequence justly censurable. The exceptionable phrases are distinguished by the character: "Wisdom and folly, the virtuous and the vile, *the learned and ignorant, the temperate and debauched*, all give and return the jest."[1] For the same reason, and it is a sufficient reason, that he said "the virtuous and the vile," he ought to have said "the learned and the ignorant, the temperate and the debauched.

I proceed to give examples in some of the other parts of speech. The construction of substantive nouns is sometimes ambiguous. Take the following instance: "You shall seldom find a dull fellow of good education, but (if he happen to have any leisure upon his hands) will turn his head to one of those two amusements for all fools of eminence, *politics or poetry*."[2] The position of the words *politics or poetry* makes one at first imagine, that along with the term *eminence*, they are affected

[9] Matthew xiii. 52. [1] Brown on the Characteristics, Ess. 1. Sect. 5.
[2] Spectator, No. 43.

by the preposition *of*, and construed with *fools*. The repetition of the *to* after eminence would have totally removed the ambiguity. A frequent cause of this fault in the construction of substantives, especially in verse, is when both what we call the nominative case and the accusative are put before the verb. As in nouns those cases are not distinguished either by inflection or by prepositions, so neither can they be distinguished in such instances by arrangement.

> The rising tomb the lofty column bore.[3]

Did the tomb bear the column, or the column the tomb?

> And thus the son the fervent sire addrest.[4]

This, though liable to the same objection, may be more easily rectified, at least in a considerable measure. As the possessive pronoun is supposed to refer to some preceding noun, which, for distinction's sake, I have here called the antecedent, though the term is not often used in so great latitude, it is always better to be construed with the accusative of the verb, and to refer to the nominative as its antecedent. The reason is, the nominative, to which it most naturally refers, whether actually preceding or not, is always conceived in the order of things to precede. If then it was the son who spoke, say,

> And thus the son his fervent sire addrest.

If the father,

> And thus his son the fervent sire addrest.

In confirmation of this, let us consider the way in which we should express ourselves in plain prose, without any transposition of words. For the first, "Thus the son addressed his father;" for the second, "Thus the father addressed his son;" are undoubtedly good: whereas to say in lieu of the first, "Thus his son addressed the father;" and in lieu of the second, "Thus his father addressed the son," are not English. By the English idiom, therefore, the possessive pronoun is, in such instances, more properly joined to the regimen of the verb than to the nominative. If this practice were universal, as it is both natural and suitable to the genius of our tongue, it would always indicate the construction wherever the possessive pronoun could be properly introduced. For this reason I consider the two following lines as much clearer of the charge of ambiguity than the former quotation from the same work:

[3] Pope's Odyssey, Book xii. [4] Ibid. Book xix.

Young Itylus, his parent's darling joy,
Whom chance misled the mother to destroy.[5]

For though the words *whom* and *the mother* are both in the accusative, the one as the regimen of the active verb *misled*, the other as the regimen of the active verb *destroy*, yet the destroyer or agent is conceived in the natural order as preceding the destroyed or patient. If, therefore, the last line had been,

Whom chance misled his mother to destroy,

it would have more naturally imported, that the son destroyed his mother; as it stands, it more naturally imports, agreeably to the poet's design, that the mother destroyed her son; there being in this last case no access for the possessive pronoun. I acknowledge, however, that uniform usage cannot (though both analogy and utility may) be pleaded in favour of the distinction now made. I therefore submit entirely to the candid and judicious the propriety of observing it for the future.

The following is an example of ambiguity in using conjunctions: "At least my own private letters leave room for a politician, well versed in matters of this nature, to suspect *as much, as* a penetrating friend of mine tells me."[6] The particle *as*, which in this sentence immediately precedes the word *a penetrating friend*, makes frequently a part of these compound conjunctions *as much as, as well as, as far as*.—It will therefore naturally appear at first to belong to the words *as much*, which immediately precede it. But as this is not really the case, it ought to have been otherwise situated; for it is not enough that it is separated by a comma, these small distinctions in the pointing being but too frequently overlooked. Alter the arrangement then, and the expression will be no longer ambiguous: "At least my own private letters, as a penetrating friend of mine tells me, leave room for a politician well versed in matters of this nature to suspect as much." In the succeeding passage the same author gives us an example of an ambiguity in the application of an adverb and a conjunction: "I beseech you, sir, to inform these fellows, that they have *not* the spleen, *because* they cannot talk without the help of a glass, or convey their meaning to each other without the interposition of clouds."[7] The ambiguity here lies in the two words *not* and *because*. What follows *because* appears, on the first hearing, to be the reason why the person here addressed is desired to inform these fellows, that they are not splenetic; on the second, it appears to be the reason why people ought to conclude that they are not;

5 Pope's Odyssey, Book xix. 6 Spect. No. 43.
7 Ibid. No. 53.

and on the third, the author seems only intending to signify that this is not a sufficient reason to make any body conclude that they are. This error deserves our notice the more, that it is often to be found even in our best writers.

Sometimes a particular expression is so situated, that it may be construed with more or less of another particular expression which precedes it in the sentence, and may consequently exhibit different senses: "He has, by some strange magic, arrived at the value of half a plum, as the citizens call *a hundred thousand pounds*."[8] Is it *a plum*, or *half a plum*, which the citizens call a hundred thousand pounds? "I will spend a hundred or *two* pounds, rather than be enslaved."[9] This is another error of the same sort, but rather worse. *Hundred* cannot regularly be understood between the adjective *two* and its substantive *pounds*. Besides, the indefinite article *a* cannot properly express one side of the alternative, and supply the place of a numeral adjective opposed to *two*. The author's meaning would have been better expressed either of these ways: "I will spend one or two hundred pounds," or, "I will spend one hundred pounds or two, rather than be enslaved." In the former case it is evident that the words *hundred pounds* belong to both numeral adjectives; in the latter, that they are understood after the second. The reference and construction of the concluding words in the next quotation is very indefinite: "My Christian and surname begin and end with *the same letters*."[1] Doth his Christian name begin with the same letter that his surname begins with, and end with the same letter that his surname ends with? or, Doth his Christian name end with the same letter with which it begins, and his surname also end with the same letter with which it begins? or, lastly, Are all these four letters, the first and the last of each name, the same letter?[2]

Sometimes the particular clause or expression is so situated that it may be construed with different members of the sentence, and thus exhibit different meanings: "It has not a word," says Pope, "but what the author religiously thinks *in it*."[3] One would at first imagine his meaning to be, that it had not a word which the author did not think to be in it. Alter a little the place of the two last words, and the ambiguity will be removed: "It has not a word *in it*, but what the author religiously thinks." Of the same kind also is the subsequent quotation: "Mr. Dryden makes a very handsome observation on Ovid's writing a letter from Dido to Æneas, *in the following words*."[4] Whether are *the following words*, the words of

[8] Tatler, No. 40. [9] Swift to Sheridan.

[1] Spectator, No. 505. O.

[2] An example of the first, is Andrew Askew, of the second, Hezekiah Thrift, and of the third, Norman Neilson.

[3] Guardian, No. 4. [4] Spect. No. 62.

Dido's letter, or of Dryden's observation? Before you read them you will more readily suppose them to be the words of the letter; after reading them you find they are the words of the observation. The order ought to have been, "Mr. Dryden, in the following words, makes a very handsome observation on Ovid's writing a letter from Dido to Æneas."

I shall conclude this section with an instance of that kind of ambiguity which the French call a *squinting construction;*[5] that is, when a clause is so situated in a sentence, that one is at first at a loss to know whether it ought to be connected with the words which go before, or with those which come after. Take the following passage for an example: "As it is necessary to have the head clear as well as the complexion, *to be perfect in this part of learning,* I rarely mingle with the men, but frequent the tea-tables of the ladies."[6] Whether To be perfect in this part of learning, is it necessary to have the head clear as well as the complexion: or, To be perfect in this part of learning, does he rarely mingle with the men, but frequent the tea-tables of the ladies? Whichever of these be the sense, the words ought to have been otherwise ranged.

SECTION III.—*The Unintelligible.*

I have already considered two of the principal and most common offences against perspicuity; and come now to make some remarks on the third and last offence mentioned in the enumeration formerly given. It was observed, that a speaker may not only express himself obscurely, and so convey his meaning imperfectly to the mind of the hearer, that he may not only express himself ambiguously, and so, along with his own, convey a meaning entirely different; but even express himself unintelligibly, and so convey no meaning at all. One would, indeed, think it hardly possible that a man of sense, who perfectly understands the language which he useth, should ever speak or write in such a manner as to be altogether unintelligible. Yet this is what frequently happens. The cause of this fault in any writer I take to be always one or other of the three following; first, great confusion of thought, which is commonly accompanied with intricacy of expression; secondly, affectation of excellence in the diction; thirdly, a total want of meaning. I do not mention, as one of the causes of this imputation, a penury of language; though this, doubtless, may contribute to produce it. In fact I never found one who had a justness of apprehension, and was free from affectation, at a loss to make himself understood in his native tongue, even though he had little command of language, and made but a bad choice of words.

[5] Construction louche.

[6] Guardian, No. 10.

PART I.—*From Confusion of Thought.*

The first cause of the unintelligible in composition is confusion of thought. Language, as hath been already observed, is the medium through which the sentiments of the writer are perceived by the reader. And though the impurity or the grossness of the medium will render the image obscure or indistinct, yet no purity in the medium will suffice for exhibiting a distinct and unvarying image of a confused and unsteady object. There is a sort of half-formed thoughts, which we sometimes find writers impatient to give to the world, before they themselves are fully possessed of them. Now, if the writer himself perceive confusedly and imperfectly the sentiments he would communicate, it is a thousand to one, the reader will not perceive them at all. But how then, it may be asked, shall he be qualified for discovering the cause, and distinguishing in the writer between a confusion of thought and a total want of meaning? I answer, that in examples of this kind the causes will, sometimes, not always, be discovered, by means of an attentive and frequent perusal of the words and context. Some meaning, after long poring, will perhaps be traced; but in all such cases we may be said more properly to divine what the author would say, than to understand what he says; and therefore all such sentences deserve to be ranked among the *unintelligible.* If a discovery of the sense be made, that it is made ought rather to be ascribed to the sagacity of the reader than to the elocution of the writer. This species of the unintelligible (which, by the way, differs not in kind, but in degree, from the obscurity already considered, being no other than that bad quality in the extreme) I shall exemplify first in simple, and afterwards in complex sentences.

First in simple sentences: "I have observed," says Sir Richard Steele, who, though a man of sense and genius, was a great master in this style, "that the superiority among these," (he is speaking of some coffee-house politicians,) "proceeds from an opinion of gallantry and fashion."[7] This sentence, considered in itself, evidently conveys no meaning. First, it is not said, whose opinion, their own, or that of others; secondly, it is not said what opinion, or of what sort, favourable or unfavourable, true or false, but in general an opinion of gallantry and fashion, which contains no definite expression of any meaning. With the joint assistance of the context, reflection, and conjecture, we shall perhaps conclude that the author intended to say, "that the rank among these politicians was determined by the opinion generally entertained of the rank in point of gallantry and

[7] Spect. No. 49.

fashion that each of them had attained." But no part of this is expressed. Another specimen: "And as to a well-taught mind, when you've said an haughty and proud man, you have spoke a narrow conception, little spirit, and despicable carriage."[8] Here, too, it is possible to guess the intention of the author, but not to explain the import of the expression.

Take the two following examples of complex sentences from the same hand: "I must confess we live in an age wherein a few empty blusterers carry away the praise of speaking, while a crowd of fellows overstocked with knowledge are run down by them: I say, overstocked, because they certainly are so, as to their service to mankind, if from their very store they raise to themselves ideas of respect and greatness of the occasion, and I know not what, to disable themselves from explaining their thoughts."[9] The other example is, "The serene aspect of these writers, joined with the great encouragement I observe is given to another, or, what is indeed to be suspected, in which he indulges himself, confirmed me in the notion I have of the prevalence of ambition this way."[1] But leaving this, which is indeed the dullest species of the unintelligible, I proceed to the second class, that which arises from an affectation of excellence.

PART II.—*From Affectation of Excellence.*

In this there is always something figurative; but the figures are remote, and things heterogeneous are combined. I shall exemplify this sort also, first in a few more simple sentences, and then in such as are more complex. Of the former take the following instances: "This temper of the soul," says the Guardian, speaking of meekness and humility, "keeps our understanding tight about us."[2] Whether the author had any meaning in this expression, or what it was, I shall not take upon me to determine; but hardly could any thing more incongruous in the way of metaphor have been imagined. The understanding is made a girdle to our other mental faculties, for the fastening of which girdle, meekness and humility serve for a buckle. "A man is not qualified for a butt, who has not a good deal of wit and vivacity, *even in the ridiculous side of his character*."[3] It is only the additional clause in the end that is here exceptionable. What a strange jumble! A man's wits and vivacity placed in the side of his character. Sometimes in a sentence sufficiently perspicuous, we shall find an unintelligible clause inserted, which, as it adds not to the sense, serves only to interrupt the reader and darken the sentiment. Of this the fol-

[8] Guardian, No. 20.
[9] Spectator, No. 484.
[1] Guardian, No. 1.
[2] Ibid. No. 1.
[3] Spect. No. 47.

lowing passage will serve for an example: I seldom see a noble building, or any great piece of magnificence and pomp, but I think how little is all this to satisfy the ambition, *or to fill the idea*, of an immortal soul."[4] Pray, what addition does the phrase *to fill the idea* make to the sense; or what is the meaning of it? I shall subjoin, for the sake of variety, one poetical example from Dryden, who, speaking of the universal deluge, says,

> Yet when that flood in its own depths was drown'd,
> It left behind it false and slippery ground.[5]

The first of these lines appears to me marvellously nonsensical. It informs us of a prodigy never heard of or conceived before, a drowned flood, nay, which is still more extravagant, a flood that was so excessively deep, that after leaving nothing else to drown, it turned *felo-de-se* and drowned itself. And, doubtless, if a flood can be in danger of drowning in itself, the deeper it is, the danger must be the greater. So far at least the author talks consequentially. His meaning, expressed in plain language (for the line itself hath no meaning), was probably no more than this: "When the waters of the deluge had subsided."

I proceed to give examples of a still higher order, in sentences more complicated. These I shall produce from an author who, though far from being deficient in acuteness, invention, or vivacity, is perhaps, in this species of composition, the most eminent of all that have written in the English language: If the savour of things lies cross to honesty, if the fancy be florid, and the appetite high towards the subaltern beauties and lower order of worldly symmetries and proportions, the conduct will infallibly turn this latter way."[6] This is that figure of speech which the French critics call *galimatias*, and the English comprehend under the general name *bombast*, and which may not improperly be defined *the sublime of nonsense*. You have lofty images and high sounding words, but are always at a loss to find the sense. The meaning, where there is a meaning, cannot be said to be communicated and adorned by the words, but is rather buried under them. Of the same kind are the two following quotations from the same author: "Men must acquire a very peculiar and strong habit of turning their eye inwards, in order to explore the interior regions and recesses of the mind, the hollow caverns of deep thought, the private seats of fancy, and the wastes and wildernesses, as well as the more fruitful and cultivated tracts of this obscure cli-

[4] Pope's Thoughts on various Subjects.
[5] Panegyric on the Coronation of King Charles II.
[6] Characteristics, Vol. III. Misc. ii. Chap. 2

mate."[7] A most wonderful way of telling us, that it is difficult to trace the operations of the mind. This may serve to give some notion of the figure which the French Phœbus (no offence to the Grecian, who is of a very different family) is capable of making in an English dress. His lordship proceeds in his own inimitable manner, or rather in what follows hath outdone himself: "But what can one do? or how dispense with these darker disquisitions, and moon-light voyages, when we have to deal with a sort of moon-blind wits, who, though very acute and able in their kind, may be said to renounce day-light, and extinguish in a manner the bright visible outward world, by allowing us to know nothing beside what we can prove by strict and formal demonstration."[8] It must be owned, the condition of those wits is truly deplorable, for though very acute and able in their kind, yet being moon-blind, they cannot see by night, and having renounced day-light, they will not see by day: so that, for any use they have of their eyes, they are no better than stone-blind. It is astonishing, too, that the reason for rendering a moon-light voyage indispensable is, that we have moon-blind persons only for our company, the very reason which to an ordinary understanding would seem to render such a voyage improper. When one narrowly examines a piece of writing of this stamp, one finds one's self precisely in the situation of the fox in the fable, turning over and considering the tragedian's mask,[9] and can hardly refrain from exclaiming in the same words:

> How vast a head is here without a brain![1]

Part III.—*From Want of Meaning.*

I come now to the last class of the unintelligible, which proceeds from a real want of meaning in the writer. Instances of this sort are, even in the works of good authors, much more numerous than is commonly imagined. But how shall this defect be discovered? There are, indeed, cases in which it is hardly discoverable; there are cases, on the contrary, in which it may be easily discovered. There is one remarkable difference between this class of the unintelligible and that which was first taken notice of, proceeding from confusion of thought, accompanied with intricacy of expression. When this is the cause of the difficulty, the reader will not fail, if he be atten-

[7] Characteristics, Vol. III. Misc. iv. Chap. 2. [8] Ibid.

[9] *Persona tragica* is commonly rendered so; but it was very different from what is called a mask with us. It was a case which covered the whole head, and had a face painted on it suitable to the character to be represented by it.

[1] O quanta species, inquit, ast cerebrum non habet. Phædrus.

tive, to hesitate at certain intervals, and to retrace his progress, finding himself bewildered in the terms, and at a loss for the meaning. Then he will try to construe the sentence, and to ascertain the significations of the words. By these means, and by the help of the context, he will possibly come at last at what the author would have said. Whereas, in that species of the unintelligible which proceeds from a vacuity of thought, the reverse commonly happens. The sentence is generally simple in its structure, and the construction easy. When this is the case, provided words glaringly unsuitable are not combined, the reader proceeds without hesitation or doubt. He never suspects that he does not understand a sentence, the terms of which are familiar to him, and of which he perceives distinctly the grammatical order. But if he be by any means induced to think more closely on the subject, and to peruse the words a second time more attentively, it is probable that he will then begin to suspect them, and will at length discover that they contain nothing but either an identical proposition which conveys no knowledge, or a proposition of that kind of which one cannot so much as affirm that it is either true or false. And this is justly allowed to be the best criterion of nonsense.[2] It is, indeed, more difficult to distinguish sentences of this kind from those of the second class of the unintelligible already discussed, in which the darkness is chiefly imputable to an affectation of excellence. But in these matters it is not of importance to fix the boundaries with precision. Sometimes pompous metaphors and sonorous phrases are injudiciously employed to add a dignity to the most trivial conceptions: sometimes they are made to serve as a vehicle for nonsense. And whether some of the above citations fall under the one denomination, or the other, would scarcely be worth the while to inquire. It hath been observed that in madmen there is as great variety of character as in those who enjoy the use of their reason. In like manner it may be said of nonsense, that, in writing it, there is as great scope for variety of style, as there is in writing sense. I shall therefore not attempt to give specimens of all the characters of style which this kind of composition admits. The task would be endless. Let it suffice to specify some of the principal.

1. *The Puerile.*

The first I shall mention is the *puerile*, which is always produced when an author runs on in a specious verbosity, amusing

[2] Of all that is written in this style we may justly say in the words of Lord Verulam (De Aug. Scient. L. vi. C. 2,) applying to a particular purpose the words of Horace,

———Tantum series juncturaque pollet,
Tantum de medio sumptis accedit honoris;

his reader with synonymous terms and identical propositions, well-turned periods, and high-sounding words: but, at the same time, using those words so indefinitely, that the latter can either affix no meaning to them at all, or may almost affix any meaning to them he pleases. "If 'tis asked," says a late writer, "Whence arises this harmony or beauty of language? what are the rules for obtaining it? the answer is obvious, Whatever renders a period sweet and pleasant makes it also graceful; a good ear is the gift of Nature; it may be much improved, but not acquired by art; whoever is possessed of it, will scarcely need dry critical precepts to enable him to judge of a true rhythmus and melody of composition; just numbers, accurate proportions, a musical symphony, magnificent figures, and that *decorum*, which is the result of all these, are unison to the human mind; we are so framed by Nature that their charm is irresistible. Hence, all ages and nations have been smit with the love of the muses."[3] Who can now be at a loss to know whence the harmony and beauty of language arises, or what the rules for obtaining it are? Through the whole paragraph, the author proceeds in the same careless and desultory manner, not much unlike that of the Critical Essay upon the Faculties of the Mind; affording at times some glimmerings of sense, and perpetually ringing the changes upon a few favourite words and phrases. A poetical example of the same signature, in which there is not even a glimpse of meaning, we have in the following lines of Dryden:

From harmony, from heavenly harmony
    This universal frame began;
    From harmony to harmony
Thro' all the compass of the notes it ran,
The diapason closing full in man.[4]

In general, it may be said, that in writings of this stamp, we must accept of sound instead of sense, being assured at least, that if we meet with little that can inform the judgment, we shall find nothing that will offend the ear.

2. *The Learned.*

Another sort I shall here specify, is the learned nonsense. I know not a more fruitful source of this species than scholastical theology. The more incomprehensible the subject is, the

ut speciem artis, nescio cujus præclaræ, sæpenumero reportent ea, quæ si solvantur, segregentur, et denudentur, ad nihilum fere recasura forent.—— As to the causes of the deception there is in this manner of writing, I shall attempt the investigation of them in the following chapter.

[3] Geddes on the Composition of the Ancients, Sect. 1.

[4] Song for St. Cecilia's Day, 1687.

greater scope has the declaimer to talk plausibly without any meaning. A specimen of this I shall give from an author, who should have escaped this animadversion, had he not introduced from the pulpit a jargon which (if we can say without impropriety that it was fit for any thing) was surely fitter for the cloister: for what cannot in the least contribute to the instruction of a Christian society may afford excellent matter of contemplative amazement to dronish monks. "Although we read of several properties attributed to God in Scripture, as wisdom, goodness, justice, &c., we must not apprehend them to be several powers, habits, or qualities, as they are in us; for as they are in God, they are neither distinguished from one another, nor from his nature or essence in whom they are said to be. In whom, I say, they are said to be: for, to speak properly, they are not in him, but are his very essence or nature itself; which, acting severally upon several objects, seems to us to act from several properties or perfections in him; whereas, all the difference is only in our different apprehensions of the same thing. God in himself is a most simple and pure act, and therefore cannot have any thing in him but what is that most simple and pure act itself; which, seeing it bringeth upon every creature what it deserves, we conceive of it as of several divine perfections in the same almighty Being. Whereas God, whose understanding is infinite as himself, doth not apprehend himself under the distinct notions of wisdom, or goodness, or justice, or the like, but only as Jehovah."[5] How edifying must it have been to the hearers to be made acquainted with these deep discoveries of the men of science; divine attributes which are no attributes, which are totally distinct and perfectly the same; which are justly ascribed to God, being ascribed to him in Scripture, but do not belong to him; which are something and nothing, which are the figments of human imagination, mere chimeras, which are God himself, which are the actors of all things; and which, to sum up all, are themselves a simple act! "Who is this that darkeneth counsel by words without knowledge?"[6] Can the tendency of such teaching be any other than to perplex and to confound, and even to throw the hearers into universal doubt and scepticism? To such a style of explication these lines of our British bard, addressed to the patroness of sophistry as well as dulness, are admirably adapted:

> Explain upon a thing, till all men doubt it;
> And write about it, goddess, and about it.[7]

Of the same kind of school-metaphysics are these lines of Cowley:

> Nothing is there *to come*, and nothing *past*,
> But an eternal *now* does always last.[8]

[5] Beveridge's Sermons. [6] Job xxxviii. 2. [7] Dunciad. [8] Davideis, Book i.

What insatiable appetite has this bastard philosophy for absurdity and contradiction! A *now* that lasts; that is, an instant which continues during successive instants! an eternal now, an instant that is no instant, and an eternity that is no eternity. I have heard of a preacher, who, desirous to appear very profound, and to make observations on the commonest subjects which had never occurred to any body before, remarked, as an instance of the goodness of providence, that the moments of time come successively, and not simultaneously or together, which last method of coming would, he said, occasion infinite confusion in the world. Many of his audience concluded his remark to be no better than a bull: and yet, it is fairly defensible on the principles of the schoolmen; if that can be called principles which consists merely in words. According to them, what Pope says hyperbolically of the transient duration and narrow range of man, is a literal description of the eternity and immensity of God:

> His time a moment, and a point his space.[9]

I remember to have seen it somewhere remarked, that mankind being necessarily incapable of making a present of any thing to God, have conceived, as a succedaneous expedient, the notion of destroying what should be offered to him, or at least of rendering it unfit for any other purpose. Something similar appears to have taken place in regard to the explanations of the divine nature and attributes, attempted by some theorists. On a subject so transcendent, if it be impossible to be sublime, it is easy to be unintelligible. And that the theme is naturally incomprehensible, they seem to have considered as a full apology for them in being perfectly absurd. In the former case, what people could not in strictness bestow upon their Maker, they could easily render unfit for the use of men: and in the latter, if one cannot grasp what is above the reach of reason, one can without difficulty say a thousand things which are contrary to reason.

But though scholastic theology be the principal, it is not the only subject of learned nonsense. In other branches of pneumatology we often meet with rhapsodies of the same kind. I shall take an example from a late right honourable writer, who, though he gives no quarter to the rants of others, sometimes falls into the ranting strain himself: "Pleasures are the objects of self-love; happiness that of reason. Reason is so far from depriving us of the first, that happiness consists in a series of them: and as this can be neither attained nor enjoyed securely out of society, a due use of our reason makes social and self-

[9] Essay on Man, Ep. i.

love coincide, or even become in effect the same. The condition wherein we are born and bred, the very condition so much complained of, prepares us for this coincidence, the foundation of all human happiness: and our whole nature, appetite, passion, and reason, concur to promote it. As our parents loved themselves in us, so we love ourselves in our children, and in those to whom we are most nearly related by blood. Thus far instinct improves self-love. Reason improves it further. We love ourselves in our neighbours, and in our friends too, with Tully's leave; for if friendship is formed by a kind of sympathy, it is cultivated by good offices. Reason proceeds. We love ourselves in loving the political body whose members we are; and we love ourselves, when we extend our benevolence to all mankind. These are the genuine effects of reason."[1] I would not be understood to signify that there is no meaning in any clause of this quotation, but that the greater part of it is unmeaning; and that the whole, instead of exhibiting a connected train of thought, agreeably to the author's intention, presents us only with a few trifling or insignificant phrases speciously strung together. The very first sentence is justly exceptionable in this respect. Had he said, "Pleasure is the object of appetite, happiness that of self-love," there had been some sense in it; as it stands, I suspect there is none. Pope, the great admirer and versifier of this philosophy, hath succeeded much better in contra-distinguishing the provinces of reason and passion, where he says,

Reason the card, but passion is the gale:[2]

this always the mover, that the guide. As the card serves equally to point to us the course that we must steer, whatever be the situation of the port we are bound for, east or west, south or north; so reason serves equally to indicate the means that we must employ for the attainment of any end, whatever that end be (right or wrong, profitable or pernicious) which passion impels us to pursue.[3] All that follows of the passage quoted, abounds with the like loose and indefinite declamation. If the author had any meaning, a point very questionable, he hath been very unhappy and very unphilosophical in expressing it. What are we to make of the coincidence or sameness of self-love and social affection produced by reason? What of parents loving themselves in their children? &c. &c.—Any thing you please, or nothing. It is a saying of Hobbes, which this author hath quoted with deserved commendation, that

[1] Bolingb. Ph. Fr. 15.

[2] Essay on Man, Ep. ii.

[3] For the further elucidation of this point, see the analysis of persuasion given in Book I. Chap. vii. Sect. 4.

"words are the counters of wise men, but the money of fools." The thought is ingenious and happily expressed. I shall only remark upon it, that this noble writer may be produced as one of many witnesses, to prove that it is not peculiar to fools to fall into this error. He is a wise man indeed who never mistakes these counters for legal coin. So much for the learned nonsense. And doubtless, if nonsense ever deserves to be exposed, it is when she has the arrogance to assume the garb of wisdom.

3. *The Profound.*

I proceed to another species, which I shall denominate *the profound*, and which is most commonly to be met with in political writings. No where else do we find the merest nothings set off with an air of solemnity, as the result of very deep thought and sage reflection. Of this kind, however, I shall produce a specimen, which, in confirmation of a remark made in the preceding paragraph, shall be taken from a justly celebrated tract of a justly celebrated pen: "It is agreed," says Swift, "that in all governments there is an absolute and unlimited power, which naturally and originally seems to be placed in the whole body, wherever the executive part of it lies. This holds in the body natural; for wherever we place the beginning of motion, whether from the head, or the heart, or the animal spirits in general, the body moves and acts by a consent of all its parts."[4] The first sentence of this passage contains one of the most hackneyed maxims of the writers on politics; a maxim, however, of which it will be more difficult than is commonly imagined, to discover, I say not the justness, but the sense. The illustration from the natural body, contained in the second sentence, is indeed more glaringly nonsensical. What it is that constitutes this consent of all the parts of the body which must be obtained previously to every motion, is, I will take upon me to affirm, utterly inconceivable. Yet the whole of the paragraph from which this quotation is taken, hath such a speciousness in it, that it is a hundred to one even a judicious reader will not, on the first perusal, be sensible of the defect.

4. *The Marvellous.*

The last species of nonsense to be exemplified I shall denominate *the marvellous*. It is the characteristic of this kind, that it astonishes and even confounds by the boldness of the

[4] Disc. of the Contests and Dissensions in Athens and Rome, first sentence.

affirmations, which always appear flatly to contradict the plainest dictates of common sense, and thus to involve a manifest absurdity. I know no sort of authors that so frequently abounds in this manner, as some artists, who have attempted to philosophize on the principles of their art. I shall give an example from the English translation of a French book,[5] as there is no example which I can remember at present in any book written originally in our own language: "Nature," says this writer, "in herself is unseemly, and he who copies her servilely, and without artifice, will always produce something poor, and of a mean taste. What is called load in colours and light, can only proceed from a profound knowledge in the values of colours, and from an admirable industry, which makes the painted objects appear more true, if I may say so, than the real ones. In this sense it may be asserted, that in Rubens' pieces, Art is above Nature, and Nature only a copy of that great master's works." What a strange subversion, or inversion, if you will, of all the most obvious, and hitherto undisputed truths. Not satisfied with affirming the unseemliness of every production of Nature, whom this philosopher hath discovered to be an arrant bungler, and the immense superiority of human Art, whose humble scholar dame Nature might be proud to be accounted, he riseth to asseverations which shock all our notions, and utterly defy the powers of apprehension. Painting is found to be the original; or rather Rubens' pictures are the original, and Nature is the copy: and indeed very consequentially, the former is represented as the standard by which the beauty and perfections of the latter are to be estimated. Nor do the qualifying phrases, *if I may say so*, and *in this sense it may be asserted*, make here the smallest odds. For as this sublime critic has no where hinted what sense it is which he denominates *this sense*, so I believe no reader will be able to conjecture what the author *might have said*, and not absurdly said, to the same effect. The misfortune is, that when the expression is stript of the *absurd meaning*,[6] there remains nothing but balderdash,[7] an unmeaning jumble of words which, at first, seem to announce some great discovery.[8] Specimens

[5] De Piles's Principles of Painting.

[6] For the propriety and import of this expression, see Ch. VII. Sec. II.

[7] The latter part of the sentence was thus expressed in the first edition. "a jumble of bold words without meaning." To this phraseology exception was taken, which, though not entirely just, appears to have arisen from some obscurity, perhaps an ambiguity in the expression. This, I hope, is removed by the alteration now made.

[8] Since writing the above observations, I have seen De Piles's original performance, and find that his translator hath, in this place at least, done him no injustice. The whole passage in the French is as follows: "La Nature est ingrate d'elle-même, et qui s'attacheroit à la copier simplement comme elle est, et sans artifice, feroit toujours quelque chose de pauvre et d'un très petit goût. Ce que vous nommez exagérations dans les couleurs, et dans les

of the same kind are sometimes also to be met with in the poets. Witness the famous protestation of an heroic lover in one of Dryden's plays:—

My wound is great, because it is so small.

The nonsense of which was properly exposed by an extemporary verse of the Duke of Buckingham, who, on hearing this line, exclaimed in the house,—

It would be greater, were it none at all.

Hyperbole, carried to extravagance, is much of a piece, and never fails to excite disgust, if not laughter, instead of admiration. Of this the famous laureate just now quoted, though indeed a very considerable genius, affords, among many other striking instances, that which follows;

That star, that at your birth shone out so bright,
It stain'd the duller sun's meridian light.[9]

Such vile fustian ought to be carefully avoided by every writer.

Thus I have illustrated, as far as example can illustrate, some of the principal varieties to be remarked in unmeaning sentences or nonsense; the puerile, the learned, the profound, and the marvellous; together with those other classes of the unintelligible, arising either from confusion of thought, accompanied with intricacy of expression, or from an excessive aim at excellence in the style and manner.

So much for the explication of the first rhetorical quality of style, perspicuity, with the three ways of expressing one's self by which it may be injured; the obscure, the double meaning, and the unintelligible.

lumières, est une admirable industrie qui fait paroître les objets peints plus véritables, s'il faut ainsi dire, que les véritables mêmes. C'est ainsi que les tableaux de Rubens sont plus beaux que la Nature, laquelle semble n'être que la copie des ouvrages de ce grand homme." Recueil de divers ouvrages sur la Peinture et le Coloris. Par M. de Piles. Paris, 1755, p. 225. This is rather worse than the English. The qualifying phrase in the last sentence, we find, is the translator's, who seems out of sheer modesty to have brought it to cover nudities. His intention was good; but this is such a rag as cannot answer.

[9] Dryden on the Restoration.

CHAPTER VII.

What is the Cause that Nonsense so often escapes being detected, both by the Writer and by the Reader?

SECTION I.

The Nature and Power of Signs, both in Speaking and in thinking.

Before quitting the subject of perspicuity, it will not be amiss to inquire into the cause of this strange phenomenon; that even a man of discernment should write without meaning, and not be sensible that he hath no meaning; and that judicious people should read what hath been written in this way, and not discover the defect. Both are surprising, but the first much more than the last. A certain remissness will at times seize the most attentive reader; whereas an author of discernment is supposed to have carefully digested all that he writes. It is reported of Lopez de Vega, a famous Spanish poet, that the Bishop of Beller, being in Spain, asked him to explain one of his sonnets, which he said he had often read, but never understood. Lopez took up the sonnet, and after reading it several times, frankly acknowledged that he did not understand it himself; a discovery which the poet probably never made before.

But though the general fact hath been frequently observed, I do not find that any attempt hath been yet made to account for it. Berkeley, indeed, in his Principles of Human Knowledge, hath suggested a theory concerning language, though not with this view, which, if well-founded, will go far to remove the principal difficulty: "It is a received opinion," says that author, "that language has no other end but the communicating our ideas, and that every significant name stands for an idea. This being so, and it being withal certain that names, which yet are not thought altogether insignificant, do not always mark out particular conceivable ideas, it is straightway concluded that they stand for abstract notions. That there are many names in use amongst speculative men, which do not always suggest to others determinate particular ideas, is what nobody will deny. And a little attention will discover, that it is not necessary (even in the strictest reasonings) significant names which stand for ideas should, every time they are used, excite in the understanding the ideas they are made to stand for in reading and discoursing, names being for the most part used as letters are in algebra, in which, though a particular quantity be marked by each letter, yet to proceed right it is not requisite that in every step each letter suggest to your thoughts that particular quantity it was appointed to stand for."[1] The same principles have been adopted by the author of a Treatise of Human Nature, who, speaking of abstract ideas, has the following words: "I believe every one who examines the situation of his mind in reasoning, will agree with me, that we do not annex distinct and complete ideas to every term we make use of, and that in talking of *government, church, negotiation, conquest,* we seldom spread out in our minds all the simple ideas of which these complex ones are composed. 'Tis, however, observable that notwithstanding this imperfection, we may avoid talking nonsense on these subjects, and may perceive any repugnance among the ideas, as well as if we had a full comprehension of them. Thus if, instead of saying that *in war the weaker have always recourse to negotiation,* we should say, that *they have always recourse to conquest;* the custom which we have acquired of attributing certain relations to ideas, still follows the words, and makes us immediately perceive the absurdity of that proposition."[2] Some excellent observations to the same purpose have also been made by the elegant Inquirer into the origin of our ideas of the sublime and beautiful.[3]

Now, that the notions on this subject maintained by these ingenious writers, however strange they may appear on a superficial view, are well founded, is at least presumable from this consideration: that if, agreeably to the common hypothesis, we could understand nothing that is said but by actually comparing in our minds all the ideas signified, it would be impossible that nonsense should ever escape undiscovered, at least that we should so far impose upon ourselves, as to think we understand what in reality is not to be understood. We should in that case find ourselves in the same situation, when an unmeaning sentence is introduced into a discourse, wherein we find ourselves when a sentence is quoted in a language of which we are entirely ignorant: we are never in the smallest danger of imagining that we apprehend the meaning of the quotation.

But though a very curious fact hath been taken notice of by those expert metaphysicians, and such a fact as will, perhaps, account for the deception we are now considering; yet the fact itself, in my apprehension, hath not been sufficiently accounted for. That mere sounds, which are used only as signs, and have no natural connexion with the things whereof they are signs, should convey knowledge to the mind, even when they excite no idea of the things signified, must appear at first

[1] Introd. Sect. 19. [2] Vol. I. Book i. Part ii. Sect. 7. [3] Part V.

extremely mysterious. It is, therefore, worth while to consider the matter more closely; and in order to this, it will be proper to attend a little to the three following connexions: first, that which subsisteth among things; secondly, that which subsisteth between words and things; thirdly, that which subsisteth among words, or the different terms used in the same language.

As to the first of these connexions, namely, that which subsisteth among things, it is evident that this is original and natural. There is a variety of relations to be found in things, by which they are connected. Such are, among several others, resemblance, identity,[4] equality, contrariety, cause and effect, concomitancy, vicinity in time or place. These we become acquainted with by experience; and they prove, by means of association, the source of various combinations of ideas, and abstractions, as they are commonly denominated. Hence mixed modes, and distinctions into genera and species; of the origin of which I have had occasion to speak already.[5]

As to the second connexion, or that which subsisteth between words and things, it is obvious, as it hath been hinted formerly, that this is not a natural and necessary, but an artificial and arbitrary connexion. Nevertheless, though this connexion hath not its foundation in the nature of things, but in the conventions of men, its effect upon the mind is much the same. For having often had occasion to observe particular words used as signs of particular things, we hence contract a habit of associating the sign with the thing signified, insomuch that either, being presented to the mind, frequently introduces or occasions the apprehension of the other. Custom, in this instance, operates precisely in the same manner as in the formation of experience formerly explained. Thus, certain sounds, and the ideas of things not naturally related to them, come to be as strongly linked in our conceptions, as the ideas of things naturally related to one another.

As to the third connexion, or that which subsisteth among words, I would not be understood to mean any connexion among the words considered as sounds, such as that which results from resemblance in pronunciation, equality in the number of syllables, sameness of measure or cadence; I mean solely that connexion or relation which comes gradually to subsist among the different words of a language, in the minds of those who speak it, and which is merely consequent on this,

[4] It may be thought improper to mention *identity* as a relation by which *different* things are connected; but it must be observed, that I only mean so far *different*, as to constitute distinct objects to the mind. Thus the consideration of the same person, when a child and when a man, is the consideration of different objects, between which there subsists the relation of identity.

[5] Book I. Chap. v. Sect. ii. Part 2. On the formation of experience.

that those words are employed as signs of connected or related things. It is an axiom in geometry, that things equal to the same thing are equal to one another. It may, in like manner, be admitted as an axiom in psychology, that ideas associated by the same idea will associate with one another. Hence it will happen, that if from experiencing the connexion of two things there results, as infallibly there will result, an association between the ideas or notions annexed to them, as each idea will moreover be associated by its signs, there will likewise be an association between the ideas of the signs. Hence the sounds, considered as signs, will be conceived to have a connexion analogous to that which subsisteth among the things signified; I say the sounds considered as signs: for this way of considering them constantly attends us in speaking, writing, hearing, and reading. When we purposely abstract from it, and regard them merely as sounds, we are instantly sensible that they are quite unconnected, and have no other relation than what ariseth from similitude of tone or accent. But to consider them in this manner commonly results from previous design, and requires a kind of effort which is not exerted in the ordinary use of speech. In ordinary use they are regarded solely as signs, or rather they are confounded with the things they signify; the consequence of which is, that, in the manner just now explained, we come insensibly to conceive a connexion among them, of a very different sort from that of which sounds are naturally susceptible.

Now this conception, habit, or tendency of the mind, call it which you please, is considerably strengthened both by the frequent use of language, and by the structure of it. It is strengthened by the frequent use of language. Language is the sole channel through which we communicate our knowledge and discoveries to others, and through which the knowledge and discoveries of others are communicated to us. By reiterated recourse to this medium, it necessarily happens, that when things are related to each other, the words signifying those things are more commonly brought together in discourse. Hence the words and names themselves, by customary vicinity, contract in the fancy a relation additional to that which they derive purely from being symbols of related things. Further, this tendency is strengthened by the structure of language. All languages whatever, even the most barbarous, as far as hath yet appeared, are of a regular and analogical make. The consequence is, that similar relations in things will be expressed similarly; that is, by similar inflections, derivations, compositions, arrangement of words, or juxtaposition of particles, according to the genius or grammatical form of the particular tongue. Now, as by the habitual use of a language (even though it were quite irregular) the signs would insensibly become connected in the imagination, wherever the things signified are connected in nature; so, by the regular structure of a language, this connexion among the signs is conceived as analogous to that which subsisteth among their archetypes. From these principles we may be enabled both to understand the meaning and to perceive the justness of what is affirmed in the end of the preceding quotation: "The custom which we have acquired of attributing certain relations to ideas, still follows the words, and makes us *immediately* perceive the absurdity of that proposition." *Immediately*, that is, even before we have leisure to give that attention to the signs which is necessary in order to form a just conception of the things signified. In confirmation of this doctrine it may be observed, that we really think by signs as well as speak by them.

I have hitherto, in conformity to what is now become a general and inveterate custom, and in order to avoid tiresome circumlocutions, used the terms *sign* and *idea* as exactly correlative. This, I am sensible, is not done with strict propriety. All words are signs, but that the signification cannot always be represented by an idea will, I apprehend, be abundantly evident from the observations following. All the truths which constitute science, which give exercise to reason, and are discovered by philosophy, are general; all our ideas, in the strictest sense of the word, are particular. All the particular truths about which we are conversant, are properly historical, and compose the furniture of memory. Nor do I include under the term *historical*, the truths which belong to natural history; for even these too are general. Now, beyond particular truths or individual facts, first perceived and then remembered, we should never be able to proceed one single step in thinking, any more than in conversing, without the use of signs.

When it is affirmed that *the whole is equal to all its parts*, there cannot be an affirmation which is more perfectly intelligible, or which commands a fuller assent. If, in order to comprehend this, I recur to ideas, all that I can do, is to form a notion of some individual whole divided into a certain number of parts, of which it is constituted, suppose of the year divided into the four seasons. Now, all that I can be said to discern here, is the relation of equality between this particular whole and its component parts. If I recur to another example, I only perceive another particular truth. The same holds of a third and of a fourth. But so far am I, after the perception of ten thousand particular similar instances, from the discovery of the universal truth, that if the mind had not the power of considering things as signs, or particular ideas as representing an infinity of others, resembling in one circumstance, though totally dissimilar in every other, I could not so much as conceive the meaning of a universal truth. Hence it is that *some ideas*, to adopt the expression of the author above quoted, *are particular in their nature, but general in their representation.*

There is, however, it must be acknowledged, a difficulty in explaining this power the mind hath, of considering ideas, not in their private, but, as it were, in their representative capacity; which, on that author's system who divides all the objects of thought into impressions and ideas, will be found altogether insurmountable. It was to avoid this difficulty that philosophers at first recurred, as is sometimes the case, to a still greater, or rather to a downright absurdity, the doctrine of abstract ideas. I mean only that doctrine as it hath been frequently explained; for if any one is pleased to call that faculty by which a particular idea is regarded as representing a whole order, by the name *abstraction*, I have no objection to the term: nay more, I think it sufficiently expressive of the sense:—whilst certain qualities of the individual remain unnoticed, and are therefore abstracted from, those qualities only which it hath in common with the order engross the mind's attention. But this is not what those writers seem to mean, who philosophize upon abstract ideas, as is evident from their own explications.

The patrons of this theory maintain, or at least express themselves as if they maintained, that the mind is endowed with a power of forming ideas, or images, within itself, that are possessed not only of incongruous, but of inconsistent qualities, of a triangle, for example, that is of all possible dimensions and proportions, both in sides and angles, at once right-angled, acute-angled, and obtuse-angled, equilateral, equicrural, and scalenum. One would have thought that the bare mention of this hypothesis would have been equivalent to a confutation of it, since it really confutes itself.

Yet in this manner one no less respectable in the philosophic world than Mr. Locke has, on some occasions, expressed himself.[6] I consider the difference, however, on this article, between him and the two authors above mentioned, as more apparent than real, or (which amounts to the same thing) more in words than in sentiments. It is indeed scarcely possible that men of discernment should think differently on a subject so perfectly subjected to every one's own consciousness and experience. What has betrayed the former into such unguarded and improper expressions, is plainly an undue, and till then, unprecedented use of the word *idea*, which he has employed (for the sake, I suppose of simplifying his system) to signify not only, as formerly, the traces of things retained in the memory, and the images formed by the fancy, but even the perceptions of the senses on the one hand, and the conceptions of the intellect on the other, "it being that term which," in his

[6] Essay on Human Understanding, B. II. C. xi. Sect. 10, 11; B. IV. C. vii. Sect. 9.

opinion, "serves best to stand for whatsoever is the object of the understanding, when a man thinks."[7] Accordingly, he no where, that I remember, defines it with some logicians, "a pattern or copy of a thing in the mind." Nevertheless he has not always, in speaking on the subject, attended to the different acceptation he had in the beginning affixed to the word; but, misled by the common definition, (which regards a more limited object,) and applying it to the term in that more extensive import which he had himself given it, has fallen into those inconsistencies in language which have been before observed. Thus this great man has, in his own example, as it were, demonstrated how difficult it is even for the wisest to guard uniformly against the inconveniences arising from the ambiguity of words.

But that what I have now advanced is not spoken rashly, and that there was no material difference between his opinions and theirs on this article, is, I think, manifest from the following passage: "To return to general words, it is plain, by what has been said, that general and universal belong not to the real existence of things, but are the inventions and creatures of the understanding, made by it for its own use, and concern only signs, whether words or ideas. Words are general, as has been said, when used for signs of general ideas, and so are applicable indifferently to many particular things; and ideas are general, when they are set up as the representatives of many particular things: but universality belongs not to things themselves, which are all of them particular in their existence; *even those words and ideas which in their signification are general.* When, therefore, we quit particulars, the generals that rest are only creatures of our own making; *their general nature being nothing but the capacity they are put into by the understanding of signifying or representing many particulars. For the signification they have, is nothing but a relation that by the mind of man is added to them.*"[8] Nothing, in my apprehension, can be more exactly coincident with Berkeley's doctrine of abstraction. Here not only words but ideas are made signs; and a particular idea is made general, not by any change produced in it, (for then it would be no longer the same idea,) but "by being set up as the representative of many particular things." "Universality," he observes, as it belongs not to things, belongs not even to "those words and ideas, which are all of them particular in their existence, but general in their signification." Again, the general nature of those ideas, is "nothing but the capacity they are put into by the understanding of signifying or representing many particulars;" and if possible, still more

[7] Essay on Human Understanding, B. I. C. i. Sect. 8.
[8] B. III. C. iii. Sect. 11.

explicitly, "the signification they have is nothing but a relation;" no alteration on their essence, "that by the mind of man is added to them."

Some of the greatest admirers of that eminent philosopher seem to have overlooked entirely the preceding account of his sentiments on this subject, and through I know not what passion for the paradoxical (I should rather say, the impossible and unintelligible), have shown an amazing zeal for defending the propriety of the hasty expressions which appear in the passages formerly referred to. Has not the mind of man, say they, an unlimited power in moulding and combining its ideas? The mind, it must be owned, hath an unlimited power in moulding and combining its ideas. It often produceth wonderful forms of its own, out of the materials originally supplied by sense; forms indeed of which there is no exemplar to be found in nature, centaurs, and griffins,

Gorgons, and hydras, and chimeras dire.

But still it must not attempt absolute impossibilities, by giving to its creature contradictory qualities. It must not attempt to conceive the same thing to be black and white at the same time, to be no more than three inches long, and yet no less than three thousand; to conceive two or more lines to be both equal and unequal, the same angle to be at once acute, obtuse, and right. These philosophers sagely remark, as a consequence of their doctrine, that the mind must be extremely slow in attaining so wonderful a talent; whereas, on the contrary, nothing can be more evident than that the power of abstracting, as I have explained it, is to a certain degree, and must be, as early as the use of speech, and is consequently discoverable even in infants.

But if such an extraordinary faculty as they speak of were possible, I cannot, for my part, conceive what purpose it could serve. An idea hath been defined by some logicians, the form or resemblance of a thing in the mind, and the whole of its power and use in thinking is supposed to arise from an exact conformity to its archetype. What then is the use or power of that idea, to which there neither is nor can be any archetype in nature, which is merely a creature of the brain, a monster that bears not the likeness of any thing in the universe.

In the extensive sense in which Locke, who is considered as the most strenuous supporter of that doctrine, uses the word idea, even the perceptions of the senses, as I had occasion lately to remark, are included under that term. And if so, it is incontrovertible, that a particular idea often serves as the sign of a whole class. Thus in every one of Euclid's theorems, a particular triangle, and a particular parallelogram, and a particular circle, are employed as signs to denote all triangles, all parallelograms, and all circles. When a geometrician makes a diagram with chalk upon a board, and from it demonstrates some property of a straight-lined figure, no spectator ever imagines that he is demonstrating a property of nothing else but that individual white figure of five inches long which is before him. Every one is satisfied that he is demonstrating a property of all that order, whether more or less extensive, of which it is both an example and a sign; all the order being understood to agree with it in certain characters, however different in other respects. Nay, what is more, the mind with the utmost facility extends or contracts the representative power of the sign, as the particular occasion requires. Thus the same equilateral triangle will with equal propriety serve for the demonstration not only of a property of all equilateral triangles, but of a property of all isosceles triangles, or even of a property of all triangles whatever. Nay, so perfectly is this matter understood, that if the demonstrator in any part should recur to some property, as to the length of a side, belonging to the particular figure he hath constructed, but not essential to the kind mentioned in the proposition, and which the particular figure is solely intended to represent, every intelligent observer would instantly detect the fallacy. So entirely for all the purposes of science doth a particular serve for a whole species or genus. Now, why one visible individual, or, in the style of the above-mentioned author, why a particular idea of sight, should, in our reasonings, serve, without the smallest inconvenience, as a sign for an infinite number, and yet one conceivable individual, or a particular idea of imagination, should not be adapted to answer the same end, it will, I imagine, be utterly impossible to say.

There is, however, a considerable difference in kind between such signs as these, and the words of a language. Amongst all the individuals of a species, or even of the most extensive genus, there is still a natural connexion, as they agree in the specific or generic character. But the connexion that subsisteth between words and things is, in its origin, arbitrary. Yet the difference in the effect is not so considerable as one would be apt to imagine. In neither case is it the matter, if I may be allowed the expression, but the power of the sign that is regarded by the mind. We find that even in demonstrative reasonings, signs of the latter kind, or mere symbols, may be used with as much clearness and success as can be conferred by natural signs. The operations both of the algebraist and of the arithmetician are strictly of the nature of demonstration. The one employs as signs the letters of the alphabet, the other certain numerical characters. In neither of these arts is it necessary to form ideas of the quantities and sums signified; in some instances it is even impossible; yet the equations and calculations resulting thence are not the less accurate and convincing.—So much for the nature and power of artificial signs.

Perhaps I have said too much on the subject; for on a review of what I have written, I am even apprehensive lest some readers imagine, that after quoting examples of the unintelligible from others, I have thought fit to produce a very ample specimen of my own. Every subject, it is certain, is not equally susceptible of perspicuity: but there is a material difference between an obscurity which ariseth purely from the nature of the subject, and that which is chargeable upon the style. Whatever regards the analysis of the operations of the mind, which is quicker than lightning in all her energies, must in a great measure be abstruse and dark. Let then the dissatisfied reader deign to bestow on the foregoing observations a second perusal; and though after that he should be as much at a loss as before, the case may not be without remedy. Let him not therefore be discouraged from proceeding; there is still a possibility that the application of the principles, which I have been attempting to develope, will reflect some light on them; and if not, it is but few minutes thrown away; for I do not often enter on such profound researches.

SECTION II.—*The Application of the Preceding Principles.*

Now, to apply this doctrine to the use for which it was introduced, let us consider how we can account by it for these phenomena, that a man of sense should sometimes write nonsense and not know it, and that a man of sense should sometimes read nonsense, and imagine he understands it.

In the preceding quotation from the Treatise on Human Nature, the author observes that "notwithstanding that we do not annex distinct and complete ideas to every term we make use of, we may avoid talking nonsense, and may perceive any repugnance among the ideas, as well as if we had a full comprehension of them." This remark generally holds. Thus in matters that are perfectly familiar, and are level to an ordinary capacity, in simple narration, or in moral observations on the occurrences of life, a man of common understanding may be deceived by specious falsehood, but is hardly to be gulled by downright nonsense. Almost all the possible applications of the terms (in other words, all the acquired relations of the signs) have become customary to him. The consequence is, that an unusual application of any term is instantly detected; this detection breeds doubt, and this doubt occasions an immediate recourse to ideas. The recourse of the mind, when in any degree puzzled with the signs, to the knowledge it has of the thing signified, is natural, and on such plain subjects perfectly easy. And of this recourse the discovery of the meaning or of the unmeaningness of what is said is the immediate effect. But in matters that are by no means familiar, or are treated in an uncommon manner, and in such as are of an abstruse and intricate nature, the case is widely different. There are particularly three sorts of writing wherein we are liable to be imposed on by words without meaning.

The first is, where there is an exuberance of metaphor. Nothing is more certain than that this trope, when temperately and appositely used, serves to add light to the expression and energy to the sentiment. On the contrary, when vaguely and intemperately used, nothing can serve more effectually to cloud the sense, where there is sense, and by consequence to conceal the defect, where there is no sense to show. And this is the case not only where there is in the same sentence a mixture of discordant metaphors, but also where the metaphoric style is too long continued, and too far pursued.[9] The reason is obvious. In common speech the words are the immediate signs of the thought. But it is not so here; for when a person, instead of adopting metaphors that come naturally and opportunely in his way, rummages the whole world in quest of them, and piles them one upon another; when he cannot so properly be said to use metaphor as to talk in metaphor, or rather when from metaphor he runs into allegory, and thence into enigma, his words are not the immediate signs of his thought; they are at best but the signs of the signs of his thought. His writing may then be called what Spenser not unjustly styled his Faerie Queene, *a perpetual allegory or dark conceit.* Most readers will account it much to bestow a transient glance on the literal sense, which lies nearest; but will never think of that meaning more remote, which the figures themselves are intended to signify. It is no wonder then that this sense, for the discovery of which it is necessary to see through a double veil, should, where it is, more readily escape our observation, and that where it is wanting we should not so quickly miss it.

There is, in respect of the two meanings, considerable variety to be found in the tropical style. In just allegory and similitude there is always a propriety, or if you choose to call it, congruity, in the literal sense, as well as a distinct meaning or sentiment suggested, which is called the figurative sense. Examples of this are unnecessary. Again, where the figurative sense is unexceptionable, there is sometimes an incongruity in the expression of the literal sense. This is always the case in mixed metaphor, a thing not unfrequent even in good writers.

[9] Ut modicus autem atque opportunus translationis usus illustrat orationem, ita frequens et obscurat et tædio complet; continuus vero in allegoriam et ænigmata exit. QUINT. L. VIII. C. vi.

Thus, when Addison remarks that "there is not a single view of human nature, which is not sufficient to *extinguish* the *seeds* of pride," he expresses a true sentiment somewhat incongruously; for the terms *extinguish* and *seeds* here metaphorically used, do not suit each other. In like manner, there is something incongruous in the mixture of tropes employed in the following passage from Lord Bolingbroke: "Nothing less than the *hearts* of his people will content a patriot prince, nor will he think his *throne* established, till it is established *there*." Yet the thought is excellent. But in neither of these examples does the incongruity of the expression hurt the perspicuity of the sentence. Sometimes, indeed, the literal meaning involves a direct absurdity. When this is the case, as in the quotation from the *Principles of Painting* given in the preceding chapter, it is natural for the reader to suppose that there must be something under it; for it is not easy to say how absurdly even just sentiments will sometimes be expressed. But when no such hidden sense can be discovered, what, in the first view, conveyed to our minds a glaring *absurdity*, is rightly on reflection denominated *nonsense*. We are satisfied that De Piles neither thought nor wanted his readers to think, that Rubens was really the original performer, and God the copier. This then was not his meaning. But what he actually thought, and wanted them to think, it is impossible to elicit from his words. His words then may justly be termed *bold*, in respect of their literal import, but *unmeaning* in respect of the author's intention.

It may be proper here to observe, that some are apt to confound the terms *absurdity* and *nonsense* as synonymous, which they manifestly are not. An absurdity, in the strictest acceptation, is a proposition either intuitively or demonstratively false. Of this kind are these: "Three and two make seven." "All the angles of a triangle are greater than two right angles." That the former is false we know by intuition; that the latter is so, we are able to demonstrate. But the term is further extended to denote a notorious falsehood. If one should affirm, that "at the vernal equinox the sun rises in the north, and sets in the south," we should not hesitate to say that he advances an absurdity; but still what he affirms has a meaning; insomuch that on hearing the sentence we pronounce its falsity. Now, *nonsense* is that whereof we cannot say either that it is true, or that it is false. Thus when the Teutonic theosopher enounces, that "all the voices of the celestial joyfulness qualify, commix, and harmonize in the fire which was from eternity in the good quality," I should think it equally impertinent to aver the falsity as the truth of this enunciation. For, though the words grammatically form a sentence, they exhibit to the understanding no judgment, and consequently admit neither assent nor dissent. In the former instances I say the meaning, or what they affirm, is absurd; in the last instance I say there is no meaning, and therefore properly nothing is affirmed. In popular language, I own, the terms absurdity and nonsense are not so accurately distinguished. Absurd positions are sometimes called nonsensical. It is not common, on the other hand, to say of downright nonsense, that it comprises an absurdity.

Further, in the literal sense there may be nothing unsuitable, and yet the reader may be at a loss to find a figurative meaning, to which his expressions can with justice be applied. Writers immoderately attached to the florid or highly figured diction, are often misled by a desire of flourishing on the several attributes of a metaphor, which they have pompously ushered into the discourse, without taking the trouble to examine whether there be any qualities in the subject to which these attributes can with justice and perspicuity be applied.

In one of the examples of the unintelligible above cited, the author having once determined to represent the human mind under the metaphor of a country, hath involved in his thoughts the various objects which might be found in a country, but hath never dreamt of considering whether there be any things in the mind properly analogous to these. Hence the strange parade he makes with *regions* and *recesses*, *hollow caverns* and *private seats*, *wastes* and *wildernesses*, *fruitful* and *cultivated tracts*, words which, though they have a precise meaning as applied to country, have no definite signification as applied to mind. With equal propriety he might have introduced all the variety which Satan discovered in the kingdom of darkness,

> Rocks, caves, lakes, fens, bogs, dens, and shades of death;[1]

or given us with Othello,

> ————All *his* travel's history.
> Wherein, *belike*, of antres vast, and deserts idle,
> Rough quarries, rocks, and hills whose heads touch heaven,
> '*T had been his* hint to speak.[2]

So much for the immoderate use of metaphor, which, by the way, is the principal source of all the nonsense of orators and poets.

The second species of writing wherein we are liable to be imposed on by words without meaning, is that wherein the terms most frequently occurring denote things which are of a complicated nature, and to which the mind is not sufficiently familiarized. Many of those notions which are called by philosophers mixed modes, come under this denomination. Of these

[1] Paradise Lost.

[2] Shakspeare.

the instances are numberless in every tongue: such as *government*, *church*, *state*, *constitution*, *polity*, *power*, *commerce*, *legislature*, *jurisdiction*, *proportion*, *symmetry*, *elegance*. It will considerably increase the danger of our being deceived by an unmeaning use of such terms, if they are besides (as very often they are) of so indeterminate, and consequently equivocal signification, that a writer, unobserved either by himself or by his reader, may slide from one sense of the term to another, till by degrees he fall into such applications of it as will make no sense at all. It deserves our notice also, that we are in much greater danger of terminating in this, if the different meanings of the same word have some affinity to one another, than if they have none. In the latter case, when there is no affinity, the transition from one meaning to another is taking a very wide step, and what few writers are in any danger of; it is, besides, what will not so readily escape the observation of the reader. So much for the second cause of deception, which is the chief source of all the nonsense of writers on politics and criticism.

The third and last, and I may add, the principal species of composition, wherein we are exposed to this illusion by the abuse of words, is that in which the terms employed are very abstract, and consequently of very extensive signification. It is an observation that plainly ariseth from the nature and structure of language, and may be deduced as a corollary from what hath been said of the use of artificial signs, that the more general any name is, as it comprehends the more individuals under it, and consequently requires the more extensive knowledge in the mind that would rightly apprehend it, the more it must have of indistinctness and obscurity. Thus the word *lion* is more distinctly apprehended by the mind than the word *beast*, beast than *animal*, animal than *being*. But there is, in what are called abstract subjects, a still greater fund of obscurity than that arising from the frequent mention of the most general terms. Names must be assigned to those qualities as considered abstractedly, which never subsist independently, or by themselves, but which constitute the generic characters and the specific differences of things. And this leads to a manner which is in many instances remote from the common use of speech, and therefore must be of more difficult conception. The qualities thus considered as in a state of separation from the subjects to which they belong, have been not unfitly compared by a famous wit of the last century to disembodied spirits:

> He could reduce all things to acts,
> And knew their natures and abstracts;
> Where entity and quiddity
> The ghosts of defunct bodies fly.[3]

[3] Hudibras, B. I. C. i.

As the manes of the departed heroes which Æneas saw in the infernal regions were so constituted as effectually to elude the embrace of every living wight; in like manner the abstract qualities are so subtle as often to elude the apprehension of the most attentive mind. They have, I may say, too much volatility to be arrested, were it but for a moment.

> ——The flitting shadow *slips* away,
> Like winds or empty dreams that fly the day.[4]—DRYDEN.

It is no wonder then, that a misapplication of such words, whether general or abstract, should frequently escape our notice. The more general any word is in its signification, it is the more liable to be abused by an improper or unmeaning application. A foreigner will escape discovery in a crowd, who would instantly be distinguished in a select company. A very general term is applicable alike to a multitude of different individuals, a particular term is applicable but to a few. When the rightful applications of a word are extremely numerous, they cannot all be so strongly fixed by habit, but that, for greater security, we must perpetually recur in our minds from the sign to the notion we have of the thing signified; and for the reason aforementioned, it is in such instances difficult precisely to ascertain this notion. Thus the latitude of a word, though different from its ambiguity, hath often a similar effect.

Further, it is a certain fact, that when we are much accustomed to particular terms, we can scarcely avoid fancying that we understand them, whether they have a meaning or not. The reason of this apprehension might easily be deduced from what hath been already said of the nature of signs. Let it suffice at present to observe the fact. Now, on ordinary subjects, if we adopt such a wrong opinion, we may easily be undeceived. The reason is, that on such subjects, the recourse from the sign to the thing signified is easy. For the opposite reason, if we are in such an error on abstract subjects, it is next to impossible that ever we should be undeceived. Hence it is, if without offence I may be indulged the observation, that in some popular systems of religion, the zeal of the people is principally exerted in support of certain favourite phrases, and a kind of technical and idiomatical dialect to which their ears have been long inured, and which they consequently imagine they understand, but in which often there is nothing to be understood.

From such causes it hath arisen, that ever since the earliest

[4] ——Ter comprênsa manus effugit imago,
Par levibus ventis, volucrique simillima somno.
ÆNEIS, lib. ii.

days of philosophy, abstract subjects have been the principal province of altercation and logomachy; to the support of which, how far the artificial dialectic of the schoolmen, nay, the analytics and the metaphysics, the categories and the topics of the justly admired Stagyrite, have contributed, we have considered already.[5] Indeed at length disputation in the schools came to be so much a mechanical exercise, that if once a man had learned his logic, and had thereby come to understand the use of his weapons, and had gotten the knack of wielding them, he was qualified, without any other kind of knowledge, to defend any position whatsoever, how contradictory soever to common sense, and to the clearest discoveries of reason and experience. This art, it must be owned, observed a wonderful impartiality in regard to truth and error, or rather the most absolute indifference to both. If it was oftener employed in defence of error, that is not to be wondered at; for the way of truth is one, the ways of error are infinite. One qualified in the manner above-mentioned could as successfully dispute on a subject of which he was totally ignorant, as on one with which he was perfectly acquainted. Success indeed tended then no more to decide the question, than a man's killing his antagonist in a duel serves now to satisfy any person of sense that the victor had right on his side, and that the vanquished was in the wrong. Such an art as this could at bottom be no other than a mere playing with words, used indeed grammatically, and according to certain rules established in the schools, but quite insignificant, and therefore incapable of conveying knowledge.

Vain wisdom all, and false philosophy.

This logic, between two and three centuries ago, received a considerable improvement from one Raimund Lully, a native of Majorca, who, by the ingenious contrivance of a few concentric moveable circles, on the borders of some of which were inscribed the subjects, of others the predicaments, and of others the forms of questions, not only superseded the little in point of invention which the scholastic logic had till then required, but much accelerated the operations of the artist. All was done by manual labour. All the circles, except the outmost, which was immoveable, were turned upon the common centre, one after another. In this manner the disposition of subjects, predicaments, and questions, was perpetually varied. All the proper questions on every subject were suggested, and pertinent answers supplied. In the same way did the working of the engine discover and apply the several topics of argument that might be used in support of any question. On this rare device one

[5] Book I. Chap. vi.

Athanasius Kircher made great improvements in the last century. He boasted that by means of a coffer of arts, divided into a number of small receptacles, entirely of his own contriving, a thousand prodigies might be performed, which either could not be effected at all by Lully's magical circles, or at least not so expeditiously.

Nothing can more fully prove that the fruit of all such contrivances was mere words without knowledge, an empty show of science without the reality, than the ostentatious and absurd way in which the inventors and their votaries talk of these inventions. They would have us believe that in these is contained a complete encyclopædia, that here we may discover all the arts and sciences as in their source, that hence all of them may be deduced *à priori*, as from their principles. Accordingly they treat all those as no better than quacks and empirics who have recourse to so homely a tutoress as experience.

The consideration of their pretensions hath indeed satisfied me that the ridicule thrown on projectors of this kind, in the account given by Swift[6] of a professor in the academy of Lagado, is not excessive, as I once thought it. The boasts of the academist, on the prodigies performed by his frame, are far less extravagant than those of the above-mentioned artists, which in truth they very much resemble.[7]

[6] Gulliver's Travels, Part iii.

[7] At what an amazing pitch of perfection doth Knittelius, a great admirer both of Lully and of Kircher, suppose that the adepts in this literary handicraft may arrive. The assiduous and careful practice will at length, according to him, fully instruct us, "quomodo de quâcunque re propositâ statim librum concipere, et in capita dividere, de quâcunque re ex tempore disserere, argumentari, de quocunque themate orationem formare, orationem mentalem per horam, dies, et septimanas protrahere, rem quamcunque describere, per apologos et fabulas proponere, emblemata et hieroglyphica invenire, de quâcunque re historias expedite scribere, adversaria de quâcunque re facere, de quâcunque materiâ consilia dare, omnes argutias ad unam regulam reducere, assumptum thema in infinitum multiplicare, ex falso rem demonstrare, quidlibet per quidlibet probare, possimus." Quirinus Kuhlmannus, another philosopher of the last century, in a letter to Kircher hath said with much good sense, concerning his coffer, "Lusus est ingeniosus, ingeniose Kirchere, non methodus, primâ fronte aliquid promittens, in recessu nihil solvens. Sine cista enim puer nihil potest respondere, et in cista nihil præter verba habet; tot profert quot audit, sine intellectu, adinstar psittaci; et de illo jure dicitur quod Lacon de philomela, *Vox est prætereaque nihil*." Could any body imagine that one who thought so justly of Kircher's device was himself the author of another of the same kind! He had, it seems, contrived a scientific machine, that moved by wheels, with the conception of which he pretended to have been inspired by Heaven, but unfortunately he did not live to publish it. His only view, therefore, in the words above quoted, was to depreciate Kircher's engine, that he might the more effectually recommend his own. "Multa passim," says Morhoff concerning him (Polyhistor, vol. I. lib. ii. cap. 5.), "de rotis suis combinatoriis jactat, quibus ordinatis unus homo millies mille, imo millies millies mille scribas vincat; qui tamen primarius rotarum scopus non est, sed grandior longe restat, nempe notitia providentiæ æternæ, orbisque terrarum motus." And again, "Nec ullus hominum tam insulso judicio præditus est, qui hac institutione libros doctos, novos, utiles, omni rerum scientiâ plenos, levissimâ operâ edere non potest."

So much for the third and last cause of illusion that was taken notice of, arising from the abuse of very general and abstract terms, which is the principal source of all the nonsense that hath been vented by metaphysicians, mystagogues, and theologians.

CHAPTER VIII.

The extensive Usefulness of Perspicuity.

SECTION I.

When is Obscurity Apposite, if ever it be Apposite, and what kind?

Having fully considered the nature of perspicuity, and the various ways in which the laws relating to it may be transgressed, I shall now inquire, whether to be able to transgress with dexterity in any of those ways, by speaking obscurely, ambiguously, or unintelligibly, be not as essential to the perfection of eloquence, as to be able to speak perspicuously.

Eloquence, it may be said, hath been defined to be that art or talent whereby the discourse is adapted to produce the effect which the speaker intends it should produce on the hearer.[8] May not then obscurity, on some occasions, be as conducive to

How much more modest is the professor of Lagado: "He flatters himself, indeed, that a more noble exalted thought than his never sprang in any other man's head," but doth not lay claim to inspiration. "Every one knows," he adds, "how laborious the usual method is of attaining to arts and sciences: whereas by his contrivance, the most ignorant person, at a reasonable charge, and with a little bodily labour, may write books in philosophy, poetry, politics, law, mathematics, and theology" (no mention of history) "without the least assistance from genius and study." He is still modest enough to require time, and some corporeal exercise, in order to the composing of a treatise; but those artists propose to bring a proficient "*statim* librum concipere," instantly, "levissimâ operâ," with little or no pains. I shall conclude with laying before the reader the opinion of Lord Verulam, concerning the Lullian art, an opinion that may with equal justice be applied to the devices of all Lully's followers and imitators. "Neque tamen illud prætermittendum, quod nonnulli viri magis tumidi quam docti insudârunt circa methodum quandam, legitimæ methodi nomine haud dignam, cum potius sit methodus imposturæ, quæ tamen quibusdam ardelionibus acceptissima procul dubio fuerit. Hæc methodus ita scientiæ alicujus guttulas aspergit, ut quis sciolus specie nonnullâ eruditionis ad ostentationem possit abuti. Talis fuit ars Lullii, talis typocosmia a nonnullis exarata; quæ nihil aliud fuerunt, quam vocabulorum artis cujusque massa et acervus; ad hoc, ut qui voces artis habeant in promptu, etiam artes ipsas perdidicisse existimentur. Hujus generis collectanea officinam referunt veteramentariam, ubi præsegmina multa reperiuntur, sed nihil quod alicujus sit pretii." De Aug. Scient. lib. vi. cap. 2. I shall only observe, that when he calls this art a method of imposture, he appears to mean that it puts an imposition upon the mind, not so much by infusing error instead of truth, as by amusing us with mere words instead of useful knowledge.

[8] Book I. Chap. i.

the effect intended, as perspicuity is on other occasions? If the latter is necessary in order to inform, is not the former necessary in order to deceive? If perspicuity be expedient in convincing us of truth, and persuading us to do right, is not its contrary, obscurity, expedient in effecting the contrary; that is, in convincing us of what is false, and in persuading us to do wrong? And may not either of these effects be the aim of the speaker?

This way of arguing is far more plausible than just. To be obscure, or even unintelligible, may, I acknowledge, in some cases, contribute to the design of the orator, yet it doth not follow, that obscurity is as essential to eloquence as the opposite quality. It is the design of the medical art to give health and ease to the patient, not pain and sickness, and that the latter are sometimes the foreseen effects of the medicines employed, doth not invalidate the general truth. Whatever be the real intention of a speaker or writer, whether to satisfy our reason of what is true or of what is untrue, whether to incline our will to what is right or to what is wrong, still he must propose to effect his design by informing our understanding; nay more, without conveying to our minds some information, he might as well attempt to achieve his purpose by addressing us in an unknown tongue. Generally, therefore, this quality of style, perspicuity, is as requisite in seducing to evil, as in exciting to good, in defending error, as in supporting truth.

I am sensible that this position must appear to many no other than a paradox. What! say they, is it not as natural to vice and falsehood to skulk in darkness, as it is to truth and virtue to appear in light? Doubtless it is in some sense, but in such a sense as is not in the least repugnant to the doctrine here advanced. That therefore we may be satisfied of the justness of this theory, it will be necessary to consider a little further the nature both of persuasion and of conviction.

With regard to the former it is evident, that the principal scope for employing persuasion is, when the mind balances, or may be supposed to balance, in determining what choice to make in respect of conduct, whether to do this or to do that, or at least whether to do or to forbear. And it is equally evident that the mind would never balance a moment in choosing, unless there were motives to influence it on each of the opposite sides. In favour of one side perhaps is the love of glory, in favour of the other the love of life. Now, whichever side the orator espouses, there are two things that must carefully be studied by him, as was observed on a former occasion;[9] the first is to excite in his hearers that desire or passion which favours his design; the second is, to satisfy their judgments that there

[9] Book I. Chap. vii. Sect. 6. See the analysis of persuasion.

is a connexion between the conduct to which he would persuade them, and the gratification of the desire or passion which he excites. The first is effected by communicating natural and lively ideas of the object; the second by arguments from experience, analogy, testimony, or the plurality of chances. To the communication of natural and vivid ideas, the pathetic circumstances formerly enumerated[1] are particularly conducive.—Now, to the efficacious display of these circumstances, nothing can be more unfriendly than obscurity, whose direct tendency is to confound our ideas, or rather to blot them altogether. And as to the second requisite, the argumentative part, that can never require obscurity, which doth not require even a deviation from truth. It may be as true, and therefore as demonstrable, that my acting in one way will promote my safety, or what I regard as my interest, as that my acting in the contrary way will raise my fame. And even when an orator is under a necessity of replying to what hath been advanced by an antagonist, in order to weaken the impression he hath made, or to lull the passion he hath roused, it is not often that he is obliged to avail himself of any false or sophistical reasoning, which alone can render obscurity useful. Commonly, on the contrary, he hath only to avail himself of an artful exhibition of every circumstance of the case, that can any way contribute to invalidate or to subvert his adversary's plea, and consequently to support his own. Now, it is a certain fact that, in almost all complicated cases, real circumstances will be found in favour of each side of the question. Whatever side therefore the orator supports, it is his business, in the first place, to select those circumstances that are favourable to his own plea, or which excite the passion that is directly instrumental in promoting his end; secondly, to select those circumstances that are unfavourable to the plea of his antagonist, and to add to all these such clearness and energy by his eloquence, as will effectually fix the attention of the hearers upon them, and thereby withdraw their regards from those circumstances, equally real, which favour the other side. In short, it is the business of the two antagonists to give different or even opposite directions to the attention of the hearers; but then it is alike the interests of each to set those particular circumstances, to which he would attract their notice, in as clear a light as possible. And it is only by acting thus that he can hope to effectuate his purpose.

Perhaps it will be urged, that though, where the end is persuasion, there doth not seem to be an absolute necessity for sophistry and obscurity on either side, as there is not on either side an absolute necessity for supporting falsehood, the case is certainly different when the end is to convince the understand-

[1] Book I. Chap. vii. Sect. 5. The explication and use of those circumstances.

ing. In this case, whatever is spoken on one side of the question, as it is spoken in support of error, must be sophistical: and sophistry seems to require a portion of obscurity, to serve her as a veil, that she may escape discovery. Even here, however, the case is not so plain as at first it may be thought. Sophistry (which hath sometimes been successfully used in support of truth) is not always necessary for the support of error. Error may be supported, and hath been often strenuously supported, by very cogent arguments and just reasoning.

But as this position will probably appear to many very extraordinary, if not irrational, it will be necessary to examine the matter more minutely. It is true, indeed, that in subjects susceptible of demonstrative proof, error cannot be defended but by sophistry; and sophistry, to prevent detection, must shelter herself in obscurity. This results from the nature of scientific evidence, as formerly explained.[2] This kind of evidence is solely conversant about the invariable relations of number and extension, which relations it evolves by a simple chain of axioms. An assertion, therefore, that is contrary to truth in these matters, is also absurd and inconceivable; nor is there any scope here for contrariety of proofs. Accordingly, debate and argumentation have no footing here. The case is far otherwise with moral evidence, which is of a complex nature, which admits degrees, which is almost always combated by opposite proofs, and these, though perhaps lower in degree, as truly of the nature of proof and evidence as those whereby they are opposed. The probability, on the whole, as was shown already,[3] lies in the proportion which the contrary proofs, upon comparison, bear to one another; a proportion which, in complicated cases, it is often difficult, and sometimes even impossible, to ascertain. The speakers, therefore, on the opposite sides have each real evidence to insist on; and there is here the same scope as in persuasory discourses, for all the arts that can both rivet the hearer's attention on the circumstances of the proof favourable to the speaker's design, and divert his attention from the contrary circumstances. Nor is there, in ordinary cases, that is, in all cases really dubious and disputable, any necessity, on either side, for what is properly called sophistry.

The natural place for sophistry is, when a speaker finds himself obliged to attempt the refutation of arguments that are both clear and convincing. For an answerer to overlook such arguments altogether might be dangerous, and to treat them in such a manner as to elude their force requires the most exquisite address. A little sophistry here will, no doubt, be thought necessary by one with whom victory hath more charms than truth; and sophistry, as was hinted above, always implies

[2] Book I. Chap. v. Sect 2. [3] Ibid.

obscurity; for that a sophism should be mistaken for an argument, can be imputed only to this, that it is not rightly understood.

As from what hath been said, we may learn to distinguish the few cases wherein a violation of the laws of perspicuity may be pertinent to the purpose of the orator, I shall next inquire what kind of violation is in such cases best fitted for answering his design. It is evident it cannot be the first, which, for distinction's sake, was denominated by the general name Obscurity. When a hearer not only doth not understand, but is himself sensible that he doth not understand what is spoken, it can produce no effect on him but weariness, suspicion, and disgust, which must be prejudicial to the intention. Although it is not always necessary that every thing advanced by the speaker should convey information to the hearer, it is necessary that he should believe himself informed by what is said, ere he can be convinced or persuaded by it. For the like reason, it is not the second kind of transgression, or any discoverable ambiguity in what is spoken, that is adapted to the end of speaking. This fault, if discovered, though not of so bad consequence as the former, tends to distract the attention of the hearer, and thereby to weaken the impression which the words would otherwise have made. It remains, that it is only the third and last kind above discussed, when what is said, though in itself unintelligible, a hearer may be led to imagine that he understands. When ambiguities can artfully be made to elude discovery, and to conduce to this deception, they may be used with success.[4] Now, though nothing would seem to be easier than this kind of style, when an author falls into it naturally; that is, when he deceives himself as well as his reader; nothing is more difficult when attempted of design. It is besides requisite, if this manner must be continued for any time, that it be artfully blended with some glimpses of meaning; else, to persons of discernment, the charm will at last be dissolved, and the nothingness of what hath been spoken will be detected; nay, even the attention of the unsuspecting multitude, when not relieved by any thing that is level to their comprehension, will infallibly flag. The invocation in the Dunciad admirably suits the orator who is unhappily reduced to the necessity of taking shelter in the unintelligible.

> Of darkness visible so much be lent,
> As half to show, half veil the deep intent.

There is but one subject in nature (if what is unintelligible can be called a subject) on which the appetite of nonsense is

[4] That they are often successful this way hath been justly remarked by Aristotle. Των δ' ονοματων, τω μεν σοφιστη ὁμωνυμιαι χρησιμοι, παρα ταυτας γαρ κακουργει. Ρητ. γ.

utterly insatiable. The intelligent reader needs not be informed that I mean what is commonly termed mystical theology; a subject whose supposed sublimity serves with its votaries to apologize for its darkness. That here indeed there may be found readers who can, not only with patience but with avidity, not only through pages but through volumes, lose themselves in wandering over a maze of words unenlightened by a single ray of sense, the translation of the works of Jacob Behmen, and our modern Hutchinsonian performances, are lamentable proofs. But this case is particular.

After all, we are not to imagine that the sophistical and unmeaning, when it may in some sense be said to be proper, or even necessary, are, in respect of the ascendant gained over the mind of the hearer, ever capable of rivalling conclusive arguments perspicuously expressed. The effect of the former is at most only to confound the judgment, and by the confusion it produceth, to silence contradiction; the effect of the latter is fully to convince the understanding. The impression made by the first can no more be compared in distinctness and vivacity to that effected by the second, than the dreams of a person asleep to his perceptions when awake. Hence we may perceive an eminent disadvantage, which the advocate for error, when compelled to recur to words without meaning, must labour under. The weapons he is obliged to use are of such a nature, that there is much greater difficulty in managing them than in managing those that must be employed in the cause of truth, and when managed ever so dexterously, they cannot do equal execution. A still greater disadvantage the patron of the cause of injustice or of vice must grapple with. For though he may find real motives to urge in defence of his plea, as wealth perhaps, or ease, or pleasure, he hath to encounter or elude the moral sentiments which, of all motives whatever, take the strongest hold of the heart. And if he find himself under a necessity of attempting to prove that virtue and right are on his side, he hath his way to grope through a labyrinth of sophistry and nonsense.

So much for the legitimate use of the unintelligible in oratory.

SECTION II.—*Objections answered.*

But are there not some subjects, and even some kinds of composition, which from their very nature demand a dash of obscurity? Doth not decency often require this? Doth not delicacy require this? And is not this even essential to the allegoric style, and to the enigmatic? As to the manner which decency sometimes requires, it will be found, on examination, to stand opposed more properly to vivacity than to perspicuity of style, and will therefore fall to be considered afterwards.

I shall now, therefore, examine, in the first place, in what respect delicacy may be said to demand obscurity. Thus much indeed is evident, that delicacy often requires that certain sentiments be rather insinuated than expressed; in other words, that they be not directly spoken, but that sufficient ground be given to infer them from what is spoken. Such sentiments are, though improperly, considered as obscurely expressed, for this special reason, that it is not by the first operation of the intellect, an apprehension of the meaning of what is said, but by a second operation, a reflection on what is implied or presupposed, that they are discovered; in which double operation of the mind there is a faint resemblance to what happens in the case of real obscurity. But in the case of which I am treating, it is the thought more than the expression that serves for a veil to the sentiment suggested. If, therefore, in such instances there may be said to be obscurity, it is an obscurity which is totally distinct from obscurity of language.

That this matter may be better understood, we must carefully distinguish between the thought expressed and the thought hinted. The latter may be affirmed to be obscure, because it is not expressed, but hinted; whereas the former, with which alone perspicuity of style is concerned, must always be expressed with clearness, otherwise the sentiment will never be considered as either beautiful or delicate.[5] I shall illustrate this by examples.

No subject requires to be treated more delicately than praise, especially when it is given to a person present. Flattery is so nauseous to a liberal spirit, that even when praise is merited, it is disagreeable, at least to unconcerned hearers, if it appear in a garb which adulation commonly assumes. For this reason, an encomium or compliment never succeeds so well as when it is indirect. It then appears to escape the speaker unawares, at a time that he seems to have no intention to commend. Of this kind the following story will serve as an example: "A gentleman who had an employment bestowed on him, without so much as being known to his benefactor, waited upon the great man who was so generous, and was beginning to say he was infinitely obliged——*Not at all*, says the patron, turning from him to another: *Had I known a more deserving man in England, he should not have had it.*"[6]

[5] This will serve to explain what Bouhours, a celebrated French critic, and a great advocate for perspicuity, hath advanced on this subject, "Souvenez-vous, que rien n'est plus opposé à la véritable delicatesse que d'exprimer trop les choses, et que le grand art consiste à ne pas tout dire sur certains sujets; à glisser dessus plutôt que d'y appuyer; en un mot, à en laisser penser aux autres plus que l'on n'en dit." Manière de bien penser, &c.

[6] Tatler, No. 17.

Here the apparent intention of the minister was only to excuse the person on whom the favour had been conferred the trouble of making an acknowledgment, by assuring him that it had not been given from personal attachment or partiality. But whilst he appears intending only to say this, he says what implies the greatest praise, and, as it were, accidentally betrays the high opinion he entertained of the other's merit. If he had said directly, "You are the most deserving man that I know in England," the answer, though implying no more than what he did say, would have been not only indelicate but intolerable. On so slight a turn in the expression it frequently depends, whether the same sentiment shall appear delicate or gross, complimental or affronting.

Sometimes praise is very successfully and very delicately conveyed under an appearance of chagrin. This constitutes the merit of that celebrated thought of Boileau: "To imagine in such a warlike age, which abounds in Achilleses, that we can write verses as easily as they take towns!"[7] The poet seems only venting his complaints against the unreasonable expectations of some persons, and at the same time discovers, as by chance, the highest admiration of his monarch and the heroes who served him, by suggesting the incredible rapidity of the success with which their arms were crowned.

Sometimes also commendation will be couched with great delicacy under an air of reproach. An example of this I shall give from the paper lately quoted: "*My Lord*," said the duke of B——m, after his libertine way to the earl of O——y, "*you will certainly be damned.*" "How, my Lord?" said the earl with some warmth. "*Nay*," replied the duke, "*there's no help for it, for it is positively said, Cursed is he of whom all men speak well.*"[8] A still stronger example in this way we have from the Drapier, who, speaking to Lord Molesworth of the seditious expressions of which he had himself been accused, says: "I have witnesses ready to depose, that your Lordship hath said and writ fifty times worse, and what is still an aggravation, with infinitely more wit and learning, and stronger arguments: So that as politics run, I do not know a person of more exceptionable principles than yourself: And if ever I shall be discovered, I think you will be bound in honour to pay my fine and support me in prison, or else I may chance to inform against you by way of reprisal."[9]

I shall produce one other instance from the same hand, of an indirect, but successful manner of praising, by seeming to invert the course of the obligation, and to represent the person

[7] Et dans ce tems guerrier et fecond en Achilles
Croit que l'on fait les vers, comme l'on prend les villes.

[8] Tatler, No. 17.

[9] Drapier's Letters, 5.

obliging as the person obliged. Swift, in a letter to the archbishop of Dublin, speaking of Mr. Harley, then lord high treasurer, afterwards earl of Oxford, by whose means the Irish clergy had obtained from the queen the grant of the first fruits and tenths, says, "I told him that, for my part, I thought he was obliged to the clergy of Ireland, for giving him an occasion of gratifying the pleasure he took in doing good to the church."[1]

It may be observed, that delicacy requires indirectness of manner no less in censure than in praise. If the one, when open and direct, is liable to be branded with the name of *flattery*, the other is no less exposed to the opprobrious appellation of *abuse*, both alike, though in different ways, offensive to persons of taste and breeding. I shall give from the work last quoted a specimen (I cannot say of great delicacy) in stigmatizing, but at least of such an indirect manner as is sufficient to screen the author from the imputation of downright rudeness. "I hear you are like to be the sole opposer of the bank; and you will certainly miscarry, because it would prove a most perfidious thing. Bankrupts are always for setting up banks; how then can you think a bank will fail of a majority in both houses!"[2] It must be owned that the veil here is extremely thin, too thin to be altogether decent, and serves only to save from the imputation of scurrility a very severe reproach. It is the manner which constitutes one principal distinction between the libeller and the satirist. I shall give one instance more of this kind from another work of the same author. "To smooth the way for the return of popery in queen Mary's time, the grantees were confirmed by the pope in the possession of the abbey-lands. But the bishop tells us that this confirmation was fraudulent and invalid. I shall believe it to be so, although I happen to read it in his lordship's history."[3] Thus he insinuates, or signifies by implication, that his lordship's history is full of lies. Now, from all the specimens I have exhibited, it will, I suppose, sufficiently appear to any person of common understanding, that the obscurity required by delicacy, either in blaming or commending, is totally distinct in kind from obscurity of expression, with which none of the examples above quoted is in the smallest degree chargeable.

The illustrations I have given on this topic will contribute in some measure to explain the obscurity that is requisite in allegories, apologues, parables, and enigmas. In all these sorts of composition there are two senses plainly intended, the literal and the figurative: the language is solely the sign of the literal sense, and the literal sense is the sign of the figurative. Per-

[1] Swift's Letters, 10. [2] Ibid. 40.

[3] Preface to the Bishop of Sarum's Introduction to the third volume of his History of the Reformation.

spicuity in the style, which exhibits only the literal sense, is so far from being to be dispensed with here, that it is even more requisite in this kind of composition than in any other. Accordingly, you will perhaps nowhere find more perfect models both of simplicity and of perspicuity of style than in the parables of the gospel. Indeed, in every sort of composition of a figurative character, more attention is always and justly considered as due to this circumstance than in any other sort of writing. Æsop's Fables are a noted example of this remark. In further confirmation of it, we may observe that no pieces are commonly translated with greater ease and exactness than the allegorical; and that even by those who apprehend nothing of the mystical sense. This sure could never be the case if the obscurity were chargeable on the language.

The same thing holds here as in painting emblems, or graving devices. It may, without any fault in the painter or engraver, puzzle you to discover what the visible figure of the sun, for example, which you observe in the emblem or the device, was intended to signify; but if you are at a loss to know whether it be the figure of the sun or the figure of the moon that you are looking at, he must have been undoubtedly a bungling artist. The body, therefore, if I may so express myself, of the emblem, or of the device, and precisely for the same reason, of the riddle or of the allegory, must be distinctly exhibited, so as scarcely to leave room for a possibility of mistake. The exercise that in any of these performances is given to ingenuity, ought wholly to consist in reading the soul.

I know no style to which darkness of a certain sort is more suited than to the prophetical. Many reasons might be assigned which render it improper that prophecy should be perfectly understood before it be accomplished. Besides, we are certain that a prediction may be very dark before the accomplishment, and yet so plain afterwards as scarcely to admit a doubt in regard to the events suggested. It does not belong to critics to give laws to prophets, nor does it fall within the confines of any human art to lay down rules for a species of composition so far above art. Thus far, however, we may warrantably observe, that when the prophetic style is imitated in poetry, the piece ought, as much as possible, to possess the character above mentioned. This character, in my opinion, is possessed in a very eminent degree by Mr. Gray's ode called *The Bard.* It is all darkness to one who knows nothing of the English history, posterior to the reign of Edward the first, and all light to one who is well acquainted with that history. But this is a kind of writing whose peculiarities can scarcely be considered as exceptions from ordinary rules.

But further, may not a little obscurity be sometimes very suitable in dramatic composition? Sometimes indeed, but very seldom; else the purpose of the exhibition would be lost. The drama is a sort of moral painting, and characters must be painted as they are. A blunderer cannot properly be introduced conversing with all the perspicuity and precision of a critic, no more than a clown can be justly represented expressing himself in the polished style of a courtier. In like manner, when the mind is in confusion and perplexity, arising from the sudden conflict of violent passions, the language will of necessity partake of the perturbation. Incoherent hints, precipitate sallies, vehement exclamations, interrupted perhaps by feeble checks from religion or philosophy; in short, every thing imperfect, abrupt, and desultory, are the natural expressions of a soul overwhelmed in such a tumult. But even here it may be said with truth, that to one skilled in reading Nature, there will arise a light out of the darkness, which will enable him to penetrate farther into the spirit, than he could have done by the help of the most just, most perspicuous, and most elaborate description. This might be illustrated, were it necessary, but a case so singular is hardly called an exception. The dramatist then can but rarely claim to be indulged in obscurity of language, the fabulist never.

CHAPTER IX.

May there not be an Excess of Perspicuity?

I SHALL conclude this subject with inquiring whether it be possible that perspicuity should be carried to excess. It hath been said that too much of it has a tendency to cloy the reader, and, as it gives no play to the rational and active powers of the mind, will soon grow irksome through excess of facility. In this manner some able critics have expressed themselves on this point, who will be found not to differ in sentiment, but only in expression from the principles above laid down.

The objection ariseth manifestly from the confounding of two objects, the common and the clear, and thence very naturally their contraries, the new and the dark, that are widely different. If you entertain your reader solely or chiefly with thoughts that are either trite or obvious, you cannot fail soon to tire him. You introduce few or no new sentiments into his mind, you give him little or no information, and consequently afford neither exercise to his reason nor entertainment to his fancy. In what we read, and what we hear, we always seek for something in one respect or other new, which we did not know, or at least attend to, before. The less we find of this, the sooner we are tired. Such a trifling minuteness, therefore, in narration, description, or argument, as an ordinary apprehension would render superfluous, is apt quickly to disgust us. The reason is, not because any thing is said too perspicuously, but because many things are said which ought not to be said at all. Nay, if those very things had been expressed obscurely (and the most obvious things may be expressed obscurely) the fault would have been much greater; because it would have required a good deal of attention to discover what, after we had discovered it, we should perceive not to be of sufficient value for requiting our pains. To an author of this kind we should be apt to apply the character which Bassanio in the play gives of Gratiano's conversation; "He speaks an infinite deal of nothing. His reasons are as two grains of wheat hid in two bushels of chaff: you shall seek all day ere you find them, and when you have them they are not worth the search."[4] It is therefore futility in the thought, and not perspicuity in the language, which is the fault of such performances. There is as little hazard that a piece should be faulty in this respect, as that a mirror shall be too faithful in reflecting the images of objects, or that the glasses of a telescope shall be too transparent.

At the same time, it is not to be dissembled that, with inattentive readers, a pretty numerous class, darkness frequently passes for depth. To be perspicuous, on the contrary, and to be superficial, are regarded by them as synonymous. But it is not surely to their absurd notions that our language ought to be adapted.

It is proper, however, before I dismiss this subject, to observe, that every kind of style doth not admit an equal degree of perspicuity. In the ode, for instance, it is difficult, sometimes perhaps impossible, to reconcile the utmost perspicuity with that force and vivacity which the species of composition requires. But even in this case, though we may justly say that the genius of the performance renders obscurity to a certain degree excusable, nothing can ever constitute it an excellence. Nay, it may still be affirmed with truth, that the more a writer can reconcile this quality of perspicuity with that which is the distinguishing excellence of the species of composition, his success will be the greater.

[4] Shakspeare's Merchant of Venice.

THE

PHILOSOPHY OF RHETORIC.

BOOK III.

THE DISCRIMINATING PROPERTIES OF ELOCUTION.

CHAPTER I.

Of Vivacity as depending on the Choice of Words.

HAVING discussed the subject of perspicuity, by which the discourse is fitted to inform the understanding, I come now to those qualities of style by which it is adapted to please the imagination, and consequently to awake and fix the attention. These I have already denominated vivacity and elegance, which correspond to the two sources whence, as was observed in the beginning of this inquiry,[5] the merit of an address to the fancy immediately results. By vivacity of expression, resemblance is attained, as far as language can contribute to the attainment; by elegance, dignity of manner.

I begin with vivacity, whose nature (though perhaps the word is rarely used in a signification so extensive) will be best understood by considering the several principles from which it arises. There are three things in style on which its vivacity depends, the choice of words, their number, and their arrangement.

The first thing, then, that comes to be examined, is the words chosen. Words are either proper terms, or rhetorical tropes; and whether the one or the other, they may be regarded not only as signs, but as sounds; and consequently as capable, in certain cases, of bearing in some degree a natural resemblance or affinity to the things signified. These three articles, therefore, proper terms, rhetorical tropes, and the relation which the sound may be made to bear to the sense, I shall, on the first topic, the choice of words, consider severally, as far as concerns the subject of vivacity.

[5] Book I. Chap. i.

SECTION I.—*Proper Terms.*

I begin with proper terms, and observe that the quality of chief importance in these, for producing the end proposed, is their *speciality*. Nothing can contribute more to enliven the expression, than that all the words employed be as particular and determinate in their signification as will suit with the nature and the scope of the discourse. The more general the terms are, the picture is the fainter; the more special they are, it is the brighter. The same sentiments may be expressed with equal justness, and even perspicuity, in the former way, as in the latter; but as the colouring will in that case be more languid, it cannot give equal pleasure to the fancy, and by consequence will not contribute so much either to fix the attention, or to impress the memory. I shall illustrate this doctrine by some examples.

In the song of Moses, occasioned by the miraculous passage of the Israelites through the Red Sea, the inspired poet, speaking of the Egyptians, says, "They *sank* as *lead* in the mighty waters."[6] Make but a small alteration in the expression, and say, "They *fell* as *metal* in the mighty waters;" and the difference in the effect will be quite astonishing. Yet the sentiment will be equally just, and in either way the meaning of the author can hardly be mistaken. Nor is there another alteration made upon the sentence, but that the terms are rendered more comprehensive or generical. To this alone, therefore, the difference of the effect must be ascribed. *To sink* is, as it were, the species, as it implies only "falling or moving downwards in a liquid element;" *to fall* answers to the genus;[7] in like manner, *lead* is the species, *metal* is the genus.

"Consider," says our Lord, "the lilies how they grow: they toil not, they spin not; and yet I say unto you, that Solomon in all his glory was not arrayed like one of these. If then God so clothe the grass, which to-day is in the field, and to-morrow is cast into the oven, how much more will he clothe you?"[8] Let us here adopt a little of the tasteless manner of modern paraphrasts, by the substitution of more general terms, one of

[6] Exod. xv. 10.

[7] I am sensible that genus and species are not usually, and perhaps cannot be so properly, applied to verbs; yet there is, in the reference which the meanings of two verbs sometimes bear to each other, what nearly resembles this relation. It is only when *to fall* means to move downwards, as a brick from a chimney-top, or a pear from the tree, that it may be denominated a genus in respect of the verb *to sink*. Sometimes, indeed, the former denotes merely a sudden change of posture from erect to prostrate, as when a man who stands upon the ground is said to fall, though he remains still on the ground. In this way we speak of the fall of a tower, of a house, or of a wall

[8] Luke xii. 27 and 28.

their many expedients of infrigidating, and let us observe the effect produced by this change. "Consider the flowers, how they gradually increase in their size, they do no manner of work, and yet I declare to you, that no king whatever, in his most splendid habit, is dressed up like them. If then God in his providence doth so adorn the vegetable productions, which continue but a little time on the land, and are afterwards put into the fire, how much more will he provide clothing for you?" How spiritless is the same sentiment rendered by these small variations! The very particularizing of *to-day* and *to-morrow* is infinitely more expressive of transitoriness than any description, wherein the terms are general, that can be substituted in its room.

Yet to a cold annotator, a man of mere intellection without fancy, the latter exhibition of the sentiment would appear the more emphatical of the two. Nor would he want some show of reason for this preference. As a specimen, therefore, of a certain mode of criticizing, not rarely to be met with, in which there is I know not what semblance of judgment without one particle of taste, I shall suppose a critic of this stamp entering on the comparison of the preceding quotation and the paraphrase. "In the one," he would argue, "the beauty of only one sort of flowers is exalted above the effects of human industry, in the other the beauty of the whole kind. In the former one individual monarch is said not to have equalled them in splendour, in the latter it is affirmed that no monarch whatever can equal them." However specious this way of reasoning may be, we are certain that it is not solid, because it doth not correspond with the principles of our nature. Indeed what was explained above,[9] in regard to abstraction, and the particularity of our ideas, properly so called, may serve in a great measure to account for the effect which speciality hath upon the imagination. Philosophy, which, strictly considered, addresseth only the understanding, and is conversant about abstract truth, abounds in general terms, because these alone are adequate to the subject treated. On the contrary, when the address is made by eloquence to the fancy, which requires a lively exhibition of the object presented to it, those terms must be culled that are as particular as possible, because it is solely by these that the object can be depicted. And even the most rigid philosopher, if he choose that his disquisitions be not only understood but relished (and without being relished they are understood to little purpose), will not disdain sometimes to apply to the imagination of his disciples, mixing the pleasant with the useful. This is one way of sacrificing to the Graces.

But I proceed to give examples in such of the different

[9] Book II. Chap. vii. Sect. 1.

parts of speech as are most susceptible of this beauty. The first shall be in the verbs.

> It seem'd as there the British Neptune stood
> With all his hosts of waters at command;
> Beneath them to *submit* th' officious flood;
> And with his trident *shov'd* them off the sand.[1]

The words *submit* and *shov'd* are particularly expressive of the action here ascribed to Neptune. The former of these verbs *submit* may indeed be called a *Latinism* in the signification it hath in this passage. But such idioms, though improper in prose, are sometimes not ungraceful in the poetic dialect. If in the last line instead of *shov'd*, the poet had used the verb *rais'd*, which, though not equivalent, would have conveyed much the same meaning, the expression had been fainter.[2]

The next examples shall be in adjectives and participles.

> The kiss *snatch'd* hasty from the *sidelong* maid,
> On purpose guardless——.[3]

Here both the words *sidelong* and *snatch'd* are very significant, and contribute much to the vivacity of the expression. *Taken* or *ta'en* substituted for the latter, would be much weaker. It may be remarked, that it is principally in those parts of speech which regard life and action that this species of energy takes place.

I shall give one in nouns from Milton, who says concerning Satan, when he had gotten into the garden of Eden,

> Thence up he flew, and on the tree of life
> Sat like a *cormorant*.[4]

If for cormorant he had said *bird of prey*, which would have equally suited both the meaning and the measure, the image would still have been good, but weaker than it is by this specification.

In adjectives the same author hath given an excellent example, in describing the attitude in which Satan was discovered by Ithuriel and his company, when that malign spirit was employed in infusing pernicious thoughts into the mind of our first mother,

[1] Dryden's Year of Wonders.

[2] In this instance Dryden hath even improved on the original he imitated; which is not often the case either of translators or of imitators. Virgil says simply, "*Levat* ipse tridenti."

[3] Thomson's Winter.

[4] Paradise Lost, B. iv.

————Him there they found
Squat like a toad, close at the ear of Eve.[5]

No word in the language could have so happily expressed the posture as that which the poet hath chosen.

It will be easy from the same principles to illustrate a remark of the Stagyrite, on the epithet *rosy-finger'd*, which Homer hath given to the morning. This, says the critic, is better than if he had said *purple-finger'd*, and far better than if he had said *red-finger'd*.[1] Aristotle hath observed the effect solely in respect of beauty, but the remark holds equally true of these epithets in respect of vivacity. This in a great measure may be deduced from what hath been said already. Of all the above adjectives the last is the most vague and general, and therefore the worst; the second is better, because more special, *purple* being one species comprehended under *red;* the first is the best, because the most particular, pointing to that single tint of *purple* which is to be found in the *rose*. I acknowledge, at the same time, that this metaphorical epithet hath an excellence totally distinct from its vivacity. This I denominate its elegance. The object whence the metaphor is taken is a grateful object. It at once gratifies two of the senses, the nose by its fragrance, and the eye by its beauty. But of this quality I shall have occasion to treat afterwards.

I proceed at present in producing examples to confirm the theory advanced. And to show how much even an adverb, that is very particular in its signification, may contribute to vivacity, I shall again have recourse to the Paradise Lost.

Some say, he bid his angels turn *askance*
The poles of earth, twice ten degrees and more,
From the sun's axle————.

If the poet, instead of saying *askance*, had said *aside*, which properly enough might have been said, the expression would have lost much of its energy. This adverb is of too general signification, and might have been used with equal propriety, if the plane of the ecliptic had been made perpendicular to that of the equator; whereas the word *askance*, in that case, could not have been employed, it denoting just such an obliquity in the inclination of these two planes as actually obtains. We have an example of the same kind in the description which Thomson gives us of the sun newly risen.

————Lo! now apparent all,
Aslant the dew bright earth, and colour'd air,
He looks in boundless majesty abroad.[7]

[5] Paradise Lost, B. iv.

[6] Arist. Rhet. L. 3. Διαφερει δ' ειπειν, όιον ῥοδοδακτυλος ηως μαλλον η φοινικοδακτυλος, η ετι φαυλοτερον ερυθροδακτυλος.

[7] Summer.

Further, it will sometimes have a considerable effect in enlivening the imagery, not only to particularize, but even to individuate the object presented to the mind. This conduct Dr. Blair, in his very ingenious Dissertation on the poems of Ossian, observes to have been generally followed by his favourite bard. His similitudes bring to our view *the mist on the hill of Cromla*, *the storm on the sea of Malmor*, and *the reeds of the Lake of Lego*. The same vivacious manner is often to be found in holy writ, *swift as a roe or as a fawn upon mount Bether*,[8] *white as the snow in Salmon*,[9] *fragrant as the smell of Lebanon*.[1] And in the passage lately quoted from the gospel, the introduction of the name of Solomon hath an admirable effect in invigorating the sentiment, not only as it points out an individual, but one of great fame in that country among the people whom our Saviour addressed; one, besides, who was universally esteemed the wisest, the richest, and the most magnificent prince that ever reigned over Israel. Now, this is a consideration which was particularly apposite to the design of the speaker.

It may indeed be imagined, that this manner can enliven the thought only to those who are acquainted with the individuals mentioned; but, on mature reflection, we may easily discover this to be a mistake. Not only do we, as it were, participate by sympathy in the known vivid perceptions of the speaker or the writer, but the very notion we form of an *individual* thing known or unknown, from its being conceived as an individual, or as one thing, is of a more fixed nature than that we form of a *species*, which is conceived to be equally applicable to several things, resembling indeed in some respects, though unlike in others: and for the same reason, the notion we have of a species is of a more steady nature than that we form of a *genus*, because this last is applicable to a still greater number of objects, amongst which the difference is greater and the resemblance less.

I mean not however to assert, that the method of individuating the object ought always to be preferred by the poet or the orator. If it have its advantages, it hath its disadvantages also; and must be used sparingly by those who choose that their writings should be more extensively known than in their own neighbourhood. *Proper names* are not in the same respect essential to the language as *appellatives*. And even among the former, there is a difference between the names *known to fame*, and the names of persons or things comparatively *obscure*. The last kind of names will ever appear as strangers to the greater part of readers, even to those who are masters of the language. Sounds to which the ear is not

[8] Cant. ii. 17. [9] Psalm lxviii. 14. [1] Hosea xiv. 6.

accustomed, have a certain uncouthness in them, that renders them, when occurring frequently, fatiguing and disagreeable. But that nevertheless, when pertinently introduced, when neither the ear is tired by their frequency, nor the memory burthened by their number, they have a considerable effect in point of vivacity, is undeniable.

This holds especially when, from the nature of the subject, the introduction of them may be expected. Every one is sensible, for instance, that the most humorous or engaging story loseth egregiously, when the relater cannot or will not name the persons concerned in it. No doubt the naming of them has the greatest effect on those who are acquainted with them, either personally or by character; but it hath some effect, even on those who never heard of them before. It must be an extraordinary tale indeed which we can bear for any time to hear, if the narrator proceeds in this languid strain, "A certain person who shall be nameless, on a certain occasion, said *so and so*, to which a certain other person in the company, who likewise shall be nameless, made answer."—Nay, so dull doth a narrative commonly appear wherein anonymous individuals only are concerned, that we choose to give feigned names to the persons rather than none at all. Nor is this device solely necessary for precluding the ambiguity of the pronouns, and saving the tediousness of circumlocution; for where neither ambiguity nor circumlocution would be the consequence, as where one man and one woman are all the interlocutors, this expedient is nevertheless of great utility. Do but call them any thing, the man suppose Theodosius, and the woman Constantia,[2] and by the illusion which the very appearance of names, though we know them to be fictitious, operates on the fancy, we shall conceive ourselves to be better acquainted with the actors, and enter with more spirit into the detail of their adventures, than it will be possible for us to do, if you always speak of them in the indefinite, the general, and therefore the unaffecting style of *the gentleman* and *the lady*, or *he* and *she*. This manner, besides, hath an air of concealment, and is ever reminding us, that they are people we know nothing about.

It ariseth from the same principle that whatever tends to subject the thing spoken of to the notice of our senses, especially of our eyes, greatly enlivens the expression. In this way the demonstrative pronouns are often of considerable use.

[2] The choice however is not quite arbitrary even in fictitious names. It is always injudicious to employ a name which, from its customary application, may introduce an idea unsuitable to the character it is affixed to. This error I think Lord Bolingbroke chargeable with in assigning the name *Damon* to his philosophical antagonist (Let. to M. De Pouilly). Though we read of a Pythagorean philosopher so called, yet in this country we are so much accustomed to meet with this name in pastorals and amorous songs, that it is impossible not to associate with it the notion of some plaintive shepherd or love-sick swain.

"I have coveted," says Paul to the elders of Ephesus, "no man's silver, or gold, or apparel; yea, ye yourselves know that *these* hands have ministered to my necessities, and to them that were with me."[3] Had he said, "*my* hands," the sentence would have lost nothing either in meaning or in perspicuity, but very much in vivacity. The difference to hearers is obvious, as the former expression must have been accompanied with the emphatic action of holding up his hands to their view. To readers it is equally real, who in such a case instantaneously enter into the sentiments of hearers. In like manner, the English words *yon* and *yonder* are more emphatical, because more demonstrative than the pronoun *that*, and the adverb *there*. The two last do not necessarily imply that the object is in sight, which is implied in the two first. Accordingly, in these words of Milton,

> ————For proof look up,
> And read thy fate in *yon* celestial sign.[4]——

The expression is more vivid than if it had been, "*that* celestial sign." "Sit ye here," saith our Lord, "whilst I go and pray *yonder*."[5] The adverb *there* would not have been near so expressive.[6] Though we cannot say properly that pronouns or adverbs, either of place or of time, are susceptible of genera and species, yet we can say (which amounts to the same as to the effect) that some are more and some less limited in signification.

To the above remarks and examples on the subject of *specialty*, I shall only add, that in composition, particularly of the descriptive kind, it invariably succeeds best for brightening the image, to advance from general expressions to more special, and thence again to more particular. This, in the language of philosophy, is descending. We descend to particulars; but in the language of oratory it is ascending. A very beautiful climax will sometimes be constituted in this manner, the reverse will often have all the effect of an anti-climax. For an example of this order in description, take the following passage from the Song of Solomon: "My beloved spake and said to me, Arise, my love, my fair, and come away; for lo, the winter is past, the rain is over and gone, the flowers appear on the earth, the time of the singing of birds is come, and the voice of the turtle is heard in our land; the fig-tree putteth forth her green figs, and the vines, with the tender grape, per-

[3] Acts xx. 33, 34. [4] Paradise Lost. [5] Matt. xxvi. 36.

[6] Le Clerc thus renders the original into French, "Asseyez-vous ici, pendant que je m'en irai prier *là*." At the same time sensible how weakly the meaning is expressed by the adverb *là*, he subjoins in a note, "Dans un lieu qu'il leur montrait du doigt." The English version needs no such supplement.

fume the air. Arise, my love, my fair, and come away."[7] The poet here, with admirable address, begins with mere negatives, observing the absence of every evil which might discourage his bride from hearkening to his importunate request: then he proceeds by a fine gradation to paint the most inviting circumstances that could serve to ensure the compliance of the fair. The first expression is the most general; "The winter is past." The next is more special, pointing to one considerable and very disagreeable attendant upon winter, *the rain;* "the rain is over and gone." Thence he advanceth to the positive indications of the spring, as appearing in the effects produced upon the plants which clothe the fields, and on the winged inhabitants of the grove. "The flowers appear on the earth, and the time of the singing of birds is come." But as though this were still too general, from mentioning birds and plants, he proceeds to specify *the turtle*, perhaps considered as the emblem of love and constancy; *the fig-tree* and *the vine*, as the earnest of friendship and festive joy, selecting that particular with regard to each, which most strongly marks the presence of the all-reviving spring. "The voice of the turtle is heard in our land, the fig-tree putteth forth her green figs, and the vines with the tender grape perfume the air." The passage is not more remarkable for the liveliness, than for the elegance of the picture it exhibits. The examples are all taken from whatever can contribute to regale the senses and awaken love. Yet reverse the order, and the beauty is almost totally effaced.

So much for that quality in proper terms which confers vivacity on the expression.

SECTION II.—*Rhetorical Tropes.*

PART I.—*Preliminary Observations concerning Tropes.*

I come now to inquire how far the judicious use of tropes is also conducive to the same end. It hath been common with rhetoricians to rank under the article of diction, not only all the tropes, but even the greater part of the figures of eloquence, which they have uniformly considered as qualities or ornaments merely of elocution, and therefore as what ought to be explained among the properties of style. It is however certain, that some of them have a closer connexion with the thought than with the expression, and by consequence fall not so naturally to be considered here. Thus all the kinds of comparison, as they imply a likeness in the *things*, and not in the *symbols*, belong properly to the thought. Nay, some com-

[7] Chap. ii. 10, 11, 12, 13.

parisons, as was remarked above,[8] are not merely illustrations of a particular sentiment, but are also arguments from analogy in support of it. And if thus comparison holds more directly of thought than of language, the same may doubtless be said of all those other figures which I have already observed are but different modes of exhibiting a comparison.

It must be owned, however, that metaphor, though no other in effect than comparison in epitome, hath at least as intimate a connexion with the style as with the sentiment, and may therefore be considered under either head. That we may perceive the reason of this peculiarity, let it be observed, that there is a particular boldness in metaphor, which is not to be found in the same degree in any of the figures of rhetoric. Without any thing like an explicit comparison, and commonly without any warning or apology, the name of one thing is obtruded upon us, for the name of another quite different, though resembling in some quality. The consequence of this is, that as there is always in this trope an apparent at least, if it cannot be called a real impropriety, and some degree of obscurity, a new metaphor is rarely to be risked. And as to ordinary metaphors, or those which have already received the public sanction, and which are commonly very numerous in every tongue, the metaphorical meaning comes to be as really ascertained by custom in the particular language as the original, or what is called the literal meaning of the word. And in this respect metaphors stand on the same foot of general use with proper terms.

What hath been now observed concerning metaphor may with very little variation be affirmed of these three other tropes, synecdoche, metonymy, and antonomasia. These are near akin to the former, as they also imply the substitution of one word for another, when the things signified are related. The only difference among them is, that they respect different relations. In *metaphor* the sole relation is resemblance; in *synecdoche*, it is that which subsisteth between the species and the genus, between the part and the whole, and between the matter and the thing made from it; in *metonymy*, which is the most various of the tropes, the relation is nevertheless always reducible to one or other of these three, causes, effects, or adjuncts; in *antonomasia*, it is nearly that of the individual to the species, or conversely. There is one trope, *irony*, in which the relation is contrariety. But of this I shall have occasion to speak when I come to consider that quality of style which hath been named animation.

On a little attention it will be found to be a plàin consequence of what hath been observed above, that though any

[8] Book I. Chap. vii. Sect. 2, on engaging attention.

simile, allegory, or prosopopeia is capable of being translated (and that even without losing any of its energy) from one tongue into another, a metaphor, a synecdoche, or a metonymy (for this holds more rarely of antonomasia), which is both significant and perspicuous in an original performance, is frequently incapable of being rendered otherwise than by a proper word. The corresponding metaphor, synecdoche, or metonymy, in another language will often be justly chargeable with obscurity and impropriety, perhaps even with absurdity. In support of this remark let it be observed, that the noun *sail* in our tongue is frequently used, and by the same trope the noun *puppis* in Latin, to denote a ship. Let these synecdoches of a part for the whole, which are so very similar, be translated and transposed, and you will immediately perceive, that a man could not be said to speak Latin, who in that language should call a ship *velum;* nor would you think that he spoke better English, who, in our language, should call it a *poop.*[9] These tropes therefore are of a mixed nature. At the same time that they bear a reference to the primitive signification, they derive from their customary application to the figurative sense, that is, in other words, from the use of the language, somewhat of the nature of proper terms.

In further confirmation of this truth it may be remarked, that of two words even in the same language, which are synonymous, or nearly so, one will be used figuratively to denote an object which it would be unsufferable to employ the other to denote, though naturally as fit for suggesting it. It hath been said, that "an excellent *vein* of satire runs through the whole of Gulliver's travels:" substitute here *artery* in the room of *vein*, and you will render the sentence absolutely ridiculous. The two words *beast* and *brute* are often metaphorically applied to human creatures, but not in the same signification. The former denotes either a *blockhead* or a *voluptuary* of the grossest kind; the latter, one in the highest degree *unmannerly* and *ferocious*. Accordingly we speak of *beastly* ignorance; we say, "gluttony is a *beastly* vice;" but we should say, "his behaviour to those unhappy people was quite *brutal*." The word *brutish*, however, though derived

[9] This doctrine might be illustrated by innumerable examples, if it were necessary. For an instance take that expression of Cicero (Pro Ligario), "Cujus latus ille mucro petebat? Here we have a synecdoche in the word *mucro*, and a metaphor in the word *petebat*, neither of which can be suitably rendered into English. "Whose side did that point seek?" is a literal version, but quite intolerable. "Whom did you mean to assail with that sword?" Here the sense is exhibited, but as neither trope is rendered, much of the energy is lost. In like manner in the phrase, "Vario Marte pugnatum est," "They fought with various success;" there is a metonymy in the word *Marte*, which no translator into any modern language, who hath common sense, would attempt to transplant into his version. See Traité des Tropes, par M. du Marsais, Art. vii. 4.

from the same root, is employed like *beastly*, to denote stupid or ignorant. Thus to say of any man, "he acted *brutishly*," and to say "he acted *brutally*," are two very different things. The first implies, he acted *stupidly;* the second, he acted *cruelly* and *rudely*. If we recur to the nature of the things themselves, it will be impossible to assign a satisfactory reason for these differences of application. The usage of the language is therefore the only reason.

It is very remarkable that the usages in different languages are in this respect not only different, but even sometimes contrary; insomuch that the same trope will suggest opposite ideas in different tongues. No sort of metonymy is commoner amongst every people than that by which some parts of the body have been substituted to denote certain powers or affections of the mind, with which they are supposed to be connected. But as the opinions of one nation differ on this article from those of another, the figurative sense in one tongue will by no means direct us to the figurative sense in another. The same may be said of different ages. A commentator on Persius has this curious remark, "Naturalists affirm, that men laugh with the spleen, rage with the gall, love with the liver, understand with the heart, and boast with the lungs."[9] A modern may say with Sganarelle in the comedy, "It was so formerly, but we have changed all that."[1] For so unlike are our notions, that the spleen is accounted the seat of melancholy and ill-humour. The word is accordingly often used to denote that temper; so that with us a splenetic man, and a laughing merry fellow, form two characters that are perfect contrasts to each other. The heart we consider as the seat, not of the understanding, but of the affections and of courage. Formerly indeed we seem to have regarded the liver as the seat of courage; hence the term *milk-livered* for cowardly.[2]

One plain consequence of the doctrine on this head which I have been endeavouring to elucidate, is, that in every nation where from time to time there is an increase of knowledge and an improvement in the arts, or where there often appear new

[9] Cornutus on these words of the first satire, *Sum petulanti splene cachinno.*—"Physici dicunt homines splene ridere, felle irasci, jecore amare, corde sapere, et pulmone jactare." In the ancient piece called the Testaments of the Twelve Patriarchs, supposed to be the work of a Christian of the first century, we find these words in the testament of Nephtali, for illustrating that God made all things good, adapting each to its proper use, Καρδιαν εις φρονησιν, ἡπαρ προς θυμον, χολην προς πικριαν, εις γελωτα σπληνα, νεφρους εις πανουργιαν. Grab. Spicil. Patrum, 1 Sec. t. i. ed. 2, p. 212.

[1] "Cela était autrefois ainsi; mais nous avons changé tout cela." Le Malade malgré lui. MOLIERE.

[2] From these things we may observe, by the way, how unsafe it is in translating, especially from an ancient language into a modern, to reckon that because the proper sense in two words of the different languages corresponds, the metaphorical sense of the same words will correspond also. In this last respect the words, as we have seen, may nevertheless be very different in signification, or even opposite. I think, in particular, that many translators

works of genius in philosophy, history, or poetry, there will be in many words a transition more or less gradual, as that improvement is more or less rapid, from their being the figurative to their being the proper signs of certain ideas, and sometimes from their being the figurative signs of one, to their being the figurative signs of another idea. And this, by the way, discloseth to us one of the many sources of mutation to be found in every tongue. This transition will perhaps more frequently happen in metaphor than in any other tropes, inasmuch as the relation of resemblance is generally less striking, and therefore more ready to be overlooked, than those relations on which the others are founded. Yet that they too will sometimes be affected by it, we have no reason to question. That in those metonymies in particular, of which some instances have been given, wherein the connexion may be justly accounted more imaginary than real, such changes in the application should arise, might naturally be expected. The transition from the figurative to the proper, in regard to such terms as are in daily use, is indeed inevitable. The word *vessel* in English hath doubtless been at first introduced by a synecdoche to signify a *ship*, the genus for the species, but it is now become by use as much a proper term in this signification as the word ship itself.

With regard to metaphor, it is certain, that in all languages there are many words which at first had one sense only, and afterwards acquired another by metaphorical application, of which words both senses are now become so current, that it would be difficult for any but an etymologist to determine which is the original and which the metaphorical. Of this kind in the English tongue are the substantives, *conception*, *apprehension*, *expression;* the first of these, *conception*, when it notes an action of the mind, and when the beginning of pregnancy in a female, is alike supported by use; the second and third terms, *apprehension* for seizure, and *expression* for squeezing out, are now rather uncommon. Yet these are doubtless the primitive significations.

It may be further remarked, that in some words the metaphorical sense hath justled out the original sense altogether, so that in respect of it they are become obsolete. Of this kind in our tongue are the verbs *to train*, *to curb*, *to edify*, *to enhance*, the primitive significations whereof were *to draw*, *to bend*, *to build*, *to lift*. And if one should now speak of the

of the Bible have been betrayed into blunders, through not sufficiently adverting to this circumstance. For instance, nothing at first appears to be a juster, as well as a more literal version of the Greek σκληροκαρδιος, than the English *hard-hearted*. Yet I suspect that the true meaning of the former term, both in the Septuagint and in the New Testament, is not *cruel*, as the English word imports, but *indocile, intractable*. The general remark might be illustrated by numberless examples, but this is not the place.

acuteness of a razor, or of the *ardour* of the fire, we could not say that to a linguist he would speak unintelligibly, but by every man of sense he would be thought to express himself both pedantically and improperly. The word *ruminate*, though good in the metaphorical sense, to denote *musing* on a subject, would scarcely be admitted, except in poetry, in the literal sense, for *chewing the cud*. Thus it happens with languages as with countries; strangers received at first through charity, often in time grow strong enough to dispossess the natives.

Now, in regard to all the words which fall under the two last remarks, whatever they were formerly, or in whatever light they may be considered by the grammarian and the lexicographer, they cannot be considered as genuine metaphors by the rhetorician. I have already assigned the reason. They have nothing of the effect of metaphor upon the hearer. On the contrary, like proper terms, they suggest directly to his mind, without the intervention of any image, the ideas which the speaker proposed to convey by them.

From all that hath been said, it evidently follows, that those metaphors which hold mostly of the thought, that is, those to which the ear hath not been too much familiarized, have most of the peculiar vivacity resulting from this trope; the invariable effect of very frequent use being to convert the metaphorical into a proper meaning. A metaphor hath undoubtedly the strongest effect when it is first ushered into the language; but by reason of its peculiar boldness, this, as was hinted already, is rarely to be hazarded, I may say it ought never to be hazarded, unless when both the perspicuity is secured to an ordinary understanding by the connexion, and the resemblance suggested is very striking. A new metaphor (and the same holds, though in a lower degree, of every trope) is never regarded with indifference. If it be not a beauty, it is a blemish. Besides, the more a language advanceth in richness and precision, and the more a spirit of criticism prevails among those who speak it, the more delicate the people become in this respect, and the more averse to the admission of new metaphors. It is even proper it should be so, there not being the same plea of necessity in such languages, as in those that are but poorly supplied with words. Hence it is that in modern times, the privilege of coining those tropes is almost confined to poets and orators; and as to the latter, they can hardly ever be said to have this indulgence, unless when they are wrought up to a kind of enthusiasm by their subject. Hence also have arisen those qualifying phrases in discourse, which, though so common in Greek and Latin, as well as in modern languages, are rarely, if ever, to be met with either in the rudest or in the most ancient tongues. These are, *so to speak*, *if I may thus express myself*, and the like.

I cannot help remarking, before I conclude this article of the origin of tropes, and of the changes they undergo, through the gradual operation of custom, that critics ought to show more reserve and modesty than they commonly do, in pronouncing either on the fitness or on the beauty of such as occur sometimes in ancient authors. For first it ought to be observed (as may be collected from what has been shown above) that the less enlightened a nation is, their language will of necessity the more abound in tropes, and the people will be the less shy of admitting those which have but a remote connexion with the things they are employed to denote. Again, it ought to be considered, that many words which appear as tropical to a learner of a distant age, who acquires the language by the help of grammars and dictionaries, may, through the imperceptible influence of use, have totally lost that appearance to the natives, who considered them purely as proper terms. A stranger will be apt to mistake a grammatical for a rhetorical trope, or even an accidental homonymy for a far-fetched figure. Lastly, it ought to be remembered how much the whole of this matter is everywhere under the dominion of caprice, and how little the figurative part of the language of any people is susceptible of a literal translation, that will be accounted tolerable, into the language of any other. If these things were properly attended to, I imagine we should, on these subjects, be more diffident of our own judgment, and consequently less captious and decisive.

So much for the nature of tropes in general, and those universal principles on which in every tongue their efficacy depends; and so much for the distinction naturally consequent on those principles, into grammatical tropes and tropes rhetorical.

PART II.—*The different sorts of Tropes conducive to Vivacity.*

I now consider severally the particular ways wherein rhetorical tropes may be rendered subservient to vivacity.

1. *The Less for the more General.*

The first way I shall mention is, when, by means of the trope, a species is aptly represented by an individual, or a genus by a species. I begin with this, because it comes nearest that speciality in the use of proper terms, from which, as was evinced already, their vivacity chiefly results. Of the individual for the species I shall give an example from our celebrated satirist Mr. Pope.

May some choice patron bliss each grey goose quill!
May every Bavius have his Bufo still![3]

Here, by a beautiful antonomasia, Bavius, a proper name, is made to represent one whole class of men, Bufo, also a proper name (it matters not whether real or fictious), is made to represent another class. By the former is meant every bad poet, by the latter every rich fool who gives his patronage to such. As what precedes in the Essay secures the perspicuity (and in introducing tropes of this kind, especially new ones, it is necessary that the perspicuity be thus secured), it was impossible in another manner to express the sentiment with equal vivacity.

There is also a sort of antonomasia to which use hath long ago given her sanction, and which therefore needs not be introduced with much precaution.

Such is the following application of famous names; a Solomon for a wise man, a Crœsus for a rich man, a Judas for a traitor, a Demosthenes for an orator, and a Homer for a poet. Nor do these want a share of vivacity, when apposite and properly managed.

That kind of synecdoche by which the species is put for the genus is used but sparingly in our language. Examples, however, occur sometimes, as when an assassin is termed a *cut-throat*, or a fiction a *lie*, as in these words of Dryden:

The cock and fox the fool and knave imply,
The truth is moral, tho' the tale a *lie*.

In like manner, slaughter, especially in battle, is by poets sometimes denominated *murder*, and legal prosecution *persecution*. Often in these instances the word may justly be said to be used without a figure. It may, however, in general be affirmed of all those terms, that they are more vivid and forcible, for this single reason, because they are more special.

There is one species of the *onomatopeia* which very much resembles the *antonomasia* just now taken notice of. It is when a verb is formed from a proper name, in order to express some particular action, for which the person to whom the name belonged was remarkable. An example of this we have in the instructions which Hamlet gave the players who were to act his piece before the king and queen. He mentioned his having seen some actors who in their way out-heroded Herod, intimating, that by the outrageous gestures they used in the representation, they overacted even the fury and violence of that tyrant. This trope hath been admirably imitated by Swift, who says concerning Blackmore, the author of a translation of some of the psalms into English verse,

[3] Prologue to the Satires.

Sternhold himself he out-sternholded.

How languid in comparison of this would it have been to say, that in Sternhold's own manner Sir Richard outdid him. But it must be owned, that this trope, the *onomatopeia*, in any form whatever, hath little scope in our tongue, and is hardly admissible except in burlesque.

2. *The most Interesting Circumstance distinguished.*

The second way I shall take notice of, wherein the use of tropes may conduce to vivacity, is when the trope tends to fix the attention on that particular of the subject which is most interesting, or on which the action related, or fact referred to, immediately depends. This bears a resemblance to the former method; for by that an individual serves to exhibit a species, and a species a genus; by this a part is made to represent the whole, the abstract, as logicians term it, to suggest the concrete, the passion its object, the operation its subject, the instrument the agent, and the gift the giver. The tropes which contribute in this way to invigorate the expression, are these two, the synecdoche and the metonymy.

For an example of this in the synecdoche, let it be observed, that by this trope the word *hand* is sometimes used for man, especially one employed in manual labour. Now, in such expressions as the following,

All *hands* employ'd, the royal work grows warm;[4]

it is obvious, from the principles above explained, that the trope contributes to vivacity, and could not be with equal advantage supplied by a proper term. But in such phrases as these, "One of the hands fell overboard;" "All our hands were asleep," it is ridiculous, as what is affirmed hath no particular relation to that part specified. The application of tropes in this undistinguishing manner, is what principally characterizes the contemptible cant of particular professions. I shall give another example. A *sail* with us frequently denotes a *ship*. Now to say, "We descried a *sail* at a distance," hath more vivacity than to say, "We descried a *ship*," because in fact the sail is that part which is first discovered by the eye; but to say "Our sails ploughed the main," instead of "Our ships ploughed the main," would justly be accounted nonsensical, because what is metaphorically termed *ploughing the main*, is the immediate action of the keel, a very different part of the vessel. To produce but one other instance, the word *roof* is emphatically put for house in the following quotation:

[4] Dryden.

Return to her? and fifty men dismiss'd?
No; rather I abjure all *roofs*, and choose
To be a comrade with the wolf and owl,
To wage against the enmity o' th' air,
Necessity's sharp pinch——— [5]

The notion of a house as a shelter from the inclemencies of the sky, alluded to in these lines, directly leads the imagination to form a more vivid idea of that part of the building which is over our heads.[6]

It was observed that the metonymy also contributes in this way to vivacity. It doth so by substituting the instrument for the agent, by employing the abstract to represent the concrete, or by naming the passion for its object, the gift for the giver, the operation for the subject. Of the first sort, the instances are very common; as when we say of a poem, that it is the production of an elegant *pen*, instead of an elegant writer. In the same way *pencil* is sometimes used for painter. It must be owned that the triteness of such expressions considerably lessens their value, and that for a reason explained in the preceding part of this section. It is however certain, that what vivacity can justly be ascribed to them, ariseth purely from the principle which hath just now been illustrated in the synecdoche; namely a coincidence in the expression with the bent of the imagination, both pointing to that particular with which the subject spoken of is immediately connected. Nay, so close is the relation between this species of the metonymy, and that of the synecdoche above exemplified, that the same expression may sometimes be considered indifferently as belonging to either trope. Thus in the quotation brought from Dryden, "All *hands* employed," it is of no consequence whether we denominate the word *hands* one or other, a part for the whole, or the instrument for the agent.

[5] Shakspeare's Lear.

[6] The Latin example quoted from Tully in a note on the first part of this section, affords a good illustration of this doctrine. "Cujus latus ille *mucro* petebat?" Mucro for gladius, the point for the weapon, is in this place a trope particularly apposite. From the point the danger immediately proceeds; to it therefore, in any assault, the eye of both the assailant and of the assailed are naturally directed; of the one that he may guide it aright, and of the other that he may avoid it. Consequently on it the imagination will fix, as on that particular which is the most interesting, because on it the event directly depends: and wherever the expression thus happily assists the fancy by coinciding with its natural bent, the sentiment is exhibited with vivacity. We may remark by the way, that the specifying of the part aimed at, by saying, *Cujus latus*, and not simply *quem*, makes the expression still more graphical. Yet *latus* here is no trope, else it had been *Quod latus*, not *Cujus latus*. But that we may conceive the difference between such a proper use of tropes as is here exemplified, and such an injudicious use as noway tends to enliven the expression, let us suppose the orator had intended to say, "He held a sword in his hand." If instead of the proper word he had employed the *synecdoche*, and said "*Mucronem* manu tenebat," he would have spoken absurdly, and counteracted the bent of the fancy, which in this instance leads the attention to the hilt of the sword, not to the point.

The second species of metonymy mentioned, the abstract for the concrete, occurs much seldomer, but hath also in the same way a very good effect. Isaac Bickerstaff, in his lucubrations, acquaints us with a visit which an eminent rake and his companions made to a Protestant nunnery erected in England by some ladies of rank. "When he entered," says the author, "upon seeing a servant coming towards him, with a design to tell him, this was no place for them, up goes my grave *Impudence* to the maid."[7] Every body must perceive that the expression would have been incomparably fainter if he had said, "Up goes my grave *impudent fellow* to the maid." The reason is obvious, an *impudent fellow* means, one who, amongst other qualities, has that of impudence; whereas, by personifying the abstract, you leave no room for thinking of any other quality; the attention is entirely fixed on that to which the action related is imputable, and thus the natural tendency of the fancy is humoured by the expression.

The last species of this trope I took notice of, if that can be called one species which is so various in its appearances, presenting us sometimes with the passion instead of its object, sometimes with the operation instead of its subject, and sometimes with the gift instead of the giver, is in very frequent use. By this trope the Almighty hath been styled "the *terror* of the oppressor, and the *refuge* of the oppressed;" which, though the same in sense, is more emphatical than "the object of terror to the oppressor, and the giver of refuge to the oppressed." "The Lord is my *song*," says Moses, "he is become my *salvation*,"[8] that is, the subject of my song, the author of my salvation. Dryden makes Lord Shaftesbury style the Duke of Monmouth,

> The people's *prayer*, the glad diviner's theme,
> The young men's *vision*, and the old men's *dream*.[9]

Here the terms *prayer*, *vision*, *dream* (for the word theme is literal) are used each for its respective subject. Nothing is more natural or more common amongst all nations, the simplest as well as the most refined, than to substitute the passion for its object. Such tropes as these, my *love*, my *joy*, my *delight*, my *aversion*, my *horror*, for that which excites the emotion, are to be found in every language. Holy writ abounds in them; and they are not seldom to be met with in the poems of Ossian. "The *sigh* of her secret soul," is a fine metonymy of this kind, to express the youth for whom she sighs in secret. As the vivacity of the expression in such quotations needs no illustration to persons of taste; that the cause of this vivacity ariseth

[7] Tatler, No. 32.
[8] Exod. xv. 2.
[9] Absalom and Achitophel.

from the coincidence of the expression with the bent of the imagination, fixing on the most interesting particular, needs no eviction to persons of judgment.

3. *Things Sensible for Things Intelligible.*

A third way wherein tropes may be rendered subservient to vivacity is, when things intelligible are represented by things sensible. There is no truth more evident than that the imagination is more strongly affected by what is perceived by the senses, than by what is conceived by the understanding. If therefore my subject be of things only conceivable, it will conduce to enliven the style, that the tropes which I employ, when I find it convenient to employ tropes, exhibit to the fancy things perceivable.

I shall illustrate this doctrine first in metaphors. A metaphor, if apposite, hath always some degree of vivacity, from the bare exhibition of likeness, even though the literal and the figurative senses of the word belong to the same class of objects; I mean only in this respect the same, that they be both sensible or both intelligible. Thus a *blunder* in the administration of public affairs, hath been termed a *solecism* in politics, both things intelligible. Again when the word *sails* is employed to denote the wings of a fowl, or conversely, when the word *wings* is adopted to signify the sails of a ship, both objects are of the same class, as both are things sensible; yet these metaphors have a considerable share of vivacity, by reason of the striking resemblance, both in the appearance of the things signified, and in their use. The last, however, is the best, for a reason which will be given in the next remark. But in general it may be asserted, that in the representation of things sensible there is less occasion for this trope: accordingly, this application of it is now almost entirely left to the poets. On the contrary, if we critically examine any language, ancient or modern, and trace its several terms and phrases to their source, we shall find it hold invariably, that all the words made use of, to denote spiritual and intellectual things, are in their origin metaphors, taken from the objects of sense. This shows evidently that the latter have made the earliest impressions, have by consequence first obtained names in every tongue, and are still, as it were, more present with us, and strike the imagination more forcibly than the former.

It may be said that if this observation be true, it is to no purpose to mention the method of enlivening the diction, the representing of intelligible things by sensible images, since it is impossible by language to represent them otherwise. To this I answer, that the words of which I am speaking I call metaphors in their origin; notwithstanding which, they may be at present agreeably to what was formerly observed, proper terms. When speaking of tropes in general, it was remarked that many words, which to a grammatical eye appear metaphors, are in the rhetorician's estimate no metaphors at all. The ground of this difference is, that the grammarian and the rhetorician try the words by very different tests. The touchstone of the former is etymology, that of the latter is present use. The former peruseth a page, and perhaps finds not in the whole ten words that are not metaphorical; the latter examines the same page, and doth not discover in it a single metaphor. What critic, for example, would ever think of applying this appellation to terms such as these, *spirit*, *evidence*, *understanding*, *reflection?* Or what etymologist would not acknowledge that to this trope solely these terms had owed their birth?

But I proceed to give examples of vivacity, by true rhetorical metaphors, wherein things sensible are brought to signify things intelligible. Of this the following is one from Pope:

At length Erasmus, that great injur'd name,
(The glory of the priesthood, and the shame!)
Stemm'd the wild *torrent* of a barbarous age,
And drove those holy Vandals off the stage.

Here the almost irresistible influence of general manners, which is an object purely of the understanding, is very appositely and vivaciously represented by a *torrent*, an object both of the sight and of the feeling. By the same vivid kind of metaphor *light* is used for knowledge, *bridle* for restraints; we speak of *burning* with zeal, being *inflamed* with anger, and having a *rooted* prejudice.

But metaphor is not the only trope which can in this way confer vivacity; metonymy frequently in a similar manner promotes the same end. One very common species of the metonymy is, when the badge is put for the office, and this invariably exhibits a sensible in lieu of an intelligible object. Thus we say the *mitre* for the priesthood, the *crown* for the royalty; for the military occupation we say, the *sword*, and for the literary professions, those especially of theology, law, and medicine, the common expression is the *gown*. Often also in those metonymies wherein the cause is put for the effect, and contrariwise, in those wherein the effect is put for the cause, we have the same thing exemplified, a sensible object presented to the mind instead of an intelligible. Of the former, the cause for the effect, the following lines of Dryden may serve as an illustration:

'Tis all thy business business how to shun,
To bask thy naked body in the *sun*.[1]

[1] Dryden's Persius.

Though the rhyme had permitted the change, the word *sunshine* instead of sun, would have rendered the expression weaker. The luminary itself is not only a nobler and distincter, but a more immediate object to the imagination than its effulgence, which, though in some respect sensible as well as the other, is in some respect merely intelligible, it not being perceived directly no more than the air, but discovered by reflection from the things which it enlightens. Accordingly, we ascribe to it neither magnitude nor figure, and scarce with propriety even colour. As an exemplification of the latter, the effect or something consequential for the cause, or at least the implement for the motive of using it, these words of scripture will serve, "The *sword* without, and terror within,"[2] where the term sword, which presents a particular and perceivable image to the fancy, must be more picturesque than the word *war*, which conveys an idea that is vague and only conceivable, not being otherwise sensible but by its consequences.

4. *Things Animate for Things Lifeless.*

A fourth way in which tropes may promote vivacity, is when things sensitive are presented to the fancy instead of things lifeless; or, which is nearly the same, when life, perception, activity, design, passion, or any property of sentient beings, is by means of the trope attributed to things inanimate. It is not more evident that the imagination is more strongly affected by things sensible than by things intelligible, than it is evident that things animate awaken greater attention and make a stronger impression on the mind than things senseless. It is for this reason that the quality of which I am treating hath come to be termed vivacity, or liveliness of style.

In exemplifying what hath been now advanced, I shall proceed in the method which I took in the former article, and begin with metaphor. By a metaphor of this kind, a literary performance hath been styled the *offspring* of the brain; by it a state or government in its first stage is represented as a child in these lines of Dryden,

> When empire in its *childhood* first appears,
> A watchful fate o'ersees its tender years.[3]

In the two last examples we have things lifeless exhibited by things animate. In the following, wherein the effect is much the same, sense, feeling, and affection are ascribed metaphorically to inanimate matter. Thomson, describing the influence of the sunbeams upon the snow in the valley, thus vividly and beautifully expresseth himself,

[2] Deut. xxiii. 25.

[3] Almanzor.

———Perhaps the vale
Relents awhile to the reflected ray.[4]

"Every hedge," says the Tatler, "was *conscious* of more than what the representations of enamoured swains admit of."[5] Who sees not how much of their energy these quotations owe to the two words *relents* and *conscious?* I shall only add, that it is the same kind of metaphor which hath brought into use such expressions as the following: a *happy* period, a *learned* age, the *thirsty* ground, a *melancholy* disaster.

There are several sorts of metonymy which answer the same purpose. The first I shall mention is that wherein the inventor is made to denote the invention. *Ceres,* for instance, to denote bread, *Bacchus* wine, *Mars* war, or any of the pagan deities to denote that in which he is especially interested, as *Neptune* the sea, *Pluto* hell, *Pallas* wisdom, and *Venus* the amorous affection. It must be owned, that as this kind seems even by the ancients to have been confined to the discoveries, attributes, or dominions ascribed in their mythology to the gods, it is of little or no use to us moderns.[6]

Another tribe of metonymies, which exhibits things living for things lifeless, is when the possessor is substituted for his possessions. Of this we have an example in the gospel: "Wo unto you, scribes and pharisees, hypocrites, for ye devour the *families* of widows."—Here the word *families* is used for their means of subsistence.[7] Like to this is an expression in Balaam's prophecy concerning Israel: "He shall eat up the *nations* his enemies."[8]

A third tribe of metonymies which often presents us with animate instead of inanimate objects, is when the concrete is made to signify the abstract; as *the fool* used for folly, *the knave* for knavery, *the philosopher* for philosophy. I shall illustrate this by some examples. Dryden hath given us one of this kind that is truly excellent:

The slavering cudden propt upon his staff,
Stood ready gaping with a grinning laugh,

---

[4] Winter.

[5] Tatler, No. 7.

[6] Even when such tropes occur in ancient authors, they can scarcely be translated into any modern tongue, as was hinted on Part First in regard to the phrase "Vario *Marte* pugnatum est." Another example of the same thing, "Sine *Cerere* et *Baccho* friget *Venus*."

[7] Matt. xxiii. 14. The noun οικιας may be rendered either *families* or *houses*. The last, though used by our translators, hath here a double disadvantage. First, it is a trope formed upon a trope (which rarely hath a good effect), the *house* for the family, the thing containing for the thing contained, and the *family* for their means of living; secondly, ideas are introduced which are incompatible. There is nothing improper in speaking of a person or family being devoured, but to talk of devouring a house is absurd. It may be destroyed, demolished, undermined, but not devoured.

[8] Numb. xxiv. 8.

To welcome her awake, nor durst begin
To speak, but wisely kept the *fool* within.[9]

The whole picture is striking. The proper words, every one of them, are remarkably graphical, as well as the metonymy with which the passage concludes. Another from the same hand,

Who follow next a double danger bring,
Not only hating David but the *king*.[1]

As David himself was king, both the proper name and the appellative would point to the same object, were they to be literally interpreted. But the opposition here exhibited manifestly shows that the last term, *the king*, is employed by metonymy to denote the royalty. The sense therefore is, that they have not only a personal hatred to the man that is king, but a detestation of the kingly office. A trope of this kind ought never to be introduced but when the contrast, as in the present example, or something in the expression, effectually removes all obscurity and danger of mistake. In the passage last quoted, there is an evident imitation of a saying recorded by historians of Alexander the Great, concerning two of his courtiers, Craterus and Hephæstion: "Craterus," said he, "loves *the king*, but Hephæstion loves *Alexander*." Grotius hath also copied the same mode of expression, in a remark which he hath made, perhaps with more ingenuity than truth, on the two apostles Peter and John. The attachment of John, he observes, was to *Jesus*, of Peter to *the Messiah*.[2] Accordingly, their master gave the latter the charge of his church, the former that of his family, recommending to him in particular the care of Mary his mother. The following sentiment of Swift is somewhat similar:

I do the most that friendship can;
I hate *the viceroy*, love the man.

The viceroy, for the viceroyalty. I shall only add two examples more in this way: the first is from Addison, who, speaking of Tallard when taken prisoner by the allies, says,

An English muse is touch'd with generous woe,
And in the unhappy man forgets *the foe*.[3]

The foe, that is, his state of hostility with regard to us at the time: for the second I shall again recur to Dryden,

A tyrant's power in rigour is exprest,
The father yearns in the true prince's breast.

---

[9] Cymon and Iphigenia.

[1] Absalom and Achitophel.

[2] Annotationes in Johan. Intr.

[3] Campaign.

The father, to denote fatherly affection, or the disposition of a father. In fine, it may justly be affirmed of this whole class of tropes, that as metaphor in general hath been termed an allegory in epitome, such metaphors and metonymies as present us with things animate in the room of things lifeless are prosopopœias in miniature.

But it will be proper here to obviate an objection against the last-mentioned species of metonymy, an objection which seems to arise from what hath been advanced above. Is it possible, may one say, that the concrete put for the abstract should render the expression livelier, and that the abstract put for the concrete should do the same? Is it not more natural to conclude, that if one of these tropes serve to invigorate the style, the reverse must doubtless serve to flatten it? But this apparent inconsistency will vanish on a nearer inspection. It ought to be remembered that the cases are comparatively few in which either trope will answer better than the proper term, and the few which suit the one method, and the few that suit the other, are totally different in their nature. To affirm that in one identical case methods quite opposite would produce the same effect, might, with some appearance of reason, be charged with inconsistency; but that in cases not identical, nor even similar, contrary methods might be necessary for effecting the same purpose, is nowise inconsistent. But possibly the objector will argue on the principles themselves severally considered, from which, according to the doctrine now explained, the efficacy of the tropes ariseth: "If," says he, "the abstract for the concrete confers vivacity on the expression, by concentrating the whole attention on that particular with which the subject is most intimately connected, doth it not lose as much on the other hand, by presenting us with a quality instead of a person, an intelligible for a sensible, an inanimate for a living object?" If this were the effect the objection would be unanswerable. But it is so far otherwise, that in all such instances, by ascribing life, motion, human affections, and actions, to the abstract, it is in fact personified, and thus gains in point of energy the one way, without losing any thing the other. The same thing holds of congenial tropes, the dole for the donor, and the rest. In like manner, when the concrete is used for the abstract, there is, in the first place, a real personification, the subject being in fact a mere quality both inanimate and insensible: nor do we lose the particularity implied in the abstract, because, where this trope is judiciously used, there must be something in the sentence which fixes the attention specially on that quality. Thus, to recur to the preceding examples, when David and the king, though known to be the same person, are contradistinguished in the same line, the mind is laid under a necessity of considering the word *king* as implying purely that which constitutes him such, namely the royal power. The same may be said of the other instances. So far indeed I agree with the objector, that wherever the trope is not distinctly marked by the words with which it is connected, it is faulty and injudicious. It both misses vivacity and throws obscurity on the sentiment.

I have here examined the tropes so far only as they are subservient to vivacity, by presenting to the mind some image which, from the original principles of our nature, more strongly attaches the fancy than could have been done by the proper terms whose place they occupy. And in this examination I have found that they produce this effect in these four cases: first, when they can aptly represent a species by an individual, or a genus by a species; secondly, when they serve to fix the attention on the most interesting particular, or that with which the subject is most intimately connected; thirdly, when they exhibit things intelligible by things sensible; and fourthly, when they suggest things lifeless by things animate. How conducive the tropes are in like manner both to elegance and to animation will be examined afterwards. They even sometimes conduce to vivacity, not from any thing preferable in the ideas conveyed by them, but in a way that cannot properly come under consideration, till we inquire how far this quality depends on the number of the words, and on their arrangement.

PART III.—*The Use of those Tropes which are Obstructive to Vivacity.*

Let us now, ere we finish this article, bestow some attention on the opposite side (for contraries serve best to illustrate each other), and make a few remarks on those tropes which either have a natural tendency to render the expression more languid, or at least are noway fitted for enlivening the diction. That there are tropes whose direct tendency is even to enfeeble the expression is certainly true, though they are fewer in number and more rarely used than those which produce the contrary effect. The principal tropes of this kind which I remember at present are three sorts of the synecdoche, the genus for the species, the whole for a part, and the matter for the instrument or thing made of it, and some sorts of the metaphor, as the intelligible for the sensible. Of the genus for the species, which is the commonest of all, *vessel* for ship, *creature* or *animal* for man, will serve as examples. Of the whole for a part, which is the most uncommon, I do not recollect another instance but that of the man or woman by name, sometimes for the body only, sometimes only for the soul; as when we say, "Such a one was buried yesterday," that is, "the body of such a one was buried yesterday;" "Æneas saw his father in Elysium," that is, his father's ghost. The common phrase "all the world," for a great number of people, and some others of the same kind, have also been produced as examples, but improperly; for in all such expressions there is an evident hyperbole, the intention being manifestly to magnify the number. Of the third kind, the matter for what is made of it, there are doubtless several instances, such as *silver* for money, *canvas* for sail, and *steel* for sword.

It is proper to inquire from what principles in our nature tropes of this sort derive their origin, and what are the purposes which they are intended to promote. The answer to the first of the queries will serve effectually to answer both. First, then, they may arise merely from a disposition to vary the expression, and prevent the too frequent recurrence of the same sound upon the ear. Hence often the genus for the species. This is the more pardonable, if used moderately, as there is not even an apparent impropriety in putting at any time the genus for the species, because the latter is always comprehended in the former; whereas, in the reverse, there is inevitably an appearance of impropriety, till it is mollified by use. If one is speaking of a linnet, and sometimes instead of *linnet* says *bird*, he is considered rather as varying the expression than as employing a trope. Secondly, they may arise from an inclination to suggest contempt without rudeness; that is, not openly to express, but indirectly to insinuate it. Thus, when a particular man is called a creature or an animal, there is a sort of tacit refusal of the specific attributes of human nature, as the term implies only the direct acknowledgment of those enjoyed in common with the brutes, or even with the whole creation. The phrases *no creature*, and *every creature*, like *all the world*, are a kind of hyperbolic idioms, which come not under this category. Thirdly, they may proceed from a love of brevity in cases wherein perspicuity cannot be hurt. Thus to say,

Your friend Alexander lies here interr'd,

is briefer, and not less perspicuous, than to say, "The corpse of your friend Alexander—." Fourthly, they may spring from a desire to find a term that will make a better counterpart, in respect either of the sense or of the sound, to some other word which the speaker or the writer hath had occasion to use, the ideas conveyed by the two words being also related. This occasions sometimes not only that the genus is used for the species, but that the matter is made to signify the thing made of it; both of which will be further illustrated when I come to consider how far vivacity may result from arrangement. Fifthly (and this is the last source that occurs to my thoughts), tropes of this kind may arise from a desire of palliating the representation, and that either from humanity, from courtesy, or from decency.

By the first of the five principles above mentioned, if used discreetly, something is done for the sake of variety, where the vivacity of the expression is little affected; by the second, even a further end, a species of animation is attained; by the third and fourth, what is lost of vivacity in one way is more than compensated in another; but by the fifth, we are led to avoid this quality as a fault.

There are some subjects of which it may be necessary on certain occasions to speak, which, nevertheless, present an object to the imagination that is either disagreeable or indecent. It is sufficient that such things be hinted to the understanding, so that the meaning may be apprehended; it is by no means fit that they be painted in the liveliest colours to the fancy. There are some things which a painter may find it expedient to introduce into a picture, and to render just discoverable, by placing them in a shade, in the back-ground, or at a corner, which it would be extremely improper to set in such a point of view as would immediately attract and fix the eye of the spectator. The like doubtless holds with regard to the orator. And it hath been chiefly to veil without darkening what the smallest degree of delicacy requires us to avoid exposing in the strongest light, that certain sorts of tropes and modes of expression have first been brought into use. To the same cause is also to be ascribed the recourse that is often had to circumlocution, which will fall to be considered in the ensuing chapter.

All such tropes and modes of expression have come under the common denomination of the *euphemism*, a name that hath been assigned purely from the consideration of the purpose for which they are employed; which is to express in terms that are inoffensive an object in some respect or other offensive. The euphemism is not a distinct trope (as it hath improperly been accounted by some critics), but a certain application of other tropes, especially of metaphor and synecdoche, and even of some of the figures of elocution, the periphrasis in particular. Sometimes we are led to this from a principle of civility, or even of affection, when the plain and direct mention of an object might either recall grief, or hurt sensibility; and sometimes from ideas of decorum.

It is by a euphemism that the words *deceased* and *departed* came at first to be used instead of *dead*, which is no other than a synecdoche of the genus for the species; *falling asleep* for *dying*, which is a metaphor, there being an evident resemblance between sleep and death, and *stopping payment* for *becoming bankrupt*, which is a metonymy of the effect for the cause. There is, indeed, in employing this figure, the euphemism, more than in any other, a natural tendency to change. The reason may easily be deduced from the general doctrine concerning tropes, explained in the first part of this section. The frequent use of any word in this manner brings it insensibly to have all the effect of the proper term whose place it was intended to supply: no sooner is this effect produced by it, than the same principle that influenced us at first to employ it operates with equal strength in influencing us to lay it aside, and in its stead to adopt something newer and still more remote. The excessive delicacy of the French in this respect has given rise to expressions which it would not be easy to trace from any known trope or figure of oratory, and which, to say the truth, have something ridiculous in their appearance. Thus a *disbanded* regiment is with them a *reformed* regiment; a *cashiered* officer is a *reformed* officer, and a man is said to *reform* his equipage, when necessity obliges him to give it up; even the hangman, through the superabundance of their complaisance, is titled *the master of the high works*.[4] In the use of this figure among the ancients, superstition, in regard to some words which were thought to be of bad omen, seems to have had as great a share as either a delicate sympathy with the feelings of others, or a very nice sense of what is decent and cleanly.

As to the nature and extent of the last source which was assigned of the euphemism, it will be proper to be a little more particular. Those things which it is indecent to express vividly are always such as are conceived to have some turpitude in them, either natural or moral. An example of this decency in expression, where the subject hath some natural turpitude, you will find in Martha's answer, as it is in the original, when our Saviour gave orders to remove the stone from the sepulchre of her brother Lazarus, "Lord, by this time he *smelleth*, for he hath been dead four days."[5] In our version it is somewhat indelicately, not to say indecently, rendered *stinketh*. Our translators have in this instance unnecessarily receded from their ordinary rule of keeping as close as possible to the letter. The synecdoche in this place answers just as well in English as in Greek: the perspicuity is such as secures the reader from the possibility of a mistake, at the same time that the expression is free from the indecency with which the other is chargeable. But if it be necessary to avoid a vivid exhibition of what appears uncleanly to the external senses, it is much more necessary in whatever may have a tendency to pollute the mind. It is not always the mention of vice as such, which has this tendency. Many of the most atrocious crimes may be mentioned with great plainness, without any such danger, and

[4] Le maître des hautes œuvres.

[5] John xi. 39, ηδη οζει.

therefore without the smallest indecorum. What the subjects are which are in this way dangerous, it is surely needless to explain. And as every person of sense will readily conceive the truth of the general sentiment, to propose without necessity to produce examples for the elucidation of it, might justly be charged with being a breach of that decency of which I am treating.

So much for the use that may be made of tropes in softening and even in enervating, as well as in enlivening and invigorating the expression; though it must be owned that the occasions are comparatively few on which the former purpose can be said to be expedient.

I shall only add a few remarks concerning the *catachresis*, which hath in like manner been improperly reckoned a separate trope. The reason that I have taken no notice of it hitherto is, that it is but rarely defensible in modern languages, which require the strictest regard to propriety. And even in a few cases wherein it is defensible, it is purely so because necessary; but it is seldom eligible, as it rarely contributes either to ornament or to strength. I shall explain myself by some instances.

One species of the catachresis is, when words are used in a signification that is very near their ordinary meaning, but not precisely the same. Examples of this would be a *high* man for a *tall* man, a *large* oration for a *long* oration, a *big* genius for a *great* genius. This, if any thing, would be classed under the metaphor, as there is a resemblance in the import of the words. Unluckily the word adopted is too near a coincidence with the right epithet to present an image to the fancy, at the same time that it is not entirely coincident, and therefore cannot be denominated a proper term. In this application the name *catachresis* is no more than another word for impropriety. Of this kind there is an example in the fifth commandment, as it runs in our version, "that thy days may be *long* (anglicè *many)* upon the land."[6]—It is impossible to avoid such blunders in translating, when one aims at being literal, without attending to the different geniuses of different tongues. In original performances they are more rarely to be met with, being just such improprieties as none but novices in the language are apt to fall into.

A second species of this figure is when words which, from their etymology, appear to be applicable solely to one kind of thing, come afterwards to be applied to another, which is nearly related in its nature or design, but with which, nevertheless, the analysis of the word will not accord. This is sometimes not only excusable from necessity, as when the language doth not furnish a proper term, but sometimes also receives the sanction

[6] Exod. xx.

of general use. And in this case, whatever it was originally, it becomes proper. I shall give some examples of this in our own tongue. As it is probable that amongst our Saxon ancestors candleholders were solely made of wood, they were properly denominated *candlesticks;* afterwards, when, through an increase of wealth and luxury, such utensils were made of metal, the old name was nevertheless retained, and at first by a catachresis applied to these. But the application is now ratified, and the word appropriated, by custom. The name *ink-horn*, denoting a portable case for holding *ink*, probably at first made only of *horn*, is a similar instance. In like manner the word *parricide* in English, like *parricida* in Latin, at first perhaps signified only the murderer of his father, but hath come to be equally applied to him who murders his mother, his brother, or his sister. In all these instances there was an excuse at first from necessity, the language not affording words strictly proper. But now having obtained the universal suffrage, which in every country gives law to language, they need no excuse. There is an instance of a catachresis of this kind in our translation of the Bible, which (not being supported by the plea of necessity) ought to be considered as a glaring impropriety; "He made the lever of brass, and the foot of it of brass, of the *looking-glasses* of the women."[7] It is however probable that the word *mirror* was not in such common use then as it is now. There are a few phrases which come under the same denomination, and which, though favoured by custom, being quite unnecessary, deserve to be exploded. Such, amongst others, are the following: the *workmanship* of God, for the work of God; a *man of war*, for a *ship of war;* and a *merchantman* for a trading vessel. The absurdity in the last two instances is commonly augmented by the words connected in the sequel, in which, by the application of the pronouns *she* and *her*, we are made to understand that the man spoken of is a female. I think this gibberish ought to be left entirely to mariners; amongst whom, I suppose, it hath originated.

The only remaining species of the catachresis, which I can recollect at present, is no other than a far-fetched and incongruous metaphor. Nothing can more justly be reduced under this class than the application of the attributes of one corporeal sense to the objects of another; as if we should say of a voice that it is *beautiful* to the ear; or of a face, that it is *melodious* to the eye. Nothing succeeds better, as hath been observed already, than metaphors taken from the objects of sensation, to denote the object of pure intellection; yet nothing generally succeeds worse than metaphors that are only transferred from sense to sense. I say *generally*, because such is

[7] Exod. xxxviii. 8

the omnipotence of fashion, in respect of language, that it is capable of conciliating us even to such applications. Thus the term *sweet* belongs properly to the sense of tasting alone; yet it hath been transferred to the senses of smelling, of hearing, and of seeing. We say a *sweet* scent, a *sweet* melody, a *sweet* prospect. The word *soft* in like manner belonged originally to the sense of touching, and to it only. Yet it hath been applied metaphorically, and (as we learn by the event) successfully to other senses. Thus we talk of a *soft* whisper, and Pope speaks of the *soft-eyed* virgin. Customary applications at length become proper, though they do not exhibit the primitive sense. For this reason, several of the aforesaid instances are not to be considered at present as examples of the *catachresis*. Sometimes, however, even a new catachresis of the last-mentioned kind, which is the most hazardous, will please the most fastidious critic. Take the following example from Young:—

> Her voice is but the *shadow* of a sound. [8]

The reason of our approbation in this case is, if I mistake not, that an allusion or comparison is suggested which exhibits more strongly the author's meaning, than it could have been exhibited by any other words in the same compass. The sentiment is, that the same relation which the shadow bears to the substance of which it is the shadow, the lady's voice bears to an ordinary sound.

Having now discussed what was proposed here concerning tropes, I shall conclude with observing that in this discussion there hath been occasion, as it were, incidentally to discover,—that they are so far from being the inventions of art, that, on the contrary, they result from the original and essential principles of the human mind;—that accordingly they are the same *upon the main*, in all nations, barbarous and civilized;—that the simplest and most ancient tongues do most abound with them, the natural effect of improvement in science and language, which commonly go together, being to regulate the fancy, and to restrain the passions;—that the sole business of art in this subject is to range the several tropes and figures into classes, to distinguish them by names, and to trace the principles in the mind which gave them birth.

The first, indeed, or rather the only people upon the earth, who have thought of classing under proper appellations the numerous tropes and figures of elocution, common to all languages, were the Greeks. The Latins, and all modern nations, have, in this particular, only borrowed from them, adopting the

[8] Universal Passion.

very names they used. But as to the tracing of those figures to the springs in human nature from which they flow, extremely little hath as yet been attempted. Nay, the names that have been given are but few, and by consequence very generical.—Each class, the metaphor and the metonymy in particular, is capable of being divided into several tribes, to which no names have yet been assigned.

It was affirmed that the tropes and figures of eloquence are found to be the same *upon the main* in all ages and nations. The words *upon the main* were added, because though the most and the principal of them are entirely the same, there are a few which presuppose a certain refinement of thought not natural to a rude and illiterate people. Such in particular is that species of the metonymy, the concrete for the abstract, and possibly some others. We shall afterwards perhaps have occasion to remark, that the modern improvements in ridicule have given rise to some which cannot properly be ranged under any of the classes above mentioned; to which, therefore, no name hath as yet been appropriated, and of which I am not sure whether antiquity can furnish us with an example.

SECTION III.—*Words considered as Sounds.*

When I entered on the consideration of vivacity as depending on the choice of words, I observed that the words may be either proper terms or rhetorical tropes; and whether the one or the other, they may be regarded not only as signs but as sounds, and consequently as capable in certain cases of bearing, in some degree, a natural resemblance or affinity to the things signified. The two first articles, proper terms and rhetorical tropes, I have discussed already, regarding only the sense and application of the words, whether used literally or figuratively. It remains now to consider them in regard to the sound, and the affinity to the subject of which the sound is susceptible. When, as Pope expresseth it, "the sound is made an echo to the sense,"[9] there is added in a certain degree, to the association arising from custom, the influence of resemblance between the signs and the things signified; and this doubtless tends to strengthen the impression made by the discourse. This subject, I acknowledge, hath been very much canvassed by critics; I shall therefore be the briefer in my remarks, confining myself chiefly to the two following points. First, I shall inquire what kinds of things language is capable of imitating by its sound, and in what degree it is capable;

[9] Essay on Criticism.

secondly, what rank ought to be assigned to this species of excellence, and in what cases it ought to be attempted.

PART I.—*What are articulate Sounds capable of imitating, and in what Degree?*

First, I shall inquire what kinds of things language is capable of imitating by its sound, and in what degree it is capable.

And here it is natural to think, that the imitative power of language must be greatest when the subject itself is things audible. One sound may surely have a greater resemblance to another sound, than it can have to any thing of a different nature. In the description therefore of the terrible thunder, whirlwind and tempest, or of the cooling zephyr and the gentle gale, or of any other thing that is sonorous, the imitation that may be made by the sound of the description will certainly be more perfect than can well be expected in what concerns things purely intelligible, or visible, or tangible. Yet even here the resemblance, if we consider it abstractly, is very faint.

The human voice is, doubtless, capable of imitating, to a considerable degree of exactness, almost any sound whatever. But our present inquiry is solely about what may be imitated by articulate sounds, for articulation greatly confines the natural powers of the voice; neither do we inquire what an extraordinary pronunciation may effectuate, but what power in this respect the letters of the alphabet have, when combined into syllables, and these into words, and these again into sentences, uttered audibly indeed and distinctly, but without any uncommon effort. Nay, the orator, in this species of imitation, is still more limited. He is not at liberty to select whatever articulate sounds he can find to be fittest for imitating those concerning which he is discoursing. That he may be understood, he is under a necessity of confining himself to such sounds as are rendered by use the signs of the things he would suggest by them. If there be a variety of these signs, which commonly cannot be great, he hath some scope for selection, but not otherwise. Yet so remote is the resemblance here at best, that in no language, ancient or modern, are the meanings of any words, except perhaps those expressing the cries of some animals, discoverable, on the bare hearing, to one who doth not understand the language.

Indeed, when the subject is articulate sound, the speaker or the writer may do more than produce a resemblance, he may even render the expression an example of that which he affirms. Of this kind precisely are the three last lines of the following quotation from Pope:—

These equal syllables alone require,
Tho' *o*ft th*e* *e*ar th*e* *o*pen vowels tire,
While expletives their feeble aid *do* join,
And ten low words oft creep in one dull line.[1]

But this manner, which, it must be owned, hath a very good effect in enlivening the expression, is not imitation, though it hath sometimes been mistaken for it, or rather confounded with it.

As to sounds inarticulate, a proper imitation of them hath been attempted in the same piece, in the subsequent lines, and with tolerable success, at least in the concluding couplet:—

Soft is the strain when Zephyr gently blows,
And the smooth stream in smoother numbers flows;
But when loud surges lash the sounding shore,
The hoarse rough verse should like the torrent roar.[2]

An attempt of the same kind of conformity of the sound to the sense, is perhaps but too discernible in the following quotation from Dryden:

O'er all the dreary coasts,
Dreadful gleams,
Dismal screams,
Fires that glow,
Shrieks of woe,
Sullen moans,
Hollow groans,
And cries of tortur'd ghosts.[3]

Milton's description of the opening of hell-gates ought not here to be overlooked.

——— On a sudden open fly
With impetuous recoil and jarring sound,
Th' infernal doors, and on their hinges grate
Harsh thunder———.[4]

The same author has, in another performance, given an excellent specimen in this way,

Grate on their scrannel pipes of wretched straw.[5]

He succeeds the better here, that what he says is evidently accompanied with a design of exciting contempt. This induceth us to make allowance for his leaving the beaten road in search of epithets. In this passage of the Odyssey—

[1] Essay on Criticism. [2] Ibid.
[3] Ode on St. Cecilia's Day. [4] Paradise Lost, B. ii.
[5] Lycidas. An imitation of a line of Virgil, Ecl. iii.
Stridenti miserum stipulâ disperdere carmen.

——————— His bloody hand
Snatch'd two unhappy of my martial band;
And dash'd like dogs against the stony floor;[6]

the sound, but not the abruptness of the crash, is, I imagine, better imitated than in the original, which on account of both, especially the last, was much admired by the critic of Halicarnassus. An excellent attempt in this way we have in a poem of Dyer;

———— The Pilgrim oft
At dead of night mid his oraison hears
Aghast the voice of time, disparting towers,
Tumbling all precipitate down-dash'd,
Rattling around, loud thundering to the moon.[7]

But the best example to be found in our language is, in my opinion, the following lines of Mr. Pope,

What! like Sir Richard, rumbling, rough, and fierce,
With arms, and George, and Brunswick crowd the verse,
Rend with tremendous sounds your ears asunder?
With gun, drum, trumpet, blunderbuss, and thunder?
Then all your muse's softer art display,
Let Carolina smooth the tuneful lay,
Lull with Amelia's liquid name the nine,
And sweetly flow through all the royal line.[8]

The success here is the greater that the author appears through the whole to deride the immoderate affectation of this over-rated beauty, with which some modern poetasters are so completely dazzled. On the whole, the specimens produced, though perhaps as good as any of the kind extant in our language, serve to evince rather how little than how much can be done in this way, and how great scope there is here for the fancy to influence the judgment.

But there are other subjects beside sound, to which language is capable of bearing some resemblance. Time and motion, for example, or whatever can admit the epithets of quick and slow, is capable in some degree of being imitated by speech. In language there are long and short syllables, one of the former being equal or nearly equal to two of the latter. As these may be variously combined in a sentence, and syllables of either kind may be made more or less to predominate, the sentence may be rendered by the sound more or less expressive of celerity or tardiness. And though even here the power of speech seems to be much limited, there being but two degrees

[6] Pope's Od. In Homer thus.
Συν δε δυω μαρψας, ὡστε σκυλακας ποτι γαιη
Κοπτ'————

[7] Ruins of Rome, Dodsley's Collection, vol. i. [8] Sat. 1.

in syllables, whereas the natural degrees of quickness or slowness in motion or action may be infinitely varied, yet on this subject the imitative power of articulate sounds seems to be greater and more distinctive than on any other. This appears to particular advantage in verse, when, without violating the rules of prosody, a greater or a less number of syllables is made to suit the time. Take the following example from Milton,

> When the merry bells ring round,
> And the jocund rebecs sound,
> Tŏ mān̆y̆ ă yōuth ănd mān̆y̆ ă māid
> Dancing in the chequer'd shade.[9]

In this passage the third line, though consisting of ten syllables, is, by means of two anapæsts, pronounced, without hurting the measure, in the same time with an iambic line of eight syllables, and therefore well adapted in sound to the airy diversion he is describing. At the same time it must be owned, that some languages have in this particular a remarkable superiority over others. In English the iambic verse, which is the commonest, admits here and there the insertion of a spondee, for protracting, or of an anapæst, as in the example quoted, for quickening the expression.[1]

But, in my opinion, Greek and Latin have here an advantage, at least in their heroic measure, over all modern tongues. Accordingly, Homer and Virgil furnish us with some excellent specimens in this way. But that we may know what our own tongue and metre is capable of effecting, let us recur to our own poets, and first of all to the celebrated translator of the Grecian bard. I have made choice of him the rather, as he was perfectly sensible of this beauty in the original, which he copied, and endeavoured, as much as the materials he had to work upon would permit him, to exhibit it in his version. Let us take for an example the punishment of Sisyphus in the other world, a passage which had on this very account been much admired in Homer by all the critics both ancient and modern.

> Up the high hill he heaves a huge round stone;
> The huge round stone resulting with a bound,
> Thunders impetuous down, and smokes along the ground.[2]

---

[9] L'Allegro.

[1] Perhaps the feet employed in ancient poetry are not in strict propriety applicable to the measures adopted by the English prosody. It is not my business at present to enter into this curious question. It suffices that I think there is a rhythmus in our verse plainly discernible by the ear, and which, as it at least bears some analogy to the Greek and Latin feet, makes this application of their names sufficiently intelligible.

[2] In Greek thus,

——————Λααν ανω ωθεσκε ποτι γοφον
Αυτις επειτα πεδονδε κυλινδετο λαας αναιδης. Od.

It is remarkable that Homer (though greatly preferable to his translator in both) hath succeeded best in describing the fall of the stone, Pope, in relating how it was heaved up the hill. The success of the English poet here is not to be ascribed entirely to the length of the syllables, but partly to another cause, to be explained afterwards.

I own I do not approve the expedient which this admirable versifier hath used, of introducing an Alexandrine line for expressing rapidity. I entirely agree with Johnson,[3] that this kind of measure is rather stately than swift: yet our poet hath assigned this last quality as the reason of his choice. "I was too sensible," says he in the margin, "of the beauty of this, not to endeavour to imitate it, though unsuccessfully. I have, therefore, thrown it into the swiftness of an Alexandrine, to make it of a more proportionable number of syllables with the Greek." Ay, but to resemble in length is one thing, and to resemble in swiftness is another. The difference lies here: in Greek, an hexameter verse whereof all the feet save one are dactyls, though it hath several syllables more, is pronounced in the same time with an hexameter verse whereof all the feet save one are spondees, and is, therefore, a just emblem of velocity; that is, of moving a great way in a short time. Whereas the Alexandrine line, as it consists of more syllables than the common English heroic, requires proportionably more time to the pronunciation. For this reason, the same author, in another work, has, I think, with better success, made choice of this very measure to exhibit slowness:

> A needless Alexandrine ends the song,
> That, like a wounded snake, drags its slow length along.[4]

It deserves our notice, that in this couplet he seems to give it as his opinion of the Alexandrine, that it is a dull and tardy measure. Yet, as if there were no end of his inconsistency on

In Latin verse, Vida, in his Art of Poetry, hath well exemplified this beauty, from his great master Virgil.

> Ille autem membris, ac mole ignavius ingens
> Incedit tardo molimine subsidendo.

Here not only the frequency of the spondees, but the difficulty of forming the elisions; above all, the spondee in the fifth foot of the second line instead of a dactyl, greatly retard the motion. For the contrary expression of speed,

> Si se forte cavâ extulerit mala vipera terrâ,
> Tolle moras, cape saxa manu, cape robora, pastor,
> Ferte citi flammas, date tela, repellite pestem.

Here everything concurs to accelerate the motion, the number of dactyls, no elision, no diphthong, no concurrence of consonants, unless where a long syllable is necessary, and even there the consonants of easy pronunciation.

[3] Rambler, No. 92. [4] Essay on Criticism.

this subject, he introduceth a line of the same kind a little after in the same piece, to represent uncommon speed:

> Not so when swift Camilla scours the plain,
> Flies o'er th' unbending corn, and skims along the main.[5]

A most wonderful and peculiar felicity in this measure to be alike adapted to imitate the opposite qualities of swiftness and slowness. Such contradictions would almost tempt one to suspect that this species of resemblance is imaginary altogether. Indeed, the fitness of the Alexandrine to express, in a certain degree, the last of these qualities, may be allowed, and is easily accounted for. But no one would ever have dreamt of its fitness for the first, who had not been misled by an erroneous conclusion from the effect of a very different measure, Greek and Latin hexameter. Yet Pope is not the only one of our poets who hath fallen into this error. Dryden had preceded him in it, and even gone much further. Not satisfied with the Alexandrine, he hath chosen a line of fourteen syllables, for expressing uncommon celerity:

> Which urg'd, and labour'd, and forc'd up with pain,
> Recoils, and rolls impetuous down, and smokes along the plain.[6]

Pope seems to have thought that in this instance, though the principle on which Dryden proceeded was good, he had exceeded all reasonable bounds in applying it; for it is this very line which he hath curtailed into an Alexandrine in the passage from the Odyssey already quoted. Indeed, the impropriety here is not solely in the measure, but also in the diphthongs *oi*, and *ow*, and *ai*, so frequently recurring, than which nothing, not even a collision of jarring consonants, is less fitted to express speed. The only word in the line that seems adapted to the poet's view is the term *impetuous*, in which two short sylables, being crowded into the time of one, have an effect similar to that produced by the dactyl in Greek and Latin. Creech, without the aid of an Alexandrine, hath been equally, if not more unsuccessful. The same line of the Latin poet he thus translates:

> And with swift force rolls thro' the humble plain.

Here the sentiment, instead of being imitated, is contrasted by the expression. A more crawling spondaic verse our heroic measure hardly ever admits.

At the same time, in justice to English prosody, it ought to be remarked, that it compriseth one kind of metre, the

[5] Essay on Criticism.

[6] Lucretius, B. iii.

anapæstic, which is very fit for expressing celerity, perhaps as much as any kind of measure ancient or modern. But there is in it a light familiarity, which is so ill adapted to the majesty of the iambic, so as to render it but rarely admissible into poems written in this measure, and, consequently, either into tragedy or into epic.

Ere I conclude what may be said on the subject of motion, I shall observe further, that there are other affections of motion beside swiftness and slowness, such as vibration, intermission, inequality, which, to a certain degree, may be imitated in the sound of the description. The expression,

Troy's turrets tottered——

in the translation of the Iliad, is an instance of the first, the vibration being represented by the frequent and quick recurrence of the same letters, ranged a little differently. In the line

Tumbling all precipitate down-dash'd,

already quoted from the Ruins of Rome, there is an attempt to imitate the motion as well as the sound. The last of the four following lines from Milton contains also a tolerable imitation of both:

Oft on a plat of rising ground,
I hear the far-off curfew sound,
Over some wide-watered shore,
Swinging slow with sullen roar.[7]

Another very natural subject of imitation is size, or whatever the terms great or little may be applied to, literally or metaphorically. Things grand may be imitated by long and well-sounding words, things bulky by long and ill-sounding words, things little by short words. The connexion here is as obvious as in either of the two former cases; but the power of our language is rather less. It affords so little variety in the choice of words in respect of length, that often the grandest objects in nature cannot be expressed with propriety otherwise than by a poor monosyllable. Bulkiness, accompanied with motion, will fall to be exemplified in the next article.

A fourth subject of imitation in language is difficulty and ease. There is a considerable difference in this respect in

[7] Il Penseroso.

the pronunciation of different words and sentences, which, if happily accommodated to the sentiment, adds to the effect of the expression. If, for instance, what is difficultly acted be difficultly pronounced, and if, on the contrary, what is performed with facility be uttered with ease, there will result a certain degree of vivacity from this slight resemblance. For it is an invariable maxim, that the ear is grated with hearing what the organs of speech find it uneasy to articulate. Several things contribute to render pronunciation difficult. First, the collision of vowels; that is when one syllable ends with a vowel, and the next (it matters not whether it be in the same word or not) begins with the same vowel, or with one which approaches to it in the sound. R*e*-*e*nter, c*o*-*o*perate, r*e*-*i*nforce, r*e*-*a*nimate, th*o*' *o*ft, th*e* *e*ar, th*e* *o*pen, are examples of this. A certain effort is required to keep them as it were asunder, and make both be distinctly heard as belonging to different syllables. When the vowels are very unlike in sound, or the formation of the one is easily accomplished after the articulation of the other, they have not the same effect. Thus, in the words var*ie*ty, c*oe*val, the collision doth not create a perceptible difficulty. Now, as difficulty is generally the cause of slowness in any operation, such a clashing of vowels is often employed to represent a tardy or lingering motion.[8] A second cause of difficulty in utterance is the frequent recurring of the aspirate (h,) especially when placed between two vowels that are both sounded. It is this which renders the translation of the passage above quoted from the Odyssey so significant of the same qualities.

> Up the *h*igh *h*ill *h*e *h*eaves a *h*uge round stone.

A like effect is produced by any of the mutes that are aspirated, as the *th* and *ph*, or *f*, especially if combined with other consonants. The following line of Chaucer is not a bad example of this:

> He through the thickest of the throng gan threke.[9]

A third cause of difficulty in pronunciation is the clash of two or more jarring consonants. Some consonants are easily combined; the combinations of such are not expressive of this quality, but it is not so with all. An instance of this difficulty we have in the following line:

[8] It is chiefly from this cause that the line in the Odyssey above quoted is so expressive of both. Λααν ανω ωθεσκε——

[9] Knight's Tale.

> And strains ´from hard bound brains´ six lines a-year.[1]

We have here once five consonants, sometimes four, and sometimes three, which are all pronounced without an intervening vowel. The difficulty is rendered still more sensible by the double pause, which occasions a very drawling movement. Another example I shall take from the same author.

> When Ajax strives some rock's vast weight to throw,
> The line too labours, and the words move slow.[2]

In the first of these lines, the harsh combination of consonants make the difficulty of pronunciation very observable; in the second, the author hath not been so successful. I know not how it might affect the more delicate ear of an Italian, but if we compare it with the generality of English verses, we shall find it remarkably easy and flowing. It has nothing in respect of sound, either in the syllables separately or in the measure, that in the least favours the sentiment, except only in its ending in a spondee, instead of an iambus. But this is too common in our poesy to have any effect that is worthy of notice. Vida's translator, in a passage extremely similar, hath been happier, if he may not be thought to have exceeded in this respect:

> If some large weight his huge arm strive to shove,
> The verse too labours, the throng'd words scarce move.[3]

First, the word *verse* is harsher than *line;* secondly, the ending is in two spondees, which, though perhaps admissible into the iambic measure, is very rare, and hath for that reason a more considerable effect. A fourth cause of difficulty in the pronunciation is the want of harmony in the numbers. This is frequently an effect of some of the fore-mentioned causes, and may be illustrated by some of the examples already quoted. In the following passage from Milton, one of the most unharmonious in the book, hugeness of size, slowness and difficulty of motion, are at once aptly imitated;

> ———— Part, huge of bulk!
> Wallowing, unwieldy, enormous in their gait,
> Tempest the ocean.[4] ————

An illustration of tardiness, difficulty, and hesitancy through fear, the same author hath also given us in the ill-compacted lines which follow:

[1] Pope, Fragment of a Satire.
[2] Essay on Criticism.
[3] Pitt.
[4] Paradise Lost, B. vii.

He came,´ and with him Eve,´ more loth,´ tho' first
To offend, discountenanc'd both, and discomposed.[5]

Several of the foregoing causes concur in the following couplet:

So he with difficulty and labour hard,
Mov'd on, with difficulty and labour he.[6]

A fifth cause of difficulty, the last I shall take notice of, is when there is a frequent recurrence of the same letters or syllables, especially where the measure requires a quick pronunciation, because then there is the greatest risk of mistake and confusion.[7]

I shall just mention another subject of imitation by sound which is very general, and may be said to comprehend every thing not included in those above mentioned. The agreeable in things may be adumbrated to us by smooth and pleasant sounds, the disagreeable by such as are harsh and grating. Here, it must be owned, the resemblance can be but very remote, yet even here it will sometimes serve to enliven the expression.

Indeed the power of numbers, or of a series of accordant sounds, is much more expressive than that of single sounds. Accordingly, in poetry we are furnished with the best examples in all the kinds; and as the writer of odes hath in this respect a much greater latitude than any other kind of versifier, and at pleasure may vary his measure with his subject, I shall take a few illustrations from our lyric poets. All sorts of English verse, it hath been justly remarked, are reducible to three, the iambic, the trochaic, and the anapæstic. In the first of these the even syllables are accented, as some choose to express it, or as others, the even syllables are long; in the second it is on the odd syllables that the accent rests; in the third, two unaccented syllables are followed by one accented. The nearer the verses of the several kinds are to perfection, the more exactly they correspond with the definitions just now given; though each kind admits deviations to a certain degree, and in long poems even requires them, for the sake of variety. The iambus is expressive of dignity and grandeur; the trochee, on the contrary, according

5 Paradise Lost, B. x. 6 Paradise Lost, B. ii.

7 An excellent example of this kind we have from the Iliad,

Πολλα δ' αναντα, καταντα, παραντα τε δοχμια τ' ηλθον.

This recurrence is the happier here, as it is peculiarly descriptive of rugged ways and jolting motion.

to Aristotle,[8] is frolicsome and gay. It were difficult to assign a reason of this difference that would be satisfactory; but of the thing itself, I imagine, most persons will be sensible on comparing the two kinds together. I know not whether it will be admitted as a sufficient reason, that the distinction into metrical feet hath a much greater influence in poetry on the rise and fall of the voice, than the distinction into words; and if so, when the cadences happen mostly after long syllables, the verse will naturally have an air of greater gravity, than when they happen mostly after the short. An example of the different effects of these two measures we have in the following lines of an admired modern, whose death lately afforded a just subject of lamentation to every good man as well as to every friend of the muses.

> Thee the voice, the dance obey,
> Temper'd to thy warbled lay.
> O'er Idalia's velvet green
> The rosy crowned loves are seen
> On Cytherea's day,
> With antic sports, and blue ey'd pleasures,
> Frisking light in frolic measures;
> Now pursuing, now retreating,
> Now in circling troops they meet;
> To brisk notes in cadence beating,
> Glance their many-twinkling feet.
> Slow melting strains their queen's approach declare:
> Where'er she turns the Graces homage pay.
> With arms sublime, that float upon the air,
> In gliding state she wins her easy way:
> O'er her warm cheek and rising bosom move
> The bloom of young desire, and purple light of love.[9]

The expression of majesty and grace in the movement of the six last lines is wonderfully enhanced by the light and airy measure of the lines that introduce them.—The anapæst is capable, according as it is applied, of two effects extremely different; first it is expressive of ease and familiarity, and accordingly is often used with success both in familiar epistles and in pastoral. The other effect is an expression of hurry, confusion, and precipitation. These two, however different, may be thus accounted for. The first is a consequence of its resemblance to the style of conversation: there are so many particles in our language, such as monosyllabic pronouns, prepositions, conjunctions, and articles, on which the accent never rests, that the short syllables are greatly supernumerary. One consequence of this is, that common chat is with greater ease, as I imagine, reduced to this measure, than to any other. The second consequence ariseth purely from its rapidity compared with other measures. This effect it is especially fitted to produce, when

[8] Rhet. Lib. iii.

[9] Gray's Progress of Poesy.

it is contrasted with the gravity of the iambic measure, as may be done in the ode; and when the style is a little elevated, so as to be sufficiently distinguished from the style of conversation. All these kinds have been employed with success in the Alexander's Feast, an ode that hath been as much celebrated as perhaps any in our language, and from which I propose to produce some illustrations. The poet, on recognizing Jove as the father of his hero, hath used the most regular and perfect iambics—

> The líst'ning crówd admíre the lófty sóund,
> A présent déitý they shóut aróund,
> A présent déitý the váulted róofs rebóund.
> With rávish'd eárs
> The mónarch heárs,
> Assúmes the gód
> Affécts to nód,
> And séems to sháke the sphéres.

But when he comes to sing the jovial god of wine, he very judiciously changes the measure into the brisk trochaic.

> Bácchus éver fáir and yóung.
> Drínking jóys did fírst ordáin.
> Bácchus bléssings áre a tréasure,
> Drínking is the sóldier's pléasure.
> Rích the tréasure,
> Swéet the pléasure,
> Swéet is pléasure áfter páin.

Again, when he describes his hero as wrought up to madness, and setting fire to the city in a fit of revenge, he with great propriety exhibits this phrenzy in rapid anapæsts, the effect of which is set off the more strongly by their having a few iambic lines interspersed.

> Revénge, revénge, Timótheus críes,
> See the fúries aríse!
> See the snákes that they réar,
> How they híss in their háir,
> And the spárkles that flásh from their eýes!—
> Behóld how they tóss their tórches on hígh,
> How they póint to the Pérsian abódes
> And glíttering témples of their hóstile góds,
> The princes appláud with a fúrious joy;
> And the king seiz'd a flámbeau with zéal to destróy——

So much for the power of numbers. It may not be amiss now, ere I conclude this topic, to make a few cursory remarks on the imitative powers of the several letters which are the elements of all articulate sounds. And first, soft and delicate sounds are mostly occasioned by an equal mixture of consonants with short and monophthong vowels; the consonants being chiefly those denominated liquids, *l*, *m*, *n*, *r*, and those among the mutes called slender, *p*, *t*, *k*, or *c*, and *ch* when they sound as *k;* to these add *v*, also *z*, and *s*, when they sound as in the two words *Zion* and *Asia*. In like manner the duplication of a consonant sounds more delicately than the combination of different consonants. Thus *ammiro* is softer than *admiro*, *fatto* than *facto*, *atto* than *apto*, and *disse* than *dixe*. Secondly, strong and loud sounds are better exhibited by diphthongs and long vowels, those of the mutes called middle, and which comparatively may be termed *hard*, *b*, *d*, *g*, in both its sounds, and *j;* especially when these are combined with liquids which render them more sonorous, without occasioning harshness, as in the words, *bombard*, *thunder*, *clangour*, *bludgeon*, *grumble*. Thirdly, to roughness the letter *h* contributes as well as the gutturals. Such is the Greek χ, to which there is no corresponding sound in English, though there is in Spanish and in German; also those of the mutes called aspirates, as *f*, or *ph*, and *th*, in both its sounds,[1] the double *r*, and all uncouth combinations. Fourthly, to sharp and cutting sounds the following letters best contribute, *s* when it sounds as in *mass*, *c* when it has the same sound, *ch* when it sounds as in *chide*, *x*, *sh*, and *wh;* from the abounding of which letters and combinations amongst us, foreigners are apt to remark I know not what appearance of whistling or hissing in our conversation. Indeed, the word *whistle* is one whose sound is as expressive of the signification as perhaps any other word whatever. Fifthly, obscure and tingling sounds are best expressed by the nasals, *ng* and *nk*, as in *ringing*, *swinging*, *twanging*, *sinking;* by the *sn*, as in *snuffle*, *sneeze*, *snort;* and even by the *n* simply when it follows another liquid or a mute, and when the vowel (if there be a vowel interposed between it and the precedent consonant) is not very audibly pronounced, as in *morn*, *horn*, *sullen*, *fallen*, *bounden*, *gotten*, *beholden*, *holpen*.—This sound formerly much abounded in English. It was not only the termination of many of the participles, but also of most plurals both of nouns and of verbs. As a plural termination, if we except a very few nouns, we may say it is now entirely banished, and very much, perhaps too much, disused in participles. The sound is unmusical, and consequently when too frequent, offensive, but may nevertheless have a good effect when used sparingly. Besides, it would be convenient, especially in verse, that we could oftener distinguish the preterite from the participle, than our language permits.

Now, of the five sorts of sound above explained, it may be remarked by the way, that the first is characteristic of the Italian, the second of the Spanish, the third of the Dutch, and

[1] Of these one occurs in the noun *breath*, the other in the verb *breathe*. The first is the roughest.

perhaps of most of the Teutonic dialects: the fourth of the English, and the fifth of the French, whose final *m* and *n*, when not followed by a vowel, and whose terminations *ent* and *ant* are much more nasal than the *ng* and *nk* of the English. I suspect too, both from their prosody and from their pronunciation, that of all the languages above mentioned, the French is the least capable of that kind of imitation of which I have been speaking. On the other hand, I think, but in this opinion I am not confident, that of all those languages the English is, on the whole, the most capable. There is perhaps no particular excellence of sound in which it is not outdone by one or other of them; the Italian hath doubtless more sweetness, the Spanish more majesty, the German perhaps more bluster: but none of them is in this respect so various as the English, and can equal it in all the qualities.

So much for the properties in things that are susceptible of a kind of imitation by language, and the degree in which they are susceptible.

PART II.—*In what esteem ought this kind of Imitation to be held; and when ought it to be attempted?*

It remains now to consider what rank ought to be assigned to this species of beauty, and in what cases it ought to be attempted.

As to the first of these inquiries, from what hath been already said it appears very plain that the resemblance or analogy which the sound can be made in any case to bear to the sense, is at best, when we consider the matter abstractly, but very remote. Often a beauty of this kind is more the creature of the reader's fancy, than the effect of the writer's ingenuity.

Another observation which will assist us in determining this question is, that when the other properties of elocution are attained, the absence of this kind of imagery, if I may express it by so strong a term, occasions no defect at all. We never miss it. We never think of it. Whereas an ambiguous, obscure, improper, languid, or inelegant expression is quickly discovered by a person of knowledge and taste, and pronounced to be a blemish. Nor is this species of resemblance to be considered as on the same footing with those superior excellencies, the want of which, by reason of their uncommonness, is never censured as a fault, but which, when present, give rise to the highest admiration. On the contrary, not the absence only, but even the attainment of this resemblance, as far as it is attainable, runs more risk of passing unheeded than any other species of beauty in the style. I ought however to except from this the imitation produced by the different kinds of measure in poetry, which, I acknowledge, is sufficiently observable, and hath a much stronger effect than any other whereof language alone is susceptible. The reason why in other cases it may so readily pass unnoticed, is, that even the richest and most diversified language hath very little power, as hath been shown already, in this particular. It is therefore evident that if the merit of every kind of rhetorical excellence is to be ascertained by the effect, and I know of no other standard, to this species we can only assign with justice the very lowest rank. It ought consequently ever to give place to the other virtues and ornaments of elocution, and not they to it.

As to the other question, In what cases it may be proper to aim at the similitude in sound of which I have been treating; those cases will appear to one who attentively considers what hath been already advanced on the subject, to be comparatively few. Hardly any compositions in prose, unless those whose end is to persuade, and which aim at a certain vehemence in style and sentiment, give access to exemplify this resemblance. And even in poetry it is only the most pathetic passages, and the descriptive parts, to which the beauty whereof I am speaking seems naturally adapted. The critical style, the argumentative, and the didactic, by no means suit it. Yet it may be said, that some of the examples above quoted for the illustration of this subject are taken from writings of the kind last mentioned, from Pope on Criticism, and Vida on Poesy. But it must be observed that the authors, in the passages alluded to, are discoursing on this very subject. An exemplification was therefore necessary in them, in order to convey to their readers a distinct idea of what they meant to recommend.

I must further observe, that even in those poems wherein this kind of resemblance is most suitable, it is only in a few passages, when something more striking than ordinary comes to be described, that it ought to be attempted. This beauty in language is not to be considered as bearing an analogy to dress by which the whole person is adorned, but to those jewels which are intended solely for the decoration of certain parts, and whose effect depends very much on their being placed with judgment. It is an invariable rule, that in every poem and oration, whatever be the subject, the language, in the general tenor of it, ought to be harmonious and easy. A deviation in a few particular passages may not only be pardonable, but even meritorious. Yet this merit, when there is a merit in introducing harsh sounds and jarring numbers, as on some occasions there doubtless is, receives great relief from its contrariety to the general flow of the style. And with regard to the general flow, as I observed already, the rule holds invariably. Supposing the subject of the piece were the twelve labours of Hercules, should the poet, in order to adapt his language to his theme, choose words of the most difficult utterance, and through the whole performance studiously avoid harmony and grace, far from securing to himself admiration, he would not even be read.

I shall only add, that though it is not prudent in an author to go a step out of his way in quest of this capricious beauty, who, when she does not act spontaneously, does nothing gracefully, a poet in particular may not unreasonably be more solicitous to avoid her opposite, especially in the expression of the more striking thoughts; as nothing in such a case can be more ungraceful in the style, than when, either in sound or in measure, it serves as a contrast to the sentiment.

CHAPTER II.

Of Vivacity as depending on the Number of the Words.

SECTION I.—*This Quality explained and exemplified.*

When I entered on the subject of vivacity,[2] I observed that this quality of style might result either from a happy choice of words, from their number, or from their arrangement. The first I have already discussed, and shown how words may conduce to vivacity, not only from their sense, whether they be proper or figurative, but also from their sound.

I come now to consider how far vivacity may be affected by the number of the words. On this article it may be established as a maxim that admits no exception, and it is the only maxim which this article admits, that the fewer the words are, provided neither propriety nor perspicuity be violated, the expression is always the more vivid. "Brevity," says Shakspeare, "is the soul of wit."[3] Thus much is certain, that of whatever kind the sentiment be, witty, humorous, grave, animated, or sublime, the more briefly it is expressed, the energy is the greater, or the sentiment is the more enlivened, and the particular quality for which it is eminent the more displayed.

Among the ancients the Lacedæmonians were the most remarkable for conciseness. To use few words, to speak energetically, and to be laconic, were almost synonymous. As when the rays of the sun are collected into the focus of a burning-glass, the smaller the spot is which receives them,

[2] Book III. Chap. i. [3] Hamlet.

compared with the surface of the glass, the greater is the splendour; or as in distillation, the less the quantity of spirit is, that is extracted by the still, compared with the quantity of liquor from which the extraction is made, the greater is the strength; so in exhibiting our sentiments by speech, the narrower the compass of words is, wherein the thought is comprised, the more energetic is the expression. Accordingly we shall find, that the very same sentiment expressed diffusely, will be admitted barely to be just; expressed concisely, will be admired as spirited.

To recur to examples, the famous answer returned by the Countess of Dorset, to the letter of Sir Joseph Williamson, secretary of state to Charles the Second, nominating to her a member for the borough of Appleby, is an excellent illustration of this doctrine. "I have been bullied," says her ladyship, "by an usurper, I have been neglected by a court, but I will not be dictated to by a subject; your man sh'n't stand."[4] If we consider the meaning, there is mention made here of two facts, which it was impossible that any body of common sense, in this lady's circumstances, should not have observed, and of a resolution in consequence of these, which it was natural for every person who had a resentment of bad usage to make. Whence then results the vivacity, the fire which is so manifest in the letter? Not from any thing extraordinary in the matter, but purely from the laconism of the manner. An ordinary spirit would have employed as many pages to express the same thing, as there are affirmations in this short letter. The epistle might in that case have been very sensible, and withal very dull, but would never have been thought worthy of being recorded as containing any thing uncommon, or deserving a reader's notice.

Of all our English poets none hath more successfully studied conciseness, or rendered it more conducive to vivacity, than Pope. Take the following lines as one example of a thousand which might be produced from his writings:—

> See how the world its veterans rewards!
> A youth of frolics, an old age of cards:
> Fair to no purpose, artful to no end;
> Young without lovers, old without a friend;
> A fop their passion, but their prize a sot:
> Alive ridiculous, and dead forgot.[5]

Nothing is more evident than that the same passage may have great beauties and great blemishes. There is a monotony in the measure of the above quotation (the lines being all so equally divided by the pauses) which would render it, if much longer, almost as tiresome to the ear as a speech in a French

[4] Catalogue of royal and noble authors.

[5] Moral Essays, Ep. ii.

tragedy; besides, the unvaried run of antitheses through five successive lines is rather too much, as it gives an air of quaintness to the whole. Yet that there is a great degree of liveliness in the expression is undeniable. This excellence is not, I acknowledge, to be ascribed solely to the brevity. Somewhat is doubtless imputable both to the words themselves, and to their arrangement; but the first mentioned is still the principal cause. The trope in the fifth line, *their passion*, for *the object of their passion*, conduceth to vivacity, not only as being a trope, but as rendering the expression briefer, and thereby more nervous. Even the omission of the substantive verb, of the conjunctions, and of the personal pronouns, contribute not a little to the same end. Such ellipses are not indeed to be adopted into prose, and may even abound too much in verse. This author in particular hath sometimes exceeded in this way, and hath sacrificed both perspicuity and a natural simplicity of expression to the ambition of saying a great deal in few words. But there is no beauty of style for which one may not pay too high a price. And if any price ought to be deemed too high, either of these certainly ought; especially perspicuity, because it is this which throws light on every other beauty.

Propriety may sometimes be happily violated. An improper expression may have a vivacity, which, if we should reduce the words to grammatical correctness, would be annihilated. Shakspeare abounds in such happy improprieties. For instance,—

> And be these juggling fiends no more believed,
> That palter with us in a double sense,
> That *keep the word of promise to our ear,*
> *And break it to our hope.*[6]

In another place,

> ————————It is a custom,
> *More honoured in the breach than the observance.*[7]

David's accusation of Joab, that *he had shed the blood of war in peace,*[8] or what Solomon says of the virtuous woman, that *she eateth not the bread of idleness,*[9] serves also to verify the same remark. Every body understands these expressions; every body that knows English perceives an impropriety in them, which it is perhaps impossible to mend without destroying their energy.[1] But a beauty that is unperceivable is no

[6] Macbeth.
[7] Hamlet.
[8] 1 Kings, ii. 5.
[9] Prov. xxxi. 37.
[1] The Hebraism in each of these quotations from Scripture constitutes the peculiarity: and as the reasons are nearly equal with regard to all modern languages, for either admitting or rejecting an oriental idiom, the observa-

beauty. Without perspicuity, words are not signs, they are empty sounds; speaking is beating the air, and the most fluent declaimer is but as a sounding brass and a tinkling cymbal.

Yet there is a sort and a degree of obscurity which ought not to be considered as falling under this censure. I speak not of those sentences wherein more is meant than meets the ear, the literal meaning being intended purely to suggest a further meaning, which the speaker had chiefly in view. I gave some examples in this way when on the subject of perspicuity, and showed that they are not to be regarded as exceptions from the rule.[2] But what I here principally allude to is a species of darkness, if I may call it so, resulting from an excess of vivacity and conciseness, which, to a certain degree, in some sorts of composition, is at least pardonable. In the ode, for instance, the enthusiastic fervour of the poet naturally carries him to overlook those minutenesses in language, on which perspicuity very much depends. It is to abruptness of transition, boldness of figure, laconism of expression, the congenial issue of that frame of mind in which the piece is composed, that we owe entirely the

> Thoughts that breathe, and words that burn.

Hence proceeds a character of the writing, which may not unhappily be expressed in the words of Milton, "Dark with excessive bright." I have compared vivacity produced by a

tion will equally affect other European tongues into which the Bible is translated. A scrupulous attention to the purity of the language into which the version is made, must often hurt the energy of the expression. Sacy, who in his translation hath been too solicitous to Frenchify the style of Scripture, hath made nonsense of the first passage, and (to say the least) has greatly enervated the second. The first he renders in such a manner as implies that Joab had killed Abner and Amasa oftener than once, "Ayant répandu leur sang" (le sang d'Abner et d'Amasa) "durant la paix, comme il avoit fait, durant la guerre." A terrible man this Joab,

> And thrice he routed all his foes, and thrice he slew the slain.

The other passage he renders "Elle n'a point mangé son pain dans l'oisiveté." The meaning is very indistinctly expressed here. Can a sluggard be said to be idle when eating? or does the most industrious disposition require that in the time of eating one should be employed in something else? Such a translation as this is too free to exhibit the style of the original, too literal to express the sense, and therefore is unlucky enough to hit neither. Diodati hath succeeded better in both. The last he renders literally as we do, and the first in this manner, "Spandendo in tempo di pace, il sangue che si spande in battaglia." This clearly enough exhibits the sense, and is sufficiently literal. The meaning of the other passage, stripped of the idiom and expressed in plain English, is neither more nor less than this—"She eateth not the bread which she hath not earned." In many cases it may be difficult to say whether propriety or energy should have the preference. I think it safer in every dubious case to secure the former.

[2] Book II. Chap. viii. Sect. 2.

happy conciseness to the splendour occasioned by concentrating sunbeams into a little spot. Now, if by means of this the light is rendered dazzling, it is no more a fit medium for viewing an object in, than too weak a light would be. Though the causes be contrary, the effects are in this respect the same. Objects in both are seen indistinctly. But the cases to which this observation is applicable are extremely few.

Indeed, the concise manner in any form is not alike adapted to every subject. There are some subjects which it particularly suits. For example, the dignity and authority of the preceptive style receives no small lustre from brevity. In the following words of Michael to Adam, how many important lessons are couched in two lines.

> Nor love thy life, nor hate; but what thou liv'st,
> Live well; how long, or short, permit to Heaven.[3]

The aphoristic style, and the proverbial, receive likewise considerable strength from the laconic manner. Indeed, these two styles differ from each other only as the one conveys the discoveries in science, and the other the maxims of common life. In Swift's Detached Thoughts we find a few specimens of this manner. "The power of fortune is confessed by the miserable; the happy ascribe all their success to merit."—"Every man desires to live long; but no man would be old."—"A nice man is a man of nasty ideas."—"The sluggard," saith Solomon, "hideth his hand in his bosom; it grieveth him to bring it to his mouth."[4]—"The desire of the slothful killeth him, for his hands refuse to labour."[5]—"A fool," says the son of Sirach, "travaileth with a word, as a woman in labour of a child."[6] It is indeed true, that a great degree of conciseness is scarcely attainable, unless the style be figurative; but it is also true, that the vivacity of the expression is not to be attributed solely to the figure, but partly to the brevity occasioned by the figure. But though the combination of the figurative with the concise is very common, it is not necessary. This will appear from some of the examples already given, wherein, though we discover a happy comprehension of a great deal of meaning in little compass, there is neither trope nor figure. Nor, indeed, is there either of these, in the picture that Swift gives of himself, where he says, "I am too proud to be vain," in which simplicity, perspicuity, and vivacity, are all happily united. An inferior writer, in attempting to delineate fully

[3] Paradise Lost.
[4] Proverbs xxvi. 15.
[5] Ibid. xxi. 25.
[6] Ecclus. xix. 11.

the same character, would have employed many sentences, and not have said near so much. Further, the writer on politics often avails himself of a sententious conciseness, which adds no little energy to the sentiments he unfolds. Of the successful application of brevity in this way, we have an excellent model in the Spirit of Laws. It hath no bad effect, if used sparingly, even in narrative.[7]

On the other hand, the kinds of writing which are less susceptible of this ornament are the descriptive, the pathetic, the declamatory, especially the last. It is, besides, much more suitable in writing than in speaking. A reader has the command of his time; he may read fast or slow, as he finds convenient; he can peruse a sentence a second time when necessary, or lay down the book and think. But if, in haranguing to the people, you comprise a great deal in few words, the hearer must have uncommon quickness of apprehension to catch your meaning, before you have put it out of his power, by engaging his attention to something else. In such orations, therefore, it is particularly unseasonable; and by consequence it is, in all kinds of writing addressed to the people, more or less so, as they partake more or less of popular declamation.

SECTION II.—*The principal Offences against Brevity considered.*

But though this energetic brevity is not adapted alike to every subject, we ought on every subject to avoid its contrary, a languid redundancy of words. It is sometimes proper to be copious, but never to be verbose. I shall, therefore, now consider some of the principal faults against that quality of style of which I have been treating.

PART I.—*Tautology.*

The first I shall take notice of is *the tautology*, which is either a repetition of the same sense in different words, or a representation of any thing as the cause, condition, or con-

[7] The *veni, vidi, vici,* of Cæsar derives hence its principal beauty; *I came, I saw, I conquered,* is not equal. So small a circumstance as the repetition of the pronoun, without which the sentence in our language would appear maimed, takes much from its vivacity and force.

sequence of itself. Of the first, which is also the least, take the following example from Addison:

> The dawn is overcast;———the morning lowers;
> And———heavily in clouds brings on the day[8]———

Here the same thought is repeated thrice in different words. Of the last kind I shall produce a specimen from Swift. "I look upon it as *my duty*, so far as God hath enabled me, and as long as I keep within the bounds of truth, of *duty*, and of decency—."[9] It would be strange indeed that any man should think it is duty to transgress the bounds of duty. Another example from the same hand you have in the words which follow: "So it is, that I must be *forced* to get home partly by stealth, and partly by *force*."[1] "How many are there," says Bolingbroke, "by whom these *tidings* of good *news* were never heard?"[2] This is *tidings* of *tidings*, or *news* of *news*. "Never did Atticus succeed better in gaining the *universal* love and esteem of *all* men."[3] Either of the two words in italics might have been used, but not both.

It is also considered as of the nature of tautology, to lengthen a sentence by coupling words altogether or nearly synonymous, whether they be substantives or adjectives, verbs or adverbs. This fault is very common, and to be found even in our best writers. "In the Attic commonwealth," says Doctor Swift, "it was the *privilege* and *birthright* of every *citizen* and *poet*, to rail *aloud* and in *public*."[4] —If he had said simply, "In the Attic commonwealth it was the privilege of every citizen to rail in public,"—the sentence would have lost nothing of the sense. And it is an invariable maxim, that words which add nothing to the sense or to the clearness, must diminish the force of the expression. There are certain synonymas which it is become customary with some writers regularly to link together; insomuch that a reader no sooner meets with one of them, than he anticipates the introduction of its usual attendant. It is needless to quote authorities. I shall only produce a few of those couples which are wont to be thus conjoined, and which every English reader will recollect with ease. Such are, *plain and evident*, *clear and obvious*, *worship and adoration*, *pleasure and satisfaction*, *bounds and limits*, *suspicion and jealousy*, *courage and resolution*, *intents and purposes*. The frequent recurrence of such phrases is not indeed more repugnant to vivacity than it is to dignity of style.

[8] Cato.
[9] Letter to Lord Lyttleton.
[1] Letter to Sheridan.
[2] Ph. Fr. 38.
[3] Spectator, No. 467. R.
[4] Preface to the Tale of a Tub.

But is there no occasion on which synonymous words may be used properly? I answer, There are two occasions; and I do not at present recollect any other. One is, when an obscurer term, which we cannot avoid employing, on account of some connexion with what either precedes or follows, needs to be explained by one that is clearer. The other is, when the language of the passions is exhibited. Passion naturally dwells on its object: the impassioned speaker always attempts to rise in expression; but when that is impracticable, he recurs to repetition and synonymy, and thereby in some measure produces the same effect. The hearer perceiving him, as it were, overpowered by his subject, and at a loss to find words adequate to the strength of his feelings, is by sympathy carried along with him, and enters into all his sentiments. There is in this case an expression in the very effort shown by recurring to synonymas, which supplies the deficiency in the words themselves. Bolingbroke exclaims in an invective against the times, "But all is little, and low, and mean among us."[5] It must be owned, that there is here a kind of amplification, or at least a stronger expression of indignation, than any one of these three epithets could have effected alone; yet there is no climax in the sentence, and in this metaphorical use of the words, no sensible difference of signification.[6] But every body must perceive that this manner suits only the popular and declamatory style, and that in those compositions which admit no species of the pathetic, it can have no place.

I observe further, that an adjective and its substantive will sometimes include a tautology. This happens when the former expresses nothing but what is implied in the signification of the latter. "Let them," says the Craftsman, "throw as much *foul dirt* at me as they please."[7] Of the same stamp are, the *verdant green*, the *umbrageous shade*, the *sylvan forest*, expressions not frequently to be met with except perhaps in the writings of some of our minor poets. *First aggressors*, *standard pattern*, *subject-matter*, and *some few*, are much commoner, but deserve to be exploded for the same reason.

Lastly, in some single words there is so much of the appearance of tautology, that they ought in prose at least to be avoided. Such are, *Most-highest*, *worser*, *lesser*, *chiefest*, *extremest;* for *Most-high*, *worse*, *less*, *chief*, *extreme*. The first occurs often in the translation of the Psalms inserted in the liturgy, and has thence acquired something venerable in

[5] Spirit of Patriotism.

[6] In these words of Cicero concerning Cataline, "Abiit, excessit, evasit, erupit," there is a stronger expression of triumph than in any of them singly.

[7] No. 232.

its appearance;[8] the second, though used in Shakspeare's time, is at present obsolete. I know not why the other three have not before now shared the same fate.

PART II.—*Pleonasm.*

Another trespass against this species of vivacity is the *pleonasm* which implies barely superfluity, or more than enough. Here, though the words do not, as in the tautology, repeat the sense, they add nothing to it. For instance, "They returned *back again* to the *same* city *from* whence they came *forth;*" instead of "They returned to the city whence they came." The five words *back*, *again*, *same*, *from*, and *forth*, are mere expletives. They serve neither for ornament nor for use, and are therefore to be regarded as encumbrances. "I went home," says the Guardian, "full of *a great many* serious reflections;"[9] much better, "full of serious reflections." "If he happens," says the Spectator, "to have any leisure *upon his hands.*"[1] To what purpose *upon his hands?* "The everlasting club," says the same author, "treats all other clubs with *an eye of* contempt;"[2] for "treats all other clubs with contempt." *To treat with the eye* is also chargeable with impropriety and vulgarism. "Flavia, who is the mamma," says the Tatler, "has all the charms and desires of youth still *about her.*"[3] The two last words are at least superfluous.

In such a phrase as this, "I wrote *a letter* to you yesterday," the French critics would find a pleonasm; because it means no more than what is clearly expressed in these words, "I wrote to you yesterday." Yet in the last form there is an ellipsis of the regimen of the active verb; and one would imagine that the supplying of an ellipsis could never constitute a pleonasm. It is at least certain, that where the supply is so unnecessary, as it is here, it is better to follow the usual mode of speaking. But when any additional circumstance requires the insertion of the noun, the nicest judge will not condemn the expression as pleonastic; as "I wrote you a long letter yesterday," "This is the third letter I have written you on the same subject."[4]

[8] It is to this, I think, solely that the approbation of those whose ears are accustomed to that expression in public worship, is to be ascribed, and not, as Dr. Lowth supposes [Introd. Adject.], to a singular propriety from the subject to which it is applied, the Supreme Being, who is higher than the highest. For if this reason were good, we should also find a singular propriety in the phrases *most wisest* and *most best*, when applied to God, because he is as certainly wiser than the wisest, and better than the best. By the same rule *the Supremest Being* would be a title much more emphatical than *the Supreme Being*.

[9] No. 34. [1] No. 43. [2] No. 73. [3] No. 206.

[4] It deserves our notice, that on this article the idiom of the tongue hath great

It may not be improper here to remark, that every word that is accounted an expletive doth not always constitute a pleonasm. For example, the *do* and the *did*, as the signs of the tenses, are frequently necessary, and sometimes emphatical. The idiom of the language renders them for the most part necessary in negation and interrogation; and even in affirmation they are found in certain circumstances to give an emphasis to the expression. For instance, "Did I object to this measure formerly? I do object to it still." Or, "What I did publicly affirm then, I do affirm now, and I will affirm always." The contrast of the different tenses, in these examples, is more precisely marked by such monosyllables as are intended singly to point out that circumstance, than they can be by the bare inflections of the verb. The particle *there*, when it is not an adverb of place, may be considered as a kind of expletive, since we cannot assign to it a separate sense. Nevertheless it is no pleonasm; for though it is not easy to define in words the import of such terms, yet if the omission of them make the expression appear either stiff or defective, they are not to be regarded as useless.

Lastly, I shall observe on this subject, that as there are some single words which have I know not what air of tautology, there are some also which have a pleonastic appearance. Such are the following, *unto*, *until*, *selfsame*, *foursquare*, *devoid*, *despoil*, *disannul*, *muchwhat*, *oftentimes*, *nowadays*, *downfall*, *furthermore*, *wherewithal;* for *to*, *till*, *same*, *square*, *void*, *spoil*, *annul*, *much*, *often*, *now*, *fall*, *further*, *wherewith*. The use of such terms, many writers have been led into, partly from the dislike of monosyllables, partly from the love of variety. The last end it hardly answers, as the simple word is still included; and as to the first, I am persuaded that this dislike hath carried some modern writers to the other extreme, and, I imagine, the worse extreme of the two. It hath proceeded on an opinion, which I shall afterwards evince to be erroneous, that a frequent recurrence of monosyllables is inconsistent with harmony. However, with regard to the words specified, it would not be right to preclude entirely the use of them in poetry, where the shackles of metre render variety more necessary, but they ought to be used very sparingly, if at all in prose.

It is worth while to remark, that the addition of a short syllable to the termination of a word, when that syllable hath

influence, insomuch that an expression in one language may contain a pleonasm, which, if literally rendered into another, would express no more than is quite necessary. Thus the phrase in French, "Il lui donna des coups de *sa* main," is pleonastic: but there is no pleonasm in these words in English, "He gave him blows with *his* hand." On the contrary, "Il lui donna des coups de main," is proper in French. "He gave him blows with hand," is defective in English. The sense however, may be expressed in our language with equal propriety and greater brevity in this manner, "He gave him handy blows."

no separate signification, doth not exhibit the appearance of a pleonasm, which any syllable prefixed, or a long one added, never fails to exhibit. Thus, *mountain*, *fountain*, *meadow*, *valley*, *island*, *climate*, are as good as *mount*, *fount*, *mead*, *vale*, *isle*, *clime*, and in many cases preferable. Indeed the words *fount*, *mead*, *vale*, and *clime*, are now almost confined to poetry. Several adjectives may in like manner be lengthened by the addition of an unaccented syllable, as *ecclesiastical*, *astronomical*, *philosophical*, *grammatical*, from *ecclesiastic*, *astronomic*, *philosophic*, *grammatic;* in all which, if the choice be not a matter of absolute indifference, it may at least be determined by the slightest consideration of variety or of sound. Sometimes custom insensibly assigns different meanings to such different formations, as in the words *comic* and *comical*, *tragic* and *tragical*, *politic* and *political*. Though the words here coupled were at first equally synonymous with those before mentioned, they are not entirely so at present. *Tragic* denotes belonging to tragedy; *tragical*, resembling tragedy. The like holds of *comic* and *comical*. We say, "the *tragic* muse, the *comic* muse;" and "a *tragic* poet," for a writer of tragedy, a comic poet for a writer of comedy; but "I heard a *tragical* story," for a mournful story, and "I met with a *comical* adventure," for a droll adventure. We say, "a *politic* man," for an artful fellow; but a *political* writer, for a writer on politics. There is not, however, a perfect uniformity in such applications, for we constantly use the phrase "the body *politic*," and not *political*, for the civil society. On the whole, however, it would seem that what is affixed, especially when unaccented, is conceived as more closely united to the word, than what is prefixed is conceived to be. In this last case the supernumerary syllable, if it make no change on the signification, always conveys the notion of an expletive, which is not suggested in the first.

But before I quit this subject, it will not be beside the purpose to observe, that there are cases in which a certain species of pleonasm may not only be pardonable, but even have a degree of merit. It is at least entitled to indulgence, when it serves to express a pertinent earnestness of affirmation on an interesting subject, as in phrases like these, "We have seen with our eyes," "we have heard with our ears," which perhaps are to be found in every language.[5] Again, in poetical description, where the fancy is addressed, epithets which would otherwise be accounted superfluous, if used moderately, are not without effect. The *azure heaven*, the *silver moon*, the *blushing morn*, the *sea-girt isle*. Homer abounds in such. They often occur also in sacred writ. The warm manner of the ancient Orientals, even in their prose compositions, holds much more

[5] Vocemque his auribus hausi. Vidi ante oculos ipse meos.

of poesy, than the cold prosaic diction of us moderns and Europeans. A stroke of the pencil, if I may so express myself, is almost always added to the arbitrary sign, in order the more strongly to attach the imagination. Hence it is not with them, *the beasts, the birds, the fish, the heaven, and the earth;* but *the beasts of the field, the birds of the air, the fish of the sea, the heaven above, and the earth beneath.* But though in certain cases there is some indulgence given to terms which may properly be styled pleonastic, I scarcely think that an epithet which is merely tautological is in any case tolerable.

PART III.—*Verbosity.*

The third and last fault I shall mention against a vivid conciseness is *verbosity.* This, it may be thought, coincides with the pleonasm already discussed. One difference however is this; in the pleonasm there are words which add nothing to the sense; in the verbose manner, not only single words, but whole clauses, may have a meaning, and yet it were better to omit them, because what they mean is unimportant. Instead, therefore, of enlivening the expression, they make it languid. Another difference is, that in a proper pleonasm a complete correction is always made by rasing. This will not always answer in the verbose style; it is often necessary to alter as well as blot.

It will not be improper here further to observe, that by *verbosity* I do not mean the same thing which the French express by the word *verbiage,* as some persons, misled by etymology, may be inclined to think. By this term is commonly understood a parade of fine words, plausibly strung together, so as either to conceal a total want of meaning, or to disguise something weak and inconclusive in the reasoning. The former, with which alone we are here concerned, is merely an offence against vivacity, the latter is more properly a transgression of the laws of perspicuity.

One instance of a faulty exuberance of words is the intemperate use of circumlocution. There are circumstances wherein this figure is allowable, there are circumstances wherein it is a beauty, there are circumstances wherein it is a blemish. We indulge it often for the sake of variety, as when, instead of *the women,* an author says *the fair sex,* or when instead of *the sun,* a poet puts *the lamp of day;* we choose it sometimes for the sake of decency, to serve as a sort of veil to what ought not to be too nakedly exposed, or for the sake of avoiding an expression that might probably offend.[6] Sometimes indeed propriety

[6] See Book III. Chap. i. Sect. ii. Part 3.

requires the use of circumlocution, as when Milton says of Satan, who had been thrown down headlong into hell,

> *Nine times the space that measures day and night*
> *To mortal men,* he with his horrid crew
> Lay vanquish'd, rolling in the fiery gulf—[7]

To have said *nine days and nights,* would not have been proper, when talking of a period before the creation of the sun, and consequently before time was portioned out to any being in that manner. Sometimes this figure serves, as it were accidentally, to introduce a circumstance which favours the design of the speaker, and which to mention of plain purpose, without apparent necessity, would appear both impertinent and invidious. An example I shall give from Swift: "One of these authors (*the fellow that was pilloried,* I have forgot his name) is so grave, sententious, dogmatical a rogue, that there is no enduring him."[8] What an exquisite antonomasia have we in this parenthesis! Yet he hath rendered it apparently necessary by his saying, "I have forgot his name." Sometimes even the vivacity of the expression may be augmented by a periphrasis, as when it is made to supply the place of a separate sentence. Of this the words of Abraham afford an instance: "Shall not *the judge of all the earth* do right."[9] *The judge of all the earth* is a periphrasis for GOD, and as it represents him in a character to which the acting unjustly is peculiarly unsuitable, it serves as an argument in support of the sentiment, and is therefore conducive even to conciseness. In this view we may consider that noted circumlocution employed by Cicero, who, instead of saying simply, Milo's domestics killed Clodius, says, "They did that which every master would have wished his servants to do in such an exigence."[1] It is far from being enough to say of this passage, that it is an euphemism, by which the odious word *killed* is avoided. It contains also a powerful vindication of the action, by an appeal to the conscience of every hearer, whether he would not have approved it in his own case. But when none of these ends can be answered by a periphrastical expression, it will inevitably be regarded as injuring the style by flattening it. Of this take the following as an example from the Spectator: "I wont say, we see often, in *the next tender things to children,* tears shed without much grieving."[2] The phrase here employed appears, besides, affected and far-fetched.

Another source of languor in the style is when such clauses are inserted, as to a superficial view appear to suggest some-

[7] Paradise Lost, B. i.

[8] Letters concerning the Sacramental Test.

[9] Gen. xviii. 25.

[1] "Fecerunt id servi Milonis,—quod suos quisque servos in tali re facere voluisset." Cicero pro Milone.

[2] No. 95.

thing which heightens, but on reflection are found to pre-suppose something which abates, the vigour of the sentiment. Of this I shall give a specimen from Swift: "Neither is any condition of life more honourable in the sight of God than another, otherwise he would be a respecter of persons, *which he assures us he is not*."[3] It is evident that this last clause doth not a little enervate the thought, as it implies but too plainly, that without this assurance from God himself, we should naturally conclude him to be of a character very different from that here given him by the preacher.

Akin to this is the juvenile method of loading every proposition with asseverations. As such a practice in conversation more commonly infuseth a suspicion of the speaker's veracity, than it engages the belief of the hearer, it hath an effect somewhat similar in writing. In our translation of the Bible, God is represented as saying to Adam, concerning the fruit of the tree of knowledge, "In the day thou eatest thereof, thou shalt *surely* die."[4] The adverb *surely*, instead of enforcing, enfeebles the denunciation. My reason is the same as in the former case. A ground of mistrust is insinuated, to which no affirmation is a counterpoise. Are such adverbs then never to be used? Not when either the character of the speaker, or the evidence of the thing, is such as precludes the smallest doubt. In other cases they are pertinent enough. But as taste itself is influenced by custom, and as, for that reason, we may not be quick in discerning a fault to which our ears have from our infancy been habituated, let us consider how it would affect us in an act of parliament, to read that the offender shall for the first offence *certainly* be liable to such a penalty, and for the second he shall *surely* incur such another. This style would appear intolerable even to one of ordinary discernment. Why? The answer is obvious. It ill suits the dignity of the British senate to use a manner which supposes that its authority or power can be called in question. That which hath misled our translators in the passage quoted, as in many others, hath been an attempt to express the import of a Hebraism which cannot be rendered literally into any European tongue. But it is evident that they have not sufficiently attended to the powers of the language which they wrote. The English hath two futures, no inconsiderable advantage on some occasions, both for perspicuity and for emphasis. The one denotes simply the futurition of the event, the other also makes the veracity and power of the speaker vouchers of its futurition. The former is a bare declaration; the latter is always, in the second person and the third, unless when used imperatively, either a promise or a threatening. No language, that I know, exactly hits this distinc-

[3] Sermon on Mutual Subjection. [4] Gen. ii. 17.

tion but our own. In other languages you must infer, not always infallibly, from the tenor of the story, whether the future is of the one import or of the other; in English you find this expressed in the words.[5]

Further, it was observed that affirmative adverbs are no less improper when doubt is entirely precluded by the evidence of the fact, than when it is prevented by the authority of the speaker. I have given an example of the latter, and shall now produce one of the former. An Israelite informing David concerning Goliath, is represented in our version as saying, "*Surely*, to defy Israel is he come up."[6] Had the giant shown himself between the camps, and used menacing gestures, or spoken words which nobody understood, this expression would have been natural and proper. But no man could have talked in this manner who had himself been a witness that every day, for forty days successively, this champion had given an open defiance to Israel in the most explicit terms, and in the audience of all the army. Such adverbs always weaken an assertion that is founded on the evidence of sense, or even of unexceptionable testimony, and are suited only to cases of conjecture or probability at most. It requires a certain justness of taste to know when we have said enough, through want of which, when we attempt to say more, we say less.

Another example, of a nature pretty similar, and arising from a similar cause, is the manner wherein our interpreters have attempted, in the New Testament, to strengthen the negation, wherever the double negative[7] occurs in the Greek, even in the most authoritative threatenings, by rendering it sometimes *in no case*, sometimes *in no wise*. It is evident that, in such instances, neither of these phrases expresseth more than the single adverb *not*, and as they partake of the nature of circumlocution, and betray an unsuccessful aim at saying more, they in effect debilitate the expression. The words "Ye shall

[5] This remark needs perhaps a further illustration, and in order to this it will be necessary to recur to some other language. The passage quoted is thus translated into Latin by Castalio, *Si ea vesceris, moriere*. He judged right not to add *certe* or *profecto* even in Latin. Neither of these adverbs could have rendered the expression more definite, and both are liable to the same exception with the English adverb *surely*. Yet take the version as it stands, and there is an evident ambiguity in the word *moriere*. It may be either the declaration of one who knew that there was a poisonous quality in the fruit, and meant only to warn Adam of his danger, by representing the natural consequence of eating it; or it may be the denunciation of a legislator against the transgression of his law. Every one who understands English will perceive immediately, that, on the first supposition, he must render the words into our language, "If thou eat thereof, thou *wilt* die;" and on the second supposition he must render them, "If thou eat thereof, thou *shalt* die." If there be any thing emphatical in the original idiom, it serves here, in my opinion, to mark the distinction between a simple declaration and the sanction of a law; which are perfectly distinguished in our tongue by the two futures.

[6] 1 Sam. xvii. 25.

[7] Ου μη.

not enter the kingdom of heaven," as they have more simplicity, have also, from the mouth of a legislator, more dignity and weight than "ye shall *in no case*," or "*in no wise* enter into it," as though there were various ways and means of getting thither. The two negatives of the Greek are precisely on the same footing with the two negatives of the French;[8] our single particle *not* is a full equivalent to both. For should a translator from the French attempt to render every double negative by such a periphrasis in English, his version would be justly accounted ridiculous. It may be thought a consequence of this doctrine, that the solemn protestation, "Verily, verily, I say unto you," so often adopted by our Lord, would rather weaken than enforce the sentiment. But the case is different. As these words enter not into the body of the proposition, but are employed solely to introduce it, they are to be considered purely as a call to attention, serving not so much to affirm the reality, as the importance of what is to be said. Or if they are to be understood as affirming the reality, it is from this single consideration, because said by him.

I add, as another cause of a languid verbosity, the loading of the style with epithets, when almost every verb hath its attendant adverb, which may be called its epithet, and every substantive its attendant adjective, and when both adjectives and adverbs are often raised to the superlative degree. Epithets used sparingly and with judgment have a great effect in enlivening the expression, but nothing has more of an opposite tendency than a profusion of them. That such profusion has this tendency, may be deduced, partly from a principle already mentioned, partly from a principle which I am going to observe. That already mentioned is, that they lengthen the sentence without adding proportionable strength. The other principle is, that the crowding of epithets into a discourse betrays a violent effort to say something extraordinary, and nothing is a clearer evidence of weakness than such an effort, when the effect is not correspondent. I would not, however, be understood to signify, that adjectives and adverbs are always to be regarded as mere epithets. Whatever is necessary for ascertaining the import of either noun or verb, whether by adding to the sense or by confining it, is something more than an epithet, in the common acceptation of that term. Thus when I say, "the *glorious sun*," the word *glorious* is an epithet, because it expresses a quality, which, being conceived always to belong to the object, is, like all its other qualities, comprehended in the name. But when I say, "the *meridian* sun," the word

[8] *Ne pas* or *non point*. Sometimes the French use even three negatives where we can properly employ but one in English, as in this sentence: "Je *ne* nie *pas* que je *ne* l' aie dit." "I do *not* deny that I said it." I believe no man who understands both languages will pretend that the negation here is expressed more strongly by them than by us.

meridian is not barely an epithet, because it makes a real addition to the signification, denoting the sun in that situation wherein he appears at noon. The like may be said of "the *rising*," or "the *setting* sun." Again, when I say, "the *towering* eagle," I use an epithet, because the quality *towering* may justly be attributed to all the kind; not so when I say "the *golden* eagle," because the adjective *golden* serves to limit the sense of the word *eagle* to one species only, and is therefore in effect a part of the name. Let it not be imagined hence, that mere epithets are always useless. Though all the essential qualities of a genus are included in the name, the scope of a discourse often renders it important, if not necessary, that some particular qualities should be specially attended to by the hearer; and these, by consequence, require to be specified by the speaker. On the contrary, a redundancy of these never fails to give a tiresome sameness to the composition, where substantives and adjectives, verbs and adverbs, almost invariably strung together, offend not more against vivacity than against harmony and elegance.[9] This vicious quality of style is sometimes denominated *juvenility*, as denoting immaturity of judgment, or an inexperience like that which would make a man mistake corpulency for the criterion of health and vigour. Besides, in young writers, a certain luxuriance in words is both more frequent and more pardonable.

There is one kind of composition, the paraphrase, of whose style verbosity is the proper character. The professed design of the paraphrast is to say in many words what his text expresseth in few; accordingly, all the writers of this class must be at pains to provide themselves in a sufficient stock of synonymas, epithets, expletives, circumlocutions, and tautologies, which are in fact, the necessary implements of their craft. I took notice, when treating of the influence which the choice of proper terms might have on vivacity, of one method of depressing their subject very common with these men, by generalizing as much as possible the terms used in the text. The particulars just now recited are not only common with

[9] I cannot help thinking that the following passage, which Rollin has quoted from Mascaron, as an example of style elevated and adorned by means of circumlocution and epithet, is justly exceptionable in this way. "Le roi, pour donner une marque immortelle de l'estime et de l'amitié dont il honoroit ce grand capitaine *(M. de Turenne)*, donne une place illustre à ses glorieuses cendres, parmi ces maîtres de la terre, qui conservent encore dans la magnificence de leurs tombeaux une image de celle de leurs trônes." *The king, that he may give an immortal mark of the esteem and friendship wherewith he honoured this great captain, gives an illustrious place to his glorious ashes, among those masters of the earth, who still preserve, in the magnificence of their tombs, an image of that of their thrones.* Bell. Lett. Liv. III. Chap. iii. Art. ii. Sect. 5. In the quick succession of such yokemates as these, *immortal mark, great captain, illustrious place, glorious ashes, magnificent tombs*, there appears a strong attempt towards the grand manner, which, after all, terminates in the tumid.

them, but essential to their work. I shall produce an example from an author, who is far from deserving to be accounted either the most verbose, or the least judicious of the tribe. But first, let us hear his text, the words of Jesus Christ: "Therefore, whosoever heareth these sayings of mine, and doeth them, I will liken him to a wise man, who built his house upon a rock; and the rain descended, and the floods came, and the winds blew, and beat upon that house, and it fell not: for it was founded upon a rock."[1] Now, let us hear the paraphrast. "Wherefore he that shall not only *hear* and *receive* these my instructions, but also *remember*, and *consider*, and *practise*, and *live according to* them; such a man may be compared to one who builds his house upon a rock; for a house founded upon a rock stands *unshaken* and *firm*, against all the assaults of rains, and floods, and storms; so the man who, in his life and conversation, *actually practises and obeys* my instructions, will *firmly* resist all the temptations of the devil, the allurements of pleasure, and the terrors of persecution, and shall be able to stand in the day of judgment, and be rewarded of God."[2] It would be difficult to point out a single advantage which this wordy, not to say flatulent, interpretation hath of the text. Is it more perspicuous? It is much less so; although it is the chief, if not the sole end of this manner of writing, to remove every thing that can darken the passage paraphrased, and to render the sense as clear as possible. But lest this censure should be thought rash, let it be observed that two things are clearly distinguished in the text, which are in themselves certainly distinct, to *hear* the commands of our master, and to *obey* them. There was the greater need that this distinction should be properly preserved, because it was the plain intention of the speaker to contrast those who heard and obeyed, with those who heard but obeyed not; as we learn from the similitude contained in the two following verses.[3] Yet this primary distinction is confounded in the paraphrase, by a multitude of words partly synonymous, partly different in signification. Thus, for *whosoever heareth these sayings of mine, and doeth them;* we have, "him that hears, and receives, and remembers, and considers, and actually practises, and obeys these my instructions, and lives according to them." I might allege, as another instance of the want of perspicuity, that the duty and the reward are strangely blended throughout the whole. A deficiency of words is, no doubt, oftener than the contrary, a cause of obscurity; but this evil, as I had occasion formerly to remark, may also be the effect of an exuberance. By a multiplicity of words the sentiment is not set off and accommodated, but, like David equipped in Saul's armour, it is encumbered and oppressed.

[1] Matt. vii. 24, and 25. [2] Dr. Clarke. [3] Verses 26 and 27.

Yet this is not the only, or perhaps the worst consequence, resulting from this manner of treating sacred writ. We are told of the torpedo, that it has the wonderful quality of numbing every thing it touches. A paraphrase is a torpedo. By its influence the most vivid sentiments become lifeless, the most sublime are flattened, the most fervid chilled, the most vigorous enervated. In the very best compositions of this kind that can be expected, the Gospel may be compared to a rich wine of a high flavour, diluted in such a quantity of water as renders it extremely vapid. This would be the case if the paraphrase (which is indeed hardly possible) took no tincture from the opinions of the paraphrast, but exhibited faithfully, though insipidly, the sense of the evangelist. Whereas, in all those paraphrases we have had occasion to be acquainted with, the Gospel may more justly be compared to such a wine, so much adulterated with a liquor of a very different taste and quality, that little of its original relish and properties can be discovered. Accordingly, in one paraphrase, Jesus Christ appears a bigoted Papist: in another, a flaming Protestant: in one, he argues with all the sophistry of the Jesuit; in another, he declaims with all the fanaticism of the Jansenist: in one, you trace the metaphysical ratiocinations of Arminius: in another, you recognise the bold conclusions of Gomarus; and in each you hear the language of a man who has thoroughly imbibed the system of one or other of our Christian rabbis. So various and so opposite are the characters which, in those performances, our Lord is made to exhibit, and the dialects which he is made to speak. How different is his own character and dialect from them all! If we are susceptible of the impartiality requisite to constitute us proper judges in these matters, we shall find in him nothing that can be thought to favour the subtle disquisitions of a sect. His language is not, like that of all dogmatists, the language of a bastard philosophy, which, under the pretence of methodizing religion, hath corrupted it, and, in less or more, tinged all the parties into which Christendom is divided. His language is not so much the language of the head as of the heart. His object is not science, but wisdom; accordingly, his discourses abound more in sentiments than in opinions.[4]

[4] I would not be understood to signify by this censure, that paraphrase can never be a useful mode of explication, though I own that, in my opinion, the cases wherein it may be reckoned not improper, nor altogether unuseful, are not numerous. As the only valuable aim of this species of commentary is to give greater perspicuity to an original work, obscurity is the only reasonable plea for employing it. When the style is very concise or figurative, or when there is an allusion to customs or incidents now or here not generally known, to add as much as is necessary for supplying an ellipsis, explaining an unusual figure, or suggesting an unknown fact or mode alluded to, may serve to render a performance more intelligible, without taking much from its energy. But if the use and occasions of paraphrase are only such as have

But I have digressed from my subject, and shall therefore return to it by observing, that another species of verbosity, and the only one which remains to be taken notice of, is a prolixity in narration, arising from the mention of unnecessary circumstances. Circumstances may be denominated unnecessary, either because not of such importance as that the scope of the relation is affected by their being known, or because implied in the other circumstances related. An error of the former kind belongs properly to the thought, of the latter to the language. For the first, when it is habitual, a man is commonly styled loquacious: for the second, verbose. Such a sentence as the following would be an instance of the second; for with the first I am not here concerned. "On receiving this information, he arose, went out, saddled his horse, mounted him, and rode to town." All is implied in saying, "On receiving this information, he rode to town." This manner, however, in a certain degree, is so strongly characteristic of the uncultivated, but unaffected style of remote ages, that in books of the highest antiquity, particularly of the sacred code, it is not at all ungraceful. Of this kind are the following scriptural phrases, "He lifted up his voice and wept." "She conceived and bore a son." "He opened his mouth and said." For my own part, I should not approve the delicacy of a translator, who, to modernize the style of the Bible, should repudiate every such redundant circumstance. It is true that in strictness they are not necessary to the narration, but they are of some importance to the composition, as bearing the venerable signature of ancient simplicity. And in a faithful translation, there ought to be, not only a just transmission of the writer's sense, but, as far as is consistent with perspicuity and the idiom of the tongue into which the version is made, the character of the style ought to be preserved.

So much for the vivacity produced by conciseness, and those blemishes in style which stand in opposition to it, tautology, pleonasm, and verbosity.

been now represented, it is evident that there are but a few books of Scripture, and but certain portions of those few, that require to be treated in this manner. The notions which the generality of paraphrasts (I say not all) entertain on this subject, are certainly very different. If we may judge from their productions, we should naturally conclude that they have considered such a size of *subject matter* (if I may be indulged this once in the expression) as affording a proper foundation for a composition of such a magnitude; and have, therefore, laid it down as a maxim, from which, in their practice, they do not often depart, that the most commodious way of giving to their work the extent proposed, is that equal portions of the text (perspicuous or obscure, it matters not) should be spun out to equal length. Thus regarding only quantity, they view their text, and parcel it, treating it in much the same manner as goldbeaters and wiredrawers treat the metals on which their art is employed.

CHAPTER III.

Of Vivacity, as depending on the Arrangement of the Words.

SECTION I.—*Of the nature of Arrangement, and the principal division of Sentences.*

HAVING already shown how far vivacity depends either on the words themselves, or on their number, I come now, lastly, to consider how it is effected by their arrangement.

This, it must be owned, hath a very considerable influence in all languages, and yet there is not any thing which it is more difficult to regulate by general laws. The placing of the words in a sentence resembles, in some degree, the disposition of the figures in a history piece. As the principal figure ought to have that situation in the picture which will, at the first glance, fix the eye of the spectator, so the emphatical word ought to have that place in the sentence which will give it the greatest advantage for fixing the attention of the hearer. But in painting there can rarely arise a doubt concerning either the principal figure, or the principal place; whereas here it is otherwise. In many sentences it may be a question, both what is the word on which the emphasis ought to rest, and what is the situation which (to use the language of painters) will give it the highest relief. In most cases, both of simple narration and of reasoning, it is not of great consequence to determine either point; in many cases it is impossible. Besides, in English, and other modern languages, the speaker doth not enjoy that boundless latitude which an orator of Athens or of Rome enjoyed, when haranguing in the language of his country. With us, who admit very few inflections, the construction, and consequently the sense, depends almost entirely on the order. With the Greeks and the Romans, who abound in inflections, the sense often remains unalterable, in whatever order you arrange the words.

But notwithstanding the disadvantage which, in this respect, we Britons labour under, our language even here allows as much liberty as will, if we know how to use it, be of great service for invigorating the expression. It is true, indeed, that when neither the imagination nor the passions of the hearer are addressed, it is hazardous in the speaker to depart from the practice which generally obtains in the arrangement of the words; and that even though the sense should not be in the least affected by the transposition. The temperament of our language is phlegmatic, like that of our climate. When, therefore, neither the liveliness of representation, nor the warmth of passion, serve, as it were, to cover the trespass, it is not safe to leave the beaten track. Whatever is supposed to be written or spoken in a cool and temperate mood, must rigidly adhere to the established order, which with us, as I observed, allows but little freedom. What is said will otherwise inevitably be exposed to the censure of quaintness and affectation, than which perhaps no censure can do greater prejudice to an orator. But as it is undubitable, that in many cases both composition and arrangement may, without incurring this reproach, be rendered greatly subservient to vivacity, I shall make a few observations on these, which I purpose to illustrate with proper examples.

Composition and arrangement in sentences, though nearly connected, and, therefore, properly in this place considered together, are not entirely the same. Composition includes arrangement and something more. When two sentences differ only in arrangement, the sense, the words, and the construction, are the same; when they differ also in other articles of composition, there must be some difference in the words themselves, or, at least, in the manner of construing them. But I shall have occasion to illustrate this distinction in the examples to be afterwards produced.

Sentences are either simple or complex; simple, consisting of one member only; as this, "In the beginning, God created the heaven and the earth;"[5] complex, consisting of two or more members linked together by conjunctions; as this, "Doubtless thou art our father, | though Abraham be ignorant of us, | and Israel acknowledge us not."[6] In the composition of the former, we have only to consider the distribution of the words; in that of the latter, regard must also be had to the arrangement of the members. The members too are sometimes complex, and admit a subdivision into clauses, as in the following example, "The ox knoweth his owner, | and the ass his master's crib;—but Israel doth not know, | my people doth not consider."[7] This decompound sentence hath two members, each of which is subdivided into two clauses. When a member of a complex sentence is simple, having but one verb, it is also called a clause. Of such a sentence as this, "I have called | but ye refused;"[8] we should say indifferently, that it consists of two members, or of two clauses.[9] The members

[5] Gen. i. 1. [6] Isaiah lxiii. 16. [7] Ibid. i. 3. [8] Prov. i. 24.

[9] The words *member* and *clause* in English, are used as corresponding to the Greek κωλον and κομμα, and to the Latin *membrum* and *incisum*.

or the clauses are not always perfectly separate, the one succeeding the other; one of them is sometimes very aptly inclosed by the other, as in the subsequent instance: "When Christ (who is our life) shall appear:—then shall ye also appear with him in glory."[1] This sentence consists of two members, the former of which is divided into two clauses; one of these clauses, "who is our life," being as it were embosomed in the other, when "Christ shall appear."

So much for the primary distinction of sentences into simple and complex.

SECTION II.—*Simple Sentences.*

With regard to simple sentences, it ought to be observed first, that there are degrees in simplicity. "God made man," is a very simple sentence. "On the sixth day God made man of the dust of the earth after his own image," is still a simple sentence in the sense of rhetoricians and critics, as it hath but one verb, but less simple than the former, on account of the circumstances specified. Now it is evident, that the simpler any sentence is, there is the less scope for variety in the arrangement, and the less indulgence to a violation of the established rule. Yet even in the simplest, whatever strongly impresses the fancy, or awakens passion, is sufficient to a certain degree to authorize the violation.

No law of the English tongue, relating to the disposition of words in a sentence, holds more generally than this, that the nominative has the first place, the verb the second, and the accusative, if it be an active verb that is employed, has the third;[2] if it be a substantive verb, the participle, adjective, or predicate of whatever denomination it be, occupies the third place. Yet this order, to the great advantage of the expression, is often inverted. Thus, in the general uproar at Ephesus, on occasion of Paul's preaching among them against idolatry, we are informed, that the people exclaimed for some time without intermission, "Great is Diana of the Ephesians."[3] Alter the arrangement, restore the grammatic order, and say, "Diana of the Ephesians is great;" and you destroy at once the signature of impetuosity and ardour resulting, if you please to call it so, from the disarrangement of the words.

[1] Col. iii. 4.

[2] Let it be observed, that in speaking of English syntax, I use the terms nominative and accusative merely to avoid tedious circumlocutions, sensible that in strict propriety our substantives have no such cases. By the nomina tive I mean always the efficient, agent, or instrument operating, with which the verb agrees in number and person; by the accusative, the effect produced, the object aimed at, or the subject operated on.

[3] Acts xix. 28 and 34.

We are apt to consider the customary arrangement as the most consonant to nature, in consequence of which notion we brand every departure from it as a transgression of the natural order. This way of thinking ariseth from some very specious causes, but is far from being just. "Custom," it hath been said, "becomes a second nature." Nay, we often find it strong enough to suppress the first. Accordingly, what is in this respect accounted natural in one language, is unnatural in another. In Latin, for example, the negative particle is commonly put before the verb, in English it is put after it; in French one negative is put before and another after. If in any of these languages you follow the practice of any other, the order of the words will appear unnatural. We in Britain think it most suitable to nature to place the adjective before the substantive; the French and most other Europeans think the contrary. We range the oblique cases of the personal pronouns as we do the nouns, whose place they occupy, after the verb; they range them invariably before, notwithstanding that when the regimen is a substantive, they make it come after the verb as we do. They and we have both the same reason, *custom*, which is different in different countries.

But it may be said that more than this can be urged in support of the ordinary arrangement of a simple sentence above explained. The nominative, to talk in the logicians' style, is the subject; the adjective, or participle, is the predicate; and the substantive verb the copula. Now, is it not most natural that the subject be mentioned before the thing predicated of it? and what place so proper for the copula which unites them as the middle? This is plausible, and, were the mind a pure intellect, without fancy, taste, or passion, perhaps it would be just. But as the case is different with human nature, I suspect there will be found little uniformity in this particular in different tongues, unless where, in respect either of matter or of form, they have been, in a great measure, derived from some common source.

The Hebrew is a very simple language, and hath not that variety, either of moods or of conjunctions, that is requisite for forming a complicated style. Here, therefore, if any where, one would expect to find an arrangement purely natural. Yet in this language, the most usual, and what would with them therefore be termed the grammatical disposition of the words, is not the disposition above mentioned. In the historic style, or when past events are related, they commonly place the verb first, then the nominative, afterwards the regimen, predicate, or attendant circumstances.[4] The freedom which Greek and

[4] Thus the very first words of Genesis, a book even among the books of Scripture remarkable for simplicity of style, are an evidence of this in the

Latin allow on this article, renders it improper to denominate one order grammatical exclusively of others. I imagine, therefore, that perhaps the only principle in which on this subject we can safely rest, as being founded in nature is, that whatever most strongly fixes the attention, or operates on the passion of the speaker, will first seek utterance by the lips. This is agreeable to a common proverb, which perhaps, to speak in Shakspeare's phrase,[5] *is something musty*, but significant

active verb: בראשית ברא אלהים את השמים ואת הארץ. The order is preserved exactly in the Vulgate: "In principio creavit Deus cœlum et terram." That the same order is observed in disposing the substantive verb, appears from the fifth verse, ויהי ערב ויהי בקר יום אחד. The arrangement here is perfectly exhibited in the Latin version of Junius and Tremellius, which is generally very literal: Sic fuit vespera et fuit mane diei primi." Yet in English we should be apt to call the order in both passages, especially the last, rather unnatural. "In the beginning created God the heavens and the earth." "And was evening and was morning day first." The same thing might be illustrated in the passive verbs, in the neuter, and in the reciprocal, if necessary. Nothing therefore can be more evident than that it is custom only which makes us Britons prefer one order of words, and others another, as the natural order. I am surprised that a critic of so much taste and discernment as Bouhours (see his *Entretiens d'Ariste et d'Eugene*, 2. *La Langue Française*) should represent this as one of the excellencies of the French tongue, that it follows the natural order of the words. It is manifest, from what has been said, that its common arrangement has no more title to be denominated natural than that of any other language. Nay, we may raise an argument for confuting this silly pretence from the very laws that obtain in this language. Thus, if the natural order require that the regimen should follow the active verb, their way of arranging the oblique cases of the pronouns is unnatural, as they always place them before the verb; if, on the contrary, the natural order require that the regimen should precede the governing verb, their way of arranging nouns governed by verbs is unnatural, since they always place them after the verb; so that, whichever be the natural way, they depart from it in the disposition of one or other of these parts of speech. The like may be urged in regard to the nominative, which, though for the most part, it go before the active verb, in certain cases follows it. This happens frequently when the verb is preceded by the oblique case of the relative, as in this sentence: Le retardement *que souffre le lecteur*, le rend plus attentif." And even in placing their adjectives, wherever use hath made exceptions from the general rule, it has carried the notion of what is natural along with it. They would call it as unnatural to say *homme jeune* as to say *gardien ange*. All therefore that can be affirmed with truth is, that the French adhere more inviolably than other nations to the ordinary arrangement established in the language. But this, as I hope to evince in the sequel, is one of the greatest imperfections of that tongue. The ease with which the Italian admits either order in the personal pronouns, especially in poetry, adds often to the harmony and the elegance, as well as to the vivacity of the expression, as in these lines of Metastasio's Artaserse;

Sallo amor, lo sanno i numi;
Il mio core, il tuo lo sa.

Bouhours, in the dialogue above-mentioned, has dropped the character of critic and philosopher for that of encomiast. He talks like a lover about his mistress. He sees neither blemish nor defect. All is beauty and excellence. For my part, if I were to prove the inferiority of French to Italian and Spanish, the two languages with which he compares it, I should not desire other or better topics for evincing the point than the greater part of those which he has employed, in my judgment very unsuccessfully, for the contrary purpose.

[5] Hamlet.

enough, "Nearest the heart, nearest the mouth." In these transpositions, therefore, I maintain that the order will be found, on examination, to be more strictly natural than when the more general practice in the tongue is followed.

As an irrefragable argument in support of this doctrine, it may be pleaded, that though the most usual, which is properly the artificial order, be different in different languages, the manner of arranging, or (if you like the term better) transposing, above specified, which is always an effect of vivacity in the speaker, and a cause of producing a livelier conception in the hearer, is the same in all languages. It is for this reason, amongst others, that I have chosen to take most of my examples on this topic, not from any original performance in English, but from the common translation of the Bible, and shall here observe once for all, that both in the quotations already made, and those hereafter to be made, our translators have exactly followed the order of the original. And, indeed, all translators of any taste, unless when cramped by the genius of the tongue in which they wrote, have in such cases done the same.[6] It may be proper also to remark, that there are some modern tongues which in this respect are much more inflexible than ours.

The next example I shall produce is very similar to the former, as in it the substantive verb is preceded by the participle passive, and followed by the nominative. In the acclamations of the people on our Saviour's public entry into Jerusalem, the historian informs us, that they cried out, "Blessed is he that cometh in the name of the Lord."[7] Instead of this, say "He that cometh in the name of the Lord is blessed;" and by this alteration in the order of the words, apparently trifling, you convert a fervid exclamation into a cold aphorism.

The third example shall be of an active verb, preceded by the accusative, and followed by the nominative. It may be proper to observe, by the way, that unless one of these is a pronoun such an arrangement is scarcely admissible in our language. These cases in our nouns, not being distinguished by inflection, as they are in our pronouns, are solely ascertained by place. But to come to the proposed example, we are informed by the sacred historian that when Peter and John ordered the cripple, who sat begging at the beautiful gate of the temple, to look on them, he looked at them very earnestly, expecting to receive

[6] Gr. Μεγαλη ἡ Αρτεμις Εφεσιων. Lat. Vulg. Erasm. "Magna Diana Ephesiorum." Castal. Beza, "Magna est Diana Ephesiorum." Ital. Diodati, "Grande e la Diana degli Efesii." How weak in comparison is the French version of Le Clerc! "La Diane des Ephesiens est une grande déesse." How deficient that of Beausobre! "La grande Diane des Ephesiens." How ridiculous that of Saci! "Vive la grande Diane des Ephesiens."

[7] Matt. xxi. 9. Gr. Ευλογημενος ὁ ερχομενος εν ονοματι Κυριου. Lat. Vulg. Eras. Bez. "Benedictus qui venit in nomine Domini." Cast. "Benè sit ei qui venit," &c. Ital. Diod. "Benedetto colui che viene nel nome del Signore." Fr. Le Clerc, Beaus., Saci, "Beni soit celui qui vient au nom du Seigneur."

something from them. Then Peter said, "Silver and gold have I none, but such as I have, give I thee; in the name of Jesus Christ of Nazareth, arise and walk."[8] Here the wishful look and expectation of the beggar naturally leads to a vivid conception of that which was the object of his thoughts, and this conception as naturally displays itself in the very form of the declaration made by the apostle. But as every thing is best judged by comparison, let us contrast with this the same sentence arranged according to the rigid rules of grammar, which render it almost a literal translation of the Italian and French versions quoted in the margin, "I have no gold and silver; but I give thee that which I have: In the name of —" The import is the same, but the expression is rendered quite exanimate. Yet the sentences differ chiefly in arrangement, the other difference in composition is inconsiderable.

There is another happy transposition in the English version of the passage under view, which, though peculiar to our version, deserves our notice, as it contributes not a little to the energy of the whole. I mean not only the separation of the adjective *none* from its substantives *silver* and *gold*, but the placing of it in the end of the clause, which, as it were, rests upon it. "Silver and gold have I *none*." For here, as in several other instances, the next place to the first, in respect of emphasis, is the last. We shall be more sensible of this by making a very small alteration on the composition and structure of the sentence, and saying, "Silver and gold are not in my possession;" which is manifestly weaker.

My fourth example should be one wherein the verb occupies the first place in the sentence, which often happens in the ancient languages with great advantage in point of vivacity. But this cannot frequently obtain in English, without occasioning an ambiguity; the first place when given to the verb, being, by the rules of our syntax, appropriated to distinguish these three things, a command, as "*Stay* not here;" a question, as

[8] Acts. iii. 6. Gr. Αργυριον και χρυσιον ουχ ὑπαρχει μοι· ὁ δε εχω, τουτο σοι διδωμι. Εν ονοματι Ιησου Χριστου του Ναζωραιου εγειραι και περιπατει. Lat. Vul. Eras. Bez. "Argentum et aurum non est mihi; quod autem habeo, hoc tibi do. In nomine Jesu Christi Nazareni, surge et ambula." Castalio hath not adhered so closely to the order of the words in the original, but hath in this and some other places, for the sake of latinity, weakened the expression: "Nec argentum mihi nec aurum est; sed quod habeo, hoc tibi do. In nomine," &c. It would seem that neither the Italian language nor the French can admit so great a latitude in arranging the words; for in these the vivacity resulting from the order is not only weakened but destroyed. Diod. "Io non ho ne argento ne oro; ma quel che ho, io t'el dono: nel nome di Jesu Christo il Nazareo, levati e camina." Le Clerc, Beausobre, "Je n'ai ni or ni argent; mais ce que j'ai, je vous le donne: au nom de Jesus Christ de Nazareth, levez-vous et marchez." Saci's is the same, except in the last member, where, by transposing the words, "au nom de Jesus Christ de Nazareth," and putting them after "levez-vous," he hath altered the sense, and made that a circumstance attending the action of the lame man, which was intended to express the authority whereby the apostle gave the order.

"*Were* they present?" and a supposition, as "*Had* I known," from an assertion, as "*Ye stay* not here;" "They *were* present;" and "I *had* known." A few trifling phrases, as *said he*, *replied they*, are the sole exceptions in the simple tenses, at least in prose. In some instances, however, in the compound tenses, the verb may precede without giving rise to any double meaning. In such cases it is not the auxiliary or the substantive verb that begins the sentence, as in supposition and interrogation, but the infinitive of the principal verb in the active voice, and the participle in the passive, as in expressions like these, "*Go* I must, whatever may ensue." "*Avoid* it he could not by any means." An instance in the passive voice hath been given in the second example. I shall here observe, that in one passage of Scripture our translators, by not attending to this small circumstance, that the import of the passive verb lies in the participle, have, without necessity, not only given up the emphatical arrangements, but, in order to be literal, have copied a figure, which, though forcible in the original, is, in the place assigned it in the translation, rather unnatural and insignificant. The passage alluded to is this, "Another angel followed, saying, Babylon is fallen, is fallen, that great city."[9] Here, as it was the event itself that chiefly occupied the angel's mind, the verb in the Greek with great propriety begins the proclamation: Again, as it was an event of so surprising a nature, and of such mighty consequence, it was natural to attempt, by repeating the word, to rivet it in the minds of the hearers, ere he proceeded any further. The words *is fallen* in our language answer to the single word by which the verb is expressed in the original. Our translators were sensible they could not say, "*Is fallen*, *is fallen*, Babylon that great city." This could convey no meaning, being neither affirmation nor interrogation, hypothesis nor wish. For this reason they have preferred the colder arrangement prescribed by grammarians, though by so doing they have also lost the effect of the reduplication. A little attention to the genius of our tongue would have shown

[9] Rev. xiv. 8. Gr. Επεσεν, επεσε Βαβυλων ἡ πολις ἡ μεγαλη. As the expression is taken from Is. xxi. 9, the same order is found in the Hebrew, נפלה נפלה בבל. All the Latin translators that I have seen, have followed the same order. "Cecidit, cecidit Babylon, urbs illa magna." Le Clerc and Saci in the French both agree with the arrangement in the English. "Babylone est tombée: elle est tombée: cette grande ville." Beausobre's version in that tongue is rather better, as it comes nearer the order of the words in the Greek. He begins with the pronoun, and puts the name after the verb. "Elle est tombée, elle est tombée, Babylone la grande ville." This, I believe, is as near the original as the idiom of the French will permit. In the Italian, Diodati hath preserved entirely the vivacity resulting both from the disposition of the words and the reduplication of the verb, and hath given the passage that turn which the English interpreters might and should have given it: "Caduta, caduta e Babilonia la gran cita." It is evident that in this matter the Italian allows more liberty than the French, and the English more than the Italian. The truth of this observation will appear more fully afterwards.

them that all the effect, both of the order and of the figure, would have been preserved by saying, "*Fallen, fallen,* is Babylon the great city."[1]

Often a particle, such as an adverb or preposition belonging to a compound verb (for it matters not in which way you consider it), emphatically begins the sentence, as in that formerly quoted for another purpose. "*Up* goes my grave Impudence to the maid." In the particle *up*, that circumstance is denoted which particularly marks the impudence of the action. By the help of it, too, the verb is made to precede the nominative, which otherwise it could not do. In negations it holds very generally, that the negative particle should be joined to the verb. Yet in some cases the expression is greatly enlivened, and consequently the denial appears more determinate, by beginning the sentence with the adverb. "*Not* every one," says our Saviour, "that saith unto me, Lord, Lord, shall enter into the kingdom of heaven; but he that doeth the will of my Father who is in heaven."[2] Vary but the position of the negative in the first member, and say, "Every one that saith unto me, Lord, Lord, shall not enter into the kingdom of heaven," and you will flatten the expression exceedingly. On so light a circumstance in the arrangement does the energy of a sentence sometimes depend. We have some admirable examples of the power of this circumstance in Shakspeare. In the conference of Malcolm with Macduff; after the former had asserted that he himself was so wicked that even Macbeth, compared with him, would appear innocent as a lamb, Macduff replies with some warmth.

————————*Not* in the legions
Of horrid hell, can come a devil more damn'd,
In ills to top Macbeth.[3]

The arrangement in this sentence is admirably adapted to the speaker's purpose; whereas, if you dispose the words in the usual manner, and say, "A more damned devil in the legions of horrid hell cannot come to top Macbeth in ills;" we shall scarcely be persuaded that the thought is the same. If it were needful to multiply examples, I might easily show that other

[1] Somewhat similar is the admirable example we have in this passage of Virgil:

Me, me, adsum qui feci, in me convertite ferrum. Æn. L. ix.

The emphasis here is even the stronger, that the pronoun so happily begun with and repeated is perfectly irregular, it being quite detached from the construction of the sentence.

[2] Matt. vii. 21. Gr. Ου πας ὁ λεγων μοι, Κυριε Κυριε, εισελευσεται εις την βασιλειαν των ουρανων. All the Latin translators, however differently they express the sense, agree in beginning with the negative particle. So also doth Diodati in the Italian; "*Non* chiunque mi dice, Signore, Signore, entrera nel regno de' cieli." Not so the French. Le Clerc and Beausobre thus: "Tous ceux qui me disent, Seigneur, Seigneur, n'entreront pas tous dans le royaume du ciel." Saci thus, "Ceux qui me disent, Seigneur, Seigneur, n'entreront pas tous dans le royaume des cieux."

[3] Macbeth.

adverbs, particularly those of time and of place, when such circumstances require special notice, may, with great advantage to the energy, appear foremost in the sentence.

I proceed to observe that when a sentence begins with a conjunction, whether it be expressed in one word or more, with naming or titling the persons addressed, with a call to attention, or even with a term that is little more than an expletive, the place immediately following such phrase, title, or connective, will often give the same advantage to the expression that fills it, as in other cases the first place will do. The first term or phrase is considered only as the link which connects the sentence with that which went before; or if it have no relation to the preceding, as an intimation that something is to be said. Of this a few examples will suffice. The place immediately after a conjunction which begins the sentence is sometimes emphatical, as in that of Milton:

———At last *his sail-broad vans*
He spreads for flight.———[4]

where the description is the more picturesque that the verb is preceded by its regimen. The possessive pronoun and the epithet, unless when a particular emphasis rests upon one of them, are regarded only as constituting parts of one complex sign with the noun. Secondly, the place after the address, as in that of the same author,

Powers and dominions, deities of heaven!
* * * * * *
Me, tho' just right and the fixt laws of heaven
Did first create your leader.————[5]

Nothing could better suit, or more vividly express, the pride and arrogance of the arch-apostate, than the manner here used of introducing himself to their notice. Thirdly, the place after a call to attention, as in that of the apostle, "Behold, *now* is the accepted time: behold, *now* is the day of salvation."[6] Lastly, the place after an expletive: "There *came* no more such abundance of spices as these which the queen of Sheba gave to king Solomon."[7] Perhaps the word *there*, in this passage, cannot properly be termed an expletive; for though it be in itself insignificant, the idiom of the language renders it necessary in this disposition of the sentence; for such is the power of this particle, that by its means even the simple tenses of the verb can be made to precede the nominative, without the appearance of interrogation. For when we interrogate we must say, "Came there—" or "Did there come—." A little

[4] Paradise Lost, B. ii.
[5] Ibid.
[6] 2 Cor. vi. 2.
[7] 1 Kings x. 10.

attention will satisfy us that the verb in the passage produced ought to occupy the emphatical place, as the comparison is purely of what was brought into the country then, and what was at any time imported afterwards. Even though the particle *there* be preceded by the copulative, it will make no odds on the value of the place immediately following. "And there *appeared* to them Elias, and Moses."[8] The apparition is here the striking circumstance. And the first place that is occupied by a significant term is still the emphatical place. In all the three preceding quotations from Scripture the arrangement is the same in the original, and in most of the ancient translations, as it is with us. The modern versions vary more, especially in regard to the passage last quoted.[9]

I shall add one example more from Scripture, wherein the oblique case of the personal pronoun, though preceded by two conjunctions, emphatically ushers the verb and its nominative. "Among many nations there was no king like Solomon, who was beloved of his God, and God made him king over all Israel: nevertheless even him did outlandish women cause to sin."[1] My remark concerns only the last clause of the sentence. It is manifest that the emphasis here ought to rest on the *him*, who, from what immediately precedes, might have been thought proof against all the arts, even of female seduction. This clause, every body must perceive, would have been much more weakly expressed, had it been arranged thus: *Nevertheless outlandish women did cause even him to sin.*

[8] Mark ix. 4. Gr. Και ωφθη αυτοις Ηλιας συν Μωσει.

[9] In Italian, Diodati renders it, "Et Elia apparue loro, insieme con Moise." In French, Le Clerc, "Ensuite Elie et Moise leur apparurent." Beausobre, "Ils virent aussi paroître Moise et Elie." Saci, "Et ils virent paroître Elie et Moise." It would seem that neither of these tongues can easily admit the simple tense to precede both its nominative and its regimen. By the aid of the particle *there*, this is done in English without ambiguity, and without violence to the idiom of the language.

[1] Neh. xiii. 26. The clause affected by this criticism stands thus in the original: גַּם־אוֹתוֹ הֶחֱטִיאוּ הַנָּשִׁים הַנָּכְרִיּוֹת. The order is exactly the same in the Greek of the Septuagint; Και τουτον εξεκλιναν αἱ γυναικες αἱ αλλοτριαι: and nearly the same in the Latin Vulgate; "Et ipsum ergo duxerunt ad peccatum mulieres alienigenæ." Junius is rather more literal. "Etiam ipsum ad peccandum induxerunt feminæ alienigenæ." Castalio, with at least equal energy, places the pronoun before the conjunction. "Eum tamen ad peccandum mulieres perduxerunt extraneæ." In all these, as in the English translation, what is principally emphatical in the arrangement is preserved, the pronoun being the first among the significant terms. It is not so in Diodati's Italian version: "E pure le donne straniere lo fuero peccare:" nor in Saci's French; "Et après cela neanmoins des femmes étrangères le firent tomber dans le péché." It is remarkable, that though the ordinary grammatical rules, both of French and of Italian, place the pronoun governed before the governing verb, the reverse of which obtains in English, the latter language is more capable of accommodating itself to such an expressive disposition of the words, as has been now exemplified, than either of the former. The reason is, though these tongues make the oblique case of the pronoun generally precede the verb, they do not admit the nominative to intervene, but for the most part, except in asking a question, place it before both.

Sometimes indeed it is necessary, in order to set an eminent object in the most conspicuous light, to depart a little from the ordinary mode of composition as well as of arrangement. The following is an example in this way: "Your fathers, where are they? and the prophets, do they live for ever?"[2] A colder writer would have satisfied himself with saying, "Where are your fathers? and do the prophets live for ever?" But who, that has the least spark of imagination, sees not how languid the latter expression is, when compared with the former? The sentiment intended to be conveyed in both, namely the frailty and mortality of man, is one of those obvious truths which it is impossible for any person in his senses to call in question. To introduce the mention of it, in order to engage my assent to what nobody ever denied or doubted, would be of no consequence at all; but it is of consequence to rouse my attention to a truth which so nearly concerns every man, and which is, nevertheless, so little attended to by any. In such cases the end of speaking is not to make us *believe*, but to make us *feel*. It is the heart and not the head which ought to be addressed. And nothing can be better adapted to this purpose than first, as it were independently, to raise clear ideas in the imagination, and then, by the abruptness of an unexpected question, to send us to seek for the archetypes.

From all the examples above quoted, those especially taken from holy writ, the learned reader, after comparing them carefully, both with the original, and with the translations cited in the margin, will be enabled to deduce, with as much certainty as the nature of the question admits, that that arrangement which I call rhetorical, as contributing to vivacity and animation, is, in the strictest sense of the word, agreeably to what hath been already suggested, a natural arrangement; that the principle which leads to it operates similarly on every people, and in every language, though it is much more checked by the idiom of some tongues than by that of others; that, on the contrary, the more common, and what for distinction's sake I call the grammatical order, is, in a great measure, an arrangement of convention, and differs considerably in different languages.[3]

[2] Zech. i. 5.

[3] All the French critics are not so immoderately national as Bouhours. Since composing the foregoing observations I have been shown a book entitled, *Traité de la Formation méchanique des Langues*. The sentiments of the author on this subject are entirely coincident with mine. He refers to some other treatises, particularly to one on Inversion, by M. de Batteux, which I have not seen. Concerning it he says, "Ceux qui l'auront lu, verront que c'est le défaut de terminaisons propres à distinguer le nominatif de l'accusatif, qui nous a forcé à prendre cet ordre moins naturel qu'on ne le croit: que l'inversion est dans nôtre langue, non dans la langue Latine, comme on se le figure: que les mots étant plus faits pour l'homme que pour les choses, l'ordre essentiel à suivre, dans le discours représentatif de l'idée des objets, n'est pas tant la marche commune des choses dans la nature que la succession véritable des pensées, la rapidité des sentimens ou de l'intérêt du cœur, la

He will discover also, that to render the artificial or conventional arrangement, as it were, sacred and inviolable, by representing every deviation (whatever be the subject, whatever be the design of the work) as a trespass against the laws of composition in the language, is one of the most effectual ways of stinting the powers of elocution, and even of damping the vigour both of imagination and of passion. I observe this the rather, that in my apprehension, the criticism that prevails amongst us at present leans too much this way. No man is more sensible of the excellence of purity and perspicuity, properly so called; but I would not hastily give up some not inconsiderable advantages of the English tongue, in respect both of eloquence and of poetry, merely in exchange for the French *netteté*.

I should next proceed to make some remarks on the disposition and the form of the clauses in complex sentences; for though some of the examples already produced are properly complex, in these I have only considered the arrangement of the words in the principal member, and not the disposition of the members. But before I enter on this other discussion, it will be proper to observe, and by some suitable examples to illustrate the observation, that the complex are not so favourable to a vivacious diction as the simple sentences, or such as consist of two clauses at the most.

Of all the parts of speech, the conjunctions are the most unfriendly to vivacity; the next to them the relative pronouns, as partaking of the nature of conjunction. It is by these parts, less significant in themselves, that the more significant parts, particularly the members of complex sentences, are knit together. The frequent recurrence, therefore, of such feeble supplements, cannot fail to prove tiresome, especially in pieces wherein an enlivened and animated diction might naturally be expected. But no where hath simplicity in the expression a better effect in invigorating the sentiments, than in poetical description on interesting subjects. Consider the song composed by Moses, on occasion of the passage of the Israelites through the Red Sea, and you will find, that part of the effect produced by that noble hymn is justly imputable to the simple, the abrupt, the rapid manner adopted in the composition. I shall produce only two verses for a specimen. "The enemy said, I will pursue; I will overtake; I will divide the spoil; my revenge shall be satiated upon them: I will draw my sword; my hand shall destroy them; thou blewest with thy breath; the sea covered them: they sank as lead in the mighty waters."[4] This is the figure which the Greek rhe-

fidélité de l'image dans la tableau de l'action; que le Latin en préférant ces points capitaux procède plus naturellement que le Français," &c. No. 22.

[4] Exod. xv. 9, 10. The word by our interpreters rendered *wind* also denotes

toricians call asyndeton, and to which they ascribe a wonderful efficacy. It ought to be observed that the natural connexion of the particulars mentioned is both close and manifest; and it is this consideration which entirely supersedes the artificial signs of that connexion, such as conjunctions and relatives. Our translators (who, it must be acknowledged, are not often chargeable with this fault) have injured one passage in endeavouring to mend it. Literally rendered it stands thus: "Thou sentest forth thy wrath: it consumed them as stubble."[5] These two simple sentences have appeared to them too much detached. For this reason, they have injudiciously combined them into one complex sentence, by inserting the relative *which*, and thereby weakened the expression: "Thou sentest thy wrath, which consumed them as stubble." They have also thought fit sometimes to add the conjunction *and* when it was not necessary, and might well have been spared.

If any one perceives not the difference, and consequently, is not satisfied of the truth of this doctrine, let him make the following experiment on the song now under review. Let him transcribe it by himself, carefully inserting conjunctions, and relatives in every place which will admit them in a consistency with the sense, and then let him try the effect of the whole. If, after all, he is not convinced, I know no argument in nature that can weigh with him. For this is one of those cases in which the decision of every man's own taste must be final with regard to himself.

But those who feel the difference in the effects, will permit such as are so disposed to speculate a little about the cause. All that comes under the cognizance of our senses, in the operations either of Nature or of Art, is the causes which precede, and the effects which follow. Hence is suggested to the mind the notion of power, agency, or causation. This notion or idea (call it which you please) is from the very frame of our nature, suggested, necessarily suggested, and often instantaneously suggested; but still it is suggested and not perceived. I would not choose to dispute with any man about a word, and, therefore, lest this expression should appear ex-

spirit and *breath*. A similar homonymy in the corresponding term may be observed, not only in the oriental, but in almost all ancient languages. When this noun has the affixed pronoun, by which it is appropriated to a person, the signification *wind* is evidently excluded, and the meaning is limited to either *spirit or breath*. When it is, besides, construed with the verb *blow*, the signification *spirit* is also excluded, and the meaning confined to *breath*. It is likewise the intention of the inspired penman to represent the wonderful facility with which Jehovah blasted all the towering hopes of the Egyptians. Add to this, that such a manner is entirely in the Hebrew taste, which considers every great natural object as bearing some relation to the Creator and Sovereign of the universe. The thunder is God's voice; the wind, his breath; the heaven, his throne; the earth, his footstool; the whirlwind and the tempest are the blasts of his nostrils.

[5] Exod. xv. 7.

ceptionable, I declare my meaning to be only this, that it is *conceived* by the understanding, and not *perceived* by the senses, as the causes and the effects themselves often are. Would you then copy nature in an historical or descriptive poem, present to our imaginations the causes and the effects in their natural order; the suggestion of the power or agency which connects them will as necessarily result from the lively image you produce in the fancy, as it results from the perception of the things themselves, when they fall under the cognizance of the senses.

But if you should take the other method, and connect with accuracy where there is relation; and, with the help of conjunctions and relatives, deduce with care effects from their causes, and allow nothing of the kind to pass unnoticed in the description, in lieu of a picture, you will present us with a piece of reasoning or declamation. Would you, on the contrary, give to reasoning itself the force and vivacity of painting, follow the method first prescribed, and that even when you represent the energy of spiritual causes, which were never subjected to the scrutiny of sense. You will thus convert a piece of abstruse reflection, which, however just, makes but a slender impression upon the mind, into the most affecting and instructive imagery.

It is in this manner the psalmist treats that most sublime, and, at the same time, most abstract of all subjects, the providence of God. With what success he treats it every person of taste and sensibility will judge. After a few strictures on the life of man, and of the inferior animals, to whatever element, air, or earth, or water, they belong, he thus breaks forth; "These wait all upon thee, that thou mayest give them their meat in due season. Thou givest them. They gather. Thou openest thy hand. They are filled with good. Thou hidest thy face. They are troubled. Thou takest away their breath. They die and return to their dust. Thou sendest forth thy spirit. They are created. Thou renewest the face of the earth."[6] It must be acknowledged, that it is not every subject, no, nor every kind of composition, that requires, or even admits the use of such glowing colours. The psalm is of the nature of the ode, being, properly defined, a sacred ode; and it is allowed that this species of poesy demands more fire than any other.

It may indeed be thought, that the vivacity resulting from this manner of composing is sufficiently accounted for, from the brevity which it occasions, and of which I treated in the preceding chapter. It is an undoubted truth, that the brevity here contributes to the force of the expression, but it is not

[6] Psalm civ. 27—30.

solely to this principle that the effect is to be ascribed. A good taste will discern a difference in a passage already quoted from the song of Moses, as it stands in our version, and as it is literally rendered from the Hebrew;[7] though in both, the number of words, and even of syllables, is the same. Observe also, the expression of the psalmist, who having compared man, in respect of duration, to a flower, says concerning the latter, "The wind passeth over it, and it is gone."[8] Had he said, "The wind passing over it, destroys it," he had expressed the same sentiment in fewer words, but more weakly.

But it may be objected, If such is the power of the figure asyndeton, and if the conjunctive particles are naturally the weakest parts in a sentence, whence comes it that the figure polysyndeton, the reverse of the former, should be productive of that energy which rhetoricians ascribe to it? I answer, the cases must be very different which require such opposite methods. Celerity of operation, and fervour in narration, are best expressed by the first. A deliberate attention to every circumstance, as being of importance, and to this in particular, the multiplicity of the circumstances, is best awakened by the second. The conjunctions and relatives excluded by the asyndeton are such as connect clauses and members; those repeated by the polysyndeton are such as connect single words only. All connectives alike are set aside by the former; the latter is confined to copulatives and disjunctives. A few examples of this will illustrate the difference. "While the earth remaineth," said God immediately after the deluge, "seedtime, and harvest, and cold, and heat, and summer, and winter, and day, and night shall not cease."[9] Every thing to which a permanency of so great importance is secured, requires the most deliberate attention. And in the following declaration of the apostle, much additional weight and distinctness are given to each particular by the repetition of the conjunction. "I am persuaded that neither death, nor life, nor angels, nor principalities, nor powers, nor things present, nor things to come, nor height, nor depth, nor any other creature, shall be able to separate us from the love of God."[1]

SECTION III.—*Complex Sentences.*

PART I.—*Subdivision of these into Periods and loose Sentences.*

I come now to the consideration of complex sentences. These are of two kinds. They are either periods, or sentences

[7] Exod. xv. 7. [8] Psalm ciii 16. [9] Gen. viii. 22. [1] Rom. viii. 38, 39.

of a looser composition, for which the language doth not furnish us with a particular name. A period is a complex sentence, wherein the meaning remains suspended, till the whole is finished. The connexion, consequently, is so close between the beginning and the end, as to give rise to the name *period*, which signifies circuit. The following is such a sentence: "Corruption could not spread with so muc hsuccess, though reduced into system, and though some ministers, with equal impudence and folly, avowed it, by themselves and their advocates, to be the principal expedient by which they governed; if a long and almost unobserved progression of causes and effects did not prepare the conjuncture."[2] The criterion of a period is this: if you stop any where before the end, the preceding words will not form a sentence, and therefore cannot convey any determined sense. This is plainly the case with the above example. The first verb being *could*, and not *can*, the potential and not the indicative mood, shows that the sentence is hypothetical, and requires to its completion some clause beginning with *if*, *unless*, or some other conditional particle. And after you are come to the conjunction, you find no part where you can stop before the end.[3] From this account of the nature of a period, we may justly infer, that it was much easier in Greek and Latin to write in periods than it is in English, or perhaps in any European tongue. The construction with them depended

[2] Bolingbroke, Spirit of Patriotism.

[3] It is surprising that most modern critics seem to have mistaken totally the import of the word *period*, confounding it with the complex sentence in general, and sometimes even with the simple but circumstantiated sentence. Though none of the ancients, as far as I remember, either Greek or Latin, have treated this matter with all the precision that might be wished, yet it appears to me evident, from the expressions they employ, the similitudes they use, and the examples they produce, that the distinction given above perfectly coincides with their notions on this subject. But nothing seems more decisive than the instance which Demetrius Phalereus has given of a period from Demosthenes, and which, for the sake of illustrating the difference, he has also thrown into the form of a loose sentence. I refer the learned reader to the book itself; Περι Ἑρμηνειας I. IA. The ancients did indeed sometimes apply the word *period* to simple but circumstantiated sentences of a certain structure. I shall give the following example in our own language for an illustration; "At last, after much fatigue, through deep roads and bad weather, we came with no small difficulty to our journey's end." Otherwise thus, "We came to our journey's *end* at *last*, with no small *difficulty*, after much *fatigue*, through deep *roads*, and bad weather." The latter is in the loose, the former in the periodic composition. Accordingly in the latter there are, before the conclusion, no less than five words, which I have distinguished by the character, namely, *end*, *last*, *difficulty*, *fatigue*, *roads*, with any of which the sentence might have terminated. One would not have expected that a writer so accurate and knowing as M. du Marsais, should so far have mistaken the meaning of the word *period* in the usage of the ancients, as to define it in this manner: *La période est un assemblage de propositions liées entr' elles par des conjonctions, et qui toutes ensemble font un sens fini.* "The period is an assemblage of propositions connected by conjunctions, and making altogether one complete sense."—(Principes de Grammaire, La Periode.) This is a proper definition of a complex sentence; and that he meant no more is manifest from all his subsequent illustrations. Take the following for an example, which he gives in another

mostly on inflection: consequently the arrangement, which ascertains the character of the sentence in respect of composition, was very much in their own power; with us, on the contrary, the construction depends mostly on arrangement, which is therefore comparatively very little in our power. Accordingly, as the sense in every sentence hangs entirely on the verb, one ordinary way with them of keeping the sense suspended, was by reserving the verb to the end. This in most cases the structure of modern languages will not permit us to imitate. An example of a complex sentence, that is not a period, I shall produce from the same performance. "One party hath given their whole attention, during several years, to the project of enriching *themselves*, and impoverishing the rest of the *nation;* and by these and other means of establishing their *dominion*, under the *government*, and with the favour of a family who were *foreigners*, and therefore might believe that they were established on the throne by the good will and strength of this party alone." The criterion of such loose sentences is as follows: There will always be found in them one place at least before the end, at which, if you make a stop, the construction of the preceding part will render it a complete sentence. Thus in the example now given, whether you stop at the word *themselves*, at *nation*, at *dominion*, at *government*, or at *foreigners*, all which words are marked in the quotation in italics, you will find you have read a perfect sentence.

Wherefore then, it may be asked, is this denominated one sentence, and not several? For this reason, that though the preceding words, when you have reached any of the stops above mentioned, will make sense, and may be construed separately, the same cannot be said of the words which follow.

In a period, the dependence of the members is reciprocal; in a loose sentence the former members have not a necessary dependence on the latter, whereas the latter depend entirely on the former. Indeed, if both former and latter members are, in respect of construction, alike independent on one another, they do not constitute one sentence, but two or more. And here I shall remark by the way, that it is by applying the observation just now made, and not always by the pointing, even where the laws of punctuation are most strictly observed, that we can discriminate sentences. When they are closely related in respect of sense, and when the sentences themselves are simple, they are for the most part separated only by commas or by

place of the same work: "*Il y a un avantage réel à être instruit; mais il ne faut pas que cet avantage inspire de l'orgueil.*" "There is a real advantage in being instructed; but we ought not to be proud of this advantage." He adds, "Le *mais* rapproche les deux propositions ou membres de la période, et les met en opposition." "The *but* connects the two propositions or members of the period, and sets them in opposition." Des Conjonctions. It is evident that the sentence adduced is no period in the sense of the ancients.

semicolons, rarely by colons, and almost never by points. In this way the passages above quoted from the song of Moses and the Psalms are pointed in all our English Bibles.

But there is an intermediate sort of sentences which must not be altogether overlooked, though they are neither entirely loose, nor perfect periods. Of this sort is the following: "The other institution," he is speaking of the eucharist, "has been so disguised by ornament, ‖ and so much directed, in your church at least, to a different purpose from commemoration, that if the disciples were to assemble at Easter in the chapel of his Holiness, Peter would know his successor as little, ‖ as Christ would acknowledge his *vicar;* and the rest would be unable to guess ‖ what the ceremony *represented* ‖ or intended."[4] This sentence may be distributed into four members. The first is complex, including two clauses, and ends at *commemoration.* The second is simple, ending at *Holiness.* It is evident that the sentence could not terminate at either of these places, or at any of the intermediate words. The third member is subdivided into two clauses, and ends at *vicar.* It is equally evident that if the sentence had been concluded here, there would have been no defect in the construction. The fourth member, which concludes the sentence, is also compound, and admits a subdivision into three clauses. At the word *represented,* which finishes the second clause, the sentence might have terminated. The two words which could have admitted a full stop after them are distinguished by italics. Care hath also been taken to discriminate the members and the clauses. It may, however, justly be affirmed, that when the additional clause or clauses are, as in the preceding example, intimately connected with the foregoing words, the sentence may still be considered as a period, since it hath much the same effect. Perhaps some of the examples of periods to be produced in the sequel, if examined very critically, would fall under this denomination. But that is of little or no consequence.

On comparing the two kinds of complex sentences together, to wit, the period and the loose sentence, we find that each hath its advantages and disadvantages. The former savours more of artifice and design, the latter seems more the result of pure Nature. The period is nevertheless more susceptible of vivacity and force: the loose sentence is apt, as it were, to languish, and grow tiresome. The first is more adapted to the style of the writer, the second to that of the speaker. But as that style is best, whether written or spoken, which hath a proper mixture of both; so there are some things, in every species of discourse, which require a looser, and some which require a preciser manner. In general, the use of periods best suits the dignity of the historian, the political writer, and the

[4] Bol. Phil. Es. iv. Sect. 7.

philosopher. The other manner more befits the facility which ought to predominate in essays, dialogues, familiar letters, and moral tales. These approach nearer the style of conversation, into which periods can very rarely find admittance. In some kinds of discourses intended to be pronounced, but not delivered to the public in writing, they may properly find a place in the exordium and narration, for thus far some allowance is made for preparation; but are not so seasonable, unless very short, in the argumentative part, and the pathetic.

PART II.—*Observations on Periods, and on the use of Antithesis in the composition of Sentences.*

I now proceed to offer some observations on the period. It hath been affirmed to have more energy than a sentence loosely composed. The reason is this: The strength which is diffused through the latter, is in the former collected, as it were, into a single point. You defer the blow a little, but it is solely that you may bring it down with greater weight. But in order to avoid obscurity, as well as the display of art, rhetoricians have generally prescribed that a period should not consist of more than four members. For my own part, as members of sentences differ exceedingly both in length and in structure from one another, I do not see how any general rule can be established to ascertain their number. A period consisting of but two members may easily be found, that is at once longer, more artificial, and more obscure, than another consisting of five. The only rule which will never fail, is to beware both of prolixity and of intricacy; and the only competent judges in the case are good sense and a good ear.

A great deal hath been said, both by ancient critics and by modern, on the formation and turn of periods. But their remarks are chiefly calculated with a view to harmony. In order to prevent the necessity of repeating afterwards, I shall take no notice of these remarks at present, though the rules founded on them do also in a certain degree contribute both to perspicuity and to strength.

That kind of period which hath most vivacity is commonly that wherein you find an antithesis in the members, the several parts of one having a similarity to those of the other, adapted to some resemblance in the sense. The effect produced by the corresponding members in such a sentence is like that produced in a picture where the figures of the group are not all on a side, with their faces turned the same way, but are made to contrast each other by their several positions. Besides, this kind of periods is generally the most perspicuous. There is in them not only that original light which results from the expression when suitable, but there is also that which is reflected reciprocally from the opposed members. The relation between these is so strongly marked, that it is next to impossible to lose sight of it. The same quality makes them also easier for the memory.

Yet to counterbalance these advantages, this sort of period often appears more artful aud studied than any other. I say *often*, because nothing can be more evident, than that this is not always the case. Some antitheses seem to arise so naturally out of the subject, that it is scarcely possible in another manner to express the sentiment. Accordingly we discover them even in the Scriptures, the style of which is perhaps the most artless, the most natural, the most unaffected, that is to be found in any composition now extant.

But I shall satisfy myself with producing a few specimens of this figure, mostly taken from the noble author lately quoted, who is commonly very successful in applying it. "If Cato," says he, "may be censured, severely indeed but justly, || for abandoning the cause of liberty, || which he would not however survive; . . what shall we say of those, || who embrace it faintly, || pursue it irresolutely, . . grow tired of it, || when they have much to hope, . . and give it up, || when they have nothing to fear?"[5] In this period there is a double antithesis, the two clauses which follow the pronoun *those* are contrasted, so are also the two members (each consisting of two clauses) which conclude the sentence. Another specimen of a double antithesis differently disposed, in which he hath not been so fortunate, I shall produce from the same work. "Eloquence that leads mankind by the ears, || gives a nobler superiority || than power that every dunce may use, || or fraud that every knave employ, || to lead them by the nose." Here the two intermediate clauses are contrasted, so are also the first and the last. But there is this difference. In the intermediate members there is a justness in the thought as well as in the expression, an essential requisite in this figure. In the other two members the antithesis is merely verbal; and is therefore at best but a trifling play upon the words. We see the connexion which eloquence has with the ears, but it would puzzle Œdipus himself to discover the connexion which either power or fraud has with the nose. The author, to make out the contrast, is in this instance obliged to betake himself to low and senseless cant.

Sometimes, though rarely, the antithesis affects three several clauses. In this case the clauses ought to be very short, that the artifice may not be too apparent. Sometimes, too, the antithesis is not in the different members of the same sentence, but in different sentences. Both the last observations are exempli-

[5] On the Spirit of Patriotism.

fied in the following quotation from the same performance: "He can bribe, ‖ but he cannot seduce. He can buy, ‖ but he cannot gain. He can lie, ‖ but he cannot deceive." There is likewise in each sentence a little of antithesis between the very short clauses themselves.

Neither is this figure entirely confined to periods. Sentences of looser composition admit it; but the difference here is the less observable, that an antithesis well conducted produces the effect of a period, by preventing the languor which invariably attends a loose sentence, if it happen to be long. The following is an instance of antithesis in such a sentence: "No man is able to make a juster application of what hath been here *advanced*, to the most important interests of your *country*, to the true interest of your royal master, and to your private interest *too;* if that will add, as I presume it will, some weight to the *scale;* and if that requires, as I presume it does, a regard to futurity as well as to the present moment."[6] That this is a loose sentence a little attention will satisfy every reader. I have marked the words in italics, at which, without violating the rules of grammar, it might have terminated. I acknowledge, however, that the marks of art are rather too visible in the composition.

Sometimes an antithesis is happily carried through two or three sentences, where the sentences are not contrasted with one another, as in the example already given, but where the same words are contrasted in the different members of each sentence, somewhat differently. Such an antithesis on the words *men*, *angels*, and *gods*, you have in the two following couplets:

> Pride still is aiming at the blest abodes;
> MEN would be ANGELS, ‖ ANGELS would be GODS.
> Aspiring to be GODS, ‖ if ANGELS fell;—
> Aspiring to be ANGELS, ‖ MEN rebel.[7]

The like varied opposition in the words *principles*, *means*, and *ends*, may be observed in the two following sentences: "They are designed to assert and vindicate the honour of the Revolution; of the principles established, of the means employed, and of the ends obtained by it. They are designed to explode our former distinctions, and to unite men of all denominations, in the support of these principles, in the defence of these means, and in the pursuit of these ends."[8] You have in the subsequent quotation an antithesis on the words *true* and *just*, which runs through three successive sentences. "The anecdotes here related were true, and the reflections made upon them were just

[6] Dedication of the Dissertation on Parties. [7] Essay on Man.
[8] Dedication of the Dissertation on Parties.

many years ago. The former would not have been related, if he who related them, had not known them to be true; nor the latter have been made, if he who made them had not thought them just: And if they were true and just then, they must be true and just now, and always."[9]

Sometimes the words contrasted in the second clause are mostly the same that are used in the first, only the construction and the arrangement are inverted, as in this passage, "The old may inform the young; || and the young may animate the old."[1] In Greek and Latin this kind of antithesis generally receives an additional beauty from the change made in the inflection, which is necessary in those ancient languages for ascertaining what in modern tongues is ascertained solely by the arrangement.[2] This obtains sometimes, but more rarely, in our language, as in these lines of Pope.

> Whate'er of mongrel no one class admits,
> A wit with dunces, || and a dunce with wits.[3]

Something pretty similar is also to be remarked, when the words in the contrasted members remain the same under different inflections, the construction varied but not inverted. And this is the last variety of the antithesis that I shall specify; for to enumerate them all would be impossible. You have an example of this kind of contrast in the last line of the following couplet.

> Leave such to trifle with more grace and ease,
> Whom folly pleases, || and—whose follies please.[4]

---

[9] Advertisement to the Letters on Patriotism.

[1] Dedication of the Dissertation on Parties.

[2] An instance of this is that given by Quint. l. ix. c. 3. "Non ut edam vivo, sed ut vivam edo." A literal translation into English, "I do not live that I may eat, but I eat that I may live," preserves the antithesis, but neither the vivacity nor the force of the original. The want of inflection is one reason of the inferiority, but not the only reason. It weakens the expression that we must employ fifteen words, for what is expressed in Latin with equal perspicuity in eight. Perhaps it would be better rendered, though not so explicitly, "I do not live to eat, but I eat to live." Another example in point is the noted epigram of Ausonius,

> Infelix Dido, nulli bene nupta marito:
> Hoc pereunte, fugis; hoc fugiente, peris.

But though it is chiefly in this sort which the ancients called αντιμεταβολη that the advantage of varied inflections appears, it is not in this sort only. In all antithesis without exception, the similar endings of the contrasted words add both light and energy to the expression. Nothing can better illustrate this than the compliment paid to Cæsar by Cicero, in his pleading for Ligarius —"Nihil habet nec fortuna tua majus quam ut possis, nec natura tua melius quam ut velis, conservare quam plurimos." This perhaps would appear to us rather too artificial. But this appearance ariseth merely from the different structure of modern languages. What would in most cases be impossible to us, the genius of their tongue rendered not only easy to them, but almost unavoidable.

[3] Dunciad, B. iv.

[4] Pope's Imitations of Horace, B. II. Ep. ii.

I shall now consider both what the merit of the antithesis is, and to what kind of composition it is best adapted. It hath been remarked already, and cannot be justly questioned, that it often contributes both to vivacity and to perspicuity; on the other hand, it hath been charged with bearing the manifest signatures both of artifice and of puerility; of artifice, because of the nice adjustment of the correspondent clauses; of puerility, because of the supposed insignificance of the task of balancing words and syllables. The latter of these charges results so entirely from the former, that an answer to one is an answer to both. It is solely the appearance of artifice that conveys the notion of a task, and thereby gives rise to the charge of childishness. If therefore in any instance an antithesis cannot be reckoned artificial, it will not, at least on account of the expression, be deemed puerile.

It was remarked, when I entered on the consideration of this figure, that it sometimes ariseth so naturally from the subject, as to appear inevitable. This particularly is the case where a comparison is either directly made, or only hinted. Samuel, we are told, said to Agag, immediately before he killed him, "As thy sword hath made women childless, so shall thy mother be childless among women."[5] The sentiment here expressed, namely, that the treatment which the tyrant was to receive, was due to him by the law of retaliation, rendered some antithesis in the words scarcely avoidable. Yet the antithesis in this passage is more in the thought than in the expression; as the words in the contrasted clauses are not opposed to each other with that nicety which many authors would have employed.

But though accuracy of opposition may on some occasions have a very good effect, this will never be the case where it gives rise to any thing that appears forced in the construction, unnatural in the arrangement, or unharmonious in the cadence. Nature, ease, and fluency, are first to be regarded. In the two following examples you have precision in the contrast, without the appearance of too much art in the expression. "Beware of the ides of March, said the Roman augur to Julius Cæsar. Beware of the month of May, says the British Spectator to his fair countrywomen."[6] Again, "I must observe, that as in some climates there is a perpetual spring, so in some female constitutions there is a perpetual May." In either instance, if the comparison itself escape censure, the expression will be pronounced faultless. An antithesis therefore doth not always necessarily imply art, and if in some instances it doth to a certain degree imply art, it ought to be remembered, that there are some kinds of composition, which not only admit, but even re-

[5] 1 Sam. xv. 33.

[6] Spectator, No. 395. X.

quire a more elaborate diction than other kinds; and that in every kind of composition there are some parts wherein even the display of art is more allowable than in other parts. The observations with regard to the proper subjects for periods will very nearly answer here, and therefore need not to be repeated.

The antithesis, it is thought, is particularly unfavourable to persuasion, and therefore quite unfit for the more vehement and argumentative parts of a discourse. This is true of some sorts of antithesis (for they differ greatly in their nature), but it is not true of all. It is true of such as are sometimes found in long and complicated sentences. But it is not true of those which sentences of a less compound nature may admit. The enthymeme itself, the common syllogism of orators, is often successfully cast into this mould. Demetrius Phalereus, in his treatise of elocution, hath given us an example of this, from one of the most eloquent orations of Demosthenes against his famous rival. The example translated into English equally suits our present purpose. "For as, if any of those had then been condemned, ‖ you would not now have transgressed;
so if you should now be condemned, ‖ others will not hereafter transgress."[7] The sentence is besides a perfect period, consisting of two members, each of which is subdivided into two clauses. I shall give the same argument with as little apparent antithesis as possible, by imitating the attempt which Demetrius hath made to express the sense in a looser manner. "Do not overlook this transgression of your laws; for if such transgressors were punished, this man would not now have acted as he hath done; nor will another do so afterwards, if he should be condemned on this occasion."[8] The argument is the same, though much less forcibly, and even less naturally expressed. But if the enthymeme is often cast into the form of antithesis, we may say of the dilemma, a species of argument in like manner frequent with orators, that it is hardly susceptible of another form, as in that given by Cicero: "If he is a bad man, why do you associate with him? if he is a good man, why do you accuse him?"[9] Nor are these the only sorts of argument that may be used in this manner. There is hardly any which may not in some cases derive both light and energy from this figure. What can be more cogently urged, or better adapted for silencing contradiction, than the answer which Balaam gave Balak, who used various expedients to induce him to turn the blessing

[7] Περι Ἑρμ. ΛΑ. *Ωσπερ γαρ ειτις εκεινων ἑαλω, συ τά δ' ουκ αν εγραψας· οὑτως αν συ νυν ἁλως αλλος ου γραψει.*

[8] Ibid. *Μη επιτρεπετε τοις τα παρανομα γραφουσιν· ει γαρ εκωλυοντο, ουκ αν νυν οὑτος ταυτα εγραψεν· ουδ ἑτερος ετι γραψει, τουτου νυν ἁλωντος.*

[9] De Inventione, lib. i. As the antithesis in the words is more perfect, and the expression more simple in the Latin, than it is possible to render them in a translation into any modern tongue; so the argument itself appears more forcible, "Si improbus est, cur uteris: sin probus, cur accusas?"

he had pronounced on Israel into a curse. Yet the prophet's reply runs wholly in antithesis. "God is not a man, ‖ that he should lie; . . neither the son of man, ‖ that he should repent. Hath he said, ‖ and shall he not do it? . . or hath he spoken, ‖ and shall he not make it good?"[1] In the same antithetic form the Psalmist disposeth his argument in support of the divine knowledge. "He that planted the ear, ‖ shall he not hear? He that formed the eye, ‖ shall he not see?"[2] He argues from the effect to the cause, the only way in which we can argue intelligibly concerning the divine attributes. But it would not be easy, I imagine, to give in so few words either a more perspicuous or a more persuasive turn to the reasoning. It is not then every kind of antithesis that either savours of artifice, or is unsuited to persuasion.

One thing to which it seems agreed on all sides that this figure is particularly adapted, is the drawing of characters. You hardly now meet with a character either in prose or in verse, that is not wholly delineated in antithesis. This usage is perhaps excessive. Yet the fitness of the manner can scarcely be questioned, when one considers that the contrasted features in this moral painting serve to ascertain the direction and boundaries of one another with greater precision than could otherwise be accomplished. It is too nice a matter, without the aid of this artifice, for even the most copious and expressive language. For a specimen in this way take these lines of Pope:

> Should such a man, too fond to rule alone,
> Bear, like the Turk, no brother near the throne,
> View him with scornful, yet with jealous eyes,
> And hate for arts that caus'd himself to rise;
> Damn with faint praise, ‖ assent with civil leer,
> And without sneering, teach the rest to sneer;
> Willing to wound, ‖ and yet—afraid to strike,
> Just hint a fault, ‖ and—hesitate dislike;
> Alike reserv'd to blame, or to commend,
> A tim'rous foe, ‖ and—a suspicious friend;
> Dreading ev'n fools, ‖ by flatterers besieged,
> And so obliging, ‖ that he ne'er obliged.[3]

With what a masterly hand are the colours in this picture blended; and how admirably do the different traits, thus opposed, serve, as it were, to touch up and shade one another! I would not be understood by this to signify my opinion of its likeness to the original. I should be sorry to think that it deserves this praise. The poet had received, or fancied he had received, great provocation. And perfect impartiality, in one under the influence of resentment, is more than can be expected

[1] Numb. xxiii. 19. [2] Psalm xciv 9.
[3] Prologue to the Satires.

from human nature. I only speak of the character here exhibited, as one who speaking of a portrait, without knowing the person for whom it was drawn, says it is well painted and that there is both life and expression in the countenance.

If there be any style of composition which excludes antithesis altogether (for I am not positive that there is), it is the pathetic. But the true reason which hath induced some critics immoderately to decry this figure is, that some authors are disposed immoderately to employ it. One extreme naturally drives those who perceive the error to the opposite extreme. It rarely leaves them, even though persons of good sense and critical discernment, precisely where they were before. Such is the repulsive power of jarring tastes. Nay, there is a kind of mode, which in these, as well as in other matters, often influences our censures without our knowing it. It is this which sometimes leads us to condemn as critics, what as authors we ourselves practise. Witness the following reproach from the author just now quoted.

> I see a chief who leads my chosen sons,
> All arm'd with points, antitheses, and puns.[4]

On the other hand it is certain, that the more agreeable the apposite and temperate use of this figure is, the more offensive is the abuse, or, which is nearly the same, the immoderate use of it. When used moderately, the appearance of art, which it might otherwise have, is veiled, partly by the energy of the expression, which doth not permit the hearer at first to attend critically to the composition, and partly by the simplicity, or at least the more artless structure, both of the preceding sentences and of the following. But if a discourse run in a continued string of antithesis, it is impossible the hearer should not become sensible of this particularity. The art is in that case quite naked. Then indeed the frequency of the figure renders it insipid, the sameness tiresome, and the artifice unsufferable.

The only original qualities of style which are excluded from no part of a performance, nay, which ought, on the contrary, to pervade the whole, are purity and perspicuity. The others are suited merely to particular subjects and occasions. And if this be true of the qualities themselves, it must certainly be true of the tropes and figures which are subservient to these qualities. In the art of cookery, those spiceries which give the highest relish must be used the most sparingly. Who then could endure a dish wherein these were the only ingredients? There is no trope or figure that is not capable of a good effect. I not except those which are reckoned of the lowest value, alliteration, paronomasia, or even pun. But then the effect

[4] Dunciad.

depends entirely on the circumstances. If these are not properly adjusted, it is always different from what it was intended to be, and often the reverse.

The antithesis in particular gives a kind of lustre and emphasis to the expression. It is the conviction of this that hath rendered some writers intemperate in the use of it. But the excess itself is an evidence of its value. There is no risk of intemperance in using a liquor which has neither spirit nor flavour. On the contrary, the richer the beverage is, the danger is the greater, and therefore it ought to be used with the greater caution. Quintilian hath remarked concerning the writings of Seneca, which are stuffed with antithesis, that "they abound in pleasant faults."[5] The example had not been dangerous, if the faults had not been pleasant. But the danger here was the greater, as the sentiments conveyed under these figures were excellent. The thought recommended the expression. An admiration of the former insinuated a regard to the latter, with which it was so closely connected, and both very naturally engaged imitation. Hence Seneca is justly considered as one of the earliest corrupters of the Roman eloquence. And here we may remark by the way, that the language of any country is in no hazard of being corrupted by bad writers. The hazard is only when a writer of considerable talents hath not perfect chastity of taste in composition: but, as was the case of Seneca, affects to excess what in itself is agreeable. Such a style, compared with the more manly elocution of Cicero, we call effeminate, as betraying a sort of feminine fondness for glitter and ornament. There is some danger that both French and English will be corrupted in the same manner. There have been some writers of eminence in both, who might be charged, perhaps as justly as Seneca, with abounding in pleasant faults.

But enough of the antithesis; I return to the consideration of periods in general. And on this head I shall only further remark, that when they consist of complex members, we must follow the same rule in arranging the clauses of each member, in order to give all possible energy to the sentence, that we do in arranging the members of the period. By doing thus, we shall never be in danger of thinking that the member is complete till it actually be so, just as by the structure of the period we are prevented from thinking the sentence finished before the end. A disappointment in the former case is of less moment, but it is still of some. In each it occasions a degree of languor which weakens the expression.

I shall give an example of a period where, in one of the members, this rule is not observed. "Having already shown how the fancy is affected by the works of Nature, and after-

[5] Instit. Lib. X. Cap. i. Abundant dulcibus vitiis.

wards considered in general both the works of Nature and of *Art*, || how they mutually assist and complete each other, || in forming such scenes and prospects || as are most apt to delight the mind of the beholder;   I shall in this paper throw together some reflections on that particular art || which has a more immediate tendency than any other, || to produce those pleasures of the imagination, || which have hitherto been the subject of this discourse."[6] This sentence is a period, agreeably to the definition formerly given. Wherever we stop, the sentence is imperfect till we reach the end. But the members are not all composed according to the rule laid down. It consisteth of three members. The first ends at *Nature*, is a single clause, and therefore not affected by the rule; the second is complex, consisting of several clauses, and ends at *beholder;* the third is also complex, and concludes the sentence. The last member cannot be faulty, else the sentence would be no period. The fault must then be in the structure of the second, which is evidently loose. That member, though not the sentence, might conclude, and a reader naturally supposes that it doth conclude, first at the word *art*, afterwards at the word *other*, both which are before its real conclusion. Such a composition therefore even in periods, occasions, though in a less degree, the same kind of disappointment to the reader, and consequently, the same appearance of feebleness in the style, which result from long, loose, and complex sentences. A very little alteration in the faulty member will unite the clause more intimately, and entirely remove the exception; as thus—— "and afterwards considered in general, how in forming such scenes and prospects, as are most apt to delight the mind of the beholder, the works both of Nature and of Art mutually assist and complete each other."

It may be thought, and justly too, that this care will sometimes make the expression appear elaborate. I shall only recommend it as one of the surest means of preventing this effect, to render the members as simple as possible, and particularly to avoid synonymas and redundancies, of which there are a few in the member now criticized. Such are *scenes* and *prospects*, *assist* and *complete*, *mutually* and *each other*. With the aid of this reformation also, the whole period will appear much better compacted as follows; "Having already shown how the fancy is affected by the works of Nature; and afterwards considered in general || how in forming such scenes as are most apt to delight the mind of the beholder, || the works both of Nature and Art assist each other;   I shall in this paper throw together some reflections on that particular art, || which has a more immediate tendency than any

[6] Spectator, No. 415. O.

other, || to produce those primary pleasures of the imagination, || which have hitherto been the subject of this discourse."

Part III.—*Observations on Loose Sentences.*

In complex sentences of looser composition, there is, as was observed, a much greater risk of falling into a languid manner. This may arise from different causes. First, even where the sentence is neither long nor complex, the members will sometimes appear disjointed. The consequence always is, that a hearer will at first be in doubt whether it be one sentence or more. Take the following for an example; "However, many who not read themselves, || are seduced by others that *do;* and thus become unbelievers upon trust, and at second *hand;* and this is too frequent a case."[7] The harmony of the members taken severally, contributes to the bad effect of the whole. The cadence is so perfect at the end both of the first member and of the second, that the reader is not only disappointed, but surprised, to find the sentence still unfinished. The additional clauses appear out of their proper place, like something that had been forgotten.

Another cause of languor here is the excessive length of a sentence, and too many members. Indeed, wherever the sentiments of an author are not expressed in periods, the end of a member or clause, or even an intermediate word, as hath been observed already, may be the end of the sentence. Yet the commonness of such sentences, when they do not exceed an ordinary length, prevents in a great measure a too early expectation of the end. On the contrary, when they transgress all customary limits, the reader begins to grow impatient, and to look for a full stop or breathing-place at the end of every clause and member. An instance of this excess you have in the succeeding quotation: "Though in yesterday's paper, we considered how every thing that is great, new, or beautiful, is apt to affect the imagination with pleasure, we must own that it is impossible for us to assign the necessary cause of this *pleasure,* because we know neither the nature of an idea, nor the substance of a human *soul,* which might help us to discover the conformity or disagreeableness of the one to the *other;* and therefore, for want of such a light, all that we can do, in speculations of this kind, is to reflect on those operations of the soul that are most *agreeable,* and to range, under their proper heads, what is pleasing or *displeasing* to the *mind,* without being able to trace out the several necessary and efficient *causes* from whence the pleasure or displeasure

7 Swift's Sermons on the Trinity.

arises."[8] The reader will observe that in this passage I have distinguished by italics all those words in the body of the sentence, no fewer than seven, at any of which, if there were a full stop, the construction of the preceding part would be complete. The fault here is solely in the length of the whole, and in the number of the parts. The members themselves are well connected.

In the next example we have both the faults above mentioned in one sentence: "Last year a paper was brought here from *England*, called a Dialogue between the Archbishop of Canterbury and Mr. *Higgins*, which we ordered to be *burnt* by the common *hangman*, as it well *deserved*, though we have no more to do with his Grace of Canterbury, than you have with the Archbishop of *Dublin*, whom you tamely suffer to be *abused openly*, and by *name*, by that paltry rascal of an *observator;* and lately upon an affair wherein he had no *concern*, I mean the business of the missionary of *Drogheda*, wherein our excellent primate was *engaged*, and did nothing but according to *law* and discretion."[9] Hardly will you find in any of the worst English writers a more exceptionable sentence in point of composition than the preceding, which is taken from one of the best. The spots which might be in it will be found, on an attentive perusal, to be no fewer than fourteen; the clauses are exceedingly unequal, abrupt, and ill-compacted. Intricacy in the structure of a complex sentence might also be here exemplified as a cause of languor. But as this error never fails to create obscurity, it hath been considered already under a former head.

PART IV.—*Review of what has been deduced above in regard to Arrangement.*

I have now briefly examined how far arrangement may contribute to vivacity, both in simple sentences and in complex, and from what principles in our nature it is, that the effect ariseth.

In this discussion I have had occasion to consider, in regard to simple sentences, the difference between what may properly be called the rhetorical and natural order, and that which I have denominated the artificial and grammatical, or the customary way of combining the words in any particular language. I have observed, as to the former, and taken some pains to illustrate the observation, that it is universal, that it results from the frame of spirit in which the sentiment, whatever it be, is spoken or written, that it is by consequence a

[8] Spectator, No. 413, O.
[9] Swift's Letter concerning the Sacramental Test.

sort of natural expression of that frame, and tends to communicate it to the hearer or the reader. I have observed also, that this order, which alone deserves the name of natural, is in every language more or less cramped by the artificial or conventional laws of arrangement in the language; that, in this respect, the present languages of Europe, as they allow less latitude, are considerably inferior to Greek and Latin, but that English is not a little superior in this particular to some of the most eminent of the modern tongues. I have shown also that the artificial arrangement is different in different languages, and seems chiefly accommodated to such simple explanation, narration, and deduction, as scarcely admits the exertion either of fancy or of passion.

In regard to complex sentences, both compound and decompound, I have remarked the difference between the loose sentence and the period; I have observed the advantages and the disadvantages of each in point of vivacity, the occasions to which they are respectively suited, the rules to be observed in composing them, and the faults which, as tending to enervate the expression and tire the reader, ought carefully to be avoided. I have also made some remarks on the different kinds of antithesis, and the uses to which they may properly be applied.

Thus much shall suffice for the general illustration of this article, concerning the vivacity which results from arrangement.

CHAPTER IV.

Of the Connectives employed in combining the Parts of a Sentence.

I AM very sensible that the remarks contained in the preceding chapter on the particular structure and the particular arrangement in sentences, whether simple or complex, which are most conducive to vivacity, however well these remarks are founded, and however much they may assist us in forming a judgment concerning any performance under our review, are very far from exhausting this copious subject; and still farther from being sufficient to regulate our practice in composing.

For this reason I judged that the observations on the nature and the management of connective particles contained in this chapter and the succeeding might prove an useful supplement to the two preceding ones (for they are connected with both), and serve at once to enlarge our conceptions on this subject, and to assist our practice. At first indeed I had intended to comprehend both these chapters in the foregoing. But when I reflected, on the other hand, not only that they would swell the article far beyond the ordinary bounds, but that, however much the topics are related, the nature of the investigation contained in them is both different in itself, and must be differently conducted, I thought it would have less the appearance of digression, and conduce more to perspicuity, to consider them severally under their proper and discriminating titles.

I need scarcely observe, that by connectives I mean, all those terms and phrases which are not themselves the signs of things, of operations, or of attributes, but by which, nevertheless, the words in the same clause, the clauses in the same member, the members in the same sentence, and even the sentences in the same discourse, are linked together, and the relations subsisting among them are suggested. The last of these connexions I reserve for the subject of the ensuing chapter; all the rest I comprehend in this. The proper subject of this is the connectives of the several parts in the sentence; the proper subject of the next is the connectives of the several sentences in the discourse.

SECTION I.—*Of Conjunctions.*

It was observed already concerning the connectives, that of all the parts of speech they are the most unfriendly to vivacity. In their nature they are the least considerable parts, as their value is merely secondary. Yet, in respect of the difficulty there is in culling and disposing them, they often prove to an author the most considerable. In themselves they are but the taches which serve to unite the constituent parts in a sentence or a paragraph. Consequently, the less conspicuous they are, the more perfect will the union of the parts be, and the more easily will the hearer glide, as it were, from one word, clause, or member of a period into another. The more observable they are, the less perfect will the union be, and the more difficulty will the hearer pass on from member to member, from clause to clause, and from word to word. The cohesion of the parts of a cabinet or other piece of furniture seems always the more complete, the less the pegs and tacks, so necessary to effect it, are exposed to view.

It is a secret sense of the truth of this doctrine with regard to language, which imperceptibly, as taste improves in a nation, influences the writers to prefer short to long conjunctions. With us, in particular, it is the more necessary to attend to this circumstance, as the nouns and the verbs, which are the most significant words, are mostly monosyllables. For as every thing is judged by comparison, polysyllabic conjunctions must appear the more cumbersome on that very account. Happily enough at present our conjunctions and relatives in most frequent use (for the last also are merely a species of connectives) are monosyllables.[1] A few which do not occur so often are dissyllables.[2] Almost all the polysyllabic conjunctions are now either disused altogether, or occur but rarely.[3]

In the ancient style which obtained in this island, the conjunctions were sometimes lengthened and rendered remarkable by combining them together. Thus the particle *that*, which is both a conjunction and a relative, was annexed to most of them. Two centuries ago we should not have said, "*After* I have spoken," but, "*After that* I have spoken." In like manner we should then have said, *because that*, *before that*, *although that*, *whilst that*, *until that*, *except that*, *unless that*, *since that*, and *seeing that*. Sometimes they even used *if that*, *for that*, and *when that*. This particle seems to have been added in order to distinguish the conjunction from the preposition or the adverb, as the word to which it was annexed was often susceptible of both uses, and sometimes of all the three.[4] But the event hath shown that this expedient is quite superfluous. The situation marks sufficiently the character of the particle, so that you will rarely find an ambiguity arising from this variety in the application. The

1 Such are the following, in several of which the constituent syllable is also short, *and, too, or, nor, nay, yea, but, yet, if, tho', lest, than, as, ere, till, since, so, for, that, whilst, when, who, whose, whom, which, what.*

2 These are, *also, likewise, before, after, because, besides, further, again, unless, whereas, altho'.*

3 These are, *however, moreover, nevertheless, notwithstanding that, insomuch that, albeit, furthermore, forasmuch as.* The three last may be counted obsolete, except with scriveners, The rest cannot entirely be dispensed with.

4 The same manner of forming the conjunctions is retained to this day both in French and in Italian. They are in French, *après que, parce que, avant que, bien que, de peur que, tandis que, jusqu'à ce que, à moins que, depuis que, lors que;* in Italian, *subito che, percio che, prima che, anchora che, per tema che, mentre che, sin tanto che, altro che, da che, gia sia che.* An effect of the improvement of taste, though not in the same degree, may be observed in both these languages, similar to that which hath been remarked in English. Some drawling conjunctions formerly used are now become obsolete, as, in French, *encore bien que, bien entendu que, comme ainsi soit que;* in Italian, *concio fosse cosa che, par laqual cosa che, gia sia cosa che.* The necessary aid of the particle *que* in French for expressing the most different and even contrary relations, hath induced their celebrated critic and grammarian Abbé Girard to style it *the conductive conjunction.* The same appellation may be assigned with equal propriety to the *che* in Italian.

disuse therefore of such an unnecessary appendage is a real improvement.

The relatives, as was hinted before, partake of the nature of conjunction, both as they are the instruments of linking the members of sentences together, and as they have no independent signification of their own. These, when in coupling the clauses of a paragraph they are joined with a preposition, form what may properly be termed a sort of complex conjunctions. Such are, according to the original form of the words, *upon which*, *unto which*, *with that*, *by which*, or, according to a method of combining entirely analogical in our language, *whereupon*, *whereunto*, *therewith*, *whereby*. In the use of such drawling conjunctions, whether in the loose or in the compound form, there is considerable risk, as is evident from the principles above explained, of rendering the sentence tiresome, and the expression languid.

Some writers, sensible of the effect, seem totally to have mistaken the cause. They have imputed the flatness to the combination, imagining that the uncompounded form of the preposition and the pronoun would nowise affect the vivacity of the style. Lord Shaftesbury was of this opinion, and his authority hath misled other writers. His words are: "They have of late, it's true, reformed in some measure the gouty joints and darning work of *whereunto's*, *whereby's*, *thereof's*, *therewith's*, and the rest of this kind; by which complicated periods are so curiously strung, or hooked on, one to another, after the long-spun manner of the bar or pulpit."[5] Accordingly several authors have been so far swayed by this judgment, as to condemn, in every instance, this kind of composition of the adverbs *where*, *here*, and *there*, with prepositions. But if we would be satisfied that the fault, where there is a fault, doth not lie in the composition, let us make the experiment on one of the long-spun complicated periods of which the author speaks, by resolving the *whereupon* into *upon which*, by saying *unto which*, for *whereunto*, and so of the rest, and I am greatly deceived, if we find the darning work less coarse, or the joints less gouty, than they were before this correction. And if in any case the combined shall displease more than the primitive form, I suspect that the disuse will be found the cause and not the consequence of its displeasing.

Compositions of this sort, with dissyllabic prepositions, are now mostly obsolete, and it would be silly to attempt to revive them. But with several of the monosyllabic prepositions they are still used. I shall therefore here offer a few arguments

[5] Misc. v. chap. 1. For the same reason we should condemn the *quapropter*, *quamobrem*, *quandoquidem*, *quemadmodum*, of the Latin, whose composition and use are pretty similar. To these a good writer will not frequently recur; but their best authors have not thought fit to reject them altogether.

against dispossessing them of the ground which they still retain. First, they occasion a little variety. And even this, however inconsiderable, unless some inconvenience could be pleaded on the opposite side, ought, in conjunctions especially, for a reason to be given afterwards, to determine the matter. Secondly, they sometimes, without lengthening the sentence, interrupt a run of monosyllables (a thing extremely disagreeable to some critics), very opportunely substituting a dissyllable instead of two of the former. Thirdly, they in certain cases even prevent a little obscurity, or at least inelegance. It was observed, on a former occasion, that when any relative occurs oftener than once in a sentence, it will seldom be compatible with the laws of perspicuity that it should refer to different antecedents. And even if such change of the reference should not darken the sense, it rarely fails to injure the beauty of the expression. Yet this fault, in long periods and other complex sentences, is often scarcely avoidable. Sometimes the only way of avoiding it is by changing an *of which*, *in which*, or *by which*, into *whereof*, *wherein*, or *whereby*. This will both prevent the too frequent recurrence of the syllable *which*, none of the most grateful in the language; and elude the apparent inaccuracy of using the same sound in reference to different things. Fourthly, more is sometimes expressed by the compound than by the primitive form, and, consequently, there are occasions on which it ought to be preferred. The pronouns *this*, *that*, and *which*, do not so naturally refer to a clause or a sentence as to a word; nor do the two first refer so naturally to a plural as to a singular; whereas the compounds of *here*, *there*, and *where*, do, with equal propriety, refer to all these. Few will pretend that the place of *therefore* would be properly supplied by *for that*, or that *with what* would be in every case an equivalent for *wherewith;* or *after this*, for *hereafter;* but even in other instances not quite so clear, we shall on examination find a difference. In such a sentence as this, for example, "I flattered her vanity, lied to her, and abused her companions, and *thereby* wrought myself gradually into her favour;" it is evident that the words *by that* would here be intolerable; and if you should say *by these actions*, or *by so doing*, the expression would be remarkably heavier and more awkward.

The genuine source of most of these modern refinements is, in my opinion, an excessive bias to every thing that bears a resemblance to what is found in France, and even a prejudice against every thing to which there is nothing in France corresponding:—

> Whose manners still our tardy apish nation
> Limps after, in base awkward imitation.[6]

---

[6] Shakspeare, Richard II.

Hence it proceeds, that we not only adopt their words and idioms, but even imitate their defects, and act as if we thought it presumption to have any words or phrases of our own, to which they have nothing correspondent. I own that this may happen insensibly, without design or affectation on the part of our writers; and that either from the close intercourse which we have with that nation, or from the great use that we make of their writings, and the practice now so frequent of translating them. But that I may not be thought unreasonable in imputing to this cause what is not justly chargeable on it, I shall specify in the margin a few instances wherein the penury of the French language hath, in the way of which I am speaking, been hurtful to the English.[7]

[7] The local adverbs are very properly classed with us, as in Latin, into three orders, for denoting rest or motion *in* a place, motion *to* it, and motion *from* it. In every one of these orders, there are three adverbs to denote *this* place, *that* place, and *what*, or *which* place, interrogatively or relatively. In French there are only two orders, the first and second being confounded. See the scheme subjoined.

	1	2	3		1 & 2	3
English.	Here	Hither	Hence.	French.	Ici	D'ici.
	There	Thither	Thence.		Là	De là.
	Where	Whither	Whence.		Où	D'où.

Since the restoration, which I take to be neither the only nor the earliest, but the most successful era, in regard to the introduction of French books, French sentiments, and French modes, into this island, the adverbs of the first order have almost always been employed in conversation, and frequently in print, for those of the second. Thus we say, "*Where* are you going?" and sometimes, "Come *here*," though the only proper adverbs, in such cases, be *whither* and *hither*. Another instance the above scheme furnishes of the absurd tendency we have to imitate the French, even in their imperfections. The local adverbs of the third order are with them distinguished from those of the first and second only by prefixing the preposition *de*, which signifies *from*. This is manifestly the origin of those pleonastic phrases in English, *from hence*, *from thence*, and *from whence*. I shall produce another evidence of the bad effect of this propensity. So many of Nature's works are known to us by pairs, the sexes for example, and the most of the organs and the members of the human body, and, indeed, of every animal body, that it is natural, even in the simplest state of society, and in the rise of language, to distinguish the dual number from the plural. And though few languages have made, or, at least, retained this distinction in the declension of nouns, yet most have observed it in the numeral adjectives. The English, in particular, have observed it with great accuracy, as appears from the annexed scheme:—

When the discourse is of	two;	when it is of several.
Collectively	Both.	All.
Distributively	Each.	Every.
Indiscriminately	Either.	Any.
Exclusively	Neither.	None.
Relatively and Interrogatively	Whether	Which.

This distinction in French hath been overlooked altogether, and in English is beginning, at least in some instances, to be confounded. Perhaps the word *every* will not be found in any good writer applied to two; but it is certain that the word *each* hath usurped the place of *every*, and is now used promiscuously by writers of all denominations, whether it be *two* or *more* that are spoken of. The pronominal adjective *whether* is now quite obsolete, its place being supplied by *which*. About a century and a half ago, *whether*

I shall only here subjoin to these observations, that if the *whereunto's* and the *therewithal's*, may be denominated the gouty joints of style, the *viz.'s*, and the *i. e.'s*, and the *e. g.'s*, for *videlicet*, *id est*, and *exempli gratiâ*, may not unfitly be termed its crutches. Like these wretched props, they are not only of foreign materials, but have a foreign aspect. For as a stick can never be mistaken for a limb, though it may, in a clumsy manner, do the office of one, so these pitiful supplements can never be made to incorporate with the sentence, which they help in a bungling manner to hobble forward.

I proceed to exemplify further in our own language the general observation made above, that an improvement of taste leads men insensibly to abbreviate those weaker parts of speech, the connexive particles. I have remarked already the total suppression of the conjunction *that* after *because*, *before*, *although*, and many others of the same stamp, with which it was wont to be inseparably combined. But we have not stopped here. This particle is frequently omitted, when there is no other conjunction to connect the clauses, as in this example, "Did I not tell you positively, I would go myself?" In order to construe the sentence, we must supply the word *that* after *positively*. Concerning this omission I shall just observe, what I would be understood, in like manner, to observe concerning the omission of the relatives, to be mentioned afterwards, that though in conversation, comedy, and dialogue, such an ellipsis is graceful, when, without hurting perspicuity, it contributes to vivacity; yet, wherever the nature of the composition requires dignity and precision in the style, this freedom is hardly to be risked.

Another remarkable instance of our dislike to conjunctions

was invariably used of *two*, as appears from all the writings of that period, and particularly from the translation of the Bible; thus, Matt. xxi. 31, "*Whether* of them twain did the will of his father?" and xxiii. 17, "*Whether* is greater, the gold, or the temple?" The rest of this class have hitherto retained their places amongst us. How long they may continue to do so, it will be impossible to say. Indeed, the clumsy manner in which these places are supplied in French, doth perhaps account for our constancy, as it will prove, I hope, our security against a sudden change in this particular. It would sound extremely awkward in our ears *all the two, or the one or the other*, and *nor the one nor the other*, which is a literal version of *tous les deux, ou l'un ou l'autre*, and *ni l'un ni l'autre*, the phrases whereby *both*, *either*, and *neither*, are expressed in French. It may be said, custom softens every thing, and what though several words thus fall into disuse, since experience shows us that we can do without them? I answer, first, change itself is bad, unless evidently for the better; secondly, perspicuity is more effectually secured by a greater choice of words, when the meanings are distinct; thirdly, vivacity is promoted both by avoiding periphrasis, and by using words as much as possible limited in signification to the things meant by the speaker; fourthly, in an abundance without confusion, there is always greater scope for variety. And to come to the particular defect which gave rise to these observations, every body must be sensible that the frequent recurrence in French to these uncouth sounds, *quoi*, *que*, *qui*, *quelque*, and the like, doth not serve to recommend the language to the ear of a stranger.

is a method, for aught I know peculiar to us; by which the particles *though* and *if*, when in construction with any of the tenses compounded with *had*, *could*, *would*, or *should*, are happily enough set aside as unnecessary. This is effected by a small alteration in the arrangement. The nominative is shifted from its ordinary station before the auxiliary, and is placed immediately after it, as in these words, "Had I known the danger, I would not have engaged in the business;" that is, "*If* I had known the danger."—"Should you remonstrate ever so loudly, I would not alter my resolution," that is, "*Though* you should remonstrate,"——The reason that this transposition cannot be admitted in the other tenses is, that in them it would occasion an ambiguity, and give the sentence the appearance of an interrogation, which it scarcely ever hath in the tenses above mentioned. Sometimes, indeed, the preterimperfect admits this idiom, without rendering the expression ambiguous; as in these words, "Did I but know his intention," for "*If* I did but know his intention."—"Were I present," for "*If* I were present." The tense, however, in such instances, may more properly be termed an aorist, than a preterite of any kind; and the mood is subjunctive.

SECTION II.—*Of other Connectives.*

Now that I am speaking of the auxiliaries, it may not be amiss to remark, that they too, like the conjunctions, the relatives, and the prepositions, are but words of a secondary order. The signification of the verb is ascertained by the infinitive or the participle which follows the auxiliar in the compound tenses of the active voice, and always by the participle in the passive. The auxiliaries themselves serve only to modify the verb, by adding the circumstances of time, affirmation, supposition, interrogation, and some others. An abridgment in these, therefore, which are but weak, though not the weakest parts of discourse, conduceth to strengthen the expression. But there are not many cases wherein this is practicable. Sometimes *had* supplies emphatically the place of *would have*, and *were* of *would be*. An instance of the first we have in the words of Martha to our Saviour. "Lord, if thou hadst been here, my brother *had* not died."[8] The last clause would have been feebler, had it been, "my brother *would* not *have* died." An example of the second is the words of the Israelites on hearing the report of the spies. "*Were* it not better for us to return into Egypt?"[9] for "*Would* it not *be* better?"

But to come to the consideration of the relatives; the first real improvement which taste hath produced here, is the dis-

[8] John xi. 21.

[9] Num. xiv. 3.

mission of the article from its wonted attendance on the pronoun *which*. The definite article could no where be less necessary, as the antecedent always defines the meaning. Another effect of the same cause is the introduction of *what* instead of *that which*, as, "I remember *what* you told me;" otherwise, "*that which* you told me." Another is the extending of the use of the word *whose*, by making it serve as the possessive of the pronoun *which*.

The distinction between *who* and *which* is now perfectly established in the language. The former relates only to persons, the latter to things. But this distinction, though a real advantage in point of perspicuity and precision, affects not much the vivacity of the style. The possessive of *who* is properly *whose;* the pronoun *which*, originally indeclinable, had no possessive. This want was supplied in the common periphrastic manner by the help of the preposition and the article. But as this could not fail to enfeeble the expression, when so much time was given to mere conjunctives, all our best authors, both in prose and in verse, have come now regularly to adopt in such cases the possessive of *who;* and thus have substituted one syllable in the room of three, as in the example following: "Philosophy, *whose* end is to instruct us in the knowledge of Nature,"—for "Philosophy, *the* end *of which* is to instruct us." Some grammarians remonstrate. But it ought to be remembered, that use well established must give law to grammar, and not grammar to use. Nor is this acceptation of the word *whose* of recent introduction into the language. It occurs even in Shakspeare, and almost uniformly in authors of any character since his time. Neither does there appear to be any inconvenience arising from this usage. The connexion with the antecedent is commonly so close as to remove all possible ambiguity. If, however, in any instance, the application should appear ambiguous, in that instance, without question, the periphrasis ought to be preferred. But the term thus applied to things could not be considered as improper, any longer than it was by general use peculiarly appropriated to persons, and, therefore, considered merely as an inflection of the pronoun *who*. Now, that cannot be affirmed to be the case at present.

Though to limit the signification of the pronouns would at first seem conducive to precision, it may sometimes be followed with inconveniences which would more than counterbalance the advantage. "*That*," says Dr. Lowth, "is used indifferently both of persons and things, but perhaps would be more properly confined to the latter."[1] Yet there are cases wherein we cannot conveniently dispense with this relative as applied to persons;

[1] Introduction, Sentences.

as first, after *who* the interrogative, "Who *that* has any sense of religion would have argued thus?" Secondly, when persons make but a part of the antecedent; "The men and things that he hath studied, have not contributed to the improvement of his morals." In neither of these examples could any other relative be used. In the instances specified by Dr. Priestley,[2] the *that*, if not necessary, is at least more elegant than the *who*. The first is after a superlative, as, "He was the fittest person that could then be found;" the second is after the pronominal adjective *the same;* as, "He is the same man that you saw before." And it is even probable that these are not the only cases.

The possessive *its* of the neuter personal pronoun *it*, hath contributed in the same way, though not a relative, both to abbreviate and to invigorate the idiom of the present age. It is not above a century and a half since this possessive was first brought into use. Accordingly you will not find it in all the vulgar translation of the Bible. Its place there is always supplied either by the article and the preposition, as in these words, "They are of those that rebel against the light; they know not *the* ways *thereof*, nor abide in *the* paths *thereof*,"[3] for "they know not *its* ways, nor abide in *its* paths;" or by the possessive of the masculine, as in this verse, "The altar of burnt-offerings with all *his* furniture, and the laver and *his* foot."[4] The first method is formal and languid; the second must appear awkward to English ears, because very unsuitable to the genius of the language, which never, unless in the figurative style, as is well observed by Mr. Harris,[5] ascribes gender to such things as are neither reasonable beings, nor susceptible of sex.

The only other instance of abbreviation which I recollect in the pronouns, is the frequent suppression of the relatives *who*, *whom*, and *which*. This, I imagine, is an ellipsis peculiar to the English, though it may be exemplified from authors of the first note; and that too in all the cases following; first, when the pronoun is the nominative to the verb; secondly, when it is the accusative of an active verb; and thirdly, when it is governed by a preposition. Of the first case, which is rather the most unfavourable of the three, you have an example in these words, "I had several men died in my ship, of calentures,"[6] for "who died." Of the second, which is the most tolerable, in these, "They who affect to guess at the objects they cannot see,"[7] for "*which* they cannot see." Of the third, in these, "To contain the spirit of anger, is the worthiest discipline we

[2] Grammar, Pronouns.

[3] Job xxiv. 13.

[4] Exod. xxxi. 9.

[5] Hermes.

[6] Gull. Trav. Honyhnhmns.

[7] Bol. Phil. Es. ii. Sect. 1.

can put ourselves to,"[8] for "to *which* we can put ourselves." Sometimes, especially in verse, both the preposition and the pronoun are omitted, as in the speech of Cardinal Wolsey, after his disgrace,

> Had I but serv'd my God with half the zeal
> I serv'd my king.[9]——————

To complete the construction of this member of the sentence, the words *with which* must be supplied immediately after "zeal." Concerning this idiom I shall only observe in general, that as it is the most licentious, and therefore the most exceptionable in the language, it ought to be used very cautiously. In some cases it may occasion obscurity; in others, by giving a maimed appearance to the sentence, it may occasion inelegance. In both these it ought carefully to be avoided.[1]

The only other part of speech which partakes of the weakness remarked in conjunctions, relatives, and auxiliary verbs, is prepositions. These are expressive of the relations which substantives, as the signs of things, bear to one another, or to the verbs, the symbols of agency with which they are construed. They answer the same purpose in connecting words, which the conjunctions answer in connecting clauses. For the same reason the shorter these particles are, they are the better. The less time you bestow on the insignificant parts of a sentence, the more significant will the whole appear. Accordingly, in all languages the prepositions are commonly among their shortest words. With us such of them as are in most frequent use consist of one short syllable only.[2] And even those which occur seldomer, rarely exceed two syllables

On this part of speech the improvements have not been so

[8] Spectator, No. 438. T. [9] Shakspeare's Henry VIII.

[1] In French, by an idiom not unlike, the antecedent is often dropped, and the relative retained, as in this example, "Il ne faut pas se fier *à qui* a beaucoup d'ambition," "A qui," for "à *celui* qui." The idiom is not the same in Italian, for though the antecedent is sometimes dropped, there is properly no ellipsis, as the relative is changed: as thus, "Lo stampatore *a chi* leggie," for *a quel che*. This is exactly similar to the English *what* for *that which*. By poetic license there is sometimes an ellipsis of the antecedent in English verse, as in this line of Dryden, Georg. 2,

> Which *who* would learn as soon may tell the sands.

Who for *he who*. More rarely when the antecedent is the regimen of a verb, as

> I gladly shun'd *who* gladly fled from me. Rom. and Juliet.

Who for *him who;* but never when it is the regimen of a preposition.

[2] Such are, *at, in, of, from, till, too, for, by, through, near, with, on, off.*

[3] Such are, *above, below, along, across, amid, around, beyond, within, without, beside, among, between, except.* It may not be amiss to observe, that though the French in the commonest prepositions have the advantage of us by reason of their frequent elisions, the coalition of some of them with the article, and their pronominal particles *y* and *en*, they have nevertheless greatly the disadvantage in the less common, which with them are not so properly denominated preposi-

considerable (nor was there equal need) as on the conjunctions and the relatives. Yet even here the progress of taste hath not been entirely without effect. The *until* and *unto*, are now almost always, and the *upon*, very often, contracted into *till* and *to* and *on*. The *to* and the *for* are in some cases, without occasioning any inconvenience, and with a sensible advantage in point of energy, discarded altogether. Thus we say, "Forgive *us* our debts," and not "forgive to *us* our debts." I have gotten *you* a license," and not, "I have gotten a license *for you*." The same manner hath also obtained in some other modern tongues. What I am next to mention is peculiar to us; the preposition *of* is frequently supplied by the possessive case of the noun. Lastly, which is a real acquisition in respect of vivacity, when two or more nouns are conjoined in the same construction, it is not necessary in English, as in French, that the preposition of the first be repeated before each of the subsequent nouns. This ought to be done only in those cases wherein either perspicuity or harmony requires it.

Now that I am on the subject of the prepositions, it will not be improper to consider a peculiarity which is often to be found with us in their arrangement. In every other language the preposition is almost constantly prefixed to the noun which it governs; in English it is sometimes placed not only after the noun, but at a considerable distance from it, as in the following example. "The infirmary was indeed never so full as on this day, *which* I was at some loss to account *for*, till upon my going abroad, I observed that it was an easterly wind."[4] Here no fewer than seven words intervene between the relative *which*, and the preposition *for* belonging to it. Besides, the

tions as prepositive phrases that supply the place of prepositions. In evidence of this take the French translation of all the dissyllabic prepositions above mentioned, except the four last. These are, *au dessus de, au dessous de, le long de, au travers de, au milieu de, autour de, au dela de, au dedans de, au dehors de.* On comparing the two languages merely in point of vivacity, the French, I think, excels in the colloquial and epistolary style, where the recurrence must be frequent to those petty aids of discourse, the prepositions first mentioned, and where there is little scope for composition, as there are almost no complex sentences. The English, on the contrary, excels in the more elaborate style of history, philosophy, and oratory, where a greater variety of prepositions is needed, and where there is more frequent occasion of recurring to the conjunctions. These indeed are rather unwieldy in French; and I am not sure but a tacit conviction of this is the cause that a sort of detached aphoristic style is getting much into vogue with their authors. I shall remark here also, that their vivacity of expression is often attained at the expense of perspicuity. "La personne qui l'aime," may mean either, "The person who loves him," "The person who loves her," or, "The person who loves it." Nay more, though there is a difference in writing between *qui l'aime*, and *qu'il aime*, there is no difference in sound, and therefore the same phrase spoken may also mean, "The person whom he loves." In Italian there are several periphrastic prepositions in the same taste with the French, as "*a lintorno di, di là di, in mezzo di, dentro di, fuori di, di sopra di, di sotto di.* There are only two prepositions in French which we are obliged to express by circumlocution. These are, *chez*, at the house of, and *selon*, according to.

[4] Spectator, No. 440. C.

preposition doth not here precede its regimen, but follow it. One would imagine, to consider the matter abstractly, that this could not fail in a language like ours, which admits so few inflections, to create obscurity. Yet this in fact is seldom or never the consequence. Indeed the singularity of the idiom hath made some critics condemn it absolutely. That there is nothing analogous in any known tongue, ancient or modern, hath appeared to them a sufficient reason. I own it never appeared so to me.

If we examine the matter independently of custom, we shall find that the preposition is just as closely connected with the word, whether verb or noun, governing, as with the word, whether noun or pronoun, governed. It is always expressive of the relation which the one bears to the other, or of the action of the one upon the other. And as the cause in the order of Nature precedes the effect, the most proper situation for the preposition is immediately after the word governing, and before the word governed. This will accordingly in all languages be found the most common situation. But there are cases in all languages, wherein it is even necessary that the word governing should come after the word governed. In such cases it is impossible that the preposition should be situated as above described. Only half of the description is then attainable; and the speaker is reduced to this alternative; either to make the preposition follow the word governing, in which case it must be detached from the word governed; or to make it precede the word governed, in which case it must be detached from the word governing. The choice in itself arbitrary custom hath determined in every tongue.

But will it be admitted as a maxim, that the custom of one language, or even of ever so many, may be urged as a rule in another language, wherein no such custom hath ever obtained? An argument founded on so false a principle must certainly be inconclusive. With us indeed either arrangement is good; but I suspect that to make the preposition follow the word governing is more suitable than the other to the original idiom of the tongue, as in fact it prevails more in conversation. The most common case wherein there is scope for election, is with the relatives *whom* and *which;* since these, as in the example quoted, must necessarily precede the governing verb or noun. But this is not the only case. Vivacity requires sometimes, as hath been shown above, that even the governed part, if it be that which chiefly fixes the attention of the speaker, should stand foremost in the sentence. Let the following serve as an example: "*The man* whom you were so anxious to discover, I have at length got information *of*." We have here indeed a considerable hyperbaton, as grammarians term it; there being no less than thirteen words interposed between the noun and the preposition. Yet whether the expression can be altered for the better, will perhaps be questioned. Shall we say, "*Of the man* whom you were so anxious to discover, I have at length got information?" Who sees not that by this small alteration, not only is the vivacity destroyed, but the expression is rendered stiff and formal, and therefore ill adapted to the style of conversation? Shall we then restore what is called the grammatical, because the most common order, and say, "I have at length gotten information of the man whom you were so anxious to discover?" The arrangement here is unexceptionable, but the expression is unanimated. There is in the first manner something that displays an ardour in the speaker to be the messenger of good news. Of this character there are no traces in the last; and in the second there is a cold and studied formality which would make it appear intolerable. So much is in the power merely of arrangement. Ought we then always to prefer this way of placing the preposition after the governing word? By no means. There are cases wherein this is preferable. There are cases wherein the other way is preferable. In general, the former suits better the familiar and easy style, which copies the dialect of conversation; the latter more befits the elaborate and solemn diction which requires somewhat of dignity and pomp.

But to what purpose, I pray, those criticisms which serve only to narrow our range, where there would be no danger of a trespass, though we were indulged with more liberty? Is it that the genius of our language doth not sufficiently cramp us without these additional restraints? But it is the unhappiness of the generality of critics, that when two modes of expressing the same thing come under their consideration, of which one appears to them preferable, the other is condemned in gross, as what ought to be reprobated in every instance. A few contractions have been adopted by some writers which appear harsh and affected; and all contractions without exception must be rejected, though ever so easy and natural, and though evidently conducing to enliven the expression.[5] One order of the words in a particular example seems worthy of the pre-

[5] About the beginning of the present century, the tendency to contract our words, especially in the compound tenses of the verbs, was undoubtedly excessive. The worst of it was, that most of the contractions were effected by expunging the vowels, even where there was no hiatus, and by clashing together consonants of most obdurate sound, as Swift calls them. This produced the animadversion of some of our ablest pens, Addison, Swift, Pope, and others, whose concurring sentiments have operated so strongly on the public, that contractions of every kind have ever since been in disgrace, even those of easy pronunciation, and which had been in use long before. Yet our accumulated auxiliaries seemed to require something of this kind. And though I am sensible that *wasn't, didn't, shouldn't,* and *couldn't,* are intolerably bad, there are others of more pleasant sound, to which our critics, without any injury to the language, might have given a pass. On the contrary, even those elisions whereby the sound is improved, as when the succession of an initial

ference; and it must be established as a rule, that no other order in any case is to be admitted.

But we are not peculiar in this disposition, though we may be peculiar in some of our ways of exerting it. The French critics, and even the academy, have proceeded, if not always in the same manner, on much the same principle, in the improvements they have made on their language. They have indeed cleared it of many, if not of all their low idioms, cant phrases, and useless anomalies; they have rendered the style in the main more perspicuous, more grammatical, and more precise than it was before. But they have not known where to stop. Their criticisms often degenerate into refinements, and every thing is carried to excess. If one mode of construction, or form of expression, hath been lucky enough to please these arbitrators of the public taste, and to obtain their sanction, no different mode or form must expect so much as toleration. What is the consequence? They have purified their language; at the same time they have impoverished it, and have, in a considerable measure, reduced all kinds of composition to a tasteless uniformity. Accordingly, in perhaps no language, ancient or modern, will you find so little variety of expression in the

to a final vowel is prevented (which in all languages men have a natural propensity to avoid by contracting), as *I'm* for *I am;* or when a feeble vowel is suppressed without harshness, as in the last syllable of the preterites of our regular verbs (which without a contraction we can never bear in verse); or when some of our rougher consonants are cut off after other consonants as *'em* for *them;* (these I say) have all shared the same fate. Some indulgence, I think, may still be given to the more familiar style of dialogues, letters, essays, and even of popular addresses, which like comedy are formed on the dialect of conversation. In this dialect, wherein all language originates, the eagerness of conveying one's sentiments, the rapidity and ease of utterance, necessarily produce such abbreviations. It appears indeed so natural, that I think it requires that people be more than commonly phlegmatic, not to say stupid, to be able to avoid them. Upon the whole, therefore, this tendency, in my opinion, ought to have been checked and regulated, but not entirely crushed. That contracting serves to improve the expression in vivacity is manifest; it was necessary only to take care that it might not hurt it in harmony or in perspicuity. It is certainly this which constitutes one of the greatest beauties in French dialogue; as by means of it, what in other languages is expressed by a pronoun and a preposition, they sometimes convey not by a single syllable, but by a single letter. At the same time, it must be owned, they have never admitted contractions that could justly be denominated harsh; that they have not, on the other hand, been equally careful to avoid such as are equivocal, hath been observed already. We are apt to imagine, that there is something in the elision of letters and contraction of syllables that is particularly unsuitable to the grave and solemn style. This notion of ours is, I suspect, more the consequence of the disuse than the cause; since such abbreviations do not offend the severest critic, when they occur in books written in an ancient or a foreign language. Even the sacred penmen have not disdained to adopt them into the simple, but very serious style of holy writ. Witness the κᾀγω for και εγω, απ' εμου, for απο εμου, κᾀκεινος for και εκεινος, and many others. No doubt desuetude alone is sufficient to create an unsuitableness in any language. I will admit further, that there is some convenience in discriminating the different characters of writing by some such differences in the style. For both these reasons, I should not now wish to see them revived in performances of a serious or solemn nature.

various kinds of writing, as in French. In prose and verse, in philosophy and romance, in tragedy and comedy, in epic and pastoral, the difference may be very great in the sentiments, but it is nothing, or next to nothing, in the style.

Is this insipid sameness to be envied them as an excellence? Or shall we Britons, who are lovers of freedom almost to idolatry, voluntarily hamper ourselves in the trammels of the French academy? Not that I think we should disdain to receive instruction from any quarter, from neighbours, or even from enemies. But as we renounce implicit faith in more important matters, let us renounce it here too. Before we adopt any new measure or limitation, by the practice of whatever nation it comes recommended to us, let us give it an impartial examination, that we may not, like servile imitators, copy the bad with the good. The rules of our language should breathe the same spirit with the laws of our country. They ought to prove bars against licentiousness, without being checks to liberty.

SECTION III.—*Modern languages compared with Greek and Latin, particularly in regard to the Composition of Sentences.*

Before I conclude this chapter, I must beg leave to offer a few general remarks on the comparison of modern languages with Greek and Latin. This I am the rather disposed to do, that it will serve further to illustrate the principles above laid down. I make no doubt but the former have some advantages in respect of perspicuity. I think not only that the disposition of the words according to certain stated rules may be made more effectually to secure the sentence against ambiguous construction, than can be done merely by inflection, but that an habitual method of arranging words which are in a certain way related to one another, must, from the natural influence of habit, on the principle of association, even where there is no risk of misconstruction, more quickly suggest the meaning, than can be done in the freer and more varied methods made use of in those ancient languages. This holds especially with regard to Latin, wherein the number of equivocal inflections is considerably greater than in Greek; and wherein there are no articles, which are of unspeakable advantage, as for several other purposes, so in particular for ascertaining the construction. But whilst the latter, though in this respect inferior, are, when skilfully managed, by no means ill adapted for perspicuous expression, they are, in respect of vivacity, elegance, animation, and variety of harmony, incomparably superior. I shall at present consider their advantage principally in point of vivacity, which in a great measure, when the subject is of such a nature as to excite passion, secures animation also.

In the first place, the brevity that is attainable in these

languages gives them an immense superiority. Some testimonies in confirmation of this remark may be obtained by comparing the Latin examples of antithesis quoted in the notes of the second part of the third section of the preceding chapter, with any English translation that can be made of these passages. And I suspect, if a version were attempted into any other European tongue, the success would not be much better. It is remarkable, that in any inscription in which it is intended to convey something striking or emphatical, we can scarcely endure a modern language. Latin is almost invariably employed for this purpose in all the nations of Europe. Nor is this the effect of caprice or pedantry, as some perhaps will be apt to imagine. Neither does it proceed merely, as others will suppose, from the opinion that that language is more universally understood; for I suspect that this is a prerogative which will be warmly contested by the French; but it proceeds from the general conviction there is of its superiority in point of vivacity. That we may be satisfied of this, let us make the trial, by translating any of the best Latin inscriptions or mottos which we remember, and we shall quickly perceive, that what charms us expressed in their idiom, is scarcely supportable when rendered into our own.[6] The luggage of particles, such as pronouns, prepositions, and auxiliary verbs, from which it is impossible for

[6] Let us make the experiment on the inscriptions of some of the best devices or emblems that are extant. I shall give a few examples for illustration's sake, from the sixth of Bouhours' *Entretiens d' Ariste et d'Eugene*, called *Les Devises*. The first shall be, that of a starry sky without the moon, as representing an assembly of the fair, in which the lover finds not the object of his passion. The motto is, "Non mille quod absens." In English we must say, "A thousand cannot equal one that is absent." Another instance shall be that of a rock in the midst of a tempestuous sea, to denote a hero who with facility baffles all the assaults of his enemies. The motto, "Conantia frangere frangit." In English, "I break the things which attempt to break me." In this example we are obliged to change the person of the verb, that the words may be equally applicable, both in the literal sense and in the figurative, an essential point in this exercise of ingenuity. The personal pronoun in our language must always be expressed before the verb. Now the neuter *it* will not apply to the hero, nor the masculine *he* to the rock; whereas the first person applies equally to both. The third instance shall be that of the ass eating thistles, as an emblem of a parasite who serves as a butt to the company that entertains him. The motto, "Pungant dum saturent." In English, "Let them sting me, provided they fill my belly." In all these, how nervous is the expression in the original; how spiritless is the translation! Nor is this recourse to a multitude of words peculiar to us. All European languages labour, though not equally, under the same inconvenience. For the French, take Bouhours' version of the preceding mottos. The first is, "Mille ne valent pas ce que vaut une absente." The second, "Il brise ce qui fait effort pour le briser." This version is not perfectly adequate. The Latin implies a number of enemies, which is not implied here. Better thus "Il brise les choses qui font effort pour le briser." The third is, "Qu'ils me piquent, pourvu qu'ils me saoüillent." These are in no respect superior to the English. The Italian and the Spanish answer here a little better. Bouhours himself, who is extremely unwilling, even in the smallest matters, to acknowledge any thing like a defect or imperfection in the French tongue, is nevertheless constrained to admit, that it is not well adapted for furnishing such mottos and inscriptions.

us entirely to disencumber ourselves, clogs the expression, and enervates the sentiment.

But it is not in respect of brevity only that the ancient tongues above-mentioned are capable of a more vivid diction than the modern. For when, in the declensions and conjugations, the inflection, as is frequently the case, is attended with an increase of the number of syllables, the expression on the whole cannot always be denominated briefer, even when it consists of fewer words. However, as was observed before, when the construction is chiefly determined by inflection, there is much ampler scope for choice in the arrangement, and consequently the speaker hath it much more in his power to give the sentence that turn which will serve most to enliven it.

But even this is not all the advantage they derive from this particularity in their structure. The various terminations of the same word, whether verb or noun, are always conceived to be more intimately united with the term which they serve to lengthen, than the additional, detached, and in themselves insignificant, syllables or particles, which we are obliged to employ as connectives to our significant words. Our method gives almost the same exposure to the one as to the other, making the insignificant parts and the significant equally conspicuous; theirs much oftener sinks, as it were, the former into the latter, at once preserving their use, and hiding their weakness. Our modern languages may in this respect be compared to the art of carpentry in its rudest state, when the union of the materials employed by the artizan could be effected only by the help of those external and coarse implements, pins, nails, and cramps. The ancient languages resemble the same art in its most improved state, after the invention of dovetail joints, grooves, and mortices, when thus all the principal junctions are effected by forming properly the extremities or terminations of the pieces to be joined. For by means of these the union of the parts is rendered closer, whilst that by which their union is produced is scarcely perceivable.

Addison, if I remember right, somewhere compares an epic poem (and the same holds, though in a lower degree, of every other literary production), written in Greek or in Latin, to a magnificent edifice, built of marble, porphyry, or granite, and contrasts with it such a poem or performance in one of our modern languages, which he likens to such a building executed in freestone, or any of those coarser kinds of stone which abound in some northern climates. The latter may be made to answer all the essential purposes of accommodation as well as the former, but as the materials of which it is constructed are not capable of receiving the same polish, and consequently cannot admit some of the finer decorations, it will not only be inferior in beauty, but its imitative ornaments will be much less lively and expressive. It may nevertheless be equal to the other both in grandeur and in utility. If the representations that have been given of the Chinese language are genuine, if all their words are monosyllabic and indeclinable, if every relation and circumstance, even time and number, must be expressed by separate particles, I should think a performance in their tongue might be justly compared to a building in brick, which may be both neat and convenient, but which hardly admits the highly ornamented finishing of any order of architecture, or indeed any other species of beauty than that resulting from the perception of fitness. But this only by the way.

If I might be indulged one other similitude, I should remark, that the difference between the ancient Greek and Latin, and the modern European languages, is extremely analogous to the difference there is between their garb and ours. The latter will perhaps be admitted to be equally commodious, possibly for some purposes more so; but with its trumpery of buttons and button-holes, ligatures and plaits formally opposed to one another, it is stiff and unnatural in its appearance; whereas the easy flow and continually varied foldings of the former, are at once more graceful, and better adapted for exhibiting nature in shape, attitude, and motion, to advantage. The human figure is, I may say, burlesqued in the one habit, and adorned by the other. Custom, which can conciliate us to any thing, prevents us from seeing this in ourselves and in one another; but we quickly perceive the difference in pictures and statues. Nor is there a painter or a statuary of eminence who is not perfectly sensible of the odds, and who would not think his art degraded in being employed to exhibit the reigning mode. Nay, in regard to the trifling changes, for they are but trifling, which fashion is daily making on our garments, how soon are we ourselves brought to think ridiculous, what we accounted proper, not to say elegant, but two or three years ago; whereas no difference in the fashions of the times and of the country can ever bring a man of taste to consider the drapery of the toga or of the pallium as any way ludicrous or offensive.

Perhaps I have carried the comparison further than was at first intended. What hath been said, however, more regards the form or structure, than the matter of the languages compared. Notwithstanding the preference given above in point of form to the ancient tongues, the modern may, in point of matter (or the words of which the language is composed), be superior to them. I am inclined to think that this is actually the case of some of the present European tongues. The materials which constitute the riches of a language will always bear a proportion to the acquisitions in knowledge made by the people. For this reason, I should not hesitate to pronounce that English is considerably richer than Latin, and in the main fitter for all the subtle disquisitions both of philosophy and of criticism. If I am more doubtful in regard to the preference, when our tongue is compared with Greek, notwithstanding the superiority of our knowledge in arts and sciences, the reason of my doubt is, the amazing ductility of that language, by which it was adapted to express easily in derivations and compositions, new indeed but quite analogical, and therefore quite intelligible, any discoveries in the sciences, or invention in the arts, that might at any time be made in their own, or imported from foreign countries. Nay, it would seem to be a general conviction of this distinguishing excellence, that hath made Europeans almost universally recur to Greek for a supply of names to those things which are of modern invention, and with which the Grecians themselves never were acquainted, such as microscope, telescope, barometer, thermometer, and a thousand others.

CHAPTER V.

Of the Connectives employed in combining the Sentences in a Discourse.

IN the preceding chapter I have discussed what I had to offer on the manner of connecting the words, the clauses, and the members of a sentence. I intend in the present chapter to consider the various manners of connecting the sentences in a discourse, and to make some remarks on this subject, for the assistance of the composer, which are humbly submitted to the judgment of the reader.

SECTION I.—*The Necessity of Connectives for this Purpose.*

It will scarcely be doubted by any person of discernment, that as there should always be a natural connexion in the sentiments of a discourse, there should generally be corresponding to this, an artificial connexion in the signs. Without such a connexion the whole will appear a sort of patch-work, and not a uniform piece. To such a style we might justly apply the censure which the emperor Caligula gave of Seneca's, that is "sand without lime,"[7] the parts having no cohesion. As to the connexion of periods and other sentences, it is formed, like

[7] Arena sine calce.

that of words, clauses, and members, mostly by conjunctions, frequently by pronouns, the demonstrative especially,[8] and sometimes by other methods, of which I shall soon have occasion to take notice.

When facts are related in continuation, or when one argument, remark, or illustration, is with the same view produced after another, the conjunction is a *copulative.*[9] If the sentiment in the second sentence is in any way opposed to that which immediately precedes, an *adversative* is employed to conjoin them.[1] If it is produced as an exception, there are also *exceptive* conjunctions for the purpose.[2] Both the last-mentioned orders are comprehended under the general name *disjunctive.* If the latter sentence include the reason of what had been affirmed in the preceding, the *causal* is used.[3] If, on the contrary, it contain an inference, it must be introduced by an *illative.*[4] Besides these, there is in every tongue a number of phrases, which have the power of conjunctions in uniting sentences, and are of great utility in composition, both for enabling the orator to hit with greater exactness the relations almost infinitely diversified that may subsist between the thoughts, and for the variety they afford in that part of speech, wherein variety is more needed than in any other.[5] It likewise deserves our notice, that several of those words which are always classed by grammarians and lexicographers among the adverbs, have, in uniting the several parts of a discourse, all the effect of conjunctions.[6] The general name of *connexive* I shall therefore apply indiscriminately to them all.

SECTION II.—*Observations on the Manner of using the Connectives in combining Sentences.*

It remains to make a few observations with regard to the right manner of using the materials above specified, for connecting sentences and paragraphs. It is not indeed by any use of them, that we can propose to add much energy to the style, for that is rarely the gift of these particles; but we may employ them so as to preclude the irksomeness and langour which invariably result from an improper use of them.

My first observation shall be, that as there are many con-

[8] *This, that, such.*

[9] *And, now, also, too, likewise, again, besides, further, moreover, yea, nay, nor.*

[1] *But, or, however, whereas.*

[2] *Yet, nevertheless.*

[3] *For.*

[4] *Then, therefore.*

[5] *Add to this, in like manner, on the contrary, in short, to proceed, to return, to conclude.* We might produce phrases, if necessary, corresponding to each of the above orders.

[6] Such are some adverbs of time, as *then,* signifying at that time, *hitherto, formerly;* of place, as *here, thus, far;* of order, as *first, secondly, finally;* of resemblance, as *thus, accordingly;* of contrariety, as *else, otherwise, contrariwise.*

junctions and connective phrases appropriated to the coupling of sentences, that are never employed in joining the members of a sentence, so there are several conjunctions appropriated to the latter use, which are never employed in the former; and some that are equally adapted to both these purposes. This distinction in connectives will be found in different instances to flow from different sources. In some it is a natural distinction arising from the very import of the words; in which case we shall always find, on inquiry, that it obtains alike in every tongue. In other instances, it is a distinction merely customary, founded on the usages which prevail in a particular language.

As to those particles which are naturally fitted for conjoining clauses and members, but not sentences, they are chiefly the comparative,[7] the hypothetical,[8] and the intentional.[9] Let it not be imagined, that because a conjunction which falls under one or other of these denominations is often found in the beginning of a sentence, it serves to couple the sentence with that which went before. Such a connexive will always be discovered, on examination, to have no reference to any thing without the sentence. Consider the following examples. "If ye love me, ye will keep my commandments." "Though I tell you what I am, ye will not believe me." "That I might save sinners, I came into the world." It is manifest that the conjunction wherewith each of these sentences begins, marks singly the relation that subsists between the two following clauses, or the nature of the dependence which the one has on the other. It is not even implied in the expression, that any thing had been said before. Accordingly, the same sense, without any variation, is expressed when the clauses are transposed; though sometimes the one arrangement will exhibit it with greater energy than the other. Thus, "Ye will keep my commandments, if ye love me;" "Ye will not believe me, though I tell you what I am;" and "I came into the world, that I might save sinners," are precisely the same sentiments with those contained in the examples produced.

But may not the subordinate part connected with the additional particle, properly constitute one sentence, and the declaration another? Impossible. Every sentence must contain the enunciation of some proposition distinctly intelligible by itself, and expressive of some judgment, desire, or purpose of the speaker. But what only points to the motive or condition of something yet untold, answers none of these ends. Thus the words, "Unless ye repent," enunciate nothing, and therefore convey to the hearer no information of judgment,

[7] *Than.*
[8] *If, though, although, when, unless, except.*
[9] *That, so that, insomuch that, lest.*

purpose, or desire. They give indeed the expectation of such information, and thereby keep up the attention, till we hear what follows. No sooner are the words "ye shall perish" added, than we have the explicit declaration of a certain judgment or sentiment of the speaker. For this reason grammarians have justly remarked, that in every sentence there must be a verb in the indicative mood either expressed or implied. In all the three examples above given, we have it expressed in the second clause of their original form; the verb in the hypothetical part, and in that which marks the intention, is properly in the subjunctive or potential. It matters not whether the mood be distinguished by inflection, arrangement, or particles. In commands, interrogations, and wishes, the indicative is not expressed but implied, and by the idiom of the tongue suggested to the understanding with sufficient clearness. The interrogative and the optative, as well as the imperative, are, in respect of sense, totally distinct from the two moods above mentioned; though in most languages distinguished only by particles or arrangement.[1] Thus, though in these three sentences, "Go away;" "Will ye go away?" and "Oh that ye would go away;" there is probably no indicative expressed, yet it is so manifestly implied, that none who understands the language can be at a loss to perceive, that each of them fully enunciates a certain affection of the speaker, a command, request, or wish. They signify neither more nor less than "I command you to go away;" "I desire to be informed whether ye will go away;" and "I wish that ye would go away."

What hath been said of the conditional and intentional particles, holds still more evidently of the comparative particle *than*, which as frequently it doth not even need to be followed by a verb in any mood, so it can never begin the sentence without a manifest hyperbaton. The particle *as* is sometimes strictly a comparative conjunction. Such it is in these words, "As your fathers did, so do ye." In this case it falls under the same predicament with the conditional connectives. Sometimes it is equivalent to *thus*, and may be still called a comparative particle, as it intimates some resemblance in that which follows to that which preceded. But this is also effected by the copulatives *likewise* and *in like manner*. Such it is in the beginning of the similitude,

> *As* when an angel by divine command.[2]

In this case it evidently connects sentences. Again, the *illative* is perfectly adapted for connecting sentences. The inference itself may very properly be expressed in a proposition

[1] See Hermes, Book I. chap. viii.

[2] Addison's Campaign.

distinctly enunciated, and, therefore, independently intelligible. The conjunction serves only to intimate that the reason or evidence of this judgment, which may also be a distinct proposition, was assigned in the words immediately preceding. This reasoning holds, in like manner, with regard to the *causal* conjunction. The relation between the sentences is the same; the order only is inverted; as we have here the consequence before the cause. And I suppose it is too clear to need illustration, that there is nothing in the import of the words to hinder *copulatives* and *disjunctives* from connecting sentences as well as members, and members as well as sentences. Yet even among those that are alike fitted for both purposes, there is some difference in point of strength. From their very nature they do not all unite the parts with equal closeness. They are like cements which differ in their degrees of tenacity. Thus the illative conjunctions and the causal, constitute a more intimate union than the adversative and the copulative. Again, that formed by demonstrative pronouns seems weaker than that effected by conjunctions. So much for the natural difference in the connectives resulting from the different import of the words.

That there is also a great, though arbitrary difference, arising from idiom, is unquestionable. In the best writers of antiquity, we often meet with sentences that begin with a relative pronoun, answering to our *who*, *whom*, or *which*. By all the most eminent writers among the moderns, not only in English, but in other European tongues, this practice is now, I think, carefully avoided. It is custom only that can make this difference. When the cause is purely natural, the effect will be found the same in all languages. Accordingly, what was observed above concerning the conditional, intentional, and comparative conjunctions, is equally applicable to every tongue. And if we consider abstractly the effect of the relatives, we shall find, that what follows the *who*, *whom*, or *which*, is often the enunciation of some judgment, purpose, or desire, which, as it may constitute a separate sentence, serves to vindicate from the charge of impropriety the usage of the ancients. Yet there is some reason also on the side of the moderns. The personal pronouns do but presuppose the subject, whether person or thing, to be known, and consequently, do no more than supersede the repetition of the name. There can be, therefore, no doubt of the propriety of beginning sentences with these. Whereas the relatives not only refer to something immediately said, that we may know the subject of discourse, but seem so closely to connect the part which follows with that which precedes, that the one makes, as it were, the description of either the nominative, or the regimen of the verb, in the other. In this view, they may be said to create a union too close to subsist conveniently between different sentences. There is at least a risk, that they will give such an ambiguous appearance to the second, as to render it doubtful whether it be a separate sentence or a member of the foregoing. For this reason the illative *wherefore*, as it includes the power of the pronoun *which*, doth not seem to be so analogically used by our writers in connecting sentences, as in connecting members.

Again, as an irrefragable evidence that there is a difference in connectives arising purely from idiom, let it be observed, that we find it sometimes taking place among conjunctions of the same order. The causal *because* forms too close a union to subsist between separate sentences. The case is different with the causal *for*, though in every other respect synonymous. This latter particle is not adapted for uniting clauses which must necessarily be included in the same sentence. As an evidence that this distinction can be attributed only to custom, we may remark, that it is variable, differing in different ages. For instance, in Shakspeare's time, the causal particles seem to have been used promiscuously. We have at least in his writings several examples, in which he uses the particle *for*, where every writer at present would say *because*, as in the following passage:

> Heaven defend your good souls, that ye think,
> I will your serious and great business scant,
> *For* she is with me.[3]

Nay, even among the copulatives, which, of all the conjunctions are the most vague in their application, there are some that use seems to have appropriated to the coupling of sentences, not of members, such as *again*, *further*, *besides;* and some to the uniting not of sentences so properly as of paragraphs, or even of larger portions of writing, that commonly fall under that denomination, such as *moreover* and *furthermore*.

The copulative *and*, on the contrary, some critics are for confining to the single purpose of uniting the parts within the sentence, and seem to imagine that there is some impropriety in using it for combining sentences. But as in this opinion, from what hath been evinced above, it is evident they are not supported by any argument from the import of the words, this conjunction being naturally on the same footing with the other copulatives, so neither have they any plea from usage in its favour. The examples for the contested use, which might be produced from all the best authorities in the language, are innumerable. But though use alone, in matters of language, is ever held a sufficient reason why things should continue in the state wherein we find them, when there is no positive ground for an

[3] Othello.

alteration, I shall, in the present case, where, indeed, I could never discover the vestige of a reason for change, produce two arguments on the opposite side against excluding this particle from a privilege it hath always heretofore possessed; arguments which, I hope, will appear satisfactory. First, being a monosyllable, it will, on a principle above explained, if not used too often, serve to smooth the current of the discourse; inasmuch as it will render the transition from sentence to sentence easier than it is possible to render it, when recourse is always had to connectives of greater length. Secondly, it adds one to the number of the copulatives, and, consequently (where variety is of importance, as it certainly is here, on a principle presently to be explained), this particle, if not absolutely necessary, is at least convenient.

My second observation is, that one of the best expedients for preventing the connexives from becoming too conspicuous, is to avoid the frequent recurrence to the same particles, especially if they consist of more than one syllable. And if so, with still greater reason must we avoid recurring often to the same conjunctive phrases.

I do not deny that there are cases wherein the repetition even of a conjunction, like other rhetorical repetitions, may add to the energy of the expression. Thus when several successive sentences bear the same relations to one that preceded, or to one that is to follow, this containing the common cause, consequence, motive, or concomitant of what is signified in those, they may be ushered more emphatically by repeating the connexive than by varying it. The common relation gives a propriety to the figure. But such cases are rare, and easily distinguished. As to those which usually occur to the composer, it may be asserted to hold universally, that nothing will contribute more to enfeeble the style, than frequently to recur to the same heavy conjunctions, or long connectives, whatever they be. The *now*, *and*, *for*, *but*, *nay*, *nor*, have this advantage from their brevity, that though often repeated they pass almost unnoticed. But who, that hath any taste, can endure the incessant quick returns of the *also*'s, and the *likewise*'s, and the *moreover*'s, and the *however*'s, and the *notwithstanding*'s? An excess in these is insupportable. It is a maxim in elocution that will not often be found to fail, that in the use of the more ignoble parts of speech there is greater need of variety than in the use of such as are of higher quality. The very significance of the nobler parts doth, as it were, support their dignity; but since the attendance of the less noble is necessary, shift them oftener, obtrude not on us always the same individuals, and we shall have less leisure to criticize them, or to advert to their insignificance.

The third remark I shall make on this subject is, that another useful expedient for answering the same end is to vary the situation of the conjunction, wherever the idiom of the tongue and the harmony of the sentence will permit the variation. The place where we should naturally expect to find it, when it connects two sentences, is doubtless the beginning of the second. But in most languages a little latitude is indulged on this article. In those cases, therefore, which admit this freedom, one, two, or more words may precede the conjunction, and serve as a cover to render it less observable. In the beginning it stands by itself; whereas, placed in the manner now mentioned, it may be said to stand in a crowd. But no tongue whatever gives this indulgence in assigning a place to every connexive.

With us in particular, no monosyllabic conjunction, except the illative *then*, can be thus transposed.[4] Our language, however, hath been abundantly indulgent (where indulgence is of greater consequence) in the power it gives us in the disposal of those which consist of more than one syllable. Thus almost all the copulatives which come under this denomination,[5] the disjunctives *however* and *nevertheless*,[6] and the illative *therefore*, may be shifted to the second, the third, the fourth place, or even further.

It would be difficult to assign a satisfactory reason for the difference that hath been made in this respect, between conjunctions of one syllable and those of more. Yet we have ground to believe that it is not merely accidental, as some traces of the same distinction are to be found in most languages.[7] It will indeed appear, from what hath been illustrated above, that the monosyllabic conjunctions need not be managed with the same address as the others, there not being the same hazard that they would soon become tiresome. On the contrary, it may be said, that being of themselves so inconsiderable, it is necessary that their situation be ascertained, in order to give them that degree of influence, with-

[4] There is another monosyllabic conjunction, which, even where it connects sentences, is not placed in the beginning of the second. But this implies no transposition, as the first place could not be assigned to it without the violation of universal practice. The particle I mean is the conjunction *too*, when it signifies *also*. Thus we say, "He *too* was included in the act of indemnity." To say, "*Too* he," would not be English.

[5] The copulative *again* cannot conveniently be transposed, as it would scarcely fail to occasion an ambiguity, and be mistaken for the adverb signifying *a second time*.

[6] The disjunctive *whereas* is never transposed.

[7] In Latin, for example, the monosyllabic conjunctions, *et*, *sed*, *nam*, when they connect two sentences, regularly maintain there place in the beginning of the second; whereas, to the dissyllables, *quoque*, *autem*, *enim*, more latitude is allowed. In French too, the monosyllables, *et*, *mais*, *car*, have invariably the same situation. It is otherwise with *aussi*, *pourtant*, *pourquoi*, though there is not so great freedom allowed in arranging them, as in the English dissyllabic conjunctions.

out which they could not answer the purpose even of conjunctions.

But it may be argued against the solution now given, and, indeed, against the whole of the precedent reasoning on this article, "How few, if any, have ever reflected on the different effects of these different arrangements? Or how could a difference, not reflected on, give rise to a difference in the laws by which their respective places are assigned them?" To this I answer, that taste alone, whose general principles are the same in every people, and which, like every appetite, seeks its own gratification, produceth insensibly, as it improves, and even where there is no direct intention, an improvement in the language as well as in the arts. It is by gradual, and what may be termed implicit compact, that the language, like the common law of every nation, hath obtained at first an establishment among them. It is to the same cause that the alterations to the better or to the worse, as knowledge and taste advance or decline among the people, are afterwards to be ascribed. That there should ever have been any formal or explicit convention or contrivance in this case, is an hypothesis, in my opinion, not only unsupported by reason, but repugnant to it. It is the province of criticism and philosophy, which appear much later than language, being of much slower growth, and to which close attention and reflection are not less requisite than taste, to investigate the latent causes in the principles of taste, by which the various changes have been actually, though in a manner imperceptibly, produced.

My fourth observation is, that though certain circumstances require that one connexive be immediately followed by another, the accumulating of these without necessity ought always to be avoided. There are some complex conjunctions which appear to be two, because in writing custom hath not combined the parts into one word, but are properly one in import and effect. Such are, *as if*, *so that*, *insomuch that*, and a few others. Of these I am not now speaking.

As to those between which, though adjoined in situation, there is no coalition in sense, let it be observed, that—there are cases in which propriety requires the aid of more than one;—there are cases in which the idiom of the language permits the use of more; that, on the contrary,—there are cases in which propriety rejects the union altogether; and lastly,—there are cases in which idiom rejects it. Each of these four cases I shall consider severally.

First, as to the cases wherein propriety requires the aid of more than one connexive, it was remarked formerly, that some conjunctions are limited to the use of connecting words and members, whilst others are employed indiscriminately for the connection of words, members, or sentences. When one of each kind meets in the beginning of a sentence, the intention of the first is generally to express the relation which the sentence bears to that immediately preceding; and the intention of the second, to express the dependence of the one clause on the other, in the sentence so introduced. Take the following passage of scripture for an example: "I go to prepare a place for you. AND *if* I go to prepare a place for you, I will come again, and receive you to myself."[8] The copulative AND connects the two sentences. The hypothetical conjunction *if* serves only to mark the first member of the last sentence, as the condition or limitation of the promise contained in the second member. The reader will observe, that I have distinguished the different applications of the two conjunctions in this example by a difference in the character in which they are printed. I intend, for the sake of perspicuity, to adopt the same method in the other examples which are to be produced. But it is not copulatives only that may be thus combined with conditional particles. The causal, illative, and adversative, may all be employed in the same way. The first of these is exemplified in the following quotation: "Let us not say we keep the commandments of the one, when we break the commandments of the other. FOR *unless* we observe both, we obey neither."[9] The above instances will serve to illustrate the observation in all other combinations with connectives of the same order. For an example of the like construction in the conjunction *that*, these words of the poet will suffice:

> If there's a power above us;
> AND that there is, all nature cries aloud
> Thro' all her works; he must delight in virtue.[1]

It is not material that the whole is here comprised in one sentence. The first conjunction serves to unite the member that precedes with that which follows; the second to exhibit the connexion that subsists between the succeeding clauses. And what relation two connected complex sentences bear to the members of each, that relation bear the members of a complicated sentence to the clauses of which they consist. It was said, that the first of two conjunctions so placed is generally the connexive of the sentences, and that the second marks the relation subsisting between the members of the sentence which ensues. This holds generally, but not always. If the connective of the sentences be one of those particles which, agreeably to the third observation, the

[8] John xiv 2, 3. [9] Hooker. [1] Addison's Cato.

idiom of the language permits us to transpose, it may properly possess the second place, and the other the first, as in the example following: "It is of the utmost importance to us, that we associate principally with the wise and virtuous. *When*, THEREFORE, we choose our companions, we ought to be extremely careful in regard to the choice we make." The second conjunction THEREFORE is that which connects the sentences. The first conjunction *when* hath no relation to any thing beyond the second sentence. The only examples I have yet produced, are those wherein one of the conjunctions is by its nature always appropriated to the subordinate use of connecting the parts of a sentence. But even where the two connectives are alike susceptible of both uses, the structure of the expression may sufficiently evince, that the one is employed solely to connect the sentence to what precedes in the discourse, and the other solely to conjoin the members, as in the following example: "Such is the probable consequence of the measure I now recommend. BUT *however* this may succeed, our duty is the same." Of the different applications of the two conjunctions in this passage, there cannot be the smallest doubt. Sometimes a decompound sentence may be ushered by no fewer than three successive conjunctions; the first being the connexive of the sentences; the second that which ascertains the relation of the members of the sentence thus introduced; the third that which indicates the connexion of the clauses of the first member of that sentence, as in the subsequent example, "To those who do not love God, the enjoyment of him is unattainable. NOW AS *that* we may love God, || it is necessary to know him; SO *that* we may know God, || it is necessary to study his works." The conjunction NOW connects this period with the preceding sentence; AS is expressive of the relation which the first member bears to the second, beginning with SO; *that* indicates the dependence of the first clause of the first member, "we may love God," on the second clause, "it is necessary to know him;" and corresponds to the conjunction *that* which follows the SO, in the beginning of the second member, and which, in like manner, indicates the dependence of the first clause of the second member, "we may know God," on the last clause, "it is necessary to study his works." But though the introduction of two conjunctions, having different references in the manner above explained, is perfectly compatible with the rules of good writing, and often inevitable, I cannot say so much for the admission of three, whose various applications must distract the attention, and so create a confusion and difficulty alike inconsistent with the principles of perspicuity, of vivacity, or of elegance.

Secondly, as to those cases wherein we cannot say propriety

requires, but the idiom of language permits, the use of more than one connexive, they are either when the connexives are of the same order; for instance, in the copulatives *and further, and in like manner;* in the adversatives *but however;* in the exceptives *yet nevertheless, yet notwithstanding.* With regard to such combinations we may safely pronounce, that if the use of synonymas even in the more significant parts of speech are for the most part incompatible with vivacity and strength, the like use in the more insignificant, and consequently weaker parts, must be still more exceptionable. Again, when the connectives are of different, but not opposite orders, idiom often permits the concurrence of two, though the reference of both is the same; that is, though both are intended merely to connect the sentence with that which preceded. Thus the copulative is often combined with the illative, *and therefore,* or with a particle expressive of order, *and thirdly;* the causal with a particle expressing opposition, *for else, for otherwise;* a disjunctive with such a particle or phrase, *or on the contrary;* an adversative with an exceptive, *but yet;* a comparative with a copulative, *as also.* It were endless to enumerate all that idiom permits us in this manner to conjoin. It is only by attending to the practice of good authors, that it can perfectly be learnt. It is not to be questioned, that in some instances, the use of two connectives, though not absolutely necessary, may be expedient both for rounding the period and for expressing more perfectly the relation of the sentences. But they are much more commonly the effect either of negligence, or of a vitiated taste in what concerns composition, and are often to be met with in the middling class of writers. The following will serve as an example of this manner: "*Although* he was close taken up with the affairs of the nation, *nevertheless* he did not neglect the concerns of his friends." Either of the conjunctions would have done better than both. An author of this stamp will begin a sentence thus, "Whereas, on the other hand, supposing that"—Who sees not, that "If, on the contrary"—would express the same connexion with more energy, as well as brevity? When a speaker interlards his discourse with such accumulated connexives, he always suggests to a judicious hearer, the idea of one that wants to gain time, till he cast about for something to say. Yet this fault is certainly more pardonable in speaking than in writing. The composer may take his own time, being under no necessity of writing faster than he can provide and dispose his materials. The slowness of his invention will not be betrayed to the reader by any method more readily than by that which the speaker is sometimes forced to use in order to conceal it.

Thirdly, as to those cases in which propriety itself forbids the concurrence of two conjunctions, it is impossible we should fall into a mistake. They are always distinguished by some repugnancy in the import of the words, which even common sense shows to be incompatible. Such are a copulative with a disjunctive, a causal with an illative, a particle expressive of resemblance with one expressive of contrariety.

Fourthly, as to those cases in which idiom alone forbids the concourse. These are to be learnt only by practice. Thus idiom permits the junction of a copulative with an illative particle, but never with a *causal*. We may say, *and therefore*, but not *and for*. We are not to seek the reason of this difference in the import of the terms, but in the custom of applying them. Again, idiom permits the use of two copulatives, but not of every two. We may say, *and also*, *and likewise*, but not *also likewise*. Two causal conjunctions are not now associated, as *for because*, nor two illatives, as *therefore then*. Yet in the dialect which obtained in the beginning of the last century, these modes of expression were common. Indeed, some of those heavy connectives which are now but little used, as *moreover*, *furthermore*, *over and above*, are all but combinations of synonymous particles, and flow from a disposition which will perhaps ever be found to prevail where style is in its infancy.

The fifth and last observation I shall make on this subject is, that it is not necessary that all the sentences in any kind of composition should be linked together by connective particles. I know of no rules that have ever been laid down for our direction in this particular. But as it always hath been, so, for aught I can perceive, it always will be, left to taste alone to determine when these particles ought to be used, and when omitted. All that occurs to me as being of any service on this head, may be comprised in the two following remarks. The first is, that the illative conjunctions, the causal and the disjunctive, when they suit the sense, can more rarely be dispensed with than the copulative. The second is, that the omission of copulatives always succeeds best, when the connexion of the thoughts is either very close or very distant. It is mostly in the intermediate cases that the conjunction is deemed necessary. When the connexion in thought is very distant, the copulative appears absurd, and when very close superfluous. For the first of these reasons, it is seldom that we meet with it in the beginning of a chapter, section, or even paragraph, except in the Bible; and for the second, that it is frequently dropt in familiar narrative, where the connexion is so obvious as to render it useless.

THE END.

INDEX